W9-CKG-972

ENCYCLOPEDIA OF

AMERICAN GOVERNMENT AND CIVICS

ENCYCLOPEDIA OF

AMERICAN GOVERNMENT AND CIVICS

MICHAEL A. GENOVESE AND LORI COX HAN

VOLUME III

Facts On File
An imprint of Infobase Publishing

Encyclopedia of American Government and Civics

Facts On File, Inc.
An imprint of Infobase Publishing
132 West 31st Street
New York NY 10001

Genovese, Michael A.
Encyclopedia of American government and civics / Michael A. Genovese and Lori Cox Han.
     p. cm.
  Includes bibliographical references and index.
  ISBN 978-0-8160-6616-2 (hc: alk. paper)   1. United States—politics and government—Encyclopedias.
2. Civics—Encyclopedias. I. Han, Lori Cox. II. Title.
  JK9.G46 2008
  320.47303—dc22   2007043813

Facts On File books are available at special discounts when purchased in bulk quantities for businesses, associations, institutions, or sales promotions. Please call our Special Sales Department in New York at (212) 967-8800 or (800) 322-8755.

You can find Facts On File on the World Wide Web at http://www.factsonfile.com

Text design by Kerry Casey
Composition by Binghampton Valley Composition
Cover design by Salvatore Luongo
Illustrations by Jeremy Eagle
Cover printed by Yurchak Printing, Landisville, Pa.
Book printed and bound by Yurchak Printing, Landisville, Pa.
Printed in the United States of America

This book is printed on acid-free paper and contains 30 percent postconsumer recycled content.

CONTENTS

PUBLIC POLICY

aging policy

Although one ages from birth throughout adulthood, the term *aging policy* describes the governmental programs and benefits aimed at senior citizens. Aging policy composes more than a third of the annual federal budget, and only defense spending surpasses it. The largest components of aging policy are SOCIAL SECURITY, Medicare and Medicaid. However, aging policy also encompasses such issues as age discrimination in employment, private pensions, taxes, Supplemental Security Income for the poor, housing and reverse mortgages, nursing home regulation, and the renewal of driver's licenses.

The age of 65 is generally used to denote one's status as a senior citizen for most programs and policies. There is nothing specific about this chronological marker that suddenly makes an individual old or elderly. Rather, the conventional use of 65 in aging policy stems from the creation of Social Security in 1935, which adopted age 65 for the receipt of benefits. In 1935, policy makers were merely following the age used in the German pension program developed in the 1880s. In addition, age 65 was considered favorable for the policy purposes of Social Security. Enough people would live to 65 so the public would willingly pay into the program on the expectation that they, too, would live to receive benefits. But given the life expectancy of 61 in 1935, not everyone would reach age 65, which was financially advantageous, as many would pay into the program who never received

benefits. Thus, age 65 developed as the nearly universal qualifier for most aging policy.

Aging policy is in much part driven by demography, which is the study of population. In 1900, the elderly numbered only 2.4 million, constituted 4 percent of the population, and had very few government policies directed toward them. In comparison, today's elderly number approximately 35 million, constitute 12.4 percent of the population, and have an entire smorgasbord of age-related policies. Many of these policies are a response to demographic trends within the elderly population. For example, the fact that older women outnumber men (65 males to 100 females over age 65) prompts the need for public policies of care giving support and nursing home regulations. Older men are likely to be married and thus have a live-in spouse available for caregiving. An older woman, on the other hand, is likely to be widowed, so she will need to look outside the family for caregiving support. Another demographic trend is that the fastest growing age group is those 85 and older. This again prompts policy needs, as this oldest group has a greater need for health care and medications, financial support due to outliving one's savings and assets, and caregiving assistance.

As a group, senior citizens are highly politically active. Seniors have one of the highest levels of VOTER TURNOUT and are the ones most likely to vote in nonpresidential as well as local elections. People over 65 are far more likely than other age groups to belong to a political party, vote in a primary election, and contribute to a political campaign. Hence, seniors are a favored target for votes and for campaign funds by politicians, who in return are more than willing to protect aging policies and benefits. At the very least, only a few politicians will risk taking on the elderly by suggesting reductions in benefits or massive reforms in aging policy and never in an election year. Aging policy has long been described as the third rail of politics.

It is not only the political activism of the elderly that promotes aging policy, but political power also stems from AARP (formerly the American Association of Retired Persons), an interest group dedicated to furthering aging issues. With 35 million members (now 50 and over) and its own zip code in Washington, D.C., AARP is the behemoth of INTEREST GROUPS. As a nonprofit, nonpartisan interest group, AARP does not support or oppose political candidates or donate financially to political campaigns. But few aging policies get enacted without the blessing of AARP, which constantly lobbies on behalf of the elderly.

As an interest group, AARP provides material, solidaristic, and purposive incentives to its membership. AARP offers unlimited material benefits including prescription drugs, travel programs and discounts, insurance, safe driver programs, and affiliated programs with companies offering discounts on their products to AARP members. Belonging to a group of like-minded people is a solidaristic benefit, and *AARP: The Magazine*, claiming the world's largest circulation, promotes the perspective of an aging community joined by common concerns, ideas, and history. The purposive benefits are those obtained increases or warded off cutbacks in aging programs achieved by AARP LOBBYING. But like any interest group, AARP suffers from free riders who benefit from AARP's political activism without having to officially become a member of AARP.

The largest public policy program devoted to aging is Social Security. Created in 1935 as part of President Franklin D. Roosevelt's NEW DEAL programs, Social Security provides financial support to retired seniors and their spouses, the disabled, and survivors of an eligible employed worker. The three requirements for receiving Social Security are that the worker paid into the program for at least 40 quarters over a lifetime, meets the retirement test of no longer working at a primary job, and meets the eligibility age (originally 65 but now gradually increasing to age 67). Roosevelt intentionally used an insurance model to create the public perspective that workers paid in and therefore were entitled to benefits, forestalling any future policy makers from eliminating the program.

Today's workers pay 6.2 percent of their salary to Social Security (up to a maximum earning of $94,200 in 2006), and their employer also pays 6.2 percent of the worker's salary, for a total of 12.4 percent per worker. Social Security contributions are compulsory and also portable, in that the worker can take contributions to this government program to his or her next job. Upon retirement and reaching the eligibility age, a worker can begin to receive Social Security benefits, which then continue for the rest of his or her life. A worker can opt for early retirement at age 62 and receive 80 percent of the full benefit amount for the rest of his or her life. The exact amount received from Social Security is based on the worker's lifetime contribution, with the maximum benefit in 2006 of $2,053 a month. The average Social Security benefit is $1,002. Individuals receiving Social Security benefits do get an annual raise with a cost of living adjustment (COLA). Social Security was never intended to be the sole or even the primary financial support in retirement. Instead, aging financial policy was conceived as a three-legged stool of private pension, savings, and Social Security.

Social Security is an intergenerational transfer whereby current beneficiaries are paid from the contributions of current workers and any surplus goes into the Social Security Trust Fund. Despite workers paying into Social Security over their employment history, the average worker earns back in benefits his or her entire contribution amount in 6.2 years. The retired person's Social Security benefits do not stop then but rather continue for the rest of his or her life.

The success of an intergenerational transfer program depends on demographics and the ratio of workers to retired beneficiaries. When Social Security was created, there were 40 workers for each retiree receiving benefits. With the decrease in the birth rate, the ratio has fallen to 3.3 workers per retiree, with further decreases projected when members of the baby boom generation (those born between 1946 and 1964) retire. Some of this decline is offset by the increase in women working, which was not adjusted for in the 1935 numbers.

Needless to say, with the coming retirement of the baby boomers (which is a huge group estimated to be approximately 76 million people and nearly 29 percent of the entire U.S. population), there are grave concerns about the future of Social Security. Once the baby boomers retire by 2020, those over the age of 65 will number approximately 54 million and could constitute 16 percent to 21 percent of the population (depending on the birth rate from now to 2020). This will dramatically shift the dependency ratio and cause great havoc with the intergenerational transfer model of Social Security. As yet, no major reforms to Social Security have been enacted. This is in part due to policy makers' reluctance to displease seniors or the baby boomers, due in part to the higher voter turnout rates for this segment of the population.

The other major aging policy is Medicare, enacted in 1965 as part of President Lyndon B. Johnson's GREAT SOCIETY programs, which is the federal program that provides health care to seniors. It is an entitlement program, which means that anyone meeting the requirements of eligibility to now receive Social Security can also receive Medicare benefits without any consideration of financial need. Current workers pay 1.45 percent of their income in a Medicare tax, with that same amount matched by their employer. Medicare beneficiaries have monthly premiums, copays, and deductibles.

As a program, Medicare is geared toward acute care of treating a temporary episodic condition and less on chronic care requiring prolonged assistance. Medicare is comprised of Parts A, B, and D. Part A is automatically available to a person eligible for Medicare benefits. It covers the costs of a hospital stay, medical tests, and medical equipment. The older patient pays a $952 deductible (as of 2006) on entering the hospital each quarter, and Medicare pays for the rest of the hospital stay. Part B covers doctor visits and is optional coverage that seniors can opt for by paying a fee of $78 a month (as of 2006) deducted from their Social Security check. The beneficiary has a $110 annual deductible and pays 20 percent of the physician charges.

Enacted in 2006, Part D provides coverage of prescription medications for those who receive Medi-care. The beneficiary pays a monthly premium for the type of coverage selected and an annual deductible of $250. Part D is described as having a donut in the policy program. Medicare pays 75 percent of drug costs from $250 to $2,850 and then 95 percent of costs after the beneficiary has spent $3,600 out of pocket on his or her prescription medications. This lack of coverage from $2,850 to $3,600 is the donut hole.

Coverage of prescription drugs under Medicare was a long-debated policy before it was enacted. One of the policy concerns is that the actual program costs are unknown. The annual cost of Part D will be determined by the health needs of the beneficiaries and the drugs prescribed by their physicians. Seniors clearly have the largest usage of prescription medications, but the extent of their prescribed drug use, and thus the cost of Part D, is yet to be determined.

While not a specific program for the older population, Medicaid has become one of the most important to seniors and their families. Medicaid, also created in 1965, is a state and federally funded health care program for the poor of all ages. This is a means-tested program, so to qualify for coverage an individual's income and assets must be below the level determined by each state. Most states use the poverty line or 150 percent above the poverty line as the income level for Medicaid eligibility. Although there are state variations, generally Medicaid covers the costs of doctor visits, hospital stays, medical equipment, and prescription drugs for those who qualify.

Medicaid has become increasingly significant for older persons because it covers the costs of continuing care in a nursing home. Medicare, on the other hand, only covers nursing home expenses for a limited stay immediately on discharge from an acute hospital. While only 4 percent of people over the age of 65 are in nursing homes at any one point in time, there is a 40 percent chance that a senior will spend some time in a nursing home during his or her lifetime.

Many older persons enter a nursing home paying out of pocket for their care. However, the average nursing home costs more than $35,000 a year, which quickly diminishes older persons' savings and assets. Often older persons will spend down (deplete their assets) paying for their nursing home costs and then qualify for Medicaid. At this point, Medicaid will pay for the nursing home and other health-care costs.

Obviously, Social Security, Medicare, and the long-term care costs of Medicaid are an enormous outlay of federal dollars for aging programs. These huge costs and the impending aging of the baby boomers into senior citizens have prompted attention to intergenerational equity. Now the questions of aging policy have become, among others, what do American citizens owe older persons, can American citizens afford to continue the same level of benefits, and how should the government allocate resources across generations. When the last of the baby boomers has its 65th birthday in 2020, there will be 54 million senior citizens. This looming magnitude of older persons assures that intergenerational equity will dictate aging policy for decades to come.

Further Reading

Altman, Stuart, and David Shactman, eds. *Policies for an Aging Society*. Baltimore, Md.: Johns Hopkins University Press, 2002; Burkhauser, Richard. *The Economics of an Aging Society*. Malden, Mass.: Blackwell Publishing, 2004; Hudson, Robert. *The Politics of Old Age Policy*. Baltimore, Md.: Johns Hopkins University Press, 2005; Koff, Theodore, and Richard Park. *Aging Public Policies: Bonding across the Generations*. Amityville, N.Y.: Baywood Publishing, 2000; Kotlikoff, Laurence J. and Scott Burns. *The Coming Generational Storm*. Cambridge, Mass.: MIT Press, 2004.

—Janie Steckenrider

arms control

In the lexicon of the new millennium, the term *arms control* is frequently equated with the "war on terrorism," defined by President George W. Bush's quest to prevent countries such as Iraq, Iran, and North Korea from developing weapons of mass destruction (WMDs) and systems for their delivery in the wake of the terrorist attacks on New York and Washington, D.C., on September 11, 2001. The United States, unable to secure approval from the UN Security Council, invaded Iraq in March 2003 with a nominal international "coalition of the willing" and ousted Iraqi dictator Saddam Hussein. Bush, supported by British prime minister Tony Blair, believed intelli-

gence information corroborated allegations that Hussein had amassed weapons of mass destruction, such as poison gas he had used against the Kurdish minority in northern Iraq in 1991, and intended to use them against America and its allies. Following the invasion, no such weapons were discovered.

A decade earlier, in the Persian Gulf War precipitated by Iraq's invasion of the emirate of Kuwait, the United States led a military coalition backed by the UNITED NATIONS that successfully restored Kuwait's independence in spring 1991. As part of the cease-fire agreement with Hussein following Operation Desert Storm, the victorious coalition imposed "no-fly zones" in the north and south of Iraq. The objective of this policy of containment was to prevent Hussein from engaging in military maneuvers and to curb his ability to threaten his neighbors or develop WMD.

The United States's successive invasions of Iraq, first in 1991 and again in 2003, accentuate a growing concern among American presidents as well as leaders of international organizations such as the United Nations, about the proliferation of nuclear, chemical, and biological weapons with the potential to devastate civilian populations, especially by Islamic fundamentalist regimes in the Middle East such as Iran, which have professed their unyielding animus towards the West and have taken steps to produce material that could be used for the production of nuclear weaponry.

Preventing the proliferation of nuclear weapons in the developing world has been a major concern of the United Nations for several decades and took on added importance after India and Pakistan, bitter rivals, each conducted their own tests of nuclear bombs in 1998. The United States was a signatory to the 1968 Nuclear Non-Proliferation Treaty (NNPT), which banned the transfer of nuclear weapons technology by the nuclear powers of that era—China, France, the Soviet Union, the United Kingdom, and the United States to developing nations. Nonetheless, the United States did not ratify the Comprehensive Test Ban Treaty of 1996, which sought to preclude all nations from conducting nuclear weapons testing. India and Pakistan also balked at signing the treaty, as did Israel. And North Korea withdrew from the NNPT in 2003 and now claims to have nuclear weapons. Neither bilateral nor multilateral

Premier Mikhail Gorbachev and President Ronald W. Reagan sign the Intermediate Nuclear Forces Treaty. *(Collection of the District of Columbia Public Library)*

talks with the Communist regime in Pyongyang have borne fruit in convincing the North Korean leadership to abandon its nuclear weapons program, and in summer 2006 the North Korean government threatened to test a long-range intercontinental ballistic missile capable of reaching U.S. territory (Alaska or Hawaii).

The Chemical Weapons Convention of 1993, signed by more than 170 countries including the United States, went into effect in 1997. The convention created an independent agency, the Organization for the Prohibition of Chemical Weapons, based in The Hague, Netherlands, to monitor stockpiles and compliance with the treaty. However, Syria and North Korea—two countries that are thought to have chemical weapons production facilities—are not signatories to the 1993 convention, which also does not cover biological weapons (e.g., viruses and other organisms, such as anthrax).

Without a doubt, the stockpiling of nuclear arms by the United States and the Soviet Union in the cold war era, which lasted from the end of World War II in 1945 to the fall of the Berlin Wall and the collapse of COMMUNISM in Eastern Europe in 1989, was of paramount importance to all U.S. presidents. Nuclear arms control dominated bilateral relations between the two superpowers for four decades. Both the United States and the Soviet Union began to amass nuclear weapons on their own soil and array such weapons in countries within their spheres of influence following World War II—for the United States the NORTH ATLANTIC TREATY ORGANIZATION (NATO) countries of Western Europe and for the Soviet Union the Warsaw Pact nations of Eastern Europe. The superpowers' mutual reliance on nuclear weaponry as their central means to deter an attack or invasion, as well as their mutual distrust of one another, led U.S. and Soviet leaders to wrestle with ways to ensure a nuclear holocaust could be avoided while simultaneously dissuading potential aggression.

Deterrence theory, based on the notion of mutually assured destruction (MAD), posited that the risk of nuclear war could be diminished if neither superpower had a strategic advantage in launching a first strike against the other. The certainty that a first strike would be met with massive retaliation and equivalent damage and civil casualties produced a stalemate, which, paradoxically, was thought to promote stability. To this end, advocates of détente—a relaxation of tensions between the superpowers—sought to negotiate treaties that would lessen the probability of a nuclear conflagration by reducing certain types of weapons, banning other types of destabilizing weapons altogether, and creating a framework of inspections in each nation to build confidence and create transparency so that the doctrine of MAD was secure.

President Dwight David Eisenhower (1953–61) led early efforts to avoid an arms race with the Soviet Union. Eisenhower, a fiscal conservative, believed that unfettered spending for nuclear weapons would bankrupt the U.S. economy. In 1953, Eisenhower announced his "New Look" policy, proposing "more bang for the buck"—investing in fewer intercontinental ballistic missiles (ICBMs) that could reach the Soviet Union but ones capable of massive retaliation should the Soviet Union decide to strike the United States. The New Look policy emphasized equipping ICBMs with nuclear warheads with substantially larger destructive potential (i.e., yields of more than 100 kilotons, about 10 times larger than the bombs dropped on Hiroshima and Nagasaki, Japan, during World War II). The policy was entirely consistent with the tenets of MAD. At the same time, Eisenhower sought to forge a relationship with Soviet leader Nikita Khrushchev, who succeeded Joseph Stalin in 1953. In 1959, Eisenhower launched a "Crusade for Peace," planned to visit the Soviet Union, and announced a summit in Paris, France, aimed at reaching an arms reduction treaty. Khrushchev walked out of the 1960 summit when Eisenhower first denied and then refused to apologize for spying on the Soviet Union through the use of high-altitude U-2 spy planes. That year the Soviets shot down a U-2 spy plane and captured its pilot, Francis Gary Powers, who was put on trial before being expelled

from the country. The failed summit was potentially one of the greatest missed opportunities for a substantial reduction in U.S. and Soviet arms.

Without a doubt, the Cuban missile crisis proved the most destabilizing moment for MAD during the cold war. The two superpowers seemingly stood on the brink of nuclear war in what is often referred to as the "missiles of October." In July 1962, the Soviet Union, in all likelihood as a response to U.S. deployment of medium-range nuclear weapons in Turkey, began a program to situate its own medium-range nuclear missiles on the island nation of Cuba, just 90 miles from the U.S. coast. In an extremely tense two weeks from October 16 until October 28, 1962, President John F. Kennedy and his advisers confirmed the presence of the Soviet missiles in Cuba and settled on a reserved though risky policy that included a naval blockade of the island. Soviet ships heading to Cuba eventually turned away. Through private channels, Kennedy eventually agreed to remove missiles from Turkey six months after the Soviets ended their missile plans for Cuba as part of a face-saving tactic for Soviet leader Nikita Khrushchev. Khrushchev did order the removal of the Soviet missiles from Cuba. In late November 1962, Kennedy ended the naval blockade of the island, and the crisis ended peacefully.

In the aftermath of the Cuban missile crisis, U.S.-Soviet arms control negotiations stalled, though some innovations, such as the establishment of a telephone "hotline" between U.S. presidents and Soviet leaders, accented the recognition by both sides of the need to avert future crises. By the early 1970s, President Richard Nixon negotiated the Anti-Ballistic Missile (ABM) Treaty with the Soviets and sought a reduction in nuclear weapons through the Strategic Arms Limitation Treaty (SALT I). The ABM Treaty ensured that neither country would construct an antimissile defense system that would potentially protect one or more cities or military sites, thereby giving a strategic advantage to one country. The ABM Treaty remained in effect for 29 years after its ratification by the U.S. Senate in 1972. President George W. Bush ultimately withdrew the United States from the ABM Treaty in late 2001, citing the need to establish a national antimissile defense system to thwart terrorists who might come into possession of nuclear weapons or other WMD.

President Ronald Reagan broke with his cold war predecessors and took a different approach to arms control issues with the Soviet Union, which he called an "evil empire." Like Kennedy in 1960, who declared a "missile gap" in terms of the United States's retaliatory capacity in the event of a first strike by the Soviet Union, Reagan campaigned for an increase in nuclear weapons stockpiles to counter a perceived Soviet advantage, particularly with respect to short-range weapons stationed against Western European countries in Warsaw Pact nations. In 1984, Reagan won German chancellor Helmut Kohl's approval to place short-range Pershing II missiles in West Germany to counter Soviet SS-20 missiles in Eastern Europe. Reagan also marshaled congressional approval for the development and deployment of MX-missiles (named after "missile experimental")—long-range intercontinental ballistic missiles (ICBMs) that could carry multiple nuclear weapons—and increased submarine-based Trident II missiles and cruise missiles.

Reagan's "reversal" of positions on the arms buildup began with Mikhail Gorbachev's accession to the post of general secretary of the Communist Party of the Soviet Union in 1985 following the death of Konstantin Chernenko. Reagan's advocacy of the Strategic Defense Initiative (SDI), a space-based anti–ballistic missile system, troubled Gorbachev immensely, as it threatened to undermine the ABM Treaty. Many analysts also believed that whether the program was achievable or not was irrelevant, as Gorbachev came to the conclusion that the Soviet Union was not able to compete technologically or economically with the program.

In the fall of 1986, Reagan and Gorbachev met for a summit in Reykjavík, Iceland. Reagan refused to concede on SDI, dubbed by the MEDIA (often pejoratively) as "Star Wars." While the summit was a short-term failure, it did pave the way for the Intermediate-Range Nuclear Forces (INF) Treaty of 1987. The INF Treaty eliminated Soviet SS-20 missiles in Eastern Europe, Pershing II missiles in NATO countries, and short-range cruise missiles. Reagan later negotiated the first Strategic Arms Reduction Treaty (START) with the Soviets in 1988, and President George H. W. Bush finalized a second round of START in 1991. Both agreements limited the number of nuclear weapons the United States and the Soviet Union could possess by phasing out stockpiles of medium- and long-range missiles.

By the time President George H. W. Bush took office in 1989, domestic upheaval in the Soviet Union was swelling. By the end of the year, with Gorbachev's announcement of the "Sinatra Doctrine"—that the Soviet Union would not intervene in the internal affairs of Warsaw Pact nations and would allow them to determine their own political and economic fates—arms control issues faded from public concern. The symbolic fall of the Berlin Wall signaled the death knell for communist regimes in Eastern Europe. Moreover, by 1991, Gorbachev's economic and political reforms—perestroika and glasnost, respectively—hastened the ultimate dissolution of the Soviet Union in late 1991.

Still, arms control remained a priority issue for the administration of George H. W. Bush. Bush brokered congressional support for an aid package for the Soviet Union to ensure that nuclear weapons under the control of the Russian military be decommissioned and not find their way to international black markets, where rogue states or terrorists might be able to purchase them. Nuclear weapons in former Soviet republics, such as Ukraine, became the purview of the newly independent countries of the Commonwealth of Independent States (CIS), with which the Bush and Clinton administrations sought bilateral dialogue.

See also DEFENSE POLICY; FOREIGN POLICY.

Further Reading
Levi, Michael A., and Michael E. O'Hanlon. *The Future of Arms Control.* Washington, D.C.: Brookings Institution Press, 2005; Maslen, Stuart. *Commentaries on Arms Control Treaties.* New York: Oxford University Press, 2005.

—Richard S. Conley

collective bargaining
Collective bargaining is the formal process of contract negotiations between an employer and representatives of its unionized employees. The goal of this process is to reach a long-term agreement regarding wages, hours, and other terms and conditions of employment. While bargaining, both parties are legally obligated to meet at reasonable times and negotiate in good faith.

However, neither party is obligated to agree to a proposal or required to make a concession that they feel is unfair. When the negotiations end in an agreement, the result is often referred to as a collective bargaining agreement. When the negotiations fail to end in an agreement, a strike or lock-out may be used by one party to gain negotiating leverage over the other. In rare cases, the employer may choose to go out of business rather than reach an agreement with its employees.

In order for collective bargaining to occur, two important criteria must be met. First, the employees must be organized under one labor union that represents them in the bargaining process. Second, there must be the need for a new collective bargaining agreement, because either the union was recently certified by the employees or the current collective bargaining agreement is about to expire.

The process of collective bargaining brings a private form of government to a unionized company. Like the government of the United States, a collective bargaining agreement results in a TWO-PARTY SYSTEM, with a legislative function, an executive function, and a judicial function. The legislative function occurs in the bargaining process itself. Just as legislators attempt to reach an agreement on new laws, the parties of collective bargaining try to reach an agreement on a new labor contract. Commonly negotiated terms involve wages, hours of work, working conditions and grievance procedures, and safety practices. The parties may also negotiate health care and retirement benefits, supplementary unemployment benefits, job characteristics, job bidding and transfer rights, and the seniority structure.

Once the parties come to an agreement, the executive function of the collective bargaining process comes to life. Both parties are legally required to execute the terms of agreement. For instance, if the agreement stipulates that new employees must be paid an hourly wage of $35.00 per hour, the employer must pay exactly $35.00 per hour, no more, no less. Similarly, if the agreement requires employees to work at least 40 hours per week, then the employees must work at least 40 hours per week.

If either party does not execute its side of the agreement properly, then the judicial function of the collective bargaining process is initiated. Both the agreement itself and the applicable laws specify what actions can be taken to resolve improper execution of the contract. These actions may include the use of grievance boards, mediators, or the state or federal courts.

There is evidence that labor unions began bargaining collectively in the United States prior to 1800. However, collective bargaining was not introduced into the American legal system until 1806, when the Philadelphia Mayor's Court found members of the Philadelphia Cordwainers guilty of conspiracy for striking. For more than 100 years, there were no formal laws that created legal boundaries of collective bargaining; there were only legal PRECEDENTs.

The first law to recognize the role of the union as a bargaining agent was the Clayton Antitrust Act of 1914. In it, Congress wrote that unions and their members shall not "be held or construed to be illegal combinations or conspiracies in restraint of trade under the antitrust laws." It was also intended to prohibit federal courts from issuing orders to stop legal strikes. Despite the intent of the Clayton Antitrust Act, the U.S. SUPREME COURT quickly negated much of the law by arguing that federal courts maintained the power to stop strikes that might eventually be deemed illegal.

The Norris-LaGuardia Act of 1932 made it much more difficult for federal courts to issue orders against a union and its leaders in order to stop strikes. It also clearly defined labor disputes and made it easier for workers to join unions and bargain collectively. It is important to note that the Norris-LaGuardia Act did not prevent STATE COURTS from issuing orders to stop strikes, only federal courts. However, many states did enact similar laws in the ensuing years that resolved this loophole.

The key piece of collective bargaining legislation was and still is the Wagner Act of 1935, better known as the National Labor Relations Act (NLRA). The centerpieces of the NLRA are the five key duties it places upon employers; employers must (1) not interfere with the employees' choice to form or run a union, (2) not interfere with the union's affairs, (3) not discriminate between union and nonunion employees, (4) not discriminate against employees who accuse the employer of unfair labor practices under the law, and (5) bargain collectively in good faith with the representatives chosen by the employees.

The NLRA provides a legal framework for employees to choose their bargaining representative via a vote by secret ballot. It also established the NATIONAL LABOR RELATIONS BOARD (NLRB), which is responsible for enforcing the NLRA and levying penalties as necessary. While the NLRA is a broad piece of legislation, it specifically excludes employees of the federal government from its protections.

The Labor Management Relations Act (LMRA), also known as the Taft-Hartley Act of 1947, established a broad set of rules for collective bargaining. While the NLRA has historically been described as prounion, the LMRA is often viewed as its proemployer successor. The latter upholds and reinforces many of the provisions of the former, but does so in a way that shifts some of the power in the bargaining process from the unions to the employers. For instance, the LMRA adds regulations that make it easier for employees to choose not to collectively bargain and to decertify their union as their bargaining representative. In addition, this act provides the right to free speech to employers, who were previously given only the opportunity to express their opinion about union elections as long as doing so was not perceived as threatening or otherwise improper. It also specifies that employees can only vote to certify a union once a year.

There are two important laws on the books that act as substitutes for the NLRA. The Federal Labor Relations Act (FLRA) of 1978 provides much more limited rights for employees of the federal government than those provided under the NLRA, with the exception of postal employees. As President Ronald Reagan once said, "Government cannot close down the assembly line. It has to provide without interruption the protective services which are government's reason for being." The FLRA provides federal government workers with the ability to bargain collectively but makes it illegal for them to strike.

The Railway Labor Act (RLA) of 1926 applies specifically to railway and airline employees. It aims to allow for collective bargaining in a way that minimizes the disruption of air and rail transportation. Collective bargaining agreements covered by the RLA never expire. Rather, the parties involved may attempt to renegotiate the contract after its ending date if they feel an inequity exists in the agreement.

The intention of this feature of the RLA is to ensure continuity of service. Without a fixed ending date, strikes and lockouts can be more easily avoided. Bargaining is completed under indirect governmental supervision, and the president of the United States has the authority to temporarily force striking or locked-out laborers back to work.

Most people are familiar with collective bargaining because of its impact on the professional sports industry. Fans of every major sport in the United States have suffered through a lock-out or a strike. Players in the National Football League struck in 1982 and then once again in 1987. Major league baseball fans were angered by a strike in 1981, then another in 1994, which caused the cancellation of the 1994 playoffs and World Series. The owners of the National Basketball Association locked out the players at the start of the 1998–99 season, resulting in a 50-game season rather than the usual 82 games. Finally, a lock-out at the start of the 1994–95 season in the National Hockey League was followed by another 10 years later, forcing the cancellation of the entire 2004–05 season.

Labor disputes in sports are far less damaging to society than those in other industries. For example, the strike called by the operators of New York City's buses and subways in 2005 was one of the most costly in history. The strike began on the morning of December 20, in the midst of the holiday shopping season, and lasted until the afternoon of December 22. By many estimates, the strike cost the city, its businesses, and its citizens in excess of $1 billion per day.

The true costs of a large strike are rarely just monetary. A 1981 walk-out by the air traffic controllers nearly shut down the nation's air transportation system and resulted in 11,359 controllers being fired. A strike by Boston's police officers on September 9, 1919, put Bostonians through a terrifying night of murders, looting, and riots before the National Guard restored order the next day. However, the number of major work stoppages per year, defined by the United States Bureau of Labor Statistics (BLS) as strikes or lock-outs involving more than 1,000 employees, has been falling since 1974. The BLS reported just 22 major work stoppages in 2005, compared to 424 in 1974.

Overall, union representation and the resulting number of employees covered by a collective bargaining agreement in the United States have been falling since the 1950s. The decline in union membership may be attributed to changing labor laws, the shifting of manufacturing jobs to countries with less expensive labor, an improvement in working conditions and wages, and a negative public perception of unions. In the airline industry, which has historically been the most organized sector of the economy, union representation has fallen from a peak near 50 percent down to about 39.5 percent. The automotive industry has also seen a significant decrease in the number of its employees covered by collective bargaining agreements, as foreign manufacturers enter the workplace and American companies outsource the manufacturing of their parts.

However, some industries have not seen a decrease in union representation of employees in recent years. Due to the changes in the American health-care system, union membership for nurses, lab technicians, medical scientists, and occupational and physical therapists are all increasing. Hotel and casino employees have experienced a steady rise in union membership as hotels and hotel chains grow larger and their demand for skilled labor grows as well. While collective bargaining is not as prominent in the American economy as it once was, it is still a fixture of the employment landscape that will be around for years to come.

See also DEPARTMENT OF LABOR; LABOR POLICY.

Further Reading

Clark, Paul F., John T. Delaney, and Ann C. Frost. *Collective Bargaining in the Private Sector.* Champaign, Ill. Industrial Relations Research Association, 2002; Herman, E. Edward. *Collective Bargaining and Labor Relations.* Upper Saddle River, N.J.: Prentice Hall, 1997; Hilgert, Raymond L., and David Dilts. *Cases in Collective Bargaining and Labor Relations.* New York: McGraw-Hill/Irwin, 2002.

—David Offenberg

Consumer Price Index

The Consumer Price Index (CPI) is a measure of the average change in the prices paid over time by urban households for a market basket of goods and services. Published monthly by the Bureau of Labor Statistics (BLS), the Consumer Price Index is calculated for two groups: households of clerical workers and wage earners (CPI-W) and for all urban consumers (CPI-U), which includes all employees in the CPI-W along with professionals, managers, technical workers, the self-employed, and the unemployed. These groups account for 32 percent and 87 percent of the population, respectively. The index is published using unadjusted and seasonally adjusted data, whereby seasonal indexes control for changes that occur at the same time and magnitude every year, such as holidays and climate patterns. In 2002, the Bureau of Labor Statistics introduced a new revisable index, the chained Consumer Price Index for all consumers (C-CPI-U), which is also published monthly but allows for two subsequent rounds of revision annually before being finalized.

The Consumer Price Index has three major uses: as an economic indicator, as a deflator of other economic series, and as a means of adjusting dollar values. As the most widely used measure of inflation, the Consumer Price Index both influences the formulation and tests the effectiveness of government economic policy, including monetary policy. As a deflator, the Consumer Price Index is used to translate retail sales, hourly and weekly earnings, and components of national income accounts into inflation-free dollars. Finally, and possibly most importantly to U.S. citizens, the Consumer Price Index functions as the basis of indexation arrangements for consumers' income payments, levels of government assistance, and automatic cost-of-living adjustments for millions of employees. According to the U.S. DEPARTMENT OF LABOR, changes in the Consumer Price Index affect the incomes of 80 million workers, 48 million SOCIAL SECURITY beneficiaries, 20 million food stamp recipients, and 4 million civil service retirees and survivors. The Consumer Price Index also influences the choice of income tax brackets, the DEPARTMENT OF THE TREASURY's inflation-indexed government debt and inflation-protected bonds, and many private labor contracts as well.

Calculation of the Consumer Price Index begins with the selection of the market basket of consumer goods and services, including food, housing, clothing, transportation fees, health and dental care, pharmaceuticals, and other items generally purchased for day-to-day living. One quarter of the market basket is updated each year, producing a full rotation of all items every four years. The prices of these goods and services are collected in 87 geographic areas across the nation, including the country's largest 31 metropolitan cities. Taxes are included in the index, as they are additional expenses incurred by consumers.

Most prices are obtained by trained Bureau of Labor Statistics representatives who make telephone calls or personal visits to approximately 50,000 housing units and 23,000 retail establishments. Retail outlets may include catalog vendors or Internet stores in addition to traditional brick-and-mortar businesses. Prices of fuel and a few select items are collected monthly in all locations, while prices for the rest of the sample goods and services are collected every month in only the three largest metropolitan cities and every other month in the remaining areas.

Each component of the Consumer Price Index market basket is assigned a weight to reflect its importance in consumer spending patterns. These expenditure weights, along with the choice of market basket items, are formed based on information assembled by the Consumer Expenditure Survey, based on a representative sample of households. The weights are updated every two years. Local data are aggregated to form a nationwide average, but separate indexes are also published by region, by population size, and for 27 local areas.

The index measures changes in price relative to a specified reference date, defining the Consumer Price Index to be equal to 100 in a reference base period. Currently, the reference base period is 1982–84. For example, the CPI-U in May 2006 was 202.5, meaning that prices had increased 102.5 percent since the reference base period. The Consumer Price Index is also used to determine the inflation rate, or the change in the price level from one year to the next. To calculate the inflation rate, the prior year's index is subtracted from the current year's index, then divided by the prior year's index, and this number is multiplied by 100 to generate a percentage. For example, the CPI-U in May 2005 was 194.4. Using this information and the May 2006 index, the inflation rate for this period can be calculated as $(202.5 - 194.4) \div 194.4 \times 100 = 4.17$ percent.

The price level has increased every year since 1975, though the rate of increase has changed from being rapid during the early 1980s to slower during the 1990s. Between 1975 and 2005, the inflation rate averaged 5 percent a year, though it occasionally exceeded 10 percent and once was as low as 1 percent. Recently, increases in the cost of oil have driven up transportation costs, with energy prices in May 2006 up 23.6 percent over one year prior. This, combined with a reported 1.9 percent increase in the price of food and 2.4 percent increase in all other items, is responsible for the 4.17 percent inflation rate.

Given that the Consumer Price Index has many practical uses with significant implications, measurement accuracy is of extreme importance. If the index is biased or provides a mismeasured rate of inflation, millions of workers and welfare recipients will be disproportionately compensated in cost-of-living adjustments. According to the Boskin Commission assigned to examine potential bias in the Consumer Price Index, if the index reported a change in the cost of living just 1 percentage point over the true value from 1997 to 2006, it would cost the government approximately $135 billion in deficit spending in 2006. Besides this cost of overcompensation, the government also uses the Consumer Price Index to maintain price stability. Costly efforts to avoid non-existent increases in inflation, along with the cost of unanticipated inflation, make a bias in the Consumer Price Index in either direction cause for concern.

Given the importance of accuracy in measuring inflation, areas of potential bias in the Consumer Price Index have been examined by numerous economic experts. The consensus is that the Consumer Price Index tends to overstate inflation, although the size of the bias has been estimated at between 0.3 and 1.6 percent. Averaged across all studies, the Consumer Price Index probably overvalues inflation by around 1 percent.

There are five main sources of bias in the Consumer Price Index: substitution, quality change, new item, new outlet, and weighting bias. Substitution bias is when the index overstates changes in the cost of living by ignoring substitutions that consumers make in response to a change in relative prices. For example, if the price of chicken rises faster than the price of beef, consumers tend to buy more beef and less chicken. This bias can occur both across items (substituting beef for chicken) and within items (substituting generics for brand-name items) and may account for roughly one-third of the upward bias in the Consumer Price Index. The Bureau of Labor Statistics has made several changes in an attempt to correct the source of its bias, such as the introduction of the Chained CPI in 2002 and using an aggregation formula that now assumes a certain amount of substitution since 1999.

The next source of bias in the Consumer Price Index is the effect of quality changes. New models of cars and televisions generally cost more than the versions they replace, although this improvement in quality is not measured by the index. Therefore, a price rise that is, in fact, a payment for improved quality might be misinterpreted as inflation. In an attempt to correct this bias, the Bureau of Labor Statistics has used econometric models to estimate the value of different item characteristics in the market. This helps to clarify the difference between an increase in price and an increase in quality and is used for items like computers, televisions, refrigerators, DVD players, and college textbooks.

The impact of new goods falls along the same lines, as it is challenging to ascertain the effect of the introduction of new items on welfare. The Bureau of Labor Statistics often faces difficulty in classifying new goods into preexisting categories, creating occasional long lags between their first appearance in the market and inclusion in the market basket. For example, the Bureau of Labor Statistics was criticized for long delays in adding cell phones and home computers to the index. The problem arises from the uncertainty of whether a newly introduced good will become a typical consumer expenditure or never amount to much, be it a new form of video recorder or a "ropeless" jump rope. The Bureau of Labor Statistics faces a trade-off between accepting a delay in the inclusion of essential new goods and incorporating new goods into the index that fail in the marketplace and must later be removed.

The next source of bias is the somewhat recent proliferation of discount outlets. As prices rise, consumers tend to shop at discount stores more frequently. Currently, when new outlets enter the Consumer Price Index sample, any difference in price between new and old is contributed to a difference in quality, which may not always be the case. The growth of discount chains itself suggests an outlet substitution, or a shift in consumer buying patterns. Thus, the Consumer Price Index may either overstate inflation by not properly accounting for the same-quality but less-costly discount alternatives, or understate inflation by dismissing the decrease in price as driven entirely by quality.

Finally, the method in which weights are assigned to goods may cause bias in the Consumer Price Index. The expenditure weights are derived from a Bureau of Labor Statistics consumer survey composed of an interview and personal diary. The interview and diary are printed on large paper and are 143 and 67 pages long, respectively. With hundreds of questions to answer, survey respondents may not provide truthful and precise information. Respondents may purposely misreport purchases to avoid subsequent questions, have inaccurate recall, and deliberately exclude unattractive purchases such as alcohol. The expenditure weights play a vital role in the calculation of the Consumer Price Index and must be as close to the true values as is feasible in order to properly estimate changes in the price level. One suggestion for improvement is the use of scanner data, which could provide information about price and quantities at the time of purchase. Scanner data would provide its own set of problems, though, as bar codes change frequently, the cost to purchase data from private firms may be prohibitive, and many goods and services do not have bar codes. Simplifying the questionnaire may also improve the quality of information, although at the cost of losing data. The Bureau of Labor Statistics is continuing to investigate this issue.

Although the Consumer Price Index is not currently a perfect measure of inflation, which may be an impossible feat, it nevertheless provides a reasonable estimate for price level changes and affects millions of people. The Bureau of Labor Statistics is dedicated to resolving sources of bias in the index and will continue to improve the accuracy of the Consumer Price Index.

See also FISCAL POLICY.

Further Reading

Abraham, Katharine. "Toward a Cost-of-Living Index: Progress and Prospects." "*Journal of Economic Perspectives* 17, no. 1 (Winter 2003); 45–58; Boskin,

M. J., E. R. Dulberger, R. J. Gordon, Z. Griliches, and D. W. Jorgenson. *Toward a More Accurate Measurement of the Cost of Living.* Final report to the U.S. Senate Finance Committee from the Advisory Commission to Study the Consumer Price Index. Washington, D.C.: U.S. Government Printing Office, 1996; Lebow, David, and Jeremy. Rudd "Measurement Error in the Consumer Price Index: Where Do We Stand?" *Journal of Economic Literature* 41, no. 1 (March 2003): 159–201; United States Department of Labor, Bureau of Labor Statistics Web site. Available online. URL: http://www.bls.gov/cpi/home.htm.

—Jennifer Pate Offenberg

defense policy

Defense policy refers to decisions and actions that seek to protect the interests of the United States. While *homeland defense,* or the protection of U.S. territory and borders, represents the most basic meaning of defense policy, the term also encompasses international actions that serve to further U.S. security. American defense policy has evolved gradually in the past 200 years, often proportionately to the expansion of the United States's role in the world that originated in the late 19th century. During the cold war, the United States institutionalized the development of defense policy by creating a formal executive bureaucracy to assist the president in making defense decisions. In the aftermath of the terrorist attacks of September 11, 2001, the United States made significant changes in its defense policy infrastructure to adapt to the needs of the 21st century.

In the century after its inception, U.S. defense policy concentrated primarily on establishing the international legitimacy of the new nation and protecting its borders, which expanded steadily throughout the contiguous United States. In 1803, Thomas Jefferson nearly doubled the territory of the United States through the Louisiana Purchase, which ensured control of the Mississippi River and its trade routes. The War of 1812 narrowly but definitively established the independence of the new nation from Great Britain. The Monroe Doctrine of 1823 expanded U.S. defense policy from the country to the hemisphere with its famous declaration that "We should consider any attempt on [the Europeans'] part to extend their system to any portion of this hemisphere as danger-

ous to our peace and safety." President James K. Polk expanded U.S. borders westward in the Mexican-American War of 1846–48 through the annexation of the territory that would become California and New Mexico. Texas and Oregon also became part of the United States in the 1840s. The expansion of the United States through the continent in this period would come to be known as Manifest Destiny.

By the end of the 19th century, the growing economy in the United States spurred a greater interest in international affairs, in part to find new markets for trade but also for political reasons. As Frederick Jackson Turner wrote, "at the end of a hundred years of life under the Constitution, the frontier has gone, and with its going has closed the first period of American history." Manifest Destiny now would extend beyond the Western Hemisphere, making the United States a world power and increasing its defense commitments. In the Spanish-American War of 1898, the United States gained control of Cuba and Puerto Rico in the Caribbean and also Guam and the Philippines in the Pacific. Yet the United States remained ambivalent over its responsibilities for collective defense vis-à-vis its allies. It did not enter World War I until 1917, three years after the global conflict began, and then only because German submarine warfare refused to recognize the rights of neutral countries such as the United States. Although American defense interests had grown, defense was still defined largely in national terms.

The first U.S. effort to incorporate collective security into defense policy failed miserably. After World War I, President Woodrow Wilson launched a grassroots campaign to build support for the Treaty of Versailles, but the treaty failed to garner a two-thirds vote in the SENATE, falling short by seven votes. Consequently, the United States did not participate in the League of Nations. For the next decade, U.S. defense policy focused primarily on protecting economic opportunities and limiting military spending. The United States hosted an international conference on naval disarmament in 1921–22, which limited the naval power of the United States, Great Britain, Japan, France, and Italy. As Adolf Hitler rose to power in Germany in the 1930s, the United States passed neutrality laws four times to ensure that it would not participate in the burgeoning conflict. After World War II began, the United States provided some aid to its allies through "cash and carry" and Lend Lease programs, but its defense policy remained narrowly focused. Only after Japan attacked Pearl Harbor on December 7, 1941, did fighting in World War II become part of American defense policy.

The Allied victory renewed questions about American global responsibilities in defense policy. While defense spending dropped sharply following World War II, U.S. security interests had expanded considerably with the origins of the cold war. The Truman Doctrine and Marshall Plan illustrated U.S. commitment to defending itself and its allies from the encroachment of COMMUNISM. To assist the president in making defense policy, Congress passed the National Security Act of 1947, which created the NATIONAL SECURITY COUNCIL, the DEPARTMENT OF DEFENSE (previously the Department of War), and the CENTRAL INTELLIGENCE AGENCY, and formally authorized the positions of the JOINT CHIEFS OF STAFF. The United States institutionalized the development of defense policy to ensure that its wide-ranging interests in the cold war would be pursued fully and systematically.

U.S. defense policy during the cold war can be defined broadly as containment of communism, though important variations emerged in different administrations. John Lewis Gaddis writes that U.S. defense policy in the cold war shifted regularly between "symmetrical" strategies, which aimed to meet any challenge posed by the Soviets regardless of cost, and "asymmetrical" strategies, which focused on selective interests and sought to control costs. The Truman administration's initial containment policy focused primarily on political and economic interests, although it did emphasize collective security with the creation of the NORTH ATLANTIC TREATY ORGANIZATION (NATO). After the Korean War began, Truman sharply increased defense spending, and U.S. interests in the cold war were more broadly defined. President Dwight D. Eisenhower reined in defense spending with his "New Look" policy, while Presidents John F. Kennedy and Lyndon B. Johnson pursued a policy of "Flexible Response" that again expanded U.S. interests and costs.

In the administration of President Richard Nixon, the United States made significant advances in reducing threats to its defense by renewing ties with both China and the Soviet Union. President Jimmy Carter tried to continue détente, but his efforts halted after the Soviet invasion of Afghanistan in 1979. President Ronald Reagan initially viewed the Soviet Union suspiciously, calling it an "evil empire" and increasing defense spending so the United States would be prepared to meet any threat posed by the communist superpower. In particular, Reagan initiated the Strategic Defense Initiative (SDI), popularly known as the "Star Wars" plan, which aimed to create a defense shield to protect the United States from attack. While Reagan steadfastly maintained his dedication to SDI, in his second term he also began to pursue ARMS CONTROL negotiations with the new Soviet leader Mikhail Gorbachev, who came to power in 1985. The two leaders eventually participated in four summit meetings and signed the Intermediate Nuclear Forces Treaty in 1987. The United States also restructured its defense policy apparatus with the Goldwater-Nichols Act of 1986, which gave more power to the chairman of the Joint Chiefs of Staff as well as to regional military commanders.

The end of the cold war prompted a reassessment of U.S. defense policy in the 1990s. The "new world order," as President George H. W. Bush famously called it, permitted nations to work together in ways not possible during the cold war. When Iraq invaded Kuwait in the summer of 1990, the United States and the Soviet Union stood together in opposing the aggression. Bush successfully negotiated a UNITED NATIONS resolution supporting the use of force against Iraq, and Congress ultimately passed a joint resolution supporting the use of force just days before the Gulf War began. Thus, the United States developed both internal and allied coalitions that viewed Saddam Hussein's actions as threats to the international order and their own defense interests.

Defense policy took a secondary role in the administration of President Bill Clinton because the public and the president were concerned foremost about the economy. Without immediate threats to U.S. security, U.S. defense policy lacked clear direction. Humanitarian interventions in Somalia and Haiti and NATO interventions in Bosnia and Kosovo served interests other than American defense and prompted many debates about U.S defense needs in the post–cold war era. The Clinton administration tried to replace the containment strategy of the cold war with a strategy of "democratic enlargement," which focused on enacting economic reform in other nations through free markets as a means of promoting DEMOCRACY. Although the phrase did not serve to replace "containment," it did illustrate how defense policy in the 1990s focused more on common economic interests with other nations than on traditional security concerns.

When George W. Bush assumed the presidency in 2001, he made some important changes in defense policy, most notably by announcing that the United States would withdraw from the 1972 Anti-Ballistic Missile (ABM) Treaty so it could pursue national missile defense freely. Bush also declared that the United States would work to contain proliferation of nuclear weapons and other weapons of mass destruction. At the same time, Bush promised to limit U.S. defense commitments, especially in the area of nation building. However, the terrorist attacks of September 11, 2001, recast the focus of defense policy to homeland security, an issue that had not commanded public attention since the cold war. Just as defense policy in the 19th century referred to protection of U.S. borders, so, too, does the term today signify foremost protection of U.S. territory. While global concerns in pursuing the continuing campaign against terrorism remain part of American defense policy, the need for homeland defense is sharply etched into the public conscience and will remain so for the foreseeable future. For this reason, the DEPARTMENT OF HOMELAND SECURITY was created in 2002, merging 22 previously independent government agencies, including the Coast Guard, Secret Service, and Customs and Border Protection. Recommendations from the commission that investigated the September 11, 2001, attacks also spurred significant changes in U.S. intelligence gathering, most notably by the creation of a Director of National Intelligence to centralize information gathering among 16 independent intelligence agencies.

The National Security Strategy (NSS) of 2002 clearly outlined the multipronged strategy of the United States to prevail in the war on terror. Most controversially, the 2002 NSS left open the possibility that the United States might respond preemptively to anticipated attacks by an enemy, "even if uncertainty remains as to the time and place of the enemy's attack." Although the United States built an international coalition to implement this strategy in waging war against Iraq in 2003, many states, including traditional U.S. allies as well as the United Nations, opposed the war. Preemption remains a component of U.S. national security strategy, though its application again in the near future is uncertain.

As presidents develop American defense policy in the coming years, they will have to balance the interests of the United States with the concerns of U.S. allies. In particular, questions about U.S. intervention, especially preemptive or preventive action, will require both domestic and international justification. While the definition of defense policy remains the same as it was in the early days of the REPUBLIC, the audience that witnesses, and participates in, the practice of American defense is much larger.

See also FOREIGN POLICY.

Further Reading

Gaddis, John Lewis. *Strategies of Containment: A Critical Appraisal of Postwar American National Security Policy*. Rev. ed. New York: Oxford University Press, 2005; LaFeber, Walter. *The American Age: United States Foreign Policy at Home and Abroad*. 2nd ed. New York: W.W. Norton, 1994; *The National Security Strategy of the United States*; September 2002. Available online. URL: http://www.whitehouse.gov/nsc/nss.pdf. Accessed July 1, 2006; *The 9/11 Commission Report: Final Report of the National Commission on Terrorist Attacks upon the United States*. New York: W.W. Norton, 2004; Schulzinger, Robert D. *U.S. Diplomacy Since 1900*. 5th ed. New York: Oxford University Press, 2001.

—Meena Bose

diplomatic policy

Diplomacy is communication between international actors that seeks to resolve conflicts through negotiation rather than war. Occasionally, this term refers to the management of international relations in general. Diplomatic policy, however, is the means by which states pursue their national interests. While some see diplomacy as attempting to achieve stability, peace, order, justice, or the distribution of wealth, many others see it as a means to instill one's IDEOLOGY or viewpoint or to cover for indiscretions or unsavory positions. Others have seen it simply as a precursor to more forceful action.

Diplomatic policy since the 17th century has generally been practiced by an elite diplomatic corps set apart from others in society. These elite spoke French and practiced the standard international relations concept of the balance of power.

After World War I (1914–18), President Woodrow Wilson sought to create a more open diplomatic system that would not lead states into war. Large state bureaucracies increasingly relied on a meritocracy approach instead of the previous reliance on social class and old school ties. These social ties, however, remained through informal networks in government.

Despite its origins in carrying reports back and forth and engaging in negotiation, diplomatic policy has come to employ persuasion and force, promises and threats, as well as what modern-day practitioners refer to as signaling. It is worth examining a few of these tools and tactics diplomacy has at its disposal as well as specific cases in U.S. diplomatic politics.

Three broad groupings of diplomatic forms include coercion, inducements, and co-option. More generally, these are frequently referred to as sticks, carrots, and soft power. Coercion, or threat of using "sticks" in international relations, involves threatening the use of hard power. Power, or the ability to get another country to do what it otherwise would not have done, is classified as hard power when military effort is involved. This is directly punishing another country for its behavior. This can be through the use of military force of differing levels or economic sanctions.

Military force runs the gamut from signaling dissatisfaction with another country by publicly displaying force, such as military maneuvers or exercises, to small air strikes and raids, to large invasions and occupations. While total war is risky and rare in international relations, lower-level threats of military power are common in diplomatic negotiation. Military threats are frequently left in the background as unspoken signals as to what is coming if countries do not agree. While condemning the American war in Iraq in 2003, French president Jacques Chirac did acknowledge that the threat of force was a necessary aspect of U.S. diplomacy.

Economic sanctions have proven to be more problematic than military force. While this may be because of their ineffectiveness, it may also be because of their misapplication. Economic sanctions, such as embargoes, blockades, or fines or levies against another country, may lack the directed threat of military power. While military force can destroy the opposing armed forces and force pain and suffering on a population, armed forces, and leadership, economic sanctions may find it more difficult to coerce all groups in a society. Economic sanctions may by necessity need to be more focused on different groups in a society in order to avoid punishing innocent civilians.

In addition, economic sanctions are difficult to maintain, especially in a multinational setting. Since there is economic profit to be made through trade and investment as well as issues of national interest at stake, countries will frequently attempt to skirt the sanctions or become exempt from their effects. During the late 1990s, when the United States and the United Kingdom sought the imposition of economic sanctions on Iraq to force the destruction of Iraq's weapons of mass destruction program, Jordan and Turkey regularly received exemptions from the UNITED NATIONS Oil for Food program. Arguing that it was a matter of vital national security, Jordan and Turkey were allowed to gain access to Iraqi oil shipments and were generally exempted from international sanctions.

Lastly, economic sanctions may be imposed with unrealistic expectations and be ill advised in many crisis situations. Economic sanctions might prevent another country from developing certain military capabilities, but they are unlikely to force a government to resign from power. Because of their misapplication, economic sanctions may be doomed to fail before they begin. It is up to the diplomat to convince other countries to cooperate with economic sanctions.

A second type of diplomatic policy involves offering inducements. Frequently referred to as "carrots," these can include trade and investment incentives as well as official foreign aid in order to persuade others to change policy positions. While this is frequently seen as an alternative to the use of military force, it can be used in conjunction with threats of military force. The "Big Three" EUROPEAN UNION countries—France, Germany, and the United Kingdom—offered Iran economic inducements to stop its uranium enrichment program, while U.S. President George W. Bush did the same in 2005. President Bush's offer of inducements—selling airplane parts and aiding Iran in its bid to join the WORLD TRADE ORGANIZATION—was coupled with the threat of censuring Iran in the UN Security Council, which entailed the possibility of economic sanctions.

The United States used inducements in the form of economic aid during the cold war to fight the spread of COMMUNISM. While two main countries, Israel and Egypt, have long maintained their position as the largest targets of U.S. foreign aid, other countries receive more or less aid based on U.S. national interests. Currently, U.S. aid has focused on countries engaged in the "Long War" or the "War on Terror." Afghanistan, Pakistan, Sudan, and Indonesia have therefore received greater attention than they previously did. Since President Bush's announcement in his 2003 State of the Union speech of a five-year, $15-billion initiative to combat AIDS, U.S. aid has flown to countries at the heart of the AIDS crisis, such as Haiti and South Africa. Previous targets for U.S. aid have been central and eastern European countries following the end of the cold war, as well as the Balkan region during the disintegration of Yugoslavia in the 1990s. Currently, the largest recipient of U.S. foreign aid is Iraq, as the United States seeks to rebuild the country after the 2003 Iraq war.

Foreign aid takes many forms, but common varieties include military aid, bilateral economic assistance, economic aid to support political and military objectives, multilateral aid, and humanitarian assistance. Bilateral development aid occupies the largest share of U.S. assistance programs and is focused on long-term sustainable progress. The lead agency involved is the UNITED STATES AGENCY FOR INTERNATIONAL DEVELOPMENT (USAID). Money frequently goes to projects involved in economic reform, DEMOCRACY promotion, environmental protection, and human health. AIDS/HIV projects also fall under this area, as does the Peace Corps.

The second-largest area of U.S. aid is military aid. Military aid peaked in 1984 and has declined since then as a percentage of the overall aid budget. Military aid can take the form of grants or loans to foreign powers to procure U.S. military hardware, training given to foreign military officers and personnel, and aid for peacekeeping operations around the world.

The third-largest area of U.S. aid is economic aid that is used in support of U.S. political and security objectives. This includes money to support Middle East peace proposals as well as those focused specifically on the war on terror. Aid has recently increased in areas including narcotics, crime, and weapons proliferation. Congressional actions such as the Nunn-Lugar Amendment have helped pay for the removal and destruction of nuclear weapons in the former Soviet Union. In addition, biological and chemical weapons are targeted for dismantling, and antiproliferation efforts have increased.

The fourth area of U.S. aid is humanitarian aid, constituting roughly 12 percent of the U.S. aid budget. This aid money is used to alleviate short-term or immediate humanitarian crises. A growing area here is food aid, carried out under the auspices of the Food for Peace program. In addition, U.S. programs send U.S. volunteers out to provide technical advice and train others in modern farming techniques.

Lastly, the United States contributes money to multilateral assistance programs. Aid is sent to the United Nations, including the United Nations Children's Fund (UNICEF) and the United Nations Development Programme (UNDP), as well as multilateral development banks such as the WORLD BANK.

A third type of diplomatic policy is to attract or co-opt other countries. Frequently referred to as soft power, this policy seeks to make other countries want what you want. Countries promote their values, culture, or political institutions in the hopes that others will emulate them. Instead of coercing countries through force, soft power attracts countries by example. Open political systems, where citizens are free to say and do what they will, are held up as examples others should copy in their own societies. Shared values, such as adherence to law, open trading systems, and respect for human rights, are also promoted as the high point of state evolution.

In order to promote soft power, countries often rely on public diplomacy. Public diplomacy is the act of promoting a country's interests, culture, and institutions by influencing foreign populations. In essence, it is a public relations campaign carried out by a country to attract like-minded countries and sway those with differing opinions. Tools used to this end include international broadcasting, such as through the Voice of America radio network, education, sports, and cultural exchanges, as well as international information programs that some have called "PROPAGANDA activities."

President Woodrow Wilson created the Committee on Public Information during World War I in order to disseminate information overseas. During World War II, President Franklin D. Roosevelt established the Foreign Information Service to conduct foreign intelligence and disseminate propaganda. In 1942, the Voice of America program was created and first broadcast in Europe under the control of the Office of War Information.

The cold war saw the mobilization of American resources with the goal of swaying other countries against communism while reassuring American allies. Granted congressional authority under the U.S. Information and Educational Exchange Act of 1948, international broadcasts accelerated to counter the Soviet information campaign in Europe. The CIA established the Radio Free Europe and Radio Liberty programs in 1950 and beamed pro-Western information into Eastern Europe and the Soviet Union.

While reorganization has cut some programs and solidified control under the State Department, Congress and others looked to increase the programs after the terrorist attacks of September 11, 2001. The war on terror pointed to the need for an information campaign. The 1990s saw a decrease in the overall level of funding for public diplomacy, while at the same time international favorable ratings of the United States were high. Since 9/11 and the wars in Afghanistan and Iraq, there has been a downturn in international opinion of the United States. Recognizing the need for a revamped international information campaign, the George W. Bush administration increased funding to the State Department, and the public diplomacy budget has seen a steady increase since 2001.

Recent information programs geared toward the Middle East include an Arabic language magazine and a Persian Web site. Cultural exchanges have been carried out with the Iraqi National Symphony as well as Arab women with activist and political backgrounds from 15 countries who traveled to the United States in 2002. In addition, the United States operates an Arabic-language television station, Al-

Hurra, and maintains radio stations in both Arabic and Persian.

Along with an increase in spending, the Bush administration attempted to address perceived shortfalls in public diplomacy with high-profile moves. Secretary of State Colin Powell made an appearance on Music Television (MTV) in February 2002, answering questions from young people from around the world. MTV reached 375 million households in 63 countries at the time. A second act was the appointment of Karen Hughes to the position of undersecretary for public diplomacy and public affairs at the State Department in July 2005. Hughes, counselor to President Bush for his first 18 months in the White House, as well as a communications consultant to the president during the 2004 election campaign, has been a long-time adviser and confidante to President Bush. Her appointment to this position was seen as a recognition by the president of the importance of combating a declining U.S. image abroad.

A frequent criticism of public diplomacy and soft power in general is whether it works and how much is needed to counter negative images. While Congress and former public diplomacy officials maintain that academic exchanges, increased through the use of scholarships, and overseas academic programs such as sponsored lectures and the building of libraries are necessary, others have pointed to the perceived lack of success. While Egypt receives one of the largest shares of U.S. aid, the Egyptian population overall has a negative view of Americans. Clearly, more needs to be done to change this perception.

Diplomatic policy does not function in a vacuum, and the different aspects of diplomatic policy, whether hard or soft power, cannot exist on their own. Striking the proper balance between inducements, coercion, and attraction is a difficult task. As many politicians have recognized, carrots without sticks may be taken advantage of, while sticks without the promise of rewards may also signal a dead-end policy.

Further Reading

Barston, Ronald P. *Modern Diplomacy*. London: Longman, 1997; Hamilton, Keith, and Richard Langhorne. *The Practice of Diplomacy*. New York: Routledge, 1994; Nye, Joseph. *The Paradox of American*

Power. New York: Oxford University Press, 2002; United States Under Secretary for Public Diplomacy and Public Affairs. Available online. URL: http://www.state.gov/r/. Accessed June 25, 2006.

—Peter Thompson

disability policy

Disability policy in the United States has followed changes in thinking about people with disabilities (hereafter PWDs). Although the stages overlap and are not distinct, a medical focus was followed by a focus on rehabilitation followed by a CIVIL RIGHTS focus. Policy used to be focused on compensation for an impairment's effects; it is now directed toward full social participation by PWDs. The changing focus affected policy debates in employment, transportation, housing, education, civil rights, health care, and other areas. Some policy makers increased emphasis on PWDs in the policy process, not just as passive recipients of public policies. Policy challenges remain, as is evident in deliberations over disaster preparedness, affordability and universal design of buildings, acute and long-term care, assistive technology, and access to recreation.

Disability is defined differently by policy makers with different purposes. Education laws and policies usually set forth a list of conditions. Civil rights laws such as the Americans with Disabilities Act (ADA) refer to "substantial limitation of a major life activity." These words were carried over from amendments to the Rehabilitation Act defining a "handicapped individual." Beyond obvious examples like inability to walk or speak, policy makers debated the meaning and application of the definitional phrase. The UNITED STATES SUPREME COURT drew a narrow interpretation, but sponsors of the ADA such as Representative Steny Hoyer (D-MD) insisted that the Supreme Court's interpretation was "not what we intended." Analysts with a social conception of disability insisted that policy must include restoration of the ADA and include citizens with a variety of physical, mental, cognitive, and sensory conditions. Policy would need to counter "disablement," by which social and economic barriers were imposed on PWDs.

Policy making was greatly affected by adoption of the Rehabilitation Act in 1973, the Individuals with Disabilities Education Act in 1975 (initially the Education of all Handicapped Act) and the Americans with Disabilities Act in 1990. Other important federal legislation included the Developmental Disabilities Act in 1963, and as recently amended and reauthorized in 2000, the Developmental Disabilities Assistance and Bill of Rights Act; the Architectural Barriers Act of 1968; the Developmental Disabilities Services and Facilities Construction Act of 1970; Project Head Start (changes in 1974 required 10 percent of participants to be disabled children); the Air Carrier Access Act of 1986; the Technology-Related Assistance Act of 1988; and the Workforce Investment Act of 1998. State and local policy making in education, employment, transportation, and medical care also affects PWDs, and most federal acts rely on state and local policy makers for their implementation.

The Rehabilitation Act's role has increased over time. Section 504 of the act has been used to advance nondiscrimination and access to government offices and to entities such as schools that receive government funding. Implementation of the Rehabilitation Act was accelerated by sit-ins at federal office buildings, first in San Francisco and later in Washington, D.C., in 1977. A more recent (1998) significant addition to the act was section 508 promoting access to electronic and information technology (e.g., requiring federal Web sites to be accessible to blind users of screen readers unless it would be an "undue burden" to do so).

The ADA has reflected the strengths and weaknesses of federal disability policy. Most policy-making debate has involved application of the first three of the ADA's five titles. Title I deals with employment and provides for nondiscrimination. Under title I, some disabled people are entitled to provision of auxiliary aids (such as adaptive telephones, listening devices, or furniture) from employers. Title II refers to nondiscrimination in services provided by state and local governments. It includes provisions promoting access to transportation. In the 1999 U.S. Supreme Court decision *Olmstead v. LC and EW,* the Court held that title II's nondiscrimination guarantee extended to the right of institutionalized individuals to live in a less restrictive community environment. Title III refers to "public accommodations" such as stadiums and shopping malls. They, too, are obligated to ensure nondiscriminatory access to services. The act was adopted on July 26, 1990, and its standards under titles II and III were applicable from January 26, 1992. It included qualifiers relating to such factors as "fundamental alteration," "undue hardship," historic buildings, and pre-ADA construction. These qualifiers have often been misinterpreted as exemptions; instead, they call for application of different standards.

Increasingly, policy recognizes many PWDs' desire to live and work with a disability. This is a change from the Revolutionary War, in which an "Invalid Corps" retained soldiers who did not prefer immediate discharge and a pension, and even from the SOCIAL SECURITY Act. Under that act, many PWDs under 65 receive payments either under the Supplemental Security Income (SSI) program or under Social Security Disability Insurance (SSDI, providing a higher degree of benefits based on years in the workforce).

Although definitions of disability used by policy makers vary widely, the PWD population has always been great, and the proportion of the population affected by disability policies (often because of employment or the disability of a family member) much greater still. In the 2000 CENSUS, 34.8 million people 16 and older in the United States reported a physical disability, 26.8 million reported difficulty going outside, 16.5 million reported a sensory disability, 14.6 million reported a mental disability, and 11.3 million reported a self-care disability. The census used overlapping categories. Below age 16, many more Americans would be in the "mental disability" category. That category combined cognitive and psychiatric disabilities. Overall, the U.S. PWD population was 19.3 percent of the 257 million people (the 5 and older noninstitutionalized population).

An active disability rights movement contributes to the shaping of policy. Centers for Independent Living work with the U.S. Rehabilitation Services Administration to provide employment services. Federally mandated protection and advocacy organizations (many affiliated through the National Disability Rights Network) interact with state and local officials. Groups such as ADAPT (initially American Disabled for Accessible Public Transit, now extended to other disability issues including personal assistant services) exert pressure on state and federal policy makers. The American Association of People with Disabilities was founded in 1995 and seeks to influence policy on behalf of the PWD community, often through mobilizing its members. Prominent public interest law firms including the Disability Rights Education and Defense Fund and Disability Rights Advocates seem to influence policy in this area.

Making of disability policy in the United States happens at every level of government. CABINET departments of Health and Human Services, Justice, Transportation, Housing and Urban Development, Labor, and Education are extensively involved; on particular issues, parts of the Homeland Security, Commerce, Defense, and State Departments are involved as well. Often, disability policy making comes from independent agencies such as the FEDERAL COMMUNICATIONS COMMISSION, the Social Security Administration, the Equal Employment Opportunity Commission, and the Access Board. Since 1978, the National Council on Disability, now an independent federal agency, has offered advice to policy makers on a wide range of disability issues.

Disability policy making has been spurred by an active disability rights movement. Within the DEPARTMENT OF EDUCATION, the Office of Special Education and Rehabilitative Services (OSERS), supplemented by state and local policy makers, plays a major role in implementing the Individuals with Disabilities Education Improvement Act (2004, IDEA). The essentials of EDUCATION POLICY under the act (and its predecessors, going back to the Education of All Handicapped Act of 1975) were zero reject (no matter how severe the disability, the federal government must ensure education); free and appropriate public education (FAPE); nondiscriminatory assessment; individualized educational program (IEP); least restrictive environment (LRE); and DUE PROCESS / procedural safeguards (involving parents' and students' participation). The federal share of funding for programs under IDEA has consistently been less than targeted. Under the Developmentally Disabled Assistance and Bill of Rights Act of 1975 (and 2000) and the No Child Left Behind Act of 2001, the federal government became involved in withdrawing or giving funds to institutions according to prescribed guidelines. Policy makers' expressed goal has become to decrease the gap between education of PWDs and education of nondisabled children.

The DEPARTMENT OF JUSTICE has a Disability Rights Section, which has brought cases on service animal access, movie theater seating, building construction, and other issues. Titles II and III of the ADA are enforced partly through complaint mechanisms. The Disability Rights Section occasionally pursues litigation or mediation on behalf of individuals who filed complaints or may institute proceedings itself. Chiefly because of resource limitations, the section is only able to pursue a small fraction of alleged ADA violations.

An interagency Architectural and Technical Barriers Compliance Board (Access Board) creates guidelines for the Architectural Barriers Act and the 1990 Americans with Disabilities Act. The Access Board was created in 1973 under the Rehabilitation Act.

The Equal Employment Opportunity Commission (EEOC) administers the ADA's title I. Complaints to the EEOC may involve discrimination in hiring or firing or a failure to provide auxiliary aids. The overwhelming majority of title I complaints have been rejected, and when complaints are pursued through litigation by the commission, they have encountered mixed success. Because of delays and limited remedies, the EEOC handles only a small portion of the cases of employment discrimination. A few others are handled by state agencies, including, for example, California's Department of Fair Employment and Housing.

The U.S. DEPARTMENT OF LABOR, along with STATE GOVERNMENTS and nongovernmental actors (for-profit and nonprofit), administer policies seeking to address high rates of PWD unemployment (40 to 70 percent, according to different sources). Programs such as the "Ticket to Work" were designed to address the disincentives to disability employment from loss of other benefits.

Since the administration of President Franklin Delano Roosevelt, policy makers have encouraged private initiatives to employ some disabled people at very low wages. A later version of earlier policies is the Javits-Wagner-O'Day (JWOD) network. Lax monitoring and occasional fraud have characterized this program designed eventually to boost disability employment. The JWOD Committee for Purchase from People Who Are Blind or Severely Disabled includes representatives from the Department of

Labor, the Department of the Army, the Department of Education, the DEPARTMENT OF AGRICULTURE, and elsewhere.

The Federal Communications Commission (FCC) shapes changes in telephone, television, and radio services. Section 255 of the Communications Act of 1934, as amended, deals with "access by persons with disabilities." The ADA's title IV addresses "services for hearing-impaired and speech-impaired individuals." The FCC administers policy on captioning of television broadcasts, telecommunications for the deaf, and other issues.

Federal HOUSING POLICY concerning PWDs focuses on nondiscrimination, especially through the Fair Housing Act Amendments of 1988. A landlord may not discriminate by demanding a higher security deposit, prohibiting necessary disability-related alterations, or prohibiting a PWD's needed service animal. Although not federally mandated, universal design and "visitability" (accessibility to visitors) are promoted by the organization Concrete Change. Visitability policy is incorporated in municipal ordinances in Long Beach, California, and elsewhere.

Disability advocates castigated the U.S. DEPARTMENT OF HOMELAND SECURITY's failure to take disability into account during the 2005 evacuations in New Orleans and the Gulf Coast area from Hurricane Katrina. Following a 2004 executive order, the Interagency Coordinating Council on Emergency Preparedness and Individuals with Disabilities was established.

The U.S. DEPARTMENT OF TRANSPORTATION has primary responsibility for implementing the Air Carrier Access Act. The act includes rules that new aircraft with more than one aisle must have accessible restrooms and rules on wheelchair storage, seating, and boarding. The act was passed in response to increased activism by such organizations as Paralyzed Veterans of America. Many of the initial piecemeal policies to promote accessible public transit became outdated with passage of the ADA. Many other concerns remain, however, including accessibility in bus and rail transportation.

Transportation policy making has thus been characterized by PWD pressure at local, state, and federal levels. The organization ADAPT's last two letters initially indicated its focus on "public transportation." Today, ADAPT's name and focus extend to other disability rights topics, but transportation access is still a major concern. The U.S. Department of Transportation issued regulations to improve transit access, first under section 16a of the 1970 Urban Mass Transit Act and later under the Rehabilitation Act. The regulations applied to recipients of federal funds. With adoption of the ADA, lifts or ramps were routinely installed on fixed-route buses.

As the 21st century began, ADAPT, CILs, and policy makers confronted the issue of long-term care, and particularly of personal assistance. At the federal and state levels, escalating Medicaid and Medicare expenditures (administered through the U.S. DEPARTMENT OF HEALTH AND HUMAN SERVICES) were consequences of institutionalization (e.g., in state hospitals and nursing homes) and a rising life expectancy. Medicaid and Medicare are used by many PWDs to obtain health care. An "institutional bias" means widespread reliance on nursing homes, mitigated by more common use of waivers.

The Social Security Administration is an independent federal agency. It administers Social Security Insurance (SSI) and Social Security Disability Insurance (SSDI), relied upon by many PWDs who are not employed or whose wages are low enough to qualify. Some PWDs receive higher income with SSDI, based on contributions during prior employment.

Disability policy is sometimes made inadvertently when other policy concerns are addressed. For example, the Deficit Reduction Act (2005) included a section on Money Follows the Person, rewarding state programs that allowed for consumer choice with Medicaid long-term care funds. Since the program might allow Medicaid recipients to live outside more expensive nursing homes, cost savings resulted. Government cutbacks enabled this disability-related program but have jeopardized others. PWDs' education remains underfunded, and programs to improve technology access, employment, and transportation have been implemented at a slower pace because of financial constraints. Many bureaus that make disability policy are inadequate to address the great social inequalities confronting PWDs. Pressure from the disability rights movement and help from key allies inside and outside government will therefore continue to play a vital role.

Further Reading
Blanck, Peter, Eve Hill, Charles D. Siegal, and Michael Waterstone. *Disability Civil Rights Law and Policy.* St. Paul, Minn.: Thomson-West, 2004; Colker, Ruth. *The Disability Pendulum: The First Decade of the Americans with Disabilities Act.* New York: New York University Press, 2005; Colker, Ruth, and Adam A. Milani. *Everyday Law for Individuals with Disabilities.* Boulder, Colo.: Paradigm Publishers, 2006; Krieger, Linda Hamilton. *Backlash against the ADA: Reinterpreting Disability Rights.* Ann Arbor: University of Michigan, 2003; O'Brien, Ruth. *Crippled Justice: The History of Modern Disability Policy in the Workplace.* Chicago: University of Chicago, 2001; Scotch, Richard K. *From Good Will to Civil Rights: Transforming Federal Disability Policy*, 2nd ed. Philadelphia: Temple University Press, 2001; Shapiro, Joseph P. *No Pity: People with Disabilities Forging a New Civil Rights Movement.* New York: Times Books, 1993; Switzer, Jacqueline Vaughn. *Disabled Rights: American Disability Policy and the Fight for Equality.* Washington, D.C.: Georgetown University Press, 2003.
—Arthur W. Blaser

drug policy

The modern fight (approximately 1980 to the present) against the selling and use of illicit drugs such as marijuana, heroin, cocaine, and methamphetamines—commonly referred to as the "war on drugs"—has been at the forefront of U.S. domestic policy for the past two and a half decades. The war on drugs, as it has been waged in the modern era, is perhaps best encapsulated in federal and state laws that have imposed more severe punishments on drug sellers and drug users and in the billions of dollars in taxpayer money used to thwart the supply of drugs in the market. The significant resources used to combat the problem are a direct result of the significant social costs illicit drugs impose on American society. Drugs and drug use are often blamed for causing criminal activity, the break-up of families, loss in work productivity, and the spread of diseases such as HIV/AIDS.

Although considerable attention is given to illicit drug use today, it was not always viewed as a major social problem. In 1900 drug use was an issue that

A member of the U.S. Coast Guard protects more than 11.5 tons of cocaine before a press conference. *(Coast Guard)*

failed to reach the government's policy making agenda, as few saw it as a serious social problem. Opium and its derivatives, morphine, heroin, cocaine, and cannabis (marijuana) were all legal substances and freely available to whoever chose to use them. For example, cocaine was a widely used ingredient in soda-pop (Coca-Cola until 1903), medicine, and alcoholic beverages such as wine. This laissez-faire approach to drugs during this period did not come without costs, as common use of such drugs led to addiction. It is estimated that 2 to 4 percent of the American population was addicted to morphine with many of those being middle- and upper-class citizens.

The political climate surrounding drugs and drug use began to change shortly thereafter as antidrug crusaders were able to make a convincing case that the growing drug epidemic was a threat to society. As a result, support grew for drug prohibition policies and policies that punished those who sold, possessed, or used cocaine or heroin. Between 1900 and the

1930s, an important political shift occurred in connection to the drug issue—for the first time, curbing the use of drugs became a legitimate goal of national government policy.

These changes in the public's perception of drugs and the social costs connected to them fostered a wave of legislation at both the federal and state levels of government aimed at reducing the sale of drugs. The first federal drug legislation, known as the Harrison Act, was enacted in 1914. The Harrison Act prohibited the sale of heroin, cocaine, and their derivatives except by a physician's prescription. In comparison with later policies, this legislation was relatively lenient on drug users themselves, as drug use was not considered a crime under the new law; users were simply asked to turn to doctors for prescriptions to buy them.

However, by the early 1930s, under considerable political pressure from the DEPARTMENT OF THE TREASURY, Congress expanded the reach of antidrug laws from those that focused solely on drug sellers to those that punished drug users as well. In 1937, Congress passed the Marijuana Tax Act, which placed federal regulations on marijuana for the first time. During the 1950s, fears about COMMUNISM and organized crime were tied in political rhetoric to the drug issue, which enabled the Boggs Act of 1951 and the Narcotics Control Act of 1956 to pass by wide legislative majorities. Both of these pieces of legislation dramatically increased the penalties for violating federal drug laws. The Boggs Act imposed a mandatory two-year sentence for a first conviction of possession, five to 10 years for the second offense, and 10 to 20 years for third time offenders. The Narcotics Control Act increased the mandatory minimum penalties even further for second and third time offenders.

Importantly, it was during this era when illicit drug use was outlawed, and the sanctions for use were slowly ratcheted up that laid the foundation for the modern-day war on drugs. The current drug war primarily follows a deterrence-based approach whereby policies are designed to limit the supply of drugs into the marketplace through increased drug enforcement efforts and to impose tough sanctions (via incarceration) to punish those who sell or use drugs. Together, these policies aim to remove drug offenders from the larger community and deter would-be drug users from becoming involved with drugs in the first place. This approach to the drug problem has led to a dramatic explosion in federal and state tax dollars spent on eradicating drug supplies in the United States, steep increases in the number of individuals arrested and incarcerated on drug-related charges, and longer mandatory sentences for drug dealers and users.

For example, following the deterrence-based approach led to dramatic increases in APPROPRIATIONS earmarked for bureaucratic agencies closely involved with drug enforcement duties. The Drug Enforcement Agency (DEA), the main federal agency charged with the eradication of drug supplies in the United States, saw its budget increase from $215 to $321 million between 1980 and 1984. Antidrug funds allocated to the DEPARTMENT OF DEFENSE more than doubled from $33 to $79 million, and the Customs Department's budget increased from $81 million to $278 million during this same period.

The focus given to eradication of drug supplies through tough enforcement had negative implications for those EXECUTIVE AGENCIES designed to reduce the demand for drugs through treatment and anti-drug education. Between 1981 and 1984, the budget of the National Institute on Drug Abuse was reduced from $274 million to $57 million, and the antidrug funds allocated to the DEPARTMENT OF EDUCATION were cut from $14 million to $3 million. By 1985, 78 percent of the funds allocated to the drug problem went to law enforcement, while only 22 percent went to drug treatment and prevention.

The Anti-Drug Abuse Act of 1986 was a major piece of legislation that symbolizes much of the deterrence-based policy approaches to the fight against drugs. This bill increased federal funds toward narcotics control efforts, instituted the death penalty for some drug-related crimes, and established tougher drug sentencing guidelines. These sentencing guidelines included new mandatory sentencing laws that force judges to deliver fixed sentences to individuals convicted of a drug crime regardless of other possible mitigating factors. Congress had initially intended for these mandatory sentencing laws to apply primarily to so-called drug "king pins" and managers in large drug distribution networks. However, analysis of sentencing records shows that only 11 percent of federal drug defendants are high-level drug offenders. During President George H. W. Bush's administration (1989–93), a record 3.5 million drug arrests were made, causing a significant strain on federal and state prison populations, as more than 80 percent of the increase in the federal prison population between 1985 and 1995 was a result of drug convictions. More recent statistics show similar trends. In 2002 (the most recent data available), approximately one-fifth (or 21.4 percent) of state prisoners were incarcerated on drug-related charges. Moreover, drug offenders, up 37 percent, represented the largest source of jail population growth between 1996 and 2002.

Given these trends, what specific set of forces helped produce U.S. drug policies that place such a heavy emphasis on reducing drug supplies and issue stringent punishments on both drug sellers and users? As mentioned earlier, part of the answer can be traced back to the first half of the 20th century, when illicit drugs were first outlawed and longer sentences were imposed for violating federal drugs laws. But the policies connected to the highly salient, modern-day war on drugs are dramatically different from those of the earlier era, both in terms of the amount of tax dollars spent on drug enforcement and in the number of people arrested and incarcerated on drug-related offenses. To better understand the current state of drug policy, it is useful to look back to presidential politics of the late 1960s. It was in the 1968 presidential election that the drug issue jumped onto the national political agenda and precipitated the build-up to the drug policies of today.

Seeking to gain stronger political support in the southern states, the REPUBLICAN PARTY along with its 1968 presidential candidate, Richard Nixon, began highlighting issues such as crime and welfare—both issues appealed to southern white voters. Using campaign symbols that had strong racial undertones, the Republicans were able to link blacks and minority groups as instigators of crime, an important social problem that Nixon pledged he could help solve if elected president. In priming social issues like crime, the Republicans were able to split much of the NEW DEAL coalition by getting many poor, rural, southern white voters with hostilities toward blacks to switch their party allegiances away from the DEMOCRATIC PARTY, which in the end helped solidify Nixon's slim electoral victory in 1968.

Using strong rhetorical language while in office, President Nixon linked drugs and drug use as major causes of criminal activity in America, and ever since, the two issues have been closely intertwined in political debate. Not only did drug use cause more crime according to Nixon, the two issues were closely connected in that they shared "root" causes that had to be dealt with in similar fashions. More specifically, Nixon and other political (ideologically conservative) leaders espoused the idea that crime and drug use were a result of individual failure—drug use was a result of poor choices made by individuals. This "individualist" nature of drug use was exemplified several years later by Republican president Ronald Reagan in a nationally televised speech in which he stated, "Drug users can no longer excuse themselves by blaming society. As individuals, they are responsible. The rest of us must be clear that we will no longer tolerate drug use by anyone." The drug and crime issues viewed from this perspective were in stark contrast to the traditional liberal Democratic perspective, which tended to blame drugs and crime on systemic factors such as poverty and homelessness.

As is the case with any public policy problem, the factors that are widely understood to cause a problem also help structure the solutions to it. Drug policy over the past two and half decades has largely been shaped in an era in which criminal activity and drug use have been viewed by many citizens and elected leaders in both the White House and Congress in very individualistic terms. Given this, it is no coincidence that deterrence-based policies such as increased drug enforcement, incarceration, and mandatory sentencing—policies that try to get people to think twice before they use drugs and punish severely those who do—have become pillars of America's drug policy.

Alternatively, others argue that incarcerating large numbers of individuals for drug possession, creating mandatory prison sentences, and spending a large proportion of funds aimed at cutting drug supplies is misplaced. Instead, it is argued that scarce resources should be used to fund drug policies that are driven by the presumption that drug abuse is a medical problem, and because of this, policies should promote treatment, not punishment.

Motivated by stresses caused by overcrowded prisons, high prisoner recidivism rates, and growth in the use of highly addictive drugs such as methamphetamine, some U.S. states appear to be rethinking their drug policies (that over the past two decades have largely followed the deterrence-based approach at the federal level of government) and have begun to place greater emphasis on drug treatment. In 2000, voters in California, the state that had the highest rate of incarceration for drug users in the nation, enacted the Substance Abuse and Crime Prevention Act (Proposition 36) using the state's INITIATIVE process. This initiative requires that individuals arrested and charged with nonviolent drug offenses be placed into drug treatment instead of prison. Estimates suggest that this policy has saved California tax payers $1.4 billion over the program's first five years largely because of reductions in prison costs resulting from fewer people being sent to prison on drug charges. The initiative remains controversial, however, as opponents argue that the law is too lenient on drug offenders and that treatment success rates have been far too low.

Using the significant discretion states have traditionally had under the U.S. Constitution to define criminal law and protect the health and safety of their citizens, U.S. states have also passed additional drug reform laws. Those state laws that have gained the most attention are those that permit the use of marijuana for medical purposes. Since 1996, a total of 11 states, including Alaska, Arizona, California, Colorado, Hawaii, Maine, Maryland, Nevada, Oregon, Vermont, and Washington have removed state-level penalties for marijuana use by medical patients who have a doctor's recommendation. These state laws allow marijuana to be used to treat certain diseases and to help cope with pain. The extent to which patients and doctors are protected under medical marijuana laws varies by state.

States' medical marijuana laws conflict with federal drug policy, which does not recognize a medical use for marijuana and mandates that the drug cannot be used under any circumstances. These differences in states' medical marijuana laws and federal drug law came to a head in 2005 when the federal government challenged California's medical marijuana law in court on the grounds that the California law violated (a higher authority) federal law. In the case of *Gonzales v. Raich* (No. 03-1454), the UNITED STATES SUPREME COURT ruled in favor of the federal government and said that the federal government could prosecute individuals for using marijuana even in those 11 states that explicitly permit it. The majority of the Court based its decision on the power of Congress to regulate interstate commerce. This ruling remains controversial, but the different approaches states have taken in their fight against drugs illustrates how drug policy in the United States, when examined more carefully, is becoming more diversified than is often believed.

Without a doubt, drug abuse and the costs it imposes on society will remain problems that the government will be asked to solve in the years ahead. However, what is not known is the direction and form drug policies will take. Will drug policy continue to place greater emphasis on punishment of drug sellers and users, or will future policy place greater emphasis on prevention and drug treatment? In the end, these are political questions that will be decided by legislative bodies at the federal, state, and local levels of government.

Further Reading

Beckett, Katherine. *Making Crime Pay: Law and Order in Contemporary American Politics.* New York: Oxford University Press, 1997; Bertram, Eva, Morris Blachman, Kenneth Sharpe, and Peter Andreas. *Drug War Politics: The Price of Denial.* Berkeley: University of California Press, 1996; Longshore, Douglas, et al. "Evaluation of the Substance Abuse and Crime Prevention Act." University of California, Los Angeles, Integrated Substance Abuse Programs, 2005; Meier, Kenneth J. *The Politics of Sin: Drugs, Alcohol and Public Policy.* Armonk, N.Y.: M.E. Sharpe, 1994; Tonry, Michael, "Why Are U.S. Incarceration Rates So High?" *Crime and Delinquency* 45, no. 4 (1999): 419–437; U.S. Sentencing Commission. "Mandatory Minimum Penalties in the Federal Justice System: Special Report to Congress." Washington, D.C.: Government Printing Office, 1991.

—Garrick L. Percival

education policy

Education policy has been one of the top domestic issues in America for most of the past two decades. Citizens, the news MEDIA, and politicians across the ideological spectrum regularly call for improvements in the nation's education system. Many states and the federal government are responding with reform proposals in the hope of improving the quality of education for all students to deal with international competitiveness concerns, as well as to address the achievement gap faced by low-income and minority students.

Education policy is significant both for its efficiency and equity dimensions. Most American concerns about competing in economic terms with other nations, which were focused on Japan in the 1980s and now on China and India in the future, emphasize the fact that education is critical to building an intelligent, flexible workforce. At the same time, the huge achievement gaps in America limit the ideal that education can be the force that propels low-income children into success in the "American Dream" in their economic futures.

One of the most significant influences on the development of the contemporary reform movement was the publication of *A Nation at Risk*, a 1983 U.S. DEPARTMENT OF EDUCATION report that indicated that the United States was falling behind other nations in educating its children. The report called for the establishment of academic standards as a means toward improving the education system and prompted widespread education reform in the states. Calls for educational reform, taking various forms, have continued since 1983. But while many reforms have been tried, few have demonstrated the ability to either improve average levels of performance or decrease the large achievement gap between higher-income students and lower-income students.

Although there is generally widespread consensus that the nation's public education system needs to be improved, the appropriate method of reform is the source of fierce political disagreements. The education system is incredibly large and fragmented and fraught with politics and various philosophical opinions regarding how children learn. Some of the most pressing current topics include FEDERALISM issues, the No Child Left Behind (NCLB) Act, standardized testing, curriculum policy, school choice, and school finance.

Control of the American education system has historically been in the hands of local governments, with the state and federal governments playing very limited roles. Although responsibility for education is ultimately vested in STATE GOVERNMENTs by their STATE CONSTITUTIONS, it is often argued that local governments are better suited to make education decisions for local students in areas such as bilingual education, special education programs, curriculum, textbooks, and funding. Over the past several decades, however, there has been an increase in state and federal responsibility for public education, both in terms of funding, especially at the state level, and more recently the establishment of standards and other requirements.

Beginning in the 1950s, the federal government increased its share of responsibility for funding public education. In the 1980s and 1990s, state governments began instituting standards-based reform, whereby states specify subject matter that students are to be taught and expected to learn. Even with such standards, local school districts were still given the discre-tion to determine how to reach such goals. In recent years, however, the federal government has passed comprehensive legislation, drastically increasing its role in the nation's education system. The No Child Left Behind Act of 2001, discussed below, is a clear example of the recent shift in power toward the federal government, even though it gets its authority through the focus of funding low-income students.

Calls for national standards or requirements, such as those mandated by NCLB, generate considerable opposition on the grounds that the local districts (or at least the states) are the more appropriate arenas for such decisions to be made. Even with these higher levels of government involved, American local school districts have more power over education than in most other countries.

The NCLB of 2001 is a reauthorization of the Elementary and Secondary Education Act (ESEA), which was initially enacted in 1965. In 2002, the Education Commission of the States called it "the most significant federal education policy initiative in a generation." The complex and comprehensive legislation requires states to pursue more stringent accountability systems and annual testing of all students in grades three through eight, as well as requiring "highly qualified" teachers. The legislation mandates school report cards and data reporting that include performance by race, income, and gender. According to the legislation, states must make progress in raising students' proficiencies in certain areas as well as in closing the gap between advantaged and disadvantaged students.

Under NCLB, there are a number of progressively more important consequences for schools and districts that do not achieve the required progress. Students whose schools are placed on "improvement status" must be given school choice options and must be provided "supplemental education services," such as tutoring services, during the second year of improvement status. Furthermore, districts must take corrective actions such as decreasing funding, restructuring, and replacing school staff. In exchange for these stringent expectations, the legislation provides increased federal funding for education and some flexibility for using such federal dollars.

The implementation of NCLB has proven quite controversial. Supporters believe that it is a major step toward focusing attention on the need for all children to achieve. Some critics are opposed to extensive testing of students, while others focus on the high costs involved with implementing the legislation. Others are concerned with the potential for adverse consequences resulting from the school choice provisions in the legislation. In any event, states and districts are currently struggling to meet the requirements imposed by the legislation.

Standardized testing refers to the use of large-scale achievement tests to measure students' mastery of designated subject matter. Such tests may also come with incentives or consequences, such as sanctions for schools with low or stagnant test scores, which add a "high-stakes" element. Examples of "high-stakes" tests include high school graduation tests, competency tests for grade level achievement, and tests used to rate schools with such categorizations as "failing" or "successful." All of these "high-stakes" tests are tied to accountability—holding students, teachers, and schools accountable for learning at a designated level.

Although standardized testing has played a role in education in the United States since at least the 1920s, current usage differs dramatically from earlier purposes. For example, the main purpose of testing in the 1950s and 1960s was to measure and monitor individual student performance and coursework. Today, the tests are also used for accountability measures, including evaluating schools' effectiveness, as noted above.

As with NCLB more generally, contentious disagreements surround the role of standardized testing. Critics object to the particular standards themselves, the federal government's role in stipulating standards, and the types of assessments used to measure the standards. Some also argue that the greater focus on test scores shifts priorities to "teaching to the test" and potentially creates incentives for cheating. The public, however, has generally been in favor of accountability standards and testing.

While certain core curriculum elements have always been part of American education—"reading, writing, arithmetic"—knowledge advances rapidly, and debates arise about what should be emphasized and how it should be taught. There is a broad notion that American education has bypassed some of the "basics" as it has become more inclusive of different perspectives and that some rigor has been lost in the

process. While the education expert Richard Rothstein and others emphasize that this comes partly from inaccurate perceptions of a prior "golden age" of American education, it has spawned a "back-to-basics" argument about what students should be taught. E. D. Hirsch's "Core Knowledge" curriculum is one manifestation of this. What began as an idea that schools should share a well-designed curriculum with proper sequencing to provide all students with a shared knowledge foundation has evolved into a curriculum outlining specific material to be taught at each grade level.

One of the features of American FEDERALISM is that there is no national curriculum. States set curriculums or allow local districts to do so. As a result, there is considerable variation compared to systems in other countries. The federal government has made attempts to create national standards in education, but such efforts are generally criticized (and thus far, neutralized) on the grounds that they go against the strong tradition of local control. Major textbook publishers probably play an implicit role in partially standardizing curriculums across states, as do the requirements of national college entrance exams such as the SAT and ACT. Curriculum policy, however, is currently undergoing a shift away from predominantly local control toward a greater influence by the states and federal government. NCLB requires that states align their standardized tests with state curriculum policy. Along with the resulting increased role of the states, there has been a noted shift toward a greater focus on math, reading, and science, the subjects at the core of NCLB. In fact, schools that fail to make "Adequate Yearly Progress" (AYP) in these areas are subject to strict sanctions, including school restructuring. Some critics have argued that NCLB's focus on these areas has resulted in a "narrowing" of curriculum in public schools, including a decline in classroom time for other areas, such as the arts, social studies, and foreign languages.

One major ongoing debate centers on whether students should be taught specific facts and knowledge, or whether more emphasis should be placed on problem solving and ways of learning to think. The former approach is likely to align more closely with standardized testing expectations. That is, agreement is easier on a set of things to know and test, while advocates of the latter approach stress that it can lead to more innovative thinkers who are more likely to be interested in "life-long learning," compared to the "drill-and-kill" approaches.

School choice generally refers to the ability of parents to select a school for their child to attend, as opposed to the traditional assignment of a public school based on residency within particular school zones. Middle- and upper-income families have long exercised a form of school choice based on residential mobility. In recent decades, a number of different school choice options have emerged across the states, including open enrollment, charter schools, and vouchers. Options such as open enrollment within the public sector are long standing and relatively uncontroversial.

More recent choices, such as charter schools and vouchers, are more controversial. Charter schools, which emerged in the early 1990s, are publicly funded schools that operate under a charter from an authorizing entity or board and may be managed by nonpublic entities such as private companies or nonprofit organizations. Charter schools are accountable to the charter granting entity but have far greater discretion in the operation of the school than traditional public schools. Their enrollment (and thus survival) is based entirely on parents choosing to send their children to the school.

Voucher programs allow parents to apply some of the public money allocated for a child's education toward private school tuition. To date, there are only a handful of voucher programs across the nation, including those in Milwaukee, Cleveland, and Washington, D.C., and they have faced significant challenges in the courts. Although voucher programs were originally advocated by free-market conservatives and Catholics, recent supporters include more minorities and parents of students attending unsuccessful urban schools. In fact, most of today's voucher programs are targeted to such students, as opposed to universal voucher programs available to all students. Voucher programs can take various forms; policy decisions include whether to include religious schools, the amount of the voucher, eligibility requirements for participation (e.g., low-income families, failing schools), and accountability standards.

School choice has a diverse mix of supporters, including individuals who view choice as a means to improve education for underserved populations (e.g., minority and low-income children), free-market conservatives opposed to the bureaucracy of public education, members of the education establishment who desire autonomy from administration, and individuals seeking to support religious education. School choice opponents argue that many of these options have a harmful effect on the public school system by taking away funds from public education or "creaming" the most successful students from traditional public school. Opponents have also argued that bureaucracy is an effective structure for managing the diverse problems and issues within public schools. Opponents of vouchers, specifically, have claimed that such programs violate the First Amendment's separation of church and state doctrine when religious affiliated schools are permitted to participate. Taken as a whole, school choice is a complex issue that has come to the forefront of education policy in recent years by emphasizing bottom-up parental accountability rather than top-down district control over student assignment.

School funding for K-12 education represents the largest component of most state budgets. The federal government, states, and local governments share the costs of financing K-12 education, with more than 90 percent of the burden typically split relatively evenly between state and local governments. One of the significant debates regarding school finance concerns the need for greater spending for education. Although there are often demands to increase education funding, increased funding does not seem necessarily to result in greater performance.

Also notable are the debates concerning "equity" and "adequacy" in school finance. Because a large portion of funding comes from local districts, there is often a gap between education spending levels in high-income versus low-income communities. Over the past 30 years, there have been calls for equity in school finance as a means to reduce or eliminate the spending gap between wealthy and low-income school districts. Although the idea of distributing education dollars equally to all schools and districts is attractive, from a political standpoint, it is difficult to put an upper limit on school districts' spending.

In recent years, there has been a subsequent shift in focus from equity to adequacy. States have faced lawsuits, which argue that spending is too low, or not adequate, for students to meet educational standards. The question then becomes whether all districts are receiving and spending sufficient funds to provide students with an education enabling them to reach achievement standards, as opposed to whether the funding is equal across districts. NCLB standards are now used to support some of these adequacy suits.

Another relatively new development in school finance is the proposal for "weighted student formulas" (WSF) as a means of distributing school finance. This concept recognizes that it costs more money to educate some students than others. For example, educating students with special needs, from low-income families, or with limited English ability may involve additional costs compared with students not facing such challenges. The idea behind WSF is that schools use specific weights, or funding dollars, based on certain student characteristics. The funding then follows that student to his or her particular school. Schools with relatively more challenging student populations are given larger sums of money to help them achieve. Proponents of WSF often suggest granting more flexibility to principals, in combination with this new method for distributing funds, as a means for improving education.

Clearly, there are a number of important debates at the forefront of education policy in the United States today. Improving the education system in general and closing achievement gaps between advantaged and disadvantaged students are worthy yet difficult goals. This article has discussed some of the major issues surrounding federalism issues, the No Child Left Behind Act (2001), standardized testing, curriculum decisions, school choice, and school finances. Prior to K-12 education, Americans are focusing more attention on the value of preschool programs, especially for low-income children, but have yet to devote significant public resources to them. At the same time, after K-12 education, American higher education remains at the forefront of the world, mainly due to strong emphases on research, competition, and choice.

Further Reading

Hochschild, Jennifer, and Nathan Scovronick. *The American Dream and the Public Schools*. New York: Oxford University Press, 2003; Moe, Terry M., ed. *A Primer on America's Schools*. Stanford, Calif; Hoover Institution Press, 2001; Peterson, Paul E., ed. *Our Schools and Our Future: Are We Still at Risk?* Stanford, Calif.: Hoover Institution Press, 2003; Peterson, Paul E., and David E. Campbell, eds. *Charters, Vouchers, and Public Education*. Washington, D.C.: Brookings Institution Press, 2001; Ravitch, Diane, ed. *Brookings Papers on Education Policy*. Washington, D.C.: Brookings Institution Press, 1998–2005; Schneider, Mark, Paul Teske, and Melissa Marschall. *Choosing Schools: Consumer Choice and the Quality of American Schools*. Princeton, N.J.: Princeton University Press, 2000.

—Aimee Williamson and Paul Teske

energy policy

As a preeminent industrial power, the United States is dependent on fossil fuels in order to meet its energy needs and to sustain its economy. Whereas petroleum remains the major source of energy for automobiles, coal is the primary energy source for electricity. While the United States is a storehouse of coal and has considerable natural gas reserves (along with a supply of natural gas from Canada), it has become heavily dependent on foreign sources of oil from unstable and problematic regions around the world. Fossil fuels constitute approximately 85 percent of total U.S. energy supplies, with petroleum accounting for about 40 percent and coal and natural gas about 22 percent. Alternative sources of energy represent only a fraction of the U.S. energy pie. While nuclear power provides less than 10 percent of U.S. energy needs, renewable energy sources (e.g., solar, wind, biomass) make up less than 5 percent of the total.

In many ways, energy policy is about conflicting goals. Policy makers must ensure that the country has a secure source of energy while focusing on development of new sources on one hand and conservation of energy sources, protection of public health, and ensuring environmental quality on the other hand. The United States has relied on a variety of domestic energy sources over its more than 200-year history, including coal, timber, and water power, among others. By the 1950s, several developments began to have a profound impact on American society, including the rise of an automobile society and the expansion of the highway system, that required more fossil

Oil rigs undergo repairs after Hurricane Katrina, Galveston, Texas. *(Getty Images)*

fuels and new consumer demands that resulted in an increase in electricity use in households and industry.

Although the United States produced twice as much oil as the rest of the world as late as the 1950s, it lost its self-sufficiency in oil production a decade later and self-sufficiency in natural gas by the 1980s. By the end of the 20th century, the U.S. was importing approximately 65 percent of its oil needs, and it is expected that U.S. imports of foreign oil will continue to increase rather than decrease in the foreseeable future.

During the 19th century until the mid-20th century, coal was a major source of energy for an industrializing United States. Historically, coal was an important energy source especially for industry and transportation. Although coal has been replaced by oil as the dominant fossil fuel used in the United States, it remains an important part of the energy mix for the nation. However, it is also a very serious source of pollution.

While natural gas has been characterized as a "clean" source of energy, it also has potential problems for environmental quality. Environmentalists

have raised concerns about the impact on wildlife and habitat, for instance, in the process of exploration and production of natural gas as a major energy source.

During the last three decades of the 20th century, the United States experienced several crises involving the security of the nation's energy supply and price increases that demonstrated the vulnerability of Americans' lifestyle that has been based on cheap energy sources. Moreover, by the early part of President George W. Bush's second term in office in 2005 and 2006, gas prices averaged close to $3 per gallon in some parts of the country. Given this background, the extent to which conservation and the use of alternative sources of energy should be used has divided Democrats and Republicans in Congress and candidates for the PRESIDENCY. Moreover, organized interests have exercised their power in the energy debate.

Over the last three decades or so, a common theme in the energy debate has been the extent to which the United States should increase or decrease its production and consumption of fossil fuels. During the Richard Nixon (1969–74), Jimmy Carter (1977–81), and Bill Clinton (1993–2001) years in the White House, there was an effort to reduce dependence on foreign oil, although each administration pursued a different approach to the problem. During the Nixon administration, the ORGANIZATION OF PETROLEUM EXPORTING COUNTRIES (OPEC) cut domestic production and exports to DEVELOPED COUNTRIES, including the United States. While Congress established a Strategic Petroleum Reserve, President Nixon proposed "Project Independence," which sought to reduce foreign imports of oil while increasing domestic production and pushing for more nuclear power. In contrast, Jimmy Carter, who also faced an energy crisis in 1979–80, pushed for a "National Energy Plan" that emphasized conservation measures and encouraged research and development of alternative sources of energy. He also worked with Congress to establish the new DEPARTMENT OF ENERGY. In a speech to the nation in 1979, he referred to the energy crisis and reducing U.S. dependence on foreign oil as the "moral equivalent of war." A decade and a half later, the Bill Clinton–Al Gore team pushed an energy policy that was concerned with the reduction of carbon emissions that had a negative effect on global climate, and they encouraged continued research and development of alternative sources of energy. In 1997, Vice President Al Gore signed the Kyoto Protocol that committed the United States and other nations to mandatory cuts in carbon dioxide emissions.

In contrast to the Nixon, Carter, and Clinton efforts to reduce the country's dependence on fossil fuels and pursue a strategy that included conservation and alternative energy sources, Presidents Ronald Reagan, George H. W. Bush, and George W. Bush emphasized development and production over conservation and alternative sources of energy. Reagan pursued a policy that encouraged continued use of fossil fuels and opening up federal lands for more exploration and production. President George H. W. Bush did little to reduce U.S. dependence on foreign oil, and he supported opening up Alaska's Arctic National Wildlife Refuge (ANWR) to oil exploration. Although he supported modest incentives for renewable energy sources, he moved the United States further along in an attempt to reduce carbon emissions when he signed the Global Climate Change Conven-

tion at the Earth Summit in Rio de Janeiro in 1992. However, he used his influence to revise the guidelines and timetables of the international environmental agreement to reflect voluntary rather than mandatory efforts. President George W. Bush has promoted an energy policy that reflects the approach of President Ronald Reagan, namely, emphasis on production and development over alternative energy sources and conservation. The Energy Bill of 2005 ensured that the United States would remain increasingly dependent on foreign oil as the president continued to push for oil exploration and drilling in ANWR, while little was done to promote conservation, improve fuel efficiency, or encourage alternative sources of renewable energy.

Although providing only a small proportion of total U.S. energy needs, nuclear power and alternative (renewable) sources of energy have the potential to become the focus of increasing attention as policy makers, INTEREST GROUPS, and citizens debate the future of U.S. energy policy. Similar to fossil fuels, both nuclear and renewable energy sources also have problems. For nuclear power, safety and storage issues are the primary concerns of opponents. Touted in the past as the energy source of the future, environmental and public health crises involving nuclear accidents at Three Mile Island in Pennsylvania in 1979 and Chernobyl in Ukraine in 1986 led to political problems for the nuclear power industry. The question of how and where to store used nuclear materials remains another issue. Nuclear materials (e.g., nuclear power plant rods) become outdated in about three decades and must be placed in a safe location in order to protect citizens and the environment. The issue of where to store these materials has been demonstrated by the political conflict that arose between federal authorities and state officials and citizens in Nevada, a federal storage site. However, in recent years, the United States, along with members of the Group of 8 (which also includes Canada, France, Germany, Italy, Japan, Russia, and the United Kingdom), indicated that nuclear energy must play a part in the mix of energy use.

Alternative, renewable energy sources have much potential since they contribute fewer harmful pollutants, and they are a relatively available source of energy. Among these energy sources are solar, wind, hydroelectric and geothermal power, biomass, and hydrogen fuel cells. Energy can be produced from the Sun (solar radiation) in several ways, including the use of solar panels on rooftops and the employment of photovoltaic cells. Although the United States was a leader in promoting solar energy, Japan and members of the EUROPEAN UNION have surpassed the United States in promoting this source of energy.

The generation of energy from wind power has been derived from the use of windmills dating back for more than a century in the United States. In more recent years, especially after the oil crisis that occurred in the early 1970s, increased federal funding was directed toward obtaining energy from this source through new wind technology. However, as oil prices stabilized in the 1980s, federal funding for continued research and development of wind power decreased. Consequently, wind power remains a fraction of total energy sources. The major source of energy for producing electricity in the United States is water. Waterways provide the energy for hydroelectric plants to produce relatively inexpensive power for homes and industry. On one hand, hydroelectric power produces little pollution; on the other hand, flora and fauna can be adversely affected by the construction of dams.

Energy obtained from underground steam is known as geothermal power. In contrast to solar and wind power, which have lacked strong federal support for research and development, geothermal power is one area of the energy pie in which the United States has assumed a global leadership position. Biomass serves as another example of renewable energy, whereby organic material (e.g., wood, plants, and animal fat) is converted into a source of energy. For instance, with the increase in prices at the gas pump for American consumers, ethanol, which is produced from corn, has assumed increasing attention as a gasoline additive since it has been found to reduce pollutants that are produced from the burning of traditional gasoline used in cars and trucks.

As a nonpolluting source of energy, hydrogen fuel cells may be the energy source of the future. In the process of producing energy from hydrogen, only heat and water are produced. Hydrogen is captured from a source such as water or natural gas and then separated, stored, and used by a battery to produce energy. However, the process needs an energy source. If fossil fuels rather than nonpolluting energy sources (e.g., solar, wind, or hydroelectric) are used as the

energy source for producing hydrogen, this new source of energy that is filled with promise will become the center of future debates about appropriate uses of energy.

Future U.S. energy policy faces four major challenges, namely, geopolitics, (political instability, competition), political conflict over oil drilling in ANWR, pollution, and global warming. First, unlike the past in which the United States could count on reliable sources of energy from oil-rich countries, existing petroleum sources are beginning to peak, and potentially new opportunities for obtaining petroleum are found in deep water near politically sensitive areas in the Caspian region and Africa. Moreover, the rise of China and India are already producing concerns about increasing demands on the world's oil supply. China, in particular, has the potential to become a major rival for the United States and the European Union as it seeks to diversify its energy sources in order to sustain its economic growth.

Second, ANWR has become an arena where political conflict between Senate Republicans on one side and Senate Democrats and environmentalists on the other side has occurred over support for oil exploration in the sensitive, pristine northern slope in Alaska. The debate involves several concerns, including the amount of oil available, the impact on the environment and wildlife, and the extent to which the oil would be used for domestic purposes rather than used for export.

Third, air pollution and acid rain will continue to be problems as long as fossil fuels constitute the majority of energy use in the United States. While progress has been made in improving air quality in major metropolitan areas, air quality problems have become conspicuous in the nation's national parks. Further, coal-fired power plants in the Midwest produce sulfuric acid (a source of acid rain) that has created environmental problems in the Northeast and Canada.

Finally, the scientific community both in the United States and internationally has produced a consensus that human activities are having a negative impact on global climate. The United States is the largest producer of greenhouse gases that contribute to global warming, a problem that scientists warn might have catastrophic consequences for the planet unless action is taken very soon. In fact, climatic

U.S. Historical Energy Consumption, 1850–2000

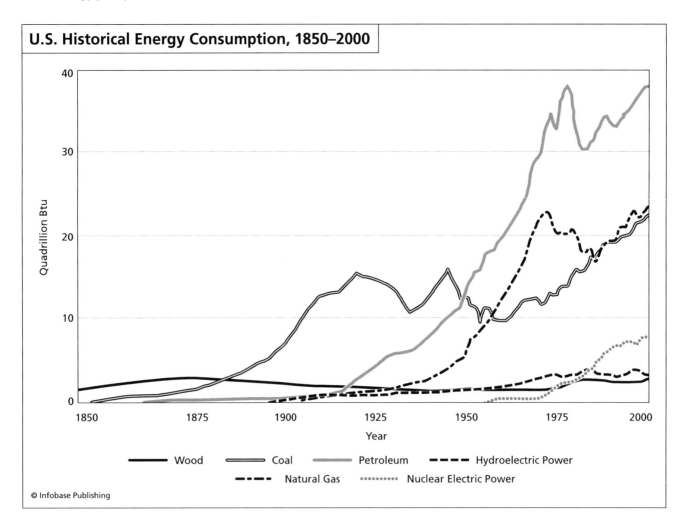

© Infobase Publishing

change is already having an effect on habitat, weather, wildlife, and coral reefs. Although the global scientific community has articulated its concerns about the impact of the continued use of fossil fuels on the global climate, President George W. Bush rejected the Kyoto Protocol in March 2001 and substituted instead a voluntary effort to address U.S. carbon emissions. There is concern among the global community that without leadership by the United States, the effort to address global warming will be difficult at best.

As U.S. policy makers move forward into the 21st century, they are faced with many difficult choices regarding energy policy. One option is to continue with more exploration and production of fossil fuels. Second, more emphasis can be placed on conservation measures. Third, alternative, renewable sources of energy might be pushed in an effort to address the energy needs of the nation. On one hand, some observers have argued that it will take a mix of these three options to sustain the economy of the United States and meet the energy needs of the American people. On the other hand, as petroleum reserves shrink, policy makers may well be forced to place more emphasis on new technologies and alternative sources of energy.

Further Reading

Duffy, Robert J. *Nuclear Politics in America*. Lawrence: University Press of Kansas, 1997; Energy Information Administration, Department of Energy. Available online. URL: www.eia.gov. Accessed June 20, 2006; Hoffman, Peter. *Tomorrow's Energy: Hydrogen, Fuel Cells, and the Prospects for a Cleaner Planet*. Cambridge, Mass.: MIT Press, 2001; Melosi, Marvin V. *Coping with Abundance: Energy and Environment in Industrial America, 1820–1980. New York: Newberry Awards Records, 1985; Morton, Rogers C. B. "The Nixon Administration Energy Policy," *Annals of the American Academy of Political and Social Science* 410 (January 1973): pp. 65–74 Prugh, Tom, Christopher Flavin, and Janet L. Sawin. "Changing the Oil Economy." In *State of the World 2005: Redefining Global Security.* Washington, DC: Worldwatch Institute, 2005; Roberts, Paul. *The End of Oil: On the Edge of a Perilous New World.* Boston: Houghton Mifflin, 2004; Smil, Vaclav. *Energy in World History.* Boulder, Colo.: Westview Press, 1994; Wirth, Timothy E., C. Boyden Gray, and John D. Podesta. "The Future of Energy Policy." *Foreign Affairs* 82, no. 4 (July/August 2003): pp. 132–155 Yetiv, Steve. *Crude Awakenings: Global Oil Security and American Foreign Policy.* Ithaca, N.Y.: Cornell University Press, 2004.

—Glen Sussman

entitlements

Entitlements are federal government programs that require payments to any individuals or organizations eligible to receive benefits defined by law. There are many different types of entitlements, though most of the entitlement expenditures of the federal government are distributed to the most vulnerable individuals in society—the poor, disabled, and elderly. Consequently, in addition to providing a legal right to payments for eligible beneficiaries, many entitlements carry a moral obligation to those in need. Moreover, some of the most costly entitlement programs, such as SOCIAL SECURITY and Medicare, are supported in PUBLIC OPINION polls by large majorities of Americans and are bolstered by powerful INTEREST GROUPS.

Since entitlements are products of legislation, entitlement benefits can only be increased or reduced either by changing existing law or by adopting new law. Reducing entitlement benefits through legislative reforms has proven to be difficult, though there is a compelling case for cutting entitlement spending. Entitlement expenditures have been largely responsible for the long-term growth in federal government spending since the mid-1960s, and the greatest budgetary effects are yet to come. Spending projections for meeting retirement and health care obligations of

the burgeoning "baby boom" generation over the next 50 years are literally unsustainable under existing law. Ultimately, entitlement benefits will need to be reduced or additional taxes will need to be raised in order to cover the expected growth of entitlement spending.

A basic understanding of entitlements requires an introduction to the variety of entitlement programs, the development of entitlement legislation and the causes of spending growth, future projections of entitlement spending, and the challenge of entitlement reform.

Entitlement programs are typically classified as either "means tested" or "non–means tested." Means tested programs take into account an individual's financial need, whereas non–means tested programs distribute benefits regardless of an individual's financial need. Means tested entitlements include such programs as Medicaid, Supplemental Security Income (SSI), food stamps, student loans, and unemployment compensation. Non–means tested programs include Social Security, Medicare, government pensions, military retirement, and veterans' benefits.

These programs vary in terms of their size, complexity, and the constituencies they serve. The largest entitlement, in terms of both cost and number of beneficiaries, is Social Security, which provides benefits for retirees and the disabled as well as benefits for their dependents and survivors. In 2005, Social Security paid benefits totaling $521 billion to more than 48 million people. Medicare, the health insurance program for people 65 years of age or older, is the second-largest entitlement program, covering benefits of more than 42 million people at a cost of $333 billion in 2005. Medicaid, the health insurance program for low-income individuals, is the third most costly program; it served 44 million people at a cost of $181.7 billion in federal expenditures. These three programs alone consumed 42 percent of all federal spending and about 71 percent of all entitlement spending in 2005.

Programs such as unemployment compensation, food stamps, government pensions, military retirement, student loans, and veterans' benefits are geared toward smaller constituent groups. All entitlement programs contain an array of details that define eligibility and benefits, though some are more complex than others.

Several programs, including Medicaid, food stamps, and unemployment compensation, depend on contributions from STATE GOVERNMENTS.

The origins and development of entitlements are as various as the programs themselves, though they typically emerge from crises, broad public concerns, and/or the innovations of policy makers or well-organized groups. Social Security began as a modest program under the Social Security Act of 1935 during the Great Depression to provide income security to aged people who could no longer work to make a living. The Social Security Act of 1935 also created Aid to Dependent Children (ADC), later changed to Aid to Families with Dependent Children (AFDC). ADC provided cash benefits to families with children who had lost a primary income earner. Social Security benefits increased with amendments to the Social Security Act in 1950 and the addition of disability insurance in 1954.

But the largest growth in entitlement programs occurred in the 1960s and 1970s during the GREAT SOCIETY era and its aftermath. Medicare and Medicaid were created in 1965, along with several smaller programs, such as food stamps and the Guaranteed Student Loan program. From 1967 to 1972, Congress and the president (both Lyndon B. Johnson and Richard Nixon) passed several increases in Social Security retirement and family support benefits. Two major enhancements in 1972 capped off this period of program expansion: Supplemental Security Income (SSI), a program to assist poor elderly, blind, and disabled individuals, and automatic cost-of-living-adjustments (COLAs) to retiree benefits. COLAs guaranteed that retiree benefits would increase with the rate of inflation, thus ensuring that the recipients' purchasing power would not be eroded by economic forces that increased prices of goods and services.

As large deficits emerged in the 1980s and 1990s, policy makers generally stopped adding new entitlement benefits. In fact, on several occasions Congress and the president enacted legislation that reduced benefits for farm subsidies, veterans, food stamps, government pensions, Medicare, Medicaid, and even Social Security. Though many of these cuts were modest, all of them were politically difficult to enact, and some amounted to very significant policy changes. In 1996, for instance, Congress and President Bill Clinton approved a welfare reform law that eliminated the entitlement status of AFDC and replaced it with a block grant to states entitled Temporary Assistance for Needy Families (TANF).

Despite attempts to control spending, one consequence of the program expansions of the 1960s and 1970s has been the growth of entitlement spending as a percentage of all federal spending. In order to make this point, it is helpful to identify three broad spending categories of the federal budget. First, discretionary spending refers to spending for domestic and defense programs that are subject to annual APPROPRIATIONS approved by Congress. Thus, if it wants to increase spending for homeland security, or raise the salaries of civil servants, or cut spending for after-school enrichment programs, it may do so. Literally thousands of line items for discretionary programs are adjusted annually through the appropriations process. A second category is mandatory spending, which covers entitlements. Mandatory programs are not subjected to annual appropriations; the amount spent on entitlement programs is determined by how many individuals or institutions qualify for the benefits defined by legislation. The third category is interest on the national debt; when the budget is in a deficit, the DEPARTMENT OF THE TREASURY needs to borrow money to pay the bills, and it must, of course, pay interest on that debt.

In 1964, prior to the creation of Medicare and Medicaid and the expansions of Social Security, mandatory-entitlement spending accounted for 34 percent of all federal spending; in 2005, mandatory-entitlement spending had grown to about 58 percent of all spending. Thus, while Congress cut some benefits in the 1980s and 1990s, it did not do nearly enough to halt the upward spending growth in entitlements.

The shift from a budget based primarily on discretionary programs to a budget driven by entitlements has profound implications for spending control. Since discretionary programs can be adjusted annually in the appropriations process, at least theoretically, Congress can control spending from year to year. But entitlement spending is uncontrollable so long as the law defining benefits does not change; spending for entitlements depends mainly on the number of eligible beneficiaries, the types of the benefits, and numerous uncontrollable forces, such as the state of the economy, demographic changes in the population, and the price of health care. If the economy goes into a recession, claims for means tested entitlements—food stamps, unemployment insurance, and Medicaid—increase. If the number of retirees increases, if people live longer, or if inflation increases, expenditures for Social Security will grow.

Medicare, one of the most expensive and fastest-growing entitlements, provides a good example of the difficulties of controlling entitlement spending. Over the past 30 years, large increases in health-care costs above the rate of inflation accounted for the dramatic increases in public health programs. When health inflation rises in a given year, the president and Congress cannot simply decide to spend less. Under existing law, doctors and hospitals are entitled to be reimbursed, and beneficiaries are entitled to medical services and treatment. Total annual spending on Medicare depends on the costs of those services and the number of eligible Medicare beneficiaries who use the health-care system. Thus, in order to reduce Medicare spending, the laws specifying eligibility must be changed first, which means reducing the benefits, increasing the costs to senior citizens, or cutting reimbursements to doctors and hospitals. Though Congress and the president have made such changes from time to time, the effects on total spending are overwhelmed by the general increase in health care spending.

Thus, the rapid growth in entitlement spending began as a result of policy changes in the1960s and early 1970s, but policy makers generally stopped adding more entitlement *benefits* by the mid-1970s. The growth in overall entitlement spending after 1974 resulted from demographic, economic, social trends, and health care cost inflation. Even though overall entitlement spending grew more than discretionary programs in the 1980s and 1990s, except for Medicare and Medicaid, it grew at a slower pace than in the 1960s and 1970s.

Entitlements are projected to grow dramatically in the future as the baby boomers retire and make unprecedented claims on retirement benefits and the public health-care system. From 2010 to 2030, the number of individuals over the age of 65 will double, and the percentage of people over the age of 65 will increase from 13 to 19 percent of the population. As a result of this demographic shift in the population, by 2030, Social Security, Medicare, Medicaid, and interest on the national debt will consume virtually every dollar of expected revenues under existing law.

The long-term budget outlook for entitlement spending was compounded in 2004, when Congress and President George W. Bush enacted the Medicare Modernization Act (Medicare Part D), which provided prescription drug coverage to Medicare-eligible individuals. As of January 2006, about 22.5 million of the 43 million Medicare recipients had enrolled in Medicare Part D, and the program is expected to cost $558 billion over the first 10 years and will grow even more rapidly thereafter.

David Walker, comptroller general of the Government Accountability Office, has been the most recent voice among public officials who have declared the projected path of entitlement spending growth "unsustainable." If nothing is done to slow the rate of growth in the big entitlement programs, the next generation of workers and their children will face massive tax increases, a reduction in their standard of living, or both. Entitlement reform advocates say it is economically, fiscally, and morally unacceptable to not change this course. The next generation should not be saddled by the excesses of the previous generations, especially when the problems are clear.

But the prospects for reining in entitlement spending are complicated by practical considerations, moral claims, and political forces. Despite the massive total cost to finance Social Security, the average monthly benefit is just over $1,000 per retiree. The good news is that a small average reduction in benefits would generate massive budget savings, but the bad news is that many retirees depend on every dollar of Social Security for subsistence. Meanwhile, Medicare and Medicaid are essential programs for millions of Americans now and in the future who will need access to the health-care system. Advocates of Social Security, Medicare, and Medicaid point out that these programs have rescued tens of millions of senior citizens from a life of poverty in old age. Any cut, particularly for low-income recipients, would be a step backward in terms of addressing the needs of the elderly.

Importantly, Social Security presents a simple set of solutions compared with Medicare and Medicaid. Demands on Social Security are fairly easy to calculate, given average life expectancies and readily available demographic data, and the alternatives for cutting spending are clear enough. Increasing the retirement age, reducing the amount of benefits, and changing the way inflation adjustments are calculated are a few notable changes that could produce savings. The costs of Medicare and Medicaid, on the other hand, are tied to the costs of health care in general. Thus, while government reforms such as reducing fraud and waste and developing a more competitive pricing structure will reduce spending, the key to controlling the costs of Medicare and Medicaid is to contain health-care costs in general, a more vexing challenge for policy makers.

The political obstacles to entitlement reform are formidable. Public opinion polls repeatedly show that Americans oppose cuts in Social Security, Medicare, and, to a lesser extent, Medicaid. Support for these programs is broad and deep; there are no clear divisions across party lines or among age groups. Younger individuals are more inclined to support private accounts as a substitute for the current Social Security program, but they do not support spending cuts. Moreover, entitlements are supported by powerful interest groups. The American Association of Retired Persons (AARP), which spearheads a coalition of senior citizen groups, has over 35 million members and amounts to one of every four registered voters. More specialized groups—hospitals, nursing homes, doctors, health maintenance organizations (HMOs), insurance companies, and now drug companies—all have a stake in the outcome of policy changes. Entitlement reform is certainly possible; after all, we have examples from the past, but the political opposition should not be understated.

Thus, we are left with a complicated and challenging puzzle: How does the federal government meet its legal obligations and deliver the necessary benefits to individual recipients of popular programs and also address the inevitable imbalance of entitlement spending to projected tax revenues? Addressing the problem will require considerable leadership in order to build a consensus that balances the claims of multiple constituencies. Indeed, the lives of virtually every American over the next 50 years will depend on the answer to this question.

See also WELFARE POLICY.

Further Reading
Derthick, Martha. *Policymaking for Social Security*. Washington, D.C.: Brookings Institution Press, 1979; Kotlifoff, Laurence J., and Scott Burns. *The Coming Generational Storm*. Cambridge, Mass.: MIT Press, 2004; Light, Paul. *Still Artful Work: The Continuing Politics of Social Security*. New York: McGraw-Hill, 1995. Moon, Marilyn, and Janemarie Mulvey. *Entitlements and the Elderly*. Washington, D.C.: Urban Institute Press, 1996; Peterson, Peter G. *Running on Empty*. New York: Farrar, Straus & Giroux, 2004; Samuelson, Robert J. *The Good Life and Its Discontents*. New York: Random House, 1995.

—Daniel J. Palazzolo

environmental policy

Environmental policy in the United States has evolved over time, as have other policy areas, but its development was hastened by dedicated activists and shifting PUBLIC OPINION that responded to an escalating environmental crisis. The United States was an early adopter of aggressive policies and institutions to control pollution, first through command-and-control regulations and later through voluntary and market-based policies.

The roots of contemporary environmental policy can be found in the nation's preindustrial past. An anthropocentric view of nature prevailed as the United States grew from an agricultural society to a fully industrialized country. The policy emphasis remained on conservation of natural resources for future extraction and continued economic growth, rather than protecting nature for its own sake. This conservation ethic led to the nation's first national parks during the late 19th century and the founding of the U.S. Forest Service in 1905. Gifford Pinchot, the director of the Forest Service under President Theodore Roosevelt, saw the environment primarily as a source of raw materials to satisfy human needs and sought to manage those materials as efficiently as possible.

As the conservation movement broadened and influenced natural resource policy decisions, a rival

A general view of the air pollution over downtown Los Angeles, California *(Getty Images)*

perspective emerged in the form of the preservation movement. An early leader was John Muir, who founded the Sierra Club in 1872 in response to the devastation of the Sierra Nevada foothills in the frenzy of the California gold rush. Preservationists promoted a biocentric approach to land management. The biocentric approach shunned the purely instrumental view of nature and sought to place human values into a larger context, whereby such goals as pristine ecosystems and saving species from extinction have inherent value. The public increasingly valued national forests and grasslands as a source of recreation and enjoyment. In response to this evolving public view, Congress directed the Forest Service to manage public lands for multiple uses and benefits in addition to sustained yields of resources.

In the area of pollution control, little progress was made prior to 1970. The patchwork of state pollution control laws was weak and ineffective, and federal attempts to give them teeth were largely unsuccessful. However, the 1960s experienced a growing appetite for government action to solve domestic problems as well as a series of ecological catastrophes, which placed the environment squarely on the national agenda by the end of the decade.

The major shift in the role of the federal government began in the 1960s, when the environment emerged as a national policy issue. Air and water quality had been in decline for decades until the urgency of the environmental crisis was raised by several focusing events, such as the publication of Rachel Carson's *Silent Spring* in 1962 and the Santa Barbara oil spill and the fire on the Cuyahoga River in 1969. These developments led to the first Earth Day in 1970. Originally conceived as a teach-in by Wisconsin SENATOR Gaylord Nelson, 20 million Americans took part in events across the country, demanding that the federal government take action to deal with the environmental crisis. After Earth Day raised the consciousness of the American public and its policy makers, the focus of the environmental movement shifted to Washington, D.C. Republican president

Richard Nixon and Democratic congressional leaders vied to demonstrate which was the "greener" of the two POLITICAL PARTIES.

Determined not to be upstaged by his Democratic rivals, President Nixon created the U.S. ENVIRONMENTAL PROTECTION AGENCY (EPA) by executive order and signed the first of several major environmental statutes into law, including the Endangered Species Act. The National Environmental Policy Act (NEPA) requires government agencies to prepare environmental impact statements before undertaking major projects and allows the public to challenge those actions on environmental grounds. Throughout the "environmental decade" of the 1970s, Congress would enact other major laws regulating different forms of pollution.

Regulation of air pollution was federalized with the enactment of the Clean Air Act (CAA) Amendments of 1970. This landmark statute authorized the EPA to set national ambient air quality standards for particulate matter, sulfur dioxide, nitrogen dioxide, volatile organic compounds, ozone (which contributes to smog), and lead. The act created 247 air quality control regions around the country and required the states to submit implementation plans to reach attainment of the standards. States were given a five-year deadline to reduce their emissions by 90 percent, although that deadline was repeatedly rolled back. The law also established auto emission standards for the first time.

Water quality was the focus of the next major environmental statutes enacted by Congress. The Clean Water Act (1972) authorized the EPA to set national water quality standards with the goal of making the nation's rivers and streams fishable and swimmable. The act established a pollution discharge permit system and funded grants to help municipalities build water treatment plants. Recognizing that the Clean Water Act did not go far enough to protect public health, Congress passed the Safe Drinking Water Act (SDWA) in 1974. The EPA was authorized by the SDWA to set drinking water standards and funded additional grants to upgrade community water systems.

After addressing air and water concerns, Congress set its sights on threats from toxic and hazardous materials. The first action was the Resource Conservation and Recovery Act of 1976. This law actually was intended to promote recycling. However, it authorized the EPA to regulate the storage, transportation, treatment, and disposal of hazardous waste. The same year, Congress enacted the Toxic Substances Control Act, which allows the EPA to ban or regulate any chemicals presenting an "unreasonable risk of harm" to human health or the ecosystem and requires the testing of new chemicals before they go on the market.

The last major environmental statute was enacted as the environmental decade closed in 1980. Congress passed the Comprehensive Environmental Response, Compensation and Liability Act (Superfund) to address the problem of abandoned hazardous waste sites, such as the New York community of Love Canal, which had been constructed on a decades-old chemical waste pit. The law required the EPA to create a list of abandoned hazardous waste sites and rank them by their risk to human health and provided a $1.6 billion fund to clean up the most dangerous sites. In 2002, more than 50,000 sites had been identified, and the Superfund National Priority List included 1,291 sites. The cost of toxic mitigation in some high-profile contamination cases, such as Glen Avon, California, and Times Beach, Missouri, contributed to a backlash against environmental regulation in the 1980s.

When President Ronald Reagan took office in 1980, he made no secret of his hostility to government regulation and used executive powers to stymie the implementation of environmental policy. Reagan issued an executive order requiring a cost-benefit analysis for every major regulatory action, cut the EPA's budget, and appointed people known for their antienvironmental views to his administration, most notably Interior Secretary James Watt and EPA Administrator Anne Burford. This decade also gave rise to the Wise Use movement. Seeking to reverse the decades-old multiple-use policy of land management, Wise Use supporters were motivated by an ideological view that the most efficient decisions about public lands were made at the local level by those who used their resources.

With the changing climate in Washington, D.C., the environmental movement went into a defensive mode. The movement's strategy shifted from legislation to litigation. With fewer allies in the White House and Congress, environmentalists turned to the courts to block the weakening of the major laws that were created during the 1970s and to fight for their enforcement. The 1980s saw a rapid growth of environmental interest group membership as well as the number of grassroots environmental organizations, which provide information to policy makers and the electorate, mobilize voters, and force implementation of environmental laws through citizen suits.

Policy makers responded to public demands for increased environmental protection during the 1990s, though not at the level witnessed in the 1970s. When the Clean Air Act was amended in 1990, the revised act reflected congressional frustration with the EPA's lack of progress in implementing the law. The 1990 amendments included specific air quality goals and deadlines for nonattainment areas, replacing the original act's language that cities make "reasonable further progress" toward attainment of their goals. Another provision required the EPA to begin regulating 189 additional hazardous air pollutants, a mandate that carried deadlines and hammer clauses to ensure its implementation.

The limitations of command-and-control policies had become apparent by the 1990s, and voluntary and market-based systems of pollution control became increasingly popular. One provision of the 1990 CAA amendments created a market for trading sulfur dioxide emissions, which contribute to acid rain. Under the trading system, industries and coal-fired utilities were given one permit for every ton of sulfur dioxide emissions, with the intent of reducing the number of permits by half over 20 years. Each participant had the freedom to reduce its own emissions ahead of schedule and sell the excess permits to others in the market. The success of the program has made it a model for tradable emissions markets on the local level and in other countries.

The focus of most environmental policy making had been on domestic problems prior to the 1990s, but Congress began to address global and transboundary problems as well. In response to the 1989 Montreal Protocol, the 1990 CAA amendments listed specific chemicals that deplete the ozone layer and included a provision to phase out their production and use. Other, more modest goals were accomplished by the decade's end: The Food Quality Protection Act was passed in 1996, stricter air quality standards for ozone and particulate matter were pro-

mulgated by the EPA in 1997, and President Bill Clinton placed large portions of public lands off limits to development by designating new national monuments and wilderness areas and designating 65 million acres of public land as roadless, a move that enraged many western politicians.

The first term of President George W. Bush (2001–05) was reminiscent of Reagan-era environmental policies, which sparked a resurgent environmental movement. After taking office, Bush reversed many of his predecessor's regulatory actions, such as a new arsenic standard for drinking water (later reinstated). Bush also reversed a campaign pledge to begin regulating carbon monoxide, a gas that contributes to global warming. He also denounced the Kyoto Protocol and withdrew the United States from the agreement to reduce greenhouse gas emissions. The administration's land management policies were just as retrograde: Bush supported initiatives in Congress to open the Arctic National Wildlife Refuge for oil exploration and initiated his Healthy Forests plan, which opened new areas of national forest to logging in the name of preventing forest fires.

Further Reading
Cahn, Matthew A. *Environmental Deceptions: The Tension between Liberalism and Environmental Policymaking in the United States.* Albany: State University of New York Press, 1995; Davies, J. Clarence, and Jan Mazurek. *Pollution Control in the United States: Evaluating the System.* Washington, D.C.: Resources for the Future, 1998; Dietrich, William. *The Final Forest: The Battle for the Last Great Trees of the Pacific Northwest.* New York: Simon & Schuster, 1992; Kettl, Donald. F., ed. *Environmental Governance: A Report on the Next Generation of Environmental Policy.* Washington, D.C.: Brookings Institution, 2002; Rosenbaum, Walter A. *Environmental Politics and Policy.* 6th ed. Washington, D.C.: Congressional Quarterly Press, 2006.
—David M. Shafie

federal debt and deficit

There is a difference between the federal *debt* and the federal *deficit*. The debt is the accumulated total of all deficits. Each year the federal government spends trillions of dollars on programs and other spending projects. When it spends more money than it takes in, that is a called a budget deficit.

The U.S. federal government began its existence with a large debt. During the Revolutionary War, the nascent government borrowed money from France and anyone else who might be of service to the colonies. (France was very willing to help finance the American Revolution because it was a heated enemy of the British, and any enemy of my enemy, so the saying goes, is my friend.) The CONTINENTAL CONGRESS also borrowed money in the form of what we today might call war bonds from the colonists themselves. It was not uncommon for a patriotic colonist to mortgage his farm or land and buy these bonds. The promise was that after the war, the new government would pay back the colonists. But after the war was won, the new federal government, under the ARTICLES OF CONFEDERATION, did not have the power to tax. When France came to the new government demanding a repayment of its debt, the U.S. government was unable to meet its responsibilities. The same was true when the farmers of the United States went to the government demanding payment of the bonds they had bought.

This caused the new government significant problems. Its major ally, France, was demanding the money that the United States owed, and the farmers were losing their property because of the failure of the new government to keep its word and repay the debt owed. In several states, minirebellions occurred. The most famous of these is referred to as Shays Rebellion. Daniel Shays was a former captain in the Revolutionary army. He led a group of disgruntled farmers to the state capital in Springfield, Massachusetts, and attempted to shut down the government. This and the minirebellions that took place in every one of the 13 states compelled the states to rethink the wisdom of the Articles of Confederation and greatly contributed to the movement to jettison the articles and write a new constitution for the nation.

In the new government created by the U.S. CONSTITUTION, taxing power was conferred to the new Congress. The new government had the means, but as one will see, not always the will, to pay the debts owed.

Almost every year (the recent exceptions were the last few years of the Bill Clinton PRESIDENCY) the federal government runs up a deficit as expenditures exceed revenues. If one were to add up all the deficits, this is what is often referred to as the national debt. The debt is the total amount of all the deficits, or the amount the government has *borrowed* and thus owes to American citizens, banks, other nations, and the bond market. The government must also pay interest on the debt. In 2005, the federal government spent $352 of each taxpayer's money on interest payments on the national debt; interest payments do not pay back the principal of the loan. Today the DEPARTMENT OF THE TREASURY's payment on the interest of the national debt alone makes that budget item the third-largest expense in the federal budget, behind only spending on the DEPARTMENT OF DEFENSE and the DEPARTMENT OF HEALTH AND HUMAN SERVICES.

Currently, the national debt is roughly $8.2 trillion (as of 2007). The per-day increase in the debt grows at roughly $2.3 billion. The population of the United States is estimated at nearly 300,000,000 people. If the national debt were divided up to estimate each citizen's share, it would come out to a bill of roughly $27,500 per person. And the debt continues to grow. There is also a concern for business and private debt. The overall debt of U.S. businesses and households is estimated to be more than the federal government's debt.

When did the debt-deficit dilemma rise to near crisis proportion? The federal government has always had difficulty living within its means. During and after World War II, the federal government, in an effort to fight first the Great Depression and then World War II, ran up huge deficits. In 1945, the federal debt and deficits were at alarmingly high rates (more than 100 percent of the gross domestic product). But this reflected emergency spending, and soon the budget deficit-debt crisis was brought under greater control. By the 1950s, the trend lines were all going in the right direction, even as the federal government continued to have difficulty keeping revenues and expenditures in line. In fact, the trend lines continued to move in the right direction until the late 1970s and 1980s. It was during the administration of President Ronald Reagan (1981–89) that an explosion of spending and cuts in taxes threw the debt-deficit balance dramatically out of line. All the trend lines started moving at a fast pace in the wrong direction. President Reagan's budget proposals as approved by

Congress, which included an increase in defense spending, a cut in taxes, and a reduction in domestic program spending, contributed to a dramatic increase in both the federal debt and yearly budget deficits. When Reagan took office in 1981, the United States was the world's largest creditor nation. When he left office eight years later, the United States was the world's largest debtor nation.

It was left to Reagan's successors to clean up the economic mess left behind. President George H. W. Bush, faced with this harsh economic reality, was compelled to break the famous campaign pledge he made in 1988 ("Read my lips: No new taxes!") and reached a compromise with the Democratically controlled Congress to raise taxes in 1990 in an attempt to reduce the national debt and deficit. This was a small but significant step in righting the economic imbalance. As economic indicators and the overall state of the economy began to improve by 1992, President Bill Clinton (1993–2001) and Congress were able to help further bring the imbalance under control, even running a budget surplus toward the end of the 1990s. And while both Bush and Clinton may have paid a political price for getting the budget crisis under control, clearly putting more discipline into federal spending programs had a very positive impact on the debt-deficit crisis.

The presidency of George W. Bush, propelled by the response to the terrorist attacks of September 11, 2001, and Bush's insistence on a substantial tax cut, once again led to large deficits and a significant increase in the national debt. Bush recommitted the economic sins of his political hero, Ronald Reagan, and called for both a huge increase in defense spending (to fight the war against terrorism) and a large tax cut. This led to negative economic consequences for the debt-deficit dilemma. Many economists were alarmed at the explosion of the deficit and warned of significant negative consequences if the U.S. government did not get it under control.

Those concerned that large deficits will be a significant drag on the overall economy argue that the deficits are unfair in that they let the current generation spend government revenues but leave the bill behind for the next generation to pay. This allows the current generation to consume more but pay less. The deficit also reduces the amount of money that is saved and invested. This means less capital and poten-

tially higher interest rates. Higher interest rates draw more foreign investment into the United States but may lead to larger trade imbalances (which are already at high rates). Those who are less concerned about the rise in the debt and deficit argue that the evidence of negative consequences is by no means clear and that the United States has nonetheless done well within the broader economic realm even while amassing large budgetary deficits.

Clearly, questions of intergenerational justice are raised when the current generation lives well but passes the enormous debt on to its children. The preamble to the U.S. CONSTITUTION states that "We the people of the United States, in Order to form a more perfect Union, establish Justice, insure domestic Tranquility, provide for the common defence, promote the general Welfare, and secure the Blessings of Liberty *to ourselves and our Posterity . . .*" (emphasis added). Many citizens would argue that the current generation should act more responsibly in regard to the economic well being of future generations and not leave them mired in debt.

See also BUDGET PROCESS; INCOME TAXES.

Further Reading
Cavanaugh, Francis X. *The Truth about the National Debt: Five Myths and One Reality*. Cambridge, Mass.: Harvard Business School, 1996; Manning, Robert D. *Credit Card Nation: The Consequences of America's Addiction to Credit*. New York: Basic Books, 2000; Rivlin, Alice M. *Reviving the American Dream: The Economy, the States, and the Federal Government*. Washington, D.C.: Brookings Institution Press, 1992.
—Michael A. Genovese

fiscal policy
Fiscal policy is the term used to describe the spending decisions governments make. When we begin to list what governments do on the domestic level or in the international arena, most government actions require spending money. Increased police protection, for example, requires spending money to hire more police officers and to provide them with the equipment necessary to do their jobs. Increasing the quality of education requires spending money for administrators to monitor levels of quality as well as spending to make certain educators are properly trained and

updated on curricula and that schools have all the resources necessary to provide an environment conducive to learning. Making the decision to go to war involves spending a good deal of money, as soldiers and other military personnel must be paid. They require equipment as well as medical supplies, food, and water; not only this, but the weapons soldiers use must be replenished or replaced, depending on the type of weapon used.

Most government actions, then, require spending money. The sources of government revenue include taxes, investments, fees, and borrowed money, otherwise known as debt. As a government begins to decide what actions to take, it must consider the sources and amounts of revenue it has. All of this, then, greatly increases the politics of fiscal policy, because taxes are not popular among citizens, and many people disagree over the direction of government actions and the allocation of resources for those actions. Generally speaking, people want government services, such as well-maintained roads and protection, but they do not want to pay taxes to support those services. Questions that are intrinsic to fiscal policy include: What actions should a government take? How much support for each action exists among the citizenry? How much money should be spent on this action? If the action requires additional revenue, from where will it come?

Another key question that must be addressed within the context of American government is what level of government should administer this policy. Our government is federalist, meaning that we have one national government and 50 subgovernment units, called STATES. Each state has many subgovernment units in turn, known as counties, parishes, or boroughs, and within those, cities and towns. The U.S. CONSTITUTION provides broad responsibilities for the national government and reserves all other powers (and responsibilities) to the states. Because of constitutional phrases that direct the national government to "promote the general welfare" and "make all laws necessary and proper" to carry out duties, citizens and political leaders debate what responsibilities belong at the national level and which should be the sole responsibility of the states. In general, the national government provides all the services directed in the U.S. Constitution and subsidizes the costs of other government services that are provided by the states. Education, some health care, transportation, welfare, and senior and children's services are examples of such government services. Some government services, are provided by cities but subsidized by the federal government, such as infrastructure preservation or renovation. Fiscal policy, then, consists of three intergovernmental relationships: national to state, national to local, and state to local jurisdictions.

When one government subsidizes the cost of providing a service, it does so through a grant. Federal grants have two main purposes: to direct policy implementation and outcomes in the states and to strengthen the fiscal capacity of states to provide services. Throughout the last century, many examinations of FEDERALISM have considered the effectiveness of federal grants. Federal grants have followed three paths: categorical grants, in which the grantor government places restrictions on and remains an active principal in grant implementation; block grants, in which the grantor government establishes parameters for the grant and monitors the outcomes of the grant; and general revenue sharing, in which the grantor government provides resources for the general use of the subgovernment, often with wide parameters established for the use of the grant. Each type of grant has its own political constituency and, necessarily, its detractors.

A categorical grant may be open or closed; that is, it may or may not have upper limits on the amount subgovernments may receive. Many categorical grants require matching funds from subgovernments or have maintenance of effort (MOE) requirements. Some grants may be established as ENTITLEMENTS, which pose a threat of budget deficits, as programs in this category, by nature, are open-ended.

Block grants enable the national government to promote goals broadly, while also funding programs in a targeted fashion, through formulas that favor states with the greatest needs. States often prefer block grants and general purpose fiscal assistance because these allow the greatest flexibility for local spending preferences. Federal officials argue from time to time for an increase in block grants in order to limit uncontrolled spending in matching funds and to reduce duplication in categorical grants. Despite trends toward block grants and general fiscal assistance, the national government continues to provide the bulk of its fiscal assistance in the form of categorical grants. Before welfare was changed to nonentitlement status and made a block grant, only 16 percent of federal domestic assistance was given in the form of block grants, and these were largely for transportation or community development.

There is considerable overlap in government grants. Within the last decade, the GOVERNMENT ACCOUNTING OFFICE (GAO) reported more than 160 programs in existence for job training and more than 90 programs for childhood development. Proposals to consolidate grants argue that the change would increase efficiency and promote state innovation to solve problems of poverty and economic development. Many studies have suggested particularly that grants geared toward poverty elimination only increase dependency and that they should therefore be eliminated or changed. Perhaps more important, when the federal government is faced with pending budget cuts, one compromise that can be reached to gain state support for reduced funding is to consolidate grants and to change their structure from categorical to block, thus allowing states dominant reign in implementing the grants.

The nature of federal funding streams tilts on a balance between allowing federal policy makers greater control of implementation and outcomes through categorical grants and increasing the efficiency and innovation of state programs, not to mention the political support of GOVERNORs and other state policy makers.

Discussion of fiscal policy should include political manipulation of grants to various congressional districts. Congress may decide the locational recipient for a grant, such as a military base, water project, or dam, but in many cases, Congress provides skeletal guidelines for a grant program (e.g., eligibility criteria, limits on grant amounts), leaving the bureaucracy to decide grant recipients, award amounts, and other conditions of the grant.

Congressional legislators can better demonstrate their efforts in the states through categorical grants and therefore have often preferred these, particularly when they are politically dependent on district constituencies, as opposed to state or local policy makers, for support. Grants may be implemented more effectively and have a greater stimulus effect when the congressional oversight committee for its authorizing agency has a greater interest in the grant. Agency

monitoring is more intense when Congress has an active interest in the policy outcomes of a grant. Increased agency monitoring subsequently has been found to trigger increased effort on the part of the subgovernment recipient to fulfill the mission of the policy.

While agency administrators have the authority to approve projects for congressional districts, skepticism exists about the influence that the president or Congress has in the decision and release of grants. Given the need to strengthen constituent support, agencies can assist members by reminding them that the support for projects of poor quality can ultimately harm, rather than garnish, constituent support. But what about political influences for granting high-quality projects? Political effects in grant distribution appear to occur most often during the initial years of a grant program and when a grant appears to be threatened. Politics affects district projects, but only in subtle ways. Bureaucrats are able to insulate their agencies from illegal political influences by allowing the release of grants to be politicized. Grants being considered in election years are usually hurried for release in the electoral season if the grants are viable and would normally have attained approval. Grants for districts of key members and members of the president's party are given priority when possible.

Fiscal policy addresses community needs in a couple of ways. The most needy metropolitan areas have their projects met regardless of the president in office because they meet grant qualifying criteria, such as having populations of 500,000 or more, being located in a targeted Northeast or Midwest frostbelt region, or meeting the economic conditions of most distressed criteria. Cities' needs are also met because of congressional district concerns and, most importantly, because these cities have a dedicated lobbyist stationed in Washington, D.C., to work to identify grants, package the grant applications, and make both federal agencies and their congressional delegations aware of the cities' needs. Cities lacking in grant writing and LOBBYING skills often are overlooked unless they meet other grant priority criteria outlined above.

Research on fiscal policy has often concentrated on the effectiveness of grants to motivate the actions of the recipient government. Much of this literature is based on the principal-agent theory, which states that the principal (in this case the government providing the grant) must understand how to motivate the agent (in this case the government receiving the grant). Considerations include whether the grants that require subgovernments to match resources or to maintain funding efforts actually create a stimulus effect, whereby the local government becomes committed to enacting the new policy and eventually internalizes the need for government involvement in the given area.

Some evidence suggests that categorical grants with matching requirements do create a stimulus effect for state and local spending. A similar theory exists with respect to block and general revenue sharing grants. This thesis is known as the flypaper effect. It postulates that the lump sum grants will trigger state and local spending. Included in this thesis is the fiscal illusion hypothesis, which states that a voter will approve of increased state and local spending, even if this results in an increase in taxes, because he or she perceives the greatest burden in providing the good to have shifted away from him or her. More explicitly, the voter believes that if federal grants are subsidizing the good, then his or her cost (via state and local taxes) is minimized.

A countertheory to the flypaper effect suggests that federal grants, whether in the form of categorical, block, or general revenue sharing, provide no stimulus, but rather are used to replace state and local funds that might have otherwise been committed to the issue area. Some evidence suggests that state and local funding have actually diminished in the areas of education and poverty relief once federal funds became available. When federal grants create incentives for increased funding on the state and local levels, those jurisdictions increase their expenditures in the given policy areas. However, when provided the opportunity to receive federal funding without matching requirements, state and local governments typically decrease their expenditures, treating federal funds as fungible resources. If a state or local government has internalized the need for a policy, it generally remains committed to funding the policy even when federal grants diminish.

Fiscal policy, then, is intrinsic to all other public policies. Fiscal policy determines the directions governments will go in taking action to provide certain services. It determines how the government will generate revenue to fund its actions. It also determines what level of government will provide the funding, or a portion of the funding, for the service, and what level of government will be responsible for implementing and monitoring the policy. In the last 20 years, the United States has moved toward block grants for social services such as welfare. It has devolved most of the policy responsibility to the states and is expanding this policy to Medicaid. The economist Richard Musgrave contends that a central question must be asked when considering fiscal policy and the responsibility for providing a government service: What is the highest level of jurisdiction that will be affected by policy outcomes? The answer, he indicates, should dictate which government should act as the principal in initiating funding and monitoring implementation and outcomes of the policy. A state may not be affected by whether a city erects a traffic light, for example. However, the nation is affected if all its citizens are not self-sustaining. Therefore, the federal government has a direct interest in education and welfare policies. As the debate continues over what level of government is appropriate for providing services, it is imperative that citizens weigh all possible outcomes before informing their representatives of their preferences for government level shifting of responsibilities.

Further Reading
Anagnoson, J. Theodore. "Federal Grant Agencies and Congressional Election Campaigns." *American Journal of Political Science* 26, no. 3 (August): 547–61; Cammisa, Anne Marie. *Governments as Interest Groups: Intergovernmental Lobbying and the Federal System.* Westport, Conn.: Praeger Publishers, 1995; Chubb, John E. "The Political Economy of Federalism." *American Political Science Review* 79 (December): 994–1015; Conlan, Timothy. *From New Federalism to Devolution.* Washington, D.C.: Brookings Institution Press, 1998; Early, Dirk. "The Role of Subsidized Housing in Reducing Homelessness: An Empirical Investigation Using Micro Data." *Policy Analysis and Management* 17, no. 4 (Fall 1998): 687–696; Hanson, Russell, ed. *Governing Partners: State-Local Relations in the United States.* Boulder, Colo: Westview Press, 1998; Hedge, David. "Fiscal Dependency and the State Budget Process." *Journal of Politics* 45 (February 1983): 198–208; Hofferbert,

Richard, and John Urice. "Small-Scale Policy: The Federal Stimulus Versus Competing Explanations for State Funding of the Arts." *Journal of Political Science* 29, no. 2 (May): 308–329; Logan, Robert R. "Fiscal Illusion and the Grantor Government." *Journal of Political Economy* 94, no. 6 (1986): 1,304–1,317; Megdal, Sharon Bernstein. "The Flypaper Effect Revisited: An Econometric Explanation." *Review of Economics and Statistics* 69, no. 2 (May 1987): 347–351; Murray, Charles. *Losing Ground: American Social Policy, 1950–1980.* New York: Basic Books, 1984; O'Toole, Laurence J., ed. *American Intergovernmental Relations.* Washington, D.C.: Congressional Quarterly Press, 2000; Rich, Michael. "Distributive Politics and the Allocation of Federal Grants." *American Political Science Review* 83, no. 1 (March 1989): 193–213; Welch, Susan, and Kay Thompson. "The Impact of Federal Incentives on State Policy Innovation." *American Journal of Political Science* 24, no. 4 (November 1980): 715–729; Wood, Dan B. "Federalism and Policy Responsiveness: The Clean Air Act." *Journal of Politics* 53 (August 1991): 851–859; Zampelli, Ernest M. "Resource Fungibility, The Flypaper Effect, and the Expenditure Impact of Grants-In-Aid." *Review of Economics and Statistics* 68, no. 1 (February 1986): 33–40.

—Marybeth D. Beller

foreign policy

Foreign policy encompasses the decisions, actions, and communications that the United States takes with respect to other nations. Foreign policy matters range from informal discussions between diplomats to summit meetings between heads of state. American foreign policy interests have expanded greatly since 1789, when the United States was most concerned about protecting its territory and borders. In the 21st century, as the United States assumes the leading role internationally in combating terrorism, it works closely with other nations to protect its political, economic, and military interests. While foreign policy in the early days of the American REPUBLIC was often a choice, today interacting with other nations is, in effect, a necessity.

American foreign policy in the 18th century is perhaps best defined by President George Washington's farewell address to the nation in 1796. Circu-lated via newspapers, the address clearly and concisely summarized the first president's views on the health and future of the American republic. In foreign affairs, Washington counseled caution foremost; while he supported trade with other nations, he warned that the United States must "steer clear of permanent alliances" with other nations. Washington did not advocate isolationism for the United States, but he did state that close ties to other nations could hinder pursuit of U.S. interests. In calling essentially for unilateralism in American foreign policy, Washington captured the unique position that the United States faced at the time with respect to other nations. Its geographic separation from the established states of the time meant that the United States possessed the luxury of choosing when it would engage in foreign affairs. Consequently, American foreign policy in the 19th century frequently overlapped with protection of U.S. national security.

When the United States did engage with other nations in the 19th century, it sought primarily to secure or expand its territorial borders. The War of 1812 with Great Britain reinforced American independence, and afterward the United States was careful not to become entangled in European politics. In 1821, Secretary of State John Quincy Adams explicitly stated in a Fourth of July address that America "goes not abroad, in search of monsters to destroy. She is the well-wisher to the freedom and independence of all." Two years later, President James Monroe announced in his annual state of the union message that any efforts by other states to gain power in the Western Hemisphere would be construed "as dangerous to [American] peace and safety." Although the Monroe Doctrine has gained popular currency as a U.S. commitment to protecting the independence of other states in the Western Hemisphere, at the time it was primarily a defensive posture to ensure that Europe did not interfere with U.S. interests. American foreign policy in the 19th century extended primarily to ensuring its own LIBERTY and independence, not to actively promoting those values for new revolutionary states.

Perhaps the most significant feature of American foreign policy in the 19th century was its focus on U.S. expansion. The Louisiana Purchase in 1803 doubled the size of the United States and opened the nation to westward expansion. Historian Frederick

Jackson Turner later identified this expansion as manifest destiny, and the concept aptly described the American perspective on the right to grow and develop as a nation. The Mexican-American War of 1846 further expanded U.S. territory, establishing the southern boundary of Texas and extending the U.S. border to California. But the Civil War of the 1860s halted manifest destiny and forced the United States to focus on ensuring its internal stability and security before engaging in foreign affairs again.

When both the Atlantic and Pacific Oceans bordered the territorial United States, the next logical step for a growing industrial power was to pursue global expansion. The United States embarked on this journey with the Spanish-American War of 1898, defeating Spain and gaining control of Cuba, Puerto Rico, Guam, and the Philippines in just four months. After the war, however, members of Congress debated whether the United States had a duty, or even a right, to take control of overseas territories, and what responsibilities would follow. In 1904, President Theodore Roosevelt unabashedly asserted the U.S. right to engage in international affairs with his statement that the United States would intervene in the Western Hemisphere whenever it saw evidence of "chronic wrongdoing" within states. The Roosevelt Corollary to the Monroe Doctrine expanded U.S. foreign policy interests greatly; whereas previously the United States had focused on defending the region from outside influence, now it was willing to act, in Roosevelt's words, as "an international peace power." Roosevelt exuberantly demonstrated his willingness to employ such power in the region and beyond, building the Panama Canal and negotiating control from a newly independent Panama; winning the Nobel Peace Prize for successfully orchestrating peace talks in the Russo-Japanese War of 1904; and showcasing U.S. naval power by sending the Great White Fleet around the world.

The U.S. role as a global power in the early 20th century was marked most clearly by its entry into World War I. Although President Woodrow Wilson had pursued diplomatic and military interventions in Latin America, particularly Mexico and the Dominican Republic, he initially sought to steer clear of the growing conflict in Europe. In fact, Wilson campaigned for reelection in 1916 with the slogan "He kept us out of war." In 1917, however, due to continu-

ing provocations, the United States declared war on Germany. In his address to Congress requesting a declaration of war, Wilson announced an agenda that went far beyond protecting U.S. interests, proclaiming that "the world must be made safe for democracy." This far-reaching goal indicated that the United States now had not only the right, but indeed also the obligation, to assist other nations in pursuing peace, liberty, and DEMOCRACY. After World War I, Wilson immersed himself in the peace treaty negotiations, focusing in particular on the creation of a League of Nations, which would prevent future world wars. But Wilson's refusal to address congressional concerns about U.S. commitments in an international organization resulted in the failure of the SENATE to ratify the Treaty of Versailles. For the next decade, American foreign policy interests would move back sharply from Wilson's ambitious agenda.

As Europe inched toward another global conflict in the 1930s, the United States again initially tried to maintain a neutral position. Congress passed several neutrality laws in the 1930s, forbidding the United States from assisting either side. Although President Franklin D. Roosevelt provided some assistance to the Allied Powers, he promised in his 1940 campaign that "Your boys are not going to be sent into any foreign wars." After becoming the first president to win election to a third (and later fourth) term, Roosevelt declared that the United States must be "the great arsenal of democracy," providing arms and supplies to the Allies without engaging directly in the war. Public and congressional sentiment favored this cautious strategy; in September 1941, a vote to extend the draft, originally enacted in 1940, passed the U.S. HOUSE OF REPRESENTATIVES by just one vote. But the Japanese attack on Pearl Harbor on December 7, 1941, galvanized the United States to enter the war, which it did the very next day.

The Allied victory over the Axis Powers in 1945 raised the question of what role the United States would play in the postwar world. Learning from the experiences of Woodrow Wilson, Roosevelt had supported the creation of an international organization to promote peace during World War II itself, and the UNITED NATIONS came into existence in 1945. The United States also was committed to rebuilding Japan and Germany for economic and security reasons. Most significantly, however, the need for a continued

U.S. presence in global affairs became evident with the origins of the cold war.

The cold war was fundamentally an ideological struggle between the United States and the Soviet Union over democracy versus COMMUNISM. From its beginnings to the dissolution of the Soviet Union in 1991, the United States practiced a policy of containment, albeit with many modifications across administrations. As defined by foreign policy expert George F. Kennan, the strategy of containment aimed to limit Soviet influence to existing areas, but it did not promote U.S. aggression against the Soviet Union. Rather, the premise of containment was that ultimately the internal flaws within communism would cause it to fall apart of its own accord. The cold war became a hot war in many places, notably Korea, Vietnam, and Afghanistan, but when the two superpowers came closest to military conflict during the Cuban missile crisis in 1962, they ultimately defused tensions. The end of the cold war is credited to many factors, including the U.S. defense buildup, with which the Soviet Union could not compete, the commitment of President Ronald Reagan to ridding the world of nuclear weapons, and the leadership of Soviet leader Mikhail Gorbachev, who loosened restrictions on the economy and public discourse, but its peaceful conclusion was by no means predictable.

The role of the United States as one of two superpowers during the cold war fostered some significant changes in the American foreign policy process. Most significantly, the National Security Act of 1947 created the NATIONAL SECURITY COUNCIL, the CENTRAL INTELLIGENCE AGENCY, the JOINT CHIEFS OF STAFF, and the DEPARTMENT OF DEFENSE (which replaced the Department of War). All of these agencies served to increase the power of the president in American foreign policy, sometimes at the expense of Congress. While Congress largely deferred to the president in the early part of the cold war, the Vietnam War prompted a resurgence of congressional engagement in foreign affairs. Most importantly, Congress passed—over President Richard M. Nixon's veto—the War Powers Resolution in 1973, which aimed to restrict the president's ability to send troops abroad for extended periods without congressional approval. But no president has recognized the War Powers Resolution as constitutional, and Congress has refrained from trying to force a president to comply with its provisions.

The end of the cold war raised many new questions about American foreign-policy power and interests. President George H. W. Bush defined the era as a "new world order," but that concept of nations working together to implement the RULE OF LAW seemed to apply primarily to the 1991 Persian Gulf War. Subsequent U.S. interventions in Somalia, Haiti, and Bosnia raised much more thorny questions about when the United States should send troops to other nations and why. In particular, the role of the United States in leading humanitarian relief efforts was widely debated, especially after U.S. soldiers were killed in a firefight in Mogadishu, Somalia, in October 1993. Just months later, the United States declined to intervene in the civil war in Rwanda, as no national security interest was at stake, though hundreds of thousands of people were killed in mere weeks. While the United States also witnessed some important foreign policy successes in the 1990s, notably the passage of the NORTH AMERICAN FREE TRADE AGREEMENT and the 1998 peace accords in Northern Ireland, the post–cold war era was largely defined by questions about America's role in the world.

The U.S. foreign policy agenda came into sharp relief with the terrorist attacks of September 11, 2001. The United States immediately condemned the attacks and quickly built an international coalition to combat terrorism. While the coalition worked together closely during the war in Afghanistan in 2001, divisions soon became evident as the United States began to consider waging war against Iraq. In the summer of 2002, President George W. Bush explicitly stated that the United States would not hesitate to take action against a potential aggressor, and the president's case for "preemptive" war was incorporated into the 2002 National Security Strategy. When the Iraq war began in 2003, the United States had the support of many allies, termed the "coalition of the willing," but it lacked support from the United Nations. This conflict raised charges of American unilateralism as well as concerns about rebuilding Iraq. In the United States, public and congressional support for PRESIDENTIAL LEADERSHIP in foreign policy was strong after 9/11, although some of that support has dissipated as the Iraq war continues.

Ultimately, American foreign policy leaders continue to wrestle with the same questions that concerned George Washington more than two centuries ago. The need to engage with other nations for commercial reasons is clear, and, of course, advances in technology mean that the United States no longer enjoys geographic isolation. Nevertheless, debates continue about how engaged the United States needs to be in world affairs and how closely it must work with other nations to pursue its aims. No president can ignore American foreign policy, but the United States enjoys the luxury of making its foreign policy choices from a position of strength and with a wide degree of independence.

See also DEFENSE POLICY; DIPLOMATIC POLICY.

Further Reading
Ambrose, Stephen E., and Douglas G. Brinkley. *Rise to Globalism: American Foreign Policy Since 1938.* New York: Penguin Books, 1997; Jentleson, Bruce W. *American Foreign Policy: The Dynamics of Choice in the Twenty-First Century.* 2nd ed. New York: W.W. Norton, 2004; McDougall, Walter A. *Promised Land, Crusader State: The American Encounter with the World Since 1776.* Boston: Houghton Mifflin, 1997; Smith, Tony. *America's Mission: The United States and the Worldwide Struggle for Democracy in the Twentieth Century.* Princeton, N.J.: Princeton University Press, 1994.

—Meena Bose

Great Society
The Great Society is the name given to a series of programs and laws established during the administration of Lyndon B. Johnson (1963–69). President Johnson called for a Great Society to be formed in a 1964 speech at the University of Michigan. In it, he stated that he wanted people from throughout the United States to come together in seminars and workshops to address social and economic problems and to form a Great Society.

The white middle class was enjoying considerable prosperity at the time of the Great Society speech. However, minorities and poor Americans were not enjoying the prosperity of their fellow citizens. The poverty rate in 1963 was 23 percent but had been as high as 27 percent in 1959. The CIVIL RIGHTS MOVE-MENT that began in the 1950s had success in making white Americans throughout the United States aware of the inequalities faced by African Americans in employment opportunities, in exercising their right to vote, and in societal segregation. As the Civil Rights movement increased awareness in the inequality of life for African Americans among whites, it simultaneously empowered many African Americans to demand government changes in order to provide EQUALITY of conditions. Urban riots over housing, employment, and education inequalities frightened many whites. Empirical evidence suggests that fear of black aggression did result in a response from policy makers to create better housing and school environments and to increase welfare benefits. The Great Society movement was not racially altruistic.

Awareness of inequalities, then, had been developing for some time before the Great Society speech. President John F. Kennedy had not experienced the devastating poverty of Appalachia until he campaigned for president in 1959 and 1960. This region of the country had a per capita income that was 23 percent lower than the national average in 1960. One-third of all Appalachians lived in poverty. As president, he formed a commission, the President's Appalachian Regional Commission (PARC), to study and make recommendations on alleviating poverty in this area. The PARC Report was presented to President Johnson in 1964.

The obvious disparity faced by the poor and minorities needed to be addressed. The national mourning of President Kennedy's death in November 1963 helped create an overwhelming Democratic victory in the 1964 election. President Johnson carried the election with 61 percent of the vote, the highest margin ever experienced in a presidential race. This gave Johnson courage to propose many policy changes to move the United States toward racial and economic equality and to expand cultural and educational quality; 96 percent of his policy proposals were passed by Congress. During the Great Society era, Congress passed several laws and established programs in the areas of racial equality, social and economic equality, education, environmental improvement, and culture. Medicare, the nation's health care program for senior citizens, was established during the Great Society era in 1965, and Medicaid, the national health care program for the poor, was expanded to include all families who qualified for Aid to Families with Dependent Children, commonly referred to as welfare. Other major pieces of legislation are outlined below.

The Civil Rights Act of 1964 banned discrimination based on race, color, religion, gender, or national origin. It ended public segregation, the practice of having separate facilities for blacks and whites, largely in the South. While enforcement of the act was not uniform, this legislation paved the way for an end to the inferior treatment that African Americans in particular had faced.

One year later, President Johnson signed EXECUTIVE ORDERS 11,246 and 11,375, further prohibiting discrimination in hiring practices (established earlier by President Kennedy under executive order 10,925 in 1961) and requiring contractors earning more than $50,000 per year from the federal government to have written AFFIRMATIVE ACTION policies for recruiting and hiring minorities in order to integrate their workforce.

The Voting Rights Act of 1965 outlawed the poll tax and literacy tests, two mechanisms that had been used in southern states to discourage African Americans from voting. The act also gave authority to the DEPARTMENT OF JUSTICE to approve or disapprove any proposal for changing voting rules in districts that were at least 5 percent African American. Moreover, the Department of Justice took control of voter registration for districts in which at least 50 percent of eligible African Americans were not registered to vote.

The Hart-Celler Act of 1965 abolished the Chinese Exclusion Act of 1882 and opened IMMIGRATION so that immigrants were no longer restricted based on race or ethnicity. Previous immigration policy gave strong preference to northwestern Europeans. This act greatly increased migration to the United States from Asia and Latin America.

In 1968, another civil rights act was passed. This act is popularly known as the Fair Housing Act because it banned discrimination in the rental, sale, or financing of property. It also prohibits threatening, coercing, or intimidating any person seeking to rent or purchase property. Prior to the Fair Housing Act, many deeds had housing codes on them stipulating that the property could never be sold to African Americans, and some even prohibited the sale of property to Jewish people.

President Johnson's War on Poverty was a critical part of the Great Society movement. This call for economic and social equality for society's disadvantaged was initially made in the president's 1964 STATE OF THE UNION ADDRESS. The speech stimulated the creation of many agencies and programs to reduce poverty. The Appalachian Regional Commission, the nation's only truly federal agency, was formed and given authority to fund projects to improve the health, economic development, highway system, water, and sewage conditions of Appalachia. The Appalachian Regional Commission is governed equally by a federal commissioner and the GOVERNORs of the 13 states that make up the Appalachian region.

The Economic Opportunity Act of 1964 helped to establish community action programs to address the needs of people for education, skill development, and employment. The Job Corps was created to help disadvantaged youths to develop skills. The Neighborhood Youth Corps helped teenagers and young adults to acquire summer employment, and Upward Bound was established to send poor high school students to college. The Food Stamp Program became a permanent program, and Head Start was expanded from a summer only to a year-round program.

Culturally, many advances were made during the Great Society years. The Corporation for Public Broadcasting, which oversees public radio and public television, was established, along with the National Endowment for the Humanities, the National Endowment for the Arts, the Kennedy Center, located in Washington, D.C., and the Hirshhorn Museum and Sculpture Garden, part of the Smithsonian Institution, also located in Washington, D.C.

The prevailing criticism of the Great Society programs is that its work resulted in an explosion in the welfare rolls. Aid to Families with Dependent Children (AFDC) was altered significantly in the Public Welfare Amendments of 1962, when Congress enacted inducements for states to provide services to AFDC clients that would lead their clients to self-sufficiency. If states provided these services, as approved by the Department of Health, Education, and Welfare, the federal government agreed to pay 75 percent of the service costs. This was a dramatic increase in AFDC funding for the states. Federal funding for normal program services was based on a formula that matched state money. In the enacting legislation, the funding match to states was one-third. Eventually, the formula was changed to provide greater assistance to poorer states: For each AFDC beneficiary, the federal government would match state spending (up to one-third of the first $37.00 in 1967; up to five-sixths of the first half of the average state payment by 1975), and then an additional proportion of state spending, depending on the state's per capita income (ranging from 50 to 65 percent).

The business community embraced the Great Society programs during the 1960s on political and economic grounds. Of political concern was the anxiety that voters would perceive an alignment between the business community and the REPUBLICAN PARTY and therefore vote in favor of liberals who wanted to expand social programs in a time of economic recession and high unemployment, such as that experienced in the 1950s. Corporate leaders such as the CEOs of Xerox, Ford, and Chase Manhattan adopted policies emphasizing corporate responsibility to assist in societal development. Many businesses aligned themselves with Presidents Kennedy and Johnson for economic reasons as well. Government programs that resulted in transfer payments often benefited the business community, particularly in the areas of housing development and job training. Additionally, as long as the tax burden for welfare came from society at large, the business community would not be targeted for assisting in unemployment or health care for the disenfranchised.

Soaring welfare rolls throughout the 1960s escalated concerns over the structure of the program and its ability to help the poor become self-sufficient. Combined state and federal expenditures on AFDC rose from $1 billion in 1960 to $6.2 billion in 1971. Changes in AFDC, from expansion of eligibility to institutionalized patients and two-parent households, as well as the elimination of residency requirements in the UNITED STATES SUPREME COURT ruling in *Shapiro v. Thompson* (1969), resulted in a tripling of the AFDC caseload between 1960 and 1974. Of particular alarm was the growing awareness that young unmarried girls were having babies and qualifying for PUBLIC ASSISTANCE and housing, often continuing a cycle of poverty as their circumstances prevented them from moving toward self-sufficiency.

Attempts to promote self-sufficiency through work requirements for AFDC clients had shown little success. The Work Incentive Initiative (WIN) Program of 1967 tied welfare benefits to work by requiring local offices to refer qualified adult participants for training and employment. Exempt from the requirements were women whose children were under six years of age, or those whose pending employment was determined to be adverse to the structure of the family, a determination that was made by caseworkers on a subjective basis. Though day care provisions were included in the same AFDC amendments that established the WIN program, funding was inadequate, the work requirements were laxly enforced, and the jobs to which clients were referred generally provided only superficial training.

Support for Great Society programs waned during the presidencies of Richard M. Nixon (1969–74) and Gerald R. Ford (1974–77). President Ronald Reagan (1981–89) curtailed a good deal of federal spending, including negotiating a 50-percent decrease in funding for the Appalachian Regional Commission. By 1996, AFDC was replaced with a block grant program, Temporary Assistance to Needy Families, which set a 60-month lifetime limit on cash assistance to poor families. Some of the programs have remained, however. Head Start and Upward Bound continue to receive funding, as does Medicare and Medicaid, although President George W. Bush signed legislation in 2005 that altered Medicare payments, and Medicaid funding on the federal and state levels continues to diminish. In 2006, Congress passed and President Bush signed legislation reauthorizing the 1965 Voting Rights Act. Funding for the arts, humanities, and public broadcasting has diminished but continues to enjoy some support at the federal level.

See also ENTITLEMENTS; WELFARE POLICY.

Further Reading

Appalachia: A Report by the President's Appalachian Regional Commission (The PARC Report), 1964. Available online. URL: http://www.arc.gov/index.do ?nodeId=2255. Accessed July 20, 2006; Blank, Rebecca, and Ron Haskins, eds. *The New World of Welfare*. Washington, D.C.: Brookings Institution Press, 2001; Derthick, Martha. *The Influence of Federal Grants*. Cambridge, Mass.: Harvard University Press, 1970; Executive Order 10925, 1961. Available online. URL: http://www.eeoc.gov/abouteeoc/35th/thelaw/eo-10925.html. Accessed July 20, 2006; Executive Order 11246, 1965. Available online. URL: http://www.eeoc.gov/abouteeoc/35th/thelaw/eo-11246.html. Accessed July 20, 2006; Fording, Richard C. "The Conditional Effect of Violence." *American Journal of Political Science* 4, no. 1 (January 1997): 1–29, Jansson, Bruce S. *The Reluctant Welfare State*. 4th ed. Belmont, Calif.: Wadsworth, 2001; Jennings, Edward T. "Racial Insurgency, the State, and Welfare Expansion: A Critical Comment and Reanalysis." *American Journal of Sociology*. 88 (May 1983): 1220–1236; Jennings, Edward T., Jr. "Urban Riots and Welfare Policy Change: A Test of the Piven-Cloward Theory." In *Why Policies Succeed or Fail*. Sage Yearbooks in Politics and Public Policy, vol. 8, edited by Helen M. Ingram and Dean E. Mann. Beverly Hills, Calif.: Sage Publishers, 1980; Noble, Charles. *Welfare As We Knew It*. New York: Oxford University Press, 1997; President L. B. Johnson's Commencement Address at Howard University, "To Fulfill These Rights," 1965. Available online. URL: http://www.lbjlib.utexas.edu/johnson/archives.hom/speeches.hom/650604.asp. Accessed July 20, 2006; Quadagno, Jill. *The Color of Welfare: How Racism Undermined the War on Poverty*. New York: Oxford University Press, 1994; Stefancic, Jean, and Richard Delgado. *No Mercy: How Conservative Think Tanks and Foundations Changed America's Social Agenda*. Philadelphia: Temple University Press, 1996; United States Bureau of the Census, Poverty Rates over Time. Available online. URL: http://www.census.gov/hhes/www/poverty/histpov/hstpov3.html. Accessed July 20, 2006; Weaver, R. Kent. *Ending Welfare as We Know It*. Washington, D.C.: Brookings Institution Press, 2000.

—Marybeth D. Beller

gun control

Gun control is one of the most enduringly controversial issues in modern American politics, yet it has long historical roots. Guns have long been a root of American violence yet are also inextricably intertwined with the Revolutionary and frontier traditions, cultural and recreational activities, and American mythology. Gun-related mayhem has been far more evident in large urban areas than in American frontier life, where fanciful images of a gun-toting, shoot-em-up existence were far less prevalent in real life than in Hollywood movies. And while most assume that gun controls (regulations pertaining to gun ownership or operation imposed by some level of government) are an artifact of the late 20th century, strict gun controls existed throughout American history, even extending back before the Revolutionary era. In recent decades, the political and policy debate over gun control and gun violence has intensified, while the nature of the controls contemplated has centered on a set of relatively modest and limited changes.

Government-enacted gun control policy extends back to the colonial era. From that point through the early Federalist period in America, firearms possession was regulated in two primary ways. One type of regulation required eligible males to own guns as part of their responsibility to their service in local militias, even though there was a chronic shortage of working firearms from the colonial period until after the Civil War. In 1792, Congress passed the Uniform Militia Act, which required a militia-eligible man to "provide himself with a good musket or firelock, a sufficient bayonet and belt, two spare flints, and a knapsack, a pouch with a box therein to contain not less than twenty-four cartridges . . . each cartridge to contain a proper quantity of powder and ball." Within the next two years, all 15 states passed similar measures, yet they lacked enforcement power, and these laws were widely ignored. In addition, states often reserved the right to take, or "impress," these guns if they were needed for defense.

The other type of early gun control law barred gun ownership to various groups, including slaves, indentured servants, Native Americans, Catholics or other non-Protestants, non–property-owning whites, and those who refused to swear oaths of loyalty to the government. Laws barring distribution of guns to Native Americans were among the first such measures. As early as the 1600s, persons discovered selling guns to Indians could be subject to death. Pennsylvania went further than other states to take guns away from citizens deemed disloyal when it passed the Test Act in 1777, which specified that those who refused to swear an oath of allegiance to the government would be disarmed, referring specifically to "persons disaffected to the liberty and independence of this state." According to one historian, this law disarmed up to 40 percent of the state's adult white male population. Further, the government conducted periodic gun CENSUSES both before and after

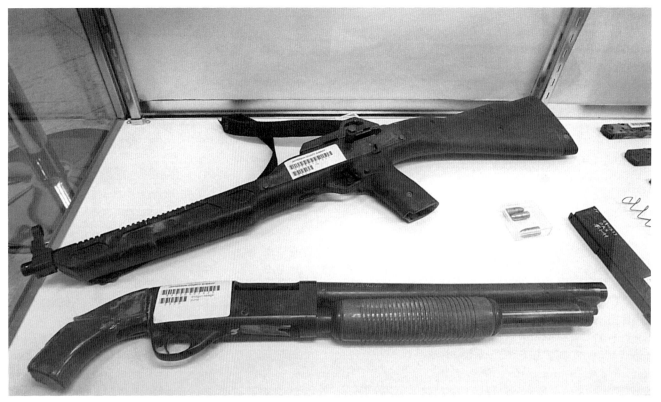

Evidence connected to the Columbine massacre on display for the first time *(Getty Images)*

the adoption of the U.S. CONSTITUTION of 1787. In 1803, for example, Secretary of War Henry Dearborn coordinated the most extensive and thorough such gun census ever conducted up until that time, concluding that about 45 percent of all militiamen had "arms," or about a quarter of the white male adult population. A similar census seven years later produced about the same results.

Two types of events spurred the frequent calls for tougher gun laws in the 20th century: the spread and fear of gun-related crime and the ASSASSINATIONS of political leaders and celebrities. Despite enduring popular support for tougher gun laws, new federal gun regulations have been infrequent and limited in scope.

The first modern push for gun control laws arose from the Progressive Era. A dramatic rise in urban crime in the late 1800s, linked to the proliferation of handguns that were heavily marketed by gun companies to urban populations, prompted citizen groups, newspaper editors, and other civic leaders to press for new regulations. In 1903, for example, the New

York City police estimated that at least 20,000 citizens in the city carried handguns on a regular basis. Gun crimes received extensive press coverage, and states and localities throughout the country enacted laws barring the carrying of concealed weapons. The federal government did not intervene in early gun control policy efforts, based on the prevailing sentiment of the time that gun regulatory decisions should be left to the states and localities. In several legal challenges to gun regulations, however, the UNITED STATES SUPREME COURT upheld the constitutionality of such regulations and established that the Constitution's Second Amendment (the "right to bear arms") only applied to citizens when in the service of a government-organized and -regulated militia (e.g., *Presser v. Illinois*, 1886; *U.S. v. Miller*, 1939). Until 2008, no gun control law had ever been declared unconstitutional as a violation of the Second Amendment.

Among the earliest and most sweeping of these new state laws was that enacted in New York State in 1911. Spurred by spiraling urban violence and the attempted assassination of New York City mayor

William J. Gaynor in 1910, the Sullivan Law (named after the STATE SENATOR who championed the bill) subjected the sale, possession, and carrying of deadly weapons to strict regulation. In particular, pistol carrying was strictly licensed, with violation elevated to a felony by the new law.

The 1920s ushered in a new era of freedom but also one of alcohol prohibition and a concomitant rise of illegal alcohol production and smuggling, which in turn accelerated the rise of organized crime, tied to highly profitable alcohol bootlegging. As rival criminal gangs jockeyed for control of the enormous illegal market, crime-related violence rose. At the same time, pressure on the national government mounted as more civic leaders demanded a coordinated federal response. In 1922, for example, the AMERICAN BAR ASSOCIATION commissioned a study that concluded that 90 percent of all murders nationwide occurred with handguns. The organization then endorsed a nationwide ban on the production and sale of handguns and handgun ammunition, except for law enforcement. As early as 1921, the Senate Judiciary Committee held hearings on a bill to bar the interstate shipment of handguns, with a few exceptions. The measure was pushed annually from 1915 until 1924, but it was always killed in committee. A similar fate met most other federal gun control efforts during this period.

By the late 1920s and early 1930s, crime escalated, the Great Depression set in, and newspapers reported gangland killings and the growing popularity among gangsters of a hand-held machine gun first developed for use in World War I, the Tommy Gun. In mob-run Chicago, for example, bootlegger Hymie Weiss and his mob attacked rival Al Capone's gang headquarters in 1926, firing thousands of rounds into the building. Capone escaped; a few weeks later he sought revenge, killing Weiss and his accomplices. In a single month in 1926, 215 Chicago gangsters were murdered, with another 160 killed by the police. The public watched with horror and fascination as events from the St. Valentine's Day Massacre to the crime sprees of Bonnie and Clyde, Pretty Boy Floyd, and John Dillinger's crime spree and subsequent shooting death at the hands of government agents covered newspaper headlines. As if to punctuate the country's gun crime worries, an unemployed anarchist fired five shots at president-elect Franklin D. Roosevelt early in 1933, who was visiting Florida at the time, narrowly missing him but fatally wounding Chicago mayor Anton Cermak. The assassin had bought his .32 caliber revolver at a local pawn shop for $8.

At the federal level, the first successful effort to enact gun policy began with a 10 percent excise tax on guns enacted in 1919 and a law prohibiting the sale of handguns to private individuals through the mail enacted in 1927. The rise of gangsterism and the election of President Franklin D. Roosevelt in 1932 spurred enactment of the first significant national gun measure, the National Firearms Act of 1934, which strictly regulated gangster-type weapons, including sawed-off shotguns and machine guns. This initial measure also included a system of handgun registration, but that provision was stripped out of the bill by gun control opponents. The Federal Firearms Act of 1938 established a licensing system for gun dealers, manufacturers, and importers.

America's involvement in World War II turned the nation's attention and resources to the war effort. After the war, millions of returning soldiers who had for the first time experienced gun use while in military service helped spawn a rise in gun ownership, mostly for hunting and sporting purposes. The relative prosperity and stability of the 1950s pushed crime issues to the back burner.

No new federal gun control laws reached the president's desk until 1968, when a five-year push for tougher laws culminated in the enactment of the Gun Control Act. Momentum for new controls took shape in the aftermath of the assassination of President John F. Kennedy in November 1963. His assassin, Lee Harvey Oswald, had purchased a rifle through interstate mail and used it to kill the president by firing three times from the sixth floor of a building along the president's motorcade route through downtown Dallas, Texas. By the mid-1960s, escalating crime rates and the spread of urban disorder raised new fears about spiraling gun violence. Such fears peaked in 1968, as urban rioting continued and when, in that same year, the civil rights leader the Rev. Martin Luther King, Jr., and Senator Robert F. Kennedy were both assassinated. Those two murders provided the final impetus for passage of the Gun Control Act. The law banned interstate shipment of firearms and ammunition to private individuals; prohibited gun sales to minors; strengthened licensing and record-keeping requirements for dealers and collectors; extended regulations to destructive devices including land mines, bombs, hand grenades, and the like; increased penalties for gun crimes; and regulated importation of foreign-made firearms. Cut from the bill was the original proposal, backed by President Lyndon Johnson, to enact blanket gun registration and licensing.

The next major gun law enacted by Congress, the Firearms Owners Protection Act of 1986 (also called the McClure-Volkmer bill), rolled back many of the provisions of the 1968 law at a time when anticontrol forces, led by the National Rifle Association (NRA), exerted great influence over Congress and the presidency of Ronald Reagan. It allowed interstate sale of long guns (rifles and shotguns), reduced record keeping for dealers, limited government regulatory powers over dealers and gun shows (in particular, limiting inspections of gun dealers to one a year), and barred firearms registration.

Highly publicized incidents of mass shootings in the late 1980s and 1990s, combined with the election of gun control supporter Bill Clinton to the presidency, resulted in a new and successful effort to enact gun laws. Yielding to public pressure, Congress enacted the Brady Law in 1993 and the Assault Weapons Ban in 1994. Named after Reagan press secretary James Brady, who was seriously wounded in the 1981 assassination attempt against Reagan, the Brady Law required a five–business-day waiting period for the purchase of a handgun, during which time local law enforcement authorities were to conduct background checks on purchasers to weed out felons, the mentally incompetent, and others barred from handgun possession; increased federal firearms license fees; financed improved record keeping; and called for implementation of the National Instant Criminal Background Check System (NICS) in 1998. Since then, handgun sales can be completed as soon as the check inquiry is cleared. Dealers have up to three days to verify that the applicant is eligible to purchase a handgun, although 95 percent of all purchases clear within two hours, according to the FBI. From 1994 to 2001, the Brady Law stopped about 690,000 handgun purchases, representing about 2.5 percent of all handgun purchases.

In 1994, Congress enacted a ban on 19 specified assault weapons plus several dozen copycat models, which were distinguished from other semiautomatic weapons by virtue of their distinctive military features, including a more compact design, short barrels, large ammunition clips, lighter weight, pistol grips or thumbhole stocks, flash suppressors, or telescoping stocks (traits that facilitate concealability and "spray fire"). The law also exempted from the ban 661 specifically named weapons. According to a U.S. DEPARTMENT OF JUSTICE study, after the ban's enactment, assault weapon crimes dropped from 3.6 percent of gun crimes in 1995 to 1.2 percent in 2002. The federal ban was imposed for a 10-year period, and lapsed in 2004. Congress failed to renew the law.

In 1997 and 1998, the country's attention was riveted by a series of seemingly inexplicable schoolyard shootings committed by school-age boys in small cities, towns, and rural areas around the country, culminating on April 20, 1999, when two high school boys brought four guns to Columbine High School in Littleton, Colorado, and began shooting. When they were done, 12 students and one teacher had been killed in the space of less than 15 minutes; 23 others were wounded. As police closed in on 18-year-old Eric Harris and 17-year-old Dylan Klebold, the two turned the guns on themselves.

In the aftermath of the incident, national shock and outrage put unprecedented pressure on Congress to respond. The leadership in the U.S. SENATE yielded to national pressure despite the fact that its Republican leaders opposed new gun control measures. On May 20, 1999, the Senate passed a bill that would have required background checks at all gun show sales, flea markets, and pawn shops (closing the "gun show loophole"), revocation of gun ownership for those convicted of gun crimes as juveniles, tougher penalties for juvenile offenders who used guns in crimes and also for those who provided such guns to juveniles, required sale of locking devices or boxes sold with all new handgun purchases, blocked legal immunity to those who sold guns to felons, and a ban on the import of high-capacity ammunition clips (those that could hold more than 10 bullets).

The Senate-passed bill was defeated in the HOUSE OF REPRESENTATIVES by a coalition of pro–

gun control representatives who considered a compromise bill too weak and anti–gun control representatives who opposed any new controls. The following Mothers Day in May 2000, more than 700,000 protestors staged the Million Mom March in Washington, D.C., in support of stronger gun laws and against gun violence.

The George W. Bush presidency was highly sympathetic to foes of stronger gun laws. The Bush administration supported the NRA's top legislative priority, enacted in 2005, a bill to grant the gun industry and gun dealers immunity from lawsuit liability, making the gun industry unique in possessing such a protection. The Bush administration also restricted access by law enforcement to gun purchase data and opposed efforts to regulate civilian access to high-powered sniper rifles. Renewed interest in stricter gun control laws increased following the shooting massacre at Virginia Tech in Blacksburg, Virginia, in April 2007. However, even in the face of such tragedies, in 2008 the Supreme Court ruled in *District of Columbia v. Heller* that the Second Amendment is protective of an individual's right to possess a firearm for personal use.

National gun control policy is implemented by the Bureau of Alcohol, Tobacco, Firearms, and Explosives (ATFE), which has had only limited success in implementing full enforcement of national gun laws. Enforcement lapses have resulted from legislative restrictions on its authority, budget cutbacks, a tarnished reputation resulting from its handling of the confrontation with the Branch Davidian compound in Waco, Texas, in 1993, and political opposition and criticism from the NRA.

Further Reading
Cook, Philip, and Jens Ludwig. *Gun Violence: The Real Costs*. New York: Oxford University Press, 2000; DeConde, Alexander. *Gun Violence in America*. Boston: Northeastern University Press, 2001; Spitzer, Robert J. *The Right to Bear Arms*. Santa Barbara, Calif.: ABC-CLIO, 2001; Spitzer, Robert J. *The Politics of Gun Control*. Washington, D.C.: Congressional Quarterly Press, 2004; Uviller, H. Richard, and William G. Merkel. *The Militia and the Right to Bear Arms*. Durham, N.C.: Duke University Press, 2002.

—Robert J. Spitzer

health-care policy
Health-care policy includes actions that governments take to influence the provision of health-care services and the various government activities that affect or attempt to affect public health and well-being. It can be viewed narrowly to mean the design and implementation of federal and state programs that affect the provision of health-care services , such as Medicare and Medicaid. It also can be defined more broadly by recognizing that governments engage in many other activities that influence both public and private health care decision making, such as funding health science research and public health departments and agencies, subsidizing medical education and hospital construction, and regulating food, drugs, and medical devices. Even environmental protection policies, such as clean air and water laws, are an important component of public health.

Health-care policy is a relatively recent endeavor for the U.S. government. What we consider to be the core of health-care policy emerged in the United States only after the 1930s, with the idea of health insurance. Individuals could take out an insurance policy, much as they did for their lives, houses, or cars, that would defray the cost of health care should an illness develop or an injury occur. Today most people are insured through their jobs, and the insurance policies cover routine medical services as well as preventive health care. Others are covered through the federal Medicare and Medicaid programs or through the Veterans' Health Care System.

The United States relies largely on the private market and individual choice to reach health-care goals. That is, most health-care services are provided by doctors and other medical staff who work in clinics and hospitals that are privately run. The U.S. government plays a smaller role than is found in most other developed nations, where national health insurance programs are common. The result is a health-care system that is something of a hybrid. It is neither completely private nor fully public. One consequence of this approach to health care is that some 45 million individuals in the United States, or 18 percent of the nonelderly population, have no health insurance.

Health care can be expensive. This affects the choices that both government and employers make in providing health care insurance and services. Moreover, general health-care costs have been rising sharply in recent years, well above the inflation rate, and drug costs have been rising even more steeply. As costs continue to increase, it is a sure bet that government health care budgets will be under severe pressure, and most employers will be forced to pass along their own added burden to employees. Those employees will likely find themselves paying more for health insurance and also receiving fewer benefits.

No other areas of public policy reach so deeply into the personal lives of Americans as health care and how to pay for it. For some, it is literally a matter of life and death, and for many more access to health care can significantly affect the quality of their lives. Government policies influence not only access to and the quality of health services across the country, but also the pace of development and approval of new drugs and medical technologies and the extent of health research that could lead to new life-saving treatments. Whether the concern is periodic medical examinations, screening for major diseases, or coping with life-threatening illnesses, health-care policy decisions eventually affect everyone, and often in ways that are not equitable.

The U.S. health-care system is widely recognized as one of the best in the world in terms of the number of physicians per capita, the number of state-of-the-art hospitals and clinics, and the number of health-care specialists and their expertise. The United States also has a large percentage of the world's major pharmaceutical research centers and biotechnology companies, which increases the availability of cutting-edge medical treatments. Despite these many strengths, however, a World Health Organization study in 2000 put the nation as only 37th among 191 nations, even though it spent a higher percentage of its gross domestic product (GDP) on health care than any other country. Such findings reflect the highly unequal access of the population to critical health-care services , from prenatal care to preventive screening for chronic illnesses. The poor, elderly, minorities, and those living in rural areas generally receive less frequent and less adequate medical care than white, middle-class residents of urban and suburban areas.

Much of the contemporary debate over health-care policy revolves around the major federal and state programs and the ways in which they might be changed to improve their effectiveness in delivery of health-care services , constrain rising costs, and promote equity. As is usually the case in American politics, there are often striking differences between liberals and conservatives and between Democrats and Republicans on these issues. Liberals and Democrats tend to favor a stronger governmental role in health-care insurance, in part to reduce current inequities in access to health-care services and because they see such access as a right that should be guaranteed by government and not subject to the uncertainties of market forces. Conservatives and Republicans tend to believe reliance on the private sector and competition among health-care insurers and providers is preferable to having government do more. Consideration of the major federal programs illustrates the challenge of changing health-care policy.

Medicare is the leading federal program. It was approved by Congress in 1965 to help senior citizens, defined as those 65 years of age and older, to meet basic health care needs. It now includes those under age 65 with permanent disabilities and those with diabetes or end-stage renal disease. As of 2006, Medicare had some 40 million beneficiaries, a number certain to rise dramatically in the years ahead as the baby boom generation (those born between 1946 and 1964) begins reaching age 65. In effect, Medicare is a national health insurance program, but only for a defined population—senior citizens.

Medicare offers a core plan, called Medicare Part A, that pays for a portion of hospital charges, with patients responsible for a copayment. Most Medicare recipients also select an optional Part B, which offers supplemental insurance for physician charges, diagnostic tests, and hospital outpatient services. In 2006, the cost to individuals was about $90 per month. Many health-care costs are not covered by either Part A or Part B of Medicare, which led Congress in 2003 to add a new Part D to cover a sizeable portion of prescription drug costs. The Republican majority in Congress designed the new program to encourage competition among private insurance companies and to promote individual choice among insurers. Critics complained, however, that the program was made unnecessarily complex and rewarded insurance companies with substantial benefits while doing little to control health-care costs. Debate over the future of Medicare is likely to continue, especially in light of projections of higher demand for its services and rising program costs. It is also likely to reflect partisan and ideological differences over health-care policy.

Medicaid is the other major federal health-care program. Also established in 1965, Medicaid was intended to assist the poor and disabled through a federal-state program of health insurance. It does so by setting standards for hospital services, outpatient services, physician services, and laboratory testing and by sharing costs of health-care services for program recipients with the states. The states set standards for eligibility and overall benefit levels for the program, and both vary quite a bit from state to state. In 2003, Medicaid provided for some 54 million people, a number expected to increase to 65 million by 2015. In 1997, Congress approved a State Children's Health Insurance Program (SCHIP), which was designed to ensure that children living in poverty had medical insurance. As is the case with Medicaid, the federal government provides funds to the states, which the states match. The states are free to set eligibility levels. Some 2 million children are covered under the SCHIP program who would not be eligible under Medicaid. Except for education, Medicaid is the largest program in most state budgets.

In response to the soaring number of Medicaid recipients and rising costs, in 2005 Congress approved broad changes that give states new powers to reduce costs by imposing higher copayments and insurance premiums on recipients. States also were given the right to limit or eliminate coverage for many services previously guaranteed by federal law. Even before the new law, many states were reconsidering how they structure their programs and what services they could afford to provide. For example, some states have tried to reduce the use of expensive nursing homes and to foster health care in the home or community. Many states also have given greater attention to detection of fraud and abuse on the part of service providers, which some analysts have estimated to cost as much as 7 percent of the entire Medicaid budget, and much higher in some states, such as New York, that have done little to control these costs.

The third major federal program is in many ways one of the most successful and yet not as visible as Medicare and Medicaid. The Veterans Health-care system is designed to serve the needs of American veterans by providing primary medical care, specialized care, and other medical and social services, including rehabilitation. The Veterans Health Administration operates veterans' hospitals and clinics across the nation and provides extensive coverage for veterans with service-related disabilities and disease, particularly for those with no private health-care insurance. In 1996 Congress substantially expanded the veterans' health programs. The new health care plan emphasizes preventive and primary care but also offers a full range of services, including inpatient and outpatient medical, surgical, and mental-health services; prescription and over-the-counter drugs and medical supplies; emergency care; and comprehensive rehabilitation services. At the request of senior military leaders, in 2000 Congress approved another health care program for career military personnel. It expands the military's health plan, known as TriCare, to include retirees with at least 20 years of military service once they become eligible for Medicare. TriCare pays for most of the costs of medical treatment that are not covered by Medicare.

This brief description of major federal health-care programs only hints at the major challenges that heath care policy faces in the years ahead. Perhaps the most important is what to do about rising costs. The Centers for Medicare and Medicaid Services estimates that health care expenditures will grow at some 7 percent annually, rising from $1.9 trillion in 2005 to $3.6 trillion by 2014. Drug costs are expected to grow at an estimated 9 to 12 percent annually over the next decade. The federal government has projected per capita expenditures for health care to rise from $6,432 in 2005 to $11,046 in 2014. Hence, there is likely to be considerable pressure on both public and private payers to cover these accelerating costs of health care. Yet such demands come at a time of substantial federal budget deficits, similar constraints on state budgets, and a public reluctance to see tax rates increase. What is the best way to deal with the predicament?

Two broad trends suggest possible solutions. One is the effort to encourage individuals in both public and private health-care insurance programs to rely on health maintenance organizations (HMOs) or other so-called managed-care programs. These are designed to promote cost-effective health-care service by encouraging regular screening exams, limiting access to costly services and specialists, and providing for lower fees that are negotiated with service providers (e.g., for physician or hospital services). Managed care now dominates the U.S. health-care system, and there is little doubt that it saves the nation billions of dollars a year in health-care costs. Despite some misgivings by the public, particularly during the 1990s, managed care is likely to continue its dominant role. Its future may well include additional economy measures, such as restrictions on drug coverage or access to specialists.

The other major solution to rising health-care costs is to encourage greater reliance on preventive health care, that is, on promotion of health and prevention of disease. If individuals are given incentives to take better care of themselves throughout their lives, they are likely to be healthier and require less medical care than would otherwise be the case. Preventive health-care measures include regular physical examinations and diagnostic tests; education and training in diet, exercise, and stress management; and smoking cessation programs, among others. For example, routine screening for serious diseases such as diabetes and high blood pressure could lead to earlier and more effective treatment. Improved health-care education could lead individuals to better control their diets and make other lifestyle choices that can improve their health.

Two of the most obvious concerns are smoking and diet. Smoking accounts for more than 440,000 deaths annually in the United States, making it the single most preventable cause of premature death. Secondhand smoke takes an additional toll, particularly in children. About half of those who smoke die prematurely from cancer, heart disease, emphysema, and other smoking-related diseases. Smoking cessation at any age conveys significant health benefits.

Diet is equally important. The U.S. surgeon general has reported that if left unabated, the trend toward an overweight and obese population may lead to as many health care problems and premature deaths as smoking. About 30 percent of those age 20 or older, some 60 million people, are obese. Another 35 percent of the adult population are overweight, and the number of young people who are overweight has tripled since 1980. Being overweight increases the risk of many health problems such as hypertension, high cholesterol levels, type 2 diabetes, heart diseases, and stroke.

What can be done to halt or reverse the trend? A change in the American diet would be one helpful action, as would other changes in lifestyle, such as regular exercise. The U.S. population increasingly has consumed foods high in calories, fat, and cholesterol, and most Americans also fall well short of the recommended levels of physical exercise and fitness. Changes in diet and exercise can come as individual choices, but governments can also help, as can private employers. Many school districts, for example, have improved nutrition in cafeterias and limited high-calorie food and drinks in their vending machines. Governments at all levels and employers as well have tried to educate people on diet and exercise, though much more could be done.

As this overview of health-care issues suggests, there is a clear need to assess the effectiveness, efficiency, and equity of all the programs and activities that constitute health-care policy in the United States. The high costs of health care alone suggest the logic of doing so, especially in terms of the standard of efficiency or costs that are applied to all public policy areas. But health-care policy also affects individuals so directly and in so many important ways that a search for better policies and programs is imperative to ensure that all citizens have reasonable access to the health care they need and that such care be of high quality. There is no one right way to change health-care policy, and solutions will emerge only after the usual process of public debate and deliberation. The suggested readings and Web sites listed below provide essential information about health-care policy. They also can assist individuals in analyzing policies and programs and seeking creative solutions to better meet these needs.

See also Department of Health and Human Services; entitlements; welfare policy.

Further Reading

American Association of Health Plans. Available online. URL: www.aahp.org. Accessed August 11, 2006; Bodenheimer, Thomas S., and Kevin Grumbach. *Understanding Health Policy*. 3rd ed. New York: McGraw Hill, 2001; Centers for Medicare and Medicaid Services, Department of Health and Human Services. Available online. URL: www.cms.hhs.gov. Accessed August 11, 2006; Hacker, Jacob S. *The Road to Nowhere: The Genesis of President Clinton's Plan for*

Health Security. Princeton, N.J.: Princeton University Press, 1997; Health Insurance Association of America. Available online. URL: www.hiaa.org. Accessed August 11, 2006; Kaiser Family Foundation. Available online. URL: www.kff.org. Accessed August 11, 2006; The Kaiser Network. Available online. URL: www.kaisernetwork.org. Accessed August 11, 2006; Kraft, Michael E., and Scott R. Furlong. *Public Policy: Politics, Analysis, and Alternatives.* 2nd ed. Washington, D.C.: Congressional Quarterly Press, 2007; Patel, Kant, and Mark E. Rushefsky. *Health Care Politics and Policy in America.* 3rd ed. Armonk, N.Y.: M.E. Sharpe, 2006

—Michael E. Kraft

housing policy

The philosophical foundation justifying the investment of public resources by government in the provision of shelter for its citizens can be found in the democratic theory of JOHN LOCKE, who argued that the fundamental purpose of government and the basis of its legitimacy to exercise authority is the protection of its citizens. Though even prior to the 20th century it was widely believed that access to some form of shelter was essential for protection, the capitalist economic system Locke embraced emphasized something more. While socialist ideologies stress communal ownership, CAPITALISM depends on the existence of private property, leading the founders of the American government, who were well versed in Locke's theory, to argue that the basis for CITIZENSHIP is property ownership, especially of a home, and it is the duty of government to protect and promote that ownership. Thus, in capitalist democracies such as the United States, an individual's material, social, and mental well-being tends to be associated with home ownership. Consequently, political leaders in the United States have developed a housing policy that not only emphasizes the widespread availability of shelter, usually affordable rental housing, but the promotion of home ownership as well.

What has made this policy contentious is the extent to which government has gone to achieve these goals by using incentives to shape the housing market and regulate the detrimental impact the market may have on society. Because middle- and upper-class individuals and families already posses the assets and credit worthiness to obtain home mortgage loans, government housing policy has necessarily been directed at low-income families, often including racial minorities, in urban centers where housing has often been scarce and expensive to obtain. Housing policy has also become deeply intertwined with issues of urban renewal, the gentrification of traditionally ethnic neighborhoods, and the overall health of entire communities because the value of property ownership not only provides individuals with financial assets, but also directly affects the value of the surrounding properties. Federal housing policy is best understood from three perspectives: provision of publicly funded rental housing, promotion of home ownership by insuring higher risk home mortgage loans, and laws requiring banks to make more mortgage loans available irrespective of income and race.

Though the provision of shelter is perhaps easier to justify as a basic human right than home ownership, the government's provision of affordable housing to the poor by dramatically increasing the availability of rental housing for low-income individuals and families has perhaps been the most controversial aspect of housing policy. A late addition to President Franklin D. Roosevelt's NEW DEAL programs, the Housing Act of 1937 sought to increase the number of affordable rental housing units in urban centers by either renovating existing units or helping to finance the construction of new units. The policy was actually designed to serve two purposes. The first was to provide shelter for the thousands of families made poor and homeless as the Great Depression put people out of work, drove up the number of foreclosures, and reduced the availability of mortgage loans. But it was also designed to stimulate the job-producing construction industry by providing money for building and renovation. To obtain widespread political support and local assistance in administration, Roosevelt chose to provide federal money directly to state approved but locally operated public housing authorities charged with identifying building sites and managing apartment complexes.

The economic boom following World War II helped fuel the construction of large numbers of public housing projects in major cities. Local control in site selection, however, allowed communities fearful of the impact low-income housing might have on property values and quality of life to use advocacy with city halls and ZONING laws to keep these projects out of the suburbs, concentrated many public housing complexes in the older inner cities rather than in middle-class neighborhoods, and is widely believed to have contributed to the emergence of ghettos. Poorly funded by Congress and most local governments, and with little effort made to make sure that facilities were well maintained or met basic safety standards, public housing projects developed reputations for terrible living conditions, poor management, urban blight, and centers of drug dealing. So widely was this believed that by the 1970s it became a social stigma to live in the "projects." In 1968, the Lyndon B. Johnson administration, as part of its War on Poverty and Model Cities programs, vastly expanded federal public housing projects under the new U.S. DEPARTMENT OF HOUSING AND URBAN DEVELOPMENT (HUD). More federal funds became available, many new units were planned to be built or renovated, and even the Federal Housing Administration was directed to begin underwriting funding for public housing.

Federal funding for housing programs and most urban renewal programs in general began to change radically with the Richard Nixon administration's greater emphasis on FEDERALISM and local policy control. The funds for these programs were pooled together into Community Development Block Grants (CDBGs) giving local politicians more flexibility to divide the money up between programs so that program priorities would match local needs. The flip side, of course, was a reduction in funding guarantees for individual programs such as public housing. Nixon's Housing and Community Development Act of 1974 also created the Section 8 Program (named after its section number in the U.S. Code) designed to subsidize the rent of low-income tenants in nongovernment-supported apartment housing, the amount of the subsidy paid to the property owner on behalf of the tenant calculated as the difference between 25 percent of the tenant's annual income (30 percent later) and the unit's fair market value.

Public housing programs and Section 8 subsidies and indeed all of HUD came under assault in 1981, when President Ronald Reagan made drastic cuts across the board in domestic spending. His actions were bolstered by a growing public perception that all public housing had done was, at best, to concentrate the poor in decaying jobless neighborhoods beset with drugs and alcohol, or, at worst, give free hand-outs that encouraged the poor to remain poor rather than try to find jobs and elevate themselves out of poverty. Though Congress later resisted deeper cuts in these programs and even restored some of what had been lost, construction of new housing projects virtually ceased in the early 1980s. President George H. W. Bush and his HUD secretary, Jack Kemp, however, took a somewhat more benign view of public housing, if still grounded in the idea of helping the poor to help themselves. Though funding for and availability of public housing was arguably far less than the demand during the Reagan and Bush years, Kemp did come into HUD with a signature self-empowerment plan. His Housing Opportunities for People Everywhere, or HOPE, program was an ambitious plan to provide federal support for tenants wishing to collectively purchase their public housing complex. He hoped that tenants would ultimately buy their own apartments and become home owners and that this would give low-income families a greater sense of commitment to both their properties and to their communities, though critics claimed that such a program could only benefit those low-income families fortunate enough to have steady incomes. The Bill Clinton administration's rather lukewarm interest in and financial support for housing policy caused this and the more traditional programs to stagnate, so that the current state of public housing policy is not dramatically different from that of the 1970s.

Even before creating public housing policy, the Franklin Roosevelt administration tried to boost the sagging housing construction industry and address the growing problem of homelessness in the 1930s by helping the battered financial industry make more mortgage loans. Falling incomes had left many individuals and families unable to qualify for standard home mortgage loans or prevent their current homes from being foreclosed, leaving a housing market so small that both the financial and construction industries were in danger of collapse. The only way to bolster the market was by reducing the risk to banks of loan default by promising that the government would cover a bank's loss if a customer did default. Thus, Congress created the Federal Housing Administration (FHA) in the National Housing Act of 1934 to use the resources of the federal government to underwrite mortgage loans considered high risk by the banking industry. To further boost the lending industry, the Roosevelt administration also created the Federal National Mortgage Association, or Fannie-Mae, to purchase FHA-secured mortgages from banks, bundle them, and then resell them in a special market to other financial institutions. By purchasing the mortgages in this "secondary" market, Fannie-Mae provided lenders with greater liquid assets that could in turn be reinvested in more loans.

Although the FHA enjoyed tremendous political support from the banking and home building industries and many members of Congress, it may have also contributed to inner-city decline and further concentration of the poor. Even with the federal government guarantee and a secondary mortgage market, financial institutions were often still unwilling to make loans to the very poor, in some cases using appraisal standards in the 1940s that bordered on discriminatory. The result was a continued neglect of the poor in the inner cities, where the only source of credit, when there was actually housing to buy, came from loan sharks. The Lyndon Johnson administration attempted to refocus the direction of the FHA in the 1960s by requiring it to help underwrite loans for the construction and renovation of subsidized rental housing in the inner cities. Johnson also sought to further expand mortgage availability by allowing FannieMae to resell non–FHA-backed loans, handing off that responsibility to the new Government National Mortgage Association (GinnieMae). Unfortunately, lax oversight of the FHA's work in subsidized housing, both in the terms of the mortgage loans and the quality of the housing produced, led to not only very poor-quality housing being built but large-scale fraud from developers and local politicians.

Johnson's attempt to refocus housing policy on ending racial segregation and providing federal assistance to the poor brought the issue of discrimination to the forefront of housing policy. The result was adding a stick to the array of carrots government already offered to the lending industry. Urban community activists organizing in the 1960s as part of the CIVIL RIGHTS MOVEMENT accused the mortgage lending industry of deliberately marking off sections of cities where racial minorities were concentrated in red marker ("redlining"). Congress responded by passing the Fair Housing Act and the Equal Credit Opportunity Act, the so-called fair lending laws, making it illegal to discriminate in the granting of mortgage credit on the basis of race and giving the U.S. DEPARTMENT OF JUSTICE and bank regulators the authority to prosecute lending institutions found to be engaging in mortgage loan discrimination.

The problem with the fair lending laws has been the identification of discrimination and enforcement. Claiming that bank regulators were unwilling to put time and resources into investigation and prosecution of the financial industry for redlining, advocates successfully persuaded Congress to pass the Home Mortgage Disclosure Act of 1975, or HMDA, requiring all lenders to document the number of mortgage loans made and where they were made. (HMDA data can be found at http://www.ffiec.gov/hmda.) The public availability of this data would, they hoped, pressure banks into making more widespread loans and pressure regulators to prosecute if they did not. When the early data appeared to show lending patterns favoring middle- and upper-income white neighborhoods, either in the suburbs or gentrified urban centers, advocates pressed their accusations of discrimination against the banking industry. Again Congress responded by passing the Community Reinvestment Act of 1977 (CRA) requiring all lending institutions to reinvest a portion of their assets, especially home mortgage loans, in all communities from which they solicited deposits, which often included low-income and minority neighborhoods. Failure to comply with the law and to document their actions with HMDA data would require financial regulators to lay sanctions on the banks and even deny applications to merge and acquire other institutions. Together HMDA and CRA have been the most effective tools urban advocates and bank regulators have to push the lending industry into increasing its efforts to make home ownership more widely available to the poor, though recent changes in banking laws under the Gramm-Leach-Bliley Act of 1999 may have undermined them by allowing banks to acquire and move assets into affiliate insurance and investment institutions not covered by these laws.

Perhaps the greatest ongoing challenge in federal housing policy is continuing to find ways to provide public funds to support programs that provide shelter to the less fortunate while at the same time providing opportunities for these same individuals to climb out of poverty and own homes of their own. At the same time, government must also balance this need against the health of the financial industry; pressuring lenders into making too many high-risk loans could have far-reaching consequences to the overall availability of credit and the viability of this industry. That said, discrimination in mortgage lending on the basis of race and income as well as the concentration of the poor into ghettos remain the paramount issues of concern for lawmakers and public housing advocates. Though large-scale statistical studies using HMDA data have not turned up clear evidence of racial discrimination in mortgage lending, it is worth noting that African Americans make up only 13 percent of the population of the United States, and whites 77 percent in 2005 (according to 2005 U.S. Census Bureau data) and that 49.3 percent of individuals and families served by public housing programs are black and only 46.5 percent are white, according to HUD's *Fiscal Year 2005 Annual Report on Fair Housing*. Furthermore, in 2003, a total of 1,793,000 families were reported living in public housing, 50 percent of whom had an annual income of less than $10,000 (the median annual income was $9,973) according to the 2003 *American Housing Survey in the United States*. The differences in home loans financed by the Federal Housing Administration are somewhat less stark. Here, 78.6 percent of all FHA-insured single-family loans in 2005 were to whites, while African Americans received only 14.1 percent. In terms of annual income, 41 percent of all families receiving government-insured mortgage loans (from the FHA and other programs) reported making less than $10,000, though the median income was $12,918. Finally, recent years have seen a growing concern regarding subprime lending to low-income urban families, or loans with high interest rates and other fees offered to customers considered to be high risk, which places a tremendous strain on families with variable income streams as they attempt to pay back loans that can border on usury. With these apparent disparities, the government's housing policy is likely to remain politically controversial well into the 21st century.

Further Reading

Bradford, Calvin. "Financing Home Ownership: The Federal Role in Neighborhood Decline." *Urban Affairs Quarterly* 14 (March 1979): 313–336; Bratt, Rachel G. "Housing for Very-Low Income Households: The Record of President Clinton, 1993–2000." Report W02-8, Joint Center for Housing Studies, Harvard University, 2002; Calem, Paul S., Jonathan E. Hershaff, and Susan M. Wachter. "Neighborhood Patterns of Subprime Lending: Evidence from Disparate Cities." *Housing Policy Debate* 15, no. 3 (2004): 603–622; Dye, Thomas R. *Understanding Public Policy*. 2nd ed. Englewood Cliffs, N.J.: Prentice Hall, 1972; Hays, R. Allen. "Ownership and Autonomy in Capitalist Societies." In *Ownership, Control, and the Future of Housing Policy*, edited by R. Allen Hays. Westport, Conn.: Greenwood Press, 1993;———. *The Federal Government and Urban Housing*. 2nd ed. Albany: State University of New York Press, 1995; Kleinman, Barbara A., and Katherine Sloss Berger. "The Home Mortgage Disclosure Act of 1975: Will It Protect Urban Consumers From Redlining?" *New England Law Journal* 12, no. 4 (1997): 957–989; Munnell, Alicia H., Geoffrey M. B. Tootell, Lynn E. Browne, and James McEneaney. "Mortgage Lending in Boston: Interpreting HMDA Data." *American Economic Review* 86 (March 1996): 25–53; Santiago, Nellie R., Thomas T. Holyoke, and Ross D. Levi. "Turning David and Goliath into the Odd Couple: The Community Reinvestment Act and Community Development Financial Institutions." *Journal of Law and Policy* 6 (Fall 1998): 571–651; Squires, Gregory D., and Sally O'Connor. *Color and Money: Politics and Prospects for Community Reinvestment in Urban America*. Albany: State University of New York Press, 2001; U.S. Census Bureau. *American Housing Survey for the United States in 2003*. Washington, D.C. 2003; U.S. Department of Housing and Urban Development. *The State of Fair Housing*. Report by the Office of Fair Housing and Equal Opportunity. Washington, D.C., 2005.

—Thomas T. Holyoke

immigration

At first, immigration to the United States was relatively unregulated, as there was plenty of room in America for newcomers and no perceived threat to those already here. In many states, especially the newer western ones, immigrants were given the right to vote and hold public office before becoming citizens (as long as the individual had declared his or her intention to become a citizen). No restrictive

The fence that runs along part of the border of the United States and Mexico *(Getty Images)*

federal immigration laws were passed until the Immigration Act of 1875, with the notable exception of the 1809 ban on the importation of slaves. As relatively large numbers of Irish and German Catholics, many of them desperately poor, began to immigrate to the United States in the late 1820s and 1830s, anti-immigrant sentiment combined with the costs of supporting the poor led cities and states to start using legislation to try to stem the tide. Some eastern states passed head taxes (e.g., $2 a head in Massachusetts) for all passengers, to be paid by the owners of immigrant vessels. Some eastern states passed immigration laws in the 1840s, usually to limit the inflow of immigrants from Ireland and Germany, but these laws were invalidated by the UNITED STATES SUPREME COURT in the *Passenger Cases* (1849), which declared the regulation of immigration to be a federal power under the COMMERCE CLAUSE.

By 1890, immigration to the United States shifted from "filling up" the new world to the importation of labor to an industrialized nation. At the same time, there was a shift in immigration from "traditional" countries (England, Ireland, Germany, France, and the Scandinavian countries) to those of east central and southern Europe. Immigration boomed at the turn of the 20th century as America recruited laborers from even more remote rural regions in eastern Europe. Because they came to work, not to live, many returned home after a relatively short period (five years or less). Nevertheless, immigration policy since the turn of the century has often aimed, either explicitly or implicitly, to encourage immigration by "desirable" races and ethnicities while discouraging or banning members of "undesirable" groups.

In the post–Civil War period, various immigration laws were passed to keep out foreigners deemed undesirable for reasons other than race or ethnicity (although some of the excluded categories had racial underpinnings): prostitutes and felons (1875); lunatics, idiots, and persons likely to become public charges (1882); victims of loathsome or dangerous diseases, polygamists, and persons convicted of misdemeanors involving moral turpitude (1891); epileptics, professional beggars, procurers, anarchists, and advocates of political violence (1903); imbeciles, feeble-minded persons, and persons with mental defects (1907); and illiterates (1917).

In the 1840s and early 1850s, anti-immigrant sentiment led to the emergence of the American (Know-Nothing) Party, whose major platform was restrictive immigration and NATURALIZATION laws. After the Civil War ended in 1865 and the subsequent ratification of the Fourteenth Amendment to the U.S. CONSTITUTION in 1868, which established a uniform national CITIZENSHIP, Congress changed the nation's naturalization laws to allow for the naturalization of "white persons and persons of African descent," pointedly excluding Asians. This was then used to bar Asians from entry to the United States on the grounds that they were ineligible for citizenship. The Page Act of 1875 added to the list of those barred from entering felons and any women "imported for the purposes of prostitution" and was particularly aimed at Asian women.

In the early 1870s, anti-Asian nativism triggered by Chinese immigration was rampant in both POLITICAL PARTIES. Racial prejudice, combined with fears of economic competition by white working men in the West, led soon afterwards to overwhelming bipartisan support for the Chinese Exclusion Act of 1882, which almost completely shut off immigration from China and also barred thousands of Chinese who had left the country temporarily from ever returning. The act was upheld by the U.S. Supreme Court, which ruled in a series of cases that the exclusion of a particular "class" of immigrant was constitutional. It was finally repealed in 1943. Asian immigration was so severely restricted that for most of America's history, Asians have represented less than 1 percent of the total population. In 1980, that increased to 1.5 percent, and by 2005 CENSUS estimates, people of Asian descent now make up 4.2 percent of the population.

In 1897, the U.S. Supreme Court ruled in *Henderson v. Mayor of New York* that the federal government, not state and local governments, had authority over immigration. Federal head taxes followed soon afterward, as did regulation to bar certain types of prospective immigrants (such as criminals, those likely to become a public charge, those suffering from contagious diseases, and those who failed to meet certain moral standards, such as polygamists). However, very few immigrants were turned away. In 1901, after President William McKinley was assassinated by an anarchist, the list of those excluded from immi-grating was expanded to include anarchists and other political radicals.

By 1920, more than a third of the U.S. population was immigrants, and anti-immigrant sentiment increased in response to perceived threats to the American way of life and economic threats to laborers, as well as racism against nonwhites and "inferior" Europeans such as Slavs and Jews. Public nativism was reflected in Congress by various attempts, led by Massachusetts congressman Henry Cabot Lodge, to require prospective immigrants to pass a literacy test. Congress approved Lodge's bill several times (1897, 1913, 1915, and 1917), and it was vetoed each time by Presidents Grover Cleveland, William Howard Taft, and Woodrow Wilson. However, in 1917, fueled by World War I nationalism, Congress voted to override the president's veto (287-106 in the House, 62-19 in the SENATE). The 1917 act required literacy, although not necessarily in English, and also barred all Asian immigrants (the "barred zone") except Filipinos (considered American nationals in the wake of the Spanish-American War) and Japanese (in recognition of the Gentleman's Agreement of 1907–08, whereby Japan agreed not to issue passports to laborers and to restrict immigration to family reunification).

After the war ended, the MEDIA warned of a coming flood of undesirable immigrants fleeing war-ravaged Europe; despite the lack of any evidence of such a flood, Congress voted to severely restrict immigration using a system of quotas based on the number of people from each nation already in the United States (the Dillingham plan, after its author, Vermont Republican Senator William P. Dillingham). The new laws were supported by domestic labor unions, which feared foreign competition, and by large firms hoping to shift from white to black labor, which they viewed as docile and unlikely to organize. President Wilson pocket vetoed the first Dillingham bill just as his second term expired, but it was quickly reenacted in special session called by the new president, Warren G. Harding, who signed it. The Dillingham plan (the Quota Law of 1921) set an overall limit on immigration of about 355,000. It allowed unlimited immigration from the Western Hemisphere (e.g., Canada and Mexico) and allowed a tiny quota for Japanese but no other Asians (except, of course, Filipinos), and Europeans were given a limit of 3 percent annually of the number of foreign-born Europeans in the country, assigned in proportion to the nationality recorded in the 1910 census. Congress extended the bill for two years in 1922. Although immigration regularly exceeded these statutory limits, it was dramatically reduced.

The 1924 Immigration Act (the Reed-Johnson Act) set up a two-stage system of quotas. Until 1929, the base was shifted from 1920 census figures to the 1890 census, and quotas were reduced from 3 percent to 2 percent, with an overall limit of only 165,000. The second phase shifted the base back to the first census of 1790 and further tightened Asian exclusion by abrogating the Gentlemen's Agreement with Japan and barring all Japanese. These shifting census dates were intended to increase quotas assigned to "desirable" nations, such as the British Isles, Germany, and Scandinavia, while reducing quotas for "undesirables."

The national-origin quota system of the Immigration Act of 1924 remained in effect until 1965, although it was changed slightly over the years. In 1943, Chinese exclusion was repealed and a quota granted. In 1946, quotas were given to the Philippines and India. All other Asians, however, were still denied admission. In 1952, Congress passed the McCarran-Walter Act, which ended racial and ethnic exclusions to immigration and naturalization law. However, national origin quotas remained in effect using the 1920 census. President Harry S. Truman vetoed the bill, objecting to maintenance of the quota system, but Congress overturned his veto. Nevertheless, between 1952 and 1965, the proportion of immigrants coming from Europe declined, while the proportion from Asia and Latin America rose considerably. Many of these were refugees. Another notable aspect of the McCarran-Walter Act, related to the anticommunist mania of the times, was a ban on immigration by lesbians and gay men, with the rationale that they were particularly vulnerable to COMMUNISM and blackmail. The exclusion was repealed with the Immigration Act of 1990 (which also removed the ban on former members of the Communist Party); homosexuals are still disproportionately barred from immigration due to exclusion based on HIV infection and cannot take advantage of family unity visas for their partners.

As the Nazis rose to power in Germany and Europe saw the outbreak of World War II, many Jews tried to immigrate to the United States to escape the Holocaust. Most were turned away. Americans tended to believe such efforts would compromise America's neutrality, and Americans also feared that a mass influx of Jews would threaten American values. Even when news of the wholesale slaughter of Jews in eastern Europe became common knowledge, politicians offered words of concern but not action to save those in the death camps. President Franklin D. Roosevelt's State Department consistently made it difficult for Jewish refugees to obtain entry into the United States, even sponsored scholars and children. Although even a much more liberal refugee policy could not have saved the 6 million individuals killed in the Holocaust, many more could have been saved with less racist and anti-Semitic policies.

The Immigration Act of 1965 ended the national origins system, instead stressing family reunification and occupational skills. Quotas by country of origin were replaced by hemispheric caps, including for the first time a ceiling on immigrants from the Western Hemisphere. A transitional component required that 40 percent of visas issued go to Irish immigrants. However, the long-term consequence has been a shift toward third world countries, including Asia, Africa, Latin America, and the Caribbean. The family reunification clauses have brought the demographic composition of immigrants closer to that of native born (more women and children). The law set aside a set portion of admissions for refugees, but large numbers of Cubans and then Southeast Asian refugees (in the wake of the Vietnam War) illustrated the unworkability of this system. In response, Congress passed the Refugee Act of 1980, which allowed refugee aliens of political and related persecution to apply for the first time for ASYLUM in the United States.

Today, most legal immigrants stay in the United States permanently rather than returning to their country of origin. Most labor immigration today is illegal, or undocumented. These laborers, like their European counterparts a century ago, tend to remain in the United States only temporarily. Some cross the border surreptitiously; others overstay their tourist or student visas. In the 1980s, nativist attitudes reemerged, this time focusing on the issue of illegal

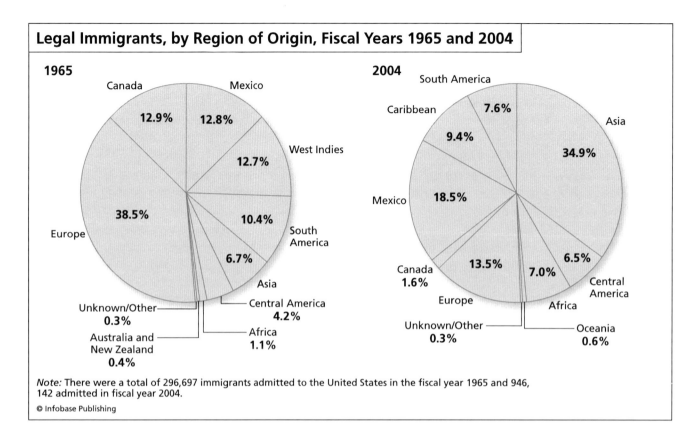

Legal Immigrants, by Region of Origin, Fiscal Years 1965 and 2004

1965

Canada 12.9%
Mexico 12.8%
West Indies 12.7%
South America 10.4%
Asia 6.7%
Central America 4.2%
Africa 1.1%
Australia and New Zealand 0.4%
Unknown/Other 0.3%
Europe 38.5%

2004

South America 7.6%
Caribbean 9.4%
Asia 34.9%
Mexico 18.5%
Central America 6.5%
Africa 7.0%
Europe 13.5%
Canada 1.6%
Oceania 0.6%
Unknown/Other 0.3%

Note: There were a total of 296,697 immigrants admitted to the United States in the fiscal year 1965 and 946, 142 admitted in fiscal year 2004.

© Infobase Publishing

immigration and specifically on the issue of economic competition from Mexicans. The 1986 Immigration Reform and Control Act (IRCA) included an amnesty provision for those who had been in the United States continuously for five years, requirements that employers verify the eligibility of all newly hired employees, sanctions for employers who knowingly hired illegal aliens, and an agricultural guest worker program for California and Texas. The enforcement provisions, however, were intentionally weak, allowing continued use of illegal immigrant labor by employers with little difficulty. IRCA granted amnesty to more than 2.7 million people, including more than 2 million Mexicans. Despite fears that IRCA would lead to more illegal immigration, evidence from border apprehensions suggests otherwise. And despite hopes that IRCA would reduce the flow of unauthorized aliens, again, data from the Immigration and Naturalization Service (INS) show no such impact. In the wake of the 9/11 terrorist attacks, Congress approved additional categories of banned immigrants as part of the USA PATRIOT Act of 2001, including aliens suspected of

being involved in terrorist activity or who have publicly endorsed terrorism.

In 2005, Congress again moved to reform immigration, with a focus on undocumented (illegal) immigrants. In the HOUSE OF REPRESENTATIVES, James Sensenbrenner (R-WI) won approval for a bill focusing on securing the border and making it a felony to help illegal immigrants. The bill sparked massive protests by immigrants across the country. In the Senate, John McCain (R-AZ) and Edward Kennedy (D-MA) pushed for an alternative approach that included an amnesty similar to that of IRCA, a new guest-worker program, and tougher enforcement of laws against hiring undocumented workers. Estimates in the spring of 2006 put the size of the unauthorized immigrant population at 11.5 to 12 million. As the election of 2006 approached, no compromise was in sight, as Democrats and Republicans squabbled over how best to reform immigration policy. The political controversy over how to regulate immigration persisted in 2007 even after the DEMOCRATIC PARTY won back both houses of Congress in the 2006 midterm elections, as this promises to be an ongoing issue in American politics for a long time.

Further Reading

Archdeacon, Thomas J. *Becoming American: An Ethnic History.* New York: Free Press, 1983; Chan, Sucheng, ed. *Entry Denied: Exclusion and the Chinese Community in America, 1882–1943.* Philadelphia: University of Pennsylvania Press, 1991. Daniels, Roger. *Coming to America: A History of Immigration and Ethnicity in American Life.* 2nd ed. Princeton, N.J.: Perennial, 2002; Daniels, Roger. *Asian America: Chinese and Japanese in the United States since 1850.* Seattle: University of Washington Press, 1988; Diner, Hasia R. *The Jews of the United States, 1654 to 2000.* Berkeley: University of California Press, 2004; Feingold, Henry. *Bearing Witness: How America and Its Jews Responded to the Holocaust.* Syracuse, N.Y.: Syracuse University Press, 1995; Johnson, Kevin R. *The "Huddled Masses" Myth: Immigration and Civil Rights.* Philadelphia: Temple University Press, 2004; Orrenius, Pia M., and Madeline Zavodny. "Do Amnesty Programs Reduce Undocumented Immigration? Evidence from IRCA" *Demography* 40, no. 3 (August 2003): 437–450; Pew Hispanic Center. "Estimates of the Unauthorized Migrant Population for States Based on the March 2005 CPS." Fact Sheet, April 26, 2006. Available online. URL: http://www.pewhispanic.org. Accessed June 23, 2006; Portes, Alejandro, and Robert L. Bach. *Latin Journey: Cuban and Mexican Immigrants in the United States.* Berkeley: University of California Press, 1985; Reimers, David M. *Still the Golden Door: The Third World Comes to America.* 2nd ed. New York: Columbia University Press, 1992.

—Melissa R. Michelson

income taxes

Income taxes are essential to modern public finance. In the United States, the federal and many STATE GOVERNMENTs depend on them as their main source of revenue. However, income taxes are more than just exactions from the earnings of individuals and corporations needed to pay for public expenditures. Politicians have come to use them to address myriad policy issues. Especially at the national level, income taxes are now the primary devices employed to both manage the macroeconomy and instill ideological principles into public policies. Indeed, few policies so arouse partisan passions and affect so many people as do income taxes. Republicans and Democrats clash routinely over who should bear the burden of such taxes as well as their imputed effects on work effort, savings and investment, entrepreneurship, and the federal budget. As such, the following discussion briefly touches on both the mechanics and the politics of income taxes. The goal is to convey their many economic, political, and ideological aspects.

The federal income tax, first made legal by a CONSTITUTIONAL AMENDMENT in 1913, did not become a "mass" tax—affecting the vast majority of income earners—until World War II, when the urgent need for revenues demanded that nearly everyone help pay for the war effort. Over the ensuing decades, as America's new role in world leadership and certain domestic issues demanded greater budgetary and other commitments, the federal income tax became not just an essential revenue source but a tool for macroeconomic and social policy making. This only complicated the two most important questions for tax policy makers, namely, what constitutes "income" and how best to tax it.

Parenthetically, these questions are relatively recent in the history of public finance. Taxes have been levied for thousands of years. For the most part, they have been excise, or sales, taxes of some sort, charged on purchases or similar transactions. The main source of revenue for the U.S. federal government prior to the income tax was tariffs, sales taxes applied exclusively to goods imported from abroad. State and local governments in the United States have long used sales taxes on domestic goods and services as well as property taxes assessed against the value of one's home to pay for their spending, namely public education and infrastructure. Only in the last century has the notion of taxing a person's annual income and accumulated wealth become accepted as legitimate at both the state and federal levels. As highlighted below, this notion arose largely out of a sense of fairness in the wake of marked income inequality wrought by the Industrial Revolution. Tariffs and other sales taxes were considered unfair, or "regressive," because they were paid largely by the poor and working classes. Today, at both the national and state levels, income taxes, often highly "progressive," with tax rates increasing with income levels, serve the dual purpose of raising revenues and redistributing tax burdens upward, or toward the wealthier income earners.

As everyone from high school and college students working part time to Fortune 500 CEO's can attest, the primary source of income open to tax stems from wages and salaries—payments for hours of labor supplied on the job. However, the federal income tax base, or the total amount of taxable sources, does not stop there. Other key sources stem from "capital," or "investment," income. These include dividends and interest paid annually by corporations and capital gains accrued on certain assets such as homes, small businesses, farms, and investment portfolios (i.e., mutual funds, stocks and bonds, etc.). In addition, such types of income as rents and royalties, alimony, unemployment compensation, SOCIAL SECURITY payments, and pensions are revenue sources for the federal government. Congress, the branch constitutionally charged with writing tax laws, regularly redefines these and other sources as "taxable" income.

This entails delineating how much of each type of income is legitimately open to taxation as well as the rate, or the percentage, at which the tax is applied. For instance, almost all wages and salaries are open to taxation. These are taxed at increasing, or graduated, rates ranging from 10 percent to 35 percent, meaning, on every additional, or marginal, dollar of wages and salaries earned, the federal tax takes anywhere from 10 to 35 cents. Conversely, 85 percent of Social Security payments are open to taxation, while only a fraction of capital gains income is subject to tax and often at noticeably lower rates. As tens of millions of taxpayers know, the annual endeavor to fill out their income tax returns involves calculating, first, their "adjusted gross income" by adding up all of the income from these many sources. Then, they subtract certain allowable deductions and exemptions for one's self and one's spouse and other dependents, thereby yielding their "taxable" income. They then apply the appropriate tax rate or rates to their taxable income, arriving at their final tax obligations. Many taxpayers find that they have overpaid during the year and are entitled to a "refund," while others find that they still owe taxes. Enforcement of the federal income tax, or

Internal Revenue, Code is the responsibility of the Internal Revenue Service (IRS).

As mundane and haphazard as all this might appear at first, the power to delineate what represents taxable income and how much to tax gives Congress enormous political power. No other public policy has come to so routinely attract the efforts of lobbyists seeking "loopholes," ideologues seeking "fairness" or "efficiency," and politicians seeking influence and reelection as has federal income tax policy, for no other public policy has come to so regularly affect hundreds of millions of income earners and voters, as well as tens of trillions of dollars in commerce. Indeed, this coalescence of political and economic forces is responsible for increasing the number of pages of the Internal Revenue Code from barely a dozen in 1913 to several thousand today.

First, lobbyists and the industries and other groups they represent are largely responsible for "loopholes," or stipulations in the tax code that exclude certain income from the federal tax base. The ability to convince Congress to grant or maintain such a legal exclusion, or deduction, from the tax code is highly prized. For instance, realtors hire lobbyists to jealously protect the ability of home owners to deduct their annual mortgage payments from their adjusted gross income, thereby reducing their taxable income. Lobbyists for restaurant owners and workers fight just as assiduously to protect the ability of corporations to deduct from their tax bills the costs of business lunches and dinners. Even state and local government representatives lobby on behalf of the deduction for interest earned on state and municipal BONDS.

Second, individuals and organizations more ideological than mercenary in nature solicit Congress to change the tax code on philosophical grounds. Those from a left-of-center, or liberal, perspective believe staunchly in the aforementioned notion of progressive taxation. For example, if someone who makes $10,000 pays $1,000, or 10 percent of his or her income in taxes, then someone making $100,000 ought to pay, not 10 percent, or $10,000, but, say, $20,000, or 20 percent in taxes. Those making several million dollars ought to pay a still higher share in income taxes. To these thinkers, income taxation, especially using progressively higher marginal tax rates, is key to redistributing income earned toward the poorer members of society. More conservative thinkers counter by arguing that such moralistic methods of taxation run the risk of becoming counterproductive. They point out that richer income earners have a higher "tax elasticity," meaning they are more sensitive than lower-income earners to higher tax rates and have the ability, through accountants and tax lawyers, to shield much of their income from higher tax rates. Or, if necessary, these wealthier income earners have the capacity to simply not undertake taxable activity in the first place. Thus, conservative thinkers argue that keeping tax rates low across all income levels is a more efficient way of helping society overall. Promoting risk-taking and entrepreneurship by allowing individuals and businesses to keep more of the rewards of their efforts leads to a bigger and wealthier economy. As will be seen below, this "equity versus efficiency" debate has largely characterized, in one form or another, the tax politics in America for more than a century.

Finally, although these diverse pressures culminate in often contradictory demands, politicians quickly discovered the benefits of indulging them. The promises of legislating legal favoritisms into the tax code can garner many members of Congress immense campaign contributions and even votes on election day. Others enjoy the ability to use the income tax to engage in "social engineering," granting benefits to or imposing costs on certain types of economic and other behavior. For example, deductions and other breaks have been granted to individuals and organizations who donate to charities, to parents with children in college, to home owners who insulate their windows and attics, and, more recently, to soldiers serving in Iraq and Afghanistan. In short, the power to tax and to exempt from tax, whether for parochial, ideological, or political reasons, remains one of the greatest prerogatives in all of policy making. It has redefined the role of the income tax from simply raising adequate revenue to fine tuning the macroeconomy and instilling social justice.

In fact, the modern federal income tax was more the product of a broad regional and ideological movement than of any economic or budgetary need. By the late 19th century, American wealth was concentrating in the Northeast as the steel, railroads, and banking industries came of age. Their benefactors in Washington, D.C., the Republicans, served their interests by keeping tariffs high, thus protecting such industries from foreign competition and shifting the burden of federal taxation onto workers and consumers. In the 1890s, Progressive Era Republicans representing farmers and ranchers in the Midwest joined forces with Democrats, largely from the agricultural South, in repeated attempts to lower tariff rates and instead enact taxes directly on the accumulating wealth in the Northeast. Indeed, for the next generation this tariff–income tax relationship would define the American political economy. After winning control of the national government in 1892, the Democrats, aided by Progressive Republicans, lowered tariff rates and introduced the first peacetime income tax in 1894. However, just a year later, the U.S. SUPREME COURT ruled the income tax unconstitutional on the grounds that its burden would not be apportioned evenly across all states. After numerous political setbacks, the Progressive-Democrat coalition finally prevailed in 1913, when the Sixteenth Amendment to the U.S. CONSTITUTION was ratified. It gave Congress the capacity to tax any kind of income without consideration to burden across the states.

Later that same year, the first constitutionally sanctioned income tax was enacted as an amendment to a much larger tariff reduction bill by the new Democratic president and congressional majority. The first federal income tax law was but a few pages and had a top rate of just 7 percent. Thanks to very high exemption levels for individual income earners and their family members, it applied to less than 2 percent of all income earners. Even after America's entry into World War I four years later, when the top rate was raised to almost 80 percent, only a small fraction of income earners paid any income tax. During the 1920s, when the Republicans returned to power, tariff rates were raised substantially, while income tax rates were sharply reduced. In the 1930s, the Democrats became the new majority party in the wake of the Great Depression and duly lowered tariffs and raised income tax rates to unprecedented levels, largely in a class war to punish the rich, whom they blamed for the economic calamity. It was not until the onset of World War II a decade later that the federal income tax became ubiquitous. The federal government needed more revenues to pay for the costs of this total war. The existing system of waiting for taxpayers to pay their annual tax bills was no longer practical.

In 1942, the U.S. DEPARTMENT OF TRANSPORTATION enacted the system we know today called "withholding." Primarily on wages and salaries, this system requires employers to withhold from each paycheck a certain amount of money that goes directly to the federal government. At the end of each year, taxpayers calculate their precise tax bills and, if they paid too much during the year, they get a refund of the difference. Otherwise, they have to pay still more by every April 15. When combined with the sharply lower exemption levels, the income tax thus became a "mass" tax, affecting upward of 80 percent of all income earners. Also, in the aftermath of the war, the Democratic Congress and President Harry S. Truman enacted the 1946 Employment Act. Following the intellectual tenets of the Keynesian economic paradigm, which argued that national governments should actively correct flaws in the private sector, this law basically committed the federal government to use all necessary fiscal (i.e., taxing and spending) and monetary policies to keep the national economy from falling back into a depression. In doing so, this act defined yet another responsibility for the income tax. Along with raising adequate revenue and redistributing incomes via top marginal rates then more than 90 percent, the federal income tax would now be used to tame the business cycle. This macroeconomic role was most thoroughly developed in the 1960s, when the Democrats, led by Presidents John F. Kennedy and Lyndon B. Johnson, used major income tax cuts to jump start an ailing economy and then tax increases to tame a growing inflation in consumer prices.

By the late 1970s, this inflation had combined with the graduated income tax to create rising real tax burdens for many Americans. While the inflation raised their incomes on paper, it forced them into higher tax brackets. This phenomenon, known as "bracket creep," thus robbed them of real buying power while increasing their real tax burdens. In 1980, Republican presidential candidate Ronald Reagan promised large cuts in income tax rates for all taxpayers as part of a conservative reaction to what was increasingly seen as a federal government grown too unwieldy and expensive. During his tenure in the White House, Reagan won enactment of two historic tax bills. Together, they reduced all tax rates, including bringing down the top marginal rate from 70 percent in 1981 to 28 percent by 1988, in exchange for the elimination of many tax loopholes. Reagan and his supporters credited these major changes in income tax policy for ushering in the booming 1980s. But his critics blamed them for unprecedented federal budget deficits. In the 1990s, Democrat Bill Clinton and a Democratic Congress reversed this downward trend in tax rates, claiming the Reagan tax cuts had unfairly favored the wealthy. Then, in 2001 and 2003, the Republican Congress worked with President George W. Bush to cut tax rates once again, claiming that lowering tax rates was more conducive to economic growth.

In short, income taxes are far more than exactions from Americans' paychecks. They are the product of many diverse political, economic, and ideological considerations. After nearly a century, the federal income tax has become part of American life. It now affects almost all income earners, and politicians have come to use it to address numerous policy issues. Its ubiquity has, in fact, caused it to become highly complex and often quite burdensome to taxpayers. In the past few years, Congress has considered replacing it with a national consumption tax, which would tax only what individuals and corporations purchase, rather than what they earn. Another option is a "flat" tax, basically the existing income tax, but with no or just a few deductions. While neither is likely to be enacted any time soon, they are the latest attempts to define "income" and prescribe how "best" to tax it.

See also FISCAL POLICY.

Further Reading

Birnbaum, Jeffrey H., and Alan S. Murray. *Showdown at Gucci Gulch: Lawmakers, Lobbyists, and the Unlikely Triumph of Tax Reform.* New York: Random House, 1987; Conlan, Timothy J., Margaret T. Wrightson, and David Beam. *Taxing Choices: The Politics of Tax Reform.* Washington, D.C.: Congressional Quarterly Press, 1990; Leff, Mark. *The Limits of Symbolic Reform: The New Deal and Taxation, 1933 39.* New York: Cambridge University Press, 1984; Pechman, Joseph. *Federal Tax Policy.* 5th ed. Washington, D.C.: Brookings Institution Press, 1987; Rosen, Harvey. *Public Finance.* New York: McGraw Hill, 2004; Stein, Herbert. *The Fiscal Revolution in America.* Chicago: University of Chicago Press, 1969; Stockman, David.

The Triumph of Politics: How the Reagan Revolution Failed. New York: Harper & Row, 1986; Wilson, Joan Hoff. *American Business and Foreign Policy 1920–1933.* Lexington: University of Kentucky Press, 1971.

—Alan Rozzi

Keynesian economics

The term *Keynesian economics* has several meanings. All stem from ideas of the British economist John Maynard Keynes (1883–1947), but not from all of his ideas. Specifically, it refers to a type of macroeconomics that rejects "classical economics" and suggests a positive role for government in steering a MARKET ECONOMY via its effect on aggregate expenditures on goods and services.

Classical economics dominated the profession from its birth until the 1930s. This school argued that rapid adjustment of prices—Adam Smith's "invisible hand"—prevents economic recessions and ends stagnation. If serious unemployment persists, it is due to nonmarket factors, such as governments or labor unions. Laissez-faire policies were recommended to allow the economy to supply as many products as possible, attaining what is now called potential output or full employment.

For many, the Great Depression sounded the death knell for classical theories: During the early 1930s, the U.S. and the world markets collapsed. In 1933, U.S. unemployment approached 13 million workers, 25 percent of the labor force. Worse, for some countries, depressed conditions began soon after World War I.

Many began to see stagnation as normal. Classical economists advocated wage and price cuts, but increasing numbers of people sought more timely solutions. Different schemes were proposed, including faster increases in the money supply, government investment in public works, fascist-style government-business cartels, and Soviet-type economic planning. In Germany, Nazi economics minister's Hjalmar Schacht's policies were "Keynesian" (broadly defined), involving government spending on infrastructure and militarism. Some others had had Keynesian ideas before Keynes, including Michał Kalecki of Poland.

The most influential was Keynes, who was very prestigious at the time. It helped that he steered a middle path, breaking with classical laissez-faire but advocating a relatively minor increase in the role of the government compared to fascism and Soviet planning.

Keynes's *General Theory* (1936) sparked a movement embraced by many of the younger generation of economists. Rejecting the classical postulate that market economies operated *only* at full employment, he aimed to understand the *unemployment equilibrium* that he saw as characterizing the 1930s. Though using theory, Keynes aimed to understand the real world. Because classicals saw economic problems as cured in the long run, he stressed that "In the long run, we are all dead."

To Keynes, price adjustment can fail to solve the problem of excess saving. The classicals saw increased saving as boosting the supply of funds available to borrow, so the price of borrowing (the interest rate) falls. In turn, businesses and individuals borrow all the new funds to finance fixed investment in new factories, housing and so on. This increases expenditure by precisely the same amount that saving rose. Any demand shortfall due to saving is thus exactly cancelled out by fixed investment expenditure.

To Keynes, fixed investment decisions were primarily determined by expectations of future profitability, not by interest rates. Investment was thus not moved significantly by saving. This breaks a key link in the classical chain. Further, it is not simply saving and investment that determine interest rates. The amount of money circulating and liquidity preference (the desire to hoard money) can be crucial: In a period of turmoil, people hold money as a safe asset, propping up interest rates and discouraging investment rises.

Excess saving means that people are abstaining from purchasing goods and services. If persistent, the demand shortfall for most products implies unwanted accumulations of inventories, so firms reduce production and employment, cutting incomes. This in turn causes saving to fall, since people are less able to save. It is thus not adjustment of interest rates but an *adjustment of income and employment*—a recession—that allows achievement of equilibrium, the equality of saving and investment. This attainment then ends any interest rate adjustment. Crucially, it occurs not at full employment, but with deficient-demand ("cyclical") unemployment, below potential.

To Keynes, uncertainty was the fundamental problem. Suppose one saves more to buy a house in the future. Nobody knows why you are saving more. Doing so lowers demand for current products *without* simultaneously creating demand for future houses (which would induce investment).

A central concept is the income-spending *multiplier*, which says that an initial change in spending (consumer demand, fixed investment, etc.) induces a *larger* change in income and output. A fall in investment, for example, reduces expenditure, revenues, and consumer incomes, pushing spending downward again. This again cuts production, employment, incomes, and so forth. Each step is smaller than the previous, so eventually the process stops at a new equilibrium level of income and output.

To Keynes, classical wage-cutting polices to end unemployment were self-defeating because they decrease income and demand. By hurting profitability and production, this decreases the demand for labor, encouraging unemployment. Further, economist Irving Fisher had argued (1933) that steadily falling prices (deflation) would deepen recessions.

Although Keynes's main book is not generally about policy, it was used to guide it. Since he had no control over his "brand name," much policy after Keynes is not "truly" Keynesian. However, our focus is on how his ideas were used, even if poorly.

If recessions do not solve themselves, the government can provide a helping hand for Smith's invisible hand. Increasing the economy's quantity of money would inspire business to spend more on investment. While classicals assumed that inflation would inevitably result, Keynesians saw that as happening primarily once full employment was achieved. But to many during the 1930s, this approach failed. One cliché was that "You can't push on a string." The special Keynesian solution was FISCAL POLICY, using the government's budget (expenditures and taxes) to change the nation's total spending. Classicals advocated a balanced budget (avoiding government borrowing). But in a recession, Keynesians argued that raising the government deficit (either by raising government outlays or cutting taxes) would stimulate the economy. After this "pump-priming" or "jump-starting," the private sector could take care of itself.

Thus, for many pundits and politicians, "Keynesianism" and "deficit spending" became synonymous. But this was not true: The "balanced budget multiplier theorem" said that a rise in government purchases stimulates the economy even if there is an *equal* rise in taxation. Second, amplifying the multiplier process, fiscal stimulus under recessionary conditions encourages private fixed investment (the accelerator effect). Business optimism, use of existing capacity, and cash flow relative to debt service obligations can all rise. Government and the private sector can be complementary rather than in conflict.

Further, the theory of functional finance, developed by Abba Lerner, argued that the government debts arising due to deficits (to solve recessions) could be reduced by raising taxes (or cutting expenditures) in periods when inflation was threatening. Finally, even with deficits, fiscal policy can have the same impact as private investment in terms of raising an economy's ability to produce. Government deficits can be used to finance projects that businesses shun, for example, investment in infrastructure (roads, airports, etc.), education, basic research, public health, disaster relief, and environmental clean up.

In practice, fiscal policy was not used to end the depression: It was not Keynes (or Roosevelt) who did so, but war. General military buildup implied expansionary fiscal policy, stimulating the U.S. and world economies. U.S. unemployment fell to 670 thousand (or 1.2 percent) in 1944. Conscious and active fiscal policy was not used in the United States until decades later, in 1964–65, after President John F. Kennedy had appointed Walter Heller and other advocates of the "new economics" (practical Keynesianism) to his COUNCIL OF ECONOMIC ADVISORS. Unfortunately, because it took so long for this policy to affect the economy, it encouraged the undesired results. It had been proposed to help the slow economy of 1960 but ended up reinforcing the inflationary results of the Vietnam War spending surge in the late 1960s.

The next active fiscal policy was contractionary: President Lyndon B. Johnson *raised* taxes in 1968, futilely trying to slow inflation. This revealed another limitation of fiscal policy: Temporary changes in government budgets may have little or no effect. Together with the long lags of the 1964–65 tax cuts, this undermined the popularity of active fiscal policy—and "fine-tuning" the economy—except during emergencies.

That, of course, does not mean that politicians avoided it. The two most important recent cases of active fiscal policy came from "conservative" presidents who might have been expected to oppose Keynesianism. Ronald Reagan's tax cuts and military buildup implied fiscal stimulus, as did George W. Bush's tax cuts and wars. On the other hand, Bill Clinton, sometimes described as a "liberal," raised taxes to create a budget surplus, even though Keynesians predicted recession. Clinton's tax hikes were followed by a demand boom. It is possible, however, that his fiscal austerity eventually contributed to the recession of 2001.

Active policy has been rare. Fiscal policy's role has mostly been *passive*. The large military budget of the cold war era and various domestic programs acted as a balance wheel, moderating fluctuations in total spending. Second, "automatic stabilization" occurs because deficits rise in a recession: Tax collections fall, while transfer payments such as unemployment insurance rise. These forces encouraged the general stability of the U.S. economy after World War II.

Almost as soon as it was born, challenges to Keynesianism arose. Many argued that the economy *would* automatically recover from depression. The "real balance effect" meant that falling prices would raise the real stock of money (real balances), raising individual wealth, causing rising expenditure, and canceling out recessions. Though most see this as too small to solve a full-scale depression, it does indicate that Keynes's unemployment equilibrium was not really an equilibrium. Movement toward the "true" equilibrium can take much too much time, however, so that Keynesian policies may still be needed. Further, it is common to simply assume that money wages do not fall quickly in response to unemployment (as seen in most evidence). Given this, practical Keynesian policies can be applied.

Another challenge was monetarism, led by Milton Friedman. Originally, the debate centered on the relative strength of monetary and fiscal policy, with Friedman favoring the former. This was mostly a false debate, since Keynes had always recognized the role of monetary policy. The problem for Keynesians was that it did not seem to work under the specific conditions seen during the depression. It did work under

the "normal" conditions seen during the 1950s and after.

In their 1963 book *Monetary History of the United States*, Milton Friedman and Anna J. Schwartz argued that the depression was a failure of monetary policy: The Federal Reserve allowed a "great contraction" of the money supply. While Keynes had blamed the market economy for the depression's persistence, Friedman blamed government (Federal Reserve) policy for its origin.

Practical Keynesianism began to decline about the time that President Richard Nixon proclaimed that "we are all Keynesians now." It had presumed that a rise in aggregate demand would not only lower unemployment but pull up prices and, if done too much, cause steady price rises (inflation). This was described by the Phillips Curve, a "trade-off" between unemployment and inflation. To some, the government could choose the best combination of these evils using demand-side policy.

But the 1970s saw both inflation and unemployment rise (stagflation), so this policy could not work. Any given unemployment rate was associated with more inflation than before (and vice-versa). The persistent inflation of the late 1960s had become built into inflationary expectations and the price-wage spiral in the early 1970s, implying inflationary persistence. Second, oil shocks of 1973–74 and 1979–80 meant higher inflation. The trade-off had not been abolished but seemed useless for achieving the best combination of evils.

Many economists embraced the "natural rate of unemployment" hypothesis that Edmund Phelps and Milton Friedman proposed in 1967: In the long run, demand-side variables (the government's budget and the money supply) have no effect on the unemployment rate. If the unemployment rate is kept below its "natural rate," this encourages rising inflationary expectations and accelerating inflation, until money's purchasing power is destroyed. If unemployment stays high, inflation expectations decreases until deflation occurs. Only at the natural rate would inflation maintain a steady pace. Demand-side efforts of any other unemployment could only work in the short run.

Friedman did not propose that policy makers try to find this rate. Rather, he suggested that a "steady as she goes" policy of constant and slow increases in the money supply would allow the economy to find it on its own, while avoiding the extremes of unreasonable inflation and depression. This was the opposite of fine-tuning.

Taking Friedman further, the new classical school of Robert Lucas et al. argued that demand-side policies could not work even in the short run: The level of output was determined by price adjustment, just as for the classicals. In response, the "new Keynesian" (NK) school arose. The new classicals had attacked the practical Keynesians' and Monetarists' assumption of price and money wage stickiness as theoretically weak. So the NKs developed theories of wage and price inertia (rejecting Fisher's and Keynes's view that price adjustment could be disastrous). On the other hand, the NKs generally opposed government deficits. The success of the NKs is seen in President George W. Bush's appointment of N. Gregory Mankiw to chair the Council of Economic Advisors.

Another limitation of Keynesianism is that demand-side policies work best for a large economy that operates relatively independently of the rest of the world, as with the United States during the 1950s and 1960s. It does not apply well at all to a small open economy: The multiplier and accelerator effects leak out to the rest of the world, while supply shocks such as those due to rising oil prices are more likely. A small country also has a very difficult time having interest rates different from those of the rest of the world. In recent decades, the United States has become increasingly like one of those economies.

Due to international exchange regime changes, monetary policy has also been strengthened compared to fiscal policy since the 1970s. Thus, macropolicy-making power has shifted from government to the Federal Reserve. Former Federal Reserve chairman Alan Greenspan was considered the economic "maestro" from 1987 to 2006. Interestingly, Greenspan maintained the activist spirit of early Keynesianism, even "fine-tuning" the economy at times.

Further Reading

Fisher, Irving. "The Debt-Deflation Theory of Great Depressions." *Econometrica* 1, no. 4 (October 1933): 337–357; Friedman, Milton. "The Role of Monetary Policy." *American Economic Review* 58, no. 1 (March 1968): 1–17; Friedman, Milton, and Anna Jacobson Schwartz. *Monetary History of the United States, 1867–1960*. Princeton, N.J.: Princeton University Press, 1963; Gordon, Robert J. *Macroeconomics*. 10th ed. Boston: Pearson, 2006; Keynes, John Maynard. *The General Theory of Employment, Interest, and Money*. Available online. URL: http://marxists.org/reference/subject/economics/keynes/general-theory/index.htm. Accessed June 22, 2006;———. "The General Theory of Employment." *Quarterly Journal of Economics* 51, no. 2 (February 1937): 209–223; Leijonhufvud, Axel. *On Keynesian Economics and the Economics Of Keynes: A Study in Monetary Theory*. New York: Oxford University Press, 1968; Mankiw, N. Gregory. "New Keynesian Economics." In *The Concise Encyclopedia of Economics.* Available online. URL: http://www.econlib.org/LIBRARY/Enc/NewKeynesianEconomics.html Accessed June 22, 2006; Meltzer, Allan H. "Monetarism." *In the Concise Encyclopedia of Economics.* Available online. URL: http://www.econlib.org/LIBRARY/Enc/Monetarism.html. Accessed June 22, 2006.

—James Devine

labor policy

A nation's labor policy may be characterized as its deliberate interventions in the labor market to accomplish national goals. Labor market interventions are considered justified because of the perceived failure of the market to achieve its major goal of efficiently allocating national labor resources and incomes to the satisfaction of policy makers or the major stakeholders in the labor market. But that goal is perceived differently by two of the major stakeholders: workers and employers. Workers perceive the legitimate goals of labor policy to be official acts to improve their tangible and intangible work conditions. Employers perceive the legitimate goals of labor policy to be official acts to help them maximize profitability by minimizing costs. As a consequence, labor policy may be seen in a more dynamic light as the prevailing balance in this struggle to achieve these conflicting perceptions of the policy goals. The outcome of the conflict between the goals of workers (which necessitates the right of workers to organize to gain increases in labor's share of production) and the goals of employers (which necessitates restrictions on the activities of workers' organizations in their attempt to enhance labor's share) has swung back and forth like a pendulum.

Some labor historians remark that unlike other industrially advanced countries, the United States had little that could be called a "labor policy" before the NEW DEAL era that began in the 1930s. The definition implicit in this use of the term, however, limits the labor policy domain to the *written* body of laws, administrative rules, and precedents employed by government to intervene in the labor market. Others broaden that domain to include all the institutions that have emerged to accommodate the government's laws and rules, including the processes by which policy proposals are created, placed on the national political agenda, and subsequently made into law or defeated. In this latter view, the labor policy domain includes not only the prevailing laws, rules, and precedents but the current official *attitudes and behaviors* that reflect *favor or disfavor* of employer or employee goals.

The above distinction is not a trivial one. In the second view, the failure of the founders of the United States to acknowledge the EQUALITY of black slaves and, to some extent, women and commoners, whom they regarded beneath their own elite station, could be considered an early "labor policy" that continues to influence the attitudes and behaviors of many toward labor, and especially the working poor, in the United States today. Labor's declining share of national income and the backlash against policies such as equal employment opportunity and AFFIRMATIVE ACTION in recent decades is considered by some as just desserts after the period of forward movement between the Great Depression of the 1930s and the decline of the CIVIL RIGHTS era in the 1970s.

A review of the state of workers' rights in those periods reveals some evidence that justifies the observation that the policy swings have been wide. Labor policies went through a cycle of initially enhancing workers' rights considerably during and after the 1930s but have reversed that trend considerably of late.

Yet, despite the elitism of the founders, most of those who fought and died in the Revolution were commoners, that is, farmers, workers, and some former slaves. Indeed, the importance of common people for the Revolution is seen in the reception of Thomas Paine's pamphlets, which were written for the masses and not for the elite. Their tremendous sales indicate the level of interest the average person had in the emerging ideology of independence. During this period, there were numerous instances of workers uniting to better their condition.

While Thomas Paine may have envisioned a social policy that ideally would have been based on greater equality, in reality the Revolution resulted in an elitist system that favored the wealthy upper classes. Major victories regarding work conditions were won by labor in the years following, especially in the northern states in the period described as Jackson Democracy, but these failed to balance the growing impact of the vast disparities between the elite and the common worker in income and wealth.

The basis for later gains in tangible labor rights at work and rights of unions to organize were laid between World War I and the New Deal. In 1913, President Woodrow Wilson signed a bill creating a CABINET-level DEPARTMENT OF LABOR whose secretary was given power to "act as a mediator and to appoint commissioners of conciliation in labor disputes." The next year saw the passage of the Clayton Act, which limits the use of injunctions in labor disputes (but the U.S. SUPREME COURT found in 1921 that the Clayton Act did not protect unions against injunctions brought against them for conspiracy in restraint of trade and, in another decision, that laws permitting picketing were unconstitutional under the Fourteenth Amendment).

In 1919, American Federation of Labor (AFL) president Samuel Gompers made a visionary recommendation for labor clauses in the Versailles Treaty that ultimately created the International Labor Organization (ILO). This was to have profound implications later for labor rights as inalienable civil rights.

One way to gain an appreciation of the increase in the scope of labor's fortunes is to review the typical labor economics textbook summary of legislation that gave form to current labor policy: the U.S. Supreme Court's decision in *Coronado Coal Co. v. UMMA* (1922), in which the United Mine Worker strike action was held not to be a conspiracy to restrain trade within the Sherman Anti-Trust Act; the Norris-LaGuardia Act of 1932, which increased the difficulty for employers to obtain injunctions and declared that Yellow Dog contracts (prohibiting employees from joining unions) were unenforceable; the Wagner Act of 1935 (also known as the National Labor Relations Act), which guaranteed labor the right of self-organization and to bargain, prohibited a list of "unfair labor practices" on the part of employers, established the NATIONAL LABOR RELATIONS BOARD with authority to investigate unfair labor practices and made strikes by federal employees illegal; the Taft-Hartley Act of 1947, which established a final list of unfair labor practices, regulated the internal administration of unions, outlawed the closed shop but made union shops legal in states without "right to work" laws, set up emergency strike procedures allowing an 80 day cooling off period, and created the Federal Mediation and Conciliation service; the Fair Labor Standards Act of 1938, which abolished child labor, established the first MINIMUM WAGE, and institutionalized the eight-hour day; and the Landrum-Griffin Act of 1959, which required regularly scheduled elections of union officers, excluded Communists and felons from holding office, held union officers strictly accountable for union funds and property, and prevented union leaders from infringing on worker rights to participate in union meetings.

The Landrum-Griffin Act already begins to reveal the reversal of the pendulum swing away from the worker organizations. In particular, business has found it increasingly easy to change work rules, especially in the older factories of the Frost Belt, and to free corporate resources for even greater southern and global expansion. These setbacks for labor were accompanied by an equally devastating reversal of the hard-won gains by civil rights leaders for African American workers that have remained so visible in the stubborn differentials in black-white wages and unemployment rates.

Before the New Deal, there was no effort to equalize opportunities for African Americans or other minorities. The government was opposed to any program of assistance to the destitute freed slaves during the Reconstruction Era and a half century thereafter. But later, the Great Depression, the maturation of civil rights organizations, and the New Deal's changes in American principles of labor policy laid the foundation for a policy shift toward a concept of proportional racial representa-

tion in employment. At the federal level, in particular, government contracting rules moved between World War II and the early 1960s from an equal treatment model of nondiscrimination to race conscious proportionalism. This era ended with the U.S. Supreme Court's application of strict scrutiny standards to racial preference in the rulings in both *Richmond v. J.A. Croson Co.* (1989) and *Adarand Constructors Inc. v. Pena* (1995) affirmative action cases.

Some writers observe that it may be time to cash in Samuel Gompers's idea of an appeal to the International Labor Organization to recognize labor rights as human rights. The U.S. reluctance to ratify ILO conventions no. 87 and 98, recommended by the secretary of labor in 1949 and the solicitor of labor in 1980, concerning the FREEDOM OF ASSOCIATION and right to bargain collectively, are considered part and parcel of the mindset that led to opposition to the International Criminal Court, the refusal to sign the Kyoto Agreement on global warming, the unwillingness to join a global ban on land mines, and the war in Iraq, all examples of American "exceptionalism," which even former secretary of state George Schultz concludes "erodes U.S. moral authority abroad."

The number of writers who continue to voice their concerns with this mindset are shrinking, and they have been overwhelmed by the large and growing number of corporately funded "think tanks" that justify the employer's view of the appropriate goals of American labor policy. The United States seems to be entering a long phase in which the view of the goal of the employee is completely deconstructed, along with all vestiges of the New Deal.

See also COLLECTIVE BARGAINING.

Further Reading

Bluestone, Barry, and Bennett Harrison. *The Deindustrialization of America*. New York: Basic Books, 1982; McConnell, Campbell, and Stanley L. Brue. *Contemporary Labor Economics*. New York: McGraw Hill, 1988; Reynolds, Lloyd G., Stanley H. Masters, and Colletta H. Moser. *Labor Economics and Labor Relations*. Upper Saddle River, N.J.: Prentice Hall, 1998; Wilson, William J. *The Truly Disadvantaged*. Chicago: University of Chicago Press, 1987.

—Robert Singleton

minimum wage

The minimum wage is the lowest hourly rate or wage that may be paid to a worker. Often, minimum wages are determined by a labor contract or union contract that is the product of COLLECTIVE BARGAINING between the employer and the employees (usually through their union). Some minimum wages are established by state laws, and the federal government also established a national minimum wage, below which it is illegal to pay employees for their work.

Should the federal or STATE GOVERNMENTs set minimum wage standards? Many business leaders assert that the only mechanism that should set wages is the free market. They argue that a government that sets wages and is intrusive in the workings of business hurts the economy. Let the free market of CAPITALISM guide wages, they argue, and a fair wage will be established.

While this position has its adherents, most today side with the federal government setting minimum wage standards, and their argument is that it is good for the worker (giving them a living wage) and good for business (because these workers reinvest their wages into the community and into the economy by buying food, clothes, appliances, cars, etc.). Today, there is widespread support for the setting of a government standard minimum wage but also widespread argument over at just what level that minimum wage should be set.

The Fair Labor Standards Act (FLSA), passed in 1938, is the overarching enabling legislation that established a national minimum wage. The U.S. DEPARTMENT OF LABOR's Employment Standards Administration is responsible for enforcement of the federal minimum wage law. In June 1933, President Franklin D. Roosevelt, early in his administration, attempted to deal with the Great Depression by, among other things, calling for the creation of a minimum wage for hourly work. He stated: "No business which depends for existence on paying less than living wages to its workers had any right to continue in this country. By business I mean the whole of commerce as well as the whole of industry; by workers I mean all workers—the white-collar class as well as the man in overalls; and by living wages I mean more than a bare subsistence level—I mean the wages of decent living." Following President Roosevelt's lead, Congress passed the National Recovery Act. However, in 1935, the U.S. SUPREME COURT declared the National Recovery Act unconstitutional, and the fledgling minimum wage was abolished. The minimum wage was reestablished in 1938 as part of the Fair Labor Standards Act, and the Supreme Court did not invalidate this effort.

In 1938, the national minimum wage was started at 25 cents an hour. In 1991, it was set at $4.25 an hour. As of 2006, the federal minimum wage was set at $5.15 an hour. Thus, a full-time worker who is the sole earner in a family of four, even though he or she is working a full-time job, still falls *below* the national poverty level.

For the most part, the politics of the minimum wage has been a partisan divide between the DEMOCRATIC PARTY, which, representing the interests of the worker, has often attempted to push up the minimum wage, and the REPUBLICAN PARTY which, representing the interests of business, often tries to keep the minimum wage down. Democratic president Harry S. Truman often said, "The Republicans favor a minimum wage—the smaller the minimum the better."

Does a higher minimum wage help or hurt the overall economy? Those who support a higher minimum wage argue that on both fairness and economic grounds, a higher minimum wage is good for the country. Fairness demands that those who work full time should earn a wage that allows them to live with dignity. If a full-time worker earns wages that are below the poverty line, that is both unfair and unwise. On economic grounds, they argue that a higher minimum wage puts more money in the hands of those who are most likely to spend it on the necessities of life, thereby putting more money into the economy, and by buying more goods, helping local businesses and thereby adding tax revenues to the public till. There is, they further argue, a widening gap between workers and managers that can be socially as well as politically dangerous if it continues to grow. It is, they argue, a win-win situation and makes moral as well as economic sense. Those who oppose a higher minimum wage argue that it is bad for business, especially small and struggling businesses, and might drive them to bankruptcy, thereby hurting the economy as well as eliminating jobs.

In what direction does the evidence point? For the most part, when the minimum wage increases slowly and steadily, it actually serves to benefit the economy. There is no solid systematic evidence to support the proposition that increases in the minimum wage have a negative impact on the economy. Who benefits from an increased minimum wage? Roughly 7.4 million workers earn minimum wages (roughly 6 percent of the workforce). More than 70 percent of these are adults, and about 60 percent are women. And while the minimum wage has not kept pace with inflation (if adjusted for inflation, the current minimum wage would have to be raised above $7.00 per hour), there is some evidence that trying to match the minimum wage to the rise in the rate of inflation would further benefit not only those earning minimum wages but the overall economy as well.

Is the minimum wage a "living wage"? That is, are those who earn the minimum wage at or above the federal poverty level? There is a difference between the minimum wage (the lowest level a full-time employee can earn) and a living wage (the amount of money needed to live by minimal standards of decency). Many scholars argue that the minimum wage is not a living wage. A full-time worker (someone who works 2,080 hours per year) earning the federal minimum wage would earn $10,712 a year, significantly below the federal poverty line of nearly $15,000 per year. When adjusted for inflation, the minimum wage reached its peak in 1968, toward the end of the GREAT SOCIETY era of President Lyndon B. Johnson, who attempted to wage a War on Poverty through his domestic policy agenda.

Some states have established minimum wages that exceed the federal standard. By law, states can set the minimum wage at whatever level they like. Today, roughly half the nation's population resides in states where the state's minimum hourly wage exceeds the federal level.

Most of the industrialized nations of the world have a minimum wage, and most of those countries have minimum wage levels that are higher comparatively than that of the United States. Most of these nations also have more expansive social welfare spending programs than exist in the United States. It is believed that New Zealand was the first nation to establish a type of minimum wage when it passed the Industrial Conciliation and Arbitration Act, allowing the government to establish wages in industries. Two years later, the state of Victoria in Australia established similar acts.

In 2006, the minimum wage issue became something of a political football, as in an election year, the Democrats pressed the Republican congressional majority to raise the minimum wage, and the Republicans, calling the bluff of the Democrats, proposed legislation to do so. But there was a catch: Attached to the minimum wage bill was a massive tax reduction measure as well. This became unacceptable to the Democrats, and eventually, the minimum wage bill failed. Then each side blamed the other for its failure. In the blame game, each party felt it had a case to make, and as the 2006 mid-term elections approached, the minimum wage issue became a source of rancor and debate. However, in 2007, the newly Democratic controlled Congress was able to pass an increased minimum wage law, signed by President George W. Bush, to increase the federal minimum wage to $7.25 by 2009.

See also FISCAL POLICY.

Further Reading
Adams, Scott, and David Neumark. *A Decade of Living Wages: What Have We Learned?* San Francisco: Public Policy Institute of California, 2005; Andersson, Fredrik, Harry J. Holzer, and Julia I. Lane. *Moving Up or Moving On: Who Advances in the Low-Wage Labor Market?* New York: Russell Sage Foundation, 2005; King, Mary C., ed. *Squaring Up: Policy Strategies to Raise Women's Incomes in the United States.* Ann Arbor: University of Michigan Press, 2001; Kosters, Marvin H., ed. *The Effects of Minimum Wage on Employment.* Washington, D.C.: AEI Press, 1996.

—Michael A. Genovese

New Deal
The New Deal refers to a series of laws passed and programs established during President Franklin D. Roosevelt's administration (1933–45) that concentrated federal government investment in the welfare of citizens. The economic devastation that occurred in the United States as a result of the Great Depression in 1929 garnered support for an increased effort on the part of the federal government. Before the New Deal, social programs had largely been the

A poster for Social Security, 1935 *(Library of Congress)*

grams operated in the form of categorical grants from the federal government to the states and local governments. The acceptance of resources by local governments often entailed conditions under which the resources were to be used and had the result of local governments relinquishing control of many policies to the national government. New Deal programs typically left the responsibility for program adjudication to local jurisdictions, requiring program accountability and often fiscal commitments from local governments. The New Deal also established laws that improved working conditions for most employees and took bold steps to save banks and improve financial investments.

One of the most dangerous effects of the Great Depression was a run on banks. In a loss of confidence when the stock market crashed in October 1929, investors withdrew their money from banks, and banks that had loaned money did not always have enough cash on reserve to provide investors with their full deposit. Knowledge of this prompted even more people to withdraw their savings, causing banks around the nation to close. By 1933, GOVERNORs in many states had ordered banks to close. Two New Deal actions saved American banks. The first was the establishment of the Federal Deposit Insurance Corporation (FDIC) to insure bank deposits. Once investors knew their money was safe, they began to deposit money in banks again. The Emergency Banking Act of 1933 provided a mechanism for reopening banks under the authority of the U.S. DEPARTMENT OF THE TREASURY, authorizing the Treasury to provide loans to banks when necessary.

The National Labor Relations Act of 1935, also known as the Wagner Act, established the NATIONAL LABOR RELATIONS BOARD and gave it authority to investigate and make determinations regarding unfair labor practices. The act also granted employees in most private sector occupations the right to organize and to engage in COLLECTIVE BARGAINING. Included in this act is the right to strike and to engage in peaceful activities in support of demands associated with workers' employment.

Another law regulating the workplace was the Fair Labor Standards Act of 1938, which established a federal MINIMUM WAGE standard and set a standard of 40 hours per week as the full-time limit for employees, with guarantees of overtime pay of one and one-half

responsibility of states and local governments. The effects of the Great Depression created widespread poverty and despair, which led the middle classes to support social programs funded on a federal level. Consider this contrast: The U.S. CENSUS reports that in 2003 (the most recently available data), 12.5 percent of all Americans lived in poverty. In 1932, nearly 17 percent of all Americans lived in poverty, and 25 percent of adults who might normally be employed were out of work.

Among the programs established during the New Deal were unemployment compensation, public housing, vocational education and rehabilitation, employment services, and aid programs for cities and rural areas. Social programs for the poor, elderly, and disabled were also established. Most of these pro-times the pay rate for employees exceeding that limit. It also established specific conditions under which children could be employed. Children under the age of 14 may not be employed by noncustodians. Between the ages of 14 and 16, a child may be employed during hours that do not interfere with schooling. The act gives authority to the secretary of labor to establish which occupations may be hazardous to the health or well-being of a child and to prohibit children under the age of 18 from being employed in those occupations.

The Works Progress Administration, generally referred to as the WPA, was established in 1935 to nationalize unemployment relief. This program created employment for largely unskilled workers, building roads, dams, sewage lines, government buildings, and so on. Females employed by the WPA were most often assigned work sewing bedding and clothes for hospitals and orphans. Both adults in a two-parent family were not encouraged to seek work with the WPA. Wages paid by the program varied depending on the worker's skill and the prevailing wage in the area in which a person lived. No one was allowed to work more than 30 hours per week. At its peak, the WPA employed 3.3 million Americans. The U.S. entry into World War II halted the WPA and other employment agencies begun during the New Deal, as men left to go to war and other men and women went to work in factories to build munitions.

Perhaps the most well-known aspect of the New Deal was the passage of the Social Security Act of 1935, which established federal social insurance programs for targeted populations on an entitlement basis. This is significant in three key ways. First, by creating entitlement programs, the government accepted responsibility for the well-being of the populations targeted in the act. Second, by establishing thresholds for assistance qualifications, the government committed to providing assistance to all people who met the threshold, thereby committing budgetary resources on a long-term basis. Third, this act took authority for poverty relief from the states. Some congressional debate took place over the loss of control faced by the states, but ultimately the act passed. The Social Security Board established regional offices to provide guidance and to monitor the states' implementation of relief programs. Program audits in the

states were required to be performed annually by accountants, causing many social workers to complain because they perceived the emphasis on poverty relief had shifted from client care to fiscal management.

The Social Security Act of 1935 divided relief into three classes: relief for the aged, relief for the blind, and relief for dependent children. Thus, the program design immediately established separate constituencies that would grow and organize individually rather than collectively. The public perception of aid preceded categorization of constituency. While the aged and blind are held in the public eye as deserving of aid, poor children are viewed as the products of undeserving parents. Therefore, aid to the poor from the beginning has met limited support.

Race was an obstacle that threatened support for the entire act. Southern Democrats threatened to break from their northern wing and join Republicans if the act was to include mandatory assistance for blacks. The dilemma was resolved by eliminating agricultural laborers and domestic workers (the dominant forms of employment for African Americans) from SOCIAL SECURITY eligibility and turning poverty assistance qualification determination over to the states.

Social Security established a pension for senior citizens over the age of 65. The pension was funded by employment taxes paid by workers and employers, based on 1 percent of the wages earned by the employees. The Social Security trust fund began to collect taxes in 1937, and benefits were released by 1940, giving the pension program time to develop a reserve.

The assistance program for needy children was called Aid to Dependent Children (ADC). It differed from other programs in the Social Security Act in that it allowed states to establish eligibility criteria as well as cash benefit levels, with no minimum set by the federal government. ADC was a categorical grant program. The federal government agreed to match state spending by 30 percent. In addition to committing funds for the program, states had to agree to have a central office and an appeals policy that would be evenly applied to applicants and clients.

Some states adopted eligibility requirements that the client home be "suitable" and that parents be "fit." Such vague criteria often resulted in elimination of African Americans from eligibility. Other southern states would end ADC subsidies to African American families during farming season or if elites were in need of domestic servants. One of the more noted criteria was the "man in the house" rule, which stated that benefits could be reduced or denied if a man not legally responsible for the children was living in the house. In extreme cases, police were often hired by the local welfare offices to visit client homes in the middle of the night to ascertain whether a man was cohabitating. By the middle of the 1970s, courts had struck down many of these regulations, suggesting issues of morality, residency requirements, and parental or housing fitness should not preclude needy children from receiving assistance because they violated federal or CONSTITUTIONAL LAW.

Many in the business community were originally reluctant to support statewide PUBLIC ASSISTANCE. As states moved to adopt widows' pensions, however, businesses joined the push for nationalization of the program. If all states were required equally to contribute, no business would suffer a tax disadvantage. One chief negotiating principle that Roosevelt established with the New Deal was that no government program could compete with the private sector. With respect to ADC and later AFDC (Aid to Families with Dependent Children), the expanded version of ADC, many businesses often supported the programs in order to demonstrate corporate responsibility for poverty assistance and thereby garner public support. Strategically, the Committee on Economic Development convinced many businesses and business organizations, including the National Chamber of Commerce and the National Association of Manufacturers, that it was a smart strategic move to increase consumer demand and to keep WELFARE POLICY nationalized because a systematic policy was more reliable than individual state plans that had formerly relied on general revenue funds for poverty assistance. Furthermore, many in private industry succeeded in increasing their business by providing support services connected to poverty relief programs.

Unions did not rally in support of federalization of antipoverty assistance or the expansions of this program that followed. Many union leaders viewed the program through the lens of territoriality: To the extent that labor was dependent on union negotia-

tions for unemployment and health compensations, the unions could remain strong. Exclusivity in many unions to whites also diminished support for poverty assistance, particularly when it was perceived that these programs might benefit African Americans at the expense of white taxpayers.

Criticisms of the New Deal are that it favored the poor and disadvantaged and was too prolabor in its outlook. Other criticisms are that it created a rise in "big government." The realities are that the New Deal altered the nature of FEDERALISM in the United States by expanding the responsibility of the federal government. The appearance of a booming national government is attributable to the decline in the gross national product (GNP) and a rearrangement of jurisdictional responsibilities. National government spending as a percentage of GNP appeared to grow because GNP fell from $97 billion to $59 billion from 1927 to 1932. The national government increased its powers in domestic policies in response to the crisis brought about by the Great Depression. In considering jurisdictional spending shares of all nonmilitary expenditures, state percentages remained relatively constant (20 percent prior to 1932 and 24 percent after 1940), while local government spending drastically decreased (50 percent prior to 1932 and 30 percent after 1940), and national government shares increased (30 percent prior to 1932 and 46 percent after 1940).

Many of the New Deal programs have continued to this day, although they have been revisited and altered by Congress from time to time. Social Security and laws protecting workers continue, as does the FDIC. ADC expanded through the 1950s up to 1996, when the program ceased to exist as an entitlement and became a time-limited block grant program known as Temporary Aid to Needy Families (TANF), which gives states considerable responsibility in deciding program rules and administration. Supplementary Security Income (SSI) continues the assistance for the aged, blind, and disabled that began with the Social Security Act of 1935.

See also ENTITLEMENTS.

Further Reading
Derthick, Martha. *The Influence of Federal Grants.* Cambridge, Mass.: Harvard University Press, 1970; DiNitto, Diana M. *Social Welfare: Politics and Public*

Policy. 6th ed. Boston: Pearson, 2007; Noble, Charles. *Welfare As We Knew It*. New York: Oxford University Press, 1997; Quadagno, Jill. *The Color of Welfare: How Racism Undermined the War on Poverty*. New York: Oxford University Press, 1994; Schneider, Anne, and Helen Ingram. "Social Construction of Target Populations: Implications for Politics and Policy." *American Political Science Review* 87, no. 2 (June 1993): 334–347; Skocpol, Theda. *Social Policy in the United States: Future Possibilities in Historical Perspective*. Princeton, N.J.: Princeton University Press, 1995; The Fair Labor Standards Act of 1938. Available online. URL: http://www.dol.gov/esa/regs/statutes/whd/0002.fair.pdf Accessed July 20, 2006; The National Labor Relations Act of 1935. Available online. URL: http://www.nlrb .gov/nlrb/legal/manuals/rules/act.asp. Accessed July 20, 2006; United States Census Bureau. Available online. URL: http://www.census.gov/. Accessed July 20, 2006; Wallis, John Joseph. "The Birth of Old Federalism: Financing the New Deal." *Journal of Economic History* 44, no. 1 (March 1984): 139–159; Weaver, R. Kent. *Ending Welfare As We Know It*. Washington, D.C.: Brookings Institution Press, 2000.

—Marybeth D. Beller

public assistance

Public assistance refers to a division of social welfare programs that are need based. In order to qualify for the benefits of these programs, then, recipients must meet minimum income eligibility standards. The term *public assistance* typically is used to mean welfare, a cash assistance program for families available only to low-income parents who have custodial care of their children. Public assistance also includes public housing programs, food stamps, reduced-price or free school meals, Medicaid, and Supplemental Security Income.

Public assistance policy in the United States has changed dramatically over the course of the last century. What began as locally funded and administered poverty assistance programs developed into federal programs, often jointly funded and jointly administered, with states retaining discretion only for eligibility and benefit determination. The current welfare program receives federal funding and has federal regulations, but the bulk of the administration has returned to the states and, in some cases, to the local

level. Throughout this change from decentralization to centralization and back again, one constant remains. Assumptions that poor personal behavior choices cause economic dependence have led to a series of attempts to control personal behavior through WELFARE POLICY regulations.

With the exception of Massachusetts, which established poverty and housing assistance as early as 1675, most states began in the 19th century to provide limited social assistance via housing for the deaf, blind, and insane as well as housing for felons. Governments held no legal responsibility for providing assistance: The 1873 U.S. SUPREME COURT case *The Mayor of the City of New York v. Miln* established that New York had the right to bar the poor from migrating into the city.

By 1911, some states started to authorize local governments to direct aid to support mothers of young children, at times providing state aid to assist in the effort. Poverty relief gained wide acceptance as a role for state or local governments through widows' pension programs. These programs were designed to keep children at home rather than in orphanages by providing subsidies to their mothers. The programs were selective in their eligibility and requirements for clients: Illegitimate and black children were often not served, and requirements could be placed on mothers for socially suitable work they might obtain to supplement the assistance. By 1920, 40 states had established some form of a widows' pension program, generally implemented at the local level. This assistance was not universally implemented and could have eligibility requirements: California, for example, established a three-year residency requirement in 1931. As late as 1934, only half of the counties in the United States provided some form of aid to mothers. Many businesses became reluctant to support these growing programs, in large part because they were not universally accepted, and, therefore, states and counties with programs disadvantaged their businesses through heavier tax burdens. Many businesses operating across state lines and those faced with competition from out-of-state companies began to lobby for a policy shift; nationalization of poverty relief for women and children would result in a level playing field for the private sector because funding APPROPRIATIONS would become universal.

The Social Security Act of 1935 established federal social insurance programs for targeted populations and did so on an entitlement basis. This is significant in three key ways. First, by creating entitlement programs, the government accepted responsibility for the well-being of the populations targeted in the act. Second, by establishing thresholds for assistance qualifications, the government committed to providing assistance to all people who met the threshold, thereby committing budgetary resources on a long-term basis. Third, this act took authority for poverty relief from the states. Some congressional debate took place over the loss of control faced by the states, but ultimately the act passed. The Social Security Board established regional offices to provide guidance and to monitor the states' implementation of relief programs. Program audits in the states were required to be performed annually by accountants, causing many social workers to complain because they perceived the emphasis on poverty relief had shifted from client care to fiscal management. The first national assistance program for needy children, Aid to Dependent Children (ADC), was established by the Social Security Act of 1935. It differed from other programs in the Social Security Act in that it allowed states to establish eligibility criteria as well as cash benefit levels, with no minimum set by the federal government.

Another NEW DEAL public assistance program was public housing. The DEPARTMENT OF HOUSING AND URBAN DEVELOPMENT (HUD) today provides funding for local governments to construct apartment complexes for the poor. Additionally, housing vouchers are made available to families who can rent HUD-approved homes and apartments, known as Section Eight housing. These vouchers pay the rent. Neither public housing apartments nor Section Eight housing is available to all who qualify or need this assistance. Waiting lists for assistance take months and even years in some cities throughout the United States.

President Harry S. Truman signed the School Lunch Act of 1946, which initiated the movement to provide meals to children. The program began as a federal categorical program, with states appropriating the bulk of the funding but matched by federal dollars. In return, states agree to provide meals that meet federally mandated nutrition guidelines and to offer reduced-price or free meals to low-income children. This has been one of the most popular public assistance programs. It has expanded over the years and now provides breakfast as well as lunch to school children who qualify.

In 1950, ADC was expanded to provide assistance for the caretaker parent. This new program was called Aid to Families with Dependent Children (AFDC). Under AFDC, administrative rules were established at the federal level, and states bore the responsibility for implementing the rules and making program decisions including the level at which the program would be administrated. Congress increased the federal match to 50 percent, up from an original grant of 33 percent, with a grant limit of $6 for the first child and $4 for each subsequent child. Congress also required that states begin to provide services to clients in order to help move them from poverty to self-sustaining employment. This requirement had no specific administrative directives, though, and implementation from the states was very weak. The program expanded again in 1961, when AFDC was changed to include two-parent families wherein one parent was unemployed but had a history of working. The new component, known as AFDC-UP, met with some contention by local office administrators who disagreed with the extension of benefits. AFDC-UP was implemented as a state option. By 1988, only 25 states had adopted the AFDC-UP provision.

The Food Stamp Act of 1964 nationalized a program that had been piloted from 1939 to 1943 and again from 1961 to 1964. Part of the New Deal included a pilot food stamp program to help the thousands who were recovering from the devastating effects of the Great Depression. The start of World War II eliminated this need, as many men joined the armed services and went to war and other men joined with women in working in munitions factories to support the war effort. After his campaign visits to West Virginia in 1960, President John F. Kennedy restarted the pilot program to alleviate the widespread poverty he found. This pilot program expanded to 22 states serving 380,000 citizens by 1964. The Food Stamp Act allowed states to determine eligibility and gave them responsibility for processing applications and monitoring the program. By 1974, when all states had implemented food stamp programs, 14 million Americans received food stamps.

AFDC was altered in another significant way in the Public Welfare Amendments of 1962, when Congress enacted inducements for states to provide services to AFDC clients that would lead their clients to self-sufficiency. If states provided these services, the federal government agreed to pay 75 percent of the service costs. This was a dramatic increase in AFDC funding for the states. Federal funding for normal program services was based on a formula that matched state money. In the enacting legislation, the funding match was one-third. Eventually, the formula was changed to provide greater assistance to poorer states: For each AFDC beneficiary, the federal government would match state spending (up to one-third of the first $37.00 in 1967; up to five-sixths of the first half of the average state payment by 1975) and then an additional proportion of state spending, depending on the state's per capita income (ranging from 50 to 65 percent).

Soaring welfare rolls throughout the 1960s escalated concerns over the structure of the program and its ability to help the poor become self-sufficient. Combined state and federal expenditures on AFDC rose from $1 billion in 1960 to $6.2 billion in 1971. Changes in AFDC, from expansion of eligibility to institutionalized patients and two-parent households, as well as the elimination of residency requirements in the U.S. Supreme Court ruling in *Shapiro v. Thompson* (1969), resulted in a tripling of the AFDC caseload between 1960 and 1974.

Attempts to promote self-sufficiency through work requirements for AFDC clients had shown little success. The Work Incentive Initiative (WIN) Program of 1967 tied welfare benefits to work by requiring local offices to refer qualified adult participants for training and employment. Exempt from the requirements were women whose children were under six years of age and those whose pending employment was determined to be adverse to the structure of the family, a determination that was made by caseworkers on a subjective basis.

Medicaid, the health insurance program for the poor, began in the 1960s. This program provides basic health care to poor children, adults, and seniors. It is a federal program in which the national government meets state appropriations on a three-to-one ratio, with states setting parameters for eligibility and determining, within federal guidelines, what services will be offered.

Further centralization of public assistance came in 1974 through the consolidation of Aid to the Blind, Aid to the Permanently and Totally Disabled, and Aid to the Elderly into a new program, Supplemental Security Income (SSI), which was assigned to the Social Security Administration for operation. This program was designed to supplement income for poor disabled adults and children as well as poor senior citizens. The federal government provided the funding for SSI, established eligibility criteria, and set benefits for SSI recipients, thus removing state authority from poverty relief for clients qualifying for this program. Many states argued that eligibility for SSI was too broad and encouraged abuse of the system because adults suffering from alcohol or drug addiction and children diagnosed with behavioral disorders could qualify for benefits.

The Food Stamp Act of 1977 streamlined the process for dispensing food stamps while establishing penalties for adult recipients who quit their jobs. The most controversial part of the act was to allow stores to return up to 99 cents in change to recipients who paid for food with a food stamp. This process did reduce the paperwork involved in reimbursing stores for the amounts that did not equal whole dollars, but it also provided a mechanism for the poor to "cash out" some of their food stamps. Many critics claimed this was an abuse of the system.

The Food Stamp Program was reduced during the 1980s by increasing enforcements and penalties. States were now allowed to require job searches by adult recipients of food stamps and to increase disqualification periods for adults who quit their jobs.

The Family Support Act (FSA) of 1988 made AFDC-UP mandatory for states, expanding benefits to include two-parent families in which the primary wage earner was unemployed. The FSA gave states the option of limiting cash assistance to six out of every 12 months for two-parent families but mandated that states provide Medicaid to these families year-round. The FSA also began the JOBS program (Job Opportunities and Basic Skills) and increased enforcement efforts for child support. In addition to benefiting two-parent families, the law benefited the states: Administration money for the JOBS program was funneled to the states, and states retained child support payments from noncustodial parents for families receiving AFDC benefits, passing through $50.00 of the support funds per month to families. The strength of JOBS was to be an emphasis on education and training, implemented through coordination of programs at the local level. The new emphasis on work activity added a component that increased the likelihood of families succeeding in maintaining economic self-sufficiency. Medicaid and child care benefits were extended to families for one full year after they left welfare. Exemptions from work activities for single mothers and mothers with children under three also reduced the effectiveness of integrating the poor into the workforce. Ultimately, AFDC rolls increased, and the JOBS program began to be viewed as unsuccessful.

President Bill Clinton came into office in 1993 having campaigned to "end welfare as we know it." While his administration did send a proposal to the 103rd Congress, the proposal did not arrive until June 1994, when election concerns, health care reform, GUN CONTROL, and other items could easily claim precedence on the legislative calendar. The 104th Congress forged two welfare reform bills that were vetoed by the president. In those two bills, the Republican GOVERNORs and congressmembers agreed to block grant welfare with a flat rate of funding for five years, end entitlement to benefits, but retain the right of states to establish eligibility criteria.

In 1996, Wisconsin governor Tommy Thompson, president of the National Governor's Association, brought the governors back together to work on a bipartisan proposal for reforming AFDC. The proposal kept the block grant and flat rate funding initiatives agreed to earlier, with an addition of federal funding to reward states that lowered their welfare rolls. Additionally, the maintenance of effort (MOE) required by states was reduced to 80 percent, and states were allowed to keep surplus funds created by declining rolls. The governors brought their proposal to Capitol Hill in February of that year and worked with Congress on a modified bill. In the end, the governors agreed to accept a provision that would apply sanctions to recipients who did not meet work requirement efforts. Requirements of the new wel-

fare program proposed in two earlier bills remained options for states to determine. These included the child cap provision, which allows states to eliminate or reduce benefits increased for children born nine months after an adult beneficiary enters the program; time limits lower than the federal 60-month limit; work requirements that exceed the federal rules; and flexibility in adopting a sanctions policy. The bill became known as the Personal Responsibility and Work Opportunity Reconciliation Act (PRWORA) that replaced AFDC with Temporary Assistance to Needy Families (TANF).

By 1994, the number of Americans receiving food stamps had grown to 28 million. The PRWORA included a provision that allowed states to restrict food stamps to three out of 36 months for healthy adults without dependent children who were not working at least 20 hours a week. The economic prosperity of the 1990s helped more Americans to become self-sufficient, and food stamp usage declined every year for seven straight years. Since 1990, food stamp usage has been on the rise. The U.S. DEPARTMENT OF AGRICULTURE reported that in 2004, 38 million Americans qualified for food stamps, although only 23 million received them.

Poverty in the United States has increased every year since 2000. The public assistance programs that are in place may not meet the demand that the poor have as affordable housing shortages increase, Medicaid services decreased, and cash assistance for poor families remains capped at a 60-month lifetime limit.

Further Reading

Blank, Rebecca, and Ron Haskins, eds. *The New World of Welfare*. Washington, D.C.: Brookings Institution Press, 2001; Cammisa, Anne Marie. *Governments as Interest Groups: Intergovernmental Lobbying and the Federal System*. Westport, Conn.: Praeger Publishers, 1995; Conlin, Timothy. *From New Federalism to Devolution*. Washington, D.C.: Brookings Institution Press, 1998; Edin, Kathryn, and Laura Lein. *Making Ends Meet: How Single Mothers Survive Welfare and Low-Wage Work*. New York: Russell Sage Foundation, 1997; Gallagher, L. Jerome, et al. "One Year after Federal Welfare Reform: A Description of State Temporary Assistance for Needy Families (TANF) Decisions as of October 1997." Available online. URL: http://www.urban.org. Accessed

June 15, 2006; Hanson, Russell, ed. *Governing Partners: State-Local Relations in the United States*. Boulder, Colo.: Westview Press, 1998; Thomas: Legislative Information on the Internet. Available online. URL: http://thomas.loc.gov. Accessed June 15, 2006; Jansson, Bruce S. *The Reluctant Welfare State*. 4th ed. Belmont, Calif.: Wadsworth, 2001; Marmor, Theodore R., Jerry L. Mashaw, and Philip L. Harvey. *America's Misunderstood Welfare State: Persistent Myths, Enduring Realities*. New York: Basic Books, 1990; Murray, Charles. *Losing Ground: American Social Policy, 1950–1980*. New York: Basic Books, 1984; Noble, Charles. *Welfare As We Knew It*. New York: Oxford University Press, 1997; Quadagno, Jill. *The Color of Welfare: How Racism Undermined the War on Poverty*. New York: Oxford University Press, 1994; Rochefort, David A. *American Social Welfare Policy: Dynamics of Formulation and Change*. Boulder, Colo.: Westview Press, 1986; Skocpol, Theda. *Social Policy in the United States: Future Possibilities in Historical Perspective*. Princeton, N.J.: Princeton University Press, 1995; United States Department of Agriculture Office of Analysis, Nutrition, and Evaluation, Food Stamp Program Participation Rates, 2004. Available online. URL: http://www.fns.usda.gov/oane/MENU/Published/FSP/FILES/Participation/FSPPart2004-Summary.pdf. Accessed June 15, 2006; Weaver, R. Kent. *Ending Welfare As We Know It*. Washington, D.C.: Brookings Institution Press, 2000; Wright, Deil S. *Understanding Intergovernmental Relations*. North Scituate, Mass.: Duxbury Press, 1978.

—Marybeth D. Beller

public debt

The "public" or "national debt" should instead be called the "government debt." This is because it is a debt owed by the government, rather than by the public or the nation (i.e., the citizens). From the perspective of citizens, much or most of the government's debt is an *asset*. That is, U.S. citizens own most Treasury bills, notes, and bonds along with the ever-popular U.S. Savings Bonds.

Most references to government debt concern only the federal debt, because STATE and local governments borrow much less than the federal government. In the early 2000s, for example, the debt of the state and local governments totaled only about 20 percent of the total for government, even though their expenditure was about 64 percent of the total. The small size of this debt arises because most states and municipalities are constitutionally required to balance their budgets (i.e., to not borrow). However, they make an exception for capital expenditure, that is, public investment in real assets such as schools and infrastructure (roads, bridges, sewers, etc.). This last point reminds us that the government has assets along with debts. At the end of 2005, the federal government's total liabilities of $9.5 trillion corresponded to $608 billion in financial assets. In addition, there are nonfinancial (real) assets, such as buildings, military bases, and mineral rights adding up to about $3.2 trillion. On balance, federal net worth equaled −$5.7 trillion.

Federal net worth (assets *minus* liabilities) is negative. Why is the government not insolvent or bankrupt, as a private business would be? As "The Budget of the United States Government: Analytical Perspectives 2007" notes: "The [federal] Government . . . has access to other resources through its sovereign powers. These powers, which include taxation, will allow the Government to meet its present obligations and those that are anticipated from future operations."

Because of its ability to tax the citizenry and the long-term strength of the U.S. economy, the federal government is extremely unlikely to go bankrupt. Further, the U.S. federal debt involves an obligation to pay using U.S. dollars. Thus, the government can (through the agency of the Federal Reserve) arrange to have paper money printed and used to pay its debts. Because the U.S. dollar is currently used as a world currency, people around the world are willing to accept its paper money. However, beyond allowing normal demand-side growth, this option is usually avoided in order to prevent excessive inflation and unwanted declines in the price of the dollar relative to other currencies.

Its abilities both to tax and to issue currency make the federal government much less likely to go bankrupt than private-sector debtors and state and local governments. During the Great Depression of the 1930s, more than 2,000 local governments became insolvent. This is one reason why these governments have positive net worth. At the end of 2005, state and local governments had $2.6 trillion in liabilities and

$2.2 trillion in financial assets. Their real assets added up to about $4 trillion.

At the end of 2005, the federal debt was about $7.9 trillion. Of this, only about 58 percent was owed to people and organizations outside the federal government, since the Federal Reserve and other government-sponsored organizations owned much of the government's IOUs. About 15 percent of this was owned by state and local governments, including their pension funds. The rest was held by banks, insurance companies, mutual funds, and individuals.

Of the privately held government debt at the end of 2005, 45 percent was directly owned by the "foreign and international" sector. The actual number may be higher to the degree that foreigners own U.S. banks and the like, which in turn own U.S. government debt. In recent years, as a result of the large U.S. balance of trade deficit, this percentage has been rising. Similarly, the percentage of U.S. private debt that is foreign-owned has risen.

Government debts should be distinguished from the similar-sounding *government deficits*. A deficit refers to the situation of the government budget, that is, to the flow of money out of the government to buy goods and services (or to transfer to individuals or corporations) *minus* the inflow of money from tax revenues and fees. A deficit occurs when spending exceeds revenue inflow, while a budget surplus occurs when revenues surpass spending.

On the other hand, the government debt refers to an outstanding pool of obligations to others. When the U.S. government runs a deficit (i.e., spends more than the revenues received), its debt increases. Government surpluses reduce its debts (as in the late 1990s). Put another way, government debts are accumulated deficits (and are reduced by surpluses). A balanced budget leaves government debt unchanged.

A federal debt of $95 trillion is extremely hard to understand. To do so, we must put it into context: The size of the government debt must be corrected for the effects of inflation and the growth of the economy. Both of these corrections are usually done by dividing the debt by gross domestic product (GDP), that is, the size of the U.S. MARKET ECONOMY during a year. This gives a rough feeling for the size of the debt relative to the potential tax collections, that is, how well the nation can cope with the debt.

Between 1946 and the late 1970s, the ratio of the privately held federal debt to GDP generally fell, mainly because of the growth of nominal GDP and secondarily because of the small size of deficits (and some rare surpluses). A small deficit makes the ratio's numerator rise less than its denominator, so that the ratio falls. The 1980s saw a rise in this ratio, primarily due to the Reagan-era tax cuts and military spending increases, along with back-to-back recessions early in the decade. (Tax revenues usually fall as incomes fall in recessions, while transfer payments such as unemployment insurance benefits rise.) This debt-GDP ratio stopped rising during George H. W. Bush's administration. Then, during President Bill Clinton's second term, the privately owned federal debt shrank compared to GDP to about 33 percent due to tax increases, budget surpluses, and a booming economy.

But under President George W. Bush, recession, tax cuts, and military spending increases meant that the federal debt rose to about 38 percent of GDP during the early months of 2004. It is expected to rise more due to promised tax cuts, further spending on the wars in Iraq and Afghanistan, and the steeply rising cost of the Medicare and Medicaid programs. In addition, rising interest rates (seen in the mid-2000s) imply that the government must make larger interest payments on its outstanding debt than in the past. However, in the near future it is not expected to attain anything close to the 106 percent reached at the end of World War II.

Should the government have a debt, especially a large one? The answer partly depends on one's political-economic philosophy. The "classical" economists (starting with Adam Smith in 1776 and persisting to this day) opposed any increase in government debt. Beyond the necessary functions of national defense, law and order, and the enforcement of contracts, the government was seen as a parasitic growth on the economy and society. Typically, however, exceptions were made during times of war, allowing deficits and rising debt. Nonetheless, advocates of classical economics are more likely to favor such ideas as adding a federal "balanced budget amendment" to the U.S. CONSTITUTION.

Modern views, influenced by KEYNESIAN ECONOMICS, are more nuanced. In "functional finance," an increase in government debt (i.e., running a government deficit) is tolerable if benefits exceed the costs. Start with the latter. The burdens of the government debt have often been exaggerated. The "burden of the debt to future generations" refers to principal and interest payments on that debt that would be paid by future generations. Because these payments are to that same generation of people (or a subset), there is no purely intergenerational debt burden.

The debt—the *principal*—does not have to be paid off. Instead of reducing the number of outstanding bonds, the federal government has such a good credit rating that it can easily borrow new money to replace the old bonds with new ones, "rolling over" the debt. This can be a problem if the government's debt is extremely high relative to its ability to tax. In this case, its credit rating falls, and the government has to pay higher interest rates on new borrowings. This has never happened to the federal government. In fact, despite the extremely high federal debt after World War II, the United States enjoyed a long boom of GDP growth. This was a period when many middle-class people owned government bonds, a very safe kind of asset, boosting their economic security and purchasing power.

The situation in which the government's debt grows too high and hurts its credit rating usually has happened due to war and civil war. It has primarily been a situation of countries other than United States, especially poor countries whose currency is not generally acceptable in the world market.

In normal times, the burden of the debt primarily consists of the *interest payments* that must be made (unless bankruptcy is declared). It is true that most of these payments are to residents of the United States. However, these payments put a restriction on the use of tax revenues. A rise in interest payments implies that a government must either cut other types of outlays or raise taxes in order to keep the budget in balance. In 2005, net interest payments represented about 7.4 percent of government outlays (and 1.5 percent of GDP). These ratios would be higher if interest rates were higher: If rates were similar to the average for 1979–2005, then the percent of payments going to net interest would be about 12.5 percent, and the percentage of GDP would be 2.5 percent.

These interest payments primarily go to those who are already wealthy (who are the main owners of federal IOUs). This can intensify existing inequality in the distribution of income, which has already been trending upward during the last 30 years or so.

Similarly, much of the interest is paid to those outside the United States. (The percentage of U.S. government interest payments going to foreigners rose steeply in the mid-2000s, attaining 34 percent in 2005.) This implies that the United States must produce more output beyond that needed for domestic use, benefiting those who have lent to our government. This is also true for interest payments to the rest of the world by private sector debtors.

It is also possible that government borrowing competes with private sector borrowing over the available supply of funds. This means that some private sector spending, including investment in factories and the like, may not happen. That is, private fixed investment can be *crowded out* by increased government borrowing (deficits), which might hurt the growth of the economy's potential. On the other hand, as the Keynesian school points out, increased government borrowing can stimulate aggregate demand. Rising incomes increase the amount of saving and thus the funds available for borrowing by both the private sector and the government. Second, if business spending on fixed investment (factories, machinery, etc.) is blocked by unused productive capacity, excessive corporate debt, and pessimistic expectations about future profitability, the rise in aggregate demand can encourage ("crowd in") private fixed investment. Thus, the problem of crowding out is crucial only when the economy is already operating near full employment.

Next, if increased government borrowing causes higher interest rates, this encourages an inflow of funds from the rest of the world to buy both U.S. dollars and U.S. assets. The resulting rise in the dollar exchange rate hurts the competitiveness of U.S. exporters while encouraging U.S. imports.

The benefits of increased debt depend on how the government uses the borrowed money. As noted, even classical economists saw winning a war as a good reason for deficits. If IOUs are incurred entirely for waste, bureaucracy, or gambling, however, it can be a disaster. If they are acquired in a way that encourages the economy and the tax base to grow, it is much like the case of private investment in a factory, since the project can pay for itself. (No one complains about private borrowing that goes into productive investment.)

Since the 1920s, many have argued that deficits should finance projects usually not profitable for private business, such as investment in infrastructure, general education, public health, cleaning up the effects of environmental destruction, basic research, and the like. In general, this investment complements private sector activities and can help the economy's ability to supply GDP (its potential output).

As noted, Keynesian economics also sees rising government debt accumulation as providing *fiscal stimulus* that helps to reverse serious recessions and end economic stagnation. This is most appropriate, as suggested, if the economy is not already near full employment, so that the crowding-out problem is minimal. This kind of policy is like an investment when it is perceived that the private sector would leave a lot of resources unused.

The new SUPPLY-SIDE ECONOMICS, on the other hand, sees tax cuts (which also increase government indebtedness) as encouraging extraordinary economic growth by unleashing the private sector, raising the economy's ability to supply. This school rejects the idea of using increased government expenditure and, in fact, wants to decrease that spending. The supply-side view assumes that "getting the government out of the private sector's business" will unleash productivity and creativity, raising potential tax revenues. In fact, some supply-siders (e.g., Arthur Laffer) argued that tax revenues may actually rise when tax cuts are instituted because this "unleashing" effect is large.

Both the Keynesian and modern supply-side schools see special tax cuts for business fixed investment as beneficial. However, most research on this subject suggests that the positive demand- and supply-side effects of such cuts are quite limited. This is because fixed investment decisions are generally made based on long-term corporate plans, in which after-tax profits play only one part.

As noted, both the supply-side and demand-side benefits of fiscal stimulus can be cancelled out if government expenditure is wasteful or benefits only the cronies of insider politicians or those politicians themselves. Government investment may be in "pork barrel" projects that benefit no one but vested interests. In fact, one of the arguments in favor of a balanced budget amendment to the U.S. Constitution is that having such a rule keeps the politicians from abusing their power in this way. Of course, such an amendment may make it extremely hard for the government to deal with depressions or such disasters as the destruction of much of New Orleans by Hurricane Katrina in 2005. Instead, many call for more popular control of and involvement in the business of governing.

See also FISCAL POLICY.

Further Reading
Eisner, Robert. *How Real Is the Federal Deficit?* New York: The Free Press, 1986; Federal Reserve, Flow of Funds, tables L.105 and L.106. Available online. URL: http://www.federalreserve.gov/releases/Z1/Current/. Accessed June 18, 2006; Gordon, Robert J. *Macroeconomics.* 10th ed. Boston: Pearson, 2006; U.S. Council of Economic Advisors. *Economic Report of the President.* Available online. URL: http://www.gpoaccess.gov/eop/ Accessed June 18, 2006; U.S. Office of Management and Budget. *Budget of the United States Government: Analytical Perspectives. Fiscal Year 2007.* Available online. URL: http://www.gpoaccess.gov/usbudget/fy07/pdf/spec. pdf. Accessed June 18, 2006.
—James Devine

public utilities

Public utilities are very large operating organizations that provide the basic infrastructures for public services, including electricity, telecommunications, natural gas, energy, water and sewage operations, and in some instances cable television (CATV). In the United States, these public services are generally provided by private firms that are regulated by the STATES and by the federal government. Often in other countries but only occasionally in the United States, these public utility organizations are publicly owned. The "public" aspect comes from the fact that most people in society receive necessary services from these organizations, often on a daily basis. In political terms, as large entities public utilities have considerable political influence themselves, and the manner in which they are regulated or operated also has important public policy consequences.

Public utilities tend to have social and economic characteristics that traditionally have differentiated them from other industries and consequently justified government involvement or regulation. Public utility firms use their networks for product and service distribution over specific geographic areas (often states or metropolitan areas in the United States). They face very large initial fixed costs to provide the facilities necessary to start providing services, which then gives them elements of a "natural monopoly," making it difficult for competitors to meet their low prices since the competitors would be faced with duplicating all of that large initial fixed investment.

Public utilities also provide what have become quite essential services for most Americans, for which there are usually no direct substitutes. As a result, in economic terminology, the demand for their services is highly inelastic, giving them at least the opportunity to raise their prices to monopoly levels absent regulation or other controls. Public utility firms often also produce what economists call significant positive and negative externalities in the course of providing their services. For example, the fact that telephone companies connect all Americans provides enormous positive network externalities to all users. On the negative side, electricity-generating public utilities have traditionally been large sources of pollutants of various kinds. The conventional pricing mechanism of the market generally fails to take account of these externalities, so it may be difficult to induce the utility to produce the level of service at a price that is socially desirable.

Over time, policy makers have also come to believe that guaranteeing universal access to a basic level of these utility services (water, communications, and energy) is essential to the protection of equal opportunity for individuals, while serving the basic necessities for modern human beings. Some utility services are also deemed critical elements of the infrastructure of local economic development.

There are two policy approaches commonly used for overcoming these economic and social concerns related to public utilities: regulation and nationalization (or municipalization). The politics of each can be complex. In the United States, in contrast to most other nations, governments' policy choices generally have been to regulate privately owned utility firms. Some American cities own their electricity firms, and U.S. water utilities are frequently publicly owned. In most other countries, however, the dominant historical pattern was to nationalize all public utilities and run them as government entities. Over the past two decades, however, more nations have adopted a U.S. model of regulating private entities and encouraging some competition among them.

Regulating the industries through rule making and administrative procedures leaves the public utility firms owned by private corporate shareholders who seek to earn profits. In the United States, based on constitutional notions of interstate commerce and the Tenth Amendment, such regulation has usually been shared by the states for the intrastate portion of public utility services and by the federal government for the interstate elements. Intrastate electricity and intrastate telecommunications services are overseen by state regulatory bodies, state public utilities commissions (PUCs). Federal regulatory bureaus, such as the FEDERAL ENERGY REGULATORY COMMISSION (FERC) and the FEDERAL COMMUNICATIONS COMMISSION (FCC), regulate public utility activities involving interstate commerce. There is not a clear line between intra- and interstate commerce, and technology and legal interpretations have moved the political agreements on where that line stands generally in a direction favoring more federal control over time. Most regulation is at the state or even local level in the case of water and sewage utilities and CATV companies.

Regulators oversee the prices that utilities can charge to various classes of customers (residential, business, and commercial); the determination of the total revenue needs so that firms can earn adequate profits to generate further capital investment; the sanctioning of entry, exit, and expansion for particular services; safety and services issues; and the territorial limits in the industry. Regulatory agencies also usually prescribe uniform accounting systems and procedures, conduct accounting and management audits, supervise utility financial practices, and examine both quantity and quality of services provided.

Governmental regulation is generally carried out through rule making and formal hearings and procedures, in which all the interested parties participate. These parties generally include consumer groups, government advocates, representatives of business user groups, but most importantly the public utility firms themselves. Some political scientists argue that public utilities have often been able to "capture" their regulators using their advantages of information and resources and that they therefore gain very favorable regulation that ensures profits and bars entry by potential competitors.

In most other nations, rather than regulating private enterprises, the political response to the rapid development of public utilities was to establish them as government-owned entities. These public utilities often became the largest employers in many countries. The utilities and their labor union organizations often wielded considerable political power, and sometimes policy decisions seemed to favor the interests of the employees over those of consumers. Thus, a literature emerged that argued that these firms should be "privatized" and regulated more like the U.S. model, so that they would provide services more efficiently. As a result of those arguments plus pressure from international trading groups such as the WORLD TRADE ORGANIZATION, in the past 25 years several large nations have privatized or partially privatized many of their public utility organizations.

Privatization has often been coupled with the growing trend toward greater competition in these industries. Some of the technological and engineering aspects that initially gave rise to public utilities as "natural monopolies" have changed over time. For example, wireless communications reduced the monopoly status of landline telecommunications utilities. As a result of these technological changes, some portions of the telecommunications and electricity industries have been "deregulated." Deregulation usually means that government allows competition in some segments of the public utilities marketplace by other firms, and in return government relaxes the degree of regulation over the incumbent public utility firm. While privatization has been the dominant trend in other advanced nations over the past 25 years, in the United States, where firms were already private, deregulation of public utilities has been the main trend. While deregulation in its most extreme form can mean the complete elimination of regulatory oversight over

private firms in these industries, in most cases it has not yet gone that far.

We can identify two distinct periods of regulatory regimes in the modern history of U.S. public utility regulation: government-oriented and market-oriented regimes. During the first half of the 20th century, the idea that a public utility is a natural monopoly and regulation is the best substitute for competition dominated legislative and regulatory practices.

The legal cornerstone for modern U.S. public utility regulation was laid in 1877 in the U.S. SUPREME COURT case of *Munn v. Illinois* regarding the right of the state to regulate rates charged by public warehouses. The *Munn v. Illinois* decision did not assert that warehousing belongs to the state function and should be nationalized through regulation. However, the Court clearly ruled that the economy would be disrupted if a monopoly firm could impose an unjust pricing burden on those customers who had no choice but to use its service. So the Court encouraged the legislature to take a larger role to regulate the rates and services in the name of the public interest.

At the federal level, Congress established the first regulatory agency in 1887, the INTERSTATE COMMERCE COMMISSION, the members of which were appointed experts. At that time, the railroads were the dominant public utility, and they had achieved monopoly pricing power as well as disproportionate political power in the United States due to their enormous wealth. Thus, the regulation of railroads was a major political and electoral question, much more so than utility regulation is today, when it is generally viewed as more of a technical issue unless prices are skyrocketing or major changes are taking place. After some initial uncertainty about the powers that Congress had actually intended to delegate to appointed regulators, in 1890 the U.S. Supreme Court affirmed that the "reasonableness of utility rates" could be the subject of regulatory and JUDICIAL REVIEW.

Several states had earlier experimented with "weak" regulatory commissions with limited powers, such as Massachusetts in the 1860s, but in 1907 the states of Wisconsin, New York, and Georgia established "strong" regulatory commissions, with jurisdiction and power over telephone, telegraph, gas, electric, and water companies. Other states followed rapidly. State regulatory commissions were widely regarded as the means by which the public was protected from excessive rates, unsafe practices, and discriminatory treatment by monopolies whose services were increasingly required by a growing American middle class.

The period from the 1920s through the 1970s was fairly stable and quiet in terms of public utility regulation in the United States. Services were expanded to reach most Americans partly because of a policy goal of achieving "universal service" and partly because prices were mostly falling during this period. New technologies lowered prices further, public utility firms earned solid profits, and, apart from some financial and regulatory issues during the Great Depression of the 1930s, public utilities prospered. Most Americans were happy with their services. This stable relationship was altered significantly in the 1960s and 1970s. In the electricity industry, many new controversies developed around nuclear power plant siting, energy shortages, skyrocketing prices, and pollution problems. At the same time, the technologies of telecommunications changed considerably, eventually leading to the break-up of the monopoly that AT&T held in 1984. In short, a series of new disruptions and issues led to greater interest in the decisions made by public utilities and focused greater political attention on these industries and their regulation.

The fallout from these events led to a more market oriented regime in the 1980s and 1990s. More policy makers became convinced that deregulation and more market oriented regulations would enhance service quality and lower prices. So-called "Chicago school" economists promoted a vision that public utilities were no longer natural monopolies and that competition could flourish in most of these industries.

More recent debates have centered on how far deregulation should go in the public utility arena and what forms of continued regulation make the most sense. Mainly due to technological changes such as wireless communications and the Internet, telecommunications has changed a great deal. Deregulation and change have been slower in electricity policy, in part due to continued problems with pollution, higher input prices for oil and other energy sources, and policy failures and scandals such as Enron that led to

the politically unacceptable blackouts of power in California in 2001.

The regulation of public utilities in the United States is a blend of political decision making and technical decisions based on expertise. Regulatory commissions, both state PUCs and federal regulatory agencies, are mostly made up of officials with some degree of expertise who are appointed, respectively, by GOVERNORs and presidents. The public utility firms often go before these regulators to seek rate increases or other changes, and then a quasi-judicial administrative proceeding takes place. Utilities hold the advantage of having the greatest stake in the decisions, leading them to spend money on LOBBYING politicians, paying high-level consultants and experts to testify, and providing the most information in the process. Utilities are also powerful politically because they are critical to future job development; they have many employees, most of whom are tied to a particular state; they have large investments in that state; and they make large campaign contributions. Their usual opponents, who may include potential competitor firms, consumer groups, and others, now can marshall more resources than they did prior to the 1960s, but they are still frequently overwhelmed by the large public utilities. The regulators, who are appointed in 39 states by the governor but elected in 11 others, are mostly insulated from direct political influences, but studies have shown that they are subject to broad political influence in some states. The outcomes of regulatory decisions are usually very complex, lengthy documents with considerable technical detail about accounting, economic, and engineering questions that are beyond the ability of most laypersons and voters to comprehend. Thus, public utility regulation can most accurately be described as a blend of political and technical decision making.

Though the services of public utilities are essential to daily survival for most Americans, they are often taken for granted, like the "pipes" and "wires" that lie underground as the infrastructure for these services. This is true except in those rare occasions when they fail, such as blackouts, when the salience of policies surrounding public utilities rises substantially. A number of policy trends, including deregulation, privatization, concern about local and global pollution, energy prices, and concerns about independence, have become intertwined with public utility issues in recent years, raising their importance to policy makers and the American political process.

Further Reading

Crew, Michael, and Richard Schuh, eds. *Markets, Pricing, and the Deregulation of Utilities.* Boston: Kluwer, 2002. Gormley, William. *The Politics of Public Utility Regulation.* Pittsburgh: University of Pittsburgh Press, 1983; Pierce, Richard. *Economic Regulation: Cases and Materials.* New York: Anderson Publishing, 1994; Teske, Paul. *Regulation in the States.* Washington, D.C.: Brookings Institution Press. 2004;

—Junseok Kim and Paul Teske

reproductive and sexual health policy

Campaigns for and against the legalization of abortion, public health interventions aimed at reducing the spread of HIV/AIDS, prosecutions of pregnant women under novel extensions of drug trafficking and child endangerment laws, and debates about the appropriateness of vaccinating teenage girls against the virus that is linked to cervical cancer, each of these examples hints at the breadth of reproductive and sexual health, as well as the intense political struggle with which it is often associated in the United States today. Yet, to understand this area of politics, attention must be paid to historical trends, connections between issues, and how larger power struggles have structured reproductive and sexual health.

While often reduced to a delimited topic or group of topics such as abortion or HIV/AIDS, reproductive and sexual health issues are many, varied, and highly interconnected in practical terms. Reproductive health issues are those that revolve around procreative capacities, while sexual health issues are primarily associated with sexual behavior and norms. Some scholars and practitioners create a conceptual distinction between these two sets of issues, yet, in practice, they are incredibly intertwined. For example, societal norms concerning sex outside of marriage, between members of different racial or ethnic groups, or between individuals of the same sex can greatly impact the extent to which funding or services are provided for those struck by sexually transmitted

infections, the way in which the children of members of those groups are viewed and potentially provided for under child welfare programs, and the degree to which these acts are socially proscribed or criminalized.

Other understandings of reproductive and sexual health are organized around the application or development of codified principles based in either U.S. constitutional doctrine or larger international human rights agreements. A focus on reproductive and/or sexual rights and duties seeks to ensure that both states and private entities respect individuals and groups' actions and needs in these areas. Many of those doing practical advocacy or theoretical work on reproductive and sexual health focus their efforts in this way, seeing reproductive and sexual rights as essential for both individual autonomy and as a necessary precondition for the exercise of a host of other CITIZENSHIP and human rights.

Understood in this broader and more practically based way, the parameters defining the set of issues thought of as related to reproductive and sexual health are not fixed, solid, nor naturally constituted, and so from a substantive perspective, vary over time and place as new issues are engaged or one issue or another gains greater salience. In the U.S. context, reproductive and sexual health includes, among other issues, contraception and family planning, prenatal care, sexually transmitted disease care (including HIV/AIDS), infant mortality, unintended pregnancy, sex education and information, abortion, sexual violence, notions of sexual pleasure, sexual behavior, adoption practices, fertility treatment, stem cell research, reproductive cloning, and cancers of the reproductive system, arguably extending as far as more general health access and beyond.

While these topics make up the substance of reproductive and sexual health, to study the politics surrounding these issues, focus must be put on the interactions of power through which various actors and institutions engage questions of reproduction, sexual behavior, and health. This can include the factors contributing to the salience of particular issues at a given historical moment, the formal policy making through which funding for particular services is determined, the processes of legalizing and/or criminalizing certain behaviors and rights, as well as the more subtle workings of power, and the means through which societies define healthy and/or moral behaviors and practices. The primary patterns of the politics of reproductive and sexual health in the U.S. context are change in salient issues over time; interconnection among issues; structuring through the social and political formations of gender, sexuality, race, class, and nation; and the harnessing of reproduction and sexuality to meet larger social and political goals.

First, in the contemporary period, a number of controversial issues have gained saliency from among the broader array of reproductive and sexual health, issues such as abortion, HIV/AIDS, and to a lesser extent, same-sex marriage and stem cell research. Other issues, such as infant mortality, broader health care access, and contraception, have occasionally received attention, but they have not consistently attained a high level of MEDIA, governmental, or popular interest in the contemporary moment. Yet, the list of the most controversial issues has not remained static over time. A long-term view allows us to see the historically specific and transitory nature of what is considered reproductive and sexual health politics.

For example, early in U.S. history, abortion was legal under COMMON LAW until the point of "quickening," that moment when a pregnant woman first felt fetal movement. Reliance on folk methods and a lack of distinction between abortion and contraception during the early stages of pregnancy did not lend themselves to abortion being a particularly salient political issue at this time. Today's notions of abortion and fetal viability would be quite foreign to early American women, who, along with most health care providers, spoke of the desire to restore a woman's menstrual cycle rather than aborting a fetus per se. In the late 1850s, however, even this early type of abortion began to be criminalized by the burgeoning medical profession and political elites in STATE GOVERNMENTS. While in many cases exceptions were made for situations in which a woman's life was at risk, doctors' policies and states' regulations as to the conditions that would justify such a therapeutic abortion varied widely. During the time abortion was largely criminalized in the United States, women and their partners still sought out and many procured abortion procedures, mostly beyond public view, from variously skilled and sympathetic doctors, midwives, and other specialized practitioners. In the mid-1950s,

women, joined by some medical practitioners, clergy, and other allies, began the modern push for access to abortion. The 1973 *Roe v. Wade* landmark decision by the U.S. SUPREME COURT located a woman's right to abortion under the RIGHT TO PRIVACY but also contributed to a relatively successful countermovement seeking to regulate and recriminalize the procedure. The attention to the fetus brought on by this powerful movement has also led to a new arena of political conflict related to reproductive and sexual health, wherein fetal rights are being asserted, most often in opposition to the rights of women. Recent years have seen new interpretations of child endangerment and drug trafficking laws, granting of benefits and services to the fetus, the creation of separate penalties for murder of a fetus, as well as an increased level of controversy in debates about stem cell research. HIV/AIDS and same-sex marriage have also become highly salient issues in contemporary U.S. politics.

As noted earlier, there is a clear practical connection between issues that concern reproductive capacity and those that deal with sexual behavior and norms. However, it is becoming clear that the interconnection goes further to the level of individual issues. It is this interconnection that is the second overall pattern in U.S. reproductive and sexual health politics.

For example, the above discussion of abortion's changing saliency through time only begins to hint at the interplay between abortion and other reproductive and sexual health issues. According to women's reports, unintended pregnancy, the necessary precursor to most abortion procedures, is the result of many factors. Economic factors include the inability to support large families, the need to work outside the home, and the lack of reliable financial support from a partner. Regardless of one's views, historians have documented the longstanding efforts of women and their partners to control procreation, albeit limited by a persisting lack of access to safe and effective contraceptive methods. These efforts notwithstanding, many American states, and with the 1873 Comstock Law, the federal government, sought to restrict access to contraceptives and family planning information. This aim was not fully invalidated for married couples until the 1965 U.S. Supreme Court case *Griswold v. Connecticut* and for single individuals through

Eisenstadt v. Baird seven years later. Notably, the link between contraception and abortion was even made through formal jurisprudence, as the right to privacy upon which the Supreme Court based its decision in *Roe* found its start in these cases concerning contraception.

Similar connections can be found between many different reproductive and sexual health issues; action or inaction regarding one issue can greatly impact others. For example, access to prenatal care can greatly affect rates of infant mortality, and public health interventions and modifications to individual sexual practices can curb the spread of not only HIV/AIDS but also rates of other sexually transmitted diseases and unintended pregnancy. Although largely occluded in mainstream political discourse and policy making, the practical interconnections of reproductive and sexual health issues persist nonetheless.

While the connection among issues within reproductive and sexual health politics must often be excavated, the connection between this politics and larger social and political formations is more easily discernable. The ways in which gender, sexuality, race, class, and immigrant status, individually and in conjunction, have served as salient factors contributing to the shape and resolution of the politics of reproductive and sexual health is the third pattern in the U.S. context. How the procreation of different groups is viewed and social norms and legislation concerning the appropriateness of various sexual behaviors among different individuals and groups, there is no default position or natural formulation; all are structured by relations of power. Decisions on whether to provide and how to regulate certain types of reproductive and sexual health services are fundamentally political acts.

Indeed, reproductive and sexual health politics are experienced and conceptualized differently based on one's position, and public health policy has not often treated these disparate situations equally. While reproductive and sexual health is relevant to men and women, the definition of this policy area as primarily a set of women's issues in a society in which women do not hold political power equal to men contributes to the shape that reproductive and sexual politics has taken in terms of funding, prioritization of problems, and more. Heterosexuality's normative status has also affected reproductive and sexual

health through the sorts of public health interventions deemed appropriate and the degree to which sexual behavior that falls outside this norm is regulated. The impact of the social and political formations of race, immigrant status, and class on reproductive and sexual health is evident in, for just several examples, the practices of breeding and family separation in America's version of chattel SLAVERY, eugenically motivated efforts to reduce the childbearing of those argued to be mentally, racially, or economically unsuitable parents, and the discriminatory policies that barred Japanese and Chinese women from emigrating to join their husbands and start families in the United States.

In addition, while the ability to terminate an unintended pregnancy is seen as the most important reproductive and sexual health guarantee, for others, the ability to bear children has also been difficult to attain. Longer-term contraception and permanent sterilization were used coercively among certain social groups, including black women, Native American women, prison inmates, and those deemed to be physically or mentally disabled. While such women have managed to find ways to use these technologies for their own family planning aims, the legacy of their coercive use remains in many communities. In the contemporary United States, a host of reproductive and sexual health disparities persists that evade individual- or group-based explanations. Infant mortality, unintended pregnancy, sterilization, HIV/AIDS diagnosis, and death all occur at disparate rates along race and class lines. As well, the focus on reproductive and sexual rights as a necessary precondition to exercising other types of rights is no panacea to those also marginalized by race, class, or immigrant status.

It is not simply that gender, sexuality, race, class, and nation impact the shape of reproductive and sexual health from a structural perspective. A fourth, related pattern throughout the U.S. history of reproductive and sexual health has been the purposeful use of this politics as an instrument to further other social and political goals. This can be seen in the way in which the procreation of certain groups has been encouraged or discouraged and in the manner in which sexual interactions and marriage have been regulated on the basis of race and sex, for just two examples.

During slavery, regulations governed the racial status and ownership of children born to African slaves. Breeding practices and other mechanisms encouraged childbearing; each furthered the economic interests of slaveholders and deemphasized the bond between enslaved parents and their children. Today, the procreation of women of color as well as poor, young, and unmarried women is not deemed by many to fulfill societal goals and thus is discouraged. Similarly, in the latter half of the 19th century, the doctors who sought to bring abortion within their purview and beyond the control of women and "irregular practitioners," such as midwives, were spurred by professional and social aims to strengthen the medical profession's place in society and by gender norms that privileged physicians' (primarily men's) judgment over women's. The efforts of their state government elite allies overlapped; their motives to restrict access were aimed primarily at reducing abortions among white middle- and upper-class women. Under this eugenic logic, it was these women's reproduction (and not that of racial and ethnic minorities, immigrants, lower-class, or disabled individuals) that was deemed essential to the progress of the American nation.

Similarly, the sexual relations and possibilities for marriage for couples who found themselves positioned on different sides of the color line have also been highly regulated by many states throughout U.S. history. These unions are often seen as potentially undermining the racial and therefore social order. Gender and sexuality factor in as well, as the sanctity of heterosexual marriage has been contested, but most often protected, as seen in recent court decisions. In addition, only recently have laws reached the books of every STATE allowing for the possibility of prosecuting men who engage in forced sexual relations with their wives. Struggle over sexual and gender norms thus characterizes recent political struggles, as reproduction and sexuality are harnessed in battles over larger social goals.

Further Reading
Luker, Kristen. *Abortion and the Politics of Motherhood*. Berkeley: University of California Press, 1984; McLaren, Angus. *A History of Contraception: From Antiquity to the Present Day*. Oxford: Blackwell Publishers, 1992; Miller, Alice M. "Sexual but Not Reproductive: Exploring the Junction and Disjunction of Sexual and Reproductive Rights." *Health and Human Rights* 4, no. 2 (2000): 69–109; Reagan, Leslie J. *When Abortion Was a Crime: Women, Medicine, and the Law in the United States, 1867–1973*. Berkeley: University of California Press, 1998; Roberts, Dorothy. *Killing the Black Body: Race, Reproduction, and the Meaning of Liberty*. New York: Vintage Books, 1997; Roth, Rachel. *Making Women Pay: The Hidden Costs of Fetal Rights*. Ithaca, N.Y.: Cornell University Press, 2000; Shapiro, Ian. *Abortion: The Supreme Court Decisions, 1965–2000*. Indianapolis: Hackett Publishing Company, 2001; Solinger, Rickie. *Pregnancy and Power: A Short History of Reproductive Politics in America*. New York: New York University Press, 2005.

—Amy Cabrera Rasmussen

secrecy
The first principle can be stated simply: Information should be kept from those who do not have a right to know it. A second principle that frequently guides the behavior of both private and governmental officials is to keep information from those who might use it to harm the official's interests. Both lead inevitably to conflicts and problems for democratic governance.

The U.S. government uses three formal categories to classify information as confidential (the lowest level of sensitivity), secret, or top secret (the most sensitive category). Individuals inside and outside the government are given security clearances that allow access to particular levels of secret materials. The standards and procedures for classifying secrets, declassifying old documents, and granting access to information were most recently defined in Executive Order 13292 issued by President George W. Bush in 2003. Most secret materials involve intelligence agencies, military plans or operations, or relations with other countries.

The major offices within the DEPARTMENT OF DEFENSE and the various intelligence agencies have developed their own detailed procedures and policies for classifying information, the specifics of which are often classified as secret. The principle of classification is straightforward: The greater the potential damage to important national interests, the more secrecy is necessary. But the application of that principle is not automatic; someone must make a judgment about how potentially damaging a piece of information is and what interests are threatened. The difference between protecting a presumed national interest, or protecting an agency of the government from looking bad, or protecting the personal or political interests of key officials is ultimately determined by people who sometimes have a vested interest in equating threats to their own interests with threats to the national interest.

An example may be the Department of Defense decision in mid-2006 to stop issuing quarterly reports to the U.S. Congress on the number of Iraqi units who were fully trained and deemed capable of operating without extensive support from U.S. forces. The Pentagon argued that this information was always meant to be secret and had been misclassified in the past. Critics in Congress argued that it was the awkward fact that the number of fully capable Iraqi units was declining and the government of Iraq seemed further away from taking over from American forces that motivated the sudden classification of the information.

The concept of EXECUTIVE PRIVILEGE is also a key to understanding government secrecy. Presidents have consistently claimed the right to keep documents and information secret from Congress on the basis of the SEPARATION OF POWERS as defined in the U.S. CONSTITUTION. While executive privilege is not directly mentioned in the Constitution or defined in laws, it has been claimed by every American president to keep information away from either Congress or the public. Claims of executive privilege also raise the question of when information really deserves to be kept secret and when the claim is being used to cover up situations or avoid political embarrassment.

While it is obvious that secrets ought to be kept secret, there are three fundamental issues that any system of secrecy necessarily raises: conflict between competing rights, confusion of political harm with danger to vital governmental functions, and efficiency. The most common and potentially explosive conflicts over who has a right to know which pieces of information occur between the EXECUTIVE BRANCH of the U.S. government and Congress and between the executive branch and the MEDIA. The right of the executive branch to formally classify information as

secret and withhold it from others is based on both constitutional and statutory law. At the same time, the right of Congress to oversee and monitor the executive is rooted in the U.S. Constitution. More often than not, Congress tends to accept executive assertions of secrecy to protect national security or the closely allied principle of executive privilege. But there are times when a congressional committee or Congress as a whole demands access to information to assure that laws are being properly executed. The result is confrontations pitting an executive branch contention that some information is too sensitive to be released to Congress, even with existing safeguards and procedures, and congressional insistence that the real secret being protected is bureaucratic bungling or misbehavior. The historical record contains a number of examples in which it is clear that executive secrecy was primarily aimed at hiding uncomfortable facts.

Congress is not the only source of challenges to executive secrecy. A corollary of the freedom granted to the press in the First Amendment is the responsibility of the media to serve as a watchdog for citizens and help make government open and transparent. The desire of the media to know what is going on and the desire of the government to keep secrets are frequently at odds.

The Freedom of Information Act (FOIA) of 1966 was an attempt to clarify the right of the media and ordinary citizens to know what the government was up to and the right of government agencies to keep secrets. While most observers feel FOIA improved public access to the workings of government, many feel that because it is the government agency that created the secret classification in the first place that interprets the requirements of FOIA in a given case, the balance of power still swings too heavily to the preservation of secrecy at the cost of transparency.

National interests, ideological or political interests, and personal interests are not clear and distinct categories; conflicts and confusions among interests are inevitable. Decisions about secrecy are made by human beings with multiple goals, from serving their country, to protecting the president and his administration, to advancing the interests of their agency or political party, to enhancing or preserving their own reputation. The guiding principle in classifying secrets is the extent to which information can be harmful to the national interest. It is all too easy for an appointed official to think that anything that might be used by political opponents to embarrass the president or the president's political party is harmful to the nation as a whole and try to use security classifications to keep embarrassing truths under cover. Managers of EXECUTIVE AGENCIES may be inclined to equate their agency's interest with the national interest and feel that anything that puts them in a bad light is a harmful secret that ought to be kept from Congress or the press.

In order for intelligence agencies to "connect the dots" and correctly analyze situations, it is necessary to first "collect the dots." Unless the relevant information flows quickly to those who have to analyze it and assemble an overall picture, it will be impossible to produce an estimate of what the real threats to the United States are in a timely and useful fashion. But a critical strategy for preserving overall secrecy is to limit access to information on a "need to know" basis. In planning a complex military operation, for example, each participant will be told only what she or he appears to need to know to carry out her or his part of the plan. The plan is compartmentalized so that only a handful of people at the top of the hierarchy have an overall picture. The more complex the plan, the more difficult it is to be sure that each participant knows what they need to know and the more difficult it is to avoid problems or even failure because critical information was not correctly shared. In a complex bureaucracy like those constituting the national security system, such as the CENTRAL INTELLIGENCE AGENCY, the Defense Intelligence Agency, the FBI, the National Security Agency, among others, the strategy of compartmentalizing information to keep secrets is referred to as "stove piping." Information and secrets travel up to the top of a bureaucratic agency rather than being broadcast across boundaries to other bureaus and agencies. The consequences can be extraordinarily serious, as detailed by the *Report of the 9/11 Commission*. The pursuit of secrecy within agencies can interfere with effective action across agencies.

Leaks, the release of information to unauthorized recipients, are endemic in complex organizations such as governments. The term *leak* is value laden and highly negative. When officials brief reporters "off the record" or "on background," or

pass on information and talking points to their friends and allies in Congress or the media, they do not define what they are doing as "leaking." A leak is a release of information that the person in charge does not appreciate. Leaks sometimes violate formal secrecy rules and most often undermine the desire of someone to keep information out of public view. Leaks can be intended to achieve one or more purposes: mobilize public opposition to (or support for) a proposed policy, embarrass political rivals within an administration, or reveal corruption or bungling within an agency. Revealing misconduct within the government is known as whistle blowing and a major source of information for both Congress and the media.

Reactions to leaks are ultimately political, depending on whether one approves or disapproves of the effects of the leak. Every administration has strenuously attempted to keep some things secret. Some presidents, for example Richard Nixon and George W. Bush, have presided over administrations that placed a particularly strong emphasis on keeping a great deal of information secret.

Further Reading
Committee on Government Reform, U.S. House of Representatives. *On Restoring Open Government: Secrecy in the Bush Administration.* Washington, D.C.: Government Printing Office, 2005; Melanson, Philip. *Secrecy Wars: National Security, Privacy and the Public's Right to Know.* Dulles, Va.: Potomac Books, 2002; National Commission on Terrorist Attacks. *The 9/11 Commission Report: Final Report of the National Commission on Terrorist Attacks upon the United States.* Authorized edition. New York: W.W. Norton, 2004; Roberts, Alasdir. *Blacked Out: Government Secrecy in the Information Age.* New York and London: Cambridge University Press, 2006.

—Seth Thompson

social security

"Social security" can encompass an enormous variety of programs to maintain income and provide for health. Abroad, it can even include education, training, and job security. In the United States, the meaning generally is considerably narrower.

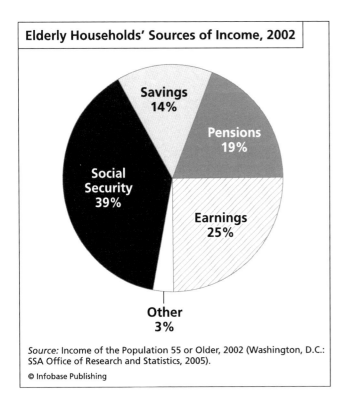

Elderly Households' Sources of Income, 2002

Savings 14%

Pensions 19%

Social Security 39%

Earnings 25%

Other 3%

Source: Income of the Population 55 or Older, 2002 (Washington, D.C.: SSA Office of Research and Statistics, 2005).

© Infobase Publishing

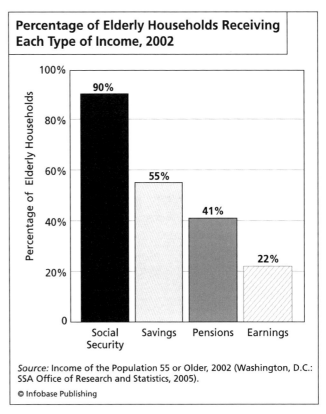

Percentage of Elderly Households Receiving Each Type of Income, 2002

Source: Income of the Population 55 or Older, 2002 (Washington, D.C.: SSA Office of Research and Statistics, 2005).

© Infobase Publishing

Technically, the federal program called Social Security could apply to any program that related to the Social Security Act of 1935 with its subsequent revisions. That, however, would include unemployment insurance and means-tested programs such as Supplemental Security Income (SSI) and Medicaid. Americans generally do not consider Social Security to include these. In both popular and professional usage in the United States, Social Security refers to contributory social insurance requiring contributions from workers and providing benefits without regard to need. Thus, it refers to the programs of the Social Security Administration (SSA) that provide old-age, survivors', and disability benefits (OASDI).

The Social Security Administration no longer administers Medicare, the program that provides health coverage largely for those 65 and over, but Medicare also, quite clearly, is contributory social insurance. Its financing mechanism is similar to that of OASDI, which involves two trust funds, one for OASI and another for disability benefits. Medicare is financed through a third trust fund. Certainly, it could be considered "social security," but it presents serious long-term financing issues that OASDI does

not. Normally, Medicare is considered separately— as it must be for any meaningful evaluation of long-range fiscal prospects. As a rule, then, *Social Security* refers to the contributory programs designed to provide income support. Thus, *Social Security* here refers specifically to OASDI, and stipulates Social Security and Medicare when the discussion includes health coverage.

Social Security funding comes through Federal Insurance Contributions Act (FICA) taxes. The worker pays 6.2 percent, while the employer matches the paycheck deductions, paying an equal 6.2 percent. The amount subject to FICA tax is capped. For 2005, the maximum amount subject to FICA taxes was $90,000. The cap rises each year based on inflation. A similar tax funds Medicare. The employee pays 1.45 percent, and the employer pays an equal amount. There is no cap; the tax is due from both worker and employer on the full amount paid.

Social Security and Medicare taxes go into trust funds, where they finance the current benefits' administrative costs. Both Medicare and Social Security operate at astonishingly low expenses for administration. For every dollar that comes in, more than 99 cents goes out in benefits. Administrative expenses of less than 1 percent of income reflect administrative efficiency that no private program can come close to matching.

Social Security taxes coming into the trust funds currently are far beyond the amount needed to pay benefits. The surplus funds by law are invested in government securities that regularly pay interest into the trust funds. The bonds in the trust funds have the same claim on the U.S. Treasury as any other Treasury bond. They are "only paper" in the sense that a $20 bill or a U.S. Savings Bond is "only paper." All have value because they have the backing of the U.S. government.

Although critics of Social Security usually portray the system as a retirement program only, it is far more. Nearly one-third of the system's benefit payments go to younger people. In addition to retirement benefits for the elderly, the system pays benefits to qualifying widows and to children of deceased workers. There are also benefits to workers who become disabled and to their dependents. Additionally, there are benefits to workers' spouses.

Social Security's benefits are protected against inflation; benefits will never lose their purchasing power. Another strength of the program is that the system provides retirement benefits for the life of the beneficiary. A retiree cannot outlive Social Security's payments.

The United States tends to be tardy in adopting social programs. When Congress passed the Social Security Act in 1935, although there had been some previous programs that were narrower in focus such as military pensions, it was America's first step toward universal social insurance. Another 30 years passed before Medicare's adoption in 1965, and its passage came only after one of the fiercest political battles in this country's history. Even then, Medicare was limited almost entirely to the elderly. Germany had put a comprehensive program in place in the 1880s, and other European countries had quickly followed the German example. To be sure, there had been pressures previously. Former president Theodore Roosevelt, in his famous Bull Moose campaign of 1912, had strongly advocated comprehensive social insurance, including health care. The

United States, however, often moves slowly on such issues.

The world's wealthiest country remains virtually alone in the industrial world in failing to provide a system of comprehensive health care for its entire population. Instead, a system of private health insurance provided through employers has evolved. As health-care costs increase, fewer employers offer such coverage, leaving more Americans without access to regular health care. The result has been that by nearly any measure of health-care results, from access, to infant mortality, to longevity, the United States suffers in comparison with other industrial countries—and in fact, it rates poorly even when compared with some countries that generally are thought to be "third world."

Companies that do offer health-care coverage are finding it increasingly difficult to do so. The costs are seriously hampering their ability to compete with other countries in which the health-care costs are widely distributed throughout society, rather than falling almost exclusively on employers. Business interests in other countries frequently were in the forefront of those who advocated for government health coverage.

In general, the American business community has yet to do so. Because a healthy workforce is essential, however, and because the burden of providing health benefits is becoming more than they can bear, it is likely that American business leaders will someday advocate government health coverage as good for business. It may even be that American business will come to confront in providing pensions what it now faces with regard to health care. As more and more corporations find it difficult or impossible to meet their commitment to provide retirement benefits to their workers, there could ultimately come to be support for increasing Social Security, rather than truncating or privatizing it.

The Social Security Act of 1935 provided only retirement benefits. Although FICA taxes started in 1937, the first retirement benefits were to be delayed until 1942. In 1939, however, Congress amended the act, changed its character, and began payments in 1940. In addition to retirement benefits, the 1939 amendments provided for benefits to spouses, dependent children, and dependent survivors of deceased workers. In 1950 with the strong support of President

Harry S. Truman, Congress expanded the program to include the self-employed. Demonstrating that support for Social Security was not limited to Democrats, President Dwight D. Eisenhower, a fiscally conservative Republican, signed into law the 1956 amendments that added disability benefits, a huge expansion. In 1965, President Lyndon B. Johnson (LBJ) signed legislation for which he and his predecessor, John F. Kennedy, had fought strenuously. LBJ's signature brought the greatest expansion in Social Security's history by adding health benefits for the aged, Medicare.

Until 1972, benefit increases depended on congressional action. That year, President Richard Nixon signed into law provisions to index benefits to inflation, providing automatic annual increases. By 1977, it had become clear that the formula used to index benefits was flawed. Because of what came to be called "stagflation" (a combination of a stagnant economy, stagnant wages, and inflation), benefits had risen too fast in relation to incoming revenues. Amendments in 1977 tried to correct the formula, protecting those who had been receiving benefits based on the old formula. This led to the so-called notch baby issue when new beneficiaries received benefits lower than their immediate predecessors.

When Ronald Reagan became president in 1981, he moved immediately to slash Social Security drastically. He had long been a foe of social insurance and had energized the opposition that had existed since the beginning. As early as the 1950s, he had argued that it should be privatized. His actions as president led to a political firestorm. Although he did succeed in trimming the program somewhat, he had to promise not to attack Social Security again. He kept his promise, but his long history of hostile rhetoric had at last made it politically possible to criticize and to some extent even to attack the program directly without paying a political price.

By 1982, a cash flow problem had developed, and there were fears that without revisions, Social Security's income would be inadequate to pay full benefits by late 1983. As many experts have noted, the system's troubles were far less severe than the news MEDIA—which often reported dire predictions from enemies of the system as though they were absolute fact—portrayed them.

Reagan honored his promise and called together a bipartisan commission to recommend action. He named Alan Greenspan as its head. The commission took only months to issue its report. The members unanimously rejected means testing or radical revisions and gave a full vote of confidence to Social Security's fundamental principles.

Among the recommendations were subjecting half of Social Security's benefits to income tax except for low-income recipients (previously, all Social Security benefits were free from income tax), with receipts to be directed to the trust funds. All new federal workers were to be incorporated into the system. The cost-of-living adjustment would be delayed for six months, and already scheduled tax increases were to take effect sooner. Congress accepted the recommendations and raised the age for full retirement gradually from 65 to 67. Those born in 1938, for example, reached the age for full retirement upon turning 65 and two months. Those born in 1960 or later had to reach age 67 to quality for full benefits.

Reagan signed the 1983 amendments, and the trustees then projected that Social Security would be sound for the full period of its long-range projection, 75 years. In 1993, President Bill Clinton signed legislation increasing the amount of benefits subject to income tax. Since then, only 15 percent, rather than 50 percent, may be excluded.

The trustees are political appointees, not unbiased experts. They include the secretary of the Treasury, the secretary of labor, the secretary of health and human services, the commissioner of Social Security, and two members from the public. Their reports for nearly two decades have made three projections: Alternative I, Alternative II (the "Intermediate Projections"), and Alternative III. Their "Intermediate Projections" for years have forecast future deficits. This is strange, because the 1983 projections called for a slight surplus, and the economy's actual performance has been far better than the 1983 projections had assumed it would be.

What, then, happened to the projected surplus? Actually, nothing happened to it. The trustees simply began to use more pessimistic calculations. Their Alternative I projections are more optimistic and call for no difficulty in the future. The economy's actual performance has consistently been much closer to the assumptions underlying the Alternative

I projections than to the Intermediate Projections, yet only the pessimistic Intermediate Projections receive publicity.

This is largely the result of a well-financed PROPAGANDA campaign designed admittedly to undermine public confidence in Social Security. The libertarian Cato Institute, funded lavishly by investment bankers and various Wall Street interests, has been quite active in this regard, as have many other organizations. Among the most successful has been the conservative Concord Coalition, which has managed to convince many in the public and in the news media that it is interested only in "fiscal responsibility" and has no political agenda.

Experts recognize that long-range projections on such complicated issues as Social Security are no more than educated guesses. Yet the news media and many policy makers assume the Intermediate Projections are precise and unquestionable. Yet the year that they project for depletion of the trust funds varies from report to report and since 1983 has never been *sooner* than 32 years away. No projection can be accurate over such a long period. It would be foolish to make radical revisions on such weak premises.

Nevertheless, there is widespread sentiment that Social Security must be "reformed." Supporters of the system have proposed a variety of measures that would increase income, such as raising or eliminating the cap on income subject to FICA taxes or reducing benefits. In the 1990s, there were many proposals to subject benefits to means tests, or to "affluence tests." Such proposals have fallen into disfavor. Supporters have come to recognize that they would destroy Social Security by converting it into a welfare system, which would have little or no political support. Social Security's enemies have turned their attention instead toward privatization, or carving "personal accounts" out of the system. Most prominently, President George W. Bush, the first president to speak openly in opposition to the principles of Social Security, favors privatization. Even Reagan had cautiously phrased his comments to disguise his opposition. George. W. Bush also has suggested radical cuts in benefits for all but the poorest Social Security recipients. His proposals have generated furious opposition.

Social Security could indeed benefit from a progressive reform, one that would protect benefits while introducing a modicum of progressivism into its funding. Benefits have always been progressive. They replace a higher portion of a low-income worker's income than of one earning more. The taxation mechanism, though, in levying a flat tax but exempting all income above a certain amount, has been regressive. This should be corrected by removing the cap on taxable income and exempting the first $20,000 of earnings from FICA taxes on workers—employers would continue to pay the tax from the first dollar of wages. Other changes could enhance the trust funds. Among them would be dedicating an estate tax to fund Social Security.

There are serious threats to America's financial future. The astronomical deficits that Presidents Reagan and George W. Bush have generated are the issue. Social Security is not the problem. The charts predicting trouble reflect Social Security, Medicare, Medicaid, and interest on the national debt. A close look reveals that Social Security's effect—even with the pessimistic projections—is tiny. The trouble comes from Medicare, Medicaid, interest on the national debt, and the assumption that "the days of 50 percent to 60 percent marginal tax rates are over."

The troubles can be made to evaporate, but that assumption must be discarded. Social Security's surplus should be dedicated to paying down the national debt (a version of the "lockbox"), thus sharply reducing interest payments. There was progress paying down that debt with Clinton's balanced budgets until Bush cut taxes and restored deficits. A reform in America's health care delivery system would provide better and more accessible care more efficiently, as other countries do, and would reduce health-care costs. It would greatly assist American business.

Eliminating President Bush's tax cuts and ensuring that the wealthy pay a greater share will be essential. Business thrived after Presidents George H. W. Bush and Clinton raised taxes. A move toward *enhancing* Social Security would also aid business. The suggested reforms could permit a doubling of Social Security benefits, thus freeing employers from the burden of providing pensions, a burden that many companies are finding it impossible any longer to shoulder. Expanding Social

Security and Medicare would not only protect America's people, it would make American business more competitive.

See also ENTITLEMENTS; NEW DEAL.

Further Reading
Baker, Dean, and Mark Weisbrot. *Social Security: The Phony Crisis.* Chicago: University of Chicago Press, 1999; Ball, Robert M., with Thomas N. Bethell. *Straight Talk about Social Security: An Analysis of the Issues in the Current Debate.* New York: Century Foundation Press, 1998; Béland, Daniel. *Social Security: History and Politics from the New Deal.* Lawrence: University Press of Kansas, 2005; Benavie, Arthur. *Social Security under the Gun: What Every Informed Citizen Needs to Know about Pension Reform.* New York: Palgrave Macmillan, 2003; Eisner, Robert. *Social Security: More Not Less.* New York: Century Foundation Press, 1998; Gladwell, Malcolm. "The Moral Hazard Myth: The Bad Idea behind Our Failed Health-Care System." *The New Yorker*, 29 August 2005, 44–49; Hiltzik, Michael A. *The Plot against Social Security: How the Bush Plan Is Endangering Our Financial Future.* New York: Harper Collins, 2005; Kingson, Eric R., and James H. Schulz, eds. *Social Security in the 21st Century.* New York: Oxford University Press, 1997; Lowenstein, Roger. "A Question of Numbers." *The New York Times Magazine*, 16 January 2005, 41ff; Skidmore, Max J. *Social Security and Its Enemies: The Case for America's Most Efficient Insurance Program.* Boulder, Colo.: Westview Press, 1999.
—Max J. Skidmore

supply-side economics

Supply-side economics may be the oldest school of modern economics. Its ideas go back to Adam Smith, whose *Wealth of Nations* (1776) emphasized the growth of the productive capacity (or potential) of a MARKET ECONOMY: Expanding the extent of the market allows greater division of labor (specialization), raising labor productivity (goods or services produced per unit of labor). Promoting a nation's prosperity thus involves unleashing markets (laissez-faire policies). Despite antagonism toward government (then run by a king), Smith suggested possible positive roles for it, for example, in education.

Both markets and government are part of supply-side economics. In fact, it is hard to define a supply-side economics "school," since *all* economics invokes supply. Many thus restrict the term to refer to views that argue for *promoting supply using tax cuts*, that is, "new" supply-side economics, associated with economist Arthur Laffer and President Ronald Reagan. Even given this definition, some quibble about what "true" supply-side economics is. Instead of that issue, this essay will focus on the contrast between new supply-side economics and "traditional" supply-side economics embraced by most economists.

This involves any government policies aimed at increasing potential or that actually does so in practice. It goes back millennia, including the Roman Republic's draining of swamps to promote health. Today it centers on the notion that many projects needed to encourage potential growth are *public goods* or other goods that private enterprise will not produce (unless subsidized) because profitability is so low. These include investment in infrastructure, public health, basic research, homeland security, disaster relief, and environmental cleanup. They might also include privatization of government services and the creation of artificial markets (as for electricity).

Such projects can also stimulate demand. If the economy starts with high cyclical unemployment, government investment lowers it, but if the economy is already near (or attains) full employment, it encourages inflation, because it typically pumps up demand much more quickly than supply. Such investment also typically raises the government deficit (all else constant), since few benefits accrue as tax revenues, especially in the short run. Most importantly, such projects (including some involving privatization) may be in "pork barrel" schemes promoting the fortunes of only a minority of politicians, their districts, and financial backers, but not those of the citizenry as a whole. So there may be unwanted distributional impacts, unfairly helping some and hurting others. Thus, traditional supply-side economics requires an active and empowered citizenry to monitor it, along with a clear consensus about national goals.

Traditional supply-side economics can involve tax cuts. Standard theory says that any tax entails two types of burdens. For a tax on a specific type of item (an excise or sales tax), there are first *direct* burdens on the buyers and sellers. This is what they pay, directly or indirectly, to the tax collector. Second, to the extent that they can avoid exchanging the items, some trades never occur. This *excess* burden loss reduces the extent of the market and can restrict specialization and hurt productivity.

Lowering taxes can thus have general benefits: For example, cutting the payroll tax workers pay could not only increase after-tax pay and (perhaps) after-tax firm revenues, but also might increase employment by abolishing some excess burden. If employment rises, so does output. Most economists see the supply response to changed wages as very low, however, so this effect is minor.

Cutting taxes implies forgoing some possible benefits. These include funds for programs that the electorate and/or politicians want; cutting taxes raises the government deficit (all else constant). Second, some taxes, called "sin taxes," are on products such as alcohol and tobacco that the government and/or voters deem undesirable. Thus, the excess burden cost must be compared to the benefits of discouraging "bad" behavior.

Regarding the new supply-side economics, this school went beyond these traditional verities. It developed during the 1970s, partly in response to stagflation, when Keynesian and monetarist policy tools were widely seen as failing. Further, inflation pushed many into higher tax brackets, provoking the "tax revolt" (e.g., California's Proposition 13 in 1978). Though some adherents were former Keynesians, new supply-side economics applied several kinds of non-Keynesian economic thought, particularly Austrian economics and new classical economics.

Different versions of new supply-side economics were developed and popularized by economists such as Laffer, Robert Mundell, and Norman Ture; journalists such as Jude Wanniski, Paul Craig Roberts, and George Gilder; and politicians such as Ronald Reagan and Jack Kemp. The term itself was coined by Wanniski in 1975, while his *The Way the World Works* (1978) presented many of its central ideas. Unlike traditional supply-side economics, new supply-side economics did not center on the specifics of government spending. Rather, the focus was on the *incentive effects* of the *tax system*. New supply-side economics argues that tax cuts can boost *aggregate* supply by reducing excess burden.

In addition, many adherents invoke Say's "law," that is, that actual and potential output always roughly coincide (because aggregate demand failure is transitory). In theory, however, new supply-side economics could instead bring in Keynesian or monetarist demand theories. Other supply-siders advocate a gold standard in international exchange, likely to impose deflationary demand constraints.

Central is the marginal tax rate of the U.S. federal personal income tax. The marginal tax rate is the ratio of the *increase* of an individual's tax obligation to the *increase* in that person's taxable income. In 2006, a single individual earning up to $7,550 in taxable income pays 10 percent of any increase to the Internal Revenue Service. For taxable incomes above $7,550 and up to $30,650, 15 percent of any rise goes to tax. The marginal tax rate rises from 10 percent to 15 percent, as for any progressive tax but unlike a "flat tax." The marginal tax rate differs from the percentage actually paid: Someone earning $10,000 pays 10 percent of the first $7,550 and then 15 percent on the next $2,450, implying an average tax rate of 11.2 percent.

To new supply-side economics, rising marginal tax rate creates an *incentive* to avoid raising one's taxable income, just as excise taxes discourage exchanging of taxed items. Increasing the marginal tax rate can cause people to leave the paid workforce (e.g., those whose spouses work for money income), stretch out vacations, retire at younger ages, and/or avoid overtime work. Some might avoid risky business opportunities while avoiding taxes via accountants and tax shelters or evading them through illegal activities.

Cutting marginal tax rates has the opposite effect, but new supply-side economics does not stress tax cuts for the poor. To James Gwartney, an economist who advocates new supply-side economics, tax cuts have larger incentive effects with higher initial marginal tax rates, as for richer folks. A 50 percent tax rate cut for a single individual in the 35 percent bracket (receiving $336,550 or more in 2006) allows him or her to keep $17.50 more of any $100 of extra income earned, but a 50 percent tax rate cut for the 10 percent bracket allows an individual to keep only $5 more of any extra $100.

Thus, to Gwartney, tax cuts for the rich mean that "given the huge increase in their incentive to earn, the revenues collected from taxpayers confronting such high marginal rates may actually increase." In sum, tax cuts, especially for the rich, can encourage work, saving, and investment, which in turn can raise potential, the tax base, and tax revenues. Laffer and other economists hoped that this would raise the total tax base so much that total revenues would *rise* despite across-the-board tax rate cuts. Gwartney argues, however, this is cancelled out by weak incentive effects of such cuts for low-income people.

David Stockman, the Reagan-era budget director, famously admitted that for the Reagan administration, new supply-side economics doctrine "was always a Trojan horse to bring down the top rate." The "supply-side formula was the only way to get a tax policy that was really trickle down," he continued. "Trickle-down theory" is simply the view that giving benefits to rich people automatically provides similar improvements to everyone. But as John Kenneth Galbraith once quipped, that theory is "horse and sparrow" economics: "if you feed enough oats to the horse, some will pass through to feed the sparrows."

But some argue that supply-side economics involves more than advocating tax cuts for the rich. Some reject the association with "trickle down." For some, Reagan was no supply-sider, and no "pure" new supply-side economics policies have ever been implemented. However, it is worth evaluating the success of pro-rich tax cuts, the main policy associated with new supply-side economics.

Before becoming Reagan's vice president, George H. W. Bush dubbed this school "voodoo economics": He saw it as ineffective, promising a "free lunch" (something for nothing). This represents the opinion of most economists. First, there is a fundamental hole in supply-side economics logic. Reducing the marginal tax rate, no matter how much, does not always increase the amount of work, saving, or investment. New supply-side economics emphasizes the *substitution* (incentive) effect: If one's after-tax wage rises by 10 percent, that increases the benefit of labor relative to leisure, encouraging more labor time. But economists' *income* effect goes the other way: Receiving more income per hour, one can get the same income

with 10 percent fewer hours. Even better, one can work the same hours as before and get 10 percent more income. The individual gets something for nothing even if society does not. The same income effect counteracts any extra incentive to save or invest due to a falling marginal tax rate.

Gwartney points to three cases in which new supply-side economics policies have been applied: during the 1920s under Treasury Secretary Andrew Mellon, after the 1964–65 tax cuts by President Lyndon B. Johnson, and under Reagan. However, other economists have pointed to other reasons, usually demand stimulus, why prosperity and tax revenue increases occurred after these tax cuts. Further, they point to very prosperous periods with high marginal tax rates (the Dwight Eisenhower years of 1953 to 1961, for example) and even after increases in taxes on the rich (the Bill Clinton years of 1993 to 2001). In the latter case, labor productivity (a key supply-side variable) grew at a clearly increased rate. Many credit the Internet and similar high-tech inventions for this surge, but these resulted much more from government programs than from tax cuts.

It is true that hours of paid work per year have generally increased between 1980 and 2000, especially for women. This may not be due to supply-side economics policies, however, since it could easily reflect efforts to "make ends meet" in the face of stagnant real family incomes (seen during this period) and the general movement of women into the paid workforce (which preceded supply-side economics). Further, increased work hours are not always desirable, as it can cut into time for leisure, family, and community activities.

Did tax cuts result in increased saving? In the aftermath of the Reagan tax cuts, it was instead consumption that rose. The era of supply-side economics in general corresponds to rising consumer spending relative to incomes. On the other hand, fixed investment (supposedly encouraged by supply-side economics tax cuts) generally fell during the Reagan (1981–89) and George H. W. Bush (1989–93) years, but then rose during the anti–supply-side economics Clinton years. In sum, the benefits of the supply-side economics program are mixed at best.

The microeconomic analysis above suggests that new supply-side economics tax cuts might cause inflation. Under Mellon, these did not happen due to gold standard discipline, while monetary policy-driven recessions prevented inflation under Reagan. Inflation did rise under Johnson, but that was partly due to increases in military spending.

Further, the government deficit rose (as a percentage of gross domestic product) under Johnson, Reagan, and George W. Bush, though much of these increases can be blamed on military buildups. Under Mellon, deficits were avoided by cutting government expenditure. On the other hand, Clinton's anti–supply-side economics tax hikes led to falling deficits—and actual surpluses.

Some advocates of new supply-side economics cite the new classical economist Robert Barro's work, arguing that deficits have no negative effect: Because they are seen as implying future taxes, that encourages saving. But as noted, the Reagan tax cuts did not encourage saving. More see deficits as imposing a needed discipline on government. Seeing any government programs beyond law enforcement and the military as inherently wasteful, these authors want to "starve the beast": Tax cuts lead to deficits and thus to spending cuts.

As a result of these and other critiques, many see supply-side tax cuts as a "special interest" program, akin to pork barrel spending, in this case benefiting only society's upper crust. They have definitely had distributional effects, reinforcing the already existing rise in the gap between the incomes of the poor and rich during the last 30 years. However, new supply-side economics does not call for "an active and empowered citizenry" or "a clear consensus about national goals." Shunning DEMOCRACY, new supply-side economics instead sees the market as the measure of all things, favoring laissez-faire over all. This survey only skimmed the surface. It is no substitute for a full-scale test of new supply-side economics theories versus mainstream alternatives.

Further Reading

Gordon, Robert J. *Macroeconomics*. 10th ed. Boston: Pearson, 2006; Greider, William. "The Education of David Stockman." *The Atlantic*, December 1981: 19–43; Gwartney, James. "Supply-Side Economics." In *The Concise Encyclopedia of Economics*. Available online. URL: http://www.econlib.org/library/Enc/SupplySideEconomics.html. Accessed June 18, 2006; Roberts, Paul Craig. "What Is Supply-Side Economics?" In *Counterpunch*. Available online. URL: http://www.counterpunch.org/roberts02252006.html. Accessed June 18, 2006; Wanniski, Jude. *The Way the World Works: How Economies Fail—and Succeed.* New York: Basic Books, 1978.

—James Devine

telecommunication policy

Who owns the broadcast airways? Why is government regulation of print MEDIA different from broadcast media? What does it mean to broadcast "in the public interest?" These questions and more lie at the core of telecommunications policy in the United States. This essay will probe these questions in order to explore the relationship between the national government in Washington, D.C., and private broadcasters, a relationship that has been in place for more than 70 years.

In the early 20th century, radio burst upon the scene as a powerful device to communicate to thousands of people widely dispersed across the country. Some radio stations could transmit their signal so that it reached audiences many states away, while a number of local broadcasters, often working from the basements of their homes, would build a transmitter that reached audiences just several blocks away. Whether the signal was powerful or weak, it became immediately clear that someone needed to police the radio transmissions, since many of these signals were crossing one another, leading to a garbled transmission at the other end. Thus, those who owned commercial radio stations found they were losing money because listeners were tuning out. The major commercial radio broadcasters began to lobby the government for some form of intervention that would set aside space on the broadcast spectrum for their use only. In exchange, government would control who received a license, and more important, it would control competition.

In an early attempt to regulate the telecommunications sector, the Radio Act of 1927 failed to address the needs of commercial broadcasters, prompting the U.S. Congress (with the backing of President Franklin D. Roosevelt) to pass the first massive legislation to deal with telecommunications. The Federal Communications Act of 1934 not only was a major consolidation of the telecommunications industry but also was notable for how quickly it was passed into law. Roosevelt requested that Congress take action on the issue in January 1934, and by June 1934, it was on his desk for him to sign. The act created a new regulatory agency that would oversee telecommunications policy in the United States. Prior to the act, oversight was shared between the DEPARTMENT OF COMMERCE and the INTERSTATE COMMERCE COMMISSION (ICC). With this act, the shared oversight was now combined into the FEDERAL COMMUNICATIONS COMMISSION (FCC), and it was charged to act in the "public interest," a term that was not defined by Congress or the president and still varies today.

The FCC is an independent regulatory agency, which ideally means that it is designed to be free from congressional or presidential political pressure. It consists of five members, three of whom are appointed by the president and two who are selected by the opposition party. All are confirmed by the SENATE and serve five-year terms, at which time they may be nominated again by the president. The president also designates one of the commissioners to serve as the chairperson of the FCC. This person will establish the agenda for the FCC, deciding whether proposed rules or changes to rules will receive one hearing or many. The chair also tends to be the public face of the FCC, often interacting one-on-one with the news media.

The FCC, as a regulatory body, has "quasi-legislative, executive, and judicial" functions. That means it has the ability to write regulations as well as to implement the laws passed by Congress and signed by the president. It executes those regulations to ensure that all entities under the FCC's jurisdiction are behaving as they should, and finally it has the judicial power to punish those who violate the rules established by the agency.

With the implementation of the Federal Communications Act and establishment of the FCC, the government became the owner of the broadcast spectrum, controlling which entities—individuals or corporations—could "use" a portion of the "public airwaves." This interaction between broadcasters and the government takes the form of licensing. Potential broadcasters must file for a license with the FCC in order to reserve a place on the broadcast spectrum (radio and television). Once a license is granted, it

must be renewed every eight years. During the process of granting a license (or even renewing one), the FCC reserves time for public comment, which allows individuals to come forward and speak in favor of or against a particular applicant. Once an application is granted, it is rarely revoked. However, when granted a broadcast license, the licensee agrees to abide by FCC rules and regulations.

As an independent regulatory agency, the FCC uses the license as a means to regulate the telecommunications sector. Those who receive a license to broadcast agree to abide by certain government regulations. There are hundreds of regulations that deal with all types of telecommunications issues—for instance, whether cable providers may offer telephone service or whether telephone companies may offer high-speed internet access. Rather than address all types of regulations, it will be more helpful to look at the major regulations that interact with the political process.

Indecency and obscenity have never been protected forms of "speech" or "press" that deserve First Amendment protections. The FCC defines indecency and obscenity in much the same way as does the U.S. SUPREME COURT. The difference, however, lies in the definition of "community standards." In general terms, the courts have ruled that when determining whether something is obscene, you needed to look, in part, at the standards of the particular community, thus leaving it to the local communities to determine for themselves what sorts of speech and press are appropriate. In the case of federal regulations, the FCC gets to determine the meaning of "community standards," which has meant that indecency and obscenity have varied greatly over time. For instance, there was a period in broadcasting when women on television were prohibited from displaying their navels on the screen. But as standards in the country changed, they often were reflected in a loosening of what was permissible on the television or radio. In the 1970s and 1980s, as more and more communities gained access to cable and then satellite television and radio, the broadcast entities that still broadcast "over the air" urged (or pushed) the FCC to relax standards in order to compete. Cable and satellite technology is largely free from FCC regulations of indecency and obscenity because consumers must pay a fee for access to the signal and do not rely on the public airwaves to reach consumers.

In the 1990s, it appeared that the FCC had completely withdrawn from oversight of indecent material on television or radio. Most notably on radio, the rise of "shock jocks" such as Howard Stern continued to push the envelope of indecency as far as possible, sometimes too far, prompting fines from the FCC. For radio personalities such as Stern, the fines that he did receive from the FCC were a drop in the bucket compared to the money he made by attracting advertising dollars because his show was so successful. In fact, most of the fines he received were displayed with pride as a marketing gimmick in order to attract more people to listen to Stern and encourage others to push the envelope of indecency.

In 2004, the upper limit was reached when pop stars Janet Jackson and Justin Timberlake, performing during the halftime at the Super Bowl (which is watched by millions), ended their performance with Ms. Jackson revealing a portion of her breast. Immediately, the switchboards at CBS (the station that broadcast the Super Bowl in 2004) lit up with protests from individuals all over the country. The next day, letters and phone calls poured in to Congress and the FCC demanding action to end the smut. The FCC immediately reacted to the public pressure. Howard Stern was run off of broadcast radio and to satellite radio (he signed a multimillion dollar deal with Sirius Satellite Radio). Clear Channel, which had profited mightily off shock jocks, was now facing enormous and unprecedented fines. For instance, the FCC leveled more money in fines during the first four months of 2004 than it had for the previous 10 years. Congress got into the act as well. In 2006, it raised the amount the FCC could fine by 10-fold over the previous amount. Congress passed and President George W. Bush signed the Broadcast Decency Enforcement Act, which raised the fines from $32,500 per incident to $325,000 per incident.

Since the news media are in private hands, access to the news media, particularly during an election, can mean the difference between winning and losing. The government worried that those who owned radio or television stations could influence the outcome of an election by either denying a candidate access to or charging one candidate less than other candidates for advertising. A requirement in receiv-ing the license is that the broadcasters not favor one candidate running for office over another. Therefore, when a candidate is sold time to air a political ad, his or her price is the same as all other candidates who bought time to run a political ad. But what happens when the news covers the incumbent during an election at staged events? Would the station be forced to provide the challenger the same amount of time for free? This issue actually did come before the FCC, and Congress amended the Federal Communications Act of 1934 to provide an exemption to news programs or public affairs interviews on Sunday talk shows such as *Meet the Press* on NBC and *Face the Nation* on CBS.

The idea behind the Fairness Doctrine was to protect those singled out by broadcasters for scorn as well as to force broadcasters to explore the complexities of controversial issues in order to create and sustain a deliberative, democratic public. The first part was challenged in 1968 when an author of a book on former presidential candidate Barry Goldwater was singled out for scorn by a conservative minister who owned a radio station. The minister believed that the book cost Goldwater the election in 1964, and he used the power of his radio station to vent his anger. The author of the book asked for an equal amount of time to reply and was denied. In the U.S. Supreme Court case *Red Lion Broadcasting v. FCC* (1968), the Supreme Court ruled that the FCC and Congress have the authority to order a privately owned broadcast station to provide an equal amount of time for rebuttal to an individual singled out by the station for scorn. There is no similar provision for the print media if it singles out an individual on its editorial page, for instance.

The second part arose from a complaint to the FCC in the 1940s against the owner of three radio stations who ordered his news staff to "slant, distort, and falsify" news against politicians he did not like. When his listeners complained, he responded that he might do whatever he wished because he owned the stations. The FCC responded with an order that required all licensees to explore all aspects of controversial issues whenever they took up discussion of political, social, cultural, and religious issues in an equal and fair amount of time.

In 1987, the Reagan administration generated a great deal of controversy when it pushed the FCC to repeal this part of the Fairness Doctrine. The administration argued, with considerable evidence, that this part of the Fairness Doctrine actually neutered most broadcast stations because rather than spending the time, money, and effort in covering all sides of controversial issues, they did not cover anything complex or controversial. Thus, rather than creating an informed citizenry, it was actually hurting it by providing milquetoast coverage that informed no one. This decision has remained controversial largely because of the effect it had on talk radio. Once this portion was removed, political talk radio proliferated throughout the country, catapulting such personalities as Rush Limbaugh, G. Gordon Liddy, and other conservatives into the center of many national debates. Conservatives and conservative ideas have flourished on talk radio since the 1987 action, with great effect on politics. For instance, when Newt Gingrich became the first Republican Speaker of the House in nearly half a century in 1995, he credited political talk radio in helping him spread the ideas of conservative Republicans along with their message throughout the country.

The Federal Communications Act continues to serve as the guiding force behind telecommunication policy in the United States. As things changed, the act would be updated from time to time by way of amendments to meet changing technological needs. In the 1990s, however, it was apparent that the law would need a major overhaul to meet dramatic changes in the ways in which Americans communicated and in the ways in which Americans listened to radio or watched television. In addition to these changes, there were also a variety of negative externalities from new technology such as the Internet that affected existing laws. For instance, the quick and easy way to view pornography online ran up against state and local laws governing obscenity. To meet these new changes, the Republican Congress and the Clinton administration worked on and finally passed the largest set of changes to telecommunication policy since the Federal Communications Act in 1934. This amendment to the 1934 law was known as the Telecommunications Act of 1996 (hereafter Telecommunications Act).

Unlike the Federal Communications Act of 1934, the Telecommunications Act took nearly a year to pass. It was introduced in Congress in March 1995 and signed into law by Clinton in February 1996. And despite the fact that this law represented the most significant overhaul to telecommunication policy in more than 60 years, most Americans saw, heard, or read very little about the changes that were being made, mostly to the benefit of the telecommunications industry. Rather, the majority of Americans, which included most of the mainstream news media in the United States, were distracted by a peripheral "dog and pony" show that in the end would matter very little to the daily lives of Americans—and certainly would matter very little compared to the massive centralization in the telecommunications industry that would create "media giants" at the expense of competition.

During the long debate over the Telecommunications Act, the media became fixed on two particular areas that generated a lot of discussion and conflict, mostly centered on the issues of indecency on television and obscenity on the Internet. The first, indecency on television, largely stemmed from parents who felt that their children were exposed to too much programming that was meant for adults. Further, because of many single parents or "latchkey" kids who were left alone at home after school, parents cried out for some method of control over what their children watched until they could get home and monitor for themselves. In response, Congress added a provision to the law that mandated a programmable computer chip, called the "V-chip," to be installed on all new television sets manufactured after January 2000. The V-chip allowed parents to lock out programming they found unsuitable for their children. The television industry also supported an industry-backed rating system for all programming that screened for violence, sexual situations, and shows suitable only for mature audiences.

The second, blocking obscenity on the Internet, received the lion's share of the coverage related to the Telecommunications Act. Congress, along with the public, faced nightly newscasts of stories involving nudity, pornography, and obscenity on the Internet, and more troublesome, all of this indecency was at the fingertips of children. There were stories in which children, innocently researching information for school projects, inadvertently put in either a wrong name or a wrong suffix (.com instead of .gov) and were taken to Web pages that featured hardcore pornography. Thus, the new Republican majority decided to do something to combat the accessible porn on the Internet. The Communications Decency Act (hereafter the CDA) had been a stand-alone act that was enveloped into the Telecommunications Act to ensure passage. The CDA made it a crime to "knowingly transmit by any telecommunications device any obscene or indecent message to any recipient under 18 years of age." It further made it a crime to transmit anything that was patently offensive to anyone under 18 or to be displayed in a way that those under 18 years of age would be able to view it. Violations of the CDA carried a possible jail term of two years.

All the time the Telecommunications Act was traveling through the LEGISLATIVE PROCESS, the focus of the press and even various public interest groups was on this tiny provision, thought to be unconstitutional if it did become law. Web pages carried a little blue ribbon displaying the owners' support for individual rights against government intrusion into what an individual reads or views in the privacy of his or her home. Once Clinton signed the Telecommunications Act into law, the CDA was immediately challenged in federal district court in Philadelphia. In the case *Reno v. ACLU* (1997), the United States Supreme Court found that the CDA was unconstitutionally broad. In an attempt to limit obscene materials, the law also made criminal perfectly legal communication. Nonetheless, the Supreme Court told Congress to rewrite the CDA in order to make it constitutional (and when it did, the CDA was challenged once again in *Ashcroft v. ACLU* [2002] and found unconstitutional a second time). After the Supreme Court rendered its decision, a cry went out among a variety of groups who were fighting the government over the potential of the CDA, and these groups were widely covered by the press.

What did not receive coverage from the press was the massive centralization in the telecommunications industry, not to mention the handover of the new digital spectrum for free. The new act would allow single companies to own radio and television stations as well as newspapers in some cities. An agreement worked out between Congress and the Clinton administration was to apply the relaxed ownership regulations to radio as a test case to determine whether competition would increase or not. The answer was almost immediately clear. Radio stations all across the country were gobbled up by large regional and national corporations. One company, Clear Channel, went from a small regional player in Texas that owned 43 radio stations prior to passage of the act to a national giant, owning 1,200 stations by 2000. If one combines Clear Channel with Viacom, another large telecommunications giant, one gets two of the largest companies that control nearly what half of the country listens to on the radio. Also, the number of communications providers in the United States rapidly declined. In the early 1980s, when communications scholar Ben Bagdikian wrote the first edition of *Media Monopoly*, he warned of the dangers to DEMOCRACY of 50 large corporations that owned the means of communications and information. After the passage of the Telecommunications Act, that number dropped to just five.

When communications and information are controlled by just a few large corporations, there are potential dangers to the needs of a democracy. Some of those dangers are the homogenization of information that creates a "sameness" wherever one goes, thus drying out the uniqueness of local culture. Further, homogenization leaves minority communities stigmatized, as they are either never represented in this communications monopoly, or their representation is skewed or negative. For instance, those who study the effects of the ways in which the local television news treats African Americans have found that night after night, crime on local television news has a black face.

In 2003, when the FCC announced that it would move to deregulate ownership of television, there was a massive outpouring from the American public who were disgusted by what happened with radio (the loss of alternative stations and the rise of shock jocks in order to make profits). Prior to the June 2003 decision (and one in which the FCC attempted to limit public input by holding just one hearing), a record 750,000 letters of protest flooded the commission. Despite these numbers, the FCC agreed to deregulate the remaining telecommunications sector. But before the regulations could be implemented, those who had sent letters to the

FCC also had begun to pressure Congress, which acted to overturn the FCC decision (along with a lawsuit in federal courts) and restore the pre-June decision, with a demand that the FCC return to the drawing board and try a second time.

Further Reading

Bagdikian, Ben. *The New Media Monopoly.* Boston: Beacon Press, 2004; McChesney, Robert. *The Problem of the Media: U.S. Communication Politics in the Twenty-First Century.* New York: Monthly Review Press, 2004.

—Christopher S. Kelley

transportation policy

The transportation system in the United States is one of the most extensive and complex in the world. It consists of a wide variety of transportation modes that currently are used to move people and commodities primarily within and between the metropolitan areas in the United States, where about 85 percent of the population lives. This enormous and complicated transportation system is the product largely of governmental policies and programs that have been the outcomes of American public policy making processes that are based on four key elements: FEDERALISM, distributive politics, the principle that taxes levied on transportation usage should be spent exclusively on that function (i.e., user fees), and controversy dealing with the desirable degree of private sector versus public sector funding and operation of the American transportation system.

The complexity of the American transportation system has been to a large extent due to the principle of federalism, which has resulted in all levels of government—national, STATE, regional, and local—becoming involved in transportation spending and decision making. At the national level, the U.S. DEPARTMENT OF TRANSPORTATION, which was created as a CABINET-level executive department in 1966 to assume the functions that had been under the authority of the undersecretary for transportation in the U.S. Commerce Department, is the primary agency in the federal government with the responsibility for shaping and administering transportation policies and programs involving all trans-

portation modes except water. For the nation's inland waterways, the U.S. Army Corps of Engineers is in charge. It operates docks and dams and maintains navigation channels throughout the nation. The U.S. Department of Transportation consists of the office of the secretary and 11 individual operating administrations: the Federal Aviation Administration, the Federal Highway Administration, the Federal Motor Carrier Safety Administration, the Federal Railroad Administration, the National Highway Safety Administration, the Federal Transit Administration, the Maritime Administration, the Saint Lawrence Seaway Development Corporation, the Research and Special Programs Administration, the Bureau of Transportation Statistics, and the Surface Transportation Board. The Homeland Security Act of 2002 authorized the establishment of the DEPARTMENT OF HOMELAND SECURITY, which in 2003 assumed the management of the U.S. Coast Guard and the Transportation Security Administration, formerly Department of Transportation operating administrations.

The administrative officials in the Department of Transportation work closely with their counterparts at both the state and local levels, including officials in each state department of transportation as well as administrative officials of transportation-related agencies in regional, county, municipal, and special district governments. The numerous interactions between the Department of Transportation administrators and the state and local transportation administrators largely involve issues related to federal categorical grants (which provide financial assistance to state and local governments for planning, building, and repairing transportation infrastructure) and administrative regulations that state and local government must follow if they are to be the recipients of these federal grants.

American transportation policy making also is complicated by its distributive rather than redistributive nature at the state and national levels. Distributive domestic policy making is considered low-level politics in that it is seldom of an ideological nature, largely involves relatively low levels of conflict, does not transfer resources from one segment of society to another, and seldom engages the focused attention of public opinion leaders in the mass MEDIA or of the highest level of state and

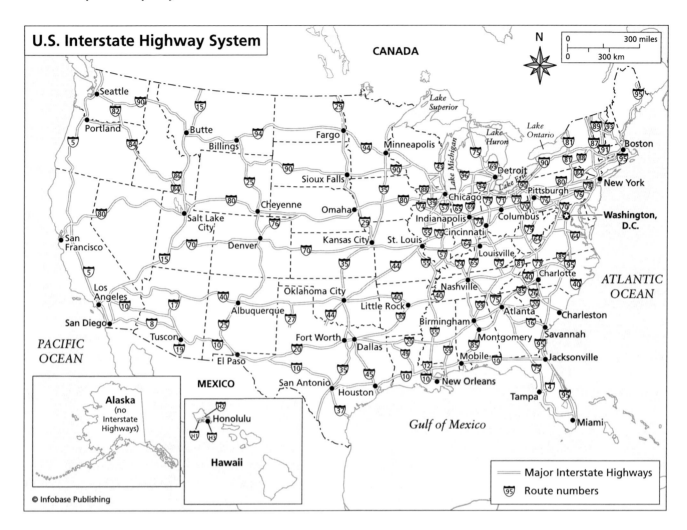

national governmental officials (i.e., the president, state GOVERNORs, top legislative leaders, or the secretaries of cabinet-level departments). In the development of transportation policies at the state and national levels, the fundamentally distributive nature of the political process features a large amount of lobbying on the part of a wide range of INTEREST GROUPS directed at both low-level government officials on legislative subcommittees and at low- to mid-level bureaucrats in transportation administrative units. The public policy outcomes of these lobbying efforts are usually compromises and largely incremental adjustments to ongoing transportation policies rather than fundamental policy changes based on systematic, comprehensive planning. To a considerable extent, state and national transportation policy can be thought of as "pork-barrel politics" in that it is largely the accumulation of many

individual monetary grants provided to lower levels of government and subsequent payments often made to private sector contractors to build and repair highways and mass transit systems.

Unlike distributive transportation policy making, redistributive domestic policy making in the United States (often involving the formulation of social welfare and environmental policies) is usually thought of as high-level politics in that it is typically characterized by high levels of ideologically based conflict; involves the transfer of resources from one group of people to another; holds the attention of major public opinion leaders in the mass media, high-level government officials, and top executives of large corporations and nonprofit organizations; and frequently is heavily influenced by the comprehensive, long-range analytical research efforts of professional planners.

Exactly how these four elements of the policy making process (federalism, distributive politics, the reliance on user fees, and disagreements concerning the proper role of the private sector versus the public sector) have affected the transportation system in the United States can be seen through an examination of the nature of the past and present American air travel, railroad, highway, and mass transit public policies and programs.

Air travel is becoming increasingly important for moving both people and commodities in the United States. Although most commodities are transported between metropolitan areas either by truck or railroad, air travel is the most frequently used mode of travel by people for nonauto trips between metropolitan areas. Each day in the United States, approximately 2 million people take more than 20,000 commercial flights. Also, overnight shipping of small packages increasingly has come to play a central role in the American economy.

Metropolitan areas depend largely on federal grants and locally generated revenues to build, expand, and operate their airports. The federal government taxes every passenger ticket, and these funds go into the airport and airways trust fund, which is a dedicated source of funds. This revenue source, exceeding $6 billion annually, includes approximately $4 billion that is used to operate the nation's air traffic control system and $2 billion for federal categorical grants for which local governments actively compete. These federal grants must be used to help fund airport improvements. Federal law also permits local governments to levy a head tax on each passenger and requires that these funds be used for airport programs.

In addition to federal assistance, metropolitan airports generate a great deal of money locally. Airlines pay local governments to land their planes, rent gates, and lease office space at metropolitan airports. Passengers pay to park their cars and to buy food and other items at the airport. Money is also collected from taxi, shuttle, and car rental companies that use airport facilities. These locally generated revenues usually are sufficient to cover all the airport's operating costs and costs related to airport infrastructure improvement and still provide enough surplus money that can be transferred to the local government's general fund to pay for other public services. Because airports are big money makers and usually thought to be essential for economic growth in a metropolitan area, many local officials, business leaders, and other local citizens promote airport improvements and expansion. However, while the economic benefits of an airport expansion tend to be widely dispersed throughout a metropolitan area, the resulting quality-of-life costs associated with noise, air pollution, and highway congestion tend to be highly concentrated in the neighborhoods immediately surrounding an airport. Consequently, most proposals to significantly expand a metropolitan airport produce intense local political controversies.

The federal government's influence on air travel in the United States has been based not only on its provision of categorical grants to local governments for airport improvements but also on its exercise of regulatory authority. The federal government began issuing administrative regulations involving air travel in 1926, when President Calvin Coolidge signed into law the Air Commerce Act. Over time, a large number of economic regulations were mandated primarily by the Civil Aeronautics Board (CAB), and air travel safety regulations were mandated primarily by the Federal Aviation Administration (FAA). The numerous economic regulations included antitrust oversight, consumer protection, airline economic fitness, the awarding of routes to airline companies, and requirements concerning the prices that airlines could charge. Because these economic regulations were widely viewed as limiting the entry of start-up airlines into lucrative air travel markets and reducing economic competition, President Jimmy Carter signed into law the 1977 Air Cargo Deregulation Act and the 1978 Airline Deregulation Act. These laws phased out the Civil Aeronautics Board's authority over fares, routes, and airline mergers. Also, pursuant to the 1978 act, the Civil Aeronautics Board itself ceased operations and shut down in 1984. In contrast to the widespread opposition aimed at the federal government's economic regulatory activity, civilian airline interest groups have tended to mobilize considerable support for the FAA's safety regulations, in that civilian airline companies tend to believe that their economic growth is based on the American public's perception that it is safe to fly. Therefore, currently the federal government's air travel regulations largely involve safety issues.

On September 11, 2001, terrorists commandeered four commercial passenger jet airliners and crashed two of them into the World Trade Center in New York City and one of them into the Pentagon in Arlington, Virginia, and the fourth airliner crashed in a field in rural Pennsylvania. Approximately 3,000 people were killed. Responding to this new form of terrorism, Congress passed and President George W. Bush signed into law in November 2001 the Aviation and Transportation Safety Act. This legislation created the Transportation Security Administration (TSA), which was charged with increasing security at the nation's airports and other transportation venues. In 2002, TSA was incorporated into the new cabinet-level DEPARTMENT OF HOMELAND SECURITY.

Prior to the 20th century, state and federal governmental efforts to develop a national transportation system focused largely on canals and railroads. One of the most important elements of the nation's transportation infrastructure during the 19th century was the Erie Canal, which opened in 1825. New York was responsible for the planning, financing, construction, and operation of the Erie Canal. Widely viewed as the most important engineering marvel of its day in the United States, the original Erie Canal extended 363 miles from the Hudson River to Lake Erie and included 83 locks, with a rise in water level of 568 feet. The Erie Canal was an immediate financial and commercial success. The toll revenue provided more than enough to pay off the canal bonds held by private investors, and the cost of transporting goods from the Midwest to the Atlantic Ocean harbors was greatly reduced. The Erie Canal was instrumental in uniting the United States from east to west and in opening European markets to American grains.

The first railroad in the United States was the Granite Railway Co. Three miles in length and pulled by horses, it began operating in 1826 and was used to carry granite blocks in Quincy, Massachusetts. The first steam locomotive was put into service by the Baltimore and Ohio Railroads in 1830. It was capable of hauling 36 passengers at 18 m.p.h. Although some STATE GOVERNMENTs provided subsidies, private corporations built, operated, and owned the railways

in the United States until the 1970s. Despite resistance by state governments and railroad companies, the federal government first began to play a major role in the development of the national railroad network in 1862. In that year, President Abraham Lincoln signed into law the Pacific Railway Act, subsidizing the construction of the Transcontinental Railroad, which was finished in 1869 and owned and operated by private corporations.

The federal government significantly increased its oversight of the evolving national transportation system in 1887, when President Grover Cleveland signed into law the INTERSTATE COMMERCE COMMISSION to regulate rates that railroads could charge for shipping freight, railroad service schedules, and railroad mergers. In the 1950s and the 1960s, the privately owned railroads in the United States decided that transporting freight was more lucrative than carrying passengers, and they began to cut back passenger service. In order that railroad passenger service between the major metropolitan areas would not be eliminated, Congress passed the Rail Passenger Service Act in 1970, creating a semipublic corporation: Amtrak (American Travel and Track). Amtrak took over nearly all intercity passenger service in the nation; with 182 trains and approximately 23,000 employees, it annually transports more than 20 million passengers between 300 American cities. Initially, Amtrak's operations were intended to become self-supporting, but this has never happened. Consequently, the federal government provides approximately $600 million in annual subsidies. The state governments also make some contributions. In return, state governments participate in deciding which routes will receive what levels of passenger services.

Because Amtrak has always run significant budget deficits and requires substantial governmental subsidies to continue operating, it has been criticized by opponents as a waste of taxpayers' money. However, supporters of Amtrak argue that focusing on its inability to be self-supporting is inappropriate in that both highways and air travel in the United States are heavily subsidized by the federal government. Criticism of Amtrak, its supporters contend, is a reflection of the disjointed nature of transportation public policy in the United States, which is biased toward auto and air travel and biased against travel by rail. They argue that travel by train should be seen as one of the essential components of a balanced, comprehensive national transportation policy.

By the early 1970s, six railroads in the Northeast and Midwest that were heavy freight haulers entered bankruptcy. Among the reasons for their economic difficulties were competition from trucks (which were indirectly subsidized through their use of the federally funded Interstate highway system) and governmental economic regulations that made it difficult for railroads to respond effectively to changing market conditions. Due to declining freight revenues, the six railroads deferred maintenance and allowed their tracks and equipment to deteriorate. As a result, increasingly business turned to trucking companies for more cost-effective transportation of freight. Recognizing the national importance of these six railroads, the federal government created the Consolidated Rail Corporation (ConRail) in 1974 and began appropriating the necessary funds to rebuild track and to either purchase new locomotive and freight cars or repair them. Also, federal government economic regulations were loosened beginning in 1980, giving railroads more flexibility to compete with trucks. By 1981, ConRail was making enough income that it no longer required federal funding. In 1987, the federal government sold its ownership interest in ConRail through a public stock offering for $1.9 billion, and the Northeast-Midwest rail freight system became a private sector, for-profit corporation.

Throughout the history of the American transportation system, there has been considerable controversy focusing on the most desirable mix of private sector and public sector control and operation of the several different transportation modes. As was the case with the airlines, by the late 1970s, pressure grew for deregulation of interstate railroad freight transportation. Until the 1950s, the railroads had been the dominant transportation mode for moving freight between the nation's cities. But the dramatic growth of the trucking industry, made possible by the development of the Interstate Highway System after 1956, resulted in a significant decline in railroad profitability as its share of intercity freight hauling eroded. The negative effects of the federal government's economic regulation of railroads, which had begun with the Interstate Commerce Act of 1887, were of increasing concern to many business groups and policy makers. The result was the enactment of the Staggers Rail Act of 1980, removing many of the federal government's controls and allowing freight-hauling railroads to have greater flexibility to change their practices by relying more on market forces. After the implementation of the Staggers Rail Act, railroad freight hauling became profitable again in that railroads were able to respond more effectively to their competition by adjusting rates eliminating unprofitable portions of track, and both integrating and consolidating rail networks. Concern by federal policy makers that railroads might charge some shippers exorbitant rates resulted in the creation of the Federal Surface Transportation Board to arbitrate disputes.

Responsibility for the enormous, complex system of roads and highways in the United States is divided among federal, state, and local governments, along with the involvement of many competing interest groups, including motorists, builders, truckers, shipping companies, automobile manufacturers, taxpayers, and others. The planning, building, and financing of major roadway and highway expansions at the local level are often the subject of vigorous debate and conflict among local governmental officials and highly mobilized interest groups (largely because of the significant impacts of such programs on local land use patterns, economic development, and quality-of-life matters). However, at the state and federal levels, highway policy making is best characterized as generally featuring low-level, distributive politics: Usually conflict levels are relatively low, mass media coverage is minimal, and the dominant actors tend to be professional transportation planners, low-level bureaucrats, members of legislative subcommittees, and interest group lobbyists. At the end of their negotiations during decision-making events, these major participants tend to reach carefully crafted agreements on highway policies that will eventually provide at least partial gratification for all of them. High-level state and federal governmental officials tend to seldom become closely involved in the formulation of highway policies, and there is usually little public awareness of the commitment to a new highway program or understanding of highway financing. Although legislative formulas usually are used to help determine which state, congressional district, or local jurisdiction will receive either a federal or state categorical grant to fund a highway project, the selection of the precise location for a highway improvement project and the awarding of a construction contract often involve partisan political considerations associated with "pork-barrel-style" politics. Two other key elements of American transportation policy making are also apparent in the design and implementation of state and federal highway policies: the heavy reliance on user fees that are dedicated (or earmarked) to fund highway projects, as well as both partnerships and tension between the private sector and public sector organizations.

In 1900, almost all the roads in the United States were local, and the rudimentary intercity roads often were toll roads owned and operated by either a state government or a private sector entity. Neighborhood streets and most county roads have been the responsibility of local governments for the entire history of the nation. Although the vast majority of the American transportation system's lane miles are local streets and county roads, state highways and Interstate highway networks currently carry a majority of the traffic volume.

Despite their relatively low traffic volumes, local streets are extremely important in the commercial and private lives of a local jurisdiction's residents. Local streets provide commercial, private, and emergency vehicles access to individual property parcels, and they also serve as the underground conduits for electrical wires and water, gas, and sewer pipes. Because local streets provide access to local properties whose owners are the primary beneficiaries, local governments in the United States always have largely financed the construction, improvement, and maintenance of local streets by levying taxes on parcels of property.

Over time, first private sector toll roads and later highways operated by state governments began to serve a complementary transportation mission to the streets financed and maintained by local governments. Before the 20th century, many of the intercity roads and rural roads in the United States were toll roads. During the 1700s, many individuals in rural areas would add gravel to stretches of nearby roads and collect fees from people who used them. Over time, companies formed to develop and maintain larger stretches of rural roadways, and they collected tolls from users to finance such ventures. The first major toll roads in the United States were the Philadelphia and Lancaster Turnpikes built in the 1790s

and the Great Western Turnpike started in 1799, which stretched across much of northern New York. The term *turnpike* originated because long sticks (or pikes) blocked passage of vehicles until a fee was paid at the toll booth, and the pikes then would be turned toward the toll booth so that the vehicle could pass. Toll roads in New England are still usually called turnpikes. In the mid- to late 19th century, numerous privately owned toll roads also were developed in the Midwest and the West, particularly in California and Nevada.

During the first decades of the 20th century, most privately owned toll roads were taken over by the state governments, which sometimes established quasi-public authorities to build and operate toll roads. With the onset of mass production of the automobile and the increased use of the automobile for travel, both within suburbanizing metropolitan areas and between metropolitan areas, faster and higher-capacity highways were needed. In the 1920s, limited-access highways, with dual-lane roadways for traffic flowing in each direction and access points limited to grade-separated exchanges, began to be developed. By the 1950s, there were limited-access highways in many of the larger metropolitan areas of the nation, and most of them were toll roads operated by state governments.

In addition to the limited-access toll roads that are funded by a dedicated revenue stream employing one type of user fee (the toll charge), state governments also have developed a much more extensive network of intercity highways that are financed largely by a second type of user fee (the gasoline tax). The state highway systems, designed for long-distance trips, higher vehicle counts, and high-speed travel, augment the enormous but relatively lightly traveled networks of local streets and county roads in the United States. While accessibility to local property parcels is the focus of the streets and rural roads controlled by local governments, travel on state highways focuses on mobility, and the primary beneficiaries are not adjacent property owners, but instead the users of the highway system—motorists, truckers, and shippers. Because the need for and costs of state highways vary largely on the basis of traffic levels, it seemed appropriate to pay for the construction and maintenance costs of the highways by charging users rather than using either property taxes or taking money from the state government's general fund. In 1918, Oregon was the first state to adopt the motor fuel tax as an alternative to the toll charge user fee. Because a fuel tax is a user fee, state governments earmarked them exclusively for transportation expenditures that primarily involved highways. This means that state transportation programs do not have to compete for APPROPRIATIONS with other public programs.

Prior to the use of the automobile, the federal government played a very small role in highway transportation and instead focused largely on the development of canals and railroads. Despite considerable resistance by state governments to relinquish any of their authority over roadways to the federal government, in 1806, President Thomas Jefferson signed into law the first federal highway program, the National Road, which became the main route west over the Allegheny Mountains into the fertile Ohio River Valley. When completed, it stretched from Maryland to Illinois. Relying on federal funding, the National Road established an important precedent, giving the federal government the constitutional authority to provide financial support for interstate highways.

In 1916, President Woodrow Wilson signed into law the Federal-Aid-Road Act, initiating the federal government's first federal aid highway program and providing states with categorical, matching grants for the construction of highways. These federal grants were aimed at helping states construct new highways to improve mail service and for the transportation of agricultural commodities to cities. This law established the basic cooperative relationship between the federal government and the state governments for expanding the nation's highway system that has existed from 1916 until today.

Aimed at creating jobs for large numbers of the unemployed during the Great Depression of the 1930s, President Franklin D. Roosevelt launched public works programs that allocated substantial increases in federal financial assistance for the construction of highways and bridges throughout the nation. Following a sharp decline in federal aid for highways during World War II, the federal government's funding for highway construction escalated dramatically in the 1950s in order to meet the need for many new and improved highways to accommo-

date postwar economic growth, to rapidly evacuate urban populations if atomic weapons were launched at American cities, and to more effectively move defense-related equipment and personnel throughout the nation during a future war. President Dwight D. Eisenhower signed into law the Federal-Aid Highway Act of 1956 and the Highway Revenue Act of 1956, authorizing the development of the National System of Interstate and Defense Highways and creating the Federal Highway Trust Fund. To finance the construction of an intercity highway program national in scale, the federal government chose a strategy that had been used by the state governments: the reliance on a user fee (the fuel tax) to generate a dedicated stream of revenues to be used for highway construction.

The federal government's creation of the nation's Interstate Highway System was of central importance in the development of the American transportation system. Once the federal government dedicated itself to building an interstate highway network, the focus of the federal, state, and local policymakers for approximately the next 50 years remained directed at the completion of a vast network of freeways (also called expressways) that would have the capacity to rapidly move large numbers of automobiles and trucks. Relatively little attention was aimed at developing a more balanced, comprehensive transportation system using other modes to move people and freight.

Confronted with the willingness of the federal government to pay for 90 percent of the construction costs of the Interstate Highway System (and the states providing only a 10 percent match), state and city governments primarily have chosen either to construct new expressways or improve existing ones to meet federal standards rather than allocating their resources for the development of mass transit infrastructure within metropolitan areas or for high-speed trains for transportation between metropolitan areas. Initially, the federal matching grants could be used only for the development of expressways between metropolitan areas, but once these federal funds became available for building an expressway within a city that would serve as a link in the Interstate Highway System, most local jurisdictions chose to construct new expressways rather than mass transit.

Currently, the National Highway Trust Fund, created in 1956, spends about $30 billion per year, and the states allocate billions more for construction and improvement of the Interstate Highway System. There continues to be strong political support in the United States for the periodic reauthorizations of federal legislation funding the Interstate Highway System. In addition to state and city government officials, who are eager to acquire these federal grants, there is extensive interest group support for building highways using federal money. The millions of drivers, automobile and tire manufacturers, oil companies, road construction contractors, and trucking companies all lobby the federal and state governments to spend generously on highways. Presently, the distribution of almost all the goods and services in the United States use sections of the Interstate Highway System's 46,837 miles of roadways, and approximately one-third of the total number of miles driven by all vehicles in the United States use the Interstate Highway System.

Although the Interstate Highway System has been financed largely by the federal government, it is the states that build, own, maintain, and operate this enormous network of highways. However, the federal government establishes standards such as pavement depth, the width of lanes, and signage design, and it also coordinates the planning of the system. Because of the dominant role that the federal government has in financing the Interstate Highway System, it has acquired considerable influence in getting state governments to enact legislation that sometimes is only indirectly related to the operation of the Interstate Highways and to the federal government's authority to regulate interstate commerce based on the COM-MERCE CLAUSE of the U.S. CONSTITUTION. By threatening to withhold federal matching grants for highways, the federal government has gotten states to pass the following laws: federal speed limits that stayed in effect between 1974 and 1995, increasing the legal drinking age to 21, requiring states to disclose the identification of sex offenders, and lowering the legal intoxication level to 0.689 percent blood alcohol. This type of federal pressure directed at state governments has been controversial. Critics argue that the federal government's threats to withhold federal highway funds unless states enact legislation that is only slightly connected to Interstate Highways, sig-

nificantly alters the balance of authority between the states and the federal government by infringing on STATES' RIGHTS and expanding the authority of the federal government. Supporters, however, maintain that this is a strategy that is effective in getting states to pass much-needed uniform legislation dealing with important domestic public policy issues. Because a state government has the option of choosing to forgo accepting federal matching grants for highways, if it decides not to pass state legislation mandated by the federal government, the U.S. SUPREME COURT has upheld this type of exercise of federal authority to be a permissible use of the Commerce Clause.

Although over the years vehicular transportation using the nation's streets and highways has become the top transportation priority of the federal and state governments, in recent years, there has been growing attention directed toward expanding and improving the mass transit infrastructure in the large metropolitan areas of the United States. As was the case historically with the ownership and operation of the nation's toll roads and railroads, the early mass transit systems (the original subways, streetcars, and buses) usually were owned by private sector companies. But as the populations in American cities became less dense and as automobiles became increasingly popular, mass transit companies could no longer attract enough riders to make a profit. By the 1960s, most of the large-city mass transit infrastructure had been abandoned by the private sector and taken over by local government jurisdictions (often mass transit SPECIAL DISTRICTS or authorities). Because the operating costs could not be met by relying only on the revenues from fares paid by the riders, and also because local governments faced considerable difficulty raising enough locally generated tax revenues to adequately subsidize mass transit, many officials of large American cities began to lobby federal and state government officials to pay for part of the costs of public mass transit by using the dedicated funds acquired through federal and state motor fuel taxes.

A coalition of urban mass transit backers was able to convince Congress to pass the Urban Mass Transportation Act of 1964, which for the first time provided some federal assistance in the form of matching grants to states and cities for the construction of urban public or private rail projects. The Urban Mass Transit Administration (now the Federal Transportation Administration) also was created. In 1974, Congress extended federal assistance to cover operating costs as well as construction costs of urban mass transit systems.

It was not until 1982, however, that Congress changed the funding formula of the earmarked gasoline tax of the Highway Trust Fund to allow these funds to be used to provide federal financial support for mass transit projects as well as highway construction. Although state governments with relatively small urban populations and relatively large rural populations, along with the highly influential coalition of highway interest groups, opposed the use of motor fuel taxes to subsidize urban mass transit systems, a strong new political movement that began to mobilize in the early 1970s was by the 1980s sufficiently strong to convince Congress that some of the gasoline tax revenues should be made available for urban mass transit. This new political movement was fueled by those who believed that the development of more mass transit in urban areas would help reduce Americans' reliance on the automobile and thereby help abate traffic congestion and air pollution. People also promoted mass transit instead of the expansion of the nation's network of urban expressways in order to save green space and reduce the loss of housing units and historic buildings in cities. Downtown business groups supported more federal funding for mass transit because they contended that expressways facilitated flight to the suburbs and the growth of suburban shopping malls. Many professional urban planners and transportation planners began to promote the development of mass transit as a means to reduce urban sprawl, regenerate blighted neighborhoods of large cities, and provide mobility to those who cannot afford or are physically incapable of using an automobile. This new political movement also included people who maintained that spending more federal funds for mass transit rather than for highways would eventually mean that the nation would be able to reduce its dependence on foreign oil.

Currently, the federal government provides approximately $6 billion a year in matching grants of up to 80 percent to state and local governments for mass transit. Most of the federal money must be spent for capital expenditures (buying new equipment or building new rail lines) for a wide range of mass transportation services, including city and suburban bus and paratransit, cable cars, subways, heritage streetcar systems, elevated rapid transit, and light rail and commuter rail services. Federal allocations, however, have not increased enough to meet many of the requests for grants by metropolitan areas intending to expand their public transit services. The competition among metropolitan areas for the receipt of federal matching grants to develop light rail lines has been particularly intense in recent years.

Federal funding for air, water, railroad, highway, and mass transit is allocated by Congress for several years at a time. These federal transportation funds presently are allotted to state and local governments using three approaches. First, most of the federal grants are allocated to state and local governments for different categories of transportation services based on relatively complex and inflexible legislative formulas. Second, some federal transportation grants are earmarked for specifically designated highway, rail, and bus projects favored by members of Congress for their districts (a decision-making approach involving distributive politics and often criticized as "pork-barrel spending"). Third, congressional reauthorizations of federal transportation funding in 1991, 1998, and 2005 have given more flexibility to state governments and local-level metropolitan planning organizations (MPOs) to determine precisely how they will allocate a portion of their federal transportation funds among a mix of different transportation programs.

This third approach was introduced in 1991 with the enactment of the Intermodal Surface Transportation Efficiency Act (ISTEA). Once-fierce competitors—trucking firms, railroads, airlines, and barges using the nation's waterways—increasingly have been cooperating in the movement of freight. In response to this intermodal trend, Congress (through enactment of the 1991 ISTEA as well as its subsequent reauthorizations in 1998 and 2005) has provided metropolitan areas with the flexibility to use a portion of their federal funds to redesign their transportation infrastructure to make for more effective air-water-rail-truck connections. The 1991 ISTEA and its reauthorizations also gave metropolitan regions more flexibility to shift some of their federal funds for highways to mass transit (or vice versa) and to use these funds for other types of special transportation programs aimed at reducing traffic congestion and air pollution. As a condition for receiving federal transportation funding, local governments since 1991, acting through their MPOs, must develop more comprehensive and more balanced regional transportation plans that provide ample opportunities for public participation and take into account land use and environmental factors.

Although local governments in metropolitan areas currently possess increased control over the use of a portion of their federal transportation funds, and although the Federal Highway Trust Fund no longer is used to exclusively fund highways, the proportion of federal funding that is spent for mass transit presently is equal to only about 25 percent of the amount of federal money allocated for highway programs. And while a diverse set of interest groups has been politically mobilized since the early 1970s presenting competing requests for federal funding to be used to finance a wide range of transportation modes, the highway interest group still appears to have formidable strength. The consequence, according to many critics of American transportation policy, is that the United States continues to rely too heavily on automobiles and trucks using a vast network of highways to move people and freight, and it remains without an adequately balanced, comprehensive transportation system.

At the beginning of the 21st century, the United States is faced with a complex and daunting set of transportation-related problems and challenges. The volume of traffic on the nation's highways continues to increase rapidly, resulting in mounting traffic congestion. Will federal, state, and local governments respond by expanding the highway network? Or will they design and implement new transportation policies that use more intelligent, computerized technologies to manage traffic flows more efficiently on existing major urban arteries and expressways? Will they also envision walking, cycling, and mass transit as viable alternatives to the automobile?

The American transportation infrastructure is aging, and the obsolescence of much of it is likely to produce substantial economic costs and reduce the quality of life throughout the nation. Presently, a majority of federal and state transportation funds is generated by the increasingly precarious approach of relying on dedicated gasoline (or fuel) taxes levied on a per-gallon basis and not as a percentage of the market price motorists pay for fuel. As a result of energy conservation measures and increased fuel efficiency of newer vehicles, federal and state gasoline tax receipts have hit a plateau and have begun to erode when adjusted for inflation. Will the state and federal governments respond by raising the gasoline tax rates? Or will they design, test, and employ new funding mechanisms, including funding transportation improvement programs through the use of general obligation BONDS, developing more toll roads, and introducing congestion pricing (charging motorists for driving on high-traffic routes or at popular times in order to obtain additional public revenues and reduce traffic volume)?

By disproportionately allocating federal and state government funds for the construction of highways, the resulting urban sprawl has reduced the amount of open space in metropolitan areas, worsened air quality, and contributed to the growing spatial mismatch between suburban job centers and low-income inner-city residents, making it very difficult for inner-city workers to gain access to metropolitan labor markets. Will urban sprawl, which has made large numbers of both residents and commuters in metropolitan areas dependent on their cars for virtually all their transportation needs, continue to be promoted by transportation policy in the United States during the early decades of the 21st century? Or will American transportation policy increasingly provide funds to build a variety of state-of-the-art mass transit systems and thereby help shape a new approach to urban land use patterns, fostering denser, more economically efficient, and more environmentally sound residential and commercial development and providing better connections between places of employment, residential units, and all the amenities of metropolitan areas?

Further Reading

Balaker, Ted, and Sam Staley. *The Road More Traveled: Why the Congestion Crisis Matters More Than You Think, and What We Can Do About It*. Lanham, Md.: Rowman & Littlefield, 2006; Dilger, Robert Jay. *American Transportation Policy*. Westport, Conn.: Praeger, 2002; Downs, Anthony. *Still Stuck in Traffic:*

Coping with Peak-Hour Traffic Congestion. Washington, D.C.: Brookings Institution Press, 2004; Hanson, Susan, and Genevieve Giuliano, eds. *The Geography of Urban Transportation.* New York: Guilford Press, 2004; Katz, Bruce, and Robert Puentes. *Taking the High Road: A Metropolitan Agenda for Transportation Reform.* Washington, D.C.: Brookings Institution Press, 2005.

—Lance Blakesley

welfare policy

Nobody likes welfare much, not even those who receive its benefits directly. Liberals criticize welfare as providing inadequate support for poor families with children and for requiring recipients to submit to intrusive investigations by zealous caseworkers. Conservatives believe welfare encourages dependency on government assistance by otherwise fully capable adults and that it offers perverse incentives leading to increased family breakups and out-of-wedlock births. Politicians from both the Democratic and Republican Parties have often sought to capitalize on the public's low esteem for welfare, and there have been many calls for reform. Perhaps none has been as memorable as Bill Clinton's 1992 presidential campaign pledge to "end welfare as we know it." With few constituencies providing political support and many calling for its overhaul, it should not be surprising that in 1996 "welfare as we knew it" was effectively dismantled and replaced with a new program of assistance for poor families with children. What should be surprising, however, is that "welfare as we knew it" remained structurally intact for 61 continuous years despite repeated efforts to "reform" it or replace it with an alternative program of federal support for the poor. Welfare represents an unusual political paradox: a program that is intensely unpopular and yet unusually resistant to efforts to reform or replace it.

To understand the roots of this paradox, one must have a basic understanding of the original structure of welfare, its place within the broader welfare state, and the impact of these origins on welfare's subsequent political development. Welfare's political development, as we shall see, was driven in great part by vast changes in the size and character of its recipients in conjunction with fundamental changes in American racial and gender relations. As the original welfare program became increasingly unfit for the challenges of a new social and political context, the calls for reform grew. Political efforts to reform welfare, however, repeatedly failed due to a number of political challenges inherent to welfare. It took a significant shift in partisan and institutional politics to lay the groundwork for a restructuring of federal welfare.

Welfare generally refers to government programs providing financial assistance to poor or low-income individuals or families. Most often, when political leaders discuss welfare they are focused on Temporary Assistance for Needy Families (TANF), the successor to the Aid to Families with Dependent Children (AFDC) program, which provides cash assistance for poor and low-income families with children, almost all of whom are fatherless families. TANF is a means-tested program, meaning that only families below a certain income level and with limited assets are eligible to receive the assistance. In addition to TANF, there are other means-tested federal and state programs for the poor, including both cash and in-kind assistance. The latter refers to the provision of directly usable goods or services that the family or individual would otherwise have to purchase. The most prominent of these is the Food Stamps program, first established in 1961 and expanded significantly in the early 1970s, which provides stamps for people who qualify because of their lack of income or low incomes and which are redeemable for groceries. The income ceiling for Food Stamps eligibility is significantly higher than for TANF, and many recipients earn incomes above the poverty line. Medicaid, established in 1965, provides health insurance for the poor and people with low incomes. The Earned Income Tax Credit (EITC), originally established in 1975 and significantly expanded in 1993 and 2001, provides low-income families who pay no federal taxes with a cash refund nonetheless, varying in amount depending on the size of the family and the level of income. Today, the EITC is larger than federal welfare under TANF, aiding more people and costing more federal dollars, and many of its recipients are above the official poverty line. The EITC enjoys political support, as opposed to welfare, because it is provided through the tax code and is connected to employment.

Aside from these better-known programs of federal assistance, there is a much less familiar network of aid, including federal tax credits, smaller federal assistance programs, state and local programs of assistance, and private nonprofit and employee benefits. The federal government provides billions of dollars in assistance for different categories of recipients through a vast array of tax credits, such as the EITC. Some of these tax credits are received by low-income and working-class populations, but most of them go to middle- and upper-class income levels. There are also a range of smaller federal programs assisting poor and low-income people with in-kind aid for basic needs such as housing and nutrition. Many states and localities (counties, cities, and towns) offer their own programs of assistance for various recipient categories, including poor single men, many of whom are homeless. Private charities also provide a range of services and assistance, ranging from small locally based organizations to large national organizations such as Catholic Charities, which has a budget larger than $3 billion annually. Finally, the vast majority of U.S. citizens receive health, disability, and retirement benefits through their private employers, benefits that are usually provided by welfare state programs in other advanced industrial democracies. The United States remains the only advanced industrial democracy that does not provide universal health insurance.

TANF, however, is the program that is generally referred to when the term *welfare* is used. TANF was established in 1996 as the centerpiece of the Personal Responsibility and Work Opportunity Reconciliation Act (PRWORA) (P.L. 104–193). It was the successor to the AFDC program, which was created as part of the PUBLIC ASSISTANCE title of the 1935 Social Security Act (Title IV). The Aid to Dependent Children (ADC) program, the original federal "welfare" program, provided assistance for fatherless children as part of this legislation. In 1959, the adult caretaker of the children assisted by ADC was included in the grant, and in 1962 the name of the program changed to Aid to *Families* with Dependent Children, reflecting this addition. ADC/AFDC provided financial assistance for poor mothers and their children as a federally guaranteed entitlement for 61 continuous years. The replacement of AFDC by TANF was much more than a simple reform of the existing welfare

program. First, the entitlement status of welfare was replaced by a federally capped block grant to states ($16.4 billion annually from 1996 to the present). Second, for the first time in the history of federal welfare, there were time limits established for receiving welfare: Recipients were limited to five years of welfare over their lifetime. In addition, the new welfare program requires that adult recipients of TANF be engaged in a state-authorized work activity after receiving welfare for two years. Third, welfare reform also devolved a great deal of administrative discretion over the design and shape of state welfare programs from the federal government to STATE GOVERN-MENTS. Aside from designing the shape of their own programs, states can decrease the lifetime limit, and almost half the states have opted for shorter lifetime limits. States are also permitted to shorten the time period before requiring recipients to work, but more than half use the federal maximum of 24 months. In 2005, as part of the Deficit Reduction Act of that year, the TANF program was reauthorized with some minor changes.

Federal welfare was established as a response to the economic collapse of the late 1920s and early 1930s. The Economic Security Act of 1935, commonly known as the Social Security Act (SSA), set up the basic structure of the new federal welfare state. The structure of the welfare state established by this landmark legislation was enormously important to the subsequent politics of welfare. The SSA established the major programs of the federal welfare state, setting up two tiers of assistance. The top tier included politically popular social insurance programs, such as SOCIAL SECURITY, and was financed and administrated completely by the federal government. The programs in this tier enjoy political legitimacy due to their financing mechanism: payroll taxes matched by employers, often viewed as contributions or even premiums. The second tier public assistance programs, in contrast, were structured as federal-state partnerships, with federal financing contingent on state government contributions. States were limited by loose federal guidelines but were given responsibility for setting benefit levels and eligibility requirements within these guidelines, resulting in wide variation in benefit levels and eligibility tests nationally. These programs required recipients to be below a basic level of income—hence their identity as means-tested programs. The original federal means-tested public assistance programs included ADC, Aid to the Blind (AB), and, after 1939, Aid to the Permanently and Totally Disabled (APTD). By the mid-1950s, ADC began to overshadow the other programs in its tier and in the 1960s totally eclipsed them in size and political significance.

The federal-state structuring of welfare was very important in shaping its political trajectory in the decades following World War II. Prior to the 1960s, many states used the administrative discretion they enjoyed as part of this structure to limit their AFDC caseloads and benefits. ADC-AFDC benefits were notoriously low in southern states and highest in the Northeast and in California. Southern states also used their administrative powers under the program to limit eligibility, keeping their caseloads artificially low while effectively discriminating against African-American families who would otherwise have been eligible for benefits based on income and family structure. These practices were successfully challenged in the political atmosphere of the mid-1960s, partly in response to the CIVIL RIGHTS revolution. As a result, the federal government increasingly exercised tighter oversight over state welfare administration, prohibiting unfair and/or arbitrary rules for determining eligibility, including those that resulted in racial discrimination. As a consequence, there were rapid increases in the size of the AFDC caseload. Between 1950 and 1970, the number of ADC recipients grew by 333 percent, with the bulk of this increase taking place in the years between 1965 and 1970. In the 1980s, President Ronald Reagan and other prominent conservatives sought to devolve federal control over numerous assistance programs to state governments. This devolution agenda accelerated considerably once the REPUBLICAN PARTY achieved majority status in the HOUSE OF REPRESENTATIVES in 1994 for the first time in 40 years. With welfare reform a central part of the new House Republican agenda—the "Contract with America"—states were to become the central authorities in designing federally funded welfare programs. This shift in the trend in administrative control is a signature aspect of welfare politics, first from the states to the federal government in the late 1960s and 1970s, and then from the federal government to the states in the late 1980s and 1990s.

In the 1960s, the characteristics of the welfare caseload changed considerably as well. ADC was originally modeled on the Mothers' Pensions programs of the 1920s. It was intended to enable primarily white widowed mothers to remain home with their children. However, the proportion of black ADC recipients increased to about 40 percent by 1961, where it remained until 1996. Since the 1996 reform, the greatest proportion of welfare "leavers," former recipients who have left the welfare rolls for work or other forms of support, have been white. This has left the remaining welfare population increasingly composed of African-American and Latino families. In addition to racial changes, today the majority of families on welfare are no longer widowed, and the percentage of out-of-wedlock births to mothers on AFDC increased 25 percent between 1950 and 1960.

Within this context, since the 1960s public criticism of welfare has increased dramatically. As a consequence, beginning with President John F. Kennedy's public assistance reforms in 1962, welfare has been the target for federal reform every four or five years. Significant reforms to AFDC were achieved in 1962, 1967, 1981, and 1988. In 1962, President Kennedy embraced a rehabilitation approach to welfare and succeeded in adding social services supports to augment AFDC. The purpose of these supports was to help move recipients successfully into employment. In 1967, a congressional coalition of conservative Democrats and Republicans sought to establish tough work requirements as part of AFDC but succeeded only partially with the establishment of the Work Incentive Program (WIN). WIN permitted states to exempt large proportions of their caseload from participation in this program of job training and work involvement, and as a result national participation rates were very low. In 1981, President Ronald Reagan was able to pass significant rule changes for eligibility determinations and other minor aspects of AFDC. These changes had a combined impact of significantly reducing the size of the welfare caseload rise for the first time in more than 20 years. Reagan achieved this success as part of a much larger budget reconciliation package. In 1982, when he sought a more direct reform of welfare—to have states assume full financial and administrative control over AFDC in exchange for the federal government assuming full control over Medicaid (also a federal-state partnership)—his proposal failed.

Indeed, more ambitious efforts to reform AFDC directly have repeatedly been met with political failure. Presidents Richard Nixon and Jimmy Carter both proposed comprehensive reforms of welfare and made these singularly important pieces of their domestic policy agenda. In both cases they failed to achieve their goals. In 1988, congressional leaders and the Reagan administration achieved what was then touted as a major welfare reform: the Family Support Act (FSA). However, in subsequent years it became increasingly clear that FSA was just another minor reform of the strangely politically persistent AFDC program. The 1988 FSA provided new federal monies to assist states in encouraging and training welfare recipients for work under the Job Opportunities and Basic Skills (JOBS) program. However, JOBS was never fully implemented. In order for states to access the federal financing for new job training programs for welfare recipients, they were required to match the financing. Because state governments were unwilling or unable to spend the voluntary matching grant monies necessary to access federal dollars available under the legislation, most of the federal financing available was never spent. Still, FSA was politically significant as a culmination of almost a decade's efforts to shift the purpose of federal welfare away from supporting poor children in fatherless families and toward encouraging self-sufficiency for poor single mothers through work. FSA was understood at the time to reflect a new consensus on welfare, emphasizing the contractual responsibilities of welfare recipients rather than the social services supports that were emphasized in the Kennedy-Johnson years. There was a growing consensus in the 1980s that welfare recipients should be required to work or prepare for work and that states should be given greater latitude in designing their own welfare programs. These principles laid the necessary groundwork for the landmark welfare reform of 1996.

Welfare's unusual capacity to resist successful reform despite its political weakness poses a unique political paradox. Welfare's political roots were from a time when women stayed home with their children, and racial segregation and other forms of discrimination were widely tolerated. The original purpose and structure of welfare accommodated these social realities. America's social context changed dramatically in the years following World War II—segregation was overturned, discrimination was rejected by majorities, and women were increasingly likely to participate in the labor force. Welfare, however, remained intact: a program structured for the world of the 1930s but somehow persisting as the federal government's main tool for addressing poverty among poor families. The conflict between the changed social context and the U.S. welfare state's original structure engendered increasing levels of political friction. But any reforms of AFDC seemed to exacerbate other problems: Increasing benefits made welfare too expensive and more attractive, and decreasing benefits made it too hard for recipients to care for their children adequately. National reformers were frustrated in their efforts to "end welfare as we knew it."

By 1996, however, riding a growing consensus concerning welfare reform and within a context of important political changes that had become manifest in Congress and in presidential politics, a policy making window, as political scientist John Kingdon might describe it, opened. The successful restructuring of federal welfare in 1996 was achieved because of the intersection of a growing consensus on welfare, reflected in FSA, with significant changes in federal politics. The establishment of a Republican majority in the House of Representatives in 1994 was of central importance. This majority was unusually cohesive and sought the ending of AFDC and a return of control over welfare to state governments. At the same time, the Democratic president, Clinton, in political trouble and facing an upcoming election, had yet to deliver on his popular 1992 campaign promise to "end welfare as we know it." Together, these circumstances catapulted welfare reform to the top of the national agenda between 1994 and 1996, altering the potential for assembling a majority congressional coalition supporting welfare reform.

The resulting replacement of AFDC by TANF in 1996 represented a watershed in U.S. welfare policy and politics. As a result of this landmark legislation, welfare is no longer an entitlement; adult recipients can no longer count on assistance being provided indefinitely, and work is a requirement for most adults receiving welfare. States have far more power in shaping welfare programs than the federal government, with a resulting wide variety of policies across the

United States. Many policy makers see this transformation as an unadulterated success, with caseloads reduced in size by more than 50 percent between 1996 and 2001. Others argue that the experience of many families making the transition off welfare to work frequently leaves that family worse off, with children in such families facing a greater likelihood of experiencing hunger, lack of needed health care, and bouts of homelessness.

TANF faces many of the old problems of the past while encountering new challenges as it moves into the future. The 1996 law mandated a reauthorization of TANF by 2002, but it took Congress until May 2005 to provide that reauthorization, partially because of difficulties in achieving legislative consensus on how strongly the federal government should require states to move larger and larger numbers of their welfare recipients into work. Moreover, at the state level, the early successes in moving large percentages of welfare recipients from welfare to work seems to have cooled off since 2002, as those who remain on welfare face multiple barriers to successful self-sufficiency: educational deficits, mental illness, substance abuse problems, experience with domestic violence, and so on. These challenges suggest that states will require additional funds to assist their remaining welfare caseloads in making successful transitions from welfare to work. The difficulties in achieving just a simple reauthorization of TANF, which is widely viewed as a virtually unalloyed success, suggest that the future of U.S. welfare policy and politics will continue to be conflict ridden, politically divisive, and resistant to effective reforms.

See also GREAT SOCIETY; NEW DEAL.

Further Reading

Cammisa, Anne Marie. *From Rhetoric to Reform? Welfare Policy in American Politics.* Boulder, Colo.: Westview Press, 1998; Gilens, Martin. *Why Americans Hate Welfare: Race, Media, and the Politics of Antipoverty Policy.* Chicago: University of Chicago Press, 1999; Gordon, Linda. *Pitied but Not Entitled: Single Mothers and the History of Welfare.* Cambridge, Mass.: The Belknap Press of Harvard University Press, 1998; Hacker, Jacob S. *The Divided Welfare State: The Battle over Public and Private Social Benefits in the United States.* New York: Cambridge University Press, 2002; Katz, Michael B. *The Price of Citizenship: Redefining the American Welfare State.* New York: Henry Holt & Co., 2001; Lieberman, Robert C. *Shifting the Color Line: Race and the American Welfare State*, Cambridge, Mass.: Harvard University Press, 1998; Skocpol, Theda. *Protecting Soldiers and Mothers: The Political Origins of Social Policy in the United States.* Cambridge, Mass.: The Belknap Press of Harvard University Press, 1992; Weir, Margaret, Ann Shola Orloff, and Theda Skocpol, eds. *The Politics of Social Policy in the United States.* Princeton, N.J.: Princeton University Press, 1988; Weaver, R. Kent. *Ending Welfare as We Know It.* Washington, D.C.: Brookings Institution Press, 2000.

—Scott J. Spitzer

STATE AND LOCAL GOVERNMENT

board of education

Boards of education, commonly referred to as school boards, were a natural development of the growth of communities and localized structures of government in the United States. School boards date back to colonial times, and as the nation grew, the education of children was viewed as a local responsibility. Kindergarten through 12th-grade education became the quintessential "public good." In the parlance of classical economics, a public good is one that is characterized by "jointness of supply" and the impossibility of excluding anyone from consumption. With regard to education, this meant that schools were typically funded by local taxation, and all children of the community were to be served by the school. Along with the need for public finance came the need for public control and accountability. The school board, which was either elected or appointed by MAYORs or other executives, became the institutionalized method of democratic oversight and control of a particular school district.

As an institution of democratic control and oversight, most school boards are popularly elected and generally function much like a legislature, taking on responsibility for bureaucratic oversight, policy development and initiatives, budget oversight, and setting broad goals for the school district. Early on, the school board was also responsible for working with teachers to ensure that the curriculum met the needs of the community. The content of education is, of course, one of the toughest questions a society must answer,

and any society that claims to be democratic must decide the best possible way to educate citizens about the values of DEMOCRACY. Because education shapes the moral character of future generations, determining who should exercise control over the curriculum is a difficult task and, at times, highly political. Parents, the STATE, and professional educators are all interested in the content of the character of a child as he or she progresses through the public school system.

By the beginning of the 20th century, there were literally thousands of school districts that had emerged throughout the United States, and virtually all of the districts were subject to local control. School boards were the principal method of governance. Despite the large number of school districts, there was surprising consistency in the subjects that were taught from community to community. As Diane Ravitch has noted, most public schools emphasized reading, writing, basic math, patriotism, CITIZENSHIP, and a moral code that was generally endorsed by the community. The schools were an integral part of the community and reflected the beliefs of the members of the community. Indeed, schools were often the focus of various kinds of community associations, and schools often served as the meeting place for various other community organizations. Thus, one would expect that there would be consensus about the instructional materials and the values taught in the schools. As in *The Music Man*, the school board was conceived to be the protector of the morality of the community. Therefore, when Professor Hill came to town, his first task was to see that the board "sang in harmony." If members of the school board were not "bickering," then they would be more likely to bring the community together.

In this idealized view, the school board merely reflects the dominant view of the community. Ravitch goes on to point out that the similarity between what was taught from district to district was reinforced by textbook publishers interested in developing texts that would appeal to the largest number of districts. However, after the turn of the century, it became clear that there were a number of competing values that the schools were being called upon to teach. Several trends contributed to the decline in the consensus over the individual values that should be taught.

First, the Progressive Era movement was interested in the professionalization of government, particularly civil service, and this concern carried over to education. Often, in cities, school boards were under the control of the political ward system, and Progressives introduced professional norms for teachers, norms for bureaucracy, unionization of teachers, and a major reemphasis on curriculum. All of these parts of the Progressive program worked against the idea of local control and the political harmony within the district that the school board was supposed to maintain.

Second, the neighborhood school, because of its extended organizations such as the Parent Teacher Association (PTA) and after-school activities, has always provided a natural meeting place for parents. In many communities, there was an overlapping membership between church, school, and neighborhoods, and dense social networks began to form. Schools naturally became a location for both social interaction and often for political organization. At the same time, as the population became more mobile, new families moved into the school districts, bringing with them different priorities and values. The consequences were often conflict over the content of the curricula and the emergence of the school as a natural base from where political action emanated. Face-to-face encounters generate, as political scientists have noted, "social capital" that fuses both norms of trust and civic awareness, thus making possible the transition from voluntary to political organizations.

Because conflicts are expressed in elections, school boards, in some communities, no longer sang in partisan harmony but were the center of intense political conflict. The school board increasingly dwelt in a vortex of multiple groups and interests that were often in conflict with one another. The political environment that the school board finds itself in consists of the following stakeholders: the state bureaucratic apparatus, teachers, local administrators, textbook companies, parents, and taxpayers in general. The effectiveness of any board is dependent on its success in marshalling political support within the community. Therefore, the school board must build political coalitions among politically diverse groups in order to maintain a smoothly functioning school system. If it is true that the conditions for democratic control over schools are a function of a strong, accountable school board, then school boards must respond to the general public interest rather than private interests. Yet, in general, because of the nature of coalition building, highly organized INTEREST GROUPS are often able to gain control over a school board. Declines in voting turnout also contribute to the dominance of particular groups and specialized interests.

Conflict within a school district is usually expressed in electoral terms, and contested elections are normally a part of a cultural conflict or a conflict over the values taught in the public schools. Low turnouts in most school board elections indicate that, most of the time, the public is willing to defer to the financial and oversight expertise of the board. Most disputed elections are about values, and curiously, voting turnout does not seem to increase during contested elections. Rather, conflict seems to occur among dominant community groups. Boards in districts where there is sharp cultural conflict normally end up being controlled by one faction or another. Under these conditions, boards can lose their sense of democratic accountability.

Most analysts over the past 20 years have identified the conflict in public schools as a conflict over precisely which values will be taught to the children. On one hand, certain groups believe that parental values should dominate the educational process. This view has led many to argue for various "voucher schemes" as a way of allowing parents to send children to schools that generally reflect their own values. The underlying idea is that the public schools have somehow abandoned a commitment to community values. The neighborhood school, so the argument goes, has increasingly become dominated by the values of professional educators, administrators, and various social engineers. On the other hand, many professionals as well as lay people adopt the view that the purpose of the public schools is to teach values that will lead children to become good citizens in a liberal polity. These values include toleration, respect for the diversity of opinion, relfectiveness, autonomy, and critical thinking.

Given the potential conflict over values, it is not difficult to see why that often, in diverse districts, school board elections become heated arenas of political conflict. The state, through the school board, is often intruding on the life of the child, particularly with respect to values. If parents within a district who are already partially mobilized disagree with the values emphasized by the school, conflict will often center on school board members. Debates over such value-based issues as sex education, the role of religion, recognition of different lifestyles, and the presumed political biases of texts are not uncommon issues in some school districts. From 1995 to 2000, there were approximately 30 recall elections in school districts nationwide. In each of these cases, some conflict over values was involved in motivating the recall movement.

In one view, the state, in order to reproduce itself, must make sure that certain democratic values are transmitted to students. On the other hand, some claim that the family unit best handles certain areas of instruction. The problem with democratic education is that it is not possible to amalgamate all possible values within a single curriculum. No single distribution of K-12 education will satisfy all parents. Voucher schemes cannot solve this embedded problem, since students who remain in the local school will still be subject to a curriculum that some feel is biased or inadequate.

School boards are instrumental in maintaining the legitimacy of the public school. This is a particularly difficult task due to the political cleavages that have developed around what values should be taught in the schools. These divisions have been made even more acute in many districts due to various social problems that confront teachers and administrators on a daily basis. The problems, in any district, may include the influx of non–English-speaking immigrants, fractured families, more mothers in the workforce, racism, the increasing influence of television

and popular MEDIA, drug and alcohol addiction, and the general decline in civic culture. The politicization of these social and cultural issues has forced school boards to deal with increasingly partisan conflict. In many instances, boards, which historically have been nonpartisan, have been forced to side with various partisan factions in order to maintain equilibrium in a school district. Under these circumstances, boards seem to function best where they are most democratic. When openness, deliberation, and compromise are values adopted by the board, the community becomes more "harmonious." The board must be able to represent broad community interests rather than particular partisan factions.

See also DEPARTMENT OF EDUCATION; EDUCATION POLICY.

Further Reading

Barber, Benjamin B. *An Aristocracy of Everyone: The Politics of Education and the Future of America.* New York: Ballantine Press, 1992; Burns, Nancy. *The Formation of American Local Governments: Private Values in Public Institutions.* Oxford: Oxford University Press, 1994; Chubb, John E., and Terry M. Moe. *Politics, Markets, and American Schools.* Washington, D.C.: Brookings Institution, 1990; Danzberger, Jacqueline P., Michael W. Kirst, and Michael D. Usdan. *Governing Public Schools: New Times, New Requirements.* Washington, D.C.: Institute for Educational Leadership, 1992; Davis, Mike. *Prisoners of the American Dream.* London: Verso Press, 1999; Friedman, Milton. *Capitalism and Freedom.* Chicago: University of Chicago Press, 1962; Fullinwider, Robert K., ed. *Public Education in a Multicultural Society.* Cambridge: Cambridge University Press, 1996; Gutmann, Amy. *Democratic Education.* Princeton, N.J.: Princeton University Press, 1987; Hirschman, Albert O. *Exit, Voice and Loyalty: Responses to Decline in Firms, Organizations, and States.* Cambridge, Mass.: Harvard University Press, 1970; Jeffe, Sherry Bebitch. "Bilingual Bellweather?" *California Journal.* (January 1998): 39; Levinson, Meira. *The Demands of Liberal Education.* Oxford: Oxford University Press, 1999; Matthewson, Donald J. *Cultural Conflict and School Board Recall Elections.* Paper presented at the annual meeting of the American Political Science Association, Philadelphia, Penn, 28–31 August 2003; McGirr, Lisa. *Suburban*

Warriors: The Origins of the New American Right. Princeton, N.J.: Princeton University Press, 2001; Peterson, Paul E. *City Limits.* Chicago: University of Chicago Press, 1981; Putnam, Robert D. *Bowling Alone: The Collapse and Revival of American Community.* New York: Simon & Schuster, 2000; Piven, Frances Fox, and Richard A. Cloward. *Why Americans Still Don't Vote: And Why Politicians Want it That Way.* Boston: Beacon Press, 2000; Ravitch, Diane. *Left Back: A Century of Battles over School Reform.* New York: Simon & Schuster, 2000; Riker, William. *Liberalism against Populism.* Lone Grove, Ill.: Waveland Press, 1982; Thoburn, Robert. *The Children Trap.* Fort Worth, Tex.: Dominion Press, 1988; Sharp, Elaine B., ed. *Culture Wars and Local Politics.* Lawrence: University of Kansas Press, 1999; Walker, Jack. *Mobilizing Interest Groups in America: Patrons, Professions and Social Movements.* Ann Arbor: University of Michigan Press, 1991.

—Donald J. Matthewson

board of elections

The board of elections (sometimes called "election commission" or "election board") is responsible for planning and implementing all stages of every local, state, and federal election held in a STATE. Boards of elections perform a variety of election-related duties, from registering voters and candidates to counting and verifying the final ballots cast. Every board has a variety of responsibilities, but the main purpose is to ensure that every primary and general election is conducted legally and uniformly across the state.

The power to determine how elections are conducted is left primarily to the states, as stated in Article I, Section 4, of the U.S. CONSTITUTION: "The times, places and manner of holding elections for Senators and Representatives, shall be prescribed in each state by the legislature thereof; but the Congress may at any time by law make or alter such regulations, except as to the places of choosing Senators." The U.S. Constitution gives states the power to determine how each will organize and implement its elections, with minimum interference from the federal government. While state legislatures create their own set of election laws, another government agency is needed to perform the administrative duties of implementing these laws. Therefore, every state (as well as

the District of Columbia) has its own board of elections to ensure that every election is held in accordance with that state's law. States may also have boards of elections at lower levels of government, such as a local or county board of elections. While many local and county election boards have many of the same duties and functions as state boards, this essay mainly focuses on those at the state level.

The state's secretary of state and/or a committee of several board members often head a state's board of elections. Appointment to a board varies from state to state depending on what the state's constitution or laws mandate. For instance, sometimes the GOVERNOR appoints all the members to the board, while in other states, members may be appointed by the two major POLITICAL PARTIES or by some combination of both GOVERNOR and party appointments.

Boards have a tremendous workload and rely on the assistance of full- and part-time staff members. Just as board memberships vary in size, so do staff sizes. The staff is responsible for the day-to-day administrative functions and assists board members in everything from answering telephones to creating reports on current election-related legislation being considered.

Because the U.S Constitution leaves the responsibility of conducting elections to the states, states' election laws vary across states. However, all must still abide by federal law. For example, consider voter registration. The U.S. Constitution grants the right to vote to all citizens over the age of 18 regardless of race, gender, or creed. However, states determine the voter registration requirements for citizens. One state may require that voters register weeks prior to an election, while another may allow registration on the same day of an election. Both registration rules are completely legal as long as the state does not impose unreasonable registration requirements, such as a literacy or aptitude test.

Every state has its own set of laws governing how elections are to be run, and each state has created a board of elections to oversee that elections are held in accordance to state (and federal) law. While states' election laws differ, the main responsibilities and duties of each state's board are the same and include (but are not limited to) the following.

Implement all state and federal election laws: Every state has its own constitution that defines how elections are to be conducted. The board's main responsibility is to oversee the election process and ensure that every election is legally conducted according to the state's law. Sometimes boards may formulate their own laws to submit to the legislature for consideration, but mostly state legislations (and sometimes the U.S. Congress) create (or revise) election laws. It is up to the board to see that these new laws are followed and to communicate to local election boards any changes that may alter how elections are conducted.

While the constitution gives states the power to determine how to run their elections, there are times when the federal government passes new legislation that all states must adopt but are given some leeway as to how the new law is to be administered. It is then the states' responsibility to implement the new federal law or act, and the boards promulgate all necessary rules and regulations to meet new federal requirements.

An example of boards implementing federal law is the National Voter Registration Act (NVRA) of 1993 (also known as the "Motor Voter Act"). To help increase the number of citizens registered to vote, NVRA requires that states register voters in one of three places: during registration for a new (or renewed) driver's license, in all offices that use state funds to provide assistance to persons with disabilities, and/or through state mail-in forms. While some states are granted exemption from this law, 44 states and the District of Columbia are responsible for meeting the requirements of the NVRA, and each state's board of elections must demonstrate to the federal government that its state complies with the act.

Register all individuals and parties involved with elections: Every state's board is responsible for maintaining current records of any person(s) and group(s) involved with elections, from registered voters and candidates to lobbyists and POLITICAL ACTION COMMITTEES. When an individual submits registration materials to become a voter or candidate for office, it is the duty of the board to ensure that all paperwork is properly completed and filed. It is also the board's responsibility to certify official lists of all candidates in a particular election. The board collects records of campaign contributions from individuals and political action committees and tracks each candidate's contributions. Boards of elections keep updated records on individuals and parties involved in elections to ensure that all participants are conducting themselves in a legal manner.

Gather and disseminate information: Boards of elections are responsible for making sure that all elections are conducted legally, and sometimes state legislatures revise or create new election laws or the courts make a ruling on how a particular election law should be executed. Because these events may significantly alter how boards operate, they must constantly monitor all proposed election-related laws and court proceedings that may impact their role. Such legal proceedings may include journals and acts of the state legislature, political practice pledges and ethics reports filed by elected state officials, or federal laws. Throughout the year, the board must then pass along this information to local election boards if the legislation and/or court rulings will alter the election process.

While boards collect information from legislatures and courts, they may also serve as an information source for them. For example, a state legislator may wish to revise an old election law and ask the state's board of elections if the proposed law adheres to current state and federal law. Board of elections members may also give their expert input as to the feasibility of various proposals and/or may testify in front of committees or legislatures when a proposed election law is being debated. They may also be asked to testify in cases involving an illegal election activity.

Boards of elections also collect information from and serve as a resource for those directly involved in elections. During campaigns, candidates, political parties, and political action committees spend thousands (sometimes even millions) of dollars on advertising, staff, travel, and numerous other campaign-related activities. To ensure that there is no illegal financial activity, all must file finance reports with the board of elections to demonstrate exactly how they spend their funds. Boards collect and file these reports and check for any suspicious activity. They may also be asked to provide this information to the public, such as community watchdog groups or the MEDIA. The board also advises potential candidates of the qualifications and requirements for running for office both prior to and during a campaign.

Boards also serve as an information source for the general public. Each board has its own Web site with information on its services, records of previous elections results, CAMPAIGN FINANCE reports, and so on. Interested individuals can obtain various election-related materials, from voter registration forms to campaign finance reports.

Monitor and certify elections: During elections, the board must monitor each voting location to ensure that the election is being run legally and uniformly. To make sure that this happens, before each election the board carefully tests voting devices and certifies that each is operating accurately. When new voting devices are proposed, such as updated machines or voting online, the board also tests these devices before approving them for use. The board also trains and certifies local election officials prior to an election. At the conclusion of an election, the board certifies the total number of ballots cast and reports any ballots that were printed and delivered to the polls, disqualified, or unused as well as any over-votes or under-votes. They certify all final election outcomes, whether it is the winner of a particular race or the result of a REFERENDUM.

Investigate cases: Sometimes allegations arise of unlawful activity that occurred during a campaign or election, such as bribery, voter fraud, illegal campaign contributions, false signatures on petitions, and so on. Such allegations must first be filed with the board, which then investigates the case. If the board finds the allegations to be false, the case is dropped; otherwise, the board moves forward with the case and takes action, whether it be disqualifying a petition or candidate or even taking court action against an individual or group.

As explained above, boards of elections have a vast variety of duties to perform. Despite the wide variety of responsibilities, the most important function that a board of elections performs is ensuring that elections are run uniformly and fairly, but sometimes states have abused their authority and used their law-making powers to prevent particular groups from participating in elections. Or there may have been widespread cases of voter fraud on an election day. At times like these, the federal government (and sometimes the U.S. SUPREME COURT) has had no choice but to interfere and impose federal election laws on the states. Such actions have created tension between the federal and state levels of government and have raised questions about the legality of lawmakers in Washington, D.C. and nonelected justices imposing new laws in an area in which the states have sovereignty. These actions have also led to problems for boards of elections in terms of implementing federal laws and programs with little financial aid to properly do so.

The most notable example of states abusing their sovereignty in elections is the period when states used election laws to prevent African Americans from voting. After the fifteenth Amendment to the U.S. Constitution was ratified in 1870, making it illegal to deny persons the right to vote on account of race, many states (especially those in the South) used their election laws as a tool to prevent minorities from voting. They created restrictions in the voting registration process, such as requiring a poll tax to be collected or a literacy test to be passed. Given the higher poverty and illiteracy rates of minorities, many African Americans could not meet the strict requirements and were prevented from voting. This went on for years with little interference from the federal government because legally, states could create their own election laws.

However, in 1965, Congress passed and President Lyndon B. Johnson signed into law the Voting Rights Act (VRA), which was designed to put a stop to states conducting elections that would prevent minorities from voting. Among the provisions of the act, states were no longer allowed to require unreasonable registration requirements, and it also required several states and counties that had a long history of racial discrimination to obtain preclearance from the U.S. DEPARTMENT OF JUSTICE before any election-related changes were made, such as redrawn district lines or voting procedures.

While many states challenged the VRA in the courts, in 1966, the U.S. Supreme Court upheld the constitutionality of the act in the case *South Carolina v. Katzenbach* (383 U.S. 301). This act was significant for state boards of elections because it is this agency that is responsible for implementing the act, from reviewing all proposed election-related changes to submit for preclearance to investigating cases of illegal activity. The VRA and its aftermath was also important for boards because this is when the federal government and court system began to become more directly involved with an area over which states previously had complete sovereignty.

This remains one of the biggest problems that boards of elections currently face and has resulted in far more federal oversight than boards have ever faced. Currently, many states' boards are struggling with implementing the Help America Vote Act (HAVA) of 2002 and adjusting to the additional federal oversight the act has brought. After the 2000 U.S. presidential election, when the outcome was delayed due to the contested vote in the state of Florida, numerous problems emerged across the nation, such as misread ballots and voter registration fraud. Voting device malfunctions in states such as Florida made many citizens and policy makers push for a new policy to make voting more uniform across states for federal elections. In 2002, Congress passed and President George W. Bush signed into law HAVA, which aims to alleviate some of the problems of 2000 and make voting more uniform and accessible. However, HAVA presents a major problem for boards of elections because now the federal government has more oversight of federal elections than ever before. HAVA established the U.S. Election Assistance Commission (EAC), which serves as a "clearinghouse" for federal elections and establishes standards each state is to abide by in order to meet the requirements of HAVA. The EAC directly reports to Congress, thus making state boards of elections more privy to federal oversight.

While it is unclear precisely what HAVA's affect on states' boards of elections will be in the future, this act signals that the federal government is continuing to take a more active role in supervising an area once completely controlled by the states—elections. For state boards of elections, this signals two things: first, that the agency now has an additional branch of government to report to and second, that the era of complete state sovereignty over elections may be over. How will boards change in their day-to-day operations, now that they must report to the federal government? If states do not meet federal objectives, will the federal government take over the board's role? Will new agencies such as the EAC be effective in their oversight? Will the national government continue to take more control over elections or return to state sovereignty in this area? In the future, boards of elections will have to address these questions and learn how to work with the federal government and agencies in order to meet new federal objectives.

See also CAMPAIGN FINANCE (STATE AND LOCAL)

Further Reading
"About the National Voter Registration Act." U.S. Department of Justice, Civil Rights Division. Available online. URL: http://www.usdoj.gov/crt/voting/nvra/activ_nvra.htm#1993. Accessed July 25, 2006; "Help America Vote Act of 2002". Federal Election Commission. Available online. URL: http://www.fec.gov/hava/hava.htm. Accessed July 25, 2006; "Introduction to Federal Voting Rights Laws." U.S. Department of Justice, Civil Rights Division. Available online. URL: http://www.usdoj.gov/crt/voting/intro/intro.htm. Accessed July 25, 2006; U.S. Election Commission Web site. Available online URL: www.eac.gov. Accessed July 25, 2006; U.S. Federal Election Commission Web site. Available online. URL: www.fec.gov. Accessed July 25, 2006.
—Carrie A. Cihasky

bonds (local government)
A bond is a certification of debt issued by a government or corporation in order to raise money. An investor who purchases a bond (bondholder) is essentially loaning money to the issuing organization (issuer) on a promise to pay a specific amount of interest periodically and a lump sum payment for the principal on the maturity date of the bond. Local government bonds are debt obligations issued by subnational government units such states, counties, cities, tribes, or other local special units (for example, school, utility, fire protection, redevelopment, or water conservation districts). Local government bonds, regardless of the actual issuing unit, are called "municipal" or "munis" by investors to distinguish them from corporate and federal Treasury bonds. Bond issues are the single most important method local governments use to acquire private funds to finance public projects. Municipal bonds are generally issued to fund long-term projects such road construction, power plants, water facilities, and education infrastructure, although they may also be used for short-term emergency spending needs such as natural disasters.

The earliest example of the use of bonds to fund public projects was by England in the 1770s for toll roads. In the United States, a revenue bond was issued in the 1800s to finance the New Orleans port, and the first recorded municipal bond was by New York City in 1812. Following a debt crisis in 1837 and widespread state bond defaults in the 1840s, municipal debt rose rapidly as restrictions were placed on state spending. The heavy reliance on municipal bonds for financing many state projects combined with a financial panic in 1873 led to widespread local government debt defaults. By the early 1900s, municipal bonds emerged as a relatively secure form of investment. In 1902, the combined debt of all state and local governments was about $2.1 billion. Local debt decreased after the Great Depression and stayed relatively low throughout the two world wars. However, after World War II, increases in population, migration to urban centers, and changes in the transportation and housing markets generated huge demands for public services. By the late 1960s, local debt had increased to $66 billion, to $361 billion in 1981, and exceeded $1 trillion in 1998. Throughout the 1990s, local government debt remained relatively level, at an annual average of $1.09 trillion. With increased devolution of federal government services to state and local levels, there has been a corresponding increase in local government debt, with total local debt rising to $1.85 trillion in 2005. Approximately 61 percent of all subnational government debt is at the state level and 39 percent with municipal or special government units.

There are two primary types of municipal bonds. They differ according to the mechanism used to commit to repay the debt. The first, general obligation bonds (also known as full-faith-and-credit), attach a legal claim by the bondholder to the revenue of the issuer. If an issuer defaults on debt obligations, the bondholder can claim payment from local revenue sources, typically local property, sales, or income tax revenues. Since they are issued against a broad revenue base, general obligation bonds are traditionally used to finance projects that benefit an entire jurisdiction, such as free-access highways, water systems, and fire protection. The second type, revenue bonds, are secured by attaching a claim to user fees or other specific dedicated tax revenues, typically directly related to the service provided by the project funded by the bond, such as higher education, toll roads, water services, and health facilities. In 2004, revenue bonds accounted for about 61 percent of all long-term municipal debt, and general obligation bonds 39 percent. Nonguaranteed, or limited-liability bonds can also be issued which lack any claim on local revenue sources. While presenting a higher risk to investors and requiring higher interest rate payment by issuers, these avoid legal claims to future revenue streams and permit projects to be funded based on their own merit. Municipalities may also use combinations of general obligation and revenue bonds to enhance the creditworthiness.

Bond issuers use a variety of credit enhancements to add additional security guarantees in order to reduce the interest rates a borrower pays. For example, bonds may include state-credit guarantee, a legal commitment by the STATE GOVERNMENT to pay the debt of a local government issuer in case of default. Private banks can also agree to provide a promise of repayment of local government debt with a bank letter of credit. Municipal-bond insurance can also be purchased by local governments to guarantee the bond repayment. Other bond varieties include structured financing, which combines traditional bonds with derivative products such as futures, options, and swaps. This allows an issuer to include expectations about long-term interest rates to improve bond marketability. Local governments may also issue what are known as municipal notes or commercial paper for short-term borrowing, typically for financing cash management needs and budget shortfalls.

The Sixteenth Amendment of the U.S. CONSTITUTION maintains a tradition of intergovernmental tax impunity, requiring that some activities of state and local governments are immune from taxation. This prevents state and federal taxes on the interest local governments pay to investors for borrowing. This tax-free income has a number of effects. Local governments can borrow at interest rates lower than those in the private market as private investment flows to tax-free municipal bonds rather than taxed private bonds. Since investors use local bonds both as a tax avoidance strategy as well as an investment, it also means there is more capital available to local governments than there would otherwise be on the merits of the project alone. Finally, the use of bond investments as a tax avoidance strategy decreases the tax revenue available to the federal government. Whether this represents a serious market inefficiency or an appropriate method of funding public projects remains a continuing area of debate. The 1986 Tax Reform Act is the most comprehensive law regulating the current municipal bond market. It created two categories of municipal bonds: those funding taxable private activities and those issued for public purposes, which remained tax-exempt. Debt issues for some privately owned assets remain tax-exempt, such as the construction of multifamily dwellings for affordable housing, hazardous waste facilities, airports and other mass commuting facilities, and some student loans. Bonds issued by any public purpose special district remain tax-exempt.

Purchasing a bond is an investment and always includes risk to the investor that the issuer will default on the debt. This risk is reflected in the interest paid to the investor, and the greater the risk, the higher the interest rate an investor expects. Investing in government bonds typically has lower risk than private corporate bonds, since governments rarely go bankrupt. A number of commercial bond ratings agencies have emerged to assess investment risk of both private and public bond issues. The three most common are Mergent's (formerly Moody's), Standard & Poor's, and Fitch Investors Services. The bond rating scale used by Standard & Poor's is as follows. AAA: (highest rating) The capacity of the bond issuer to repay debt is extremely strong. AA: Bond issuer's repayment capacity is high. A: While the bond issuer's repayment capacity remains strong, it is susceptible to fluctuations in the health of the general economy. BBB: Generally adequate financial commitment by the issuer, but bonds in this category are subject to changing economic conditions. BB, B, CCC, CC, and C: Significant risk, and the financial capacity of issuers to repay is limited. D: Bond payment is in default.

Bond ratings are based on a variety of factors, including the debt repayment history of the issuer, the degree of professionalism within a local government unit, its overall financial health, the amount of political control over spending, the health of the local economy, and the size of potential revenue sources. U.S. Federal Treasury Bonds are regarded as fully secure (AAA) since there is little likelihood that the federal government will go bankrupt. In 2004, the ranking for major metropolitan areas according to Standard & Poor's ranged from AAA for cities such as Indianapolis, Indiana, Seattle, Washington, and Min-

neapolis, Minnesota, to a low of BBB- for Pittsburgh, Pennsylvania, and Buffalo, New York. Bond ratings signal the financial health of a local government and have important political consequences. The 2003 recall election of California governor Gray Davis was partially spurred by Fitch Investor Services lowering the state's bond rating from A to BBB due to fiscal mismanagement and a $38.2 billion budget deficit. Having a good rating, however, is no guarantee to an investor. In 1994, despite a high bond rating, Orange County, California, filed for bankruptcy in the largest-ever municipal bankruptcy.

While there are disagreements among public finance scholars, there are some general guidelines regarding what constitutes appropriate issuing of debt by local governments. Since a commitment of funds today with a promise of repayment with interest in the future places a burden on future budgets, it is generally considered good practice for the users of a public project to be the ones who bear the burden of the debt. As a rule, bonds should not be issued over a time period beyond the life of the project that the debt funds. Because of this intertemporal element, bonds can be politically attractive as a way to fund services for constituents today while placing the financial burden of repayment on future generations. To control this, many jurisdictions require general obligation bonds to be approved by voters. Another mechanism to control political overuse is the requirement of pay-as-you-go financing, whereby projects are paid for out of annual appropriations rather than bond issues. However, this can be just as problematic as the misuse of the bond market. Pay-as-you-go financing may place a heavy tax burden on current residents of an area, even if some may leave a jurisdiction and no longer receive the benefits from a project. Since annual appropriation budgets cannot typically afford the large up-front construction cost of many public works, it may discourage otherwise useful projects. Funding high initial construction costs from annual funds can produce tax rate instability, with high rates during the early construction phase of a project and lower rates afterward, even though the project produces the same level of benefits over its lifespan.

Municipal bonds are not listed along with corporate and stock investments in most financial sections. In order to check a bond price, it is often necessary to consult a specialized bond dealer or association.

There are a number of critical pieces of information necessary for understanding the municipal bond market. Below is an illustration of the information given in a typical bond price quote.

Issue	Coupon	Mat.	Price	Chg.	Bid yield
Okla	7.700	01-01-22	104¼	...	7.35

While corporate and federal bonds are typically sold in $1,000 denominations, municipal bonds are issued in increments of $5,000, though the prices are quoted as $1,000 issues for the purpose of comparison. This $1,000-value for bonds is known as the par (or face) value of the bond. On the date of maturity, this is the amount that will be repaid in full by the issuer. In the example, "Issue" indicates the bond issuing entity, in this case the Oklahoma Turnpike Authority (Okla), a regional transportation special government unit. "Coupon" reports the coupon rate as a percent of par value. The bond is paying a 7.700 coupon, so it pays 7.7 percent of $1,000, or $77. "Mat." reports a maturity date of 01-01-22, meaning that the bond expires on January 1, 2022. "Price" is the current price to purchase one bond issue and is likewise expressed as a percent of par value. The reported price of 104¼ represents a current price of 104¼ percent of $1,000, or $1,042.50. "Chg." is the change in price from the previous day, with "..." meaning that the bond did not change value. When change does occur, it is rounded to increments of 1/8th of a percent (0.125 percent) and reported as positive or negative values. "Bid yield" refers to the current yield when holding the bond until maturity.

The market value of a bond is composed of two components: The present value of the coupon (a periodic payment made to the bondholder) plus the value of the amount initially borrowed (the principal paid as a lump sum at maturity). The value of both components depends on the interest rate (the amount the issuer pays for using the money) and the maturity date (the time when the bond expires). Calculating the present value of a bond is done with the bond-pricing equation, expressed as

$$\text{Bond Value} = C\left[\frac{1 - \frac{1}{(1+r)^t}}{r}\right] + \frac{F}{(1+r)^t}$$

where C = coupon payment, r = interest rate, t = periods to maturity, and F = par value. Suppose a bond pays an annual coupon of $40, an interest rate of 8 percent, has 10 years to maturity, and has a par value $1,000. The value of that bond is then calculated as

$$\text{Bond Value} = 40\left[\frac{1 - \frac{1}{(1+0.08)^{10}}}{0.08}\right] + \frac{1,000}{(1+0.08)^{10}} = 731.59$$

It is worth $731.59 to an investor purchasing that bond today.

There are a number of contemporary debates about and challenges to municipal bond markets. A perennial controversy is the division between private and public activities. The most recent example is the practice of funding sports stadiums for attracting private sports teams using PUBLIC DEBT. Other researchers have commented on the relative ease of using the bond markets to fund new projects that have high returns, compared to the difficulty in maintaining existing services. Thus, new cities with expanding public works find capital easily, while older cities are forced to look for other revenue sources. State legislation that places limits on local property tax revenues has forced local governments to innovate new means of raising capital at the same time more service responsibilities, such as welfare and health services, are being devolved to local governments. The tax-free nature of municipal bond investments also continues to generate debate. Bond investments are particularly appealing to investors in high tax brackets as a tax shelter, which creates an incentive to lobby local government officials to pursue particular bond investments.

Municipal bonds have played an important role in the United States system of FEDERALISM by allowing local government units both the power and the responsibility to take on debt for public purposes. This interaction between private financial markets and public economies has had important implications for the incentives of local political officials. The system of bond ratings compels local officials to maintain fiscal discipline and reputation within the private market. Because of its long history of federalism, the U.S. municipal bond market is the most sophisticated and developed in the world. To increase the funds for infrastructure development as well as improve governance by local officials, other countries are increasingly looking at the U.S. municipal bond market as a model. Municipal bonds will continue to evolve in both form and function in reaction to fluctuations in the availability of funds from state and national government, constituent demands, legal structures, and private capital markets.

See also BUDGETS, STATE AND LOCAL.

Further Reading

Fortune, P. "The Municipal Bond Market, Part 1: Politics, Taxes and Yields." *New England Economic Review* (Sept./Oct 1991): 13–36;———. "The Municipal Bond Market, Part II: Problems and Policies." *New England Economic Review* (May/June 1992): 47–64; Hillhouse, A. M. *Municipal Bonds: A Century of Experience.* New York: Prentice Hall. 1936; Mikesell, J. L. *Fiscal Administration: Analysis and Applications for the Public Sector.* Belmont, Calif.: Thompson/Wadsworth. 2007; Monkkonen, E. H. *The Local State: Public Money and American Cities.* Stanford, Calif.: Stanford University Press, 1995; Wesalo Temel, J. *The Fundamentals of Municipal Bonds.* New York: Wiley & Sons. 2001.

—Derek Kauneckis

budgets, state and local

For STATE and local governments, as Alexander Hamilton noted, money is the lifeblood of politics. State and local budget decisions determine how much one pays for a parking ticket or for property taxes on a business. State budgets determine how strong a reputation one's public schools and state university will enjoy. Budget choices determine whether potholes will be fixed, whether a road will be increased to four lanes, and whether one will pay admission to city, county, or state parks. Budgets are an accounting of revenues collected from different sources and expenditures on various items. A budget is at the same time a proposal, a plan of action, and a means for accounting for money already spent. Budgets at the state and local government levels are determined by politics such as election results, state and local political cultures, and a variety of other factors such as the wealth of a state, the health of the economy, and demographic trends.

Under the U.S. CONSTITUTION, FEDERALISM guarantees that states have independent political power and their own constitutions. Under most STATE CONSTITUTIONS, local and regional government (such as counties) are created by the state and can be changed by the state. Some large cities such as New York, Chicago, and Los Angeles have budgets bigger than some of the smaller states. While sharing a number of characteristics with the U.S. federal budget, state and local budgets are different in several meaningful ways. First, the federal budget is proportionately larger than all state and local governments combined. In the early 21st century in the United States, federal spending at the national level constituted about 20 percent of gross domestic product (GDP), the sum of goods and services produced by the economy. All state and local spending combined made up approximately 10 to 12 percent of GDP, meaning the public sector in the United States was about one-third of the total economy. One main difference is the responsibility of the federal government for national defense, which cost more than $400 billion annually in 2006–07. Another main difference between the different levels of budgeting is that the federal budget is a tool for managing the economy. At the state and local levels, budgets rarely are large enough to shape the overall economy of the state. However, policies on taxes and spending can determine the level of state services, the favorability of the state toward businesses, and other factors that influence the state and local economies.

State budgets differ from the federal budget in terms of rules and procedures as well. In Washington, D.C., Congress has constitutional control of the power of the purse. While the balance shifted to a stronger presidential role in budgeting in the 20th century, the president does not have the degree of budget power of state GOVERNORs. Most governors possess the "line-item veto." That means that a governor can veto a small part of a spending bill rather than have to veto an entire bill like the president. This is an important power for governors, often envied by presidents. Along another dimension, however, states are more constrained than the federal government. Most states have a balanced budget requirement, which means they are not allowed to spend more than they take in except for borrowing for some capital projects such as university buildings or infrastructure projects. The federal government, however, can spend more than it takes in and supplement it by borrowing from the public (U.S. Savings Bonds, for example) and foreign nations. Unlike the states and most local governments, the U.S. government has a large national debt as a result of running budget deficits over the years.

Budget processes in state and local governments generally run on annual or biennial cycles, including regular steps that determine where revenues will come from and how they will be spent. Because one year's budget looks similar to the budget the year before, some scholars have suggested that budgeting is "incremental." However, when examining budgets over periods of several years or following major changes or crises such as Hurricane Katrina in 2005, budgets can change quite quickly and dramatically. About half the states have a biennial budget—that is, a budget that last two years. The other states and most local governments have an annual budget. The budget cycle at the state and local levels generally consists of executive formulation, legislative approval, and administrative implementation, possibly followed by an audit. This entire cycle can take as much as three years, meaning that at any one time, several budgets are in different stages of development, enactment, and approval.

Budget formulation is generally controlled by the executive branch: the governor or MAYOR and staff. Most states have a central budget office that assists the governor in assembling the budget proposal to send to the legislature. Citizens can check the Web site of their state or city government to find out what entity is responsible for budget preparation. Important parts of state and local budgeting are economic estimates and revenue projections. Since state and local governments are generally limited to spending what comes in, the most important thing is to determine how robust tax collections will be. During an economic boom, with housing prices soaring, revenues can grow rapidly, allowing spending on new programs. In times of economic downturn, however, revenues may plummet, requiring painful cuts in education, health care, and other popular programs. Most state and local governments try to maintain some kind of "emergency," or "rainy day," fund for

such contingencies, but it is difficult to resist the current spending pressures from various interests.

As the budget is being prepared in the executive branch, agencies, departments, and various public entities such as universities make requests for allocations for the coming year or biennium. These entities generally are advocates for greater spending— "claimants"—and they are supported by various interests in the state or local jurisdiction. Much of what government does helps people (health and senior citizen programs), protects people (police, fire departments, and the National Guard), or makes their lives easier (transportation, highways) and is therefore popular with constituencies. As a result, there are heavy political pressures for greater spending in the budget process. That makes it necessary for the governor or mayor and budget office to act as guardians, or "conservers," in the process and say "no" to increased spending. That is necessary because although many programs are popular and effective, people generally do not like to pay taxes, and some programs are wasteful and ineffective. Budgeting, then, is a struggle between the parts and the whole of the budget. Many participants are trying to increase their piece of the pie, while those who have responsibility for the totals must try to resist pressures to spend more and more.

This dynamic between spenders and savers takes place both in executive formulation and legislative approval. When the governor, mayor, or county executive finally prepares a set of budget requests, they are submitted to the legislative body: the state legislature, city or county council, or board of aldermen. At this stage of state and local budgeting, legislative hearings are usually held in which the administration is called on to defend its requests, and various interests can testify for or against the budget. Law enforcement leaders may show up to argue for more money for police. Local activists may oppose cutbacks in day care programs or senior citizen activities. This is the stage at which politics and partisanship become important. In the states, governors usually have greater success with their budgets if one or both houses of the state legislature are of the same political party. Many municipalities are nonpartisan, but the political relationship between the mayor and the town council can be crucial in determining whether the executive proposals are accepted or amended.

Individual budget rules are very important and vary between states and municipalities. These can be researched online by examining the budget process in a specific jurisdiction or state.

In virtually all states and municipalities, the legislative body must give final approval to the budget. At that point, it goes back to the executive for the execution of the budget—actually cutting the checks, filling the potholes, and spending the money. At the state level, there are different agencies and departments, including the central budget office, that participate in the implementation of the enacted budget. The state or city treasurer's office often plays an important role in this. Revenues must be collected, whether from property taxes, state INCOME TAXES, speeding tickets, or lottery ticket proceeds, and deposited in the treasury. Again, budgeting is very dependent on estimates, which are informed predictions of what money will come in and what must be spent. State and local governments have procedures for monitoring budgeting and making slight adjustments if necessary. Running a shortfall can make the next budget cycle very difficult.

What forces shape state budgets, and how can differences be explained? The 50 states have different histories, levels of wealth and population, and political cultures. States such as Wyoming and Alaska are resource-rich, and state coffers overflow when energy prices are high. In Alaska, citizens pay low taxes, and each receives a check from the state each year from oil and gas royalties. Compare that to California, the most populous state, which often runs shortfalls as large as many billions of dollars in an economic downturn. Some states are more politically liberal than others and may be willing to extend state services even if it means higher taxes. In more conservative states, it is usually more difficult to start new programs. State electoral laws are an important factor in budgeting. Western states that allow citizen ballot measures such as the REFERENDUM and INITIATIVE have in recent years seen the rapid growth of "ballot box" budgeting. Voter-approved measures that either limit how states can raise revenues or mandate spending for certain popular purposes, such as health care or education, have proliferated in recent years. While often well intentioned, the result is to make budgeting much harder for the elected representatives in both the executive branch and legislative branch.

In the early 21st century, state and local budgeting remains highly influenced by what goes on in Washington, D.C. Federal mandates, which involve Congress passing laws requiring states to do certain things, often without supplying the money, have become more prevalent and more resented by states. No factor is more influential on state budgets than the Medicaid program. Medicaid helps low-income and indigent citizens receive health care, but the costs are increasing so rapidly that they are crowding out other important outlays in state budgets. Mandates affect local governments as well, such as the No Child Left Behind Act, which required changes in education spending by state and local governments without receiving what was promised from Washington. Fiscal federalism, along with the close financial interrelationship among the budgets of all levels of governments, is the reason that state and local budgets cannot be understood without understanding the role of the national government. Despite constitutional guarantees of independent political power, Congress often uses money (or the threat of withholding it) to get states to do what it wants. This was the case when the federal government threatened to withhold federal highway funds from any state that did not raise its legal drinking age to 21 during the 1980s. State and local governments retain ultimate control over their own budgets, but those budgets are also highly determined by what the federal government does and the larger national political and economic climate.

Further Reading
Rubin, Irene. *The Politics of Public Budgeting*. Washington, D.C.: Congressional Quarterly Press, 2005; National Conference of State Legislatures, "Fundamentals of Sound State Budgeting Practices." Available online. URL: www.ncsl.org/programs/fiscal/fpfssbp.htm. Accessed July 16, 2006; Kelley, Janet M., and William C. Rivenback. *Performance Budgeting for State and Local Government*. Armonk, N.Y.: M.E. Sharp, 2003.

—Lance T. LeLoup

campaign finance (state and local)
For the most part, state and local governments are free to set their own campaign finance regulations.

Federal laws apply only to candidates for Congress and the PRESIDENCY, although states and localities are bound by the First Amendment and U.S. SUPREME COURT decisions applying it to campaign finance regulations. Given this latitude, states vary significantly in the types of rules governing campaign finance. Some of this variation is due to differences in running for office. For example, campaigning for the Wyoming state legislature is quite different from campaigning for MAYOR of New York City. But much of the variation is a result of differences in the willingness to implement reforms; some states and localities have been more amenable to experimentation with campaign finance regulations to make elections fairer and to limit either the appearance or reality of CORRUPTION that can stem from contributions to candidates for public office.

The most common campaign finance regulation is disclosure—requiring candidates to state contribution and expenditure information. All states and localities have some type of disclosure requirement, although what is required to be disclosed varies significantly. For example, about half the states require the occupation and employer of the contributor to be listed, while the other half require only his or her name and address. Also, about 10 states do not require independent expenditures to be disclosed. Some states require campaign disclosure statements to be filed electronically—making the data easily available—while others require paper filings, severely limiting the utility of the data for the press, public, and researchers.

Beyond simply requiring candidates to disclose their campaign finance activity, many states and localities also place limits on the amount of money an individual, labor union, or business can contribute to candidates and POLITICAL PARTIES. For example, Los Angeles limits contributions to city council candidates to $500 during primary elections and $500 during runoff elections. Contribution limits often vary across different offices (for example, gubernatorial candidates usually have different limits than state legislative candidates) and sometimes vary across the type of contributor (for example, individuals and businesses may have different limits). Unlike on the federal level, in most states, corporations and labor unions can give directly to candidates and parties.

Contribution limits are meant to reduce the overall amount of money spent in elections, diminish the influence of large donors, and force candidates to rely on small contributions from "average" citizens rather than large contributions from wealthy donors and POLITICAL ACTION COMMITTEES. Research on contribution limits has generally found that they are not effective at accomplishing these goals. There are many ways donors get around contribution limits, the most prominent of which are independent expenditures that cannot legally be limited. Also, contribution limits, rather than forcing candidates to seek funds from "average" citizens, may prompt them to rely on lobbyists who will assist in fundraising by collecting large numbers of relatively small donations from their clients and delivering them to the candidate (a process referred to as "bundling"). Thus, there is minimal evidence that contribution limits reduce the overall amount of money raised by candidates or prevent wealthy individuals and organizations that wish to spend large sums of money influencing elections from doing so.

A less common reform, but one that has more promise than contribution limits, is the public financing of campaigns. The basic idea is to replace privately raised money with public money in order to eliminate the corrupting influence of the former. All public financing programs are voluntary; as the Supreme Court ruled in *Buckley v. Valeo* (1976), government cannot prevent candidates from raising funds or using their own money to finance their campaign.

A common form of public financing is through a system of matching funds, whereby private money raised by candidates is matched with public money in exchange for candidates agreeing to certain restrictions. This is partial public funding, in that candidates still raise some of their funds from private sources. The cities of New York and Los Angeles, along with a handful of states, have matching funds programs. In Los Angeles, candidates who join the matching funds program agree to a limit on expenditures, agree to a limit on the use of personal funds, and also are required to participate in debates. To qualify, a city council candidate must raise $25,000 from individuals in sums of $250 or less (there are higher requirements for mayoral candidates). Once they qualify, they can have contributions from individuals matched on a one-to-one basis, meaning if they receive a $250 contribution, they can receive $250 in matching funds from the city. There is a limit to the overall amount of matching funds the candidate can receive that varies depending on the office and whether it is a primary or runoff election. New York City structures its program in a similar way, except they have a four-to-one match: for every $250 contribution, candidates can receive $1,000 in matching funds. Like Los Angeles, New York City imposes an expenditure limit on participants and will match funds only up to a certain amount.

The record on matching funds programs has been mixed. On one hand, both Los Angeles and New York City have high participation rates: The majority of serious candidates in both cities accept matching funds. Further, there have been examples of candidates who would not have been able to mount a serious campaign without public funding. So matching funds programs have increased the number of candidates able to run for office (although exactly how many is hard to tell). On the negative side, some candidates have rejected public funding with few negative repercussions. Most notable were Richard Riordan and Michael Bloomberg, successful mayoral candidates in Los Angeles and New York, respectively. Both men financed their own campaigns with personal wealth and significantly outspent their publicly funded opponents. While both New York City and Los Angeles have provisions that benefit program participants when faced with a high-spending opponent, these provisions simply were not enough. Mike Woo, Riordan's main opponent in the 1993 mayoral election, was outspent by $4 million, while Mark Green, Bloomberg's 2001 opponent, was outspent by more than a 4 to 1 ratio. Further, it does not appear that matching funds programs have reduced the overall amount of private money raised; public money has been used to supplement private money rather than replace it. That said, it is unclear whether matching funds programs have altered the sources from which candidates receive funds or whether they rely less on "established interests" and more on "average citizens."

Another way public financing has been implemented is through "clean money" programs. These are similar to matching funds programs in that they provide public money to candidates in exchange for their agreement to abide by certain restrictions. The difference is that private donations do not get matched; all private money (except for a handful of small donations) is prohibited, and candidates receive a lump sum to run their campaigns. In other words, it is a full public financing program rather than just a partial one. The program works like this: To qualify for public funds, candidates need to raise a certain number of small (typically $5) contributions from individuals within the jurisdiction. This requirement is meant to demonstrate public support for the candidate (justifying the use of public funds) as well as weed out "vanity" candidates who are not serious about the election. Once candidates raise enough $5 contributions, they are given a lump sum of public funds to run their campaigns. The amount they receive varies depending on the type of election (primary or general), the level of opposition they face, and whether their opponents are also participating in the clean money program. They are prohibited from raising additional private money or using their own funds during the campaign (although sometimes they are allowed to raise small sums at the beginning of the campaign).

Maine was an early adopter of clean elections in 1996, and other states (e.g., Arizona and Vermont) have followed suit. Most states limit clean money to state legislative races. Early indications from Maine and Arizona were promising: There appeared to be more candidates running for office, and elections were generally more competitive, one of the central goals of clean money reforms. However, isolating the effects of clean money from other factors (such as TERM LIMITS, which can also increase competitiveness) is problematic, and some studies have found that clean elections have a minimal effect on competitiveness. Also, many candidates choose not to accept clean money and usually are able to raise significantly more than their clean money opponents (although the percent of candidates refusing public money varies significantly from state to state). If candidates sense that accepting clean money puts them at a disadvantage to their opponents, they are less likely to participate in the program even if they support its goals. Independent expenditures may also create problems for clean money regimes. While some states provide additional money to clean money candidates when they are opposed by independent expenditures, the existence of substantial independent expenditures—both in favor of and opposed to clean money candidates—may create anomalies in the funding formula that undermine the fairness of the system.

In general, public financing programs suffer from two major problems. First, because they are required to be voluntary, candidates can opt out, limiting the effectiveness of the program. None of the existing public financing programs prevents candidates from raising large sums from INTEREST GROUPS and wealthy individuals if they so choose. Second, most of the public financing programs are underfunded, creating a competitive disadvantage for candidates who accept public funds. There is often significant public opposition to using taxpayer money to fund political campaigns, and thus politicians are often stingy with funding these programs. Even when they initially fund public financing programs at appropriate levels, they often lose their value over time through inflation. For example, the amount of public matching funds candidates in Los Angeles can receive is the same now as it was in 1993, when it was first implemented, despite the fact that the cost of CAMPAIGNING has increased significantly. Without adequate funding, not only do candidates have an incentive to reject public funding, but those who do join are likely to be significantly outspent by their nonparticipating opponents. If states and localities increased funding for their public financing programs, it could provide incentives for more candidates to participate and level the playing field between candidates who are publicly funded and those who are not.

In conclusion, states and localities have experimented with different types of campaign finance regulations in an effort to increase competition, reduce the cost of elections, and limit the influence of wealthy donors and interest groups. There have been laboratories in which different types of campaign finance regulations have been tried and tested. Assessing whether these experiments are successful, however, is quite difficult due to the difficulty of isolating the effects of various reforms and a lack of usable data. Despite these hurdles, as more research is conducted on state and local campaign finance reform, we will gain a better understanding of the impact of these reforms and their effectiveness at accomplishing their goals.

See also CAMPAIGN FINANCE.

Further Reading
Gierzynski, Anthony. *Money Rules: Financing Elections in America*. Boulder, Colo.: Westview, 2000; Gross, Donald A., and Robert K. Goidel. *The States of Campaign Finance Reform*. Columbus: Ohio State University Press, 2003; Malbin, Michael J., and Thomas L. Gais. *The Day after Reform*. Albany, N.Y.: Rockefeller Institute Press, 1998; Schultz, David, ed. *Money, Politics, and Campaign Finance Reform Law in the States*. Durham, N.C.: Carolina Academic Press, 2002; Thompson, Joel, and Gary F. Moncrief, eds. *Campaign Finance in State Legislative Elections*. Washington, D.C.: Congressional Quarterly Press, 1998.

—Brian E. Adams

charter, municipal and town
City, county, and town charters are legal documents adopted by governments, usually through a public vote that grants the local government limited autonomy to manage the public's affairs. The presence of a charter is referred to as "home rule." (For the purposes of this essay, city and COUNTY GOVERNMENTs are referred to as MUNICIPAL GOVERNMENTs.) Charters must be permitted by STATE law. Five states, including Alabama, Hawaii, Nevada, New Hampshire, and North Carolina, have no provisions for home rule. Nine other states limit home rule to certain categories of cities only. States also permit counties home rule, though only 28 states permit county home rule. County charters are also frequently limited to certain categories of counties.

Municipal charters appear to be similar to the U.S. CONSTITUTION. Both establish the powers of their respective governments. Both describe the structure of the government and generally establish limits of governmental authority. They also determine fundamental questions concerning elections and the duties of major officeholders.

However, there are fundamental differences between municipal charters and the U.S. Constitution. City charters have very limited legal standing. Municipalities are always subordinate to state laws and rules. States reserve the right to take away city and county charters, and the state retains significant control over local governments through legislation. It is common, for instance, for the state to limit the taxing authority of cities and counties. Certain classes of city employees are often governed by state laws rather than city ordinances. Police officers, for instance, are often governed by state codes, and the city is often limited in its ability to hire and fire police chiefs. State and federal legislation often requires cities and counties to follow prescribed rules and regulations. California cities, for example, are required to meet state requirements for the recycling of refuse material, and federal and state legislation provides rules for health standards, air pollution control, and AFFIRMATIVE ACTION.

Cities and counties are best viewed as "creatures" of states, whereas the federal government is sovereign. The powers of municipalities are limited to those described in state law and subject to state review. The legal basis for limited autonomy, referred to as Dillon's rule, was first enunciated in 1868 and is generally unchallenged today. As stated by Judge John Dillon of the Iowa Supreme Court, the powers of municipalities are limited to "(f)irst those granted in expressed words; second those necessarily or fairly implied in or incident to the power expressly granted; third those essential to the accomplishment of the declared objects and purposes of the corporation." While challenges to this notion occur, the principle appears to be well established in case law.

One might ask, therefore, of what value are city and county charters? They provide municipal governments with control over some important matters, such as the form of government, the duties of elected and appointed officials, and the structure of election districts. At the city's options, other provisions can and generally are included. This essay examines the major provisions of municipal charters and looks at the advantages and disadvantages of charters.

City charters have several common features. They describe the form of government, which includes the powers of major appointed and elected officials. Particularly significant is the presence of several very different forms of government reflected in city charters. Because of the presence of charters, the organization of government in cities contains greater variety than occurs at other levels of government. Normally,

cities and counties follow one of four generally established structures of government.

The earliest and still a major form of municipal government is referred to as the weak MAYOR plan. In weak mayor governments, an elected city council is the major policy making body. A mayor is separately elected with some independent powers described in the charter, but major decisions remain with the council. Major appointments of appointed officials, for instance, are the prerogative of the council. In most weak mayor cities, the mayor is elected citywide. Council members are elected either citywide or in election districts.

The strong mayor form of government provides an elected mayor with significant control over the day-to-day running of city government. This includes appointment of city employees and significant discretion over the organization of departments within the city. The city council in a weak mayor city exercises general oversight of important public policies and can pass ordinances subject to the mayor's veto.

The commission form of government elects city department heads directly and creates a city council composed of the elected heads. Thus, voters elect a police chief, fire chief, public works chief, and so on. The charter creates a council composed of these officials and gives them major responsibility for running the affairs of the city. Under a commission charter, there is usually no mayor.

The council-manager form of government, which elects a city council, is few in number and grants it major oversight of city policy but not of city administration. Day-to-day management is delegated to an appointed CITY MANAGER, who is expected to be a professional administrator selected for his or her knowledge and skills. The council-manager structure assumes that city council members are part-time officials. They are expected to have very limited powers over city management and frequently are not involved in the hiring and firing of city employees. Usually, city council members are elected at large on a nonpartisan ballot. The mayor is a member of the council selected by council members with no duties beyond presiding at city council meetings and representing the city at public functions.

Each city adopts its charter with these general models in mind but often with significant variations. Some cities, for instance, refer to the major appointed official as the "city administrator" and reserve some of the powers usually held by the city manager to the council. Cities often vary the kinds of election districts and choose to add other elected administrators.

A second feature of charters describes the election systems of the city. Some cities permit partisan elections, while others require that elections be explicitly nonpartisan. Nonpartisan elections are required in all council-manager cities and are common in all but the largest cities. The nature of election districts also varies. Traditionally, city council members were elected in wards, small divisions of the city designed to reflect differences in racial and ethnic composition. Proponents of the council-manager structure advocate at-large elections whereby each city council member is elected by the entire city electorate. The number of city council members also is described in the charter. Some cities elect more than 50 city council members, other cities as few as five. Council-manager cities generally contain five to seven council members. Some cities elect the council members at large but require some or all to live in prescribed districts.

Cities frequently elect some staff members in addition to the city council and mayor. City treasurers are commonly elected separately. Some cities elect their city clerks and city attorneys. The city charter describes these positions and often includes the qualifications for officeholders.

City charters are often long and detailed documents that usually include numerous additional provisions. Charters describe the structure and duties of various city commissions and SPECIAL DISTRICTS. The charter of Los Angeles, for example, describes a system of advisory neighborhood councils. Charter provisions frequently respond to special interests of particular politicians or citizen groups. The City of Milwaukee charter states that "Depots, houses or buildings of any kind wherein more than 25 pounds of gun powder are deposited, stored or kept at any one time, gambling houses, disorderly taverns and houses or places where spirituous, ruinous or fermented liquors are sold without license within the limits of said city are hereby declared and shall be deemed public concerns or common nuisances." The Houston, Texas, charter until recently included a provision banning the playing of hoops in city streets, a common form of children's play in the 1890s.

Charters are legally subordinate to STATE CONSTITUTIONS and legislation, and in most states, the state legislature and the courts severely curtail city powers. Despite these limitations, charters serve a number of important purposes and are often of significant benefit to the residents. Charters do permit some degree of response to the interests of the citizens. They can provide greater representation of neighborhoods or more significant influence of the city as a whole. By varying the kind of charter system, the city can respond to varying goals and interests.

Variations in charters have encouraged innovation in government management. The council-manager government is frequently credited with improving efficiency and generating innovations, particularly in public management. The city manager profession has often been in the forefront of changes in public administration practice. Without the centralized authority and tradition of hiring professional city managers, cities would be less able to attract skilled practitioners.

The flexibility of charters and the ability of cities to change them has allowed cities to respond to pressures for changes in the policy process. As demands for neighborhood representation come to the fore, charters can be changed to encourage greater diversity of representation. With increasing concern for central policy direction and more central management, cities have changed their charters to provide the mayor with more authority. Commission and council-manager structures have often followed evidence of corruption and mismanagement in some cities.

Last, the presence of different forms of city organization has permitted analysts to evaluate different structural arrangements and thereby test some basic propositions of political science. Does the representation of racial and ethnic minorities increase with more city council members or district elections? Does efficiency improve with central authority and professional management? Do nonpartisan elections encourage different kinds of decisions than partisan elections? By testing such propositions, political scientists know more about the effects of different forms of organization and representation on public policy.

Critics cite several problems that occur because of the charter system. The charter system places emphasis on the city as defined by city boundaries, not the urban area of which it may be a part. Because of the emphasis on the interests of specific residents, it encourages the creation of smaller cities rather than metropolitan governments. Critics argue that the home rule system encourages separating cities within an urban area, and it makes cooperation among cities more difficult. Suburbs, for instance, often use the presence of a charter to attack attempts to share the burdens of policies that are regional in nature. Taxing residents to pay for areawide problems, for instance, can be viewed as an infringement on home rule. Because the creation of small communities is relatively easy, the home rule system promotes the separation of residents within communities, encouraging communities that are stratified by wealth, race, and ethnicity.

The presence of the charter and the term *home rule* may give residents the impression that the city has more control over its destiny and more autonomy than is actually present. This may lead to disillusionment on the part of residents when they attempt to change policy.

Municipal charters determine the primary organizational features of American cities. They spell out the important structural features of the government and the election system. They provide the residents with some degree of control over public policy, though it must be emphasized that control ultimately resides with the STATE GOVERNMENT. Charters have encouraged innovation and provided a variety of kinds of city government that permit one to analyze the value of different structural arrangements. The charter system, however, is often cited as an impediment to intergovernmental cooperation, and it may encourage the stratification of cities by class and race.

Further Reading
Frug, Gerald E. *City Making: Building Communities without Walls*. Princeton, N.J.: Princeton University Press, 1999; Ross, Bernard H., and Myron Levine. *Urban Politics: Power in Metropolitan America*. 6th ed. Itasca, Ill.: Peacock, 2001; Saltzstein, Alan. *Governing America's Urban Areas*. Belmont, Calif.: Wadsworth-Thompson, 2003; Syed, Anwar. *The Political Theory of American Local Government*. New York: Random House, 1966.

—Alan Saltzstein

city manager
Under a council-manager structure of government, the city council (legislative branch) appoints a city manager to serve as the chief executive and administrative officer of the city. The city council also oversees the city manager and has the ability to fire him or her. The city manager appoints and removes department heads and sees that a city's ordinances are enforced. In addition, the city manager is usually highly educated and trained and is considered a professional. In fact, 63 percent of all city managers held at least a master's degree by the turn of the 21st century. Most city managers hold master's degrees in public administration, urban planning, or public policy.

In the classic council-manager structure of government, there is no separately elected MAYOR to function as chief executive. In such traditional council-manager cities, the city council selects the mayor, who is also a member of the city council. Change has occurred, however, whereby many mayors in council-manager cities are now directly elected.

The council-manager structure of government was part of Progressive Era reforms in the early 20th century. Ending boss rule and electing honest men to city office were the original goals of the reformers. Reformers also desired the council-manager form of government because they believed a city manager would impartially and rationally administer public policy established by a nonpartisan city council. Thus, they believed that the city manager would be apolitical. Also, during this time period business and corporate ideals were very popular, and the council-manager structure of government reflected these ideals. Many saw the council-manager structure as introducing businesslike efficiency in government. Early writers compared a community's citizens to stockholders in a business, the city council to a firm's board of directors, and the city manager to a corporate manager.

In addition, Woodrow Wilson argued that a politics-administration dichotomy existed. Therefore, in a traditional council-manager system, the city council should dominate politics and policy, and the city manager should dominate the administration and implementation of policy. In fact, the council-manager system does not work in this way, and city managers themselves as well as others discredit the politics-administration dichotomy. City councils do not focus exclusively on politics or policy, and city managers do not focus exclusively on administration or implementation. For a long time, city managers have been pulled between the roles of technician and agent of the council on one hand and politician and policy leader on the other.

Although Progressive Era reformers viewed the traditional city manager as a politically neutral administrative expert, the modern city manager is not apolitical. In fact, the modern city manager is deeply involved in policy making and politics. The policy role includes control over the council agenda and policy initiation and formulation. There has been a significant increase in the percentage of city managers who perceive the policy role to be the most important of three roles of policy, politics, and administration.

However, the city council does have final say over policy making. The city manager influences public policy but should not determine it. For example, it would be inappropriate and in some cases unethical for a city manager to take policy making credit away from the council. Likewise, city councils expect the city manager to accept blame for a failed policy.

City managers also serve a political role as brokers or negotiators of community interests. In this role, city managers spend most of their time sharing knowledge, educating, negotiating among various nongovernmental groups and individuals within the city, and encouraging communication by linking people. They attempt to resolve conflicts and create compromises. Therefore, city managers are not political in the sense of building a constituency, but they are political in the sense of trying to build consensus.

Currently, the boundary line between the roles of the city manager and city council is increasingly blurred, but the two continue to have shared but distinct responsibilities. Their interaction might be referred to as an activist-initiator pattern. In other words, city council members are active policy proponents. City managers are actively involved in developing middle-range, broad-range, long-term, and citywide proposals. City manager involvement in policy is not new. What is new is the need for city managers to be the source of broad policy initiation.

At times, city managers may be bureaucratic entrepreneurs who create or exploit new opportunities to push their ideas forward. Bureaucratic entrepreneurs promote and implement policy innovations. If a community has a mayor, it is significantly less likely that a city manager will emerge as an entrepreneur. In addition, entrepreneurial city managers are more likely to emerge in cities whose local public sector workers are highly paid. A more heavily unionized local municipal workforce reduces the chances that an entrepreneurial manager will emerge. Finally, very weak taxpayer groups or very weak municipal unions increase the probability that an entrepreneurial manager will emerge.

Leadership is the key factor that pushes entrepreneurial city managers to promote their ideas. The dominant approach used by most entrepreneurial city managers is teamwork. Handling issues quietly, behind the scenes, is the main strategy employed. Entrepreneurial managers need to be salespeople for new policies both to elected officials and citizens.

Another key aspect of the city manager's role involves whether the city council can maintain control over him or her in an efficient manner. Principal-agent theory is helpful in examining this issue. Under principal-agent theory, the city council—the principal—has political incentives to control the city manager—its agent. According to principal-agent theory, an agent is passive and undynamic. In addition, some may view the city manager also as a principal, because he or she has responsibility for subordinate employees, his or her agents. Examining the city manager's power as agent, one finds that he or she has the power of policy implementation and also participates deeply in other aspects of the policy process. The power that the city manager has to appoint and remove department heads varies. City managers often discuss these decisions with the city council. In addition, the city manager is likely to develop the budget in consultation with the city council. Most city managers have significant autonomy in managing administrative operations and making staffing decisions.

The city council may also influence the city manager. The council's ability to hire, retain, and fire the city manager is a key example. The council also has authority over city managers through performance evaluations. Likewise, the council has authority to make adjustments to the city manager's salary. In reality, however, few city councils monitor city managers to any sizeable degree. As a result, city managers may be agents, but their principals (city councils) appear to exercise little formal oversight. In fact, the relationship between the city manager and city council is often viewed as cooperative.

James M. Banovetz asserts that four sets of public attitudes toward government have profoundly affected city managers. These sets of public attitudes include an early 20th-century idea that "government is corrupt," which stemmed from machine politics. From 1915 to 1935, the public believed that "government should be limited." During this period, the council-manager plan was sold to the public on the basis of its parallels with contemporary business models and the politics-administration dichotomy. Progressive Era reformers made the case for needing a city manager. The public believed that "government is paternalistic" from 1935 to 1965. During this period, city managers supervised a growing list of programs and responded to a wider set of citizen demands. In addition, the council-manager plan's popularity grew rapidly during this and the following period. From 1965 to the present the public has believed that "government is excessive." During this period, people have viewed the government's role in society as too pervasive.

Banovetz also offers the possibility that future city managers will represent a synthesis of the administrative officer and the policy activist-leader. This is a much different conception than others vision that the city manager's focus will continue to move further toward policy and political roles.

Opponents of the council-manager plan question whether the plan and, therefore, the city manager can survive. Critics contend that the council-manager form of government is elitist, unresponsive, and insulated with a leadership void and no capacity to manage conflict, among others. The criticism that this structure of government is elitist stems from its characterization during the Progressive Era reform movement. During the reform movement, elected officials were drawn from the upper strata of the community, and the mayor was not directly elected. Currently, the mayor is usually directly elected, albeit this may lead to a decline in the power of the city manager. Changes in the council-manager structure of government to increase responsiveness have also been made. In addition to a directly elected mayor, the council is more diverse, with many cities switching from at-large to district council elections. Proponents of the council-manager form of government argue that its key features can remain intact. Although the city council now does more administration and management and the city manager does more in the way of mission formulation, the basic division between the city manager and city council is not being lost. City managers continue to look to the city council for direction, even though they must do more to frame options and press the council for resolution. City council members continue to rely on the city manager and staff for professional support at the same time that they want to be broadly involved themselves. The council also respects the manager's position as head of the municipal organization. In addition, the council seeks to be informed about administrative and managerial decisions.

As a third argument, Frederickson, Johnson, and Wood contend that the council-manager label has become meaningless, because the direct election of a mayor in a traditional council-manager structure of government adds a powerful element of political leadership. It also changes the role and functioning of the city manager and the relationship between the city manager and city council. For this reason, they call council-manager cities with directly elected mayors "adapted administrative" cities. In addition, they categorize council-manager cities with more than half of their council elected by district as "adapted administrative" cities. This essay has addressed the role of the city manager, changes in the city manager's role, and changes in the council-manager structure of government. Council-manager cities will likely continue to evolve, and, therefore, so will the role of the city manager.

Further Reading
Banovetz, James M. "City Managers: Will They Reject Policy Leadership?" *Public Productivity and Management Review.* 17, no. 4 (1984): 313–324; Caraley, D. *City Governments and Urban Problems: A New Introduction to Urban Politics.* Englewood, N.J.: Prentice Hall, 1977; Frederickson, H. George, Gary Alan Johnson, and Curtis Wood. "The Evolution of Administrative Cities." In *The Adapted City: Institutional Dynamics and Structural Change.* Armonk, N.Y.: M.E. Sharpe,

2004; Nalbandian, John. "The Contemporary Role of City Managers." *American Review of Public Administration.* 19, no. 4 (1989): 261–278; Newell, Charldean, and David N. Ammons. "Role Emphases of City Managers and Other Municipal Executives." "*Public Administration Review* 45 (May–June 1987): 246–253" Selden, Sally, Gene A. Brewer, and Jeffrey L. Brudney. "The Role of City Managers: Are They Principals, Agents, or Both?" *American Review of Public Administration* 29, no. 2 (1999): 124–148; Stillman, Richard J. "The Origins and Growth of the Council-Manager Plan: The Grass-roots Movement for Municipal Reform." In *The Rise of the City Manager: A Public Professional in Local Government.* Albuquerque: University of New Mexico Press, 1974; Svara, James H. "Is There a Future for City Managers? The Evolving Roles of Officials in Council-Manager Government." *International Journal of Public Administration* 12, no. 2 (1989): 179–212;———. "The Shifting Boundary between Elected Officials and City Managers in Large Council-Manager Cities." *Public Administration Review* 59, no. 1 (1999): 44–53; Teske, Paul, and Mark Schneider. "The Bureaucratic Entrepreneur: The Case of City Managers." *Public Administration Review* 54, no. 4 (1994): 331–340; Watson, Douglas J., and Wendy L. Hassett. "Career Paths of City Managers in America's Largest Council-Manager Cities." *Public Administration Review* 64, no. 2 (2004): 192–199.

—Susan E. Baer

constitutions, state

A constitution is an official document that establishes the rules, principles, and limits of a government. While Americans largely revere the U.S. CONSTITUTION as sacrosanct, most are completely unaware that every STATE in the union has its own constitution as well. The general purpose of state constitutions is similar to the federal Constitution. They describe the structure of government, the powers of officials, and the process of amending the document itself. They also delineate the individual rights recognized by the state, while conferring various obligations and responsibilities on the state. Like the U.S. Constitution, state constitutions shape the environment in which government takes place by establishing what governments must do and what they may not do. However, state constitutions differ substantially from the U.S. Constitution, and they differ considerably from one another.

The basic framework, however, is fairly uniform. Like the U.S. Constitution, most state constitutions begin with a preamble. Minnesota's is typical: "We, the people of the state of Minnesota, grateful to God for our civil and religious liberty, and desiring to perpetuate its blessings and secure the same to ourselves and our posterity, do ordain and establish this Constitution." They are intended as broad statements of general purpose, and efforts to add more specific goals have not been successful. In 1976, for example, South Dakota voters overwhelmingly rejected a proposal that would have added the phrase "eliminate poverty and inequality" to its constitution's preamble.

The first actual article of most state constitutions contains a list of fundamental individual rights. This is a clear contrast to the U.S. Constitution, in which nearly all rights have been added as amendments to the original document. Most of the rights listed are similar to those in the U.S Constitution, such as FREEDOM OF SPEECH and FREEDOM OF RELIGION, or restrictions forbidding cruel and unusual punishment. However, many state constitutions contain more rights than those listed in the federal Constitution. A total of 19 states specifically provide for equal rights by gender, and nearly 40 states recognize various guarantees to victims of crime. At least 11 states clearly establish a RIGHT TO PRIVACY (which has been a thorny issue at the federal level) by including passages like this from Montana's constitution: "The right of individual privacy is essential to the well-being of a free society and shall not be infringed without the showing of a compelling state interest." Some rights were recognized by states long before they were legally established nationally. Wyoming, for example, extended voting rights to women in 1869, more than half a century before the Nineteenth Amendment to the U.S. Constitution was ratified in 1920. Even more notably, Vermont's prohibition of SLAVERY—"All persons are born equally free and independent . . . ; therefore no person . . . ought to be holden by law, to serve any person as a servant, slave or apprentice . . . unless bound by the person's own consent"—appears in its constitution of 1777.

Declarations of rights are typically followed by a statement addressing the division of powers. All states share the same essential SEPARATION OF POWERS framework as the national government, but whereas the U.S. Constitution largely implies this division, most state constitutions express it clearly, as in Idaho's: "The powers of the government of this state are divided into three distinct departments, the legislative, executive and judicial, and no person . . . charged with the exercise of powers properly belonging to one of these departments shall exercise any powers properly belonging to either of the others."

Lengthy descriptions of the functions, structure, powers, qualifications, and selection process of the three branches usually follow. Every state but one establishes a BICAMERAL LEGISLATURE; only Nebraska's constitution specifies that "the legislative authority of the state shall be vested in a Legislature consisting of one chamber." The number of legislators, their terms of office, and their qualifications for office are all spelled out in state constitutions, and there is wide variance in all of these areas. The structure of the executive branch varies across states, as well. In many states, GOVERNORs are elected separately from other executive officials, such as the secretary of state and the U.S. ATTORNEY GENERAL, effectively creating a plural executive. Likewise, state constitutions establish matters such as whether GOVERNORS (and other executive branch officials) shall be term limited. Finally, the rules pertaining to the judicial branch are spelled out, including the important matter of selection. Unlike FEDERAL JUDGES, most STATE JUDGES are elected to office, as prescribed by the rules in the state constitution, though the actual election procedures vary substantially. In some states, there is an ordinary election with competing candidates; in others, judges are initially appointed to office and later face a retention election, in which voters decide whether to remove him or her from the bench. State constitutions also contain provisions for the impeachment of public officials. Even here, though, there is some variance, as the constitution of Oregon does not permit ordinary impeachment but notes that "incompetency, corruption, malfeasance or delinquency in office may be tried in the same manner as criminal offenses, and judgment may be given of dismissal from office."

The institutional differences between the states and the federal government can be consequential, but the purposes of these sections in the constitutions themselves are essentially the same. That cannot be said of the substantive provisions pertaining to policy matters found in every state constitution. Unlike the U.S. Constitution, state constitutions commonly address rules of taxation (and exemptions to taxation), health care and welfare issues, environmental issues, and a host of other policies, from abortion to lotteries. Providing education is a constitutional obligation in nearly every state; passages such as this one in Kentucky's constitution are almost universal: "The General Assembly shall, by appropriate legislation, provide for an efficient system of common schools throughout the State." By contrast, the U.S. Constitution generally avoids any mention of specific issues. Political scientist Christopher Hammons has found that 39 percent of state constitutions deal with these kinds of subjects, compared to only 6 percent of the U.S. Constitution. State constitutions also establish procedures of DIRECT (PARTICIPATORY) DEMOCRACY (if any), and they determine the rules regarding local governments.

Finally, like the U.S. Constitution, state constitutions outline the process for amending the documents themselves. There are several methods for amending state constitutions, but the most common by far is the legislative proposal. If both chambers of the legislature agree to an amendment (usually by a supermajority vote of two-thirds or three-fifths), the measure is placed before voters for their approval. (Voter approval is not required in Delaware.) Some 18 states permit voters to amend their state constitutions directly, without involving the legislature at all, through a constitutional initiative process. In recent years, this procedure has resulted in a number of constitutional bans on gay marriage, similar to the one in Ohio's constitution: "Only a union between one man and one woman may be a marriage valid in or recognized by this state and its political subdivisions." A number of states take the amendment process even further and require that voters be asked every 10 or 20 years whether to hold a constitutional convention to review the entire document. While wholesale changes to constitutions are infrequent, amendments are quite common, and the vast majority of those proposed by legislatures are ratified.

The typical state constitution is more than three times longer than the federal one; even the shortest state constitution (Vermont's) is longer than its national counterpart. The specific policy provisions discussed above explain at least part of the reason for the greater length. These provisions can be quite narrow and precise; from the Alabama constitution: "The legislature may . . . provide for an indemnification program to peanut farmers for losses incurred as a result of Aspergillus flavus and freeze damage in peanuts." New York's constitution meticulously details the maximum length and width of ski trails on specific mountains. Another reason for the length of state constitutions is that they are so frequently amended. While the U.S. Constitution has been amended only 27 times, the average state constitution has roughly 120 amendments. California's constitution has been amended more than 500 times since its inception in 1879. Another key difference is longevity. Most states have replaced their entire constitution at least once since their entry into the union, and many states have done so multiple times. Louisiana's current constitution is its 11th.

Conventional wisdom has long held that the lack of permanency is an inevitable by-product of excessive specificity, the argument being that such constitutions rather quickly become obsolete and must be replaced. The "father" of the U.S. Constitution himself, James Madison, was an advocate of a short constitution focusing on institutions and more general principles. He believed that brevity was essential for the document to be durable and therefore to provide for the necessary stability of the government. But Christopher Hammons has recently argued that longer constitutions are actually *more* durable than shorter ones, demonstrating convincingly that the state constitutions that have been lengthier and more specific have actually survived *longer* than the briefer versions. He concludes that "a particularistic constitution may better represent the people that live under it, reflecting the changing policy preferences of a diverse people." If true, it would suggest that political stability is actually enhanced by constitutions that address narrower issues than what Madison believed prudent.

There is indeed wide variation across state constitutions, a result of differences in history, culture, politics, and even geography. In New Mexico, where more than 40 percent of the citizens are Latino, the constitution contains a provision dealing with bilingual education. The constitution of Illinois was written in 1971 and distinctly reflects the environmental consciousness of the time: "The duty of each person is to provide and maintain a healthful environment for the benefit of this and future generations." Colorado's constitution has an entire article dealing with mining and irrigation, while Hawaii's mandates that "the state shall provide for a Hawaiian education program consisting of language, culture and history in the public schools." Even broader institutional differences across state constitutions can sometimes be explained by such factors. State constitutions written during the Progressive Era are the most likely to permit direct democracy, such as the recall of elected officials. Similarly, the New England tradition of town hall democracy is evident in the constitution of Vermont, the only state that mandates biennial elections for the governor and both chambers of the state legislature. Still, despite the fact that the differences across state constitutions can be quite significant, their similarities are far greater. The specifics may vary in nontrivial ways, but the framework described above is fairly standard, and that is the more important point to emphasize.

State constitutions will never receive a fraction of the attention that the U.S. Constitution does, and it is hard to argue that it should be otherwise. States are important in our federal system, but the U.S. Constitution is the key document in American democracy. State constitutions do not have its historical value nor its status as a model for nascent democracies worldwide. Moreover, as Saffell and Basehart correctly point out, they are "painfully boring documents," lacking "stirring phrases" or "eloquent prose." Nevertheless, for the same reasons that American government cannot be understood apart from the U.S. Constitution, an appreciation of state constitutions is essential for understanding government and politics at the state level.

Further Reading
Hammons, Christopher W. "Was James Madison Wrong? Rethinking the American Preference for Short, Framework-Oriented Constitutions." *American Political Science Review* 93 (1999): 837–849; Maddex, Robert L. *State Constitutions of the United States.* 2nd ed. Washington, D.C.: Congressional Quarterly Press, 2005; Rutgers Center for State Constitutional Studies. Available online. URL: http://www-camlaw.rutgers.edu/statecon/. Accessed June 20, 2006; Saffell, David C., and Harry Basehart. *State and Local Government: Politics and Public Policies.* 8th ed. Boston: McGraw Hill, 2005; Smith, Kevin B., Alan Greenblatt, and John Buntin. *Governing States and Localities.*

Washington, D.C.: Congressional Quarterly Press, 2005; Tarr, G. Alan. *Understanding State Constitutions*. Princeton, N.J.: Princeton University Press, 1998.
—William Cunion

correction systems

Correction systems are an integral part of the criminal justice system in the United States and involve agencies and personnel at the national, STATE, and local levels of government. However, the bulk of law enforcement duties in the United States is carried out by state and local agencies and officials. Prisons and jails are the twin pillars of state correction systems but can also be extended to include STATE COURTS of law and probation and parole agencies. The primary purpose and function of state correction systems is to help protect public safety and welfare by arresting and charging individuals involved in criminal activity and placing under supervision or removing from the larger community individuals who have been convicted of committing a criminal offense in a court of law.

At the local level of government, sheriffs, city police, and other law enforcement officials play a critical role within states' correctional systems. These officials' primary job is to arrest those believed to be perpetrators of crimes or civil violations. County and district attorneys prosecute those charged with crimes, and state courts decide the guilt or innocence of those charged with criminal violations. After conviction in a state court of law, criminal offenders are placed under the supervision of probation departments or, in many cases, sentenced to incarceration in state prisons.

In 2004, nearly 7 million people in the United States were under some form of correctional supervision; the greatest numbers of these are on probation. Probation is court-ordered community supervision of criminal offenders by a probation agency that requires offenders to adhere to specific rules of conduct. Another type of community supervision is called parole. Parolees are individuals who are conditionally released to community supervision by a parole board decision or by mandatory conditional release after serving a prison term. Parolees are subject to being returned to jail or prison for rule violations or other offenses.

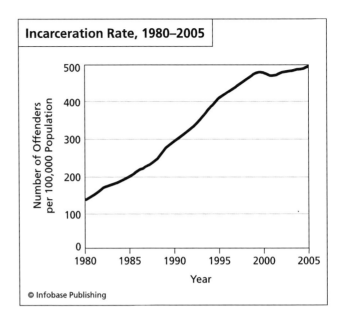

Incarceration Rate, 1980–2005

© Infobase Publishing

A more severe criminal sanction involves incarceration, or the confinement of criminal offenders in prisons or jails. Prisons are federal or state correctional facilities that confine offenders serving a criminal sentence of more than one year. Jails are correctional facilities found at the local level of government (typically COUNTY GOVERNMENTs) that are reserved for confining individuals awaiting trial or sentencing or those who are waiting to be transferred to other correctional facilities after conviction. According to the most recent statistics available (2003), there are just under 700,000 people confined in jails, while 1.25 million are confined in state prisons. Although each state's correctional system is designed to maintain public safety and welfare, which is a much-valued and popular goal in any democratic society, corrections-related policies have been at the center of domestic political disputes over the past three decades. The crux of the political debate involves concern over the increasingly punitive nature of corrections policies since the 1980s. The punitive nature of corrections policies is perhaps best exemplified by the use of the death penalty and the enactment of mandatory sentencing and three strikes laws. Those in favor of tough correctional policies argue that threats of long-term incarceration or execution help reduce crime by deterring potential criminals and repeat offenders from committing criminal acts because they can be certain of their sentence if caught. Others suggest that punitive measures do little to deter crime, have led to overcrowding in jails and prisons, and place a large strain on states' fiscal resources.

One of the defining characteristics of correction policies in the Unites States is the high rate of imprisonment. Incarceration rates in federal and state prisons, 738 per 100,000 persons in 2005, have reached unprecedented levels, making imprisonment much more likely in the United States than in any other Western democracy. According to the Bureau of Justice Statistics, if incarceration rates remain unchanged in the United States, an estimated one of every 15 persons will serve time in prison in their lifetime.

Not only are imprisonment rates in the United States the highest among Western democracies, correction policies across the United States also tend to be more punitive in other aspects. Among advanced Western democracies, only the United States retains and uses the death penalty. At the state level, the presence and use of the death penalty varies across state correction systems because STATE GOVERN-MENTS have significant discretion in deciding not only whether to enact a death penalty law, but among those states that have such a law, how often criminal offenders are sentenced to death. These differences in states' propensity to enact death penalty laws and the rate in which executions are carried out is largely determined by the level of political support for the death penalty among citizens, elected officials, and judges within each STATE. Currently, 38 of the 50 U.S. states retain the death penalty, and combining each of the states' death row inmates brings the total to more than 3,000. Of the 16 states that carried out death penalty executions in 2005 (all by lethal injection), Texas had the greatest number, with a total of 19, while Connecticut, Florida, Maryland, Delaware, and Mississippi each executed the fewest, with one each.

The increasingly punitive nature of corrections policy in the United States is also reflected in the growth and diffusion of mandatory sentencing and three strikes laws. The move toward mandatory minimum sentences for specific crimes began as early as the 1970s, gained speed during the "drug war" of the 1980s, and culminated in the spread of three strikes legislation in the 1990s. Under mandatory sentencing, judges are required to impose minimum periods of incarceration for a specific crime. By 1994, all 50 states had adopted some version of mandatory sentencing laws for certain crimes.

In a similar vein, three strikes laws require judges to sentence criminal offenders convicted of three felonies to a mandatory and extended period of incarceration. The severity of sanctions imposed by three strikes laws is perhaps best exemplified in California, which enacted its three strikes law in 1994. Under the California law, a criminal offender convicted of a felony but who also has two prior convictions for "serious or violent felonies" is sentenced to three times the normal presumptive term (to be served consecutively), or 25 years to life, whichever is longer. Three strikes laws diffused dramatically across the U.S. states during the early to mid-1990s; 24 states adopted three strikes laws between the end of 1993 and the end of 1995.

If the rise in imprisonment rates, three strikes and mandatory sentencing laws, and the use of the death penalty are indicative of an overall trend toward tougher sanctions and punishments for criminal behavior in the United States since the early 1980s, a key question remains: What exactly is driving these punitive policies? One strong possibility is that crime rates have significantly increased in the United States over the past two decades, leading policy makers and citizens alike to support greater efforts at putting criminal offenders behind bars and expanding the use of "get tough on crime" policies. However, research suggests that this is not the case. In fact, the rise in punitive correction policies has been largely independent of the crime rate in the United States.

Thus, if the rise in punitive corrections policies is not directly connected to the crime rate, what is the answer? The driving force appears to be political in nature. To better understand how politics has played such a critical role in the rise in tougher corrections-related policies, it is helpful to take a look back at recent political history.

Corrections and public safety policy before the early 1960s were generally viewed as a subject for practitioners and technocrats—those who had the greatest amount of expertise on the subject—while elected leaders gave it little public attention. However, as crime rates began to rise during the early 1960s, the issue became central to national partisan politics in the 1964 presidential election. During this time, the Democratic and Republican Parties appeared to follow two divergent paths over how best to solve the crime problem. Republicans, focusing on "wedge" issues such as crime and welfare in an attempt to secure votes from politically leaning Democratic voters, tended to blame rising crime rates on bad choices made by individuals, lenient judges, and soft punishments. Because of this, the Republican policy prescription followed a deterrence and incapacitation approach that promoted increased arrests, higher rates of incarceration, stricter probation monitoring, and mandatory sentencing aimed at dissuading criminal activity by removing offenders from the larger community. In contrast, liberal Democrats viewed rising crime as a result of structural problems such as urban poverty and lack of job skills. They promoted policies aimed at the "root" causes of crime and not tougher sanctions.

When Ronald Reagan was elected president in 1980, crime control policy got further detached from its technical, less political roots of the 1950s and came front and center in America's "morality politics" fight of the 1980s. In the process, the crime issue became closely connected to an ongoing cultural debate in the United States about what social ideals were most valued and what it meant for citizens to lead "just" and "righteous" lives. As part of this debate, the crime issue has often been portrayed by elected leaders, INTEREST GROUPS, and the MEDIA in broad, politically polarizing ways and has been used to help define what it means for individuals to act responsibly or irresponsibly and what constitutes moral and immoral behavior. Moreover, there was a renewed dissatisfaction with what were perceived to be the leniency of judges and the sense that convicted felons were not receiving sufficiently harsh treatment for the crimes they were committing. In short, the debate surrounding the crime issue became emotionally charged, and, as a result, support for punitive policies such as increased arrests, more incarcerations, and longer sentences, all driven by emotional and symbolic rhetoric, became the norm.

Not wanting to be caught on the "wrong" side of a salient political debate laced in moralistic terms, risk-averse Democrats concluded that the only way to defend against law and order politics as defined in the 1980s and into the 1990s was to "get to the right of Republicans." In other words, many Democrats felt that in order to gain public support on the crime issue and win elections, Democrats had to be as tough as or tougher than Republicans on the issue. This shift created a convergence on the crime issue among Democrats and Republicans, lending enough political support to form legislative majorities in support of tough corrections policies at both the federal and state levels of government.

The rise in the number of people behind bars in the United States, a growing number of whom are serving mandatory sentences, has important spillover implications for states' correctional systems. One of the most prevalent problems is overcrowding in prisons and jails. With more prisons across the states filled beyond their designed capacity, some have argued that states need to allocate more money for new prison construction. This is much easier said than done, however, as construction of new prisons often comes to a grinding halt due to local political concerns and the NIMBY (not in my back yard) problem. The NIMBY problem occurs in situations in which the public supports a policy in a general sense—for example, the building of a new prison—but does not want a new prison built in its neighborhood. Thus, in many local communities, building new prisons is widely unpopular because of concerns about local public safety. Some states' inability to sufficiently increase prison capacity to meet the demand has forced prisons to release some less-violent prisoners back to the community before they have served their full sentences.

Many argue that simply building more prisons to ease the problem of overcrowding is misguided. Critics of new prison construction often point to the high fiscal costs connected to state correction systems, whereby rising prison costs have helped drain state coffers strapped for money needed to pay for other valued public services such as education, health care, and protecting the environment. Instead of building more prisons, it is argued that policy makers need to find ways to reduce existing prison populations. High rates of recidivism among offenders released from prison after serving their sentences is one area that has received attention recently. Although tracking recidivism rates can be technically difficult, the latest data from the Bureau of Justice Statistics shows approximately 25 percent of prisoners released from prison are rearrested and returned to prison with a new sentence three years after being released. To help reduce this "revolving door" effect, advocates of corrections reform suggest that correction systems need to do a better job of preparing prisoners for reentry into community life by providing prisoners greater access to drug rehabilitation, job training, and other education programs while serving out their sentences. Raising the likelihood that released prisoners will become productive members of society may serve as a long-term solution to the prison overcrowding problem.

The extent to which prisons provide rehabilitation and reentry programs to prisoners varies widely. Some prisons have high-quality reentry programs that are used by a large number of prisoners, others have programs that are poorly run and underused, while still others have no programs at all. States' fiscal capacities and support for rehabilitation programs among elected leaders and prison officials explain much of the variation in access to prisoner reentry programs across states' correctional systems. Whether status quo correctional policies remain or whether significant reform is in the making is, in the end, a highly emotional political question that will continue to play a prominent role in domestic policy debates in the United States in the coming years.

Further Reading

Beckett, Katherine. *Making Crime Pay: Law and Order in Contemporary American Politics*. New York: Oxford University Press, 1997; Lin, Ann Chih. *Reform in the Making: The Implementation of Social Policy in Prison*. Princeton, N.J.:, Princeton University Press, 2000; Pastore, Ann L., and Kathleen Maguire, eds. *Sourcebook of Criminal Justice Statistics*. 31st ed. Available online. URL: http://www.albany.edu/sourcebook/. Accessed July 29, 2006; Smith, Kevin B. "The Politics of Punishment: Evaluating Political Explanations of Incarceration Rates." *Journal of Politics* 66, no. 3 (2004): 925–938; Tonry, Michael, "Why Are U.S. Incarceration Rates So High?" *Crime and Delinquency* 45, no. 4 (1999): pp. 419–437.

—Garrick L. Percival

county government

The county is a unit of local government. Other local units include cities, towns, townships, and SPECIAL DISTRICTS. Unlike cities and towns, counties are not municipal corporations. They are not formed by means of local residents sending forth petitions to the STATE GOVERNMENT. Counties are subunits of states, with their territorial limits and governmental powers defined by state governments. There are 3,034 counties in the United States. County-type governments are called parishes in Louisiana and boroughs in Alaska. There are no county governments in Connecticut and Rhode Island. In addition, there are 34 consolidated city-county governments. Examples of this type include Baltimore, Maryland; Denver, Colorado; Indianapolis, Indiana; Jacksonville, Florida; Nashville, Tennessee; New York, New York; Philadelphia, Pennsylvania; Saint Louis, Missouri; and San Francisco, California. There is a mixture of form and scope among the counties in the United States.

Counties vary greatly in physical size and population. The smallest county in terms of physical size is Arlington County, Virginia, which occupies 26 square miles. The biggest is North Slope, Alaska, which occupies 87,860 square miles, which is slightly larger than Great Britain. In terms of population, the smallest is Loving County, Texas, which has 67 residents. The largest is Los Angeles County, California, which has 9,519,338 inhabitants. If Los Angeles County were a STATE, it would rank ninth in population. Despite this great range in physical size and population, the average county contains approximately 600 square miles—a square with 24 miles on each side—and less than 50,000 inhabitants.

The modern county in the United States has its origin in the English shire. An earl ruled the shire with the assistance of the shire court. The principal officer of the shire court was the "shire reeve," the ancestor of the modern office of "sheriff." The sheriff collected taxes and presided over the shire court. After the Norman Conquest in 1066, the shires took on the French name *counties*, and earls were stripped of their office, leaving the title as one signifying nobility and not necessarily the holding of an office. Further change greeted the English county when King Edward III (1312–77) added the office of JUSTICE OF THE PEACE. A justice of the peace exercised executive powers in a county, replacing many of the duties previously performed by the sheriff.

When English government was transferred to the American colonies, the county government structure was stronger in the South than in the Mid-Atlantic and New England colonies. While many county officials in the colonial period were appointed, the early 19th century saw significant reforms of county officer selection. Commissioners, clerks, coroners, sheriffs, and justices of the peace became elected offices in many states. This development continued to the point that many counties have several directly elected executives today.

The relationship between the county and state was firmly established by what came to be known as Dillon's rule. In the Iowa case of *Merriam v. Moody's Executors* (1868), Justice John Dillon of the Iowa Supreme Court established the doctrine that counties and all other local units of government had no inherent sovereignty and were subject to the will of the state legislature for their power and authority.

The Progressive Era of the late 19th and early 20th centuries had as one of its goals the modernization of county government. This could be achieved, so the argument went, through the replacement of many directly elected officers with appointed professionals, increased reliance of county officials on salaries instead of collected fees for income, and the advancement of the concept of "home rule." The home rule movement was a response of sorts to Dillon's rule. A state legislature could choose to allow a county the opportunity to exercise home rule, through which the county could exercise broad governing powers. California was the first state to adopt home rule provisions, and in 1913 Los Angeles County became the first county to exercise home rule. Today, approximately 2,300 counties in 38 states exercise some form of home rule.

The next great change came in the form of the automobile and the post–World War II rush into suburbia. As people moved in great numbers to unincorporated areas of counties, they came to expect the same level of services they received in cities. This forced counties to enter into policy areas that went beyond those normally associated with counties. County governments got into the business of building parks, libraries, and even hospitals and expanded their role in other policy areas.

The post–9/11 era has brought great challenges to county government as well. The county is a natural level of government for emergency planning, since it has the potential to coordinate the responses of many municipalities and act as an intermediary between smaller local units and the state and federal governments. The aftermath of Hurricane Katrina revealed all too well a fundamental truth about local government: When things go well, very few notice a job well done. When things go poorly, national attention can be thrust upon officials who, before the incident, were probably unknown outside a county. The cooperation of all local units in the face of disaster is vital. Such cooperation can be useful in day-to-day affairs of county governments as well.

Many counties are also members of regional associations, such as a council of governments. For example, most counties in California belong to regional associations. These organizations are quasi-governmental units devoted to cooperation and discussion on issues of regional concern, with mass transit being a prominent example. Counties within a regional association send representatives to serve on a board of directors, share research data, conduct studies, and resolve intercountry disputes. The two largest associations in California are the Southern California Association of Governments and the Association of Bay Area Governments. The Southern California association is composed of representatives from Imperial, Los Angeles, Orange, Riverside, San Bernardino, and Ventura Counties. The Bay Area group is composed of representatives from Alameda, Contra Costa, Marin, Napa, San Francisco, San Mateo, Santa Clara, and Solano Counties.

There are three main types of county government. The most common is the commission model. Approximately 1,600 counties have a commission form of government. Such counties are governed by a board of commissioners, also known as supervisors in some states. This board typically has the power to enact ordinances, approve budgets, and appoint nonelected county officials. The standard board has three to five members who are elected to four-year terms. This type of government is generally found in counties with smaller populations.

The second-most-frequent form of county government is the commission-administrator model. This form of government is similar to the council-manager form of government adopted by many cities and is a result of the reform-oriented mission of the Progressive Era.

The goal of this movement—with respect to local government—was to replace the tangled intricacies and intrigues of partisan political machines with technically adept cadres of professional administrators, thus hoping to separate the politics of local government from the policy outputs of local government. The Progressive belief was that formally trained experts would make better allocation decisions than elected officials who might be compromised by close ties to special interests. In fact, departments of political science, as they exist in colleges and universities in the United States, owe their origins to the desire by the Progressives to create an academically trained elite devoted to policy implementation.

Accordingly, in the commission-administrator form of government, the administrator is not elected. The administrator is selected—and removed, if necessary—by the county commission. While the commission sets the overall goals, the administrator is in charge of the day-to-day affairs of policy implementation. Like CITY MANAGERs, however, county administrators often find themselves tangled in the web of local politics. While the Progressive Era formed, in part, as a response to corrupt local practices, the rise in appointed positions since the advent of the Progressive Era has bureaucratized most of the local government system and placed local constituents even further from the decision-making process. The third and final form of county government addresses, to some extent, this concern by providing for an elected executive.

Approximately 400 counties use the commission-executive form of government. This form is a prominent one in counties with larger populations. In addition, Arkansas, Tennessee, and Kentucky require counties to elect executives. A county executive is elected directly by the voters. Like a president or GOVERNOR, the executive prepares the budget, appoints and removes nonelected county officials, makes policy recommendations, and has a veto power over ordinances passed by the county commission.

In addition to the commission, administrator, and executive, there are other officials common to county government in the United States, whatever form the government may take. The traditional county officials trace the origins of their offices back to Great Britain and are as follows: sheriff, prosecutor, attorney, clerk, treasurer, assessor, and coroner. Quite often, these officials are directly elected and hold significant autonomy to make and implement policy. In addition, counties may avail themselves of further offices, which can be either appointed or elected. Some examples of which are as follows: register of deeds, auditor, road commissioner, surveyor, engineer, and school superintendent.

The desire by counties to have several directly elected executive officials, known as a plural executive, stems from a movement known as Jacksonian Democracy, named after President Andrew Jackson (1829–37), who is credited with inspiring the rise of mass POLITICAL PARTICIPATION in the United States. Local and state governments that have plural executive structures, in which there are several directly elected executive officers, are legacies of Jacksonian Democracy. In fact, the Progressive movement formed, in part, to deal with the perceived excesses of Jacksonian Democracy. In some county governments, an appointed administrator—a legacy of the Progressive movement—serves alongside an elected sheriff, prosecutor, or clerk, officials whose legacy is derived from Jacksonian Democracy. The very structure of county government reveals the history of American democracy and the tensions that have developed along the way.

The functions of county government have changed over the years as well, but many areas for which counties are responsible today have remained similar to those that existed in the colonial period: courts, jails, law enforcement, records, roads, social services, and taxes. New areas of county responsibility in the 21st century include, but are not limited to, the following: consumer protection, economic development, fire protection, health care, recreation, sanitation, transportation, and water quality. In addition, some counties have contracts with local governments within their boundaries to share the costs for certain services. This is called the Lakewood Plan, after the California city that initially adopted this method of providing services. The most common policy areas that fall under the Lakewood Plan are fire and police services.

The state or federal government mandates most of a county's policy responsibilities. Social services account for more than 60 percent of county expenditures while education is next, with a little more than 10 percent. This mandated spending restricts the budget flexibility of the modern county, and even though state aid often does not cover the costs of state mandates, state revenues are a significant source of county funds. A recent study by the U.S. Census Bureau estimates that 46 percent of county revenue is derived from state governments. Property taxes account for 20 percent of revenues. Charges and fees account for another 20 percent, while sales taxes account for 5 percent. Federal aid and other revenue sources make up the balance. In order to maintain the flow of state and federal aid, many counties are even willing to retain the services of professional lobbyists who will bring a county's needs to the attention of key policy makers. In addition, the National Association of Counties, founded in 1935, represents the broader interests of counties at the federal level.

The modern American county faces a variety of challenges. Counties are forced to confront the frightening possibility of terrorist attacks, yet, at the same time, counties must also consider the most desirable location for a park or library. On one hand, they may be dealing with the aftermath of a natural disaster while, on the other hand, dealing with the complexity of water drainage and its effect on an endangered species. While it is true that cities, states, and the federal government deal with complex issues as well, no other level of government is required to do more while strapped with a frustrating web of constraints imposed on it by other levels of government. In many ways, county governments are the unsung heroes of the American political system.

Further Reading
Austin, David. "Border Counties Face Immigration Pressure: Locals Shoulder Growing Law Enforcement Costs." *American City and County* 121, no. 4 (2006): 24; Benton, J. Edwin. "An Assessment of Research on American Counties." *Public Administration Review* 65, no. 4 (2005): 462–474; Bowman, Ann O'M., and Richard C. Kearney. *State and Local Government.* 3rd ed. Boston: Houghton-Mifflin, 2006; Coppa, Frank J. *County Government: A Guide to Efficient and Accountable Government.* Westport, Conn.: Praeger, 2000; "Local Leaders Lean on D.C. Lobbyists." *American City and County* 118, no. 2 (2003): 10; National Association of Counties. *An Overview of County Government.* Available online. URL: http://www.naco.org/Content/NavigationMenu/About_ Counties/County_Government/Default271.htm. Accessed July 25, 2006; National Association of Counties. *History of County Government.* Available online. URL: http://www.naco.org/Template.cfm?Section=History_of_County_Government&Template=/ContentManagement/ContentDisplay.cfm&ContentID=14268. Accessed July 25, 2006; Ostrom, Vincent, Robert Bish, and Elinor Ostrom. *Local Government in the United States.* San Francisco: ICS Press, 1988; Swartz, Nikki. "Housing Boom Spells Property Tax Gloom: Local Governments Try to Give Residents Some Relief." *American City and County* 120, no. 11 (2005): 20–22; Wager, Paul. *County Government across the Nation.* Chapel Hill: University of North Carolina Press, 1950.

—Brian P. Janiskee

county manager (executive)

COUNTY GOVERNMENT has a long and important history in the American political system and can be traced back even before the American founding to its use in England as the administrative arm of the national government (known in England as the "shire" rather than the "county"). The first county government in the United States was formed at James City, Virginia, in 1634; 48 of the 50 states now use the county form of government, although Alaska calls them "boroughs" and Louisiana calls them "parishes." The remaining two states, Connecticut and Rhode Island, although divided into geographic, unorganized areas called "counties" for the purposes of elections, do not have functioning county governments according to the U.S. Census Bureau.

As in England, counties in the United States operate primarily as the administrative arm of the STATE in which they are found, but many also function as local public service providers with responsibilities for economic development, hospitals, parks, libraries, and many other traditional local services. According to the most recent CENSUS, there are 3,033 counties across the country, with Hawaii and Delaware having the fewest (three each) and Texas the most (254). In addition, currently there are 33 consolidated city-county governments whereby cities and counties have combined their governments for a variety of reasons, including economies of scale, elimination of duplicated services, and the simple fact that some cities have grown so large that their boundaries are practically coterminous with the surrounding county. (Jacksonville-Duval, Florida, is an example of this consolidated type of structure.)

Further, counties vary widely in geographic size and population. Counties range in area from 26 to 97,860 square miles (Arlington County, Virginia, represents the former, and the North Slope Borough, Alaska, represents the latter) and from populations of 67 to more than 9.5 million (Loving County, Texas, and Los Angeles County, California, respectively). Despite the range in size, the majority of counties (75 percent) still have populations less than 50,000.

Three primary forms of county government exist in the United States: commission, commission-administrator/Manager, and council-executive. (The last of these is the focus of this entry, but it cannot be fully understood without some attention paid to the other two.) The commission form is the oldest and most traditional model for county government. This model is characterized by an elected county commission (sometimes known as a board of supervisors) that has both legislative authority (e.g., adopt ordinances, levy taxes, and adopt a budget) and executive or administrative authority (e.g., hire and fire employees and implement policy). Importantly, many significant administrative responsibilities are performed by independently elected constitutional officers such as the county sheriff, county clerk, and county treasurer. In short, the commission form embraces an elected board that has both legislative and administrative authority alongside a number of other elected positions that possess independent administrative authority in specific task areas.

The second form, the commission-administrator, is similar to the standard commission form in many respects with the exception that the elected board of county commissioners appoints an administrator (or manager) who serves at the pleasure of the elected commission. As part of the municipal reform movement of the late 1800s and early 1900s, government reformers argued for increased professionalism in county government, with more effective administration and clearer accountability to the voters. This, it was noted, could be accomplished by hiring a professional administrator who would separate him- or herself from many of the political functions of county government and, instead, would concentrate his or her energies on service management. This appointed administrator relieves the commission from many of the day-to-day responsibilities of running county government and is often vested with significant powers to hire and fire department heads, oversee policy implementation and coordination, and develop and implement the county budget. This new form of county government was first adopted by Iredell County, North Carolina, in 1927.

The third form of county government, the council-executive, has as its most distinguishing feature an elected executive (or administrator). Among all three models, the principle of SEPARATION OF POWERS is most clearly reflected in this governing structure. In its purest form, there are two distinct "branches" of county government, the legislative and the executive. The elected county commission heads the legislative branch of county government and, as a result, maintains legislative authority. In the second branch, there is an elected executive who heads the executive branch and maintains executive or administrative authority but who also traditionally has the ability to veto ordinances passed by the county board of commissioners. This form of government most closely resembles that found at the national level, where Congress has legislative authority and the president has executive authority who can veto legislation found unacceptable. Here, too, the county commission (similar to Congress) can override an executive veto, typically by a supermajority vote.

Not unlike the commission-administrator form, the county executive has general responsibility for the day-to-day operations of county administration (again, outside those areas for which other elected constitutional officers have responsibility, e.g., the elected sheriff or county assessor). In addition, the executive often represents the county at ceremonial events, has responsibility for providing expertise and advice to the larger elected commission, and must oversee implementation of county policy more generally defined. Again, similar to the commission-administrator, the elected executive has the power to hire and fire department heads under his or her control (often with the consent of the commission).

Although the standard commission form is in use in the majority of counties in the United States, many are shifting their structure to include either an appointed administrator (commission-administrator) or an elected executive (commission-executive). In part, this is due to the increasingly complex local government landscape, in which the needs of a professional administrator are becoming more apparent. No longer in larger, more densely populated and urban counties can all day-to-day administrative functions be effectively handled by an elected board of commissioners. Indeed, Arkansas, Kentucky, and Tennessee mandate that counties have a separate executive elected by voters.

Supporters of the commission-executive form of county government argue that there are several distinct advantages to this institutional arrangement. Among the most prominent is the idea that an elected executive is more responsive to the public interest than an appointed (or absent) chief administrative officer. Because they are answerable at the next election, an elected county executive will be more mindful of the public's concerns. Second, an elected executive provides much-needed political leadership in a diverse community. This executive is less likely to resign (or be fired) during a political crisis. Third, this model contains the best reflection of a system of CHECKS AND BALANCES available. Through the veto (and veto override), each "branch" can express its vision of policy that it believes is in the best interest of the community. Fourth, counties with an at-large elected executive have a single individual (the elected county executive) who represents the entire county. For good or for bad, this single individual can be a powerful voice of community government.

Among the arguments against an elected executive, one of the most important is that it is often difficult to find a single individual who has both excellent political and administrative skills. Although not mutually exclusive, as the demands placed on county governments increase, it is often a full-time job to keep up with the latest public management practices and technology developments. In order to address this challenge, many counties provide a professional administrative staff that can offer support to the elected executive. This institutional arrangement combines many of the advantages of the elected executive along with the skills of a professional administrator.

Counties, regardless of form, remain a valuable feature of American government. When citizens demand more political responsiveness and increased administrative professionalism and expertise from their public officials, the elected county executive will remain an important option in county government.

Further Reading

Braaten, Kaye. "The Rural County." In *Forms of Local Government*, edited by Roger L. Kemp. Jefferson, N.C.: McFarland & Co., 1999; DeSantis, Victor S. "County Government: A Century of Change." In *International City Managers Association Municipal Yearbook 1989*. Washington, D.C.: ICMA; Duncombe, Herbert Sydney. "Organization of County Governments." In *Forms of Local Government*, edited by Roger L. Kemp. Jefferson, N.C.: McFarland & Co., 1999; Fosler, R. Scott. "The Suburban County." In *Forms of Local Government*, edited by Roger L. Kemp. Jefferson, N.C.: McFarland & Co., 1999; National Association of Counties. "The History of County Government." Available online. URL: http://www.naco.org/Content/NavigationMenu/About_Counties/History_of_County_Government/Default983.htm. Accessed July 17, 2006; Salant, Tanis J. "Trends in County Government Structure." In *ICMA Municipal Yearbook 2004*.

—Robert A. Schuhmann

governor

The governor is a STATE's chief executive officer, directly elected by the people in all 50 states and in most cases for a four-year term. Generally speaking, governors play the same role within their states that the president plays on the national stage, setting the state's agenda, acting as its main spokesperson, and managing crises. However, the wide variance across states in terms of the formal powers of governors makes it somewhat difficult to generalize about the office.

In the country's early years, most governors had few powers, a clear reflection of the suspicion of executive power shared by most Americans at the time. Under English rule, the king had appointed colonial governors, who could essentially ignore the legislative will of the people's representatives. Between the perceived abuses by the British Crown and his appointed governors, many early Americans equated executive power with tyranny and sought to limit the opportunity for such abuses. As a result, the early STATE CONSTITUTIONS invested the legislative branch

Governors Tim Pawlenty (speaking, R-MN), Joe Manchin (D-WV), and Jennifer Granholm (D-MI) at a meeting of the National Governors Association, July 21, 2007 *(National Governors Conference)*

with nearly all power; in nine of the original 13 states, the legislature itself elected the governor (and in most cases for one-year terms). In only three states, South Carolina, New York, and Massachusetts, did governors have the authority to veto legislation, and South Carolina rescinded that authority by 1790. In addition, governors had little control over state agencies, as most legislatures retained the power to appoint individuals to these posts. Most indicative of the widespread distrust of executive power, in both Georgia and Pennsylvania, the first state constitutions established a committee to constitute the executive branch.

The rise of Jacksonian Democracy in the 1820s reestablished some legitimacy to executive power, and the populism associated with this movement led to the direct election of governors in most states. This change provided governors with a base of power outside the legislature and generally added to the prestige of the office, though officeholders continued to face significant institutional restraints, including the inability to veto legislation in most states. Somewhat ironically, the populist reforms also undermined gubernatorial power by establishing separate elections for other state executive positions, such as U.S. ATTORNEY GENERAL and secretary of state, a tradition that continues to the present in most states.

Nearly every state has rewritten its constitution since this era, and the powers of governors have waxed and waned according to the mood of the electorate at the time. During periods of perceived legislative inefficiency, governors were granted greater authority. At times, when CORRUPTION was seen as a key problem, governors were stripped of powers that could potentially be abused. There may also be cultural factors that led some states to expand or restrict executive power independently of the broader trends of national public opinion. As a result, state constitutions vary widely in terms of the specific powers of governors, and these differences make it difficult to generalize about governors' powers presently. Nevertheless, it is clear that governors have far more power than their early American counterparts did.

Scholars have identified several formal powers (those that are constitutional or granted by statute) shared by all governors to varying degrees. Among these are tenure potential, APPOINTMENT POWERS, budgetary authority, veto power, and judicial power.

Regarding tenure potential, balancing the need for a strong executive against the risks of abuses by that individual creates a challenge in determining the appropriate length of a governor's term in office and whether he or she should be limited in the number of terms he or she can serve; 48 states currently establish four-year terms for governors, modeled after the PRESIDENCY. New Hampshire and Vermont allow governors to serve only two-year terms, consistent with the "town hall" democratic spirit in those states. A large majority of states (36) limit their governors to two consecutive terms, and Virginia permits the governor only a single four-year term. The remaining 11 states, which can be found in all regions of the country, allow an unlimited number of four-year terms for officeholders. The increasing powers of governors can be seen clearly in the trends pertaining to tenure potential. As recently as 1960, 15 states limited governors to a single four-year term, and another 16 states established only two-year terms for their chief executives. All else being equal, longer terms mean more independence and provide more opportunities for leadership.

Although most of the early governors lacked the authority of the appointment power entirely, all governors today have some ability to appoint individuals to administrative agencies. Even here, though, substantial disparities exist across states. For example, the governors of New Jersey and Hawaii appoint officials as significant as attorney general and treasurer, major positions that are elected separately in most states. Other governors have much less discretion in this area. In North Carolina, for instance, top officials in the departments of labor, education, and agriculture are all elected statewide. Even in that case, the governor does hold substantial appointment powers, as North Carolina's governor appoints individuals to serve on more than 400 boards and commissions. And all governors are empowered to appoint temporary replacements to fill vacancies in a wide variety of offices, including the U.S. Congress. In nearly all cases, gubernatorial appointments require the approval of the state legislature or some other body acting on its behalf. The importance of the appointment power is often underappreciated. The people who head such agencies inevitably retain some degree of discretion, and their administrative choices can sometimes produce very different outcomes. A governor with strong ideological views on welfare, for example, will find that his or her policy vision is more fully realized if he or she can appoint a like-minded individual to direct those programs. The logic is most clearly seen with respect to judicial appointments. Unlike FEDERAL JUDGES, most state-level judges are elected to office, but in six states, governors have the power to nominate individuals to judgeships. Although these nominees must be confirmed by the state legislature, it is easy to see how a governor could have a strong influence on the legal process as a result of his or her powers of appointment.

When considering a governor's budgetary authority, the growth of the role of the governor in the BUDGET PROCESS strongly mirrors the same pattern at the federal level. Legislative bodies long held the responsibility for submitting a budget to the executive, who could then accept or reject the offer from the legislature. Governors possessed limited authority in such a process. In the 1920s, around the same time that Congress delegated the budgetary responsibility to the president, most STATE LEGISLATURES were likewise assigning budgetary power to governors. By centralizing the process in the governor's office, the budget is arguably more coherent but certainly more closely reflects what the governor's priorities are. There is again some variance across states. The state legislature in West Virginia, for example, may not increase the amount of the governor's proposal. But there is much less variance across states in this area than in other areas of power. For the most part, governors present a budget to the legislature, which is then authorized to modify it as the majority wishes. Of course, the legislature is constrained by the fact that governors may reject the legislature's counterproposal.

The veto power, which is the ability to reject legislative acts, is probably the most significant formal power held by governors. Although all legislatures have the authority to override a veto, the supermajority that is in most cases required means that overrides rarely occur. An extreme example of this was in New Mexico, where Governor Gary Johnson had pledged to veto any bill that increased the size of government; of the more than 700 bills he vetoed in the 1990s, the legislature was able to override only *one*. By itself, the veto power is incredibly strong, but the governors of 43 states have an additional power to veto portions of bills, a power known as the line-item veto. This authority emerged in response to budgetary crises during the Great Depression, intended to have the effect of controlling excessive spending. In recent years, the line-item veto has extended far beyond mere APPROPRIATIONS, and governors have been remarkably bold and creative in exercising this authority. Most notably, Wisconsin governor Tommy Thompson (1987–2001) wielded his veto pen very freely, striking brief passages or even single words such as "not" from legislation, essentially reversing the meaning. In 2006, Governor Ernie Fletcher of Kentucky vetoed a portion of a budget bill that would have required the election of judges in that state; by doing so, Fletcher retained for himself the power to nominate judges. Whether he should have been praised for his clever exercise of the line-item veto or criticized for subverting the will of the people through the legislature is largely a matter of perspective, one that illustrates the contradictions of executive power.

In a sense, governors also have the ability to veto decisions of the judiciary by issuing pardons or reprieves for crimes. Strictly speaking, governors possess the power of clemency, which encompasses a family of actions that reduce the penalties for a crime. The most extraordinary recent example of this authority was the 2003 decision by Illinois governor George Ryan to commute the sentences of all 167 death row inmates in that state to life in prison. The risk of

abuse here is obvious and not at all hypothetical: In 1923, Oklahoma governor John Walton pardoned hundreds of criminals and was later convicted for taking bribes from most of them. Walton's case is unusual but not unique. A series of Texas governors granted thousands of pardons between 1915 and 1927, eventually prompting lawmakers to establish a Board of Pardons and Paroles to review such cases. Even today, there is an independent clemency board in that state that can reject any gubernatorial act of clemency. Other states established similar restrictions on governors. In California, the state supreme court must approve any reprieves granted to recidivist felons. Additionally, many states require that governors provide the legislature with a written explanation of every act of clemency. While governors have a substantial amount of latitude in this area, most of them face some restrictions or regulations regarding their clemency power.

While there are substantial differences across states in terms of the powers of governors, there is considerably less variance in terms of the expectations of the officeholder. Generally speaking, the key responsibilities of a governor include being its chief legislator, its crisis manager, and its main spokesperson.

As the chief legislator, the governor's role in the legislative process is very similar to the president's. Formally, governors recommend legislation through a "state of the state" address, and as explained above, they propose the state's budget and possess the powerful tool of the veto. But their actual responsibilities in lawmaking are much greater than these formal powers suggest. As former North Carolina governor Terry Sanford (1961–65) explained, "Few major undertakings ever get off the ground without his support and leadership. The governor sets the agenda for the public debate; frames the issues; decides on the timing; and can blanket the state with good ideas by using his access to the mass media." Though legislators obviously initiate most bills, major proposals are likely to begin in the executive branch. While representatives often focus on more narrow concerns affecting their own districts, governors have a less parochial perspective that centralizes the legislative agenda in that office. Additionally, since many legislatures are part time, governors in those states have an increased opportunity to dictate the state's agenda. To be sure, governors do need the support of legislatures to enact their programs, which is often a difficult task, particularly if the legislature is controlled by the opposing party. Nevertheless, just as the president is the political center of the national government, governors are the most important political figures in their states, and productive lawmaking depends on their leadership.

Governors must also play the role of crisis manager. From natural disasters to urban riots, governors often find themselves facing situations they had not anticipated. As with presidents, governors are often defined by their responses to such crises. Formally, governors have the authority to act as commander-in-chief of the state's National Guard (though the guard may be federalized, in which case the governor is no longer in charge). Ideally, the governor can employ the guard to quell disturbances, provide emergency supplies, and generally to restore peace. However, the most well-known examples of such actions are now seen quite negatively. In 1957, Arkansas governor Orval Faubus (1955–67) ordered units of the National Guard to Little Rock's Central High School to maintain peace in the town by preventing African American students from entering the building, as had been ordered to do by the U.S. SUPREME COURT. Several years later, Ohio governor James Rhodes (1963–71, 1975–83) installed nearly 1,000 National Guard troops on the campus of Kent State University to restore order following several days of antiwar protests. On May 4, 1970, confused troops opened fire on student protestors, killing four. Though both of these governors would serve additional terms in office, their historical reputations are defined by these events, which were largely beyond their control.

The role of chief spokesperson has both substantive and symbolic significance, occasionally at the same time. On the substantive side, as explained above, the governors are expected to propose solutions to the major problems facing the state and to articulate those proposals to lawmakers and citizens. They are also expected to negotiate with companies and even foreign countries to locate businesses in their states, and most governors now have offices in Washington, D.C., for the purposes of LOBBYING the federal government to advance the state's interests, as well. Symbolically, governors represent the state at major ceremonial functions, such as dedications of new hospitals and social events for distinguished guests. While such functions may seem trivial, they are very time consuming and an indispensable part of the job. The substantive and symbolic aspects of this role sometimes merge when a state faces a crisis. During the CIVIL RIGHTS MOVEMENT, southern governors such as Ross Barnett of Mississippi (1960–64) actively led the (unsuccessful) attempt to prevent James Meredith from becoming the first black student to enroll at the all-white University of Mississippi. By contrast, Georgia governor Jimmy Carter (1971–75) signified a new era of CIVIL RIGHTS by declaring in his inaugural address that "the time for racial discrimination is over."

Like presidents, governors have considerable political power, which has increased substantially since the early days of the country, but also like presidents, governors ultimately have more responsibility than formal powers. They are expected to do far more than they can do alone and depend heavily on a cooperative legislature to enact their programs. Some governors, however, have more powers to facilitate governing than others due to factors such as longer tenure potential or a greater line-item veto authority. Regardless of their formal powers, though, governors' leadership skills matter tremendously, as they are positioned to set the state's legislative agenda and to establish the moral tone for the state. Thus, it may be appropriate that they are the ones held responsible for a state's well being, even if they are not fully invested with the power to do so.

Further Reading

Behn, Robert D., ed. *Governors on Governing*. New York: Greenwood Press, 1991; Beyle, Thad. "The Governors." In *Politics in the American States: A Comparative Analysis*. 8th ed., edited by Virginia Gray, Russell L. Hanson, and Herbert Jacob. Washington, D.C.: Congressional Quarterly Press, 2003; Beyle, Thad L., and Lynn R. Muchmore, eds. *Being Governor: The View from the Office*. Durham, N.C.: Duke Press Policy Studies, 1983; Dresang, Dennis L., and James J. Gosling. *Politics and Policy in American States and Communities*. 6th ed. Boston: Allyn & Bacon, 2006; Ferguson, Margaret R., ed. *The Executive Branch of State Government*. Santa Barbara, Calif.: ABC-CLIO, 2006; Saffell, David C., and Harry

Basehart. *State and Local Government: Politics and Public Policies*. 8th ed. Boston: McGraw Hill, 2005; Smith, Kevin B., Alan Greenblatt, and John Buntin. *Governing States and Localities*. Washington, D.C.: Congressional Quarterly Press, 2005. National Governors Association. Available online. URL: www.nga.org. Accessed May 23, 2006.

—William Cunion

initiative (direct democracy)

Historically, institution of an initiative process and other tools of DIRECT (PARTICIPATORY) DEMOCRACY were responses to corrupt politicians who demonstrated that they could not be trusted to promote the public good. Initiatives and REFERENDUMs were first adopted in South Dakota in the mid-1880s, and early use of these political innovations was championed by what were considered radical political groups at the time, such as the Populist Party and the Socialist Party. In the next two decades, these came to be advanced by politicians and others associated with the Progressive Era, a chief concern of which was the intrusion of big business into the political process to the detriment of working people. Other turn-of-the-century concerns advanced through the initiative process included Prohibition and women's suffrage. While the actual use of these tools declined during the 20th century, they have recently experienced a significant comeback, with around 100 now appearing during each two-year election cycle. It is no longer the case that initiatives are the tools of the average citizen. Rather, they seem increasingly to receive their support from big business and other special interests, from which the people once sought protection through these means.

The initiative is a tool of direct democracy whereby citizens can voice their preferences on issues of public concern directly through their votes on ballot initiatives, rather than through their representatives; other tools include referendums, or plebiscites, and recall elections. Use of mechanisms of direct democracy initiated by citizens serves to strengthen popular sovereignty, though these tools also present challenges to good governance in the pluralist setting, because directly appealing to and giving expression to the wishes of the people constitutes populism, not necessarily DEMOCRACY.

The initiative process allows citizens to raise legislative proposals and place them on the ballot. In about 24 states and the District of Columbia, an initiative may be placed on the ballot by an organized group with a sufficient number of citizens' signatures or by the state legislature or GOVERNOR. A direct initiative provides the public with the ability to raise legislative proposals and vote to approve them, bypassing the legislature, whereas indirect initiatives are submitted by the voters to the legislature and can be submitted directly to the voters only thereafter. In many cases, legislators or the governor have the power to sponsor ballot initiatives to further those ends they believe would not command a majority in their legislative assembly. When the government sponsors a ballot initiative, it risks the vote turning into a popular plebiscite on the government itself, especially when it goes down to defeat. As many as 17 states allow constitutional initiatives whereby the people can amend the state constitution. In all cases where the citizens propose legislation, there is a numerical requirement for getting the issue placed on the ballot, usually expressed as a percentage of the electorate or voters in the most recent regular general election. Article I of the U.S. CONSTITUTION prohibits popular initiatives in regard to federal legislation, as this is a congressional power that cannot be delegated.

A referendum, or plebiscite, is a form of direct democracy in which legislative or constitutional measures are proposed by a legislator to the voters for ratification. This is the usual form in which amendments to STATE CONSTITUTIONS occur and often the manner in which important categories of local government regulations such as high budget items or redevelopment plans are approved. The referendum allows for greater POLITICAL PARTICIPATION and can provide opportunities to educate and inform voters regarding important public issues. However, the referendum process relies on popular will, which may not be educated beyond how the referendum has been marketed to them and can be manipulated by officeholders to advance a favored political agenda, avoid responsibility for crafting sound legislation, or stall their political opponents.

Ballot initiatives and referendums are often used to pass laws regulating conduct that is disapproved by many people, such as drinking, drug use, or sexual behavior. While initiatives and referendums may on occasion supplement REPRESENTATIVE DEMOCRACY in cases of persistent congressional gridlock on important issues, such as taxation, for example, the populism of these tools may lead to abuse by unscrupulous politicians who seek power for themselves and not necessarily to effect sound public policy. In the past, democracy by plebiscite has provided a fig leaf for demagogueries and dictatorships because of the appearance of political leaders appealing and responding to popular will, which they have already formed to suit their unjust and undemocratic aims.

The right to recall elected government servants gives the public an additional degree of control over them beyond the ability to vote them out of office at each regular election and per their terms of office. A successful recall election dismisses an elected politician from office before his or her term of office has expired and so provides a potent tool of control over politicians in the democratic setting. Any serious threat of a recall gives a politician a clear warning of popular dissatisfaction with him or her and a clear indication of intent to remove him or her from office. Still, there may be a political motive behind encouraging a recall, one that only later becomes clearly apparent.

The initiative and other tools of direct democracy do, however, present challenges to orderly government by the people. While some people may believe that majority rule, in some form the standard by which direct democracy works in the United States, is always appropriate and legitimate, constitutional expert Cass Sunstein argues that it is, in fact, a caricature of rule by the people. In Sunstein's opinion, democracy works best when it is deliberative, and the role of the Constitution and its scheme of ACCOUNTABILITY in government is to ensure that constitutional protections of individual rights are respected even in the face of popular will to the contrary. While democracy implies rule of the people, deliberative democracy insists that a self-governing citizenry form and promote its preferences in an orderly way, one with the LIBERTY and EQUALITY of all citizens in mind. Hence, some of the issues of public morality that are often the subjects of popular initiatives and referendums are constitutionally troublesome because there may well be no filter in place to refine popular opinion to ensure it is in keeping with the

constitutional order. This becomes particularly vexing when popular will is moved to act on behalf of tradition, when the constitutional order would be better served by interrogating a traditional practice or understanding.

When initiatives are passed that exceed constitutional limits, it becomes the job of the courts to check the popular will, though this resolution brings the courts into the political arena, where their perceived legitimacy is at its lowest. In the republican democracy the founders worked out, sovereignty rests with the people, though this power is exercised through a system of governmental institutions that share this one fount of power and are characterized by CHECKS AND BALANCES. While the initiative and other tools of direct democracy are not inimical to the American political regime, when the system is working properly, recourse to them need only be made infrequently.

Further Reading

DuBois, Philip L., and Floyd Feeney. *Lawmaking by Initiative: Issues, Options, and Comparisons.* New York: Algora Publishing, 1998; Ellis, Richard J. *Democratic Delusions: The Initiative Process in America.* Lawrence: University Press of Kansas, 2002; Sunstein, Cass R. *Designing Democracies: What Constitutions Do.* Oxford: Oxford University Press, 2001.

—Gordon A. Babst

intergovernmental relations

For many years, government practitioners, the public, and even those in the academic community frequently used the terms *FEDERALISM* and *intergovernmental relations* interchangeably. However, conventional wisdom about the supposed synonymous meaning of these two terms eventually gave way to the understanding that they each refer to and describe two different, albeit related, phenomena. On one hand, federalism refers to the legal relationships between the national government and the states. On the other hand, intergovernmental relations can be conceptualized as the relations that occur or result from the interaction (both formal and informal) among popularly elected and/or full-time employed officials of different levels of government. Indeed, both William Anderson and Deil Wright emphasize that the concept

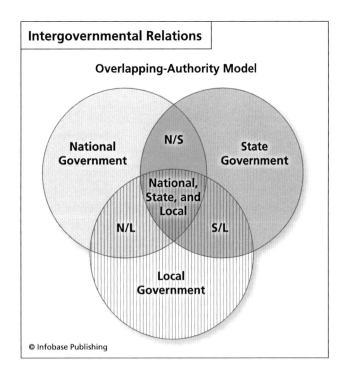

Intergovernmental Relations

Overlapping-Authority Model

National Government

N/S

State Government

National, State, and Local

N/L

S/L

Local Government

© Infobase Publishing

of intergovernmental relations has to be understood in terms of human behavior. More precisely, there are no intergovernmental relations but only relations among the officials in different governing units. In its simplest terms, intergovernmental relations are the continuous, day-to-day patterns of contact, knowledge, and evaluations of the officials who govern.

Other reasons exist for preferring intergovernmental relations to federalism. First, intergovernmental relations both recognize and analyze interactions among officials from all combinations of governmental entities at all levels, while federalism (although not precluding state-local links) has historically emphasized national-state relationships. Second, the intergovernmental relations concept transcends the mainstream legal focus found in federalism and includes a rich variety of informal and otherwise submerged actions and perceptions of officials. In addition, the concept contains no hierarchical status distinctions. That is, although it does not exclude the existence of such power differences, neither does it imply, as the concept of federalism often does, that the national level is the presumed superior. Finally, the concept of intergovernmental relations is more conducive to understanding and explaining how public policy is formulated and implemented.

In an effort to understand how the intergovernmental relations concept plays out or to simplify the complexities and realities of governance where several governments are involved, scholars have developed three models. These include the coordinate-authority, inclusive-authority, and overlapping-authority models. It would appear, based on endorsements from scholars, that the overlapping-authority model is the most representative of intergovernmental relations practice. The overlay among the circles suggests three characteristic attributes of the model: Large areas of governmental operations involve national, state, and local units (or officials) concurrently; the areas of autonomy or single-jurisdiction independence and full discretion are relatively small; and the authority and influence available to any one jurisdiction (or official) is considerably restricted. The restrictions create an authority pattern best described as bargaining.

Bargaining typically is defined as "negotiating the terms of a sale, exchange, or agreement." Within the framework of intergovernmental relations, sale is much less pertinent than exchange or agreement. More specifically, many areas of intergovernmental relations involve exchanges or agreements. A case in point is when the national government makes available a myriad of assistance programs to states and their local governments in *exchange* for their *agreement* to implement a program, carry out a project, or engage in any one of a wide range of activities. Naturally, as part of the bargain, the government receiving assistance (usually financial, but not necessarily) must typically agree to conditions such as the providing of matching funds or in-kind work and the satisfaction of accounting, reporting, auditing, and performance stipulations.

Students of American government and politics have identified seven phases, or periods, of intergovernmental relations. Each of these phases (some of which overlap) will be briefly described below with reference to the following: What policy areas dominated the public agenda? What dominant perceptions or mindsets did the chief intergovernmental relations participants have? What mechanisms or techniques were used to implement intergovernmental actions and objectives?

What is known as the conflict phase (the 1930s and before) is the early period of intergovernmental relations that focused on pinpointing the proper areas of governmental powers and jurisdiction and identifying the boundaries of officials' actions. This emphasis operated at the state and local levels as well as between national and STATE GOVERNMENTs. During this period, Dillon's rule became synonymous with state supremacy in state-local matters and was used to identify the exact limits of local government authority. The national, state, and local government officials who sought exact specification of their respective powers assumed that the powers would be mutually exclusive. Furthermore, officials appeared to have expected opposition and antagonism to be part of the usual process of determining who was empowered to do what.

Identifying roles and spelling out clear boundaries (typically through court interpretation of statutes and regulatory authority) were major features of the conflict period. The well-known U.S. SUPREME COURT case of *McCulloch v. Maryland* (1819), for instance, early on clearly instituted the conflict-oriented pattern in one policy area with specific relevance for intergovernmental relations—finances.

Although this case is perhaps better known for its interpretation of the U.S. CONSTITUTION's Necessary and Proper Clause and particularly for sustaining the power of the national government to establish a bank, it firmly established the PRECEDENT that state laws are invalid (null and void) if they conflict with the national government's delegated powers, laws enacted by Congress, or federal treaties. The preoccupation with separating or sorting out powers gave rise to the metaphor "layer-cake federalism" to describe exclusive or autonomous spheres for national, state, and local governments.

What is known as the cooperative phase occurred between the 1930s and the 1950s. Although there was always some degree of intergovernmental collaboration during the 19th and 20th centuries, such collaboration typically was not a significant or dominant feature in American political history. However, there was one period in which complementary and supportive relationships were most pronounced and had notable political consequences. That period is the cooperative phase, which was prominent for about two decades.

The principal issues of concern to the country during the period were the alleviation of the wide-spread economic suffering that occurred during the Great Depression and responses to international threats such as World War II and the Korean Conflict. Therefore, it was logical and natural for internal and external challenges to national survival to result in closer contact and cooperation between public officials at all levels of government. This increased cooperation took several and varied forms, but especially such innovations as national planning, tax credits, and formula-based grants-in-aid.

The principal intergovernmental relations mechanism as well as the main legacy of this period was fiscal. Substantial and important financial relations were firmly established and were the harbingers of more to come. Subsequently, these relations inspired a new metaphor of intergovernmental patterns—the much-publicized "marble cake" expression (popularized and elaborated on by Morton Grodzins)—as contrasted with the layer cake conception of the previous period.

Morton argued that government operations in the United States were wrongly depicted as a three-layer cake. "A far more accurate image," he said, "is the rainbow of marble cake, characterized by an inseparable mingling of differently colored ingredients, the colors appearing in vertical and diagonal strands and unexpected whirls [sic]." From Grodzins's perspective, the U.S. system of governance should be viewed as one of shared functions in which "it is difficult to find any governmental activity which does not involve all three of the so-called 'levels' of the system." Supportive of these shared functions was an implicit (and sometimes explicit) mood and pattern of behavior among participants—collaboration, cooperation, and mutual and supportive assistance.

What is known as the concentrated phase occurred between the 1940s and 1960s. During the presidencies of Harry S. Truman, Dwight D. Eisenhower, and John F. Kennedy, intergovernmental relations became increasingly specific, functional, and highly focused, that is, concentrated. Between 1946 and 1961, 21 major new grant-in-aid programs were created, nearly doubling the total enacted in the Great Depression era. With this expansion of categorical grant programs, greater attention was increasingly paid to service standards. To that end, administrative rules and regulations rather than statutes began to govern such things as award criteria, reporting, and performance requirements.

These expanded grant-in-aid programs focused on two prominent problem/needs areas: capital works, public construction, and physical development; and middle-class service needs. Examples include airports, hospitals, highways, slum clearance and urban renewal, schools, waste treatment, libraries, and urban planning. Despite the fact that there was a substantial federal government involvement in local affairs via such programs, substantial local political control was both encouraged and practiced. In this respect, the techniques of grants, service standards, construction projects, and the like matched the local tradition of initiative and voluntary participation. Moreover, intergovernmental relations techniques were consistent with middle-class values of professionalism, objectivity, and neutrality and therefore gave the appearance that objective program needs rather than politics were being served.

These major political values coincided in 1946 with the reorganization of Congress and the creation of congressional standing committees with explicit program emphases. The latter of these happenings was to have significant intergovernmental relations implications. Simply stated, these congressional committee patterns soon became the channels for access and leverage points for influencing program-specific grants.

Some have used the "water taps" metaphor to describe the intergovernmental relations process during this period. Because of the flow of influence combined with the concentrated, or focused, flow of funds in the 1946 to 1961 period, the national government had become an established reservoir of financial resources to which a rapidly increasing number of water taps were being connected. Funds could be made to flow best by those most knowledgeable (the program professionals) at turning on the numerous "spigots," and federal funds typically went directly to states that could then release them in part or in whole to local governments. Although cooperation was commonplace during this period, it occurred in concentrated and selectively channeled ways. And it was during this phase that the interconnectedness and interdependency of national, state, and local relations were confirmed and solidified.

What is known as the creative phase occurred during the 1950s and the 1960s. The foundation for the creative phase can be traced back to the cooperative and concentrated periods of intergovernmental relations, in that it stressed the need for decisiveness in politics and policy as well as the articulation of national goals. The term *creative* is commonly associated with this period partly because of President Lyndon B. Johnson's use of the slogan "creative federalism" and partly because of the many new innovative programs in intergovernmental relations. Three intergovernmental relations mechanisms were characteristic of this period. First, comprehensive local, areawide, or statewide plans had to be submitted and approved prior to the receipt of any federal grant funds. Second, extensive use was made of project grants, whereby grant proposals had to be submitted in a project type format. Project grants not only involve extensive and often elaborate proposals or requests but also give much greater discretion to grant administrators than do formula grants, in which statutory or administrative formulas determine recipient entitlements. In addition, public participation was strongly encouraged through the insertion of the "maximum feasible participation" requirement in legislation. This involvement of clients in program operations and administrative decisions often introduced a significant and unsettling disconcerting element into intergovernmental programs.

The period is perhaps best known for the proliferation of the number of grant programs, hence the employment of the metaphor "flowering." The chief policy issues and major themes addressed by this creative activism were two-fold: an urban-metropolitan focus and attention to the disadvantaged through antipoverty programs and aid-to-education funds. By 1969, there were an estimated 150 major programs, 400 specific legislative authorizations, and 1,300 federal assistance activities. Of the 400 specific authorizations, 70 involved directly funneled money to local governments, thus bypassing the states. In dollar magnitude, federal grants jumped from $4.9 billion in 1958 to $23.9 billion in 1970. Over this same time span, state aid to local governments also increased from $8.0 billion to $28.9 billion.

The significant increase in project grants and the amount of money accompanying them compared to formula grants led to a noticeable change in the attitudes and behavior of intergovernmental relations participants. Specifically, a grantsmanship perspective grew rapidly and widely. Playing the federal grant "game" became a well-known but time-consuming activity of MAYORS, CITY MANAGERS, county administrators, school officials, GOVERNORS, and particularly program professionals.

The competitive phase of intergovernmental relations occurred during the 1960s and the 1970s. This phase was distinguished by the escalation of tensions that was fueled by the proliferation of federal grants, the clash between program professionals and participation-minded clients, and the intractability of domestic and international problems. In addition, by the late 1960s, it was becoming increasingly apparent that much of the whirlwind legislation of the GREAT SOCIETY had fallen far short of achieving the lofty goals set for it. Issues related to bureaucratic behavior, administrative competence, and implementation became dominating concerns. Perhaps the most daunting concern was the lack of coordination within and among programs and within and among levels of government. Other festering concerns related to program accomplishment, effective service delivery, and citizen access. In such a political climate, candidates for public office at the national, state, and local levels focused attention on organizational structures and relationships that either hindered or helped the provision of goods and services.

The period was also marked by a sharply different approach with regard to appropriate intergovernmental relations mechanisms. Pressure mounted to change and even reverse previous grant trends. One idea put forward was the consolidation of the many grant programs under the rubric of block grants and "special" revenue sharing. General revenue sharing was proposed by President Richard M. Nixon as a means of improving program effectiveness and strengthening state and local governments, especially elected officials in their competition and disagreements with national bureaucrats. Nixon also sought mightily to slow down or even reverse the flow of grant funds by the frequent use of impounding. On the national administrative front, efforts were made to encourage metropolitan and regional cooperation (under Office of Management and Budget circular A-95) and reorganize government agencies.

The unwarranted disagreement, tension, and rivalry that earned this period the label of *competitive intergovernmental relations* was summarized best by the late senator Edmund Muskie (D-ME): "The picture, then, is one of too much tension and conflict rather than coordination and cooperation all along the line of administration—from top Federal policymakers and administrators to the state and local professional and elected officials." Yet the competition differed in degree, emphasis, and configuration from the interlevel conflict of the older layer cake phase. First, there was competition between professional program specialists or administrators (national, state, and local) and state and local elected and appointed officials. Second, there was competition among several functional program areas (e.g., highways, welfare, education, health, urban renewal, etc.), whereby like-minded program specialists or professionals, regardless of the level of government in which they served, formed rival alliances. These cross-cutting rivalries and fragmentation prompted former North Carolina governor Terry Sanford to suggest the "picket fence" metaphor as descriptive of this period of intergovernmental relations.

The calculative phase of intergovernmental relations occurred during the 1970s and the 1980s. This period was marked by the out-of-control finances and near-bankruptcy of New York City during the mid-1970s. But these problems were not confined to just NYC but rather were reflective of broader societal and political problems across the nation. The problems included lack of accountability of public officials, bankruptcy and fiscal stress, unwise and heightened dependency on federal aid, a perceived overbearing and meddlesome role of federal authorities, and the loss of public confidence in government and government officials generally.

While intergovernmental relations during this period still tended to revolve around federal aid to state and local governments, it was practiced, according to Deil Wright, from a calculative perspective and contained only the surface trappings of federalism. State and local governments had the appearance of making important choices, but the choices in reality were few and elusive. The major choice was whether to participate in federal assistance programs. Simply stated, there was a greater tendency to estimate the "costs" as well as the benefits of getting a federal grant. If they decided to take part in federal programs, a larger array of more limited options was available. These choices, however, were constrained mainly, if not exclusively, by nationally specified rules of the game. This is why "façade federalism" has been chosen as a metaphor characterizing this phase of intergovernmental relations.

The perceptions of intergovernmental relations participants of this period can be summarized as gamesmanship, fungibility, and overload. Gamesmanship means that intergovernmental relations players used various strategic "games" to achieve desired ends. One case would be grantsmanship that, although identified with the creative phase, was perfected through the competitive and calculative phases to the point that some of the rules (see Wright for examples) by which local officials played the game had been codified. Fungibility refers to the ability of state and local governments to shift or exchange resources received from the federal government for one purpose to accomplish another purpose. State and local governments often used general revenue sharing and block grants to reduce the amount of their own resources devoted to nationally assisted programs. Finally, overload refers to the belief that democratic governments have been expected to do more than they are capable of doing in an effective, efficient, and low-cost manner. Moreover, this also implies an increase in excessive regulation on the part of all governments.

Several mechanisms were used to implement intergovernmental relations activities in the calculative phase. One was the channeling of more federal aid on a formula basis as ENTITLEMENTS and in the form of general aid and block grants to states and their local governments. Associated with the mechanism of general aid is the technique of bypassing, whereby federal funds would go directly to local governments without having to pass through state coffers. Loans (e.g., to New York City and to students) constituted a third intergovernmental relations mechanism in the calculative phase. Regulation (in the form of grant guidelines in the *Federal Register*, grant law, and crosscutting requirements) was the final implementing mechanism.

The contractive phase of intergovernmental relations began during the 1980s and continues today. This most recent period will probably be remembered as one in which federal aid was shrinking, local autonomy was eroding, and court decisions and congressional legislation constricted the range of action of state and local governments. It is also likely that this time will be associated with the increasing tendency of governmental agencies at all levels to enter into contracts for the purchase and delivery of services. At present, it is uncertain whether this phase is still evolving or if it has come to a close and a new phase is emerging.

Four major intergovernmental relations problems seem to have confronted public officials during this period. First, all levels of government have been preoccupied with borrowing and budget balancing as the size and persistence of the federal deficit has loomed large and has cast a foreboding shadow over the current and long-term intergovernmental relations fiscal scene. Second, federal deficits and conservative politics have resulted in significant cuts and changes in federal aid to state and local governments. Third, the federal courts and nonelected officials have increasingly directed their attention to detailed, specific, and judgmental policy actions of state and local officials (e.g., schools, prisons, and mental health facilities) and have found numerous faults with their actions. Moreover, these nonelected, nonconstitutional officials have sought to convene, cajole, and convince popularly elected officials into following the "best courses of action" in resolving disputes. Fourth, federal mandates in the form of court orders, congressional statutes, and administrative regulations abound and are identified by Joseph Zimmerman, "as the principal irritant of American intergovernmental relations" in recent years. Managing and complying with these mandates have presented state and local officials with a significant challenge both administratively and financially.

Several terms seem to capture the perceptions of participants during this most recent phase of intergovernmental relations. Contentiousness, disagreement, and even confrontation between federal and state and local officials often characterize these interactions. Furthermore, state and local officials have come to the realization that the "good old days" of bountiful federal grant money and a nonintrusive federal government are over and that they should be wary of an overbearing federal government. These perceptions have produced a sense of defensiveness and distrust on the part of officials at all levels of government and subsequently have resulted in more litigation. In response to an obvious deterioration of intergovernmental relations, President Ronald Reagan was aggressive in efforts to reshape, reform, and restore national-state relationships through decentralization of the federal system.

The instruments by which intergovernmental relations activities were implemented during the contractive phase reveal some novel elements as well as some links to prior intergovernmental relations phases. Statutes and court decisions were prominent in the first phase of intergovernmental relations, and it is no surprise to see them during the last phase, given the strong sense of "us against them" perceptions held by all participants. Three intergovernmental relations mechanisms (information sources, negotiated dispute settlement, and privatization) appear to be new. Problem solving has been revolutionized as a result of changes in computer technology (particularly the sharing of information among liked-minded intergovernmental relations actors) and the development of new social technology (for example, mediation). Finally, privatization, through the encouragement of competition and innovation, has given especially state and local officials the opportunity to provide services in a more efficient, effective, and cost-effective manner.

While it is uncertain whether we have entered into an eighth phase of intergovernmental relations, it is certain that intergovernmental relations are destined to evolve and change in the years ahead. Moreover, it is a given that the tone of intergovernmental relations will have a significant and lasting effect on policy making at all levels of government. Will state and local governments be restored as equal or near-equal partners and exert more influence on their destinies? What impact will looming national and international events and problems have on shaping the basic contours of American intergovernmental relations? No crystal ball can provide answers to these and other questions, but we can say with some modicum of certainty with history as a predictor that intergovernmental relations will continue to vacillate between varying levels of cooperation and conflict.

Further Reading

Anderson, William. *Intergovernmental Relations in Review*. Minneapolis: University of Minnesota Press, 1960; Benton, J. Edwin, and David R. Morgan. *Intergovernmental Relations and Public Policy*. Westport, Conn.: Greenwood Press, 1986; Elazar, Daniel J. *American Federalism: A View from the States*. 3rd ed. New York: Harper & Row, 1984; Glendening, Parris N., and Mavis Mann Reeves. *Pragmatic Federalism: An Intergovernmental View of American Government*. 2nd ed. Pacific Palisades, Calif.: Palisades Publishers, 1984; Nice, David, and Patricia Fredericksen. *Politics of Intergovernmental Relations*. Chicago: Nelson-Hall, 1995; O'Toole, Laurence J. Jr., ed. *American Intergovernmental Relations*. 4th ed. Washington, D.C.: Congressional Quarterly Press, 2007; Sanford, Terry. *Storm over the States*. New York: McGraw-Hill, 1967; Wright, Deil S. *Understanding Intergovernmental Relations*. 3rd ed. Pacific Grove, Calif.: Brooks/Cole Publishing, 1988.

—J. Edwin Benton

justices of the peace

A justice of the peace is a judge of a court that has limited jurisdiction. These positions are occasionally called municipal or magistrate judgeships, but they are functionally the same. A justice of the peace usually presides over a court that hears traffic violations, misdemeanor cases, and other petty crimes. In some states, the justice of the peace is given authority over cases involving small debts, landlord and tenant disputes, and other small claims court proceedings. They are also known to perform weddings. The justice of the peace position differentiates itself from nearly every other legal role in society in that its practitioners do not need to have a law degree or any formal legal training.

The history of the justice of the peace begins in 1195, when Richard I ("the Lionheart") of England first commissioned knights to keep the peace in troublesome areas. They were responsible for making sure the laws were upheld. They were commonly referred to as keepers of the peace. In 1327, an act declared that "good and lawful men" were to be appointed to "guard the peace." These men were called conservators of the peace or wardens of the peace. It was not until 1361, during the reign of King Edward III, that the position became known as justice of the peace. The position was primarily occupied by the gentry, or land-owning nobles, and to a lesser extent those of a good family.

As the English immigrated to North America, many of their institutions were recreated and established to simulate the motherland. Aiding this process was the fact that the indigenous inhabitants were either integrated into the new society or ejected from the area and that they did not already have formal systems of law in place. Many of these early immigrants were entrepreneurs from the English upper class, which meant that they tended to be considered gentry. Others came because they were more interested in the adventure of the New World, particularly the younger generation.

Soon after the first groups of English came over, James I granted charters that would establish the colonies of North America. These charters dictated that English COMMON LAW and institutions would be established. Within the colonies, the English gentry usually administered law and government. Many of these colonial leaders had already served as justices of the peace in England and felt it blasphemous to suggest governing the colonies in a manner unlike those used in England. The first justice of the peace in North America was appointed in Virginia in 1634.

These justices of the peace closely resembled their counterparts in England. They were expected to be "men of substance and influence" and "impartial to rich and poor . . . and free from hatred or malice." Justices of the peace were not paid for their services and were often men of great respect. Their word alone held authority. They were often officers in the militia and also wardens in the local church. Few were educated in law but used their knowledge of the world and their neighbors to make judgments they deemed fair. Justices, particularly in the early years, could also serve as coroners and responded to a variety of complaints and demands of every nature. In Massachusetts, a justice of the peace was also expected to organize the local militia.

Of course, this was not the case in every colony. In some colonies, justices of the peace were not "men of substance and influence" even though that was the expectation. The justices of the peace in New Hampshire, Georgia, and North Carolina were renowned for their ignorance of law. Colonial records in New Hampshire and Georgia indicate that there were only a few qualified lawyers in the colonies throughout the 18th century. New York suffered from problems of a different nature. Originally a Dutch colony until officially ceded in 1667, judicial chaos reigned as the colony debated which country's laws were to be followed. Additionally, a number of New York's justices of the peace could not read or write, causing concern over the fairness of their decisions.

Throughout their history, justices of the peace have been primarily laymen not specifically trained in the legal profession. In the period of colonial development, lawyers were highly despised. For instance, Georgia wanted to be a "happy and flourishing colony . . . free from that pest and scourge of mankind called lawyers." The people wanted someone from within their own region whom they respected to serve as justice of the peace. Historical records indicate that areas where the justice of the peace was a local resident had the fewest complaints about the quality and decisions of their justice of the peace.

Part of the reasoning behind appointing laymen as justices of the peace was that colonies, counties, and towns could not afford to pay someone with a legal background. Of course, this assumed that there were even enough legal minds available to fill the positions. Justices of the peace were also expected to be close to the public they adjudicated. The common person had a rudimentary understanding of law, and justices of the peace were no different. As a result, they based their decisions on what they thought was right and wrong and their knowledge of the individuals involved.

As the colonies grew, the role of justice of the peace became more localized. By the end of the American Revolutionary War, counties were resisting unilateral control over the justices of the peace by the colonial, or state, GOVERNORs and/or legislatures. Indeed, county and local leaders resented that they were left out of the decision-making process, particularly because a number of the new justices of the peace were not from the region, thus not knowing local culture and expectations. In some locales, justices of the peace were so inept that colonial or state governments were being buried in complaints.

Associated with a more localized system came a shift whereby the American justices of the peace no longer resembled their counterparts in England. The position gradually became increasingly commercialized, which caused it to decline in the social scale. Plus, as the country continued to grow, each new state ushered in new cultural experiences that ultimately influenced the role of the justice of the peace. Following the Civil War and during the Industrial Revolution, the public began to demand the right to elect their own justices of the peace, as opposed to the governor or legislature making those determinations. Of course, this resulted in more commercialization and an even greater decline in the prestige of the position.

As the country spread west, formal law was virtually nonexistent. The West was commonly known to be a wild and, at times, dangerous place, and in many areas, the justice of the peace was the only source of order and protection for miles. The federal government eventually recognized that justices of the peace were not sufficient to keep order in the western states and territories. Many of the justices of the peace were functionally replaced by federal marshals who shared many of the same powers as the justices of the peace but had the backing of the national government.

By the time America entered World War II, 47 of the 48 states still had justices of the peace. Because the new states did not have landed gentry from which to pick justices of the peace, many altered their expectations so that the position essentially required no qualifications. Indeed, in 1940, only two of the 47 states that still used justices of the peace had specific qualifications for the job. This trend continues today for states that still use a justice of the peace. For instance, in Texas, the only qualifications for an individual to hold this office are be a citizen of the United States; be at least 18 years of age on the day the term starts or on the date of appointment; not have been determined mentally incompetent by a final judgment of a court; not have been finally convicted of a felony from which the person has not been pardoned or otherwise released from the resulting disabilities; as a general rule, have resided continually in Texas for one year and in the precinct for the preceding six months; and must not have been declared ineligible for the office.

With the proliferation of the automobile, the position of justice of the peace began to lose its status quickly. Justices of the peace were responsible for adjudicating traffic violations, and the public hated this. As a result, the public began to view the justice of the peace with less and less admiration. In small towns, they were often seen as tyrants and corrupt.

There has been a push, primarily organized by the AMERICAN BAR ASSOCIATION, to abolish the office of the justice of the peace. The American Bar Association, which is an organization of America's attorneys, believes that nonlawyer judges are no longer necessary because there are more people with formal legal training than ever before in American history. Many states have responded by either abolishing the position or incorporating it into other courts. Currently, the following states still rely on justices of the peace or their functional equivalent: Arizona, Arkansas, Connecticut, Delaware, Georgia, Louisiana, Massachusetts, Montana, New Hampshire, New York (in small towns and villages), South Carolina, Texas, Vermont, West Virginia, Wisconsin (depends upon locality), and Wyoming.

Recently, the function of the justice of the peace that always provided the least controversy, their ability to conduct weddings and civil unions, has become a hot-button issue. In Massachusetts, a justice of the peace can perform same-sex marriages if religious officials are unwilling to do so. Interestingly, a Massachusetts justice of the peace is legally not allowed to refuse to perform a same-sex marriage. In Connecticut, they can preside over same-sex civil unions.

Further Reading

Graham, Michael H. *Tightening the Reins of Justice in America: A Comparative Analysis of the Criminal Jury Trial in England and the United States*. Westport, Conn.: Greenwood Press, 1983; Skyrme, Sir Thomas. *History of the Justices of the Peace: England to 1689, Volume I*. Chichester, England: Barry Rose Law Publications, 1991; Skyrme, Sir Thomas. *History of the Justices of the Peace: England 1689–1989, Volume II*. Chichester, England: Barry Rose Law Publications, 1991; Skyrme, Sir Thomas. *History of the Justices of the Peace: Territories Beyond England*. Vol. 3. Chichester, England: Barry Rose Law Publications, 1991; Wunder, John R. *Inferior Courts, Superior Justice: A History of the Justices of the Peace on the Northwest Frontier, 1853–1889*. Westport, Conn.: Greenwood Press, 1979.

—James W. Stoutenborough

legislative process, state and local

The last few decades have witnessed great change regarding legislative bodies at the state and local levels. A report published in 1968 by the nonpartisan public affairs forum American Assembly noted that "state legislatures have failed to meet the challenge of change because they have been handicapped by restricted powers, inadequate tools and facilities, inefficient organization and procedures." Some 30 years later, a much different picture was drawn; David Hedge wrote in 1998 that "few political institutions have experienced as much fundamental and far-reaching change in such a short period of time as have state legislatures."

An instigating cause of STATE LEGISLATURES' enhanced power is the U.S. national government. One result of President Richard Nixon's and President Ronald Reagan's new FEDERALISM, combined with President Bill Clinton's policy of devolution (particularly with respect to WELFARE POLICY) has been to increase the power and responsibilities of STATE GOVERNMENTS. At times, the devolution of power has not stopped at the state governmental level; Clinton's welfare reform allowed states to further devolve responsibility for programs down to the local level.

According to the Tenth Amendment of the U.S. CONSTITUTION, "powers not delegated to the U.S. by the Constitution . . . are reserved to the States . . . or to the people." Hence, as a result of a combination of constitutional amendment, statutory directive, political ideology, and practical necessity, state and local governments have assumed added significance in recent years.

State legislatures share many features with the U.S. Congress. Mostly, they are bicameral bodies. To be more precise, 49 states have legislatures comprised of two legislative chambers; Nebraska is unique in that it is a unicameral legislature. All state legislatures use a COMMITTEE SYSTEM; this facilitates the lawmaking process. The average state legislature is made up of 10 to 20 committees in the upper chamber and 15 to 30 in the lower chamber. It is in these smaller assemblies that legislation is written and oversight hearings are held. Local legislative bodies, whether they be city councils or county commissions, are nearly always unicameral in nature. They do, however, share a similarity with Congress and with state legislative bodies in their use of committees as a way to divide the workload among the members. The number of committees at the local level rarely equals that at the state level.

State legislators and members of Congress perform similar functions: writing legislation, representing constituents, and overseeing the executive and judicial branches. Like members of Congress, they spend much of their time engaged in CONSTITUENCY service, also known as CASEWORK, and bringing home pork to the district (that is, they obtain governmentally funded projects that benefit their constituents). These two tasks are often done with an eye toward reelection. At the local level, particularly in the case of county commissions but also in the case of some city councils, legislative bodies also perform executive and administrative duties. These may include appointing employees, supervising road work, and heading departments.

One stark difference that exists among legislatures pertains to what is known as professionalism. This concept refers to the extent to which legislators are full time versus part time, how much they are paid, and how much staff support they have. In no state or local government does the level of professionalism equal that of Congress. However, there is great variation among states and localities regarding the components of professionalism. First consider state governments. At the upper end of the scale are the so-called professional legislatures. Legislators in states such as California and Ohio and in about seven other states are paid $50,000 to $100,000 annually for what is a full-time legislative job; they are also assisted by full-time staff. In the middle of the scale are roughly 20 states, such as Tennessee and Washington. In those states, the legislators tend to work half time, earning $12,000 to $45,000 annually. While they are assisted by professional staff, their staffers are more likely to be session-only staff (that is, the staffers are employed only when the legislature meets in session). At the lowest end of the professionalism scale are about 10 states, including Nevada and New Mexico. These also employ part-time legislators, with the pay ranging from a $144 per diem expense in New Mexico to $27,300 annually in Indiana. Staff assistance in these states can be exceptionally small. For example, Wyoming in 2003 had only 29 full-time staffers serving a legislature of 90 members. The variation that is apparent at the state level is magnified at the local level. Not surprisingly, higher levels of professionalism are more likely to be seen in the nation's most highly populated cities and counties.

The membership of state legislative bodies represents one area in which the greatest amount of change has been seen in recent decades. In terms of the male-female breakdown, the late 1960s witnessed state legislatures consisting of approximately 4 percent women. Today that figure is greater than 22 percent. In terms of the racial breakdown, roughly 8 percent of all state legislators are African American, whereas about 3 percent are of Hispanic heritage. Similar changes are apparent with respect to local legislative assemblies. For example, in 2002 there were nearly 5,500 African-American and 2,000 Hispanic local level legislators. Finally, across state and local legislatures there are about 200 openly lesbian and gay officeholders.

One of the most contentious issues concerning legislatures at any level of government concerns reapportionment and redistricting. Several factors necessitate the redrawing of district lines. These include population changes, changes in partisan control of redistricting commissions, and the impact of court cases. In the early 1960s, two key U.S. SUPREME COURT cases—*Baker v. Carr* (1962) and *Reynolds v. Sims* (1964)—had a dramatic impact. These cases had the cumulative effect of bringing to an end the gross malapportionment of legislative districts. For example, at the time, one STATE SENATOR in California represented 14,000 rural residents while another represented 6 million residents of Los Angeles County. The Warren Court based its decision on the principle of "one man, one vote," thereby rejecting the notion of drawing district lines based on geographic and/or governmental boundaries. The practical outcome of these decisions was to increase the representation of urban and suburban residents; these individuals had historically been underrepresented, while rural residents had been overrepresented. In the case of *League of United Latin American Citizens et al. v. Perry et al.* (2006), the Court reaffirmed a commitment to not allowing gerrymandered districts that corral minorities into one oddly shaped district. In the same case, the justices permitted those who control the redistricting process to redraw district lines in the middle of a decade (the traditional redistricting timeframe had been once at the beginning of a decade).

As is the case in Congress, POLITICAL PARTIES play important roles in many state and local legislatures. Specific functions typically revolve around the following: the organization and leadership of the legislature, the recruitment of candidates to run in elections, and the provision of services to legislative candidates. State legislatures vary in the extent to which one or two (or more) parties have organizational strength. For example, states such as New Jersey and Michigan exhibit strong parties on both sides of the aisle. Other states, such as Alabama and Mississippi, have only one political party that exhibits anything resembling organizational strength and political power. While parties are certainly important components of the political scene in most local governments, the nature of their involvement varies quite dramatically from that at the state level. For instance, many local elections are nonpartisan affairs. One result of this is the fact that electoral ballots may not cite a candidate's political party affiliation, something that Americans expect to see on ballots for national-level offices.

Relations with the executive help explain the amount of power that state and local legislatures wield. At the national level, Americans are accustomed to electing only a president and a VICE PRESIDENT, the former having significant veto, appointment, and budget-making powers. In the vast majority of states, there are several elected executive officials, and the GOVERNOR may or may not have powers similar to those of the president. What this means is that in many states, the legislature holds as much or more formal power as does the governor. However, state legislative bodies are disadvantaged compared to the governor in those states where the legislature meets less than full time and has a small amount of staff assistance.

Perhaps no single issue other than welfare policy better illustrates the changes that have occurred over the past few decades with respect to the power of state and in some cases local government. When President Clinton signed the Temporary Assistance for Needy Families (TANF) Act in 1996, he gave great new powers to state governments. Individual states were granted the power to determine program qualifications and requirements that were tailored to their particular circumstances. Furthermore, more than a dozen states devolved power to regional and/or county jurisdictions. Devolution of the welfare system has led to enhanced powers for lower levels of governments; it has also necessitated an expansion in the capacity of those same governments. Finally, it has necessitated greater cooperation between state and local governments, private businesses, and nonprofit organizations in an area that was once the sole province of the national government.

Finally, a discussion of state and local legislatures that is focused on change must include mention of recent efforts centered on TERM LIMITS and ethics reform. The term limit movement became especially pronounced in the 1990s. During that decade, 21 states saw the advent of legislative term limits through constitutional amendment, voter INITIATIVE, or other means. Legislators are only recently experiencing the impact of that movement. Proponents argue that term limits have inhibited the careers of allegedly corrupt politicians; opponents argue that term limits have served to shift power to governors, agencies, legislative staff, and others.

Term limits are in some ways related to a larger effort directed at ethics reform. This is an area that encompasses various potential actions. One such action is the prohibition of the receipt of gifts from individuals, lobbyists, and others. One assessment (Goodman et al., 1996) of all 50 state legislatures ranked only four states—Hawaii, Kentucky, Tennessee, and West Virginia—as having a strong code of ethics guidelines for their legislators; 16 states ranked at the low end of the scale.

Local governments are also going through extensive changes, albeit due to different pressures and in different contexts than is the case with state governments. Urbanization causes friction among adjacent local governments—cities, townships, counties, and school districts—as the demands of their individual jurisdictions affect one another. This has led to a movement toward so-called shadow governments (such as home owners' associations and development corporations) and regional governments. The former engender questions related to accountability and equity, while the latter bring up contentious notions of regional versus local cultures and perspectives.

It is a good bet that states and localities will assume additional powers, their populations will increase, they will continue to sprawl across political boundaries, and those both within and outside legislative institutions will clamor for change. As a result, these legislative bodies will evolve in unforeseen ways as the 21st century progresses.

Further Reading

Beyle, Thad L, ed. *State and Local Government 2004–2005*. Washington, D.C.: Congressional Quarterly Press, 2004; Goodman, Marshall, Timothy Holp, and Karen Ludwig. "Understanding State Legislative Ethics Reform." In *Public Integrity Annual*, edited by James S. Bowman, Lexington, Ky.: Council of State Governments, 1996; Hedge, David. *Governance and the Changing American States*. Boulder, Colo.: Westview Press, 1998; Jewell, Malcolm E., and Marcia Lynn Whicker. *Legislative Leadership in the American States*. Ann Arbor: University of Michigan Press, 1994; Morehouse, Sarah McCally, and Malcolm E. Jewell. *State Politics, Parties, and Policy*. Lanham, Md.: Rowman & Littlefield, 2003; Rosenthal, Alan. *The Decline of Representative Democracy: Process, Participation, and Power in State Legislatures*. Washington, D.C.: Congressional Quarterly Press, 1998; Van Horn, Carl E., ed. *The State of the States*. Washington, D.C.: Congressional Quarterly Press, 2006.

—Barry L. Tadlock

legislatures, state

All 50 STATES have legislative bodies similar in form and function to the federal legislature. All state legislatures except one (Nebraska) are bicameral in nature. Meeting in the state capital either annually or biannually, state legislatures propose and pass laws, provide oversight of the executive branch, and serve constituents. This discussion will emphasize features that all or nearly all 50 state legislatures have in common as well as emphasize a few key differences.

The existence of state legislatures predates the American Revolution. Following the English parliamentary model, each of the colonies (later states) adopted elective legislative bodies to govern internal matters. The oldest of these, the Virginia General Assembly, has roots dating back to 1619. For most of the 18th and 19th centuries, these bodies served as the main and sometimes only conduit for representing the will of the people. During the late 19th and early 20th centuries, the franchise was expanded, the U.S. CONSTITUTION was amended to allow for direct election of SENATORS, and the size and scope of the federal government expanded greatly, all factors that contributed to the relative decline in the importance of state legislatures as the primary voice of the people in American government.

As the 20th century progressed, however, state legislatures experienced a revival. This reemergence can be traced to two key factors. First, as the world of state politics became more complex, states increasingly turned their legislatures into full-time, professional bodies. The typical legislature at the beginning of the 20th century met every other year for 2 to 3 months and was made up of citizen-legislators who were either unpaid or received a very small stipend. Today, about two-thirds of states have semiprofessional or professional legislatures that meet every year for a significant period of time; their legislators receive a salary and have a paid staff. Even today, though, it is typically only the largest states that have all the features of a fully professionalized legislature.

A second key component to change resulted from the 1962 U.S. SUPREME COURT decision *Baker* v. *Carr*. Prior to this Court decision, many state legislatures were unprofessional bodies dominated by rural interests. Despite increases in urbanization, many state legislatures tended to be apportioned based on a population distribution that was often many decades out of date. Since state legislatures were in charge of their own apportionment, and since entrenched rural blocs wanted to maintain their grip on power, legislatures simply refused to redraw district boundaries in a way that would more accurately reflect population changes. In many states, this led to urban areas being allotted the same number of representatives as rural regions even though the former had a population several times as large. This malapportionment was particularly bad in Tennessee, where some urban districts were 19 times more populous than the most rural ones. Based on the Tennessee experience, the *Baker* decision held that such a representational structure violated the Fourteenth Amendment's equal protection clause. As a result of this "one person, one vote" ruling, state legislatures are now apportioned based on formulas that are much more in line with current populations. Thus, legislatures have become more responsive to the needs of the state populations as a whole, making them more relevant to the lives of citizens.

The contemporary state legislator is likely to be college educated and have a professional background, such as law or business. According to the National Conference of State Legislatures, about 23 percent of state legislators are women, about 8 percent are African American, and about 3 percent are Latino. The average age for a state legislator is 53, and nationwide 50 percent are Republicans, 49 percent are Democrats, and

the remaining members are independents or members of THIRD PARTIES. While some legislators see their position as a stepping-stone to higher political office, many wish to retain their present position or return to the private sector after a few years in public office. Legislative campaigns vary greatly by state. According to the Institute on Money in State Politics, in New Hampshire, a state with a part-time, citizen legislature, the average campaign for the state house of representatives in 2004 raised $495. At the other end of the spectrum, that year's races for the highly professionalized California State Senate cost an average of $438,495, an amount greater than the total raised by all 815 New Hampshire House candidates combined. Compensation and responsibilities, of course, also vary. The New Hampshire representatives receive $200 per two-year term and represent about 3,100 citizens each, while the California senators receive more than $110,000 per year and represent about 850,000 Californians. New Mexican legislators receive no salary at all.

The life of the typical state legislator is a busy one. Whether a citizen legislator or full-time professional, all legislators must focus on three aspects of the job: considering BILLs, overseeing state agencies, and serving constituents. Scrutinizing, amending, and ultimately passing or rejecting laws are the primary tasks of legislators. Most legislators run for office with a particular agenda in mind—perhaps they want to increase the quality of public schools or state highways, or they may want to change or want to rein in what they see as excessive state spending. Whatever the issues, this small number of items often becomes the subject matter for legislation the member will draft. Legislators reach the state capital with ideas for change that they developed during their campaign and are likely to find some other like-minded legislators. Although there is no formal requirement for cosponsorship of legislation, members often find it beneficial to develop their legislation in conjunction with other legislators in order to form a base of support. This is particularly necessary for large-scale and controversial legislation. Since nearly all state legislatures are bicameral, they need to find allies in the other chamber as well. Shouldering the responsibility for drafting and sponsoring a bill, seeking support for it, and seeing it through to passage is often referred to as "carrying" a bill. Without a cadre of dedicated bill carriers, most legislation dies a quiet death in committee.

While any given legislator is responsible for authoring and sponsoring only a tiny fraction of the total legislative output, he or she must weigh-in on hundreds or even thousands of potential laws each legislative session. Since no individual can develop expertise in the myriad fields of state law, legislators seek assistance and input from legislative staff and other interested parties. When considering the merits of bills, legislators often meet with lobbyists and other individuals who share their perspectives. For example, when considering a measure to fund a new state university campus, a legislator may hear from professional lobbyists representing building contractors, citizen lobbyists representing a teachers' union, and local constituents concerned about the location of the proposed facility. Though much is made, quite rightly, of those occasions when lobbyists and legislators overstep the bounds of professionalism and enter into bribery, the vast majority of interest group activity in the legislative process is beneficial to legislators and ultimately results in laws that have been thoroughly vetted by all interested and affected parties prior to passage.

Though shaping legislation is the central function of the legislator's job, oversight and CONSTITUENCY service are also crucial. Legislative oversight, typically handled at the committee level, is the process of making sure that the laws passed are indeed being carried out as intended. A typical oversight activity is auditing, making sure that monies allocated by the state are being spent responsibly and in the manner prescribed by the state budget.

A legislator's constituency is the population residing in the district he or she represents. These are the people the legislator has been elected to represent, and he or she must be attuned to their needs or risk being turned out of office in the next election. In order to best understand the wishes and concerns of the constituency, a legislator often maintains an office in the home district and/or assigns staff the responsibility of responding to constituents' concerns. These issues, ranging from the adverse effects of a law on a single constituent to the road and infrastructure needs that affect the economy of an entire community, cannot be overlooked by a responsible legislator. Responding to these needs, whether in the form of legislation or simply listening or providing needed information, can be the most personal part of a legislator's job.

In addition to the tasks of rank-and-file legislators, legislative leaders have additional powers and responsibilities. Every legislative body elects a presiding officer, often called a speaker or president, to run the legislative process. Presiding over floor activity and implementing and following the parliamentary rules of the chamber, this individual is often responsible for making committee appointments, assigning bills to committee, setting the legislative calendar, and doling out resources such as office space and staff budgets. In some states, he or she is also a party leader, but in nearly all states the presiding officer is in communication with the elected leadership of both parties in order to identify areas of agreement and hammer out compromises when necessary. Though TERM LIMITS have rendered seniority a less important qualification for leadership posts in several states, the presiding officer must be able to work well with others and must have earned the respect of his or her peers.

At the heart of the legislative process lies what is arguably the most significant source of legislative power, the presiding officer's ability to oversee the COMMITTEE SYSTEM. Virtually every bill must pass through one or more committees on its way to becoming a law. The strength of committees is often a function of party strength. In other words, states with a stronger party system tend to have weaker committee powers and vice-versa. Standing committees are designed to provide expertise in revising bills before they are brought to the floor. Such expertise sometimes occurs, such as when farmers serve on an agriculture committee. The presence of term limits in many states, however, and the shifting composition of committees from one session to the next make policy expertise less important and the gatekeeping function—the decision about when, whether, and how (favorably or unfavorably) to report bills to the chamber—becomes primary.

In addition to standing committees, most chambers have one or more leadership oriented committees, typically dominated by the majority party. Such committees have one or more of the following functions: assigning membership to all other committees, shaping the legislative agenda by applying rules to bills, and planning policy strategy for the majority party. These functions highlight the importance of being the majority party in a legislature. For example, an important issue, such as health care reform, may become the topic of legislation introduced by dozens of legislators from each political party. The decisions about which committee to send a bill to, under what rules, and in what order are often crucial factors in determining which bills will become law and which will wither away in committee.

Though representing a separate branch of government, GOVERNORs interact with state legislatures in important ways. While in all states the governor presents a budget to the legislature for review and approval, in some states, budget control is merely perfunctory because the governor is given primary budgetary responsibility. In other states, though, it is a lengthy process of give and take between the executive and legislative branches that can be one of the legislature's most important functions. The governor also has veto power in nearly every state (North Carolina excepted), and in most states the veto is rarely overridden due to supermajority requirements (Alabama requires only a simple majority). In 43 states, the governor also has a form of line item veto on spending bills in addition to the general veto.

One of the most significant changes in the functioning of state legislatures in recent decades has been the adoption of term limits in several states. Public scandals, mostly at the federal level, led to a national wave of anti-incumbent sentiment in the 1980s and 1990s. This resulted in 21 states adopting some form of term limit legislation between 1990 and 1995. These laws prevent an incumbent from running for reelection after a few terms in office (typically two to four terms totaling six to 12 years). Though limits on federal terms were found unconstitutional by the U.S. Supreme Court, most of the state restrictions withstood legal challenge. As a result, by the early 2000s, 16 state legislatures were affected by limitations on the length of time an individual could serve in office. The National Conference of State Legislatures notes that in 2006 alone, 268 legislators were prevented from running for reelection due to term limits. There have likely been some positive effects to these restrictions, such as driving corrupt officials from office, breaking up "good old boy" networks, and providing additional opportunities for women and minorities.

Along with these positives, however, have come a slew of unintended consequences. Though the measures were designed in part to limit the influence of special interests on the political process by preventing long-term relationships between legislators and lobbyists, the practical result has often been a career path in which termed-out legislators move into the ranks of lobbyists, using their personal contacts and knowledge of the legislative process to push their clients' interests. Moreover, critics note that the high turnover in state legislatures has led to a lack of institutional memory and an inefficiency of process. Unelected legislative staff members are increasingly relied upon to help novice legislators figure out their jobs, and legislatures have to re-solve the same problems every few years simply because no one serving was in office the last time the issue was addressed. Finally, the evidence suggests that term limits have done little to eliminate the presence of career politicians. Those who want to remain in politics simply move from one venue to the next—from the lower chamber to the upper chamber, from elected to appointed office, and sometimes back again. It remains to be seen whether states will continue to accept these negative consequences of a well-intentioned reform, modify their term limit laws, or follow the lead of Idaho and repeal their term limits entirely.

Because of their vital role in the American political process, state legislatures have become an important topic for empirical research. Though this entry has provided a brief sketch of the role of state legislatures, one can find out more about history, trends, and up-to-date statistics by consulting the work of professional political scientists such as Malcolm E. Jewell and Alan Rosenthal, academic journals such as *State and Local Government Review* and *Publius*, and the magazines *Governing* and *State Legislatures* (along with their corresponding Web sites).

Further Reading

Carey, John M., Richard G. Niemi, and Lynda W. Powell. *Term Limits in the State Legislatures*. Ann Arbor: University of Michigan Press, 2000; Jewell, Malcolm E. *The State Legislature: Politics and Practice*. 2nd ed. New York: Random House, 1962; Moncrief, Gary F., Peverill Squire, and Malcolm E. Jewell. *Who Runs for the Legislature?* Upper Saddle River, N.J.: Prentice Hall, 2001; Morehouse, Sarah McCally, and Malcolm E. Jewell. *State Politics, Parties, & Policy*. Lanham, Md.: Rowman & Littlefield, 2003; National Conference of State Legislatures. Available

New York City mayor Michael Bloomberg at the 40th Annual West Indian–American Day Parade, September 3, 2007 *(Getty Images)*

online. URL: http://www.ncsl.org/index.htm. Accessed June 19, 2006; Rosenthal, Alan. *Heavy Lifting: The Job of the American Legislature*. Washington, D.C.: Congressional Quarterly Press, 2004; Rosenthal, Alan. *The Decline of Representative Democracy: Process, Participation, and Power in State Legislatures*. Washington, D.C.: Congressional Quarterly Press, 1998; The Institute on Money in State Politics. Available online. URL: http://www.followthemoney.org/index.phtml. Accessed June 19, 2006; Wright, Ralph G. *Inside the Statehouse: Lessons from the Speaker*. Washington, D.C.: Congressional Quarterly Press, 2005.

Charles C. Turner

mayor

A mayor is the head of a city or MUNICIPAL GOVERNMENT. Depending on the form of municipal government, a mayor can wield extensive power or play a mostly ceremonial role. Mayors are appointed by the city council or elected by the population to serve a term (usually from two to six years). In a city with a strong mayor-council form, the mayor is usually elected at large by the population and acts as executive, administrator, and titular head of the city. The council, which is also elected by the population, forms and suggests policy but is considered weak because its decisions can be vetoed by the mayor. Also, the policy that the council forms is carried out by administrators, usually appointed by the mayor. In a weak mayor-council form of government, the council has ultimate say in the direction and administration of policy. In this form, the mayor may be selected from among the council and not elected by the population. Therefore, the council has predominant power, and the mayor acts more as a coordinator. In the council-manager form, the mayor is mostly a ceremonial figure, and the manager performs the role of the administrator, who theoretically is not a political figure but is hired as a CEO to run a large corporation. It is the city council that maintains the role of forming policy. This form of government is usually found in medium to small cities, and one problem with this form of government is that it does not provide public figures with strong political power to unite citizens. In large cities, such as New York and Chicago, however, a strong mayor is usually present.

The responsibilities of mayors vary based on how strong the mayors are. A strong mayor will help set policy and also serve as an administrator. Weak mayors, as noted, will often be appointed by the council but will still hold their seat on the council, giving them some oversight but remaining as a peer. One main distinction is that a strong mayor will often have veto power over the council, but a weak mayor will not. Strong mayors appoint administrators to head the various departments in a city, such as the police, waste management, and education, as well as other positions such as treasurer and city clerk. Weak mayors do not have this appointing power, but instead the council as a whole does this. In fact, strong mayors have recently begun to take even more control. One prime example is in the field of education, where some mayors have taken over some political power in the area of public education. In most cities, the school board is elected, but poor performance in many city schools has created community pressure for mayors to become more active. In some cities, such as Chicago and Boston, the mayor has extended city control over the school districts (and this has been attempted recently in Los Angeles as well). Certainly, such moves are not seen as being beneficial in all communities and remain controversial.

The role of the mayor is also a function of the structure of the U.S. system of FEDERALISM. The federal government has its own constitutional power that is specific to it, as do the states, and there is also shared power—areas where the federal and STATE GOVERNMENTs both play a role. Cities may share some political power with the states in some aspects, but they normally must yield to state power. In practice, this political balance can be very difficult in big cites; the mayor and the GOVERNOR must test their boundaries and come up with a balance between the large city and the state power. This line is also becoming more blurry with large cities within larger county areas, and once again a balancing act must be struck between the city government and the COUNTY GOVERNMENT in order to avoid overlap and to incur the least amount of confrontations.

One way to determine the effectiveness of mayors is to examine what is considered a successful mayor. Typically, the success of mayors was measured in their ability to draw support from and also to provide services to their urban citizens. This can especially be seen in the success for years of machine-style urban politics. Bosses of machines were successful because they helped bring jobs to people, brought them support when they needed it, and also were personable—the people could relate to the bosses and also could have personal relationships with them, something that not many people can say about mayors in big cities today.

Some political scientists argue that mayors' political personality is the key to measuring their success. To be more specific, the ability to relate to people and to solve their problems and to be popular and reelected is the trademark of a successful mayor. However, others view this as being too simplistic. Another theory of mayors' success is to consider how the mayor has governed the city and how his or her governing effectiveness changes over time. In this way, for example, a mayor who has strong support and also one who has a strong ability to govern may be successful for a period of time, until support wanes with the public as funding to carry out his or her vision runs dry. This theory is criticized because it posits the idea that most mayors will ultimately fail because a city is too complex,

too much of an urban jungle, to govern successfully. A third theory examines mayors within the context of their cities. The political, economic, and social environments of cities are all different. Each city is unique, and some cities are more governable than others. Therefore, taking that into account as well as the personality and the ability of the mayor, this context theory determines how successful mayors are by figuring these aspects together.

More recently, scholars have begun to examine the mayoralty in comparison to the PRESIDENCY, using the same types of studies and considerations. Mayors have the same responsibilities as presidents but on a different scale in many respects: They are the symbolic figure of the city, they manage or administer policy, and they also act as mediators between the city and the state and the city and the federal government, much like a president acts as a foreign ambassador. Presidents are often examined in terms of the time period in which they served—presidents who serve in a crisis and handle it well are often viewed more favorably and have more potential to be successful than those who do not have such a sensational event to prove their worth. This theory divides time into four periods when mayors serve: reconstructive, articulation, disjunction, and preemption, which then cycle over time. Reconstructive mayors will be most likely to be successful; they are innovators, changing the system that was in place before them. Articulation mayors will be less successful, as they uphold the legacy that was installed before them by the innovator, or reconstructive, mayor. Disjunction mayors will be least likely to be successful, as they serve when the current system is being attacked and criticized from all sides, and they are holding on to a sinking ship. Finally, preemption mayors have some chance for success, as they challenge the existing regime before it is completely defunct, but their success or failure is not guaranteed.

Fiorello La Guardia, mayor of New York between 1934 and 1945, can be seen as one of these preemption mayors who was very successful; in fact, he has been ranked as one of the top mayors in recent history. Frank Rizzo, mayor of Philadelphia between 1972 and 1980 as well as Dennis Kucinich, mayor of Cleveland between 1977 and 1979, on the other hand, are often ranked as two of the worst mayors, although they, too, fall into the category of a preemptive mayor.

This is because their tactics to change the system failed. To be sure, the success of this type of mayor is more dependent on the factors of the city as well as the persona of the mayor.

The Daley's of Chicago are also often considered successful mayors. Richard J. Daley was mayor from 1955 to 1976 and governed basically from machine politics—he controlled the city but did so as more of a mediator, following the will of the people and not instigating policy himself. His oldest son, Richard M. Daley, as an elected mayor beginning in 1989, has a much different style. He is considered to be a part of the "new breed" of mayors in a way. Daley's taking over of the Chicago public school system in 1995 has been heralded as a success and also vouches for the changes in mayoral leadership since the 1990s. Many other mayors have adopted this take-charge attitude. Mayor Mike White of Cleveland also initiated the takeover of the public schools, which was inspired by Daley. These big city mayors of the 1990s and beyond are marked by their desire for efficiency in government. They have initiated reforms to cut down on wasteful spending, often turning to a market-driven approach based on competition. This can be seen in Mayor John Norquist of Milwaukee, who forced the city's Bureau of Building and Grounds to compete with private contractors; the bureau ultimately won the bids by eliminating wasteful practices and spending. Many Democrats, such as Norquist, are turning to these right-wing policies of market forces, while many Republicans, such as Michael Bloomberg of New York, have turned to liberal tactics. This blurring of the line between parties has changed mayoral politics to focus more on the candidates and the issues instead of parties and INTEREST GROUPS. While this can be problematic, as not having a political base to work from can be dangerous and alienating, it appears to be the new trend. Bloomberg was reelected in 2005 despite having made many enemies of conservatives and liberals alike. These mayors seem to function more as managers do in a council-manager form, focusing on the precise administration of services and running cities like businesses.

Further Reading

Dye, Thomas R., and Susan A. MacManus. *Politics in States and Communities*. 12th ed. Upper Saddle River, N.J.: Pearson Prentice Hall, 2007; Flanagan, Richard M. *Mayors and the Challenge of Urban Leadership*. Lanham, Md.: University Press of America, 2004; Holli, Melvin G. "American Mayors: The Best and the Worst since 1960." *Social Science Quarterly* 78 (1997): 149–156; Stein, Lana. "Mayoral Politics." In *Cities, Politics, and Policy: A Comparative Analysis*, edited by John P. Pelissero. Washington, D.C.: Congressional Quarterly Press, 2003.

—Baodong Liu and Carolyn Kirchhoff

militias, state

At the founding of the REPUBLIC, *militia* meant a citizen army of the STATE, what we would today refer to as a National Guard (the guard was founded in 1916). However, today, the term *militia* usually refers to a right-wing, antigovernment or paramilitary organization.

The word *militia* comes from Latin meaning "military service." The original understanding of militia as a volunteer army made up of citizen-soldiers from each state formed the bedrock of both national defense in the new republic as well as a temporary method of organizing a military or police force to maintain civil order in cases of threat or emergency. In this sense, a militia is distinct from the regular or permanent army.

The Second Amendment to the U.S. CONSTITUTION (a part of the BILL OF RIGHTS) guarantees each state the right to form a militia and that the militia could "keep and bear arms." Today, some read the Second Amendment as guaranteeing individuals the right to bear arms, but the original understanding and the words of the U.S. Constitution refer to the maintenance of a militia and that militia's right to keep and bear arms. Some of the framers believed that the presence of state militias was a way to keep the federal government in check and might serve as an antidote to the accumulation of tyrannical power by the central state. If, the belief went, the states were armed and could resist the potential of encroachment by the power of the central government, this might serve as a check on federal power.

In *Federalist 29*, Alexander Hamilton wrote that "The power of regulating the militia and of commanding its services in times of insurrection and invasion are natural incidents to the duties of superintending the common defence, and of watching over the internal peace of the confederacy." He further dismissed warnings of some of the ANTI-FEDERALISTS that this militia might become a threat to the republic, arguing that "There is something so far-fetched and so extravagant in the idea of danger to liberty from the militia that one is at a loss whether to treat it with gravity or with raillery; whether to consider it as a mere trial of skill, like the paradoxes of rhetoricians; or as a disingenuous artifice to instill prejudices at any price; or as the serious offspring of political fanaticism. Where in the name of common sense are our fears to end if we may not trust our sons, our brothers, our neighbors, our fellow citizens? What shadow of danger can there be from men who are daily mingling with the rest of their countrymen and who participate with them in the same feelings, sentiments, habits, and interests?"

The framers of the Constitution feared a standing army. They believed it would be a threat to the republic, could be used by despots to take over the government, and might tempt ambitious leaders to venture out on imperial adventures. Therefore, the framers cautioned against maintaining a standing army. Thus, after every major military encounter in the first 150 years of the republic, the United States demobilized its military and reintegrated the armies back into the community. It was only in the past 60 years, with the advent of the cold war, that the United States maintained a standing army of any size. However, in the early years of the nation, there were still threats to safety and stability that on occasion had to be met with force. Thus, a militia was authorized to form and defend the state. Not a standing, but a temporary, army, the militia was to be called together in times of threat and quell the emergency, and then these citizen-soldiers were to return to their normal lives having served their community.

In peacetime, the militias of each state were under the control of the state GOVERNOR. In wartime or during a national emergency, Congress may call up the National Guard, and it is then under the control of the president of the United States. When the National Guard is "nationalized," it is no longer under the control of the state governor but of the federal government. Today, the National Guard is funded by federal government monies. The National Guard is often called into the service of a state during natural disasters such as floods or hurricanes (e.g., in 2005 during Hurricane Katrina), during threats of civil disturbance (such as the Watts Riots in Los Angeles in 1965 as well as the riots throughout Los Angeles in 1992), and at times to serve overseas during a crisis, war, or threatened emergency (for example, in the 2003 war in Iraq). In 1990, the U.S. SUPREME COURT, in *Perpich v. Department of Defense*, held that Congress may authorize the National Guard to be put on active federal duty for training and use outside the United States (in this case, in the Persian Gulf) without the consent of the state governor and without a formal declaration of war or national emergency.

Given that the term *National Guard* has replaced *militia* to signify the state citizen-soldiers, the term *militia* has taken on a wholly new meaning. Today, *militia* refers to paramilitary organizations, usually right-wing and anti–federal government in sentiment, that oppose the power and reach of the federal government. These new militias became more prominent in the late 1980s and early 1990s. They communicate extensively over the Internet but also have a presence at gun shows, rallies against the government, and in newsletters and extremist right-wing politics. Three of the seminal events in the development of the militia movement during the 1990s involved high-profile standoffs between federal government officials and antigovernment separatists.

The first, in 1992, occurred in Ruby Ridge, Idaho, at the home of white separatist Randy Weaver, who had initially failed to show up in court on a gun-related charge. Weaver's wife was killed when federal agents stormed the home. The second standoff occurred in 1993 just outside of Waco, Texas, at what was known as the Branch Davidian Complex. An exchange of gunfire when federal agents attempted to deliver a search warrant led to the killing of four federal agents and six members of the religious sect living in the complex. After a 51-day standoff with federal authorities, Branch Davidian leader David Koresh set the entire complex on fire, which killed all 79 people inside. The third, in 1997, occurred in Texas when the Republic of Texas separatist movement, led by Richard McLaren, held a husband and wife hostage in the west Texas town of Fort Davis in an attempt to force state officials to release two members of the group who had been arrested. McLaren and his followers claimed that the state of Texas had been illegally annexed to the United States and was still a sovereign nation.

These incidents had a powerful symbolic resonance for the militia movement, served to encourage these movements' members to identify the federal government as "the enemy," and helped persuade members that there was a conspiracy in the federal government to destroy the freedoms (especially their perceived right to keep and bear arms) enjoyed by "free Americans." The federal government continues to monitor these groups, and occasional confrontations erupt into violence and disorder.

In the modern world with the methods of modern warfare, is the militia necessary or even functional? Or is it an anachronism of a far different era? While constitutionally protected, militias in the traditional sense may be politically unnecessary in our age. As such, the nation might be better served by eliminating them altogether or modifying militias to perform more modern tasks. But such changes would require a change in the U.S. Constitution, and Americans are very reluctant to change the Constitution. For this reason, whether militias make political and military sense in the 21st century is secondary to the larger conundrum of America's deeply felt reluctance to change the Constitution.

Further Reading
Abanes, Richard. *American Militias: Rebellion, Racism & Religion*. Downers Grove, Ill.: InterVarsity Press, 1996; Cornell, Saul. *A Well-Regulated Militia: The Founding Fathers and the Origins of Gun Control in America*. New York: Oxford University Press, 2006. Hamilton, Neil A. *Militias in America: A Reference Handbook*. Santa Barbara, Calif.: ABC-CLIO, 1996. Whisker, James B. *The Rise and Decline of the American Militia System*. London: Associated University Presses, 1999;

—Michael A. Genovese

municipal courts
Municipal courts are authorized by village, town, or city ordinances (laws) and are funded by these local units of government. The courts possess limited powers and JURISDICTIONS. More persons, citizen and noncitizen, come into contact with municipal courts than all other STATE and federal courts in the United States. Thus, an individual's impression of a state's judicial system may depend on that individual's experience with municipal courts. More MEDIA attention and research inquiries are focused on federal and state district, appeals, and supreme courts than on municipal courts. This is unfortunate, since munici-

pal courts help to protect peace, dignity, and civilized behavior in most states.

Past and present authors of STATE CONSTITUTIONS and city, town, and village charters have been generally suspicious of governmental powers. Therefore, legal and political limits are placed on the legislative, executive, and judicial departments of government. Each branch or department is expected to play a significant role, however varied, in the checking and balancing of the power of the other branches in the governing of communities. Thus, municipal courts' powers tend to be limited and shared with city councils and boards (legislative bodies). Their powers are also shared with CITY MANAGERs, police departments, city attorneys, and other administrative agencies and executive bodies. Political and legal powers are widely dispersed and not concentrated in any one branch of state or local government.

Sharing of power occurs when municipal court judges are appointed by a MAYOR (an executive) with the advice and approval of the city council or town board (the legislative branch). Those judges usually serve a term of between two and four years (although some terms may be longer) as determined by the state (or local) legislative and executive branches. Limits on tenure in office also act as a check on the courts' and the judges' power. CHECKS AND BALANCES are present when a state legislature sets a fixed annual salary for municipal judges to help prevent two potentially "bad" things from occurring. First, an annual fixed salary policy prevents an angry or vindictive municipal board and/or executive from reducing a judge's pay to punish that judge's court decisions. Second, a fixed salary prevents an enterprising judge from padding his or her salary by imposing, collecting, and pocketing more fines and fees than would be appropriate.

The political interplay of differing personal values and ambitions, the economic status of communities, and the different branches of government encroaching on the powers of each other result in different authority and jurisdiction granted to municipal courts. Some states, such as South Carolina, have laws that prevent municipal courts from having jurisdiction over civil disputes. But these same courts do have jurisdiction over violations of municipal ordinances, such as motor vehicle violations and disorderly conduct. Some states limit the municipal court's ability to fine or incarcerate violators by setting maximum limits of $500 for fines or 30 days for jail time or both. In this case, the legislative body is clearly checking the power of the judicial branch. On the other hand, the Philadelphia, Pennsylvania, municipal court has argued for expanded jurisdictional powers and has been granted such authority. The municipal court in Philadelphia, is responsible for adjudicating civil cases in which the amount being contested is $10,000 or less for small claims, unlimited amounts in landlord and tenant cases, and $15,000 in school tax or real estate disputes. Philadelphia's municipal courts may also resolve criminal cases that carry a maximum sentence of jail time of five years or less.

Fines are the most common form of punishment handed down by municipal judges. Municipal courts, in general, deal with less serious crimes or misdemeanors. In Texas, when municipal ordinances relating to fire safety, public health, or ZONING are violated, fines of up to $2,000 may be charged, but only if authorized by the local governing unit within the municipality. This introduces yet another check on a municipal court's ability to balance a diverse community's needs with the public's interests.

Some portion of the monies assessed by each municipal court in fines or fees goes into the MUNICIPAL GOVERNMENT's general fund. Some of these same dollars help to fund the municipal court and, perhaps, improve its efficiency. Therefore, there is a sharing of economic resources, legal jurisdictions, and discretion by these policy-making institutions. While municipal courts share authority in balancing and checking power, for the most part the judiciary is different from the other branches of government in a most important way. Municipal courts may not set their own legal and political agenda. Mayors, town or village board members, and municipal administrators can initiate new policies, but judges cannot. Moreover, municipal court judges cannot introduce or file lawsuits, civil actions, and misdemeanor violations cases on their own initiative. Municipal judges can resolve conflicts and legal infractions only in cases brought before the bench by others. This is a significant check on judicial power.

The Tennessee state legislature both gives and takes away legal jurisdiction to and from municipal courts, as do other states at different times. In 2006, the Tennessee General Assembly legislated that munic-

ipal offenses, also contained in many municipal codes across the United States, may no longer be enforced in the municipal courts of that state. Thus, Tennessee municipal courts may not hear cases for violations of municipal ordinances such as requiring drivers to yield to emergency vehicles, preventing cruelty to animals, vandalism, window peeping, or possession of an abandoned refrigerator. The same legislature, however, allowed municipal court judges to issue inspection code warrants to building enforcement officers when probable cause exists that a code violation may be occurring on an individual's private property. Legislative bodies can curb municipal judges or, on the other hand, increase their power and jurisdiction. This dynamic process balances the state and local prerogatives, at the same time checking judicial power.

In other situations, however, municipal court judges may expand their powers by checking and balancing the local and state legislative and executive branches. One of the first actions taken by a newly appointed municipal court judge from Wilmington, Delaware, in 1946 was to abolish the segregated seating he found in his courtroom. Before this decision, a police officer would stand at the entrance to the municipal courtroom and direct members of the public to one side or the other depending on the color of their skin. This judicial action of racial integration upset state and local customs. It also checked legislative mandates and executive decisions heretofore imposed on municipal courts in Delaware.

Municipal courts can be limited laboratories of experiment within a state. Municipal court judges obtained volunteer counsel for indigent persons accused of municipal code violations (a crime) even before the U.S. SUPREME COURT did so in 1963. The former municipal court system in Wilmington, Delaware, even helped set up a probation system and permitted first-time offenders to be freed on their own recognizance. Later, these procedures, initiated by the municipal courts, became state law. These events demonstrate that a balancing of power within one branch of government may provide checks and balances on other branches of government in that state.

The issue of judicial independence in the SEPARATION OF POWERS system arises in several ways concerning municipal courts. A 2004 Missouri survey revealed that most municipal court administrators and/or clerks said they wanted greater separation from the executive branch. It seems that many court employees not only have to report to the municipal judge but also to another member of the city government's executive branch (city manager, director of finance, city clerk, or chief of police). Some court officers hold additional titles such as police dispatcher, city clerk, or even city collector. Still others may be full-time city or village employees but do not work full time within the municipal courts. Municipal courts depend on local community funding and operate with mostly part-time judges and part-time staff. An outside observer might contend that such courts do not have sufficient capacity to manage their own internal workings. Such limitations may ultimately undermine the independence of the judicial branch at the municipal level. Under these circumstances, the responsibility (if not the obligation) of the municipal court to be an independent check on the other branches of government is jeopardized. The separation of powers principle is violated when executive branch officers disallow training funds for judges, court administrators, and clerks.

Another check on judicial independence occurs when, in states such as Colorado, residency is required by a municipality. This may deprive the community of a more meritorious judge who happens to have chosen to live outside the confines of that municipality. Municipal judges in Wisconsin are required to run in an at-large community election, presumably to be accountable to the electorate. Some argue that elections make for a more independent judiciary because legislative and executive preferences may be negated or checked by voters. Others maintain that litigants in municipal courts may consist of groups or classes of people who might be unpopular with vast segments of the electorate. It could be argued that municipal judges up for reelection and mindful of the electorate's biases might subject such litigants to maximum fines and jail sentences or discriminate against them in some other way. The influence of voters then can check and balance, at times, all three branches of government.

Legitimacy, trust, and confidence in municipal courts is necessary to both the RULE OF LAW and to the strengthening of the judicial branch within the checks and balances system. It is important that states and localities measure the current level of confidence in municipal and STATE COURTS. The nation's most populous state, California, recently conducted a survey that disclosed that about two-thirds of the public had an overall positive opinion of the state's courts (including municipal courts). The results signified an improvement in the opinion of courts in the eyes of average people, because in 1992, only 50 percent of Californians polled viewed the courts favorably. When challenged by the other branches of government, the courts might be able to point to the public support of their performance. During 2006, Las Vegas, Nevada, made an evaluation of its municipal court judges that provided supportive evidence to bolster an overall positive assessment of judicial performance. Around 70 percent of respondents believed that nearly all municipal court judges were familiar with the records and documents of a case. They also believed that the judges weighed all the evidence and arguments judiciously before handing down fair verdicts. The professional conduct of these Nevada municipal court judges is said to indicate that their courtrooms are characterized by a lack of bias with regard to race, gender, religion, and the contending parties. These reports from California and Nevada seem to show public support for municipal courts.

On the other hand, New York State's 300-year-old municipal court system, present in many villages and towns, has been criticized for putting up with less than adequately trained judges and a lack of professional facilities. These failings diminish the judiciary's standing in the community and limit its ability to check and balance the other two branches of government. It might even be suggested that some municipal courts are simply unable to command enough respect within their communities to bring the judiciary up to par. It has been reported that in some rural areas and smaller towns, municipal judges hold court in highway department garages, fire stations, or their homes. Moreover, these part-time judges are said to occasionally jail people illegally or deny fundamental court procedural guarantees. Some defendants allege that they were subjected to other kinds of discrimination based on race or gender. Such criticism indicates the potential for a flawed municipal court system in New York. What accounts for these fissures in the judicial branch at the local level? Most small town municipal court judges are poorly paid, and up to three-fourths are not lawyers. Some have light caseloads, but others with heavy caseloads may be able to spend only little time with each case that comes before them. Under these conditions, it may appear that justice is not being well served in municipal courts and that these courts function badly in the checks and balances framework.

In situations similar to those mentioned above, it appears that municipal judges need more frequent training and to be required to pass more examinations before taking the bench. Requirements that municipal judgeships transition to full-time lawyers instead of nonlawyers and a call for improved supervision of municipal court judges by the state's district or supreme court commissions seem appropriate. In some jurisdictions, providing municipal courts with more computers, digital recorders, improved facilities, annual audits, and additional staff seems justified.

Municipal courts were originally installed to settle local disputes in rural, small town America. There was less need for full-time judges, support staff, or well-equipped courtrooms in the early days of the REPUBLIC. In the 21st century, however, with the increased or even excessive caseloads, there is more work for the municipal courts and their personnel. Many municipal judges handle 6,000 to 10,000 cases per year. If municipal courts are to remain flexible and perform the role of checks and balances within a state's system of justice—a major contribution to the maintenance of law and order—then municipal courts must continue to be evaluated with a critical eye and supported with adequate resources by their diverse municipalities.

Further Reading

Gambitta, Richard A. L., Marlynn L. May, and James C. Foster. *Governing through Courts*. Beverly Hills, Calif.: Sage Publications, 1981; Karlen, Delmar. *The Citizen in Court: Litigant. Witness. Juror. Judge*. New York: Holt, Rinehart, & Winston, 1964; Meyer, Jon'a, and Paul Jesilow. *"Doing Justice" in the People's Court: Sentencing by Municipal Court Judges*. Albany: State University of New York Press, 1997.

—Steve J. Mazurana and Paul Hodapp

municipal government

The U.S. CONSTITUTION established a framework in which American governments have separate but not completely independent authorities. Certain functions, such as interstate commerce and national defense, are assigned to the national government, while many others are left to the STATES. The Tenth Amendment in the BILL OF RIGHTS asserts that "the powers not delegated to the United States by the Constitution, nor prohibited by it to the States, are reserved to the States respectively, or to the people." However, the INTERGOVERNMENTAL RELATIONS among federal, state, and local governments in the United States are extremely complex. Traditional FEDERALISM (dual federalism) suggests that federal and STATE GOVERNMENTs operate interdependently within their separate jurisdictions without relying on each other for assistance or authorization. In order to cope with complicated economic and social issues, there have been several waves of institutional and ideological changes in the implementation of federalism in the United States. The NEW DEAL period began a continuous increase in the importance of intergovernmental relationships in the United States, followed by creative federalism in Lyndon Johnson's presidency, new federalism under Richard Nixon, and recent devolution of federal involvement. The pressures from a new global economy further complicate the relationship between different levels of government. Federal, state, and local governments are continuously looking for the optimal mechanism by which they can cooperate and serve the public interest.

There are several different forms of local government in America, such as COUNTY GOVERNMENT, city or municipal government, SPECIAL DISTRICTS (e.g., school, fire, and sewage), and special authorities (e.g., transit and port). Municipal governments are local governments established to serve residents within an area of concentrated population. As the United States became a highly urbanized country, with more than 80 percent of its populations living in urbanized areas, its local governments have assumed a critically important role to directly serve the needs of local residents, providing a wide range of services from police, fire protection, and garbage collection to housing, transportation, and planning. According to the 2002 Census of Governments, in addition to the federal and 50 state governments, there were 87,849 units of local governments as of June 30, 2002. Of these, 38,971 were general purpose local governments—3,034 county governments and 35,937 subcounty governments, including 19,431 municipal governments and 16,506 township governments. The remainder, which constituted more than half the total, were special purpose local governments, including 13,522 school district governments and 35,356 special district governments.

To carry out the functions of local government, cities are chartered by states, and their charters detail the objectives and authorities of the municipal government. Traditionally, the state legislature is recognized as having plenary (complete) control over municipal governments except as limited by the state or federal Constitution, which is commonly referred to as "Dillon's law," named for Judge John Forest Dillon, the chief justice of the Iowa Supreme Court more than 100 years ago, after he authored two seminal opinions establishing the modern RULE OF LAW by which the powers of local governments are evaluated. Dillon's law requires that localities obtain express permission from the state before enacting certain kinds of legislation. Legislation required by Dillon's law is often called "enabling" legislation. Under Dillon's law, STATE LEGISLATURES had to devote attention to the details of local government issues and found insufficient resources and time to deal with substantial matters of state policy. On the other hand, local government did not possess sufficient authority to deal with complicated local issues. Therefore, in some states, municipal reformers created a new concept of local control, which incorporated part of the inherent right to local self-government rule yet retained a part of the sovereignty of the states. That new principle became known as home rule. In very general terms, home rule can be defined as the transfer of power from the state to units of local government for the purpose of implementing local self government. Home rule has taken various forms around the country in the more than 40 states that have adopted it. In most states, home rule provides those local governments with some measure of freedom from state interference as well as some ability to exercise powers and perform functions without a prior express delegation of authority from the state.

While their powers are derived from the state constitution and laws enacted by the legislature, municipalities themselves are created only by the request and consent of the residents within the municipal area. Communities may incorporate as cities if their residents initiate a petition conforming to state laws. For example, in California, incorporation may be initiated by resolution of a county board of supervisors or by citizen petition, which must be signed by at least 25 percent of the locally registered voters. The petition is then submitted to the Local Agency Formation Commission (LAFCO), which reviews the proposed plan for incorporation, conducts a hearing, and then approves or denies the proposal. If the petition is approved, the board of supervisors conducts a hearing and, if without majority protest, call an election. The incorporation must be approved by a majority of the voters living within the proposed municipality. A municipality can also be disincorporated if petitioned by more than 20 percent of the voters, and a majority of those voting in a special election will determine the outcome. Municipal governments may legislate to protect the safety, welfare, and health of their residents. Municipal governments safeguard lives and property through fire and police protection; provide public facilities such as water, roads and sewage; and determine local land use in a way that is most compatible with community economic, environmental, and social goals by planning and ZONING.

Most local governments rely heavily on intergovernmental transfers, property taxes (sometimes INCOME TAXES), and miscellaneous charges to provide services to their residents. According to the 2002 Census of Governments, intergovernmental revenue made up about 25 percent of the total revenue for municipal governments, 18.5 percent of which came from the state government, 4.5 percent from the federal government, and the remaining 2 percent from other local governments. General revenue from their own sources made up about 60 percent of the total revenue for municipal governments, 36 percent of which came from taxes and the rest from charges and miscellaneous fees. The rest of municipal finance came from utility revenues. As local government responsibilities have increased but their own revenue sources have not kept pace, partially due to declining state support and receding federal aid, some municipal governments have started looking for alternative service provision to reduce their financial burdens. Some municipalities seek formal or informal intergovernmental service agreements, and others try to control costs while maintaining a high quality of services by privatizing public services, although the results of privatization or contracting out have turned out mixed. In order to secure a city's revenue base, urban policy making has been argued to be largely determined by economic forces. Cities must compete for mobile wealth in the intergovernmental marketplace or face perpetual fiscal crises and must pursue "developmental policies"—policies that provide incentives for investors and higher-income residents to locate in the jurisdiction. Economic growth is often viewed as a compelling city interest that all citizens share, as it enhances the tax base and increases economic opportunity. Local government is primarily concerned with economic growth, and many cities have formed an apparatus of interlocking progrowth associations and government units, which is commonly referred to as "growth machines." Local business communities are the major participants in growth coalitions, with their continuous interaction with public officials giving them systemic power, and they are assisted by lawyers, syndicators, and property brokers.

There are three general types of municipal government: the mayor-council, the commission, and the council-manager. Some cities may have developed a combination of two or three of these forms.

A mayor-council is the traditional form of municipal government in the United States and was used by nearly all American cities until the early 20th century. The structure of a mayor-council municipal government is similar to state and federal governments and preserves the basic SEPARATION OF POWERS between the legislative and executive branches, with an elected MAYOR as chief of the executive branch and an elected council representing the legislative branch. There are two variations of mayor-council government: the weak-mayor and strong-mayor forms. Under the weak-mayor form, the council possesses both legislative and executive authority and may appoint important administrative officials and approve the mayor's appointees. The council also exercises primary control over the municipal budget. The mayor lacks administrative power, and the

authorities are fragmented. The weak-mayor form suits only smaller and simpler governments. Under the strong-mayor form, the mayor appoints heads of city departments and other officials, has the power of veto over ordinances, and is responsible for preparing the city's budget. The council passes city ordinances, sets tax rates, and apportions money among city departments. The strong-mayor form makes the mayor the dominant force in city government and is very popular in many large American cities.

A commission form of government combines both the legislative and executive functions in one group of commissioners, usually three or more in number and elected citywide. Each commissioner supervises the work of one or more city departments. One of the commissioners may be named chairperson of the body or mayor, but the mayor normally has no more authority than other commissioners. This form provides for no separation of powers, lacks internal CHECKS AND BALANCES, and lacks a strong chief executive. The commission form first evolved in response to a major hurricane in Galveston, Texas, as an emergency recovery mechanism and is rarely used today in American cities.

A council-manager form of government consists of a small city council, usually five to seven people, that is often elected citywide and responsible for making a budget, passing ordinances, and supervising the administration of municipal government. A professional CITY MANAGER is hired with full responsibility for day-to-day operations. A mayor may exist but only performs strictly ceremonial duties and has no involvement in the city's administrative affairs. Similar to the commission form, all executive and legislative powers reside in the council alone, and no separation of powers or checks and balances is provided. The professional administrator carries out the decisions of the council, produces a budget, and supervises most of the departments. Usually, there is no set term, and the administrator serves as long as the council is satisfied with his or her work. Bringing in such a business manager–like professional administrator appears to improve the efficiency of local government, and the model has been adopted in more and more upper- and middle-class suburban cities.

The last half of the 20th century witnessed significant changes of population settlement in many advanced countries, symbolized by population spreading to low-density suburbs. In the United States, the rate of population growth in the suburbs has been more than twice that of the cities. The global economy imposed another strong challenge for localities to compete in the international marketplace. All these transformations have profound consequences for local government. New regionalism has been developed as one major mechanism that helps cities to solve issues such as city-suburb disparity, unbridled sprawl, and global competition from a regional perspective. Municipalities across the United States have used various new regionalism approaches to expand their jurisdiction or reach beyond formal borders, including city-county consolidations, annexations, interlocal agreements, extraterritorial jurisdiction, and multitiered governments.

New regionalism requires that communities look outward to the larger metropolis and consider their collective future. City-county consolidation and forming a unified municipal (metropolitan) government have been one of the most debatable approaches to achieve economies of scale by reducing the number of local government units.

Since the consolidation of New Orleans in 1805, there have been hundreds of local government consolidation attempts, but only 34 of them succeeded. The 1960s witnessed some significant successful consolidation efforts, including the Nashville-Davidson, Tennessee, consolidation in 1962, the Jacksonville-Duval County, Florida, consolidation in 1967, and the Indianapolis-Marion County, Indiana, consolidation in 1969. There had not been a consolidation at the magnitude of these three cities until the Louisville-Jefferson County, Kentucky, governments merged into a metropolitan government in 2000. Pittsburgh, Pennsylvania, Albuquerque, New Mexico, Fort Wayne, Indiana, Buffalo, New York, Topeka, Kansas, and Des Moines, Iowa, are among several areas that have recently tried and failed to pass such legislation or are considering city-county consolidation. The proposals to consolidate a city and county government have not achieved a high rate of success (less than 15 percent) due to the reason that consolidation alone does not guarantee effectiveness, efficiency, and equity in municipal governments. Many times, consolidation is just used as a political mechanism to alter

a territorial boundary and political structure for different INTEREST GROUPS.

Besides city-county consolidation, there are other ways in which the agenda of new regionalism can be achieved. For example, the twin cities of Minneapolis and St. Paul, Minnesota, applied a multitiered approach. A tiered approach is more agile than consolidation because it allows for some problems to be managed at their most appropriate local level and for regional problems to be addressed by a metropolitan authority. A linked function approach, as was attempted in Charlotte, North Carolina, is another experiment to include a city and its county under the rubric of governance by functions. Unlike consolidation or multitiered systems, linked functions are flexible and require no new levels of government. Another route to new regionalism lies in the notion of "complex networks," which advocates large numbers of independent governments voluntarily cooperating through multiple, overlapping webs of interlocal agreements. The Pittsburgh area has adopted various kinds of intergovernmental agreements in order to maximize efficiency through complex networks.

Further Reading

Leland, Suzanne M., and Kurt Thurmaier, eds. *Case Studies of City-County Consolidation: Reshaping the Local Government Landscapes.* Armonk, N.Y.: M.E. Sharpe, 2004; Logan, John R., and Harvey L. Molotch. *Urban Fortunes: The Political Economy of Place.* Berkeley: University of California Press, 1987; Peterson, Paul. *City Limits.* Chicago: University of Chicago Press, 1981; Savitch, H. V., and Ronald K. Vogel. "Paths to New Regionalism." *State and Local Government Review* 32, no. 3 (2000): 158–168; Wilson, Woodrow. "The Study of Administration." *Political Science Quarterly* 2 (1887): 197–222; Wright, Deil S. "Federalism, Intergovernmental Relations, and Intergovernmental Management: Historical Reflections and Conceptual Comparisons." *Public Administration Review* 50, no. 2 (1990);168–178.

—Lin Ye and Hank V. Savitch

municipal home rule

Home rule refers to the concept of self-governance and the extent to which a particular level of government has authority to govern its own affairs. Synonymous with sovereignty and autonomy, the notion of home rule can be applied to any level of government. In the context of American MUNICIPAL GOVERNMENT, home rule refers to the extent to which municipalities (commonly referred to as cities) govern their own affairs, free from interference by STATE or national authorities. In recent decades, municipalities in the United States have seen a tremendous erosion of their powers of home rule, particularly over fiscal matters. Today, the regulation of land use remains the primary area over which municipalities retain substantial autonomy.

The U.S. CONSTITUTION makes no mention of the governments of cities, instead establishing spheres of authority for state and national governments. Prior to the mid-19th century, the debate over the status of cities remained obscure, as events in sparsely populated and geographically isolated cities and towns usually had limited importance beyond their borders. However, as cities began to industrialize in the middle to late 19th century, new economic, social, and political conditions emerged. In particular, industrialization and rapid IMMIGRATION from Europe as well as internal migration from American farms overwhelmed cities with crowding, pollution, and disease, placing tremendous strain on city services and infrastructure. In order to respond adequately, cities began to petition their STATE GOVERNMENTs for new powers of taxation to pay for services such as infrastructure development, public safety, and education. The crisis spawned a debate over the inherent powers of cities and forced the first serious appraisal of the legal status of cities in the American political system.

Although a few legal scholars had previously wrestled with the question of municipal home rule, an 1868 ruling by Iowa Supreme Court justice John F. Dillon has largely framed subsequent debates over municipal sovereignty. Known as Dillon's rule, the principle established that cities are legally "creatures of the state," possessing no sovereignty independent of what their state governments permit. According to Dillon, "Municipal corporations owe their origin to, and derive their powers and rights wholly from, the Legislature. [The Legislature] breathes into them the breath of life without which they cannot exist. As it creates so it may destroy. . . ." Although Judge Dillon's decision relegated cities to the status of supplicants to

their state governments, his argument was not well supported by the historical record. Defenders of municipal autonomy pointed out that the sovereignty of numerous American cities during the colonial period preceded the creation of their state governments. Nevertheless, the principle of Dillon's rule became the dominant legal paradigm governing relations between states and municipalities.

The question of why Dillon's rule came to define relations between states and cities has been addressed by a number of scholars. Most agree that state supremacy was ultimately decided and enforced for political rather than constitutional reasons. Urban historian Stephen Elkin argues that Dillon's underlying purpose was "to protect private property [from the] kind of democracy developing in cities." For Elkin, state judicial oversight and other constraints on cities, including the requirement of balanced budgets, limits on taxing authority, and restrictions on borrowing, were imposed to protect corporate interests from the emergence of countervailing regulatory power by some reform-minded municipal governments. In addition, state officials argued that state regulations were needed, in their view, to rid cities of corrupt practices by immigrant-run urban political machines.

In analyzing the politics of the home rule debate, scholars also highlight ethnic and religious conflict between Protestant native-born citizens operating at the state level and mostly Catholic and Jewish immigrants from Ireland and southern and eastern Europe who had assumed political control of cities such as Boston, New York, and Chicago. In short, Dillon's rule enabled largely Protestant rural interests that controlled STATE LEGISLATURES to contain emerging political power in America's cities and to thwart potential government interference in capital and labor relations. In doing so, these interests could ensure that cities would remain primarily instruments of unregulated CAPITALISM rather than agents of social reform.

By the early 20th century, however, urban reformers had mounted a counteroffensive. In making their case for greater home rule, urban reformers drew upon a cultural history of self-governance and deeply rooted traditions of American local control. Known as the "home rule movement" and led by disaffected urban middle-class Protestants, the effort resulted in allowing cities to write their own constitutions (called charters) to permit increased home rule. As a result, cities in many states—mostly large cities—gained greater leeway to set up their own forms of government, conduct municipal elections, and engage in other initiatives not otherwise prohibited by state law. For example, today, cities with home rule charters will probably have greater leeway in passing living wage ordinances and establishing public financing of municipal elections than cities without home rule charters. Perhaps the most significant legal victory for the municipal home rule movement came in the 1926 U.S. Supreme Court decision *City of Euclid v. Ambler Realty Co.,* which essentially placed the power to regulate land use under the purview of local governments. Today, the power to regulate land development remains the most important area over which municipalities exercise home rule.

As part of their strategy to win greater latitude to govern themselves, cities also pushed to establish a legal distinction between issues considered "municipal affairs" from those of "statewide concern." However, problems quickly arose in clearly defining whether an issue was of municipal or statewide concern. For example, policy areas such as education and housing do not easily lend themselves to rigid classification as either solely municipal or statewide concerns. In practice, significant gray areas emerge in determining which level of government should ultimately decide a particular issue. What has emerged in most states is a political tension between issues of statewide concern and municipal affairs, similar to ongoing political turf battles between federal and state governments. Historically, STATE COURTS have intervened on a case-by-case basis to draw these lines, usually erring on the side of Dillon's rule.

Although the home rule movement dates from the 19th century and saw its zenith during the 1920s, several states have granted their cities home rule fairly recently, including Massachusetts (1965), North Dakota (1966), Florida (1968), Pennsylvania (1968), Iowa (1968), and Montana (1972). In 1970, Illinois gave home rule status to all cities with populations of more than 25,000 and made provisions for smaller cities to achieve home rule by citizen petition and voter approval. Some form of home rule now operates in more than half the states and two-thirds of cities with populations of more than 200,000, although its extent varies from state to state.

In recent decades, cities have seen a substantial erosion of their home rule authority, particularly over fiscal matters. For example, in 1978 California voters passed Proposition 13, which capped property taxes at 1 percent of assessed value, severely limiting the ability of cities and other local governments to raise money. Soon after, states such as Massachusetts and later Colorado passed similar laws constraining the ability of local governments to raise money. Moreover, in order to address budgetary crises during the 1990s and early 2000s, some states simply withheld funds allocated to local governments in order to cover their budget shortfalls, forcing drastic service reductions. The decline of fiscal home rule has led to a number of consequences, some predictable, some unintended. In addition to overall declining service levels, cities in California have scrambled to find alternative revenue sources. In order to maximize their tax revenue, California cities are now far more inclined to approve commercial developments, which generate the highly coveted sales tax, rather than housing, a practice known as the "fiscalization land use." The unforeseen result has contributed to both a shortage of affordable housing in the state and fueled historically high property values.

Although cities have been most active in pressing state governments for home rule, a modest home rule movement for counties has been under way. Today, 37 states permit counties some form of home rule charter, usually more limited than that for cities. Nationwide, only about 80 of the nation's 3,086 counties enjoy even such limited home rule. Most of these are large, urban counties, and 11 are in California.

Although home rule seems inherently good in terms of DEMOCRACY and local control, critics point out that it contributes to social inequality by making municipal governments responsible for policies that often have wider social implications. For example, critics especially blame home rule over land use as a primary factor in the lack of affordable housing and in particular the economic and ethnic segregation of housing patterns. In addition, in parts of the country where municipalities also govern public schools, home rule over land use has led to gross inequalities in access to adequate education for minorities and the poor. Armed with unfettered home rule authority over land use, many cities simply refuse to provide any affordable housing at all. However, in a few states, such as Oregon and Washington, state governments have imposed fairly strict conditions that require most cities and counties to build affordable housing. Critics respond that such state interference violates local government home rule, so far to no avail. Ultimately, the ideal of home rule, a cherished tradition of American local government, remains in perpetual tension with the notion of local governments as "creatures of the states" and the need to provide statewide solutions to issues of regional or statewide importance.

Further Reading

Christensen, Terry, and Tom Hogen-Esch. *Local Politics: A Practical Guide to Governing at the Grassroots*. Armonk, N.Y.: M.E. Sharpe, 2006. Danielson, Michael N. *The Politics of Exclusion*. New York: Columbia University Press, 1976; Davis, Mike. *City of Quartz*. New York: Vintage Books, 1990; Elkin, Steven. *City and Regime in the American Republic*. Chicago: University of Chicago Press, 1987; Gottdeiner, Mark. *The Social Production of Urban Space*. Austin: University of Texas Press, 1985; Judd, Dennis R., and Todd Swanstrom. *City Politics: Private Power and Public Policy*. New York: Longman, 2002; Linowes, R. Robert, and Don. T. Allensworth. *The Politics of Land Use*. New York: Praeger Publishers, 1973; Logan, John R., and Harvey L. Molotch. *Urban Fortunes: The Political Economy of Place*. Berkeley: University of California Press, 1987; Ross, Bernard H., and Myron A. Levine. *Urban Politics: Power in Metropolitan America*. Belmont, Calif.: Thompson Wadsworth, 2006; Weiher, Gregory R. *The Fractured Metropolis: Political Fragmentation and Metropolitan Segregation*. Albany: State University of New York Press, 1991.

—Tom Hogen-Esch

planning boards

Planning boards, also known as planning commissions, ZONING commissions, and zoning boards, serve an important local and regional government function. Boards work to advise local legislative bodies and planning departments on a wide range of land development, zoning, and land use planning issues. Additionally, planning boards are often delegated power to make decisions on site plans and other development decisions. They are intended to serve as a link between the community at large, developers, planning professionals, and elected officials. The origin of planning boards in the United States dates back to the 1920s. Most localities in the United States today have zoning ordinances, comprehensive plans, and planning boards.

Land use planning in the United States was and is largely a local matter. However, the forces that have shaped land use planning and the structure and powers of planning boards are national in scope. Land use controls have a long history in the United States. They began as soon as cities emerged in the American colonies. For example, farms, cemeteries, and similar uses of land that were once outside the city became a problem once cities grew. Farms produced animal waste that became a public health concern when city dwellers moved closer, and cemeteries were thought to produce unhealthy vapors. Cities passed laws that prohibited these land uses.

Beginning in the 1890s, the Progressive movement sought to change the way cities were governed and to improve the conditions of urban life. Modern land use planning in the United States emerged out of these goals, and the creation of planning boards was part of this movement. As the conditions of urban slums were exposed, efforts were made to make cities more pleasant places to live. Parks, both large and small, emerged in cities during this time as efforts to create beautiful places and to meet the recreational needs of urban populations. These efforts, known as the City Beautiful movement, sought to improve the aesthetics of buildings in addition to building parks.

Improvement of city government was also a focus of both the Progressive and City Beautiful movements. City planners emerged early in the 20th century to shape American cities, and zoning ordinances were created to define the ways that property could be used. For example, a typical zoning ordinance defines residential, recreational, commercial, industrial, and agricultural areas. The first comprehensive zoning ordinance in the United States was developed in New York City in 1916. Zoning ordinances spread quickly through American cities and developing suburbs, and by 1930 zoning had emerged as a powerful tool for planners to use in shaping the physical and human landscape of communities.

Zoning and comprehensive planning remain controversial. Supporters of zoning ordinances urge that these rules create a blueprint for the development of a community. Specifically, they promote public safety and public health, discourage overcrowding of land and overpopulation, and provide for good public services and PUBLIC UTILITIES. Furthermore, zoning protects the integrity of neighborhoods. A good example is the attempt to keep residential areas safe from the encroachment of factories and other businesses. Critics of zoning have two basic concerns. First, opponents argue that zoning, by limiting the use of land, was and continues to be a violation of PROPERTY RIGHTS. A second criticism of zoning is that the regulations are set up to preserve middle- and upper-class enclaves at the expense of the rest of the community. Zoning can be used to exclude unwanted people or uses of property. The U.S. SUPREME COURT upheld the constitutionality of zoning in *Village of Euclid v. Ambler Realty* (272 U.S. 375, 1926).

The basic structure of zoning and planning in the United States today still follows the recommendations developed in the 1920s by the U.S. DEPARTMENT OF COMMERCE's 1922 A Standard State Zoning Enabling Act (SSZEA) and the 1928 A Standard City Planning Enabling Act (SCPEA). By 1930, 35 states had passed versions of the SSZEA, and eventually all 50 states passed laws that allowed local and regional governments to zone property. In 47 states, the SSZEA still serves as the basis of state enabling legislation. The SCPEA proved less popular but was passed in many states, and it is still a basis of city planning throughout the United States. These two model laws recommended that states give local governments the authority to regulate land use through zoning in conformance with a comprehensive plan, recommended that public hearings be required before zoning laws were created and enforced, and recommended the establishment of planning boards to develop zoning laws and enforce them.

The nation's first planning board, the Los Angeles County Planning Commission, was created in 1922. After the U.S. Department of Commerce's model state laws were issued, planning boards spread quickly as zoning ordinances were created. As modeled in the SSZEA and the SCPEA, a typical planning board serves a locality—a city or town—and has seven to nine members who serve three- to four-year staggered terms. They meet twice a month, and members serve without compensation.

There is a great deal of variation outside the typical structure, however. Boards also serve counties or other regional areas. Boards can be as small as five members, while others can have as many as 20 members. Terms of office range widely as well, with some serving only two years and other serving six or more years. Some planning boards meet weekly, but most meet at least once a month. When planning members are paid, they do the work for modest sums generally intended to cover only the costs associated with service.

Boards are appointed by the community's elected leaders and are made up of community members. Some boards include one member from the local legislative body, the city council or the town board. Planning board members often come from the business community. It is not uncommon for members to have experience in development and construction, such as builders, real estate agents, architects, and engineers. Other common professional backgrounds include lawyers and teachers. As with other public officials, the percentage of women on planning boards has grown in recent years. In most instances, planning board members are not required to get training. Training is most likely to be available in more populous communities. Planning boards members also get training by attending regional or national conferences and workshops.

Planning boards work with local government planning departments to do their work. These professional staffs vary in size and expertise. The planning department is responsible for giving advice to planning boards and processing the range of documents that are part of developments and comprehensive planning.

Land use planning is still primarily a local government function undertaken with the authority of the state. The powers of planning boards vary significantly across the states and between localities within states. In some instances, planning boards serve largely in an advisory capacity to local legislative bodies, while in others, boards serve as the final decision makers on most, if not all, land use issues. Sometimes planning boards also hear appeals from property owners who are not satisfied with decisions made by other boards, but in most localities, a separate zoning board of appeals serves this function.

When planning boards emerged in the 1920s through the 1940s, they were limited to creating and administering zoning laws that restricted the use of land in a variety of ways, including primary uses of the land, the size of building lots, and how close buildings could be to the edges of lots. In recent decades, the issues that planning boards must be concerned with have changed to reflect the evolution of social beliefs and economic realities. For example, many communities have zoning for "single-family" homes. As the notion of the family has expanded, defining what a single family is has become more complex for communities. Similarly, as more Americans work for themselves and telecommute, home offices have become more prevalent. Zoning usually precluded such arrangements in areas zoned residential. A third example is the emergence of group homes and how towns can work them into zoning. Each of these examples challenges existing notions of what was acceptable traditional zoning. As zoning is a way to maintain the status quo, these new arrangements present challenges.

Planning boards have also been forced to react to new social goals, often mandated by state and federal legislation, such as environmental regulation and historic preservation. Zoning laws have had to be updated with state and federally mandated environmental requirements concerning clean water and waste management. Many states require environmental impact statements for any new development. Many communities have also sought to preserve their historic assets encouraged by the passage of the National Historic Preservation Act of 1966 and other similar laws. This law created the National Register of Historic Places and required states to participate in creating the register. As a result, many local governments have created historic zoning districts that limit the ability of property owners to change historic structures and grounds.

Finally, states and localities have recognized that the actions of individual communities have an impact beyond their own borders. Since 1990, nine states have instituted integrated statewide planning. This has impacted and sometimes superseded the work of local planning boards. In addition, some metropolitan areas have instituted regional planning and eliminated local boards in favor of regional planning boards.

Planning boards serve an important function in land use planning and development issues. At their best, they guide communities toward making well-informed choices on future development both in terms of comprehensive planning and on individual projects. But planning boards do not always work in this fashion. Boards can be so busy with the day-to-day work of reviewing development plans that they do not have time to consider the long-range implications of their actions. At times, boards can work to serve the interests of only segments of the community by thwarting all development, or in contrast they can be aligned too closely with developers. Even well-meaning boards can be overwhelmed by the financial resources of developers. Planning board members are volunteers, and localities often have only small professional development staffs.

Further Reading

Cullingham, Barry, and Roger W. Caves. *Planning in the USA*, 2nd ed. New York: Routledge, 2003; American Planning Association. Available online. URL: http://www.planning.org. Accessed March 2, 2007.

—William R. Wilkerson

property rights

Few concepts have generated as much debate across the study of politics, law, economics, and philosophy as that of property rights. The commonly understood definition of a property right is the relationship between an individual and a physical object. However, scholars have long understood property rights as a bundle of rules that define the relationship between individuals and access to, control over, and use of virtually anything that produces a benefit to people, from natural resources, to written text, manufactured products, processes, and even ideas. Property rights are defined and enforced in a variety of ways, from social norms to courts, constitutions, and legislation.

Examining the variety of ownership relationships in something even as simple as a plot of land helps illustrate the complexity of property rights. Generally, with land, an owner has the right to use, occupy, cultivate, transfer to others, share, rent, lease, or trade.

However, depending on the jurisdiction and resource, it may or may not include the right to extract and sell subsurface resources (such as minerals), or the right to sell the right to use a resource (such as leasing timber rights), or include rights to water that lies under, within, or flows over the land. Rights may be permitted to the quantity of water, but there may be controls over the quality (such as the responsibility not to pollute), and restrictions may be placed on its use (agricultural versus residential use). Rights to water may be allowed to be sold for some purposes (such as agriculture) but not for others (such as habitat restoration). If it is a parcel under the riparian rights system, it would not include rights to use the land under a navigable river, although it would include the land to the river's edge. Wildlife is probably regarded as state property and requires a permit to harvest. The title may include easements permitting neighbors access across the land and probably PUBLIC UTILITIES the right to inspect power lines. ZONING may place restrictions on the type of activities allowed, and if in an urban area, it may not include air rights (the ability to build additional levels) and view rights (the right to prevent another property owner from obstructing a view).

There is no universally accepted definition of a property right. Scholars typically examine some combination of five types of rights; access, withdrawal, management, exclusion, and alienation. Access rights are those that permit decision making about who may physically enter an area. Withdrawal rights determine how a physical unit of the resource is obtained. Management is the right to decide on the type of inputs and use patterns of an area. Exclusion refers to the right to determine who may have an access right. Alienation is the right to transfer a right via sale, leasing, or trade. There are four standard property right types, typically defined according to who holds the majority of rights. The most commonly discussed is that of private property. Private property rights are those that designate the majority of rights to an individual decision maker. For legal purposes, private property can be assigned to individuals or group entities such as corporations and government units. This legally defines the rights in relationship to other claims, so a city government may have private rights in relationship to another city government claiming the same resource, even though in both cases the property is owned by a public entity.

Private property is often contrasted with the situation of open access. Under open access systems, there are no effective rules regulating the access to a resource. Garrett Hardin famously outlined the problem of open access property regimes in his article "The Tragedy of the Commons" (1968). Every individual has an incentive to use a resource before anyone else, leading to overuse and eventual ruin for all. He characterized resources such as forests, fisheries, and the global atmosphere as suffering from the tragedy of the commons. For Hardin, the tragedy could be averted only by making it public property under the control of a state that would then manage it according to the public good or by assigning private rights, so individuals could wastefully overuse it and/or manage to maximize profits.

Various scholars have pointed out that many of the resources viewed as open access are actually common property. Under a system of common property, rights exist but are shared among a community of users rather than with an individual. The global atmosphere has very exact rights regarding use in terms of national air pollution laws, although the atmosphere is held in common among all nations. The important distinction is that if a resource is being overused, it is not that property rights do not exist, but that there may be a problem with the design or enforcement of existing rights. The same can occur with private property as well. Systems of common property are pervasive in both traditional societies as well as modern capitalist systems, and it is difficult to imagine effective alternative property structures for some types of resources, such as the atmosphere, outer space, many fisheries, and some hydrological resources.

The final property type is that of public property, whereby the majority of rights belong to a legally recognized political unit, such as a city, county, state, or country. In some cases, public property is similar to other property right types, such as when a government unit is recognized as having the full legal rights of private property or when a resource owned by a government unit is shared among its citizens in a common property situation, such as a national park. Public properties are important for supplying resources that are regarded as necessarily open to all citizens and in many cases present their own unique management challenges.

The Supreme Court has ruled that cities can seize homes for private developers. *(Getty Images)*

Defining a property right is not merely an empty academic exercise. Much of political history can be fundamentally understood as a struggle over property right relationships and the role of the individual, community, and government in maintaining, enforcing, and distributing rights. There are two fundamental issues of debate. The first is the equity of the distribution of rights against the efficiency of an economic system to generate wealth and the second the rights of individuals against the responsibilities owed to broader society.

Thinking about these issues extends as far back as Plato advocating common ownership as a means of overcoming distributional conflict in *The Republic* (370 B.C.), and Aristotle's rebuke in favor of private property. Property was considered so important that Aristotle devoted much of *Politics* (350 B.C.) to discussing the benefits of individual ownership and the limits necessary to promote the public good. Likewise, Roman law recognized an elaborate system

of individual private ownership alongside a system of public duties. During the Middle Ages, the lack of separation between church and state meant that all things were considered subject to the king's ruling under authority ordained by God. The feudal land rights systems were transferred by the right of primogeniture, which required passing lands to one's first-born son, leading to land consolidation and the system of tenant farmers legally bound to the land known as serfdom.

Modern property rights thought begins with Thomas Hobbes's *Leviathan* (1651), in which property rights were the output of a sovereign whose authoritative command guaranteed the resolution of conflict and enforced rights. He writes, "my own can only truly be mine if there is one unambiguously strongest power in their realm, and that power treats it as mine, protecting its status as well." The first break with the idea that rights are bestowed by a sovereign authority occurs with JOHN LOCKE's *Two*

Treatises of Civil Government (1690). Locke formulates the idea of NATURAL RIGHTS that holds that each person owns himself and has certain liberties that cannot be expropriated by others, not even the sovereign authority. The input of labor toward a productive end establishes an inherent property right. This is later know as the labor theory of property and is incorporated into the work of authors as diverse as David Ricardo and Karl Marx. The sanctity of individual rights is echoed in William Blackstone's *Commentaries on the Laws of England* (1765–69), in which he postulates that property rights are a unified bundle under the exclusive authority the right holder. This provides the conceptual foundation for the modern legal protection against trespass and the base of nuisance laws. Blackstone's work was important in informing many of the writers of the U.S. CONSTITUTION and continues as a reference in judicial studies.

David Hume (1711–76) rejected the idea of natural rights and proposed that property rights emerge from the legal practice, social custom, and economic necessity to limit access to scarce goods. This became known as the pragmatic approach, and is extended by the work of Immanuel Kant (1724–1804), who posits that since property rights place a claim on resources that limits the freedom of others and require respect of that claim, all rights are reliant on the mutual consent of the community and are therefore acquired, not innate. Anyone claiming a right to property necessarily accepts the legitimate right of a community to place limits in order to ensure sufficient equitable distribution and gain general consent. The pragmatic approach is found in the American legal tradition through the work of U.S. SUPREME COURT associate justice Oliver Wendell Holmes. In his classic text *The Common Law* (1881), he rejects the natural law tradition of a comprehensive unit of absolute ownership and distinguishes the right of possession, which imposes responsibilities on others not to contradict the possessor's control over the resources, and the right of title, which imposes the expectation that others will recognize control rights, even when not in immediate possession.

The debate over the appropriate role of the individual property owner in relationship to society occurs in its most visible form in constitutional definitions over the use of EMINENT DOMAIN and takings compensation. The Fifth Amendment of the U.S. Constitution requires that private property not be expropriated by government without compensation. Eminent domain is the legal right of a government to force the sale of a private property in order to pursue public purposes. A taking occurs when government action has deprived an individual of a recognized property right and is therefore owed compensation. Limits on property rights when they impose a cost on others have long been recognized as a legitimate exercise of police power (which is the necessity of government to prevent harm to its citizens). The defining case, *Hadacheck v. Sebastian*, 239 U.S. 394 (1915), ruled that an owner of a brickyard was not entitled to compensation because zoning by Los Angeles had prohibited the activity, establishing that when a property owner's use is harmful, the use may be banned even if it reduces the value of a property. In *Village of Euclid v. Ambler Realty Co.*, 272 U.S. 365 (1926), the use of zoning restrictions were determined not to constitute a taking, even when reducing the overall value of a property. *Miller v. Schoene*, 276 U.S. 272 (1928), elaborated on what activities encompassed a nuisance and ruled that the higher economic value of orchards justified the destruction of ornamental cedars that hosted a fungus that damaged the orchards, even though it did not harm the cedars. In *Penn Central Transportation Co. v. New York City*, 438 U.S. 104 (1978), refusal to grant a permit to build office space on top of an existing building due to its historic landmark designation was ruled as not a taking but supporting a community's authority to adopt regulations to protect the quality of life even if it decreases the value of a property. In *Lucas v. South Carolina Coastal Commission*, 505 U.S. 1003 (1992), the Court ruled that even though a property owner had purchased a beachfront parcel prior to the existence of land use controls prohibiting development, as long as the regulation was designed "to prevent serious public harm," no compensation was due regardless of the size of impact on the property value. The general understanding today is that government action to legitimate public interest that reduces the value of a property right is not a taking as long as the owner retains some viable use. While public projects such as highways, railroad lines, utilities, and military bases have long been allowed, the definition of public interest has been expanded in recent years. In *Hawaii Housing Authority v. Midkiff*, 466 U.S. 229 (1984), the Court ruled that an act by the state legislature intended to redistribute what it saw as an oligopoly in land ownership inflating land values (with up to 72 percent of private land on one island owned by 22 individuals) did satisfy the public use doctrine and was within the state's right to intervene to correct market failures. *Kelo v. City of New London*, 125 S. Ct. 2655 (2005), ruled that private land could be forcibly sold for a city industrial park, even though it included constructing a plant for a private company, since stimulating economic growth was a justifiable public end.

Today, research is less concerned with broad ideological ideas than with the practical impact of property rights and their performance within political and economic systems. Most researchers would agree that when market prices closely reflect the values in society and there are functioning markets of voluntary exchange, a system of private rights will tend to be more efficient than other forms. However, when prices do not fully reflect a society's values (such as in the case of many environmental resources or the value of equity) or when there are market failures (such as high transaction costs to exchanging goods), then private property rights can be suboptimal, and other forms of property may be preferred. With the increasing complexity of society, property rights are understood as flexible bundles that can be used innovatively by private firms, markets, courts, legislatures, and communities toward socially desirable ends. Contemporary approaches are more aware than ever of the economic, political, and ethical implications of different rule structures governing resource use.

Further Reading

Achian, Armen, and Harold Demsetz. "The Property Rights Paradigm." *Journal of Economic History* 33 (1973): 16–27; Anderson, Terry, and Fred McChesney. *Property Rights: Cooperation, Conflict, and Law.* Princeton, N.J.: Princeton University Press. 2003; Becker, L. C. *Property Rights: Philosophic Foundations.* Henley, U.K., and New York: Routledge & Kegan Paul, 1977; Bromley, Daniel. *Environment and Economy: Property Rights and Public Policy.* Oxford: Oxford University Press. 1991; Cole, Daniel "New Forms of Private Property: Property Rights in Environmental Goods." In *Encyclopedia of Law and Economics, Civil Law and Economics*, edited by Boudewijn Bouckaert, and Gerrit de Geest. Cheltenham, U.K.: Edward Elgar, 2000; Cribbet, John, and Corwin W. Johnson. *Principles of the Law of Property.* Westbury, N.Y.: Foundation Press, 1989; Ellickson, R. C.. "Property in Land." *Yale Law Journal* 102 (1993): 1,315–1,400. 1993; Ely, James E. *The Guardian of Every Other Right: A Constitutional History of Property Rights.* New York: Oxford University Press, 1992; Epstein, R. A. *Taking: Private Property and the Power of Eminent Domain.* Cambridge, Mass.: Harvard University Press, 1985; Hohfeld, W. N. *Fundamental Legal Conceptions as Applied in Judicial Reasoning.* Westport, Conn.: Greenwood Press, 1978; Libecap, Gary D. *Contracting for Property Rights.* Cambridge: Cambridge University Press, 1989; North, Douglass. *Institutions, Institutional Change, and Economic Performance.* Cambridge: Cambridge University Press. 1990; Ostrom, Elinor. *Governing the Commons: The Evolution of Institutions for Collective Action.* Cambridge: Cambridge University Press, 1990;———. "Private and Common Property Rights." In *Encyclopedia of Law and Economics, Civil Law and Economics*, edited by Boudewijn Bouckaert, and Gerrit de Geest. Cheltenham, U.K.: Edward Elgar, 2000; Radin, Margaret Jane. *Contested Commodities: The Trouble with Trade in Sex, Children, Body Parts, and Other Things.* Cambridge, Mass.: Harvard University Press, 2001; Rose, C. "The Several Futures of Property: Of Cyberspace and Folk Tales, Emission Trades and Ecosystems." *Minnesota Law Review* 83 (1998): 129–182; Sax, Joseph. "The Public Trust Doctrine in Natural Resource Law: Effective Judicial Intervention." *Michigan Law Review* 68 (1970): 471–566; Weingast, Barry R. "The Economic Role of Political Institutions: Market-Preserving Federalism and Economic Development." *Journal of Law, Economics, & Organization* 11, no. 1 (1995): 1–31.

—Derek Kauneckis

recalls

A recall election is one in which an elected official is subjected to removal from office by voters before his or her term is complete. It is the least common type of DIRECT DEMOCRACY, available for statewide officials in only 18 states. (It is, however, fairly common at the local level). Generally, the recall works as follows: Citizens unhappy with an elected official collect signatures on a petition calling for the special election; if a sufficient number of signatures are collected, voters are asked to cast a ballot on a question such as, "Shall Governor X be removed from office?" If a majority of voters answer in the negative, the officeholder in question retains his or her seat. If the voters answer in the affirmative, the officeholder is immediately stripped of his or her position. The procedures that govern choosing a replacement vary, though the most common mechanism involves a subsequent special election. (The well-known 2003 recall election in California used a different procedure to select a replacement; it is discussed below.)

Under the U.S. CONSTITUTION, federal officials are not subject to recall elections. Members of Congress may be expelled only by a vote of their colleagues, and other officeholders (e.g., the president and U.S. SUPREME COURT justices) can be removed from office only following IMPEACHMENT. The founders' disdain for direct democracy and their corresponding desire for independence on the part of elected representatives prevented them from instituting a recall procedure at the federal level. For them, periodic elections were the appropriate means of popular control of lawmakers. Some states have laws that appear to allow the recall of their federal officials, though it is unlikely that federal courts would permit such an effort.

Even at the state level, recall procedures are fairly recent. Oregon was the first state to establish the recall possibility to statewide office, adding the provision to its state constitution in 1908. Since then, the recall has been a rarely used device at the state level. Voter dissatisfaction may be high, but the key challenge appears to be the signature requirement to place the question on the ballot. In order to guard against excessive recall elections, most states require a significant number of signatures to be collected within a specified period of time. In Kansas, for example, sponsors of a recall must obtain signatures amounting to 40 percent of those voting in the previous gubernatorial election, and they may circulate the petition for no more than 90 days—enormous barriers that have yet to be crossed, as no statewide official has ever faced a recall election in Kansas.

Additionally, a few states limit the grounds for a recall and mandate that a court determine whether the charges against the official comply with the state's law. Minnesota's constitution requires that a recall be permitted only in the event of "serious malfeasance or nonfeasance during the term of office in the performance of the duties of the office or conviction during the term of office of a serious crime." In most recall states, the matter is considered a political question rather than a legal one. Regardless, statewide recall elections very rarely occur.

In fact, until 2003, only one GOVERNOR had been successfully recalled from office: Lynn Frazier of North Dakota in 1921. (It is worth noting that Governor Evan Meacham was likely to be recalled by Arizona voters in 1988, but the state legislature impeached and removed him from office before voters had the chance.) In 2003, California voters held Governor Gray Davis accountable for a number of problems in that state. The language of the petition revealed the broad frustration with his administration; following a list of specific grievances, the petition closed by charging Davis with "failing in general to deal with the state's major problems until they get to the crisis stage. California should not have to be known as the state with poor schools, traffic jams, outrageous utility bills, and huge debts . . . all caused by gross mismanagement."

The signature requirements in California for placing a recall vote on the ballot are relatively low compared to other states; those seeking the recall must obtain the signatures of 12 percent of the number who voted in the previous statewide election (in this case, about 900,000). Moreover, California does not limit the grounds on which a recall may be held. Even these modest requirements are normally stringent enough to keep the question off the ballot. More than 100 previous attempts had been made to recall California governors, but every one had failed due to lack of signatures. In the 2003 case, an enormous contribution of $2 million by Congressman Darrell Issa provided the means to collect the necessary signatures.

The special election took place on October 7, 2003, and voters faced a two-part ballot. First, voters were asked, "Shall Gray Davis be recalled (removed) from the Office of Governor?" Second, voters were asked to select one name from a list of 135 potential replacements. (In the event that a majority of voters answered no to the first question, the second question would be ignored.) Some 55 percent of voters answered the first question in the affirmative, and 49 percent of voters (a plurality) selected actor Arnold Schwarzenegger to replace Davis.

Other notable recall elections occurred at the local level. In 1978, Cleveland voters initiated a recall petition to oust mayor Dennis Kucinich after he fired the city's police chief live on local television. Kucinich survived the recall by less than 250 votes out of more than 120,000 cast. San Francisco mayor Dianne Feinstein faced a recall election in 1983 after proposing a ban on handguns. A handful of activists took advantage of the city's lenient recall procedures—the petition required the signatures of only 10 percent of those who voted in the previous election—to bring the matter to the voters. Feinstein shrewdly fought the effort by arguing that the recall was "an invitation to chaos" and added that "there is no candidate against whom to compare my record." Her campaign worked; more than 80 percent of voters elected to keep her in office.

Gray Davis notwithstanding, most successful recalls involve acts of malfeasance rather than issue differences. Even many supporters of the recall device concede that it should be used only in unusual cases, not for mere policy differences. Feinstein alluded to this in her campaign to retain her seat: "Orderly government cannot prevail on the shifting sands of a recall brought, not because of any corruption or incompetence, but because of a difference of opinion on an issue." A notable recent example of a successful recall illustrates the point. In 2005, voters in Spokane, Washington, recalled Mayor Jim West amid charges of having offered internships and other perks to teenagers via the Gay.com Web site. Other charges surfaced that West had been accused of molesting young boys in the 1970s and 1980s. Following a campaign that focused entirely on these matters rather than policy issues, 65 percent of Spokane voters opted to remove West from office.

Arguments for and against the recall device are fairly straightforward. On the plus side, the recall provides voters with a method of ensuring continuous accountability. Since many elected offices are for rather long terms—most governors serve four-year

terms, for example—there is ample opportunity for them to ignore the will of the voters between elections. Supporters of the recall argue that elected officials are obliged to follow the wishes of their constituents and that the long period between elections inappropriately allows those wishes to be ignored. If elections are about placing individuals in office to represent the voters, recall advocates argue, it follows that the voters should not have to wait until a predetermined date to remove unresponsive officials. Voters are especially justified in removing corrupt or incompetent officials as soon as possible.

In addition, some maintain that the recall reduces the influence of special interests, mainly by keeping officials' loyalties tethered to the general public even between elections. As with other forms of direct democracy, however, there is competing evidence that organized interests increasingly dominate the recall process; a very small number of wealthy individuals were certainly crucial in securing the necessary petition signatures in California, for example. Less-common arguments in favor of the recall include the claim that it is a more efficient process than impeachment, since it is unencumbered by partisanship. Finally, some argue that it encourages healthy CITIZENSHIP by giving voters a strong incentive to monitor public affairs regularly. All of these arguments speak broadly to the desirability of maximizing the democratic control of elected officials.

Opponents of the recall process tend to focus on a model of representation that permits independence on the part of the elected official. Governing, the argument goes, requires difficult choices whose benefits are often evident only in the long run. If officeholders are constantly worried that each and every decision they make might subject them to the immediate judgment of the voters, they might be less inclined to take the appropriate political risks. This is essentially the argument that prevailed among the founders at the time of the drafting of the U.S. Constitution.

There are a number of lesser arguments against the recall, also. Some contend that there is a moral hazard that results from not forcing voters to live with their mistakes. Political scientist Larry Sabato articulated this point in an interview with *Campaigns and Elections* magazine shortly after the California recall: "It is a good lesson for people, elections matter, you need to cast your ballot carefully. It is not a bad thing to force people to live through the consequences." Others have pointed out that recall election procedures can invite genuinely bizarre outcomes. In the California election, the large number of candidates made it possible for Davis to be removed from office with more votes of support than his successor. Additionally, a group of political scientists reported in *PS* that language barriers make it very difficult for non-English-speaking voters in such elections; evidently, *recall* is a word that does not translate easily. They also found that voter competence to handle the recall question was not high, even among those who do speak English. In their survey, they discovered that 6 percent of those who preferred Davis nevertheless expressed support for the recall, leading these researchers to conclude that "some voters believed that in order to vote *for* Davis, they needed to vote *yes* on the recall." Clearly, there are some oddities and challenges associated with recall elections that add to the controversy.

But the central argument remains the philosophical one involving representation, and how one views the desirability of the independence of elected officials will generally mirror one's opinion about the recall device. The recall is sometimes characterized as "the gun behind the door." Supporters use this terminology to imply that the recall can effectively keep lawmakers in line, as the threat is ever present. But opponents could just as easily use the phrase to illustrate the danger of the recall, particularly if voters become "trigger happy."

The recall is clearly an effective means of removing corrupt officials, but it presents problems for effective government if it is used lightly. If the grounds for a recall involve policy differences, most observers would prefer that voters make their decision at the next scheduled election rather than holding a special recall vote. Political scientist Thomas Cronin, one of the foremost experts on direct democracy, contends that the proper regulation of the recall procedure can maximize its benefits while reducing the potential for abuse. He specifically calls for "stiff signature requirements," which have indeed been the primary obstacle for most of these efforts. He adds that the best mechanism to regulate the recall is an educated electorate, for which there is no substitute as a means of guarding against "gullibility and undue haste." One might add

optimistically that an educated electorate might also minimize the need for recall elections by making wise selections in the first place.

Further Reading

Bowler, Shaun. "Recall and Representation: Arnold Schwarzenegger Meets Edmund Burke." *Representation* 40, no. 3 (2004): 200–212; Cronin, Thomas E. *Direct Democracy: The Politics of Initiative, Referendum, and Recall.* Cambridge, Mass.: Harvard University Press, 1989; Felchner, Morgan E. "Recall Elections: Democracy in Action or Populism Run Amok?" *Campaigns and Elections* 1 (June 2004); Maskell, Jack. "Recall of Legislators and the Removal of Members of Congress from Office." Report of the Congressional Research Service, 2003. Available online. URL: http://lugar.senate.gov/CRS%20reports/Recall_of_Legislators_and_the_Removal_of_Members_of_Congress_from_Office.pdf. Accessed May 20, 2006; Saffell, David C., and Harry Basehart. *State and Local Government: Politics and Public Policies.* 8th ed. Boston: McGraw Hill, 2005.

—William Cunion

referendums

A referendum is a type of ballot measure, a special kind of election in which voters decide directly on an issue rather than voting for candidates for office. Referendums are similar to but distinct from, INITIATIVES. Both involve direct votes on issues, but referendums are held in response to an act of a legislature, while initiatives are citizen-driven proposals that do not involve the legislature. There are two major types of referendums. A popular referendum occurs when citizens collect signatures on a petition to refer a specific piece of legislation to the people for them to accept or reject. A legislative referendum occurs when lawmakers submit a legislative act for voter approval. Popular referendums are available to voters in 24 states, while legislative referendums can be held in all 50 states.

The U.S. CONSTITUTION does not permit referendums (or initiatives) at the national level. Most of the founding fathers were highly skeptical of DIRECT DEMOCRACY, preferring a representative system that allows lawmakers to act somewhat independently of public opinion. James Madison most clearly defended this argument in his essay *Federalist 10*, in which he claimed that the effect of delegating decision making to representatives would be to "refine and enlarge the public views, by passing them through the medium of a chosen body of citizens, whose wisdom may best discern the true interest of their country, and whose patriotism and love of justice will be least likely to sacrifice it to temporary or partial considerations. Under such a regulation, it may well happen that the public voice, pronounced by the representatives of the people, will be more consonant to the public good than if pronounced by the people themselves, convened for the purpose."

Like many of the founders, Madison was concerned about the possibility of the "tyranny of the majority" and more generally that the passions of the people would interfere with their reason. Some opponents of the Constitution, however, pointed out that the Revolution itself was the product of ordinary citizens and contended that more DEMOCRACY is always the essential tool to control the tyrannical impulses of elected officials. The debate continues to resonate to this day, as arguments for and against direct democracy reflect these competing concerns.

The primary argument in favor of direct democracy is very simple: It gives the people more control over the decisions of their government. Referendums provide an opportunity for citizens to reject decisions of their representatives. In an age in which elected officials are widely seen as unresponsive or "out of touch," it is not surprising that most people strongly support the referendum process. The Initiative and Referendum Institute reports the results from a 2000 survey that found that those who supported the process outnumbered opponents in all 50 states by at least 30 percent and in 17 states by a margin of more than 50 percent. Moreover, they found that the highest level of support occurred in states in which ballot measures are most frequent. Support for the process is not merely abstract; a number of studies have found that VOTER TURNOUT is higher in elections in which an initiative or referendum appears on the ballot.

Along the same lines, supporters of direct democracy often contend that the process curbs the excessive power of organized INTEREST GROUPS. The argument begins from the premise that legislators are more beholden to so-called special interests than to voters, and as a result, laws reflect the small but pow-

erful groups rather than the electorate as a whole. Direct democracy, according to this line of thinking, provides a vital opportunity for voters to protect their own interests. As a rationale for direct democracy, this logic was a favorite of Progressive Era reformers in the early 20th century; as Robert LaFollette explained, "The forces of the special privileges are deeply entrenched. Their resources are inexhaustible. Their efforts are never lax. Their political methods are insidious. It is impossible for the people to maintain perfect organization in mass. They are often unaware and are liable to lose at one stroke the achievement of years of effort. In such a crisis, nothing but the united power of the people expressed directly through the ballot can overthrow the enemy."

More recently, some have argued that organized interests have subverted this goal by seizing control of the process. From the cumbersome process of obtaining signatures on petitions to the expense of television advertising, such groups are able to "buy" elections. Journalist David Broder sums up this perspective: "Though derived from a reform favored by Populists and Progressives as a cure for special-interest influence, this method of lawmaking has become the favored tool of millionaires and interest groups that use their wealth to achieve their own policy goals."

This is still a matter of some controversy in the literature, though in the most comprehensive study of the initiative process, John Matsusaka concluded flatly that he was "unable to find *any* evidence that the majority dislikes the policy changes caused by the initiative." Thus, if the critics are correct, interest groups have not only hijacked the tools of direct democracy, they have taken control of democracy itself.

So if voters like the opportunity to vote directly on issues, and it gives them more of what they want, what could possibly be the problem? One potential concern involves the rights of minorities, though this is less of a concern with referendums than with initiatives, since referendums require the legislature to act first. Thus, referendums threaten the rights of minorities only if the legislature has already chosen to expand rights. Initiatives more clearly jeopardize minorities, as there is no intermediary body to resist a tyrannical majority—just as Madison warned. Because the legislature must act first, referendums generally do not pose an unusual threat to those in the minority. A rare example of this possibility nearly occurred in Alabama in 2000. An anachronistic provision of the state's constitution prohibited interracial marriage, and lawmakers in both chambers unanimously agreed to amend the constitution to remove the ban. Although the provision had been unenforceable since the U.S. SUPREME COURT's ruling in *Loving v. Virginia* (1967), the constitutional change had to be ratified by the state's voters, just as any other amendment to the constitution. Voters approved the repeal, but with only 60 percent of the vote; two of five Alabama voters elected to keep the unenforceable ban on interracial marriage in their state's constitution. Although the effect would have been merely symbolic, a modest change in the vote would have demonstrated the risks that referendums pose to minorities.

Other arguments against referendums require less speculation and raise significant questions about the desirability of this process. The key concern expressed by most opponents of direct democracy is that voters lack the competence to make rational decisions on complex policy issues. A wide body of political science literature has repeatedly affirmed that most citizens are highly uninformed about political issues and that they often hold extremely inconsistent opinions based on very few considerations. With this in mind, critics argue that such voters will be susceptible to manipulation by clever ad campaigns or slogans and will ultimately support measures that "sound good" without having seriously considered the potential costs of the proposal. In this light, reconsideration of Matsusaka's optimistic conclusion is warranted. After all, just because voters are happy with their decisions does not necessarily indicate that they would have made the same choices were they fully aware of the competing arguments. Voter ignorance may simply continue beyond the election itself.

The problem of voter competence is not merely abstract. The terminology used in ballot measures can easily result in voter confusion. Consider the Alabama example again. This is the language as it appeared on the ballot: "Proposing an amendment to the Constitution of Alabama of 1901, to abolish the prohibition of interracial marriages." To the careful, educated reader, the meaning is clear, but it is not hard to imagine how the double negative in this sentence might confuse some voters. Such problems are a unique danger of direct democracy; REPRESENTATIVE DEMOCRACY may have problems, but legislators at least know what they are voting on.

Some scholars, however, have found that voters are surprisingly successful at employing various information shortcuts to make smart decisions on even the most complicated ballot measures. In a widely cited article, Arthur Lupia demonstrated that California voters were able to navigate a multitude of insurance reform proposals not by acquiring a large amount of information about the proposals themselves, but by making use of various cues in the public debate. For example, an otherwise uninformed voter might correctly oppose a measure supported by the insurance industry even if he or she does not know its details. Endorsements from trusted public officials and established groups might have the same effect, and the warnings of an utterly irrational electorate may well be overstated. Nevertheless, if voters must rely on elected officials and interest groups for the referendum process to work properly, the key arguments in favor of the direct vote are severely compromised.

Direct democracy, including the referendum, is becoming increasingly popular. There were more than four times as many ballot measures at the state level in the 1990s as there were in the 1960s, and there is no sign that this trend is waning. It is not uncommon for voters in some states to cast ballots on more than a dozen separate measures; the voter "pamphlet" for the 2004 election in California ran more than 150 pages, driven mainly by analysis of 15 ballot measures. There is even renewed interest in the idea of a national referendum. One subject that has long been a popular one with supporters of direct democracy is war. During the period between the world wars, a number of prominent Americans advocated a CONSTITUTIONAL AMENDMENT that would require a popular vote before committing the country to war. President Franklin D. Roosevelt put a quick end to the proposal in 1938 by expressing strong opposition to the idea. During our current time of war, this idea serves as a tangible case illustrating the pros and cons of the referendum process. If Americans were to vote directly on our involvement in a foreign war, the outcome might well result in a decision that more accurately reflects current public opinion, but it is easy to see how such a vote might not be "more consonant to the public good."

Further Reading

Broder, David. *Democracy Derailed: Initiative Campaigns and the Power of Money.* New York: Harcourt, 2000; Cronin, Thomas E. *Direct Democracy: The Politics of Initiative, Referendum, and Recall.* Cambridge, Mass.: Harvard University Press, 1989; Gerber, Elisabeth R. *The Populist Paradox: Interest Group Influence and the Promise of Direct Legislation.* Princeton, N.J.: Princeton University Press, 1999; Lupia, Arthur. "Shortcuts Versus Encyclopedias: Information and Voting Behavior in California Insurance Reform Elections." *American Political Science Review* 88 (1994): 63–76; Madison, James. Essay 10, *The Federalist Papers.* New York: Bantam Books, 1982; Matsusaka, John G. *For the Many or the Few.* Chicago: University of Chicago Press, 2004.

—William Cunion

special districts

Local governments can be placed into two broad categories. There are general purpose governments and special district governments. General purpose governments are responsible for an array of public services. Examples of general purpose governments include counties, cities, towns, and townships. Special district governments have narrow jurisdictions and are quite often funded through special taxes. They provide such services as electrical power, economic development, fire protection, higher education, hospitals, parks, libraries, utilities, mosquito control, real estate development, school construction, sanitation, and transportation.

There are approximately 35,000 special district governments in the United States. Special districts that have the ability to charge fees for their services are known as enterprise districts. Those that must rely on general revenues alone, such as property taxes, are known as nonenterprise districts. However, in addition to their fee-based revenue, enterprise districts can also receive APPROPRIATIONS from the general revenue fund of counties or cities. Special districts that have their own governing boards are known as independent districts, while those that are governed by an existing general purpose government are known as dependent districts.

Special districts are a major component of the American federal system. Their influence has increased over the past 40 years. The scope of their activity increased more than 150 percent from 1957 to 1992, more than any other type of government.

State laws vary, but for the most part, a city or county may create a special district according to provisions detailed by statute. Private citizens may also, of their own accord, petition the STATE GOVERNMENT for the creation of a district. Special districts are created for a variety of reasons. It may be the case that a general purpose government has failed to provide a certain service. On the other hand, there could be a desire to take a policy issue out of the controversial arena of local politics and make policy making less visible. Another reason for the creation of special districts is the need to allow unincorporated areas to provide services usually associated with urban areas or to provide for regional services whose provision does not fit into the framework of existing municipal boundaries. A special district could also be created to satisfy conditions of a federal grant. The most pressing reason for the creation of special districts, however, is the desire of local officials to get around tax and expenditure limitations (TELs) that have been placed on them by state governments or through citizen INITIATIVES. Political analyst Donald Axelrod refers to special districts as "political bomb shelters." They operate below the surface and provide shelter for government activities that would otherwise come under greater public scrutiny.

Given the low visibility of special districts, it is not surprising that voter participation in elections for special district governing boards is generally quite low, with 5 percent turnout being considered high. In addition, special districts can be difficult to monitor for those who are supposedly in charge of them. The directors of the Brentwood Recreation and Park District in Contra Costa County, California, did not discover that the government of which they were technically in charge went out of existence until seven months after the fact.

The sheer amount and variety of local governments is breathtaking. An American would achieve no small feat by simply locating all the different units of local government that exercise authority in a given area, which could be more than a dozen. As opposed to city or county limits that are marked by road signs, the boundaries of special districts are not obvious to passersby. Locating and charting the special districts that have jurisdiction over one's life and property could be a daunting task, and even if one did have a professional background in surveying or geography and were able to identify and draw the boundaries for all the governments in one's area, there is no guarantee that the results of one's labors would provide a clearer picture. It is not uncommon for the boundaries of special districts to have unusual shapes and confusing boundaries.

On the other hand, special districts can provide public services according to the unique characteristics of local demand. In addition, the costs of public services are directly linked to the benefits. Furthermore, because they are specific entities devoted to particular concerns, they are responsive to their constituents.

It can be argued, however, that the myriad special districts in America contribute to an inefficient and overlapping system of providing public services. They hinder regional planning and due to the sheer number of governmental units lessen accountability. This is especially apparent when one ponders the massive reserves that have been accumulated by many special districts.

There are four main schools of thought with respect to the proliferation of special districts. These are the institutional reform, critical political economy, public choice, and metropolitan ecology schools.

The institutional reform school is a legacy of the Progressive Era movement, which was most active from the late 19th to the early 20th centuries. Theorists in this area call for the integration of smaller units of local government into larger and more efficient macrogovernments. Institutional reform theorists prefer strong regional governments—metropolitan or county—that would provide an efficient and accountable means to implement administrative polices. Of course, this would involve the elimination of special districts.

Special districts led to the fragmentation of government, which, so the argument goes, leads to a decrease in both the capabilities of general purpose governments and public ACCOUNTABILITY. Most citizens are not aware of the special district governments

in their area until a tax bill arrives. Even then, it is quite possible that taxes for special districts are hidden in consolidated bills of another government that serves as the collection agency for the special district. In this way, according to John C. Bollens, a leading expert on government reform, special districts are "phantom governments." Another manifestation of this lack of accountability is the potential for corruption. Special districts may be created with the sole purpose of providing employment opportunities for governing body members and their relatives and friends.

The approach of the critical political economy school closely resembles that of the institutional reform school. The main differences are the greater emphasis of the critical political economy scholars on questions of equity and a lower level of concern over bureaucratic efficiency. Most critical political economy scholars write from a Marxist perspective that looks on the proliferation of special districts as another manifestation of the overall capitalist structure. In other words, it is the desire for capital development that drives the creation of special districts. Like the institutional reform scholars, critical political economists look on special districts as phantom governments designed to hide the true source of power within a community. The desired reform of the critical political economy theorists would be a stronger government that would address social inequalities in a direct manner.

Those in the public choice school look on the large number of special districts from a decidedly more positive perspective. The thousands of special districts—many overlapping and duplicating one another—allow citizens to enjoy an enormous level of choice when it comes to the desired amount and type of public services. The prevailing theoretical perspective of the public choice school is that the LIBERTY of the individual is the paramount concern of the community. Accordingly, local government should become a political marketplace in which citizens act as consumers of government services and select from a variety of special districts that provide particular services.

The most influential work in the public choice school is Charles Tiebout's groundbreaking 1956 article "A Pure Theory of Local Expenditures." Tiebout argued that, given the proper conditions, society would benefit from a large number of local governments competing with one another for residents. In his "pure theory," Tiebout assumed that consumers had perfect information regarding the revenues and expenditures of each local government. In addition, he assumed that each community had some idea regarding its optimum size. And, finally, he assumed that each community would seek to attain its optimum size. To the extent that these conditions are present in a system of local government, it is possible, so the argument goes, that a society could benefit from a marketplace of many local governments.

The main tenet of the metropolitan ecology approach is that a system of government is the result of a community's political culture, the institutional and legal framework within which governments are created. Each community's political culture is somewhat unique and has an inherent dignity and identity. If one starts with Alexis de Tocqueville's premise that the tendency toward a centralized administration—as embodied in both the institutional reform and critical political economy positions—is irresistible in a DEMOCRACY, short of a countervailing attachment to local communities, the only possible alternative to centralized soft despotism is some variant of the metropolitan ecology approach. In short, one must recognize the clear political fact that special districts will be created where the rules favor their creation.

Despite the scholarly controversies over special districts, these narrow-purpose governments are embedded within the American system of FEDERALISM. Eliminating special districts would require a sustained political movement that would rival the great reform movements in American history. It is unlikely that such a movement will take hold in the near future. Special districts offer local policy makers—and perhaps groups of private citizens—financial flexibility, political cover, and the appearance of decentralized decision making. Special districts serve a pressing need in today's political environment.

Further Reading

Axelrod, Donald. *Shadow Government: The Hidden World of Public Authorities—and How They Control Over $1 Trillion.* New York: John Wiley & Sons, 1992; Bollens, John C. *Special District Government in the United States.* Berkeley: University of California Press, 1957; Bollens, Scott A. "Examining the Link between State Policy and the Creation of Local Special Districts." *State and Local Government Review* 18 (1986): 117–124; Blair, George S. *Government at the Grass Roots.* Pacific Palisades, Calif.: Palisades, 1981; Burns, Nancy. *The Formation of Local Governments.* New York: Oxford University Press, 1994; Danielson, Michael N. *Metropolitan Politics.* Boston: Little Brown, 1965; Foster, Kathryn A. "Specialization in Government: The Uneven Use of Special Districts in Metropolitan Areas." *Urban Affairs Review* 31 (1996): 283–313; Hawkins, Robert B., Jr. *Self Government by District: Myth and Reality.* Stanford, Calif.: Hoover Institution Press, 1976: MacManus, Susan A. "Special District Governments: A Note on Their Use as Property Tax Relief Mechanisms in the 1970s." *Journal of Politics* 40 (1981): 1207–1214; Stephens, G. Ross, and Nelson Wilkstrom. "Trends in Special Districts." *State and Local Government Review* 30 (1998): 129–138; Tiebout, Charles M. "A Pure Theory of Local Expenditures." *Journal of Political Economy* 64 (1956): 416–424; Tocqueville, Alexis de. *Democracy in America.* Translated, edited, and introduced by Harvey C. Mansfield and Delba Winthrop. Chicago: University of Chicago Press, 2000.

—Brian P. Janiskee

state courts

When discussing policy making, the courts rarely come up, unless it is the U.S. SUPREME COURT. Much confusion abounds when it comes to discussions of state courts, what they do, their structures, and their role in the policy process. The United States has a two-pronged judiciary, the national and the state, which reinforces the principle of FEDERALISM at the heart of the U.S. CONSTITUTION and the Tenth Amendment. This essay will discuss the organization and JURISDICTION of state courts and the different selection and retention methods in the states.

There are no two state judicial structures that are identical, but there are some similarities that the states share. First, like the national scheme, there is a hierarchy in the state judicial structure. There is the trial level, which has original jurisdiction in civil and criminal matters. The trial level also offers jury trials to those who do not choose to enter plea agreements. If there is a decision handed down by the trial court that one of the sides does not agree with, the decision may be appealed. In 39 of the 50 states, there is an intermediate appellate court that a case from the trial court is appealed to. In the 11 remaining states, an appealed case goes directly to the state court of last resort, which is similar to the U.S. Supreme Court. In all cases of CAPITAL PUNISHMENT, there is a mandatory appeal that goes directly to the court of last resort, regardless of a state's intermediate appellate court. (In two states, Texas and Oklahoma, there are two distinct courts of last resort, one for criminal matters and one for civil matters.)

There are three types of jurisdiction: geographical, subject matter, and hierarchical. Geographical jurisdiction simply states that a court has jurisdiction over a particular case if that case is within that court's geographic area. For instance, a court of last resort in California has geographical jurisdiction over the entire state, whereas a trial court in California has geographic jurisdiction only in a particular city or county. Subject matter jurisdiction divides courts between civil law and criminal law. Civil law covers matters in which a dispute exists between private individuals, and criminal matters are those in which a law has been broken and the government is a party in the case. Hierarchical jurisdiction ranks the courts according to their authority. The highest court in the state's hierarchy is the state court of last resort, followed by the intermediate appellate court, followed by the trial courts. Of course, the highest court in the United States is the Supreme Court.

There are five primary ways vacancies on a state court are filled. The first is through direct partisan election, in which the voters elect judges to office for a fixed term. The second is the nonpartisan election; this method of selection is the same as the first except the candidates are not allowed to disclose their party affiliation. Third, the merit selection, or the Missouri plan, has become the most popular form of judicial selection and retention. The first stage of merit selection occurs when the GOVERNOR or judicial nominating commission appoints a judge for a fixed term, usually four years. After the initial term is over, the judge faces a retention election. A retention election is when the voters choose, by voting for or against the candidate, if they want that judge to continue serving. In a retention election, the judge does not face an opponent. Instead, the voters choose to either retain or expel the current judge. The last two methods of

judicial selection are gubernatorial and legislative appointment. That is, either the governor or the state legislature will appoint a judge to the bench for a fixed term or in some cases until the age of 70. Because there are generally three levels to the state judiciary, each level can have its own method of selection. Some states select judges to the intermediate appeals court by a different method than their state court of last resort. There is an interesting history of why different states have different methods of selection and retention, which is discussed below.

The method by which judges take their offices is a contentious issue at the state and national level. There have been a number of debates, especially recently, about the role the AMERICAN BAR ASSOCIATION (ABA) plays in Supreme Court appointments and in the way the president selects appointments. But at the national level, there is no move to revise the system in any dramatic way, such as allowing the population to vote for the newest nominee. At the state level, however, reform efforts are more dramatic. In 1878, the American Bar Association began working for a fair and just judiciary by seeking to reform the method of judicial selection. Before American independence, the king of England chose the judges in the colonies. As a move away from MONARCHY, the STATE LEGISLATURES began appointing judges once independence was won. But by the 1830s, Jacksonian Democracy took hold, and states began to elect their judges through popular election.

Election was the popular form of judicial selection, particularly for judges in the court of last resort, until the end of the Civil War, when dissatisfaction set in among the constituency who felt that judges were making their decisions along partisan lines. The late 1800s saw a shift toward nonpartisan judicial elections and systems that were precursors to the current merit plan. In 1906, the ABA, in reaction to legal scholar Roscoe Pound's speech at the annual meeting of the ABA, began looking for a better solution than nonpartisan elections, and momentum gained for the merit plan. The merit plan began taking form in 1913 with the Kales plan, named after Albert M. Kales, who was one of the founding members of the American Judicature Society, which involved a nominating commission and noncompetitive retention elections. Although California was the first state to use retention elections, it was not until Missouri adopted a merit plan in 1940 that the selection method gained popularity. The merit plan continues to be the centerpiece for judicial reform movements.

Bar associations began to spring up wherever there was corruption or the perception of an unfit judiciary. This was particularly true in New York, whose infamous Tammany Hall political machine would commonly place party loyalists in judge seats. In fact, the involvement of the St. Louis Bar Association, the Missouri State Bar Association, and the Lawyer's Association of Kansas City that led to Missouri adopting the merit plan was in response to what was felt was a corrupt judicial selection process. This story is replicated across the country and recounted in many case studies. State and local bar associations play a large role in reforming the method of judicial selection.

The importance of the varying state legal structures is seen in how judges make decisions. What we know is that the institutions within which an actor operates play a large role in determining what gets done. Thus, a judge who is elected will hand down different decisions or act differently than a judge who is appointed for life tenure. Furthermore, the selection and retention method of a state has political implications for the legislature and the governor, in that appointed states often seem more partisan in disputes over judgeships and thus judges are more ideologically motivated than those judges in an elected system. And while judges in an elected system may be more responsive to voter preferences, these judges may not be qualified to make difficult legal decisions.

State courts are an often ignored component of the American political system, yet ignoring the state courts is to ignore a vital component of the system. Collectively, the state courts decide far more cases than courts in the federal system and thus potentially have a greater impact on policy and the day-to-day operation of individuals' lives.

Further Reading
Gray, Virginia, and Russell L. Hanson, eds. *Politics in the American States*. 8th ed. Washington, D.C.: Congressional Quarterly Press, 2004; Langer, Laura. *Judicial Review in State Supreme Courts: A Comparative Study*. Albany: State University of New York Press, 2002.

—Kyle Scott

state courts of appeals
State courts of appeals represent the second of three tiers within most state judicial systems. In total, 39 states use an intermediate appellate court to help resolve appeals originating from trial level courts. In states without intermediate appellate courts, appeals fall entirely on state supreme courts. Through their existence, state appellate courts serve to relieve the burden that state supreme courts once confronted as they sought to settle challenges to lower court decisions. Looking across the states, state appellate courts have become an important institution in an era when STATE COURTS have had difficulty responding to rising quantities of civil and criminal appeals.

Originating with judicial reforms initiated in the 1960s, state courts of appeals represent attempts by state reformers to alter the professionalization of state courts. Reformers argued that state courts were overloaded and slow, additionally criticizing the level of efficiency in confronting legal challenges. At the same time that reformers of state judiciaries directed their attention toward state methods of judicial selection, they also sought reforms throughout the states that restructured the process of appeals. Today, state courts are highly professionalized institutions collectively handling the demands of more than 100 million cases a year. Federal courts, in comparison, process just over 1 million cases per year, suggesting that state courts are much more integral to the lives of most Americans.

Changes adopted in the 1960s were an effort to increase the level of professionalization of state courts, both making state courts more efficient and increasing their ability to handle a greater capacity of cases. Intermediate appellate courts provided a new structure within state judicial systems for accomplishing both objectives. The impact has been greater authority for many STATE JUDGES, from the trial level to state supreme courts, and greater ability to handle legal demands as they arise. Another impact has been the reorganization of state court systems. Prior to reforms, many state court systems were inconsistently structured with overlapping JURISDICTIONs and no uniform order of appeal. Problems originating from nonconsolidated courts included trial courts with overlapping boundaries, varying rules of procedure by individual courts, and limited jurisdiction over lower courts. With confusing litigation procedures, both inefficiency and slowness developed, leading to efforts by reformers to create additional procedures or structures to alleviate these problems. Intermediate appellate courts affected the judicial landscape by providing increased direct supervision over trial courts with both limited and general jurisdiction. State appellate courts imposed judicial hierarchy and provided judicial structure so appeals could proceed in a logical order. Additionally, as state appellate courts developed in many states, they limited the autonomy of lower court judges and helped provide stricter boundaries for trial courts. Through streamlining the litigation process and providing clear paths for appeal from trial courts to state supreme courts, state courts have become vastly more efficient.

Related to case quantity, the judicial framework in many states faced crises of management. State judicial systems were overburdened by large quantities of lawsuits and unable to process appeals in a timely or efficient manner. Prior to reforms, state supreme courts represented the last and only appellate courts in most states. By creating a new tier between lower trial courts and state courts of last resort, a lower form of appellate court was created, allowing state supreme courts to implement discretionary dockets. Thereafter, state supreme courts accepted only cases that deserved consideration at the highest level of review. Additionally, state courts of appeal allowed direct and more immediate oversight of lower trial courts, ensuring more efficiency and stricter standards. Effectively, this intermediate review has substantially relieved caseload pressures, allowing state supreme courts to concentrate on controversial areas of law, while lower appellate courts have assumed the responsibility for most appeals.

In 1962, only 14 states operated lower appellate courts. By 1980, reflecting the reforms of the 1960s and 1970s, 27 states had established lower appellate courts. Today, two-tier appellate systems are the norm, operating in 39 states. Additionally, lower appellate courts now hear every form of policy common to state courts. From criminal appeals ranging from embezzlement to sexual assault to civil appeals including First Amendment claims and employee injury claims, lower appellate courts are responsible for hearing and often resolving a variety of judicial policies. Importantly, lower appellate courts typically decide cases using three-judge panels as an alternative

to sitting en banc, when the entire court is present, unlike state supreme courts. Therefore, where lower appellate courts are composed of six or more judges, this allows different cases to be simultaneously resolved while placing fewer burdens on the entire court.

While the federal courts are largely uniform, with structural similarities within each level of the judiciary, state courts vary substantially. Whether evaluating state supreme courts, intermediate appellate courts, or trial courts, the states offer a variety of arrangements. In no more controversial area is this evident than with state methods of judicial selection. While FEDERAL JUDGES are selected by the president of the United States with the ADVICE AND CONSENT of the SENATE, the states offer five primary forms of judicial selection. Broadly, these forms of judicial selection divide between forms of election and appointment.

Elective forms of selection include both partisan and nonpartisan elections. Partisan elections are similar to most other elections, with candidates using party identification. Generally, candidates are designated as a Republican, Democrat, or a third party identifier and benefit from such identification during elections. While popular during the 19th and early 20th century, today only seven states use purely partisan judicial elections. Nonpartisan elections differ by not allowing party identification. Candidates for office are forbidden from mentioning their partisan affiliation and must run for office by focusing on issues rather than partisan platforms. Preferences for nonpartisan elections emerged as opponents to political party activity within judicial selection sought to remove corruption and political accountability from judicial service. Currently, nonpartisan elections are the more popular form of judicial election, with 12 states using elective methods that exclude partisan activity.

Appointive methods of selection include three primary types. Traditionally, the most popular appointive method of selection was executive appointment Very similar to selection within the federal judiciary, GOVERNORs are responsible for selecting candidates, often with the required consent of the upper house of the state legislature. Like the president, governors select nominees based on several criteria, including partisanship, policy preferences, and familiarity. Today, just three states use executive forms of appointment, and these states are entirely located in the Northeast. Another traditional form of selection is legislative appointment. Now limited to Virginia and South Carolina, legislative appointment involves selection of judicial candidates by the state legislature. Candidates are generally former or current state legislators, causing a close relationship between the state legislature and the judiciary. Merit selection represents the final form of state judicial selection. Currently the most popular form of selection method and used in 17 states, merit selection formats seek to balance both independence and accountability. Judges in this method are typically selected by a judicial nominating commission that delivers three nominees to the state executive. The state executive then selects one candidate who serves an initial term of one or two years. Following this initial term, judges run unopposed in a retention election. If reelected by a majority of the electorate, judges then serve an extended term. Advocated since the 1930s, states have increasingly turned toward merit selection. In total, each form of judicial selection represent attempts by state actors, including POLITICAL PARTIES and INTEREST GROUPS, to create some balance between independence and accountability for judges while in office.

Other characteristics of state courts of appeals include size of office, the number of circuits or divisions, jurisdiction, term length, selection of chief judges, and mandatory retirement. As noted above, court size remains important for state courts because office size relates directly to the number of appeals processed each year. Across the states, the sizes of state courts of appeals range from three judges in Alaska and Idaho to 105 judges in California. In the 39 states with lower appellate courts, the demand on appellate courts varies. Accordingly, the comparative difference between states such as Alaska and California is very different based on population and the number of appeals filed.

Related to office size is the quantity of circuits or divisions that each intermediate appellate court must oversee. Many state appellate circuits administer the entire state. However, 20 states have multiple divisions. Beyond a single circuit, several courts of appeals have five or six circuits, with New Jersey operating 15 separate circuits. The purpose of multiple circuits, much like the U.S. courts of appeals, is to provide specific channels of appeals based on territory or geography. Territorial differences may also affect the operation of lower appellate courts, as each court may retain a unique approach to judicial policy. Larger states such as California and Texas may contain substantial regional differences within the state that emerge within the courts based on judge or court preferences. Where consolidated, states with specific geographical circuits provide designated places to file appeals.

In addition to office size and the division of labor, state courts of appeals also divide responsibilities based on policy jurisdiction. Four states have appellate courts that focus entirely on criminal appeals. Of these states, both Texas and Oklahoma have created separate criminal courts of last resort. In Oklahoma, criminal appeals move directly from trial level courts to the court of criminal appeals. Additionally, Alaska's court of appeals hears only criminal appeals, while civil appeals move directly to the Alaska Supreme Court. States with courts of appeals that are entirely civil in nature are the Alabama and Oklahoma Courts of Appeals.

Tenure of service also varies dramatically throughout the states. The most common term length for lower appellate court judges is six years, yet the minimum term is four years and the maximum term is life tenure in Massachusetts. Additionally, in several states, primarily those with merit selection, judges must first serve a shorter initial term. Overall, term lengths vary substantially, with some states favoring shorter terms and others with longer terms. Like methods of selection, length of term has a substantial effect on the approach that judges take toward service. Where shorter, judges may reflect on political pressures related to reselection, while longer tenures afford greater freedom from external pressures.

Like the federal courts, state courts of appeals designate individual judges to lead their respective courts. Often designated the "chief judge," these individuals are responsible for managing the court, including how cases are heard, which judges hear each case, and how opinions are structured. Related to the selection of chief judges, states use several approaches. The most common method for selecting chief judges is peer voting, used in 21 states. Chief judges in these states are selected by a vote of the state court of appeals. In many states, the eventual judge selected is the most senior judge on the court. Chief judges are also chosen by standard forms of selection including executive appointment, legislative appointment, merit selection, and elections. States also use seniority and appointments by the prior chief judge as sources of selection. Once a chief judge, length of tenure ranges from one year to the remainder of a chief judge's tenure in office, with elected courts generally allowing shorter terms as chief judge than appointed courts. Terms for chief judges, like associate judges, matter greatly for the approach they take toward office. When serving longer terms, chief judges are granted the authority to shape policy and the direction of the court with few threats of reprisal by those external to the court.

In relation to retirement, judges on state courts of appeals leave both voluntarily and nonvoluntarily. Almost 60 percent of lower appellate courts have mandatory retirement rules, whereby judges may serve until a specific age. In the 23 states with age restrictions, 70 years of age is the most common mandatory age of retirement, with an additional three states allowing service until 75 years of age.

Acting as the center tier of 39 state judicial systems, state courts of appeals are granted the important responsibility of resolving many legal conflicts. This important task allows intermediate appellate courts to place their imprint on the legal rationale of cases that follow. When areas of law are unclear and when state supreme courts or the U.S. SUPREME COURT have yet to become involved in an area of policy, substantive doctrine is shaped by the actions and opinions of intermediate appellate courts. As important is the impact of lower appellate courts on state supreme courts. In the 11 states without intermediate appellate courts, state supreme courts serve as the first and only outlet for appeal. In these states, state high courts are given the task of resolving all legal disputes as they emerge on appeal. Without a discretionary docket, state supreme courts are obligated to evaluate a greater percentage of appeals than in states with discretionary dockets, potentially overburdening a state supreme court. On the other hand, in states with lower appellate courts, state supreme courts are granted the ability to determine which appeals are most important. This factor more than any other means that lower appellate courts are valued for their ability to

make the appellate system more efficient and reduce the burdens previously imposed on state supreme courts. As mentioned above, following reforms and reorganization, state courts of appeals provided a mechanism for addressing a growing quantity of legal appeals while reducing pressures on other tiers of the judiciary. Additionally, state courts of appeals possess varying structures, ranging from method of selection to the quantity of judges present within an appeal. Related to these factors, state laws and constitutional provisions have created systems of the judiciary that vary throughout the states, allowing appellate courts and judges to become more or less adept at handling legal challenges as they emerge.

Further Reading

Hall, Melinda Gann. "State Judicial Politics: Rules, Structures, and the Political Game." In *American State and Local Politics: Directions for the 21st Century*, edited by Ronald E. Weber and Paul Brace. New York: Chatham House Publishers, 1999; Meador, Daniel J., and Frederick G. Kempin. *American Courts*. St. Paul, Minn.: West Publishing, 2000; Segal, Jeffrey A., Harold J. Spaeth, and Sara C. Benesh. *The Supreme Court in the American Legal System*. New York: Cambridge University Press, 2005; Sheldon, Charles H., and Linda S. Maule. *Choosing Justice: The Recruitment of State and Federal Judges*. Pullman: Washington State University Press, 1997; Tarr, G. Alan. *Understanding State Constitutions*. Princeton, N.J.: Princeton University Press, 1998.

—Brent D. Boyea

state government

In the United States, the bulk of responsibility for governing and executing policies originally lay with the various STATES. States, being outgrowths of the English COLONIAL GOVERNMENTS, were seen as the entities to which citizens and elected officials turned when conducting their political affairs. This is not to say that the national government played no role in governing the newly formed nation, but initially, especially under the ARTICLES OF CONFEDERATION, the states were dominant in terms of seeing to it that citizens' needs were met. As it became clear that the confederacy that was created under the Articles of

Confederation was in jeopardy of breaking up because of the disproportionate strength given to the state governments, it was decided that a new form of national government was needed. This new form of government, organized under the U.S. CONSTITUTION, granted the central government considerably more power as the confederal form of government was replaced with the federal system we are familiar with today. Immediately following the adoption of the U.S. Constitution and in concert with various broad interpretations of the new powers of the federal government, the state governments began to slowly cede control over the formulation and design of public policy in the new nation.

With the adoption of the Constitution, however, the states did not sit back and obediently accept the actions and policies of the federal government. Competing philosophies concerning the proper roles of the state and federal governments led to a number of clashes during the early 1800s, most notably regarding the federal government's stance on the Alien and Sedition Acts, various tariffs, and a series of decisions surrounding the issue of SLAVERY. The philosophical differences between those who favored stronger state governments and those who favored a stronger federal government were loosely tied to partisan affiliations and were largely resolved with the Civil War and the Union victory in that conflict. Following the Civil War, the federal government again exerted its influence over the states, particularly in the South, where the short-lived experience with Reconstruction served to remind state governments in the South that they were subordinate to the federal government in Washington, D.C.

The late 1800s saw the maturation of the Industrial Revolution in the United States. A new economy based on new technology and rapid change began to replace the more agrarian and rural society with which Americans had been familiar. Because of the pluralistic nature of American government, these new industries and corporations were able to significantly influence governmental policy at both the national and state levels. Citizens in various regions of the nation, particularly in the West, in the Midwest, and on the Plains, began to react to the influence wielded by these new players by organizing locally, with the ultimate goal of influencing state government so that their interests would be heard. The populist and Progressive Era movements were the outgrowths of these local organizing activities, and the citizens of these regions ultimately had notable successes in regulating the new economy. Specifically, the newly formed groups were able to infiltrate local and state governments, subsequently regulating the railroads and other large industries. Furthermore, these reform movements led to the adoption of DIRECT DEMOCRACY at the state level, as exemplified by the adoption of the INITIATIVE, REFERENDUM, and RECALL in a number of states. These modes of direct democracy gave citizens much more control over their state governments than they had had in the past. While the federal government remained relatively strong during this period, and while the move toward direct democracy was not adopted at the national level, state governments were central to producing and maintaining the atmosphere of reform that slowly percolated up to the federal government in the early 1900s.

With the advent of two major international conflicts, World Wars I and II, the United States again experienced great changes socially and politically. In order to succeed in these two conflicts, it was necessary for the federal government to further centralize its powers so that a truly national war effort could be made. The national income tax was imposed as a way for the U.S. government to support its expansion and growth; very few states imposed similar taxes, and the states' powers in relation to the federal government continued to slip as a result. Along with the two world wars, the United States was also faced with the Great Depression. The Great Depression furthered the need for the federal government to expand its scope so that the United States would be able to pull itself out of the disastrous economic situation of the late 1920s and early 1930s. State governments were virtually bankrupt, and it was up to the federal government to provide relief to the people of the states. The Federal Emergency Relief Act, through which the federal government provided millions of dollars to the cash-strapped states, was implemented. Also, federal programs such as the Agricultural Adjustment Act and the Civilian Conservation Corps were set up to help the American people by providing economic opportunities for citizens. Thus, state governments were forced to accept supporting roles in the recovery process, and the Great Depression effectively served to secure into the future the federal government's dominance over the states as a multitude of federal programs were put in place.

The power of state governments in relation to the federal government reached low tide in the 1960s as the federal government put forth policies that obligated states to adhere to a range of federal laws. U.S. SUPREME COURT rulings such as *Brown v. Board of Education*, which was handed down in 1954 and enforced throughout the 1960s and 1970s, forced state and local governments to reform and integrate their public schools so as to give children of all races equal opportunities in school. Additionally, Congress passed the Civil Rights Act of 1964 and the Voting Rights Act of 1965, both of which were designed to ensure fair treatment of racial minorities by state governments. An earlier U.S. Supreme Court decision in 1962, *Baker v. Carr*, compelled states to reapportion their state and national legislative districts to guarantee equal representation of citizens in the nation's legislatures, and state governments worked throughout the decade to conform to the Supreme Court's decision. While most of these policies were specifically aimed at reducing the levels of segregation and discrimination in American society, these federal government mandates, taken together, served to directly influence the activities of state and local governments as the federal government oversaw the execution of these policies at the state level. In fact, state governments to this day are expected to comport to the federal government's guidelines put forth in all of the aforementioned policies.

Since the late 1960s and early 1970s, there has been a reaction to the seemingly relentless expansion and growing authority of the federal government. Generally associated with the REPUBLICAN PARTY, the movement to reduce the influence of the federal government over state government affairs was aided by the election of Ronald Reagan to the presidency and the relative successes of the Republican Party at the national level throughout the 1980s. This decade saw the federal government collapse a large number of categorical grants into a smaller number of block grants. This was seen as a victory for state governments, as block grants give states much more discretion over the ways in which they spend and use the money they receive from the federal government.

Also in the 1980s, there was a push to give control over such large programs as Medicaid and welfare to the states, though this push stalled and ultimately failed. Republican candidates for office in the 1990s consistently advocated STATES' RIGHTS in their campaigns as a way to appeal to those voters who viewed the federal government as bloated and overly intrusive in state affairs. With the adoption of such policies as welfare reform in 1996, passed by a Republican Congress and signed by Democratic president Bill Clinton, it appeared that the nation was ready to return substantial governmental responsibilities to the states. Termed devolution, or new FEDERALISM, the movement to give more power back to the states seemed an inevitability in the late 1990s. Since then, however, some scholars have cast doubt over the federal government's actual willingness to return control over policies to the state governments, as it seems that welfare reform in 1996 was the only substantial policy in which control was devolved. Especially after the terrorist attacks of September 11, 2001, this criticism has become more pronounced because of the subsequent growth of the federal government following that event. Nonetheless, policy scholars and political scientists have continued to view devolution as a real phenomenon that has altered the balance of power, once again, between the federal and state governments.

The brief, oversimplified description of historical trends in state government given above provides the context for discussing states at the beginning of the 21st century. The philosophical rift between those who favor states' rights and those who view the federal government as superior continues to frame politics and government in the United States. Undoubtedly, state governments play a much more prominent role in the everyday lives of ordinary citizens than the federal government, though their impact is not always acknowledged by scholars and the news MEDIA. The overall size of state governments and their associated budgets are considerably larger than the federal government, and the frequency with which citizens come into contact with their state governments far surpasses the frequency with which citizens come into contact with the federal government. Anyone who has obtained a driver's license, who has been pulled over for speeding, who has had to obtain state certifications, or who has personally met a STATE REPRESENTATIVE can attest to this fact.

Part of the reason for the relatively large size of state governments has been the move toward professionalization in recent decades. Professionalization refers to the movement by state governments to modernize their political affairs and conduct them in a more efficient and standardized fashion. Theoretically, a more professionalized government will produce and execute policies in a manner that is fair and equitable, as government officials are given more resources with which to work. Also, government officials are expected to be more accountable in a professionalized government, as citizens are provided with the tools to oversee their government. Features of government that signify professionalization include, among others, long terms of office, high pay for those in government, increased funding for staffing and research, clear ladders of hierarchy, clear leadership, open meeting laws, high levels of technology usage, and the efficient provision of services to citizens. The increased professionalization of state governments has generally been associated with the increasing number of responsibilities that have been thrust upon the states; that is, in order to meet demands, the states have had to upgrade their operations. Partly for this reason, political scientists as well as other social scientists have begun to view state governments as not only interesting but also very important in terms of policies and their impacts on the people of the states.

Thus, the interaction of devolution and increased state government capacity has enhanced the image and standing of state governments. As a result, particularly in the field of political science, some researchers have begun to refocus their efforts to study government and politics at the state rather than national level. Devolution and the centrality of state government to the lives of citizens are not the only factors that have drawn researchers to state government, however. Political scientists have also begun to rediscover the benefits of studying state governmental institutions and state politics with a comparative approach. The 50 states provide researchers with 50 similar but somewhat unique political environments with which to make comparisons and draw conclusions, giving researchers statistical and theoretical leverage when asking important questions about government and politics. For instance, a researcher interested in studying legislative behavior has the option of focusing on the U.S. SENATE and the U.S. HOUSE OF REPRESENTATIVES and drawing conclusions based on the actions of 535 members from the two chambers. Alternatively, that same researcher could research STATE LEGISLATURES, which altogether have more than 7,000 members, and could also have 99 different legislatures from which to base assumptions and draw conclusions (49 of the 50 states have a bicameral state legislature; Nebraska is the lone state with a unicameral state legislature). Statistically speaking, the researcher studying state legislatures has much more power and theoretical validity than the researcher studying the U.S. Congress because of the ability to work with larger sample sizes. This same logic applies also to researchers interested in studying executives, courts, and bureaucracies. Of course, this is not to say that researching government and institutions at the national level does not provide us with an understanding of government in general; obviously, the national government is very important, and researching it helps scholars better understand government and politics. However, studying state governments helps us understand government and politics much more fully due to our ability to compare across states and institutions.

The American states occupy a unique position in the American political system. Originally designed to serve as the loci of government activity in the United States, states have experienced periods and eras in which they have seen their powers expand and contract. Though the federal government today is dominant, the relative powers of state governments are on the rise. In response to their new responsibilities, the states have modernized and professionalized their governments and the delivery of services to citizens to meet new demands. Surely, if historical trends are any indication, the powers of the state governments will continue to fluctuate into the future; regardless of the directions in which state governmental powers move, the states will undoubtedly maintain their distinct position in the American federal system. For this reason, the states will provide an ideal location for political scientists to research government and politics in the years to come.

Further Reading
Brace, Paul, and Aubrey Jewett. "The State of State Politics Research." *Political Research Quarterly* 48 (1995): 643–681; Jewell, Malcolm E. "The Neglected World of State Politics." *Journal of Politics* 44 (1982): 638–657; Mooney, Christopher Z. "Why Do They Tax Dogs in West Virginia? Teaching Political Science through Comparative State Politics." *PS: Political Science and Politics* 31 (1998): 199–203; Smith, Kevin B., ed. *State and Local Government 2005–2006.* Washington, D.C.: Congressional Quarterly Press, 2006; Van Horn, Carl E. *The State of the States.* 4th ed. Washington, D.C.: Congressional Quarterly Press, 2006; Weber, Ronald E., and Paul Brace, eds. *American State and Local Politics: Directions for the 21st Century.* New York: Chatham House, 1999.

—Mitchel N. Herian

state judges

By some estimates, there are more than 30,000 judges in the United States. The vast majority of those judges serve on STATE COURTS of some type. In the United States, almost all judges are lawyers first before becoming a judge. The 50 states (plus the District of Columbia) have each established their own system of state courts, with each state choosing its own court organizational structure and judicial selection system. This essay will explore some of the various methods for categorizing state judges.

Both state and FEDERAL JUDGES in the United States can first be divided into two very broad categories: judges who serve on trial courts and judges who serve on appellate courts. In the United States, only one trial judge presides over each case in a trial court. Although the states differ greatly in whether they have a simple or complex organization for their trial courts, all cases enter the state court system through a trial court. If there is a jury present, the jury determines the primary questions of fact at a trial. If there is no jury, then the trial judge determines both questions of fact and questions of law that arise at the trial. A trial in the United States is usually a public event in which the attorneys for each side present their evidence and question witnesses in order to determine the facts of the case.

Trial courts and the judges who serve on them can be further divided into courts of general JURISDICTION and courts of limited jurisdiction. The term *jurisdiction* refers to the power of a court to hear a case. Around 90 percent of state trial courts are courts of limited jurisdiction, which means that the judge hears a very narrow range of cases. Some examples of state courts of limited jurisdiction include traffic courts, small claims courts, juvenile courts, family courts, housing courts, probate courts, drug courts, courts for minor crimes, and other courts with narrowly defined jurisdictions. Depending on the court and the specific state, some judges serve on these courts of narrow jurisdiction for their entire careers, but many judges rotate among these courts of limited jurisdiction. There are more than 9,200 judges on state courts of general jurisdiction that generally hear major criminal and civil cases. Courts of general jurisdiction can hear any case that is not specifically assigned to a court of limited jurisdiction. There are more than 14 times as many judges on state courts of general jurisdiction as there are federal trial judges.

Judges who serve on appellate courts hear appeals filed by those who have lost cases in a trial court. Most states have a two-tiered system of state appellate courts, with the court of last resort in the state generally referred to as the state supreme court. Oklahoma and Texas have two state supreme courts, one for criminal cases and one for civil cases. The courts of last resort in Maryland and New York are called the courts of appeals, while the court called the "supreme court" in the state of New York is actually a trial court. Between the trial courts and the state courts of last resort are the intermediate appellate courts, although not all states have this middle layer of appellate courts.

State appellate judges serve on panels to hear appeals. Judges on intermediate state appellate courts usually hear cases in panels of three judges, while generally state supreme courts (courts of last resort) have seven judges who all hear each case. Appeals are filed through written briefs, and generally all communication with an appellate court is done in writing. Appellate judges may hold oral arguments on their cases, but the purpose of these oral arguments is for the judges to clarify the assertions made in the written briefs submitted to the court. Appellate judges communicate their decisions through written opinions. One judge generally writes the opinion for the majority on the appellate court, while those judges with minority views often file dissenting opinions. If an appellate judge agrees with the majority's outcome in a case, but for different reasons, he or she can also generally file a concurring opinion clarifying their reasoning in the case. For the most part, appellate judges determine questions of law that become PRE-CEDENT for all trial judges hearing cases within the appellate court's jurisdictional boundaries. For example, the majority decision of a state court of last resort on a question of state law is binding precedent for all trial and appellate judges within that state. Judges on state appellate courts spend a great deal of time researching the law and writing their opinions, with far less time actually spent on the bench hearing oral arguments in the cases before them.

States differ a great deal in the selection system they use for state judges. There are generally five models of state judicial selection systems. Some states use several models of judicial selection, depending on the level of judge being selected. These models of judicial selection approach the main principles of judicial independence and judicial accountability differently. Models that favor judicial independence give the state judges long terms and attempt to insulate them from political pressures. In models that favor judicial accountability, the judges face the voters after serving relatively short terms. Thus, these judges are accountable to political majorities in their communities. The five general categories of state judicial selection systems are appointment by the GOVERNOR, appointment by the state legislature, partisan election, nonpartisan election, and the so-called Missouri plan, including retention elections. Unlike their federal counterparts, who are appointed by the president and confirmed by the SENATE for life terms, the American Judicature Society in 2004 estimated that 87 percent of the nation's 1,243 state appellate judges must stand for some type of election.

The first model for state judicial selection, appointment by the governor, most resembles the federal judicial selection system. In states such as Massachusetts and New Hampshire, the governor appoints all judges in the state system, with confirmation by the elected but obscure governor's council. In these states, judges serve life terms until the mandatory retirement age, usually 70. In states such as South Carolina and Virginia, state judges are appointed by the state legislature. In neither of these models do the judges face any type of election system. These models promote the principle of judicial independence.

The second two models for state judicial selection involve the direct election of judges. In a partisan election system such as those used in Texas and Pennsylvania, candidates for judge run on a partisan ballot just like candidates for any other elected office in the state. These judges serve short terms, typically four years. The candidates for judge must campaign and raise campaign funds just like any other candidate, and the POLITICAL PARTIES play a key role in these contests. Reelection rates are generally high for these judges, but their reelection efforts can turn on the decisions they made previously in cases before them. In nonpartisan elections such as those held in Wisconsin and Minnesota, the party affiliations of the candidates for judge do not appear on the ballot. However, the candidates for judge who appear on the general election ballot are often chosen through partisan primary elections. In states such as Ohio, even though the party label for each judicial candidate does not appear on the general election ballot, the political parties widely advertise which judicial candidates are members of their parties. Thus, the differences between partisan and nonpartisan elections seem small. These models promote the principle of judicial accountability.

The final model attempts to balance the often conflicting goals of judicial accountability and judicial independence. The so-called Missouri plan is a product of the Progressive Era and is the model of judicial selection most used by the states today. Under this model, the governor appoints a judicial selection commission, usually made up of members from each political party and from the state bar association. For each judicial opening, the commission typically submits a list of three names to the governor, and the governor must appoint one of these individuals to be the judge. The new judge then serves a set number of years on the bench, typically seven years. At the end of that fixed term of years, the judge then faces a retention election. The only question on the ballot for the voters is whether or not to retain that judge on the bench. If the voters choose not to retain a judge or if there is an opening for any other reason, the whole process begins anew with the judicial selection commission. Although the so-called merit selection commissions can be used with any of the five models of state judicial selection, the key difference between the Missouri plan and the other models is the fact that under the Missouri plan judges must face a retention election. The Missouri plan therefore attempts to promote both judicial independence and judicial accountability. It is seen as a compromise between these two competing goals.

In general, state judges spend most of their time on a variety of tasks and duties. These responsibilities include adjudication tasks such as presiding over trials, legal research, and legal writing. Judges also are involved in a variety of negotiation procedures as they try to settle cases before them without formal litigation. Judges also have administrative responsibilities, including hiring and supervision of staff in many states. Judges also must reach out to the other branches of government and to the community at large for a variety of reasons. In states that promote the value of judicial accountability, the judges must also spend part of their time raising campaign funds and other election-related tasks. State judges generally receive little special training for their often difficult and stressful jobs.

Further Reading

Baum, Lawrence. *American Courts: Process and Policy.* 5th ed. Boston: Houghton Mifflin, 2001; Brace, Paul R., and Melinda Gann Hall. "Is Judicial Federalism Essential to Democracy? State Courts in the Federal System." In *The Judicial Branch,* edited by Kermit L Hall and Kevin T. McGuire, New York: Oxford University Press, 2005; Langer, Laura. *Judicial Review in State Supreme Courts: A Comparative Study.* Albany: State University of New York Press, 2002; Tarr, G. Alan. *Judicial Process and Judicial Policymaking.* 4th ed. Belmont, Calif.: Thomson Wadsworth, 2006.

—Mark C. Miller

state representative

A state representative is an elected official whose responsibility is to help make public policy that will best meet the needs of the citizens of the district from which he or she is elected. The state representative helps to make public policy through the legislative process as a member of the STATE LEGISLATURE.

The position of state representative is constitutionally mandated. The U.S. CONSTITUTION declares in Article IV, Section 4, that each state shall have a republican form of government. It refers to state legislators' duties twice. In Article I, Section 4, the Constitution states that the state legislature shall designate the "times and places and manner for holding elections for [federal] Senators and Representatives." In Article II, Section 1, it states that the state legislature shall direct the manner in which electors to the ELECTORAL COLLEGE shall be selected.

STATE CONSTITUTIONS direct the process for electing state representatives, including the length of term in office, TERM LIMITS, if any, the length of the legislative session, and the process for determining compensation. All states except Nebraska organize their state legislature into two groups, an upper house, called the senate, and a lower house, called the house of delegates, house of representatives, general assembly, or assembly. State representatives, then, are given a title corresponding to the legislative house to which they are elected. Representatives elected to the upper house are referred to as senators, and representatives to the lower house are referred to as delegates, representatives, or assemblypersons, depending on their state. For the remainder of this article, members of the lower houses will simply be referred to as delegates, and the lower houses will be referred to as houses.

STATE SENATORS generally have longer terms than delegates. In 34 states, senators are elected for four-year terms, while delegates are elected for two year terms. The remaining 16 states have identical lengths of terms for both houses, although the length of those terms vary: 11 states have two-year terms for all state representatives, and five states (including Nebraska) have four-year terms for all representatives. A total of 18 states have imposed term limits for their state representatives. Arizona, Colorado, Florida, Maine, Montana, Ohio, and South Dakota allow representatives in either house to serve eight consecutive years, while Louisiana, Utah, and Wyoming have a 12 consecutive year limit. Idaho also has an eight-year consecutive limit, but within a 15-year period. Arkansas, California, Michigan, Missouri, Nevada, Oklahoma, and Oregon impose term limits ranging from six to 12 years, with a lifetime ban on serving in that office again.

The size of the legislative body also differs from state to state. Generally, the senate is one-third the size of the house. The average senate has 40 members, and the average house has 112 members. New Hampshire has the largest house, with 400 members, while Nebraska, the only state with a unicameral legislature, also has the fewest number of state representatives, 49. It should also be noted that Nebraska is the only state that elects state representatives in a nonpartisan race.

State representatives are classified into three categories that reflect the state constitutional design of the legislature: professional, hybrid, and amateur, or citizen, legislators. These categories refer to the length of time that a legislature is in session each year, the salary paid to legislators, and the amount of staff each legislator has. Six states, Massachusetts, Michigan, New Jersey, Ohio, Pennsylvania, and Wisconsin, have annual legislative sessions that exceed 300 calendar days. On the other end of the spectrum are six states whose legislatures are biennial: Arkansas, Montana, Nevada, North Dakota, Oregon, and Texas.

Staff load can vary widely among legislatures. New York employs nearly 4,000 people to staff its legislature, while Vermont employs fewer than 60 legislative staff. Professional legislatures typically have nine personnel per representative; hybrid legislatures have three, and amateur legislatures have on average one staff member per representative.

The level of professionalization of a state legislature is critical to understanding the ability of the state representative to make public policy and to understanding the attraction that the position of state representative has for citizens contemplating public service. Longer legislative sessions provide more time for legislators to debate public policy. Therefore, a wider variety of policies may be considered, and more time can be spent on the details of the policy when a legislative body is full time. Staffing is also very important. Staff can help legislators by researching policies that exist in other states and researching the federal rules regarding policies that states are mandated to support, such as Medicaid and Temporary Assistance to Needy Families. Staff can also research the various facets of policy proposals so that the state representative can be more informed of decisions he or she is about to make.

The level of staff and the length of session can increase the capacity of the legislature to act as an equal branch of government to the state GOVERNOR in terms of policy making. When the legislature and governor are both fully informed about policies and policy alternatives, each branch is better equipped to debate what outcomes are best for the state. Full-time state representatives are also able to engage in greater oversight of state agencies to ensure that the bureaucracy is implementing policy in the manner prescribed by the legislature.

Staffing levels are critical to a state representative in another way. In addition to making public policy, many state representatives engage in constituency services. These services include helping constituents in their interactions with state agencies and submitting requests for district area APPROPRIATIONS. Often referred to as "pork," such appropriations help to construct or maintain schools, senior citizen centers, parks, bridges, and roads as well as a host of other projects that benefit the public. State representatives with more personnel can provide increased support to constituents who need help with state agency interactions. The staff can also meet with constituents and research the needs for appropriations.

Compensation is a critical issue in the case of professional legislatures. State representatives who have careers outside the legislature are not able to spend as much time performing legislative duties as those whose sole employment is as a state representative. Compensation may also help to determine the incentive candidates have for seeking office. Research has found that full-time legislatures with moderate to high salaries may provide a greater incentive for middle-class citizens to seek office. The reason for this is that a person who commands a high salary may not be willing to sacrifice that income in order to become a full-time legislator at a lower salary. Legislatures that meet for shorter sessions may be more attractive to professionals who are self-employed or who can take extended leaves of absence for public service. Business professionals, attorneys, and some state teachers fall into these categories. The average salary paid to representatives in professional legislatures is $68,599 a year; in hybrid legislatures the average falls to $35,326 per year, and amateur legislatures on average pay their representatives $15,984 per year.

Because there is a class bias between the parties, Morris Fiorina, a political scientist, has argued that full-time legislatures become disproportionately Democratic. Even while the trend clearly is toward professionalizing legislatures, in 2005 20 states had a majority of Republican state representatives, and another 12 states were evenly split between Democratic and Republican representatives.

As in most sectors of the United States, white men have dominated the field of state representatives. This, too, is changing. Women now make up 22 percent of all state legislators. In Arizona, Colorado, Delaware, Nevada, Vermont, and Washington, women hold more than 33 percent of the state representative seats. African Americans hold 8 percent of all state representative seats, while Hispanics make up only 2 percent of state legislatures. Given that women make up 51 percent of the population, African Americans represent 12 percent of the population, and Hispanics make up nearly 13 percent of the population, it is obvious that minorities continue to be underrepresented.

The nature of representation must be considered when discussing state representatives. A good deal of research and theory has been devoted to studying representation. The most obvious concern for equal representation comes in the form of geographic representation. This idea posits that the needs of people differ from area to area. Farmers have different needs than miners, for example. Each state forms specific districts for the purpose of electing representatives. Each district has approximately the same number of people and must have contiguous and natural boundaries, so that fairness exists in selecting a state representative and that no groups are favored or rendered unlikely to be able to elect the representative of their choice. States have outlawed the practice of GERRY-MANDERING, which is constructing a district to disproportionately favor a political party or group of people.

In addition to geographic representation, symbolic representation is also a concern. It was noted above that state representatives are primarily white males. If a state had true symbolic representation, the demographics of that state would be mirrored in the legislature. For example, given the national demographics noted above, to be symbolically representative the U.S. Congress would have the following composition: 51 percent would be women, 12 per-cent would be African American, 13 percent would be Hispanic, 1 percent would be American Indian, and 4 percent would be Asian American.

The underlying assumption of the necessity for symbolic representation is that state representatives who are female or Hispanic will have different points of view than representatives who are male or white. Research on symbolic representation has shown that minorities do change the nature of legislative bodies. An increased presence of women state representatives results in additional introductions of bills addressing the needs of children, health care, and education. Little research exists on the effect of Hispanics in state legislatures. What is known about African-American state representatives is that when they are elected, it is typically from urban districts. African-American support for a candidate is generally translated as a tip that the candidate is liberal, and therefore conservatives fail to support the candidate. African Americans do not enjoy broad symbolic representation, but in districts where they are politically active, evidence suggests that their representatives, regardless of race, do respond to their demands.

The style of a representative's policy decision making has also been given considerable thought in the literature on representation. It was noted at the beginning of this essay that a state representative is charged with making public policy that will best meet the needs of the district he or she represents. This process has been classified in two categories. The first, the delegate style of representation, relies on constant interaction between a representative and his or her constituency. Through this interaction, citizens inform their representative of their policy preferences. The state representative then introduces legislation desired by constituents and votes according to the demands of the majority of those people in his or her district. The second form of active representation is known as trusteeship. In this mode, a state representative makes decisions based on what he or she considers best for the district and the state. The relationship that this type of representative enjoys with constituents is one of trust. Citizens do not play an active role in the formation of policy but provide feedback on their approval of the representative's actions at the ballot box.

State representatives, then, are constitutionally mandated positions in which people are elected by specific districts to make public policy on behalf of their constituents. The representatives are elected to the senate or house in the state legislature, where they meet in session to make policy and conduct constituent services. Most state representatives are white males who have professional backgrounds as attorneys or businessmen, although increasingly minorities and people from other professional and nonprofessional backgrounds are being elected into public service.

See also STATE AND LOCAL LEGISLATIVE PROCESS.

Further Reading

Dresang, Dennis L., and James J. Gosling. *Politics and Policy in American States and Communities.* 5th ed. New York: Pearson Longman, 2006; Fiorina, Morris P. "Divided Government in the American States: A Byproduct of Legislative Professionalism?" *American Political Science Review* 91 (1994): 148–55; Gray, Virginia, Russell L. Hanson, and Herbert Jacob. *Politics in the American States: A Comparative Analysis.* 7th ed. Washington, D.C.: Congressional Quarterly Press, 1999; Herring, Mary. "Legislative Responsiveness to Black Constituents in Three Deep South States." *Journal of Politics* 52 (1990): 740–758; Hill, Kim Quaile, and Patricia A. Hurley. "Dyadic Representation Reappraised." *American Journal of Political Science* 43, no. 1 (January 1999): 109–137; National Conference of State Legislatures, Full and Part Time Legislatures. Available online. URL: http://www.ncsl.org/programs/press/2004/backgrounder_fullandpart.htm. Accessed July 22, 2006; National Conference of State Legislatures, Legislative Budget Procedures. Available online. URL: http://www.ncsl.org/programs/fiscal/lbptabls/lbpc2t2.htm. Accessed July 22, 2006; Pitkin, Hanna F. *The Concept of Representation.* Berkeley: University of California Press, 1972; Ray, David. "The Sources of Voting Cues in Three State Legislatures." *Journal of Politics* 44 (1982): 1074–1087; Thomas, Sue. "The Impact of Women on State Legislative Policies." *Journal of Politics* 53 (1991): 958–975; United States Constitution. Available online. URL: http://www.law.cornell.edu/constitution/constitution.overview.html. Accessed July 22, 2006; U.S. Bureau of the Census, Population Factfinder. Available online. URL: http://factfinder.census.gov/. Accessed July 22, 2006; Weber, Ronald. "Presidential Address: The Quality of State Legislative Representation: A Critical Assessment." *Journal of Politics* 61, no. 3 (August 1999): 609–627; Weisburg, Herbert, Eric Heberlig, and Lisa Campoli, eds. *Classics in Congressional Politics.* New York: Longman Publishing Group, 1999; Weissburg, Robert. "Collective v. Dydactic Representation." *American Political Science Review* 72, no. 2 (June 1978): 535–547.

—Marybeth D. Beller

state senator

Americans are both blessed and cursed to be represented by three levels of government—local, STATE, and national—to say nothing of the numerous SPECIAL DISTRICTS and other governments that fall somewhere in between. Most Americans are familiar with at least the name of their representatives at the national level. Likewise, their local representatives may be familiar to them because they are physically closer to them and may have even had direct contact with them. State legislators, however, are often caught somewhere in between. They do not have the personal connection with their constituents that local representatives have, and they do not receive the volume of MEDIA coverage that their national counterparts enjoy. Despite their relative anonymity, state legislators are extremely powerful figures in American politics. Particularly in the face of devolution, a movement to return power to the states, state legislators will only increase in power in the future.

In all states but one, legislators are elected into one of two houses, either the state house (sometimes called the assembly or legislature) or the state senate. (The exception to this rule is Nebraska, which has a unicameral rather than a BICAMERAL LEGISLATURE.) This essay will consider the people who serve in the senates, people who are generally called state senators. Unlike the U.S. SENATE, where all senators serve under identical institutional structures, state senate structures vary across states. As a result, examining state senates allows us to better understand how institutional structure affects senator behavior. Consequently, the essay will focus on the ways senators are similar across contexts as well as the ways in which they vary across states. In the end, this should provide a better understanding of the motivations and actions of state senates than could be achieved by examining similarities alone.

Most people are familiar with the basic structure of the U.S. Senate. Exactly 100 senators represent all 50 states and serve for six-year terms. In contrast, state senate terms are no longer than four years, and in many states, senators serve for two-year terms. State senates are also much smaller than their national counterpart, ranging from 20 members in Alaska to 67 in Minnesota. Chamber size is always lower in the state senate than in the lower house of the legislature. Because of wide variations in population and chamber size, the number of constituents per senate district varies considerably from state to state, ranging from a low of about 13,000 in North Dakota to a high of almost 878,000 in California. While the goals and basic jobs of state senators look similar across states, these different institutional contexts provide very different constraints and incentives.

In most legislative bodies, the three most important institutional structures for keeping order are legislative leadership, committees, and POLITICAL PARTIES. State senates include all three of these structures, although their particular functions and powers vary considerably from state to state. For instance, all state senates have leaders, but the number of senate leaders and their specific powers vary from state to state. Similar to the U.S. Senate, most state senates are headed by a single leader elected from the general population, not the senate membership. Generally, the lieutenant governor (similar to the VICE PRESIDENT of the United States) occupies this position. While in most states the lieutenant governor holds little power, in some states, he or she can exercise tremendous power over the legislative process. In a sizeable minority of states, senate leaders are elected by the entire body.

Similarly, while every state senate has committees, the number of committees, their specific powers, and their rules regarding their make-up vary from state to state. In some states, they are the key to the legislative process, while in other states, committees are comparatively less powerful. Finally, most studies of the U.S. Senate suggest that parties help form ready-made coalitions and structure voting patterns. Recent work suggests that in the 49 states where senators are elected with party labels (Nebraska has nonpartisan elections for state legislators), these party labels help organize government in much the same way they do in Washington.

Three of the most important ways that the legislative environment for state senators varies are in session length, salary, and staff. In some states, such as California, the senate stays in session throughout the year, whereas in other states, such as New Hampshire, the legislature meets for only a few days every year. In states with longer sessions, senators tend to make higher salaries. For instance, in California, where senators are in office year round, they receive about $99,000 a year in salary. New Hampshire senators, with their short sessions, receive only $100 a year. Senators and legislators from the lower house make identical salaries except in Virginia where senators make an additional $360.

These trends are not only interesting by themselves but affect the occupational makeup of the senate. In legislatures with longer sessions and higher salaries, senators can afford to not hold other jobs—they are more likely to be professional politicians. This trend is particularly pronounced among women, who are less likely to hold outside careers than their male counterparts. Although there is considerable variation in the types of outside careers held by state senators, occupations that allow greater flexibility, such as lawyers, farmers, and professors are generally the best represented in the state senates.

State senators also vary considerably in their staff resources. Some states, such as California, New York, and Florida, give their senators considerable staff resources to aid them with CASEWORK, reelection, and lawmaking. Other states, such as Vermont, New Hampshire, and New Mexico, offer no personal staff, instead spreading very few staff members across all senators and senate committees.

Staff resources, salary, and session length generally vary together and are frequently combined to form a measure of legislative professionalism that can be used to summarize the institutional capacity of the legislature. Many scholars have noted the increasing professionalization of state senates (and STATE LEGISLATURES more generally). More and more states are adding more staff, increasing session length, and raising salaries to meet the increasing demands of serving in the state senates. Like many political reforms, the professionalization trend has both intended and unintended consequences. Professionalism increases the capacity of state senators and legislators, much as intended. Professionalism also increases contact between senators and their constituents, leads to policies that are more representative of public opinion, increases legislative efficiency, and increases per capita government spending.

Although most of the institutional features that affect state senators remain constant over years, TERM LIMITS stand as a notable exception. Term limits were introduced in California, Colorado, and Oklahoma in 1990 to remove the ills of election from the senate and to reduce careerism in state politics. Since then, 21 states have passed INITIATIVES to limit the terms of state senators and representatives; six of these have since been repealed, leaving 15 states that currently employ some type of term limit. The maximum number of terms a senator can serve in term limited states varies from eight on the low end to 12 on the high end. In 1996 (the first year senators were affected by term limits), four senators were termed out. The numbers picked up to 22 by 1998. By 2006, 76 senators were termed out and forced to either move onto other political bodies or retire from political careers altogether.

There is little doubt that term limits have changed the incentives for running for office as well as the behavior of senators who serve. The early evidence suggests that these incentives do little to alter the demographic makeup of the senate—they do not create an environment more (or less) conducive to electing women, minorities, younger people, or people from different occupations. Term limits do, however, shift representational patterns in noticeable ways. Senators who serve in term limited senates can more easily ignore constituent opinion because they do not depend on constituents for reelection. As a result, policy coming out of these senates may not reflect the will of the people in the same way it would in a non–term limited senate. In addition, the reduced institutional memory of term limited senators increases the power of other political actors, including INTEREST GROUPS, GOVERNORs, and the media.

All U.S. SENATORS are elected in the same manner. As most Americans know, U.S. Senators run in traditional first-past-the-post single-member district elections with staggered terms. In other words, candidates from each party run in a primary. If they win the primary, they then run for the general election. Voters have the choice to vote for one of the candidates running for office. While most state senate elections work similarly, all the senators in West Virginia and most of the senators in Vermont are elected differently. These senators are elected in multimember districts where voters vote for more than one legislator at a time. They are used less often than they once were, but multimember districts are still an important part of state senate electoral politics in some states. The evidence suggests that multimember districts increase the representation of women and decrease the representation of minorities. In addition, because of the different incentives for voting, multimember districts tend to produce more ideologically extreme senators. Multimember districts not only affect voters but also affect the ways senators do their jobs. They alter patterns of representation and lead to partnership between senators who share district boundaries, even if they are of different parties.

The final important consideration in state senate elections is the cost of CAMPAIGNING. Campaign costs in state senate elections, like in most political campaigns, has skyrocketed in recent years. This has occurred as state senate elections have shifted from being relatively unprofessional, inexpensive, localized affairs to expensive races that are taking on increasing national importance. For instance, Joel Thompson and Gary Moncrief note that POLITICAL ACTION COMMITTEE contributions to candidates for the North Carolina legislature jumped more than 400 percent in a 10-year period. The overall cost of campaigning has risen by a similar magnitude. These staggering increases in campaign costs produce different incentives to run for office and may lead to fewer nonprofessional politicians running for office. To combat this trend, many states have passed stricter CAMPAIGN FINANCE laws to reduce the cost of campaigning and attempt to return state senate campaigns to their less expensive pasts.

Thus far we have discussed the institutions state senators operate in, but we have left the demographic makeup of state senators unaddressed. Although the American political system generally does a poor job of representing the demographic makeup of America, STATE GOVERNMENTs are slightly more representative than their federal counterparts. Approximately 21 percent of senators are women, as opposed to a slightly more representative 24 percent of legislators in the lower house. According to data from the Center for the Study of American Women and Politics, these numbers have been increasing over time. Not only have women been elected in greater numbers in state senates than in the U.S. Senate, they have also been represented in greater numbers within the leadership. Indeed, women have served in leadership positions in state senates since the 1930s, much sooner than they achieved leadership roles within the U.S. Senate.

These data about representation beg the question of whether gender makes a difference in the attitudes and behaviors of state senators or their constituents. The evidence generally reveals that it does. Female legislators propose different bills and exhibit different voting patterns than their male counterparts. Female legislators also perform more casework and place more emphasis on communicating with their constituents. Finally, there is some evidence that electing female state senators can increase the political efficacy of women in the state. The data on the representation of African Americans and other minority groups reveal similar patterns. Virtually no minority group is elected with numbers approaching parity with its numbers in the general population. Further, because the state senate represents the upper house of the state legislature, state senators are less likely to hail from minority groups than their counterparts in the lower chamber. Nonetheless, by 2002 there were more than 150 African American and 59 Hispanic state senators—far surpassing the numbers in the U.S. Congress. Despite these gains, black state legislators report a lower quality of legislative life than their white counterparts.

Once again, there is evidence that minority representation matters for the way minorities view state government and for the ways legislators act in office. Black state senators propose and pass different policies than their white counterparts. Similarly, Latino senators act differently in office and are more likely to introduce bills of interest to the Latino community—even when controlling for other factors.

State senators range considerably in age. While some are young and at the early stage of a long political career, others serve in the legislature during the end of their professional lives. One factor that affects age is the minimum age one can run for the senate, which varies considerably from state to state. The minimum age ranges from 18 in some states to 30 in others. These minimum ages are often higher than and never lower than the requirements to serve in the lower house of the legislature. In addition to age requirements, state senators are required to be residents of the district they plan to serve, although the length of that residency varies from state to state.

In the end, state senators are politicians who share similar goals across contexts but whose actions are systematically affected by the interplay of institutions found in the state. While they may appear similar to U.S. senators at first glance, the accuracy of this statement varies by state.

See also STATE AND LOCAL LEGISLATIVE PROCESS.

Further Reading

Hamm, Keith E., and Gary F. Moncrief. "Legislative Politics in the States." In *Politics in the American States: A Comparative Analysis.* 8th ed., edited by Virginia Gray and Russell Hanson, Washington, D.C.: Congressional Quarterly Press, 2004; Button, James, and David Hedge. "Legislative Life in the 1990s: A Comparison of Black and White State Legislators." *Legislative Studies Quarterly* 21 (1996): 199–218; Jewell, Malcolm E. *Representation in State Legislatures.* Lexington: University Press of Kentucky, 1982; Rosenthal, Alan. *The Decline of Representative Democracy.* Washington, D.C.: Congressional Quarterly Press, 1998; Rosenthal, Alan. *Heavy Lifting: The Job of the American Legislature.* Washington, D.C.: Congressional Quarterly Press, 2004; Squire, Peverill, and Keith Hamm. *101 Chambers: Congress, State Legislatures, and the Future of Legislative Studies.* Columbus: Ohio State University Press, 2005; Thompson, Joel A., and Gary F. Moncrief. *Campaign Finance in State Legislative Elections.* Washington, D.C.: Congressional Quarterly Press, 1998.

—Christopher A. Cooper

taxation, state and local

A tax is an involuntary fee assessed to persons or businesses as required for financial support of a government. Taxes have deep roots in American history and culture and are often at the center of contemporary politics. In a variety of forms, taxes provide the primary source of revenue for all levels of government. Even state and local governments, which rely heavily on intergovernmental transfers of funds for numerous purposes (from highways to Medicaid), derive the majority of their revenues from taxes. It may be too much to say that society could not exist without taxes, but it seems clear that society as we know it would not exist without them.

Governing an industrialized state in the modern world is an enormously costly endeavor, and the federal system places much of the burden on states and localities. Currently, state and local governments spend approximately 2 trillion dollars on thousands of programs and services, and lawmakers face two separate challenges in their efforts to raise the necessary funds to pay these staggering costs. The most obvious is the fiscal challenge: how to raise sufficient revenue. Simply raising tax rates does not always produce the desired effect. While economists disagree sharply on the specifics, most agree that too high a tax burden can actually decrease revenues, especially at the state and local levels, since individuals and businesses may respond to high taxes by relocating to places with lower rates. States and communities frequently take advantage of this dynamic by offering tax incentives to attract industry. As a result, fiscal issues alone make setting tax policy a very difficult task for officials.

Making it even more difficult is the political challenge. Though no one likes to pay taxes, Americans are unusually hostile to them. This cultural trait may date back to early American history. Not only was American society built on a philosophical foundation of PROPERTY RIGHTS, but a number of key events of that era, including the Boston Tea Party, Shays' Rebellion, and the Whiskey Rebellion, were all tax revolts. Less dramatically, this legacy survives, as large majorities of Americans believe that their taxes are too high, even though the typical tax burden in the United States is lower than in most other developed nations. Recent political battles over taxes have essentially been debates about which candidate would cut taxes more. One rare exception reveals why: After 1984, Democratic presidential nominee Walter Mondale unequivocally declared during the campaign that he planned to raise taxes and went on to lose all but one state (his home state of Minnesota) in the subsequent election. Historically, politically, and even culturally, Americans are fiercely antitax.

One is tempted to say that Americans cynically oppose any tax that they are required to pay, but a more honest assessment suggests that their main concern is fairness, though what is "fair" is not at all obvious. Broadly speaking, taxes can be progressive, proportional, or regressive. A progressive tax is one in which an individual pays a higher percentage of his or her income in taxes as income increases. A tax that levies a 10 percent charge to a person making $25,000 a year but a 20 percent charge to a person making $50,000 a year is an example of a progressive tax. A proportional tax, sometimes called a flat tax, is one that assesses the same percentage to all individuals regardless of income. For example, a community that required its residents to pay 1 percent of their income to the local government would be assessing a proportional tax; wealthier people would pay far more in terms of absolute dollars (a person making $100,000 would pay $1,000, while a person making $10,000 would pay only $100), but the percentages themselves are flat. Finally, a tax is considered regressive if it costs a greater percentage of income as one's income decreases. A $50 tax to renew a driver's license is sharply regressive; even though they pay the same amount, the fee represents a much greater percentage of the income of a typical college student than it does for billionaire and Microsoft founder Bill Gates.

While Americans generally support the concept of progressive taxes, their deeply held value of property rights limits their confiscatory tendencies. Proportional taxes have a growing and committed group of supporters, but somewhat surprisingly, most kinds of taxes are at least potentially regressive. It is beyond the scope of this essay to fully consider the reasons why Americans have such a complex view of tax fairness, but it is worth mentioning the effect: Americans generally consider something to be unfair about every kind of tax, and the resulting hostility is tangible and widespread.

Lawmakers thus face a terribly difficult puzzle trying to find ways to raise the necessary funds to pay for the goods and services people expect from their governments while satisfying the political pressures to keep taxes low. A 2002 public opinion poll of Pennsylvania voters illustrates the problem: Majorities favored increasing spending on education and for prescription drug coverage for the elderly but also opposed *any* increases in sales taxes or INCOME TAXES. The response has been the creation of a dizzying array of taxes at the state and local levels and, more recently, an increasing reliance on games of chance to generate revenue.

There are dozens of kinds of taxes, but the vast majority of revenues is generated from three main types: sales, income, and property. On the whole, the bulk of state tax revenue comes from the sales tax, which is a percentage surcharge attached to the purchase of a consumer good. The typical state tax is around 5 percent, though variance across states is very wide; five states (Alaska, Delaware, Montana, New Hampshire, and Oregon) have no state sales tax whatsoever. In total, state sales taxes account for about a third of all tax revenue at the state level. Additionally, most states allow localities to assess an additional sales tax, and thousands of communities do add an extra percent or two to finance local government operations. In major cities, a total sales tax of 8 percent or more is not uncommon.

Most critics of sales taxes argue that they are regressive, and indeed a pure sales tax hits the poor especially hard. A 5 percent tax on a $100 worth of groceries might be negligible to most people but would be quite burdensome to a family living below the poverty level. Hence, most states exclude "necessities" from sales taxes, including food, prescription drugs, and utilities, and in some cases, clothing, as well. But too many exemptions would interfere with the fiscal goal of raising sufficient revenue, and the results of such choices are often comical. In New York, Kool Aid is taxable, but Ovaltine is not. The tax commissioner of Ohio told *Governing* magazine that he keeps two bottles of Snapple on his desk to illustrate the absurdity; the fruit punch is taxable, but the iced tea is exempt, as only the latter is classified as food. Even with the exemptions for necessities, most economists contend that the sales tax is at least somewhat regressive. Wealthier people may pay more sales tax in absolute dollars as a result of more spending on consumer goods, but the net effect is disproportionate, as middle- and lower-income individuals pay a greater percentage of what they earn. Hence, the sales tax is politically unpopular, and attempts to increase it are usually rejected by voters.

The sales tax faces other fiscal and political challenges as well. Despite the potential for revenue, very few states tax services, and everything from legal work to haircuts is largely free from taxation. Business owners have successfully argued that taxing such services would discourage their use and thereby harm the economy. Lawmakers have also expressed concerns about the possibility that such taxes would put their state at a competitive disadvantage. Internet sales have also drastically cut into state sales tax revenues. As a result of a 1992 U.S. SUPREME COURT ruling, Internet sales are largely free from sales taxes. Some states attempt to collect such taxes voluntarily by asking citizens to report such purchases on their tax return form, but it is hard to imagine that is an effective means of collecting in full. But whatever the problems with the sales tax, the alternatives are even less attractive.

The other primary source of tax revenue for states is the income tax. This is, of course, the tax levied on the income of an individual (or on the profits of a business), assessed as a percentage of that income. This is the main source of tax revenue for the federal government and for about 25 percent of state tax revenue as well. Although the income tax is a staple of modern American life, the complex rules make the federal income tax difficult for many Americans to understand; add to that the variety of tax systems across the states, and the state income tax is almost incomprehensible. Many states have graduated, progressive tax rates that mirror the federal system, though the rates themselves are substantially lower than the federal rates. In Louisiana, for example, the first $10,000 of income is taxed at 2 percent, the next $40,000 is taxed at 4 percent, and anything more than $50,000 is taxed at 6 percent. A handful of states have flat (proportional) rates of income taxation. Residents of Illinois, for instance, are required to pay the state 3 percent of their income, regardless of how much they earned. Finally, there are several states that do not tax individual incomes at all, including Alaska, Florida, Nevada, South Dakota, Texas, Washington, and Wyoming, while New Hampshire and Tennessee limit their state income taxes to dividends and interest income only.

The income tax is the most likely tax to be progressive, and to the extent that Americans believe that it is equitable for wealthier individuals to pay a greater share of the tax burden, it may be the closest thing to a "fair" tax. But even so, the politics are very complicated—how progressive is *too* progressive? Is it excessive for an individual to pay 20 percent of his or her income to the state? What about 40 percent?

And at what point does that individual make the decision to move to a state with lower taxes? The corporate income tax is especially vulnerable to this problem. Even though it is probably the most politically palatable tax, competition among states makes it difficult for lawmakers to impose high tax burdens on corporations for fear that they will relocate to a tax-friendlier state. As a result, the corporate income tax is not a major source of revenue for states. A very small number do generate significant revenue from the corporate income tax, but the national average is less than 6 percent.

Both the sales and income taxes are constrained by fears of interstate competition, but at least one tax is exempt by definition from that concern. The property tax is the most significant source of revenue at the local level. It is levied as a percentage of the value of real property, such as a house. The value of the property is determined by a tax assessor who typically bases his or her appraisal on the selling price of nearby similar homes. It is a crucial tax in nearly all states because it is usually the main source of funds for public education. But it is *enormously* unpopular, with the federal income tax as its only rival for "worst tax," according to recent PUBLIC OPINION polls. Not only is it complicated, but since most people pay it in a lump sum, it is considerably more painful than an income tax that is paid through weekly withholdings. Moreover, the property tax is potentially very regressive. Since homes tend to increase in value at a rate far exceeding increases in income, the same percentage rate of the property tax will result in consistently higher tax bills for home owners. Seniors on fixed incomes are unusually vulnerable, and many states have instituted caps that will freeze a property's tax rate based on a formula tied to its purchase value. In addition, nearly all states provide other kinds of exemptions to low-income or disabled home owners.

Frustration with property taxes in California in the late 1970s was so high that it led to an open revolt at the ballot box. In 1978, voters there approved a ballot measure that cut property tax rates dramatically and limited the ability of the state legislature to reverse the decision at any future date. Several other states soon followed suit, and revenues from property taxes declined sharply. In the 1950s, localities generated approximately 50 percent of their total revenues

through property taxes; today that figure is less than 30 percent and dropping steadily. Even with the protections for the poor, Americans seem to have a special antipathy for the property tax.

Lawmakers do have other tax options available to them, such as the excise tax, which is a special kind of sales tax that adds an additional surcharge to specific items, most commonly cigarettes, alcohol, and gasoline. Such taxes are used in every state, though the rates vary widely. Rhode Island assesses a tax of $2.46 on every pack of cigarettes, while South Carolina charges only seven cents (the national average is 79 cents). A few states also benefit from the severance tax, which is a fee charged to industries for the extraction of natural resources, such as oil, coal, and timber. Alaska is so rich in such resources that its severance tax finances most of the cost of governing the state, and there is no sales tax or income tax there. States also tax most licenses and permits, large cash gifts, and even death (the estate tax). These are just a sample of the numerous other kinds of taxes that states and localities use.

Ultimately, though, no matter how the tax burden is distributed and no matter what or who is taxed, Americans are extremely suspicious that they are paying more than their fair share. They still want the government to provide services, but they oppose nearly every effort to pay for them.

Games of chance have provided lawmakers with a way out of this paradox. In the past 30 years, all but a few states have legalized lotteries and/or casinos as a way of generating revenues without raising taxes. In 2001, Americans legally gambled more than $700 billion; taxes on gambling receipts are so high in Nevada that it does not need to tax the income of its residents. Lotteries are even more common. Americans spend roughly $25 billion a year on lotteries, producing sizable revenues for states. Critics contend that games of chance are seductive, short-term solutions that carry their own hidden costs, such as increases in bankruptcies and divorces. But supporters counter that unlike taxes, games of chance are completely voluntary. It is beyond the scope of this essay to elaborate on that debate, but in an antitax society, even if the long-term problems are severe, it is unsurprising that lawmakers would gravitate toward such a solution. Walter Mondale can attest to the perils of the alternative.

Further Reading
Barrett, Katherine, et al. "The Way We Tax: A 50-State Report." *Governing*. Available online. URL: http://governing.com/gpp/2003/gp3intro.htm. Accessed June 19, 2006; Brunori, David. *State Tax Policy: A Political Perspective*. Washington, D.C.: The Urban Institute Press, 2005; Saffell, David C., and Harry Basehart. *State and Local Government: Politics and Public Policies*. 8th ed. Boston: McGraw Hill, 2005; Slemrod, Joel, ed. *Tax Policy in the Real World*. New York: Cambridge University Press, 1999; Smith, Kevin B., Alan Greenblatt, and John Buntin. *Governing States and Localities*. Washington, D.C.: Congressional Quarterly Press, 2005; Thorndike, Joseph J., and Dennis J. Ventry, Jr., eds. *Tax Justice: The Ongoing Debate*. Washington, D.C.; The Urban Institute Press, 2002.

—William Cunion

town meeting

The town meeting is the purest, most direct form of democracy practiced in the United States. Town meetings have been used for more than 300 years and are most often practiced in small towns in the New England area.

The town hall meeting raises several key questions about both the proper functioning of DEMOCRACY and the effective functioning of modern government. At what level is politics most democratically and most effectively practiced? Can a nation that is serious about political democracy reject the small town, small government model on which the town hall meeting is based? Can a large or extended REPUBLIC truly embrace democratic methods and means? Can a superpower truly be a democracy? And at what level is democratic politics best practiced, the local or the national level?

A democracy is more than merely VOTING from time to time. And while this minimalist view of democracy is easy to practice and asks very little of citizens, most of those who study democracy argue that such a narrow definition does a disservice to the more robust and comprehensive view of democracy that the town hall meeting symbolizes. A pure, or participatory, democracy asks a lot of citizens, including time, attention, thought, and commitment. That is why many citizens prefer the minimalist view of democracy—it is easy to practice and asks very little of the citizen. But if the minimalist view asks little, it returns little as well. The more robust, or participatory, definitions of democracy may demand more of the citizen, but they come with the promise of delivering more as well.

To participatory democrats, the value of democracy is not merely in the way it sets up and guides power, but in the effect it has on the citizen who practices democracy. A fully practicing participant in the community is enlivened, developed, and enhanced by the very practice of democracy. He or she becomes more self-aware, more in command of life, more involved with the community, in short, more wholly and fully enriched by the experience of self-governing. He or she becomes more independent and more alive, more in touch with neighbors, and more in touch with the concerns of the community. A fully practicing democrat is a whole person. That is the way the ancient Greeks imagined the impact of democracy on the citizens of Athens. It is the goal of the town meeting form of democracy as well.

When the fever of revolution caught hold in the American colonies in the late 1700s, democracy was more an abstract idea than a tangible product. The ideas and ideals that animated the American Revolution were democratic in sentiment but never fully articulated or tangibly described. Democracy was an ideal, something to strive for, but no clear roadmap existed. The revolutionary and democratic sentiments presented by Thomas Paine in his influential pamphlet *Common Sense* (first published in January 1776) and elaborated on by Thomas Jefferson in the DECLARATION OF INDEPENDENCE (July 1776) contained grand but vague references to what form this new democratic government they were advocating might take. After the Revolution had been won, the hard work of translating these bold ideas into a workable form of government took center stage. How democratic should this new government be? What role should the common man play in this new government? Who should rule, and by what rules?

With the Revolution won, the framers were first governed by the ARTICLES OF CONFEDERATION, a distinctly STATES' RIGHTS document that left the federal government feeble. Later, a new federal Constitution was adopted giving the central government new and more significant powers. But lost in this transition was the ideal of democracy. This new Constitution was decidedly not democratic. In fact, it created a republic. So what happened to the notion of democracy?

If the framers abandoned the hope of democracy, there were others who kept the dream alive. In fact, virtually from the beginning of the republic, many, especially in the small towns of New England, kept democracy alive and well in the form of what were called town meetings, the truest and in some ways last form of pure democracy still practiced in the United States.

There is no "one size fits all" town meeting. And while the basic concept of the town hall or town meeting is the same—gather together the citizens in a small area, talk about the issues of the day, and make decisions by directly voting on public policy issues—the format of the meetings varies significantly. Different towns have different rules and regulations, usually found in the city bylaws or charter. Usually these rules are written, but in some cases they are a function of tradition and customs and are thus less formal.

Generally, the town meeting format is restricted to towns with fewer than 12,000 inhabitants. They mimic the forms of Athenian democracy practiced more than 2,000 years ago. With few exceptions, anyone may speak as long as he or she is a registered voter in the town, and voting is also open to all registered voters. There is usually an agenda that is called a "warrant" that is distributed before any town meeting so that citizens may know what decisions will be made at the town meeting.

Most town meetings are open to all citizens who live in the town. They usually decide three things: the salaries of elected officials, the town budget, and the local statutes or laws. While town meetings are fairly common in small towns in New England, they are rarely practiced in other regions of the nation.

There is a significant difference between representative government and DIRECT DEMOCRACY. In representative systems, the citizens elect others to serve as representatives or intermediaries who are to work on their behalf. In direct democracy, of which a town meeting is but one example, the people are personally and directly responsible for decision making. Proponents of the town meeting stress the participatory elements of the meeting and the democratic elements of the practice. It truly is the purest form of democracy practiced in the United States and speaks to a more genteel and nostalgic view of the potentialities of democracy in America. These town meetings allow citizens to become decision makers, bringing democracy up close and personal. They make the citizens responsible for the government. At their best, they encourage participation and responsibility taking by citizens and thus develop a more sophisticated democratic citizenry.

Critics of town meetings argue that even with this more direct form of participation, special interests tend to dominate communities, as they are better organized, better funded, and more committed to getting the "goods" that government hands out. Critics also claim that participation in town meetings tends to be low, undermining the core belief that these town meetings are about participation of the citizens in government. James Madison, in *Federalist 55*, argued that "In all numerous assemblies, of whatever characters composed, passion never fails to wrest the scepter from reason. Had every Athenian citizen been a Socrates every Athenian assembly would still have been a mob." This fear of the mob, of the potential for the passions of the citizens to become inflamed, animated the framers to eschew direct democracy and embrace instead a form of REPRESENTATIVE DEMOCRACY whereby the whims and passions of the citizens would be filtered through the representative assemblies and might thus temper the whims and passions of the mob.

While it is true that only occasionally do these town meetings exhibit the highest forms of participation, rhetoric, and decision making, they do represent a form of democracy worth maintaining. For all their faults—and every form of democracy and every form of government have their faults—they represent part of the tradition and heritage of democracy as practiced in its many forms and varieties in the United States. Faults notwithstanding, the town meeting is an honored and honorable form of direct democracy and one of the few still practiced in the United States today.

Further Reading

Fishkin, James S. *Democracy and Deliberation: New Directions for Democratic Reform.* New Haven, Conn.: Yale University Press, 1991; Goebel, Thomas. *A Government by the People: Direct Democracy in*

America, 1890–1940. Chapel Hill: University of North Carolina Press, 2002; Haskell, John. *Direct Democracy or Representative Government? Dispelling the Populist Myth.* Boulder, Colo.: Westview Press, 2001.

—Michael A. Genovese

urban development

The term *urban development* encompasses myriad theoretical orientations on the origin and evolution of cities. Urban development is interdisciplinary in nature because of the many academicians and professionals who work within it and who bring to it their unique expertise from diverse fields—sociology, psychology, criminology, ecology, political science, history, economics, finance, planning, engineering, landscape, architecture, and geography. While this specialization causes fragmentation, it also has led to enriched approaches to understanding the city, its inhabitants, and its problems.

At the turn of the 20th century, the United States was moving from an agrarian society toward industrialization. Production by individual skilled craftsmen and artisans lessened as mass production increased. Cities faced rapid growth, in part as a result of people moving from farms to cities and due to an increasing influx of immigrants. At the same time, improvements in electricity, transportation, and communication were occurring. Demands were placed on cities, and individual cities dealt with those demands such as overcrowding, pollution, and public health concerns in a variety of ways. Physically, the cities grew and developed in a variety of directions, some more orderly than others.

If we try to explain or understand that growth or the patterns of development, we have many models of urban development to consider. Among the models are classic location theory and central place theory. Classic location theory suggests firms locate based on how best to minimize costs of land, labor, and capital. Cities vary in their locational advantages. Central place theory is based on a hierarchical ordered classification of cities. High-population areas with greater demand will have higher-order industries or facilities present or will have a greater range of these available. So, for example, we will not find a museum or a hospital in every city, but even the smallest of cities will have a post office and grocery store. Other theorists have developed typologies, or classification systems, to describe cities based on specific factors such as whether the city has an economic focus on manufacturing, mining, government, business, high-tech industries, education, military, tourism resorts, retirement, or some combination of two or more of these sectors.

Other models suggest that cities compete in a competitive marketplace and must strive to promote economic growth. Therefore, decision makers must give priority to policies that promote growth and are very constrained in their choices. Yet another approach suggests that internal political forces shape urban development choices, and what occurs is no more than the outcome of which political leader is successful in winning support for his or her agenda. Under this scenario, there is assumed to be great decision making latitude given to those political leaders. Under regime theory, it is suggested that in addition to local elected officials, there are more complicated public-private interactions at work that involve informal arrangements between and among business leaders, church leaders, union interests, the MEDIA, and other INTEREST GROUPS that in turn affect urban development. Thus, with regime theory it is through the study of community power structures that one gains an understanding of the decisions involved in shaping the urban form. Another more comprehensive model suggests urban development is shaped by a combination of market conditions—attracting investment; intergovernmental support—planning, land use controls, infrastructure, and housing; popular control systems—public participation; and local culture—what the citizens value.

Urban development depends on the action or lack of action by others—on choices and on choices forgone. At the most local level, it involves all aspects of regulation, annexation, investment, and the location and availability of social services and schools. The actions taken by investors, citizens, and elected officials affect the outcomes of urban development. At the local level, the role of government in urban development includes the functions of planning, regulating, historic preservation, farmland preservation, developing desirable patterns of development, and reducing disparities among citizens. A city must plan and consider whether the results of its plans will have the intended outcomes. A city must anticipate change and be ready to match available actions with impending problems or opportunities. A city must recognize the interdependent nature of its actions and that there are some things it cannot change.

A look at any city of even modest size reveals the presence of a ZONING ordinances, subdivision regulations, and a comprehensive plan, all of which help guide local officials in keeping pace with development demands and maintaining a high quality of life for their citizens. Typically, a comprehensive plan will include an analysis of the future demands of demographics, housing, and economic conditions; an analysis of environmental and cultural elements unique to the community; an analysis of community facilities and services, such as fire stations, schools, parks and recreation facilities, libraries, and hospitals; an analysis of infrastructure, including PUBLIC UTILITIES, water supply, waste management, and technology; an analysis of transportation, including roadways, rail, water, and air travel; and an analysis of land use patterns.

Usually, 20-year projections and recommendations for addressing each of these elements will be described in the comprehensive plan. This plan may include how local programs, activities, and land development regulations will be initiated, modified, or continued, and the plan usually addresses how each of these elements may complement or conflict with plans by single or SPECIAL DISTRICTS within the municipality, such as water, sewer, and fire districts; adjacent local governments; and regional and state agencies. Most importantly, a comprehensive plan must involve public participation in order to reconcile the long-term needs of its citizens with the short-term wants of its elected officials. It must be recognized that not all citizens will be in the same position to participate. Ideally, the comprehensive plan will serve to enhance or create vibrant neighborhoods within a city that are sustainable, diverse, democratic, socially and environmentally just, and well balanced.

At the state level, urban development is affected by the state's policies on taxation, regulation, education, economic development, and transportation. Often the state serves to administer funds that are passed through from the federal government to the local jurisdictions, which in turn affects urban development.

In other instances, the state may provide direct funding for infrastructure improvements, for example, or may institute a policy that has direct implications on the climate for doing business within that state.

Historically, after World War II, the United States saw the development of federal programs that helped with improving home ownership rates through financing and housing construction and road construction that increased migration to the suburbs. More recently, at the federal level, there has been a focus on urban renewal through planning, housing, and community development programs. Federal funding through the DEPARTMENT OF HOUSING AND URBAN DEVELOPMENT supported programs to improve communities through, for example, community development Block Grants, the HOME program (which provides a federal block grant to state and local governments designed exclusively to create affordable housing for low-income households), and the Low Income Housing Tax Credit program. Depending on the particular program, aid may be to communities for infrastructure improvements or to individuals in the form of housing vouchers or rehabilitation of housing, or in the form of tax incentives to leverage private investment. Other funding programs are focused more toward economic development projects through, for example, the designation of enterprise zones (which help to promote job creation and capital investment in areas of economic distress).

As demographic and economic changes—such as increased IMMIGRATION, an aging population, the formation of smaller households, decline in manufacturing jobs, decentralization, and GLOBALIZATION—continue to occur in the United States, it will be important for all levels of government to continue to play a role in assisting cities to reach their economic potential. It is also important that government address the inequalities that continue to exist among cities and among citizens. Government must think about the services it provides, the mix of services provided, and where these services are provided.

A list compiled of core concerns in the study of cities includes evolution; culture and society; politics and government; economics, finance, and regional science; space and city systems; megacities; planning, design, landscape architecture, and architecture; race, ethnicity, and gender relations; and problems, including politics, poverty, overcrowding, discrimination, and crime. Suggestions to address some of these concerns include enhancing innovative sectors of the urban economy, transforming the physical landscape, growing the middle class through educational opportunities, revitalizing cities through support of low-wage workers, and creating neighborhoods of choice.

Over time, the study of urban development has focused on or been entwined with patterns of development, the environment, design and planning, growth, suburbanization, renewal and redevelopment, sprawl, sustainability, resurgence, and the inequities in society, such as poverty and racial segregation, that result from the realities of urban development. While this list is not exhaustive, future trends will indubitably include or build upon studying and understanding all of these issues and their influences on urban development as it continues to shape how we live, learn, work, and play.

Further Reading

Hopkins, Lewis D. *Urban Development: The Logic of Making Plans.* Washington, D.C.: Island Press, 2001; Hudnut, William H. III. *Halfway to Everywhere: A Portrait of America's First-Tier Suburbs.* Washington, D.C.: ULI-The Urban Land Institute, 2004; Katz, Bruce. *Diverse Perspectives on Critical Issues: Six Ways Cities Can Reach Their Economic Potential.* Washington, D.C.: Brookings Institution, 2006; Kotkin, Joel. *The City: A Global History.* New York: Modern Library, 2006; Legates, Richard T., and Frederic Stout, eds. *The City Reader.* New York: Routledge, 2003; Logan, John R., and Harvey L. Molotch. *Urban Fortunes.* Berkeley: University of California Press, 1987; Peterson, Paul. *City Limits.* Chicago: University of Chicago Press, 1981; Savitch, H. V., and Paul Kantor. *Cities in the International Marketplace: The Political Economy of Urban Development in North America and Western Europe.* Princeton, N.J.: Princeton University Press, 2002; Sharp, Elaine. *Urban Politics and Administration: From Service Delivery to Economic Development.* New York: Longman, 1990; Stone, Clarence N. *Regime Politics: Governing Atlanta, 1946–1988.* Lawrence: University Press of Kansas, 1989; Wheeler, Stephen M., and Timothy Beatley, eds. *The Sustainable Urban Development Reader.* New York: Routledge, 2004.

—Victoria Gordon and Jeffery L. Osgood, Jr.

zoning

In the United States, zoning is a power vested in local governments to designate areas of a city or county for specific land uses (or zones). Zoning regulates the use of land as well as the size, bulk, and placement of buildings on lots. Constitutionally, zoning is considered a police power that cities and counties derive from their STATE GOVERNMENTs. Zoning decisions are usually made by city or county planning departments staffed by professionals trained in urban planning, usually with oversight by an elected city or county board. Zoning laws are administered by building inspectors, who determine whether buildings are in compliance with zoning laws.

The general idea behind zoning is to create an orderly development of land and to separate land uses thought to be incompatible. Examples include setting aside specific areas of a city or county for single-family homes, multifamily dwellings, commercial areas, industry, and agriculture. Critics of traditional, or Euclidean, single-use zoning argue that the practice limits flexibility and creativity and often leads to sterile urban environments. Zoning is the primary tool in a larger effort by local governments to regulate land development, known as general planning. General plans are documents that attempt to regulate a community's future development. In addition to zoning areas of a city or county for specific land uses, general plans consider the need for infrastructure such as sewers, streets, and lighting as well as parks, libraries, and other public facilities.

Because zoning places limits on private PROPERTY RIGHTS, zoning decisions are among the most contentious issues for local governments. The granting of exceptions to zoning laws, known as variances, can sometimes set off political firestorms. Zoning decisions often pit INTEREST GROUPS with an interest in land development against one another. Groups typically fall into one of two camps: progrowth or slow growth. Interest groups such as developers, real estate agents, local newspapers, the business community, and public employee unions often make up powerful progrowth coalitions that seek to promote land development through permissive zoning laws. These interests typically argue that the intensification of land use will result in economic development that benefits the community as a whole.

On the other hand, home owner groups, sometimes aligned with environmental interests, tend to pursue a slow-growth (and sometimes no-growth) agenda. Slow-growth interests typically argue for restrictions on land development in order to protect themselves from quality-of-life threats such as traffic, pollution, noise, and density. Environmental interests seek to block zoning changes that threaten open space, endangered species, and other aspects of the environment.

Since the 1970s, home owners and environmentalists have become increasingly important players in zoning decisions. Historically excluded from decision making that had been dominated by progrowth insiders, slow-growth activists have sought to make land use decision making more democratic. "Ballot box zoning," whereby zoning decisions are left up to local voters instead of planning bureaucrats, is an increasingly popular way of making some land use decisions. During the 1990s, Ventura County, California, north of Los Angeles, became the poster child for ballot box zoning, with a number of municipalities adopting requirements for voter approval of important land use decisions.

In 1916, New York City became the first city in the United States to adopt a comprehensive zoning law, modeled on zoning laws in Europe. Advocates of zoning in New York argued that externalities resulting from the city's burgeoning population and industrial economy needed to be better managed. Soon after, cities around the nation began to adopt zoning as a mechanism for regulating land use. The 1926 U.S. SUPREME COURT case *Village of Euclid, Ohio v. Ambler Realty Co.* set an important PRECEDENT upholding the practice of zoning. The plaintiff in the case, a realty company, intended to develop land that it owned for commercial purposes. When the Village of Euclid rezoned the property to make it compatible with a nearby residential district, Ambler Realty Co. filed suit, arguing that its property had been taken without DUE PROCESS of law. In its decision, the Supreme Court argued that Euclid's zoning law represented a constitutional use of government authority to protect public health and safety and promote order. As the Euclid case illustrates, zoning exposes a tension between a government's duty to both protect private property and promote public health and safety. Unlike the power of EMINENT DOMAIN, for which the

taking of private property requires compensation, courts have ruled that zoning's limitations on private property do not require that property owners be compensated.

Scholars cite three main historical reasons for the emergence of zoning in the United States. First, zoning authority emerged within a context of a deeply rooted tradition of strong local government in the United States. In most other developed nations, land use authority is largely vested in state or national governments. Urban historians cite America's frontier and colonial experiences and federal political structure as underlying reasons for the nation's tradition of strong local government. Today, Houston, Texas, is the only major American city to not employ zoning, although the city's many deed restrictions perform essentially the same function as zoning.

Second, zoning emerged within the context of rapid industrialization that took place in America's cities in the late 19th and early 20th centuries. Meatpacking, steelmaking, and a host of other heavy industries were popping up in cities, sometimes in the middle of residential neighborhoods. Combined with the absence of environmental regulation, the proximity of residential areas to severe industrial pollution prompted civic leaders to consider ways of separating homes from the workplace.

Third, widespread zoning also coincided with efforts on the part of white Anglo-Saxon Protestants (WASPs) to establish moral order in American cities during a period of rapid IMMIGRATION from southern and eastern Europe. During this period, known as the Progressive Era (1900 to 1925), WASP reformers succeed in passing prohibition laws, immigration restrictions, and a number of other measures intended to uphold Protestant moral values. Modern zoning laws that ban the sale of alcohol or outlaw sex shops trace their origins to this era and illustrate the relationship between zoning and morality.

Much of the academic literature on zoning focuses on the use of zoning power to segregate populations by class and race, or what scholars call "exclusionary zoning." Classic examples are suburbs that are zoned exclusively for single-family residences. Cities that ban multifamily dwellings are thus able to exclude residents who are unable to afford the price of a single-family home. Other types of exclusionary, or "snob," zoning include large lot zoning, where homes can only be built on large lots, usually between one-half and two acres, but sometimes more. Some zoning laws restrict the number of residents who may live in a house and even limit the number of unrelated persons who can live in a home. Ultimately, critics say, exclusionary zoning allows independent suburban jurisdictions to effectively wall themselves off from minorities and the poor, resulting in metropolitan areas characterized by unequal access to housing, jobs, and education.

In 1977, the Supreme Court upheld a Chicago suburb's zoning ordinance that prohibited multifamily housing throughout much of the city. The plaintiff in the case was a local church group that wanted to build subsidized housing in the mostly white and affluent suburb. Known as the Arlington Heights case, the Court ruled that zoning restrictions are legal if there is no intent to discriminate on the basis of race. The court found that zoning laws that produced only the effect (as opposed to the intent) of racial discrimination were legal. Opponents of exclusionary zoning point out that proving discriminatory intent is an almost impossibly high legal threshold.

Although federal courts have been less inclined to overturn local zoning ordinances, opponents of exclusionary zoning have won limited victories in a few states. In a series of cases in New Jersey during the 1970s and 1980s known as the Mount Laurel decisions, housing rights advocates successfully argued that the State of New Jersey could require communities to build affordable housing. Although the Mount Laurel decisions received much attention, they did not result in the construction of much affordable housing. In the end, communities simply devised creative ways of shirking their court-ordered affordable housing requirements.

Not all zoning is exclusionary. In recent years, the concept of "inclusionary zoning" has been adopted in a number of communities as a way of increasing the supply of affordable housing. Inclusionary zoning requires developers to set aside a particular number of housing units, usually between 10 percent and 20 percent, for low- and moderate-income people. In exchange, cities often give developers "density bonuses," which allow a greater number of total units to be built than existing zoning allows. In recent years, planners around the country have sought to increase densities, or "up-zone,"

some communities in an attempt to implement a planning strategy known as "smart growth." Smart growth represents a fundamental departure from traditional urban planning in that it attempts to integrate, rather than segregate, various land use elements into a community. The idea is to make communities more livable by creating mixed-use neighborhoods consisting of dense housing close to commercial districts, jobs, and public transit. Although smart growth planning has caught on in places such as downtown Portland, Oregon, and San Diego, California, it is unlikely that a downtown condo will ever replace the single-family home as the embodiment of the American dream.

Because much of the literature on zoning focuses on the politics of exclusion, still another branch of scholarship advocates the participation of higher levels of government in land use decision making. For example, rather than leaving land use decisions solely up to cities and counties, the state governments of Oregon and Washington mandate that city and county general plans adhere to a number of statewide goals, including the provision of affordable housing and the prevention of urban sprawl. In both states, opposition to state interference in land use decisions remains fierce in some circles, and there is evidence that efforts to protect open space and farmland have limited the supply and affordability of housing. However, despite these and other efforts to oversee local land use decisions, the vast majority of state governments—many of which are dominated by suburban and rural interests—allow their local governments virtually complete control over land use decision making.

Further Reading

Babcock, Richard F. *The Zoning Game Revisited.* Madison: University of Wisconsin Press, 1990; Burns, Nancy. *The Formation of American Local Governments.* New York: Oxford University Press, 1994; Christensen, Terry, and Hogen-Esch, Tom. *Local Politics: A Practical Guide to Governing at the Grassroots.* Armonk, N.Y.: M.E. Sharpe, 2006; Danielson, Michael N. *The Politics of Exclusion.* New York: Columbia University Press, 1976; Davis, Mike. *City of Quartz.* New York: Vintage Books, 1990; Gottdeiner, Mark. *The Social Production of Urban Space.* Austin: University of Texas Press, 1985; Judd, Dennis R., and Todd Swanstrom. *City Politics: Private Power and Public Policy*. New York: Longman, 2002; Linowes, R. Robert, and Don. T. Allensworth. *The Politics of Land Use*. New York: Praeger Publishers, 1973; Logan, John R., and Harvey L. Molotch. *Urban Fortunes: The Political Economy of Place*. Berkeley: CA: University of California Press, 1987; Plotkin, Sidney. *Keep Out: The Struggle for Land Use Control*. Berkeley: University of California Press, 1987; Ross, Bernard H., and Myron A. Levine. *Urban Politics: Power in Metropolitan America*. Belmont, Calif.: Thompson Wadsworth, 2006; Weiher, Gregory R. *The Fractured Metropolis: Political Fragmentation and Metropolitan Segregation*. Albany: State University of New York Press, 1991.

—Tom Hogen-Esch

INTERNATIONAL POLITICS AND ECONOMICS

capitalism

Capitalism in the United States has attracted the attention of scholars and commentators across various disciplines. Perhaps no other general topic and its myriad ramifications has witnessed such diverse proliferation and application among researchers, practitioners, advocates, and critics. The idea and significance of capitalism have presented themselves through writings in economics, history, literary criticism, political science, sociology, philosophy, law, business, psychology, and many others. This is so because capitalism, as both idea and practical reality, is a fundamental component that defines and is simultaneously defined by almost everything that is American. The ways we conceptualize and animate most, if not all, of our political, economic, social, and cultural institutions are inextricably linked to the ways we conceptualize and practice capitalism.

Because societal and individual notions of capitalism are so pervasive and America's devotion to capitalism is ostensibly unshakeable, discussions of capitalism, even among scholars, are frequently based on unreflective self-affirmation. So as a nation, Americans largely assume that capitalism is intrinsic and that its emergence and development in the United States were inevitable. However, the ascendancy of capitalism in the United States, though partly the product of specific structural and situational advantages that have inhered in American society since the 18th century, has not been inevitable or predictable. Indeed, contrary to long-held beliefs among econo-

mists, economic and business historians, and many political scientists, many historians and social scientists have instead argued that America's roots were decidedly precapitalist, if not actually anticapitalist.

Over the past four decades, an overwhelming amount of scholarship has fueled an academic debate about the emergence and eventual development of capitalism in the United States. On one hand, a liberalist camp led by economists, economic and business historians, and their intellectual supporters has asserted that America was "born" capitalist and that even the earliest colonial settlements were suffused with an ethos based on an eagerness to acquire property and capital (what some would call greed) that promoted success through profit seeking and free markets. On the other hand, a republicanist group of scholars most prominently represented by social and labor historians, Marxist and neo-Marxist social scientists, and their acolytes has emphasized the centrality of civic humanist and classical-republican principles among colonists and the existence of a communitarian culture that promoted common civic and economic ideals and prioritized communal enterprise over individual interest. Pursuantly, capitalism was not imminent but arose from specific circumstances created by industrialization during the 19th century, circumstances that undermined and prevented the further evolution of communitarian ideologies in the United States.

Recently, despite ongoing academic controversies over the nature of capitalism in the United States, certain interpretations have been more firmly established than others, and the definitional features of the history of capitalism in America have been elucidated. Those interpretations and the aforementioned debates have acknowledged that inquiries into the history of capitalism in the United States revolve around two basic questions. First, what is capitalism, or, more specifically, what are the defining characteristics of American capitalism? And second, when and how did capitalism develop in the United States? As should be obvious, the second question presupposes a proper and adequate answer to the first, not least because American capitalist dynamics can differ widely from those of other industrialized nations.

By and large, economists agree that capitalism is an economic system dedicated to private enterprise, free markets, and the creation of profit. Some would add that an absence or minimum of governmental regulation or control is indispensable, though this notion is more an outcome of the nexus of capitalism and politics than of capitalism itself. Arguably, the sine qua non of capitalism is profit, so the fundamental impulse in capitalist societies is profit maximization. Profit is the most significant incentive for private ownership and the production of surplus value, whose eventual reinvestment enables continued growth and expansion. Although the generation of profit is conceivable and can be achieved in nonprivate environments, it is secured and logically warranted by private ownership.

Capitalist economic principles have been incorporated by different cultures in numerous settings over the course of Western history, with varying results. A common theme that characterizes most of these settings has been the rise of mass industry and the dominance of the corporation, so that today's industrial capitalism is only a remote cognate of the earliest forms of capitalism depicted by its earliest exponents. The purest forms of capitalism, something akin to the network of small-scale productive ventures envisioned by Adam Smith, generally manifested themselves during the earliest stages of capitalist development in just a handful of countries, but the realities of an industrialized world have rendered Smith's deceptively simple vision irrelevant and almost meaningless.

America in the 21st century is typical of this trend and has probably traveled further than any other industrialized nation from Smith's portrayal of capitalism as a system of unencumbered markets governed by efficient and equitable exchanges of goods among small-scale, proprietor-managed enterprises and rational consumers. The U.S. economy is dominated by networks of multinational conglomerates that support markets with monopolistic or oligopolistic rather than capitalist traits. In today's America, ownership and management have long been divided and separate, so that the link between private ownership and profit has grown increasingly complicated. In fact, the traditional coupling of ownership and profit has been supplanted by a much stronger tie between management and profit.

More than any other single factor, the modern corporation has allowed this transformation of American capitalism. The formation and acknowledgment of the modern corporation and its legitimization through COMMON LAW doctrine and statutory provision have allowed and promoted the creation of professionally managed, externally capitalized megastructures with disproportionate power and influence over markets and market dynamics. America's conglomerates and its executives enjoy political and economic privileges that belie the equity and balance necessitated by the original proponents of capitalism in the 18th century. This should not be construed as a suggestion that the power and status enjoyed by American corporations are symptoms of a Marxist theory of conspiracy between government and business. Nevertheless, leading businesses and their executives have access to and control over market dynamics and political processes that far outstrip their numerical or even theoretical significance.

Moreover, despite the fact that capitalism seemingly demands minimal regulatory interference with markets and correspondingly necessitates governmental neutrality and objectivity toward individual competitors in the marketplace, the reality in the United States has deviated considerably from that ideal. Macroeconomic circumstances and political relationships in the United States have offered some top corporations in crucial industries protections and incentives whose purpose has been to ensure the continued viability and dominance of those corporations. For example, bankruptcy laws and proceedings reveal a decided bias that allows larger corporate entities unusual latitude in their reorganization procedures, whereas private individuals and smaller businesses are often handicapped by those laws. At times, the government has even taken a direct role in the resuscitation of troubled industries, as evidenced by its bailouts in the automobile, transportation, energy, and banking industries—to name only a few.

Subsidies to farmers, steel manufacturers, and a host of other entities prolong their longevity yet distort the balance and competitive fairness that an unfettered, equitable marketplace should confer. Preferred providers of goods and services to the government, such as government contractors and subcontractors that are considered vital to the implementation and propagation of government programs, rarely compete for lucrative contracts according to the laws of supply and demand. Those contracts are awarded in an artificially restricted marketplace that favors institutional inertia and a business-as-usual environment designed to limit free competition and traditional marketplace variety. Again, this is not intended to insinuate that government and industry actively collude to control markets in the way Marxist and neo-Marxist critics have contended, but it does demonstrate that American capitalism has evolved, or maybe derogated, from its origins to a form that bears little resemblance to the 18th-century ideal. Of course, even early American society did not precisely conform to that ideal, but, in its infancy, American capitalism manifested more of the trappings of veritable capitalism than it does today.

A central focus of investigation for economists and economic historians has been the determination of when specific societies become capitalist. Many economists have argued that a society is capitalist if it exhibits sustainable per-capita income growth, and, according to that standard alone, America was indeed born capitalist. Although useful and meaningful statistical indexes are difficult to compute for the colonial period, economic data gathered by historians over the past 40 years indicate more or less consistent per-capita income growth starting during the second third of the 17th century. Such evidence notwithstanding, many scholars are loath to conclude that America was capitalist at this stage just from one statistical index based on admittedly incomplete economic data.

For this and other reasons, whether America truly was born capitalist is still an open question that will serve as intellectual fodder for ongoing debates among scholars. However, scholars now agree that even those colonial communities customarily considered communitarian havens exhibited at least some of the trappings of capitalism quite early. Stephen Innes, among others, has ably documented the presence and pervasive expansion of an acquisitive mentality among 17th-century Puritan settlements. His studies of colonial Massachusetts and Connecticut portray Puritan manufacturing and trading ventures motivated by profit and dedicated to the establishment of viable business pursuits across a region previously thought to have been concerned primarily with the implementation of a specific socioreligious vision opposed to profit seeking. Land speculation, sophisticated trading networks, and aggressive capitalization strategies were some of the hallmarks of these early communities, and, by the mid-18th century, the New England region was characterized by widespread entrepreneurship.

In the middle colonies, where religious motives were less pronounced and outright economic motives for settlement in North America were more evident, the development of an entrepreneurial spirit was also obvious. Trade, shipping, and farming were especially important to the region, as were the small manufactories that emerged in cities by the latter half of the 18th century. In this area and New England, most residents were still producers, cultivating their own land and trading surplus commodities and goods produced on their farms with neighbors, merchants, and regional trading businesses. Many of the rest, located primarily in and around urban areas, were artisans who practiced a marketable skill that enabled them to survive or at least supplement farm income. At this time, up to and including the late 18th century, employer-employee relationships of the sort that evolved out of the Industrial Revolution were not a significant factor, inasmuch as the overwhelming majority of Americans, perhaps as many as 80 percent of white freemen, owned farms or at least some physical property.

In the upper and lower South, the situation was problematic from an analytical perspective. Following a few generations of indentured servitude mostly in Virginia, SLAVERY gradually replaced a system that was decreasingly attractive both to landowners and indentured servants. During the seminal period from the 1670s to the 1720s, black slaves became the dominant source of labor for plantation owners who produced tobacco in Virginia, Maryland, and North Carolina, rice and indigo in South Carolina and Georgia, naval stores throughout the upper South, and sugar in the West Indies. American slavery, though supporting a broader economic system devoted to profit and private ownership, was hardly capitalist. It was based on exploitation and the suppression of free labor markets, and the production of agricultural staples in the South inherently favored large landowners over small farmers. With its manorial settlement patterns and paternalistic social networks based on deference and submission, the economic system in the South, especially after the advent of widespread cotton cultivation in the early 19th century, was reminiscent of feudalism.

As accustomed as we have become to stories of the inevitable dominance of slavery in the antebellum South, slavery's eventual domination of the southern economy was anything but predictable. By the 1780s, the vast profits once enjoyed by tobacco planters had shrunk severely, so that the future of tobacco cultivation in North America was in doubt. At the end of the 18th century, it would not have been unreasonable to conclude that slavery would soon disappear due to the declining viability particularly of tobacco cultivation. Of course, the invention of the cotton gin and the consequent spread of the cotton plantation throughout the deep South resurrected slavery and enshrined it as the centerpiece of the South's economic system. In addition, cotton highlighted and further entrenched the noncapitalist features of the southern economy.

The antebellum South was marked by a high concentration of wealth and income among a small percentage of large plantation owners, which produced a rigid class structure with a de facto white aristocracy increasingly alienated from the rest of southern society. Contrary to popular lore, less than 25 percent of white southerners owned slaves, and no more than 1 percent owned large plantations. Most southern whites were small farmers who, by modern standards, lived in poverty and did not benefit economically from slavery. Moreover, industrialization made comparatively little impact on the pre–Civil War South, which simply accentuated its precapitalist character. Transportation networks were substandard, so the expansion of markets experienced in the North was reserved mainly for the large planters who sold cotton to international traders and foreign textile manufacturers.

During the late 18th and early 19th centuries, the situation in the North and also the West could hardly have been more different. Beginning in the New England and mid-Atlantic regions, a gradual process of urbanization facilitated the foundation of small factories in leading manufacturing sectors, such as textiles and clothing. Capitalization schemes became more sophisticated with the growth of more mature financial markets, and markets expanded through the proliferation of transportation networks. The steamboat and railroad enabled manufacturers to reach an ever-increasing pool of consumers. And the continued movement of residents to burgeoning cities provided the labor needed for industrial growth and diversification.

By the late 19th century, most of the prerequisites for perhaps the most transformative phase of capitalist development in the United States were present in the North and West. During the first three quarters of the century, the bulk of economic growth in the United States had been underwritten by family-owned entrepreneurial ventures whose vulnerability to liabilities and relatively limited ability to raise capital governed their growth. The next phase of America's capitalist development necessarily involved the provision of tools and mechanisms through which business entities could overcome the boundaries that had traditionally defined their growth. As such, the Gilded Age galvanized a period of legal and managerial innovation that culminated in the emergence of the modern corporation. It was during this time and the decades that followed that the types of capitalist megastructures previously described in this article became the norm.

In the South, the transition to industrial capitalism was not so simple or linear. Despite the abolition of slavery mandated by the end of the Civil War through the Reconstruction amendments to the U.S. CONSTITUTION, the cultural and economic vestiges of slavery were palpable for decades thereafter and are, sadly, still recognizable. Physically, much of the South was destroyed by war, and its capacity for industrial development was minimal. Reconstruction proved to be a political failure, and the integration of millions of new African-American citizens into southern society was thwarted at every turn by the southern populace and STATE GOVERNMENTS dedicated to segregation at all costs. Eventually, the economic integration of nascent southern industries, such as textiles and mining, into national economic networks promoted the movement of the southern economy toward standards established through industrialization, but this did not happen quickly or easily.

Today, state-of-the-art manufacturing centers in the automobile and defense industries, for instance, can be found throughout the South, and southern cities such as Houston, Texas, and Atlanta, Georgia, compete with their northern counterparts as economic hubs. But the twin specters of slavery and industrial backwardness still cast a conspicuous shadow over southern economic development. Poverty levels are high, and lack of modernization is pervasive in too many parts of the rural South. Many residents, especially African Americans, are structurally prevented from competing fairly in the marketplace, with capital, material resources, and access to broader markets unavailable to them. Whether industrial capitalism truly exists in the American South is debatable, as is the related question of whether the South has successfully overcome its precapitalist past.

Further Reading

Bailyn, Bernard. *The New England Merchants in the Seventeenth Century*. Cambridge, Mass.: Harvard University Press, 1955; Chandler, Alfred D. *The Visible Hand: The Managerial Revolution in America*. Cambridge, Mass.: Harvard University Press, 1977; Galambos, Louis. *The Rise of the Corporate Commonwealth: U.S. Business and Public Policy in the Twentieth Century*. New York: Basic Books, 1988; Innes, Stephen. *Creating the Commonwealth: The Economic Culture of Puritan New England*. New York: W.W. Norton, 1995; Kulikoff, Allan. *The Agrarian Origins of American Capitalism*. Charlottesville: University Press of Virginia, 1992; Martin, John Frederick. *Profits in the Wilderness: Entrepreneurship and the Founding of New England Towns in the Seventeenth Century*. Chapel Hill: University of North Carolina Press, 1991; Montgomery, David. *Citizen Worker: The Experience of Workers in the United States with Democracy and the Free Market during the Nineteenth Century*. Cambridge: Cambridge University Press, 1993; North, Douglass C. *The Economic Growth of the United States, 1790–1860*. New York: W.W. Norton, 1966; Wilentz, Sean. *Chants Democratic: New York City and the Rise of the American Working Class, 1788–1850*. Oxford: Oxford University Press, 1984.

—Tomislav Han

command economy

In a command economy, the government takes direct control of the economy instead of relying on individual firms or entrepreneurs to make basic economic decisions and the market to provide feedback. This economic strategy is most closely associated with communist regimes such as the former Soviet Union, China, and North Korea but has some relationship to the policies of African and Asian socialist regimes.

In the comprehensive version of the command economy developed in the former Soviet Union and then exported to China, North Korea, Vietnam, and Cuba, all economic decisions are centralized in government agencies. The original goal was to avoid the exploitation believed inherent in unrestrained CAPITALISM by assuring that economic activity met human needs. Command economies were also believed to be necessary to consolidate a revolution by giving a communist party, through the government, control over much of everyday life.

A full-blown command economy, such as the one the Soviet Union attempted to create, relies on formal planning and hierarchical decision making for all economic activity. At the heart of the economy is a comprehensive five- or ten-year plan. The big plan is translated into smaller and more detailed provisions down to the level of an individual factory or collective farm. The government employee in charge of a shirt factory, for example, would be told how many shirts of various types the factory was expected to produce in the coming year, where the cloth and thread were going to come from (and how much they would cost), how many workers would be hired and what they would be paid, where the completed shirts were to be sent, and how much they were going to cost.

Over time, a number of apparently unsolvable problems have emerged in command economies that have crippled their economic performance. Chief among these have been inadequate planning, supply chain bottlenecks, quality of goods, and the phenomenon of storming.

When all economic activity is driven by a central plan, a staggering array of decisions must be consciously made. Planners at various levels must establish a specific price for every raw material, semifinished product, finished product, and each component of the manufacturing process. This raises two fundamental challenges. The first is simply making all the decisions that need to be made by the central bureaucracy before anything can happen. The second fundamental flaw in the planning process was a lack of information. Decisions about how much of what kinds of goods were required, where the raw materials could be obtained and how much they were worth, how production should be distributed, and how much the final consumer would pay for a given item, to name just a few, all require a great deal of information about complex economic and human interactions. At least some of that information is unknowable ahead of time, and plans thus had to rely on guesswork and imagination. In addition, the huge bureaucracies that were necessary to make and implement plans and monitor the economy became both a physical and economic drag on the economy.

Individual factories found themselves at the mercy of flawed plans. All the factories that needed coal to fire their boilers, for example, had to wait until the coal mines had been told how much coal to mine and where to ship it before they could hope to get their share. And if a factory needed cloth to make shirts, it had to wait and hope that the knitting mill got its raw materials in time and sent enough of the right kind of cloth.

Quality was always a major problem for command economies. Producers were typically credited with meeting their quotas when the goods left the factory. It did not matter if the production was shoddy or did not meet the needs of the consumer, because feedback from consumers was not part of the plan. A tractor that never ran quite right and fell apart in a year counted the same as a well-built, long-lasting tractor. If the plan did not credit a factory for making spare parts, they did not get made, which made repairing broken equipment or even replacing items such as windshield wipers on cars a major headache.

Quotas for production were set for each quarter and on an annual basis. If production had lagged during the period, everyone was pressured to go all out to meet the quota, a practice known in the Soviet Union as "storming." Workers who would normally be doing maintenance or other jobs were put on the assembly line and machinery was run overtime in an effort to meet the quota. At the end of that big push, production often slowed dramatically as machinery was taken out of service for maintenance and repairs, workers took time off to compensate for their overtime efforts, and other workers took care of various routine tasks that had been neglected. Almost inevitably, production lagged at the start of the new plan period, and storming became part of the routine.

The apparently inherent fatal flaws in command economies have led most countries to pursue some level of reform. The primary motives behind the reform programs introduced in the Soviet Union by Mikhail Gorbachev and the waves of reforms beginning with Deng Xiaoping in China were to increase economic efficiency without undermining the political system. While the Soviet attempt ended in the destruction of the Soviet Union, the Chinese experiment in "market Leninism" is still evolving.

Command economies are distinctive features of communist regimes. Other types of governments engage in varying degrees of economic planning and management but do not attempt to plan and regulate all the details of economic life. This important distinction is sometimes overlooked in political debates about American economic policy.

Further Reading
Gregory, Paul R. *Behind the Facade of Stalin's Command Economy.* Stanford, Calif.: Hoover Institution Press, 2001; Pei, Minxin. *China's Trapped Transition: The Limits of Developmental Autocracy.* Cambridge, Mass.: Harvard University Press, 2006.

—Seth Thompson

communism

The communist ideology stemmed from the socialist doctrine envisioned by the German economists Karl Marx and Friedrich Engels. In their writing of the *Communist Manifesto* in 1848, Marx and Engels demanded the elimination of the economic inequality

In Vilnius, Lithuania, the statue of Russian Marxist revolutionary Vladimir Ilyich Lenin is dismantled on August 23, 1991. *(Getty Images)*

(unequal wealth distribution) between the lower class and the upper class. According to their theory, the only way to accomplish such elimination is through a revolution led by the poor (workers/proletariats) against the rich (bourgeoisie), since the latter would never give up their wealth. The consequence of this revolution would bring social and economic justice with the achievement of a classless society. The Marxist theory of SOCIALISM was highly advocated by the Russians at the beginning of the 20th century. The first and foremost communist regime in the world started in the Soviet Union after the successful Bolshevik (which is the Russian word for "majority") revolution led by Vladimir Lenin against the autocracy of the czar's political regime. In 1917, the Bolshevik Party, which was renamed the Communist Party, established Soviet power. This power was rooted in the principle of the dictatorship of the proletariat (dictatorship of the many over the few). The Russian Communist movement became a model to other Communist Parties all around the world (e.g., Cuba, North Korea, Nicaragua, and Vietnam) after World War I. Among the communist parties were the Chinese, Yugoslav, Hungarian, and Czechoslovakian parties that followed Russia's lead. Communism reached the height of its influence during the leadership of Joseph Stalin in the Soviet Union from the late 1920s to the beginning of the 1950s. Stalin imposed the principles of imperialism, agrarian collectivism, industrial centralism, and TOTALITARIANISM. During this period and after the end of World War II, the cold war started between the two superpowers, the United States and the Soviet Union. This led to the emergence of an anticommunist wave in the democratic bloc that was supported by the American government. By the end of the cold war, the power of communism ultimately collapsed and was defeated by the ideals of CAPITALISM in 1991.

Communism is a belief and political practice based on Marxist socialism and further developed by Lenin and Stalin. Although Marx stated that communism must be practiced in economically advanced and industrialized societies, the Soviet leaders put communism into practice despite the fact that their empire was not highly advanced economically. In fact, none of the states that employed communism at the time were industrialized. By contrast, industrialized societies such as the United States use capitalist values. Communists believe that they must abolish capitalism through the dictatorship of the proletariat (the working class), and that will happen through the spread of socialist ideals around the world in order to create a strong communist bloc. The basic principles of communism are 1) religious atheism. This means that the communist society must not believe in God, but only in the Communist Party. Because of this, religious groups are not free to practice their religions in communist countries. This is in direct opposition to the United States; the American government often stresses the belief in God, and it grants freedom to practice any religion; 2) dialectical materialism. As explained by Marx, this means that economic factors determine social relations, and people are subject to the process of change. Throughout the historical process, the proletariat class struggles over material goods; and 3) socialism. This refers to the government ownership of the means of production. The communist government, in this regard, maintains central control over banking, business, housing, education, industry, medical care, and the military. Private property and rights of inheritance are abolished by the government. Property, thus, is publicly owned, and each person is paid according to his or her needs.

Contrary to the principle of socialism, capitalist states advocate the individual ownership of property and means of production, but under some governmental regulations and protections against any foreign threat. Capitalism is defined as an economic system based on private ownership in all business and trade fields. Such ownership is conducted under competitive conditions and ruled by the neoliberal and free market principles (i.e., decisions of production, distribution, and pricing are made by the private owners and influenced by the forces of the international market). Capitalism is characterized by an emphasis on self-interest to maximize gain either by the owner or the worker. Its ethics were first set forth by the Scottish philosopher Adam Smith. Ironically, the term *capitalism* was first introduced by Marx as he attempted to define communism as both its cause and opposite.

In a communist state, the Communist Party is the only ruling party. Hypothetically, it represents the majority of the proletariat, but in reality it is just a representation of the leaders of the party itself. Membership in the party provides many privileges that average citizens do not enjoy. For example, in the Soviet Union, party members could have access to foreign merchandise, travel to capitalist states, live in the best housing, and obtain prestigious educations and jobs for their children. The power of the party is of a totalitarian (nondemocratic) nature, since its main function is to exercise unlimited control over the society in all fields of life and to suppress opposition. As communist leaders believe, the party must be tightly controlled and disciplined to be able to lead the revolt against the capitalists. Stalin attempted to put this into practice by creating a repressive bureaucratic system that lasted until the end of the communist era. The hierarchy of the Communist Party began from the general secretary at the highest level and went down to the politburo, central committee,

national party congress, republic congress, district congress, and the party cells as the lowest level. The most powerful policy-making bodies of the party were the general secretary, the politburo, and the central committee. The party employed the communist concept of "democratic centralism." This means that the decisions of the higher party bodies are imposed on the lower bodies. The absolute power, nonetheless, is in the hand of the general secretary (the president).

Unlike the Communist Party, American POLITICAL PARTIES have no official power to get involved in governmental policy making, and their major focus is to ensure the winning of their candidates in elections. Moreover, the American president does not have absolute power due to the practice of CHECKS AND BALANCES by the other governmental branches. The communist system, on the other hand, lacks such checks and balances. Returning to the example of the Soviet Union, the judicial branch was under the direct control of the Communist Party, since there were no independent courts. The legislative members also were parts of the Communist Party who could not regulate the activities of the executive branch, including the party itself. Contrary to American legislators, communist legislators came directly from the nomination of the party, and, hence, they were not elected by the citizens.

With the official dissolution of the Soviet Union in 1991, which had consisted of 15 republics under the Russian federation, the prominence of communism ended mainly due to economic reasons. During the era of communism, the Communist Party adopted the model of the centrally planned economy, known also as a COMMAND ECONOMY. This type of economy is completely directed by the state, which has a monopoly on making decisions regarding production and allocation of goods and services. A communist economy has some advantages to the nation as a whole, such as providing social welfare by the state (e.g., free education, free health care, and free housing to all citizens). In the case of the Soviet Union, the main resource of such welfare came directly from capital investment by the government in building heavy industry. Although the Soviet Union was one of the top world manufacturers, it still lagged far behind the capitalist states that adopted the economic model of the free market. In such a market, firms compete against each other by increasing their production in order to gain more profit. The communist economy, on the other hand, has only one big firm (owned by the government) that produces its goods in accordance with the needs of the consumers. Because the needs of the consumers were unknown, the main economic problem in the Soviet Union during the 1980s was shortages of supplies. For instance, people used to stand in long lines just to buy a pair of shoes or one piece of bread before the supply ran out. As a result, people increasingly turned to the black market. This weakened the national economy and the position of the government.

Mikhail Gorbachev, the last communist president of the Soviet Union, tried to check this decline by introducing some reforms in 1987 through a program named glasnost that was already specified in his perestroika (reconstruction of the Soviet economy and politics). The basic idea of this program was to turn the communist economy from central planning to free market (e.g., allowing private ownership and foreign investments). However, it was implemented without any prior transitional plan. This led to the governmental loss of control over the national economy, particularly after the decline in tax revenues due to decentralization, and the quality of life regressed. The economic instability caused great public unrest and resentment. The resulting anger came to a head in the August coup in 1991 against Gorbachev. By the end of that year, the Soviet Communist Party had dissolved, crippling Communist Parties elsewhere. While communism still exists, it is weakened to the point of impotence. Currently, most postcommunist states are undergoing economic stagnation and facing new challenges of democratization such as multicandidate elections and FREEDOM OF THE PRESS. Perhaps these nations can work with the United States and other democratic entities to rebuild and flourish.

See also IDEOLOGY; SOCIALISM.

Further Reading

Daniels, Robert V. *The Nature of Communism*. New York: Random House, 1962; Edwards, Lee. *The Collapse of Communism*. Stanford: Calif.: Hoover Institution Press, 2000; Hyde, Douglas. *Communism Today*. South Bend, Ind.: University of Notre Dame Press, 1973; Ketchum, Richard. *What Is Communism?* New York: E. P. Dutton, 1955; Kornai, Janos.

The Socialist System. Princeton, N.J.: Princeton University Press, 1992; Meyer, Alfred G. *Communism*. New York: Random House, 1962; Salvadori, Massimo. *The Rise of Modern Communism*. New York: Holt, Rinehart, & Winston, 1963; Yoder, Amos. *Communist Systems and Challenges*. New York: Taylor & Francis, 1990.

—Muna A. Ali

developed countries

A developed country is a country that enjoys a high standard of living and an advanced, diversified economy. A high standard of living may encompass societal factors, such as high literary rates, education levels, and long life expectancy. An advanced, diversified economy consists of multiple sectors within a country reaching high levels of production, having a high gross domestic product (GDP), as well as generally possessing a high per capita GDP. However, a high GDP does not automatically enable a country to attain the label *developed*, as this economic achievement may have been attained through natural resource extraction, which is more of a short-term situation and does not reach across multiple sectors of the economy. In short, developed countries possess both economic and noneconomic factors that propel them to higher levels of development than less-developed countries.

Former descriptors of developed countries include the terms *first world, industrialized countries*, or even the more constraining *Western countries*, which leaves out developed countries in Asia and elsewhere. While these terms are still in use, the current phrase *Global North* creates a more neutral environment when discussing these countries. Likewise, DEVELOPING COUNTRIES that were once referred to as "Third World" or "nonindustrialized countries" are now known as the "Global South."

While international organizations have created their own definitions or categorization of which countries are or are not developed, there is little agreement on exactly what factors are the most important in determining whether a country is developed. The UNITED NATIONS does not have an established convention for designating a country "developed." However, most international organizations that study and label countries according to their levels of economic development are in close agreement as to which countries fall into which categories.

A list of which countries are and are not developed can be broadly stated. Western European countries are generally all developed countries, with Norway and Finland included on that list. The smaller countries in Europe, such as San Marino, Andorra, Liechtenstein, Monaco, and the Holy See (Vatican City) are also included as developed countries. The United States and Canada are developed, as are the Asian and Pacific rim nations of Japan, South Korea, Singapore, Australia, and New Zealand. In the Middle East, only Israel is frequently classified as a developed country.

Many other countries may claim the title of developed countries, but for various reasons, international organizations differ on their classification. Russia, while large and belonging to international groups such as the Group of Eight (G8) most developed countries, has rampant corruption and a per capita income that places it in the category of a developing country. Russia's inclusion in the G8 and other groups is largely a cold war legacy and not an accurate appraisal of its current developmental level.

Likewise, South Africa and Turkey have low per-capita incomes, even though other factors may indicate that these countries should be labeled developed countries. Turkey, as a NORTH ATLANTIC TREATY ORGANIZATION member and possible entrant into the EUROPEAN UNION, has internal security problems and a less developed economy, while South Africa faces one of the world's highest AIDS infection rates and a less-developed economy as well.

Many of the Persian Gulf states, such as Bahrain, Kuwait, Oman, Qatar, Saudi Arabia, and the United Arab Emirates, have a high per-capita income level. However, their economies are focused on a single commodity, oil, and their noneconomic factors are generally at low levels. Similarly, many of the Caribbean nations, such as the Bahamas, Barbados, Antigua and Barbuda, Trinidad and Tobago, and Saint Kitts and Nevis, have high per capita incomes, but their economies are also concentrated in one area, tourism, and thus do not meet the requirement for a diversified economy.

Lastly, Hong Kong, Taiwan, and Macau all lay claim to high levels of economic development and high per capita income levels, but their ongoing disputes with China, in which China claims these territories as part of mainland China, complicate the political and economic situation.

These discrepancies point to the need for a holistic approach to the classification of countries into developed and developing categories. While certain countries, such as China, Sri Lanka, Poland, and Cuba, might fare better under societal means of classification, such as literacy and life expectancy rates, other countries, such as Saudi Arabia and Kuwait, as mentioned above, suffer from lower rankings in these areas while maintaining higher levels of economic achievement. An outgrowth of the realization that noneconomic factors are of great importance to a country's level of development is the connection made between development and a country's regime type.

There is a clear, empirical relationship between development and DEMOCRACY, yet there are questions as to the direction of the causal relation. In one study, gross national product, or the value of goods and services produced by citizens of a country no matter where they are located, was cited as the key explanatory variable for whether a country will become a democracy. Economic development is not the only factor leading to democratic development, but among the countries with the lowest economic development, only a handful of them qualify as free or democratic. As the level of economic development increases, so does the likelihood that the countries will be democracies. But outside influences such as war, domestic instability, cultural factors, leadership, and social movements can all steer a country in a different direction.

The connection between democracy and a country being developed is a difficult one that leaves open many avenues for further research. Many authors believed that as more countries grew economically, they would also become freer in the political arena. However, many of the states that constituted the fastest-growing economically were not democracies, which belied the idea that the gradual transition and development of states would lead to their accepting greater POLITICAL PARTICIPATION and rights, as well as a stronger commitment to democracy. Instead, political repression and the concentration of political control among political elites have been used by many states to further their economic goals. States argue that the repression of labor groups or the suppression of political liberties to ensure domestic stability are necessary in order to attract foreign investors who can bring needed technology, capital, and skills to developing countries. Countries such as Singapore and South Korea had long been under more oppressive regimes, if not outright martial law.

On the other hand, many authoritarian states have never developed market economies or political stability. Others have achieved political stability and even some level of economic development but have seen them disappear in domestic upheavals such as coups and civil wars. Military governments are often the culprits in African and Latin American countries, as their ascension to power usually entails harsh crackdowns and a corresponding retaliation by the population, leading to domestic instability and the loss of any gains made in development.

A second case has been made concerning the confluence of development and democracy. This idea holds that while economic development is not necessarily the most important cause for achieving democracy, it is necessary to maintain democracy. Thus, democratic countries that achieve and maintain high levels of economic development will not "regress" to lower levels of development or fail as democracies. Adam Przeworksi notes that no democracy with a per capita income higher than $6,055 has ever fallen. At the same time, he notes that since 1946, 47 democracies have collapsed in poor countries. While external invasion, civil war, economic depression, or crises can test a country, high levels of economic development can buffer the fallout from these incidents.

Some developing countries that are seeking higher economic growth and higher standards of living are concerned with issues that arise out of dependency theory. This idea, developed in the 1960s and 1970s, blames the developed countries for taking advantage of developing countries and keeping these developing countries in a perpetual state of exploitation. In this model, the developed core of countries, such as the United States and western Europe, purposefully exploited the natural resources and populations of the developing countries in order to enrich themselves and prevent competition to their established positions. While many developing countries have not fully accepted this theory, they have undertaken policies to try to prevent this from occurring, frequently with unfavorable consequences.

Many of these same countries have attempted to put themselves in the developed country category by using the import substitution industrialization method. Here, developing countries attempted to become self-sufficient by increasing tariffs and producing many of the goods they previously imported as well as focusing on native natural resources such as mining and agriculture. However, corruption, inefficiency, and an inability to secure stable high prices for these commodities led most of these import substitution programs into ruin. By the 1990s, many developing countries had abandoned these policies in favor of export-led programs, such as those practiced by the "Asian tigers"—Singapore, Taiwan, South Korea, and Hong Kong. The tigers followed the example of Japan, produced manufactured goods for export to the world market, and were generally successful in becoming developed countries, although China's claim on both Taiwan and Hong Kong has occasionally thrown their political stability into question.

Societal factors make up a second component that helps determine whether a country is developed. The United Nations Development Programme designed the human development index (HDI) as a combination of life expectancy, educational attainment, and economic measurement of GDP per capita. GDP per capita is a measure of the value of goods and services produced per person within the borders of a country in a given year. Much of the focus in the HDI is on societal factors and the distance between developed and developing countries. For example, expenditures on public health as a percentage of a country's GDP in the developed world is three times that of the developing world, while life expectancy is nearly 15 years more in developed countries.

Many societal factors are not equal among the genders, so international agencies have broken down the HDI further by gender for the gender development index. Literacy rates, a basic indicator of educational level, are frequently lower among women than men. In addition, health-care services that primarily affect women, such as prenatal care and health care for infants, are frequently not available. As women assume greater responsibility for family and household maintenance through their roles as wage earners and landowners, gender-specific issues will increasingly come into focus.

The United States has long supported international development efforts through such groups as the UNITED STATES AGENCY FOR INTERNATIONAL DEVELOPMENT. This agency, created by the 1961 Foreign Assistance Act and tracing its roots back to the Marshall Plan for post–World War II Europe, combines economic aid for development assistance with attempts at promoting stability and peace. Among the many policies it carries out are training and scholarship programs, distributing food aid, helping build infrastructure, and providing small business loans. While Congress provides the money for this and other development groups, the State Department and the White House help set the policy directions for this foreign assistance program.

The Overseas Private Investment Corporation (OPIC) is another U.S. agency that provides insurance and aid to U.S. corporations looking to invest abroad. Created in 1971, this agency helps protect U.S. businesses while ensuring that they are able to invest in developing countries. The risk of political instability in developing countries is a frequent barrier to investment, so OPIC was created to manage this risk in the hope of realizing profits for American corporations while bringing much needed technology and capital to developing countries.

Further Reading

Dahl, Robert A. *Polyarchy: Participation and Opposition.* New Haven, Conn.: Yale University Press, 1971; Diamond, Larry. "Economic Development and Democracy Reconsidered." In *Reexamining Democracy*, edited by Gary Marks and Larry Diamond. Newbury Park, Calif.: Sage Publications, 1992; Huntington, Samuel P. *Third Wave: Democratization in the Late Twentieth Century.* Norman: University of Oklahoma Press, 1991; Kegley, Charles W. *World Politics: Trends and Transformation.* 11th ed. Belmont, Calif.: Thomson Wadsworth, 2007; Przeworski, Adam. "Democracy and Economic Development." In *Evolution of Political Knowledge: Democracy, Autonomy, and Conflict in Comparative and International Politics*, edited by Edward D. Mansfield and Richard Sisson. Columbus: Ohio State University Press, 2004; United Nations Development Programme. *Human Development Report.* New York: United Nations, 2005.

—Peter Thompson

developing countries

The term *developing countries* usually refers to countries that have not experienced economic development to the scale of societies in western Europe and the United States. Most developing countries are in Asia, Africa, and Latin America. They were, at one time or another, colonized by a European power in the modern era. The colonial experience, resulting in exploitation of peoples and resources in these societies, often accounts for the low but varying levels of economic, social, and political development in these countries. In the postcolonial era, as the following essay shows, they have grappled with problems such as political corruption, inefficient governments, a high level of poverty, lack of industrialization, ethnic conflict, and social fragmentation. Nevertheless, a few of these countries also exhibit high economic growth rates, resilient political institutions, and vibrant social and cultural life.

The table on page 1003 shows the vast economic and demographic differences between the developed and developing world. Most strikingly, while the low-income countries contain 36.5 percent of the world's population, their share of total world income is only 3 percent. Furthermore, 39 percent of the children under five in these countries are chronically malnourished.

In the postcolonial era (after World War II), developing countries have been called by different names: poor societies, underdeveloped countries, industrializing countries, and third world countries The last designation, in particular, was in popular usage and distinguished them from the democratic and industrialized first world and the communist second world. After the fall of COMMUNISM in Eastern Europe, the term *Third World* became problematic.

The colonial era coincided with Europe's lead in military and navigation technologies. Beginning in the late 15th century, the two factors enabled European explorers such as Christopher Columbus and Vasco Da Gama to travel great distances and establish commercial links, soon followed by political and military domination. The colonial era also coincided with the commercial and Industrial Revolutions in Europe. The newly established colonies, or commercial links, became sources of raw materials and indentured labor, especially from Africa. Existing empires or

KEY INDICATORS OF DEVELOPMENT

	Population (2005)		Gross National Income			% of Malnourished Children under 5	Adult Literacy (% Ages 15 and Older) 2000–04
	Total Millions	% of World	$ Billion	% of World	$ Per Capita		
Low Income	2,353	36.5	1,363.9	3.03	580	39	62
Middle Income	3.073	47.7	8,113.1	18	2640	11	90
High Income	1,011	15.7	35,528	79	35,131	3	NA
World	6,438	100	44,983.3	100	6.987	25	80

political entities, such as the Incas, the Mayas, and the Aztecs in Latin America and the Mughals in India, were destroyed by colonialism and replaced either with direct European rule or indirectly through their commercial arms, such as the East India Company, which operated in South Asia. The Spanish and Portuguese granted independence to territories in Latin America in the early part of the 19th century, but colonial rule continued elsewhere. However, immigrant populations from Europe ruled these countries, and this period is often characterized as semicolonialism. The 19th century was the colonial century when most of what now constitutes the developing world came under colonial rule or, as in the case of China, was greatly affected by it. The so-called 'scramble for Africa' took place in the latter half of the century, when European powers such as France, Britain, Spain, Belgium, and Holland vied with one another to occupy this continent.

The United States, itself a British colony until 1776, was not a colonizer except for notable exceptions in countries such as the Philippines (1902–42), but indirectly it asserted its dominance in various places. President James Monroe in 1823 declared to the European powers that the Americas were under U.S. influence. This move later came to be called the Monroe Doctrine. Declarations from President Theodore Roosevelt in 1904, President William Howard Taft in 1912, and President Franklin D. Roosevelt in 1933 widened the sphere of U.S. influence in the region. The United States also began to support dictatorships in Latin America and the Caribbean from the 1930s and in other parts of the world after World War II, as long as these dictators were supportive of the United States. The cold war with the Soviet Union also meant that if the United States did not support

these regimes, it would lose their allegiance, as was the case with the Cuban revolution of 1959, when Fidel Castro emerged as Cuba's leader.

Meanwhile, nationalist movements emerged at the end of the 19th century and sought political freedom and sovereignty from Europe. Beginning with freedom from Dutch rule in Indonesia in 1945 and freedom from British rule in India and Pakistan in 1947, other colonial countries soon achieved independence. Most sub-Saharan African countries became independent in the 1960s. Many American ideas and historical events facilitated the nationalist movements. Of particular note were the American independence movement in the 18th century, the Civil War featuring the abolition of slavery, President Woodrow Wilson's principles for world peace, and the CIVIL RIGHTS MOVEMENT of the 1960s. The Harlem Renaissance influenced Leopold Senghor's vision of nègritude, which argued for a distinct African identity, and people such as Martin Luther King, Jr., were received as heroes in the developing world.

The post–colonial governments of developing countries, or semicolonial in Latin America, built their sense of commanding purpose and legitimacy on the mandate that their elites received from leading the nationalist movements. The consensus domestically and internationally was that it was the government that would be entrusted to carry out the political and economic tasks that were necessary to improve the livelihood of people. Despite their failures and shortcomings, there was near total reverence accorded to postcolonial leaders such as Getulio Vargas in Brazil, Lazaro Cárdenas in Mexico, Kwame Nkrumah in Ghana, Julius Nyerere in Tanzania, Leopold Senghor in Senegal, Jawaharlal Nehru in India, and Ahmed Sukarno in Indonesia.

There were great expectations about the performance of these "commanding heights" governments. Most of these governments distanced themselves from Western style CAPITALISM, which they equated with colonial exploitation of the past, inasmuch as private agricultural plantations and industries in the former colonial territories were in the hands of Europeans. Many developing countries thus drew inspiration from Soviet-style central planning, in which the government owned and controlled many means of economic production and distribution. These governments also argued that imports would make them dependent on Western countries again. Instead, they encouraged industries in their own territories to produce import substitutes or like-products. This economic strategy came to be known as import substitution industrialization, or ISI. A few countries, especially in East Asia, also experimented simultaneously with earning high revenues from their exports while restraining their imports, so that they would not lose their hard-earned foreign exchange reserves too rapidly. This strategy, styled on the high growth rates generated by Japan in the 20th century, came to be known as export oriented industrialization (EOI). It led to rapid industrialization in countries such as Singapore, Taiwan, and South Korea, which came to be known as the "Asian tigers" or newly industrializing countries (NICS). To a limited extent, Malaysia and China also mimicked this strategy.

Developing countries adopted the ISI and EOI economic strategies in an effort to mimic the modernization and industrialization seen in the United States and western Europe. However, these strategies were mandated by governments instead of arising spontaneously through free market forces. Indeed, both ISI and EOI were led by the "visible hand" of governments rather than the "invisible hand" of markets. Postcolonial leaders believed that governments could help deliver to their societies modernization and industrialization experiences more rapidly than in western Europe. The following statement by India's Nehru in 1957 is typical of this period: "Now India, we are bound to be industrialized, we are trying to be industrialized, we must be industrialized."

Quite soon, though, postcolonial countries ran into economic and political obstacles as a result of their economic strategies. ISI prioritized industry over agriculture, resulting in food shortages and,

more important, neglect of farmers, who made up almost two-thirds of total employment in these countries. Food shortages, famines, and inflation followed in many countries. ISI itself needed imported machinery and technology to be successful, which many of these countries could not afford. Countries in Latin America, for example, borrowed large sums of money from international banks to finance ISI. By the early 1980s, they reneged on these loans. The Latin American debt crisis, which began in 1982, showed the limits of ISI strategy.

The political costs of the economic strategy were perhaps even higher. As governments could not meet the rising economic demands, they became increasingly populist or authoritarian. CORRUPTION among government officials became common, and military coups followed in many countries. The United States and the Soviet Union supported many of these dictatorial regimes as their pawns in the cold war.

The social fabric of many countries, already weakened by colonialism, became perhaps even more weakened in the postcolonial era. A few scholars argue that dictatorships and authoritarianism were the only instruments available to curb the civil unrest and rising demands in these countries. If so, the costs were high, indeed. Old ethnic hatreds also surfaced, especially in the "artificial" countries European powers created by joining together ethnic groups and territories that had never coexisted before. The Biafra war in Nigeria from 1967 to 1970 and the conflict between the Kikuyus and Luos in Kenya in the late 1960s are examples. Dictatorships arose, such as General Idi Amin in Uganda in 1971 and Pol Pot in Cambodia in 1975, that decimated entire populations. As many as 25,000 to 30,000 people disappeared under the military regime in Argentina in the late 1970s.

By the mid-1980s, the failure of the ISI and EOI economic strategies, the developing world debt crisis, and the end of the cold war induced shifts in the politics and economics of the developing world. Politically, the last 20 years or so have witnessed the end of dictatorships in most parts of the developing world. However, fears remain that unless poverty is reduced and economic growth rates take off, these countries will revert to political instability.

Economically, the import substitution strategy failed the developing world. The fall of communism also ensured that the developing world would no longer turn to central planning for economic control. Since the late 1980s, the developing world has, therefore, undertaken a number of market liberalization measures, either selling off formerly government-run enterprises to private enterprises or giving incentives to private investment, including multinational corporations. INTERNATIONAL TRADE also received a boost. These measures are often termed the Washington Consensus, after the blessing they received from the WORLD BANK, the INTERNATIONAL MONETARY FUND, and the U.S. government—all based in Washington, D.C. The early results from the implementation of the Washington Consensus are mixed. While most of the developing world has generated high growth rates, it is unclear if poverty has been reduced. A few scholars believe that the new policies have lifted middle classes and urban areas and depressed rural areas further. Nevertheless, countries as disparate as Brazil, Costa Rica, Botswana, and India are now generating very high growth rates.

The last holdouts of dictatorships and monarchies are found in the Middle East and the Arab world. The events of 9/11 and thereafter have brought Americans increasingly close to and enmeshed in this part of the developing world. Whereas in the colonial and cold war days, the United States could exercise almost uncontested dominance in international affairs, the ironic twist of the post–cold war era is that the instability in the Arab world now continually threatens the peace of the Western world.

Meanwhile, countries in East Asia that had practiced EOI have done well for themselves. A few of them, such as Singapore, Taiwan, and South Korea, are no longer termed developing countries and are counted as developed. China, with an export-oriented strategy but an authoritarian government, generates double-digit growth rates, too, but fears remain about the stresses on its political system.

The best hope for peace in the developing world and its relations with the developed world lie in economic development. The goal remains elusive. Unfortunately, nearly half the world's population still lives in poverty.

Further Reading

Calvert, Peter, and Susan Calvert. *Politics and Society in the Third World*. 2nd ed. New York: Longman, 2001; Harrison, Paul. *Inside the Third World*. New York: Penguin Books, 1990; Sen, Amartya. *Development as Freedom*. New York: Anchor Books, 2000; World Bank. *World Development Report 2008*. Washington, D.C.: The World Bank, 2007.

—J. P. Singh

distributive justice

Distributive justice concerns the fair, just, and equitable distribution of benefits and burdens. These benefits and burdens span all dimensions of social life and assume all forms, including income, economic wealth, political power, taxation, work obligations, education, shelter, health care, military service, community involvement, and religious activities. Thus, justice arguments are often invoked in connection with MINIMUM WAGE legislation, AFFIRMATIVE ACTION policies, public education, military conscription, and litigation as well as with redistributive policies such as welfare, Medicare, aid to the developing world, progressive INCOME TAXES, and inheritance taxes. Distributive justice enjoys a long and honored tradition in political, economic, and social thought. It is central to Aristotle's *Nichomachean Ethics* and *Politics*. In modern political philosophy, it has been construed in broad terms and seen as a foundation for policy formation and analysis. Michael Walzer, for example, writes that "Distributive justice is a large idea," and for John Rawls, "Justice is the first virtue of social institutions." Thus, it is widely regarded as an important concept and influential force in philosophy and the social sciences.

This description begs the question, however, of what, exactly, constitutes a "fair," "just" and "equitable" distribution (these terms are interchangeable). It seems that justice terminology employed with considerable flexibility, and fairness arguments are sometimes even made by both parties on opposite sides of a dispute. There are at least three reasons for this. A large part of the literature on justice involves prescriptive theories, theories that attempt to characterize a phenomenon in general terms and that concern what "ought to be." They can be contrasted with descriptive theories, which seek to describe in general terms what "is." Philosophers and social scientists typically propose prescriptive theories of justice as a guide for how people should behave and what policies should be enacted. One characteristic of prescriptive theories is that they are not verifiable; since they deal with values and what one believes to be just, they cannot be empirically tested. Although good theories should have a coherent internal logic, they otherwise have great latitude to proceed from any assumption and can lead, therefore, to a wide variety of very different conclusions.

A second source of variation in justice terminology refers to everyday usage and is more patterned than the differences in prescriptive theories of justice. There are different senses of justice that pertain to the specificity of ethical principles being addressed. This distinction can be traced as far back as Aristotle, who wrote that "justice and injustice seem to be used in more than one sense." He identified justice that "is not a part of virtue but the whole of excellence or virtue" versus "justice as a part of virtue." In other words, in a very general sense, justice refers to the whole of ethics such that "fair" can be equated with "good" and "unfair" with "bad." Justice in this most general sense, then, is about more than the distribution of benefits and burdens but also the whole of ethics, including virtues such as honesty, courage, loyalty, and generosity. The focus here, however, is on the more narrow definition introduced at the start, both in light of the fact that most actual usage is more specific and in order to restrict attention to a tractable subject matter.

Finally, justice arguments are often put forth, not to promote justice but rather to further the interests of the party employing them. Indeed, skeptics of justice often cite such self-serving arguments as evidence that justice is nothing more than a cloak for self-interest. Nevertheless, the fact that fairness arguments are regularly advanced is evidence of their moral force: If they were merely subterfuge without any independent ethical content, surely they would cease to carry moral weight. It is now well documented that fairness biases result from the tension between justice and self-interest and that these even lead to self-deception, that is, people often form false beliefs about what is fair in order to align those beliefs more closely with their self-interest. Thus, it is important to distinguish biased views of justice associated with stakeholders, or those who have stakes in the distribution they are judging, from the unbiased justice of impartial spectators, or people who have no such stakes and evaluate fairness from a more or less neutral stance. Whereas stakeholder views can be extremely heterogeneous due to the wide range of opposing interests that mold them, mounting research indicates that unbiased views of justice converge to fairly well defined categories. In the mid-1960s, social scientists began serious efforts to describe attitudes toward justice and their behavioral effects. This research agenda has intensified more recently and now includes work in psychology, economics, political science, and sociology. The remaining discussion is based on four elements (or forces) of justice that have been proposed to describe the existing social science evidence on unbiased views of justice. They form not only a descriptive theory of justice, but the four elements can also serve as the organizing framework for categorizing various prescriptive and descriptive theories of justice.

The category EQUALITY and need includes theories that incorporate a concern for the well-being of the least well-off members of society. The most basic and probably oldest concept equates justice with equality, including equality of opportunity, proportions, and rights. The strongest notion of equality is egalitarianism, or equality of outcomes. This serves as the foundation for various prescriptive theories of justice, as well as, more recently, for descriptive theories based on experimental findings. Nevertheless, numerous studies of the distributive preferences of people demonstrate almost universal opposition to equality or near equality of income. The equality sometimes found in experimental studies in the laboratory appears to be an artifact of contextually lean experiments rather than a general preference. Nevertheless, some researchers believe equality is one of several principles people value.

Much of the modern interest in justice can be attributed to the publication of John Rawls's major work, *A Theory of Justice*, in 1971. This book builds on the theory of the SOCIAL CONTRACT associated with JOHN LOCKE, Jean Jacques Rousseau, and Immanuel Kant, and equality, duty, and need are central to it. Rawls conceives of a hypothetical original position in which people are behind a "veil of ignorance" of their places in society. Under these conditions, Rawls claims that people would unanimously choose a particular conception of justice. The greatest attention has been paid to his so-called difference principle, according to which all goods are distributed equally unless an unequal distribution is to the advantage of the least favored. Some economists have criticized the difference principle on theoretical grounds, but various surveys and experiments also suggest that his theory is not a good description of actual values.

Although Marxism is commonly thought to be concerned with injustices, equity was actually a controversial concept for Karl Marx and Friedrich Engels, who seemed to consider it a bourgeois construct. To the extent there is a Marxist theory of justice, it seems to be best summed up in the communist distributive principle that Marx (1875) endorsed, namely, "From each according to his ability, to each according to his needs!"

Empirical studies reveal an expressed concern for helping those in need and demonstrate a willingness of people to sacrifice materially to realize that goal. Collectively, they suggest that the themes of equality and need can be integrated in the need principle: just allocations provide for basic needs equally across individuals. Specifically, the evidence suggests that need is one of several principles and that it tends to dominate when basic needs are endangered.

The second category of theories is consequentialist. These theories share the property of reflecting a concern for the overall consequences of allocations or allocation schemes (as opposed, for example, to the intentions of the actors). These include utilitarianism and welfare economics. The former is the dominant consequentialist theory in moral philosophy, and the latter is the dominant approach in prescriptive economics. Utilitarians such as Jeremy Bentham and John Stuart Mill advocated acting so as to promote the greatest aggregate happiness. Welfare economics is derived from utilitarianism and is based on evaluating choices in terms of their consequences for "social welfare," which, in turn, typically depends on a composite evaluation of individual welfare, or "utility." The most widely embraced concept in economics is the Pareto principle, which endorses any change that makes someone better off without making anyone else worse off. A weaker version, called the compensation principle, approves of any change in which the gains of some are more than sufficient to compensate any and all losses of others, even if the prescribed compensation does not actually occur. The usual definition of equity in welfare economics, however, is the absence of envy criterion. In the simplest form, an allocation is envy-free if no agent prefers the bundle of another.

A review of the literature on distributive preferences indicates that people care about the happiness or subjective value derived from allocations. There is also qualified support for the Pareto and compensation principles, although this support is significantly compromised when it conflicts with other distributive goals. Absence of envy, on the other hand, is at most a second-order concern. Together, these studies show that people often seek to maximize surplus, sometimes at a monetary cost, and that this is regarded as "fair." Efficiency in this sense does not necessarily conflict with justice but instead is itself a kind of justice, as in the efficiency principle.

The common feature among the third category of equity and desert is the dependence of fair allocations on individual actions. Desert concerns which individual characteristics are relevant to justice, and equity is what the functional relationship is of individual characteristics to just allocations. The political philosopher Robert Nozick is situated at one extreme. In *Anarchy, State and Utopia*, he argues that justice is exclusively concerned with rights that are determined by the historical acquisition by and transfer of property among individuals. For Nozick, individual choice trumps social choice, and he believes in a limited role for government. Individuals are held responsible for everything. At the other end of the political spectrum, individual responsibility is seen as minimal and state redistribution as necessary to remedy unjust inequalities occasioned by arbitrary factors such as birth and brute luck. Although effort is commonly accepted as a reasonable basis for different allocations, John Roemer, for example, sees even effort partially as something for which a person should not be held entirely accountable. Numerous field, experimental, and survey studies have verified the importance of desert for views of justice and have established that when disagreements arise about what justice requires in specific circumstances, these can often be traced to differences in perceived responsibility.

Another approach that relates individual actions to desired outcomes is equity theory. Equity theorists often trace their origins to the *Nicomachean Ethics*, in which Aristotle proposed proportionality as the foundation for justice. Specifically, fair outcomes for individuals are in proportion to their inputs. Inputs are usually thought of as a participant's contributions and outcomes as the consequences, potentially positive or negative, that a participant incurs in this connection. A significant advance for both desert theory and equity theory came with their merger, which specified that fair outcomes are in proportion to the inputs for which agents are responsible. This version, which has been called the accountability principle, or simply the equity principle, has demonstrated considerable robustness in explaining a wide range of attitudes and behaviors.

These three elements of justice helped organize theories around three distinct principles of justice: the need principle, the efficiency principle, and the accountability principle. The fourth element of justice is context, which is not a principle at all but rather the means by which the relative importance of each principle is determined. The idea is that unbiased justice is a multicriterion concept that obeys general principles, but that it is also context dependent, that is, the principles of justice require a set of people and variables that the context provides. This approach provides the means to reconcile a wide range of values and behaviors that are otherwise difficult to explain. For example, in DEVELOPING COUNTRIES, a greater emphasis on need relative to efficiency and accountability has been identified. This is surely consistent with both the perception and reality of greater material need in those countries.

The rapid growth of empirical research on distributive justice has provided a rich source of data that has informed and helped advance descriptive theories of justice. Stimulated by this work, prescriptive theorists are now beginning to employ these findings to evaluate their own theories and even to draw on empirical results to construct prescriptive theories of justice. Distributive justice can no longer be considered as an amorphous or hopelessly differentiated subject matter. Much work remains, especially in identifying the effects of context and in designing prescriptive theories, but justice has proven to be an important force that can be understood and can help decision makers understand and form policy.

Further Reading
Aristotle. *The Nicomachean Ethics*. Translated by J. A. Thomson. London: Penguin Books, 1976; Aristotle. *Politics*. Edited by David Keyt. Oxford: Clarendon Press, 1999; Babcock, Linda, and George Loewenstein. "Explaining Bargaining Impasse: The Role of Self-Serving Biases." *Journal of Economic Perspectives* 11, no. 1 (1997): 109–126; Konow, James. "Which Is the Fairest One of All? A Positive Analysis of Justice Theories." *Journal of Economic Literature* 41, no. 4 (2003): 1,188–1,239; Marx, Karl. "Critique of the Gotha Programme." In *Justice*, edited by Alan Ryan. Oxford: Oxford University Press, 1993; Rawls, John. *A Theory of Justice*. Cambridge, Mass.: Belknap Press of Harvard University Press, 1971; Walzer, Michael. *Spheres of Justice: A Defense of Pluralism and Equality*. New York: Basic Books, 1983.

—James Konow

European Union

In the aftermath of World War II, the French foreign affairs minister Robert Schuman laid the first bricks for the construction of the European Union (EU) in 1950 by declaring the necessity of establishing European economic unification as an initial step toward larger federation. The objectives of such unification were to promote peace and stabilize the economy as well as to enhance the sense of cultural similarity. As a result, a new treaty was signed in Paris in April 1951 by France, Germany, Luxembourg, Belgium, Italy, and the Netherlands. In March 1957, these countries initiated an organizational union in the form of the European Economic Community. Thereafter, several treaties were signed to guide shared economic policies, and the membership expanded to include Denmark, Greece, Spain, Portugal, Ireland, and Britain.

A deeper unification was created in February 1992, when the 12 countries extended the economic arrangement to a political one by signing the Treaty of Maastricht. In October 1997, several amendments to the Treaty of Maastricht and to the previous treaties were made by the signing of the Treaty of Amsterdam. After the expansion of the membership of the EU to include 25 member states in 2001, a new treaty known as the Treaty of Nice dealt with the issues of reforming the EU institutions. Since the EU has been guided by a series of treaties, there was a demand to construct a formal constitution for Europe. Although proposing a new constitution was not easy due to cul-

European Union, 2008

Legend:
- European Union member
- Applying for European Union status

0 — 500 miles
0 — 500 km

N

ICELAND

ATLANTIC OCEAN

SWEDEN

NORWAY

FINLAND

RUSSIA

ESTONIA

LATVIA

LITHUANIA

RUSSIA

UNITED KINGDOM

DENMARK

BELARUS

IRELAND

NETHERLANDS

POLAND

UKRAINE

GERMANY

BELGIUM

CZECH REPUBLIC

SLOVAKIA

MOLDOVA

LUXEMBOURG

LIECHTENSTEIN

AUSTRIA

HUNGARY

ROMANIA

Black Sea

SWITZERLAND

SLOVENIA

FRANCE

CROATIA

MONACO

SAN MARINO

BOSNIA AND HERZEGOVINA

SERBIA

BULGARIA

MONTENEGRO

KOSOVO

MACE.*

PORTUGAL

SPAIN

ANDORRA

ITALY

ALBANIA

TURKEY

GREECE

Mediterranean Sea

CYPRUS

MALTA

* Former Yugoslav republic of Macedonia

© Infobase Publishing

tural and political factors, a draft of the constitution was ratified by the leaders of the member states in June 2004. It defines the main objectives as the advancement of peace, the union's values, and the well-being of its people. Compared to the U.S. CON-STITUTION as drafted in 1787, the EU constitution is a contract among the governments, whereas the American one is a contract between citizens and the government that defines the political, economic, and social values of both sides. While the American constitution is short and flexible, the EU constitution is long and extensively detailed.

The EU constitution uniquely combines confederalism and FEDERALISM while retaining its supranational nature. Within the confederal system, the central government derives its authority from two or more sovereign states. This government has no direct effect on the citizens of these states. An example of confederalism is the United States during the period from 1781 to 1788. The original 13 states formed an agreement known as the ARTICLES OF CONFEDERATION, or the League of Friendship. The role of the central government was to announce war and to approve treaties. However, it did not have the authority to impose taxation, amend articles, or endorse treaties without the consent of the 13 states. Likewise, the political system of the EU is weak relative to the power of the member states (national governments), and it has no direct relationship with ordinary citizens. The EU, therefore, has no higher authority above the national governments, but it has a higher sense of mutual trust and cooperation.

Several aspects of federalism also characterize the EU. The federal system is a political entity that is divided into two levels: central (national government) and local (states). Each level has independent functions in some areas but still shares common interests with the other level. The central government sets the foreign and security policy. The local states set policies such as education and land use. The federal regime is characterized by a directly elected central government, single currency, formal constitution, common military, supreme court, and common tax structure. The central government, thus, has direct relationship with the citizens at the local level. The present system of the United States is the best example of federalism. Although the central government of the United States has higher authority, it cannot amend the constitution without the consent of two-thirds of the states, change the number of senatorial representation, redefine the borders of the states, or change the tax policy of the states. Correspondingly, the EU cannot exercise central power over such issues. The federal scheme of the EU involves a single currency (the Euro), the ability to negotiate with non-European countries, the directly elected legislature in the European parliament, the application of common policies, and the supremacy of EU law over national law.

The EU has five major supranational institutions through which decisions are made. Although these institutions have governing power, they still do not resemble the domestic model of governments such as the U.S. government with its formal CHECKS AND BALANCES. Each of these institutions has its own organizational structure and functions.

The European Council is a legislative institution that makes broad policy decisions during its meetings. The meetings are held in Brussels twice a year for two-day summits. They are attended by prime ministers and ministers of foreign affairs of the member states and by the president of the European Commission and one of his or her vice presidents. Such meetings allow greater understanding of different member states' opinions and help in bringing them together before deciding certain policies.

The European Parliament is the most democratic institution within the EU framework. Its members (currently 732) are directly elected by European citizens for five-year renewable terms. They meet in Strasbourg each month excluding August. The Parliament is responsible for checking the activities of the other EU institutions. It meets biannually with the Council of Ministers to make joint decisions regarding budgetary issues and proposed amendments. The seats of the parliament are divided among the member states based on population.

The European Commission is an institution that resembles the cabinet of ministers at the national level. It is directed by a College of Commissioners, which currently consists of 25 members appointed by the governments of the member states. The members serve five-year terms, and one of them becomes a president for the commission. The key role of the members is to prepare proposals for new laws and policies and to ensure their enforcement. The commission's main office is in Brussels. Under the college, the commission has directorate-generals who play the role of bureaucrats.

The Council of Ministers is the major decision-making body of the EU. It has a colegislative role in conjunction with the European parliament. It consists of ministers from each member state who decide policies that are directly related to their ministries during their meetings in Brussels. It has nine subcouncils, each of which specializes in a particular policy area. Ministers (or secretaries) of agriculture, for example, have their own council known as the Agriculture Council. This institution also has the Council of Presidency that is held by ministers of the member states. The presidency council represents the EU at the international venue, organizes conferences, and sponsors cultural events. The Council of Ministers is also served by the Committee of the Permanent Representatives of the Member States, known as COREPER, which is run by civil staff.

The European Court of Justice, which parallels the U.S. SUPREME COURT in some ways, makes judgments regarding the implementation of national and EU laws. Such laws must be consistent with the EU treaties and reinforced in all the member states. The court looks over disputes concerning the EU institutions, the member states, and individuals. Nevertheless, it is not responsible for making decisions relative to the citizens' affairs, such as cases of criminal or family law. Its membership currently includes 25 appointed judges for six-year renewable terms; each represents a different member state. Through a majority vote, the judges elect a president for their institution from among themselves each three years.

The EU has undergone a series of expansions in its membership. It had 12 member states in 1992. This membership extended to include Finland, Austria, and Sweden in 1995. Thereafter, the EU membership was opened up to any European state that can prove capability to satisfy the membership conditions, known as the Copenhagen Criteria. In order to meet the conditions, the states must have democratic government, respect for human rights, adherence to the RULE OF LAW, a strong MARKET ECONOMY, and strong public administration. By the fulfillment of these criteria, Cyprus, the Czech Republic, Estonia, Hungary, Latvia, Lithuania, Malta, Poland, Slovakia, and Slovenia joined the EU in 2004. Romania and Bulgaria were granted membership in the EU in 2007, but Turkey was not. Further enlargement is expected to include countries within the Balkan region as long as they meet the membership requirements.

The process of enlargement entails some privileges to both old and new members. The new member states provide a larger market for western European products. The old member states, on the other hand, support the newer members financially (western investments and EU funding of social development).

Nonetheless, the membership of the eastern and central European countries entails several disadvantages for the older members. This is mainly because of the economic and cultural gap between both groups. The countries that are considered rich among the new members still remain poorer than the poorest old members. This heightens the concerns of the western members about the migration influx of unskilled laborers. Since most of the new members were communist, their embedded culture differs from the western one. This complicates the process of compromising the diverse opinions of the member states vis-à-vis certain policies.

EU CITIZENSHIP is automatically granted to any citizen of the member states. Although it does not add obligations to the citizens at the supranational level, it confers certain rights. Among these rights are the right to free movement within the EU territory (e.g., individuals are not subject to IMMIGRATION rules), to SOCIAL SECURITY, to fair payment for workers, and to participation in the electoral process of the European parliament. These rights require the national governments to treat citizens from other member states as equals to their own in the application of local policies. By the enjoyment of these political rights, citizens are able to take part in political decisions at the EU level. They participate in the national referendums by voting for whether to join the EU and whether to accept new treaties. They can also vote and run for candidacy for the European parliament. Voters must be 18 years old and must meet local requirements that differ from one state to another. The POLITICAL PARTICIPATION of the European citizens can also be indirect through the role of INTEREST GROUPS. Like American interest groups, European interest groups play an influential role in determining certain policies. They represent various societal interests that are concerned with issues such as the environment, business, and consumerism.

To advance the union's objectives and to face internal and external challenges, the European leaders (through the EU institutions) have set out joint policies in various fields. These policies are divided into three main areas called "pillars." The first pillar involves economic, social, and environmental policies. The second pillar concerns military and foreign policies. The last pillar consists of security policies. Regardless of their classifications, all these policies are of great advantage to EU citizens. Among these, the economic policies are the most vital and the first to be considered. The European single market, which has been in operation since 1993, is an impressive reflection of such policies. This market eliminates all the barriers to trade and the free movement of capital, goods, labor, and services within the member states so as to be able to compete with the international market and to promote economic growth. After the establishment of the single market in 1999, the European Central Bank introduced the Euro as a new currency in a policy known as monetary union. Since 2002, the euro has replaced the previous national currencies of 12 members (Belgium, Germany, Spain, France, Ireland, Italy, Luxembourg, the Netherlands, Austria, Portugal, Finland, and Greece). Along with the economic policies, other policies have been adopted to instill a sense of "shared European identity," such as the unified European passport and driver license. These are among many other successful policies.

The EU and the United States are major allies. The United States played a significant role in protecting the EU's security after World War II. It participated in the economic reconstruction process in Europe through its investments under the Marshall Plan. It also advocated the idea of the European Economic Community, and it was a defender of the western European states against the threat of Soviet invasion during the cold war. This protection was under the umbrella of the NORTH ATLANTIC TREATY ORGANIZATION (NATO). After the collapse of the Soviet Union, the first Bush administration adopted a New Transatlantic Agenda and Joint EU-US Action Plan, updated in 1995, to promote peace and DEMOCRACY in Europe and around the world and to expand world trade. Since then, biannual meetings are held between the presidents of the United States, the commission, and the European Council. The meetings are also held between EU foreign ministers and the U.S. secretary of state and between the commission and the U.S. cabinet members. Despite such strong ties, there is a growing demand in the American Congress to dissolve NATO. The rationale for this demand is grounded in the fact that the EU is now more united than ever before, and there is no longer a threat from the Soviet Union that requires American engagement. In Europe, on the other hand, there is

disagreement about U.S. FOREIGN POLICY in the Middle East. While Britain and eastern European members support the United States, others such as Germany and France disagree with the U.S. policy. Their concern is that the United States is endangering Europe (e.g., the Madrid train bombings). Such clashing views between the United States and the EU, nevertheless, should not take place since they both need each other to challenge the common threats of terrorism.

See also DIPLOMATIC POLICY.

Further Reading

Archer, Clive, and Fiona Butler. *The European Union: Structure and Process*. New York: St. Martin's Press, 1996; EUROPA. "Overviews of the European Activities: Enlargement."Available online. URL: http://europa.eu/pol/enlarg/overview_en.htm. Accessed January 9, 2007; Gerven, Walter. *The European Union: A Polity of States and Peoples*. Stanford, Calif.: Stanford University Press, 2005; McCormick, John. *Understanding the European Union*. New York: Palgrave, 2005; McGiffen, Steven. *The European Union: A Critical Guide*. Ann Arbor, Mich.: Pluto Press, 2005; Nugent, Neill. *The Government and Politics of the European Community*. Durham: University of North Carolina Press, 1991; Roney, Alex. *EC/EU Fact Book*. London: Kogan Page, 1998; Warleigh, Alex. *European Union the Basics*. New York: Routledge, 2004.

—Muna A. Ali

globalization

Globalization refers to the worldwide diffusion of modes of human culture, society, economic transactions, and politics and the greater interconnectedness of the world's peoples. It has become widely accepted that humanity has entered into a globalized era, indicating that the old division into a capitalist first world, a communist second world, and a developing third world no longer applies. Because it is a complex of different processes with a great capacity to unite, divide, and re-create all manner of human relationships and interactions, it is hard to judge whether its overall effects are benign or harmful, and in which ways. Both detractors and supporters of globalization can cite empirical evidence to bolster their claims—the former, the fact that the number of people living in poverty has not appreciably decreased, nor has the intensity of poverty, especially in rural areas and urban slums; the latter, the fact that aggregate economic data have been improving. However, the persistence of concentrations of immiseration, environmental degradation, disease, and other issues of human mortality all suggest that inequality of access to important resources remains the burden of peoples living in underdeveloped countries. The social, economic, political, and environmental consequences of contemporary globalization have already been deemed controversial yet are presently unknown. Some of the most significant questions surrounding globalization include whether it is, in truth, a new phenomenon; whether it threatens the traditional sovereignty of the nation-state and current international political practice; whether economic globalization is outpacing political globalization to the detriment of the world's poor; and identity issues such as whether social and cultural aspects of globalization are really Americanization or Westernization in disguise, thus remaking the world in the image of its dominant countries.

Globalization is not itself a new phenomenon when understood merely as the extension of long-standing patterns of interaction, albeit intensified and much more fluid, but nonetheless a quantitative and not a qualitative change. Human societies have interacted with one another often over great distances for most of recorded history, though in modern times globalization has seemed driven by predominant states, cultures, and ways of conducting business. Some international political economists argue that concerns about the negative effects of globalization are greatly exaggerated, by which is meant not merely that the beneficial effects far outweigh the negative, but that globalization is itself a misnomer because it is not at all something new but the logical outgrowth of patterns of interaction that began in premodern times. Furthermore, they argue that the greater the economic integration and the lesser the degree of political regulation, the better. But the political situation today is very different than it was during the mercantile era, for example, and calls to mind Aristotle's admonition that relations of trade are no substitute for political agreement and community.

The difference today is that the processes of globalization occurred in an international context largely determined in the wake of World War II, whereupon ensued a widespread agreement to attempt an international legal regime that extended basic human rights to all the world's peoples and to conduct affairs between nation-states peaceably, an effect that conditioned both superpowers during the cold war despite their stated mutual animosity. Economic integration might not even have reaped the benefits it so far has been able to were it not for the relatively peaceful, stable international system, politically speaking. By itself, an increase in commerce does not address those fundamentally divisive issues such as territorial and ethnic disputes that are arguably fed as much as abated by the accumulation of wealth on one or more sides of entrenched, historic disagreements. Globalization as the expansion of neoliberal ideology regarding economic policy recalls the old debate between followers of Adam Smith and Karl Marx, regarding whether the free market provides a sufficient form of social regulation and so makes politics irrelevant, and whether the free market will reach an exploitative zenith at which point it will be desirable to craft a global political regime encompassing all humanity to ensure that all peoples both contribute to it and are benefited by it. At present, widening trade liberalization has progressed alongside widening income disparities and ecological destruction.

Understood as increasing economic interactions across international borders undertaken by private entities rather than governments, the relevance of the nation-state is seen to be in decline. Globalization today is often regarded as posing a threat to the sovereignty of the nation-state, whereas earlier globalization can be said to have enhanced it, albeit at the expense of peoples not yet organized into recognizable states. Globalization is criticized by some because it seems to have displaced politics from the driver's seat in what counts in international affairs in favor of large corporations and their interests. By the 1990s, the economic turnover of several multinationals exceeded the gross national product of many states, calling into question the ability of those principally developing world states to control their own destiny. In addition, the control over resources such as oil and other vital commodities by multinational companies can be viewed as a new form of imperialism that threatens smaller nations' control over their domestic economies, making them vulnerable to world market fluctuations that they have little or no ability to control and diminishing their bargaining position. Likewise, in the absence of effective and enforceable INTERNATIONAL TRADE law, those large corporations that seem to have no specific country location outside of known off-shore tax havens may present resource, environmental, and other threats even to developed economies. In this context, developing world nations are dependent on already-established capital and financial markets, even as they attempt to use global communications and information networks to their advantage. The liberal-democratic inclinations of the evolving global order, however, have the potential to condition any runaway CAPITALISM and channel its benefits to the least advantaged, which are understood to have political and economic rights that ought to be recognized regardless of the capacity of any particular state to secure them.

Use of the term *globalization* to describe an interconnected world in which no corner of the globe has not been penetrated by the financial institutions and multinational corporations of the industrialized West became widespread during the 1990s. Globalization today is generally taken to be driven by the expansion of free market capitalism such as characterizes advanced industrial countries into the developing world, and it is generally criticized for occurring without the benefit of a political envelope or legal regime adequate to the task of managing events and multiple actors in the fast-paced environment of the international economy. Especially in the developing world, the imposition of economic restructuring has led to peasant dispossession and displacement, just as it has weakened states and lessened their ability to effect economic regulation to secure for themselves the benefits and profits of their own resources and industries.

One growing feature of globalization is the movement of peoples, whether they are professionals, refugees, migrant workers, or travelers, thus integrating habits of culture such as religion, art, and popular culture. The increasingly borderless aspect of the human community allows for a myriad of novel interactions and fusions, some of which are resisted in the name of local or regional traditions. The sociologist George Ritzer delineates two processes involved in globalization, which he terms grobalization and glocalization, each with its own subprocesses and characteristics. Grobalization, the globalization of forms of growth, is a complex of capitalism in financial affairs, Americanization in culture, and "McDonaldization" of workplaces, which seem geared toward enhancing the profit, power, and influence of nation-states and corporations in the already DEVELOPED COUNTRIES. Here, the global is driving out the local and replacing indigenous processes with nothing particularly special. Glocalization, the globalization of forms of local modes of human interaction, is characterized by diversity and stresses the local independence of persons, places, things, and services from global processes. Here, the local or regional is mixing with the global to produce unique hybrids that are dispersed to other areas of the globe. These two broad processes of globalization are resulting in both more uniformity across the globe and increased attention to a Western–non-Western divide in the case of grobalization and novel forms of human interaction in the case of glocalization. The notion of multiculturalism could be analyzed from both perspectives, as the growth of a heterogenous culture that has been contributed to by a variety of local, regional, and foreign cultures, yet a homogenous worldwide culture that looks pretty much the same anywhere. Globalization is producing both complexity and variety at the same time as it is producing commonality.

While through the ease of travel and the desperation for economic opportunity globalization has brought many peoples to the United States and individual Americans to all corners of the globe, it has also brought American and Western dominance to the rest of the world, a dominance in science and culture, for example, that may be as unwelcome as it is perceived to be threatening. To many, the United States represents the Western world and so has become the target of terrorist organizations that seek to abate its influence and maintain the dominance of non-Western ways, unfortunately through destructive acts facilitated by globalization, such as electronic networks of information, financial backers, and arms merchants. Power is no longer centralized in capital cities, and the importance of the center-periphery relationship within nation-states has been eclipsed by networks of power that increase people's capacity to access power, just as they increase a country's security vulnerabilities to the coercive use of power. Defense against aggression such as guerrilla attacks is a feature of daily life in many places, one that challenges traditional forms of governance, encourages new political alliances, and bolsters regional interdependencies.

It is unclear whether the diffusion of increasingly common habits of culture will produce a recognition of our common humanity and a political understanding to match that will benefit the world's peoples, especially those who at present are not able to contribute to the transformations but instead are being remade by them, if not ignored owing to their economic poverty, political oppression, or lack of interest in their situation for one reason or another. Perhaps globalization's interruptions of the ordinary, accepted, or longstanding, and multiplications of difference alongside uniformity in modes of human existence ultimately raise the most contentious sort of issue of all, identity. As even indigenous peoples are being challenged to get on board to at least have their economic activity conditioned by world demands and practices, just as those sorts of effects are increasingly perceived to present political and ethical challenges to inhabitants of the already developed countries, such as the thorny issue of sweatshops, national and other forms of identity are revealing themselves to be not as well settled as some have believed, but far more fluid and subject to conscious choice. This new space for freedom may be only slight in many cases, including places in the developed world already accustomed to certain lifestyles, prerogatives, expectations, and lacks of concern, but the potential is there for energetic supranational bodies and conscientiously chosen collective forms of determination that will work as an improvement of the human condition.

Further Reading

Bhagwati, Jagdish. *In Defense of Globalization.* Oxford: Oxford University Press, 2004; Dunning, John H., ed. *Making Globalization Good: The Moral Challenges of Global Capitalism.* Oxford: Oxford University Press, 2003; Pirages, Dennis Clark, and Theresa Manley DeGeest. *Ecological Security: An Evolutionary Perspective on Globalization.* Lanham, Md.: Rowman & Littlefield, 2004; Ritzer, George. *The Globalization of Nothing.* Thousand Oaks, Calif.: Pine Forge/Sage, 2004; Steger, Manfred B., ed. *Rethinking Globalism.* Lanham, Md.: Rowman & Littlefield, 2004; Wolf, Martin. *Why Globalization Works.* New Haven, Conn.: Yale University Press, 2004.

—Gordon A. Babst

international law

International law in the United States has undergone changes back and forth from a marginal role, to manipulation for reasons of national interest, to respect and observation. Policy makers have given radically different interpretations of what international law is depending on how or if they sought to use it in determining U.S. policy.

The U.S. CONSTITUTION includes specific mention of the "law of nations" in Article 1, Section 8, giving Congress power to "punish . . . offenses against the law of nations"; Article VI provides that treaties are the "supreme law of the land." Beginning in the 20th century, international law has been used in U.S. courts, often along with such statutes as the Alien Tort Claims Act of 1789 (used extensively by human rights advocates after the 1970s), and the Torture Victims Protection Act, enacted in 1992 . The Foreign Sovereign Immunities Act of 1976 was used by Congress to limit the immunities that foreign sovereigns could claim under international law.

At varying times, policy makers have called attention to the different sources of international law that are detailed in Article 38 (1) of the Statute of the International Court of Justice. These sources are international agreements, custom, general principles, and, as "subsidiary means" for international legal interpretation, judicial decisions and publicists' teachings. By Article 59 of the Statute, though, the court's own decisions are to be applied only to the particular case at issue and not to serve as PRECEDENTs. So unlike in U.S. courts, where judges must make decisions consistent with mandatory precedents, judges in the International Court of Justice are not similarly obligated.

How and whether analysts, advocates, and policy makers invoke international law depends on their approach to international relations. Advocates of liberal or idealist approaches argue that at its best that the United States fulfill a leadership role by invoking international law. Advocates of realist approaches argue that international law should have a limited role in U.S. FOREIGN POLICY and should be used only to the extent that it serves U.S. national interest, defined as power. Advocates of critical, world order approaches argue that the United States often narrowly interprets international law in its self-interest. The United States should conform to changing notions of what is required, notions established by an emerging civil society.

Law that is "international" is usually, but not always, distinguished as being between "states" with sovereignty over a population and territory. It may include agreements made in a region, or bilateral agreements binding two countries. It may be distinguished from "supranational" or "community" law, by which a higher organ can bind states. Terms such as *world* and *global* may describe envisioned orders that go beyond international law. "Domestic," or internal, law is often contrasted with international law, and "comparative" law examines internal relations of two or more states. "International" law is often designated as "public" or "private," connoting rules on cross-border, primarily commercial, transactions, often also designated "transnational law." A Hague Conference on Private International Law, first meeting in 1893, continues to deal with torts, contracts, trusts, and family legal matters. The remainder of this entry focuses on public international law. Public international law consists of formal and informal rules on war and peace, the environment, territory, human rights, the sea, and other matters.

Law means rules that go beyond morality, although compliance may come from reciprocal and voluntary agreements rather than from a central authority. The agreements may be written, for example treaties with provisions on "entry into force." The Vienna Convention on the Law of Treaties of 1969 (entry into force, 1980) is a "treaty on treaties" that sets forth rules usually also followed by nonparties. (As with the other treaties mentioned in this essay, the convention "entered into force" became legally binding on parties, only after gaining ratification by a prescribed number of parties. In the United States,

the EXECUTIVE BRANCH may "ratify" a treaty only after it has been approved in the SENATE by a two-thirds vote.)

Within the UNITED NATIONS, the International Law Commission seeks to codify (place in written form) unwritten understandings. Those understandings on matters ranging from ocean navigation to property rights reflect common obligations, not just common practices. International legal obligations may be reflected in general principles of law, for instance, that interpretation of treaties should assume an intention to obey them, and in the writings and teachings of scholarly analysts.

Most agreements made across boundaries involve economic enterprises and consist of private international law. Modern public international law includes overlapping fields: law of (and during) war, international criminal law, international economic law, human rights law, international environmental law, law of the sea, territorial law, humanitarian law, refugee law, economic law, and so forth.

Some accounts of public international law go back to before the Common Era and others to the origin of the European state system in the Treaty of Westphalia in 1648. Global changes with the creation of the United Nations in the mid-20th century and with economic and political GLOBALIZATION toward the end of the 20th century led to new ways of thinking about international law. Liberation movements and the emergence of "civil society" (characterized by nonprofit, nongovernmental actors) also challenge traditional conceptions of international law. The 20th and 21st centuries are replete with attempts to create international law. Many of the first institutions reflected Europe's world dominance; some advocates have sought to redress previous imbalances. The Hague Agreements in 1899 and 1907 brought together European and North American governments in controlling contemporary weaponry. Under the 1899 Hague Convention, the Permanent Court of Arbitration (PCA) was established at The Hague, Netherlands The PCA continues to provide arbitrators for disputes between states, with five cases pending as of July 2006. In 1921, the Permanent Court of International Justice was founded at The Hague under Article 14 of the Covenant of the League of Nations. The Pact of Paris, or Kellogg-Briand Pact, which outlawed war as an "instrument of national policy," was a product of the optimism of the period around the year of its adoption, 1928.

The outbreak of World War II resulted in pessimism about international legislation that was divorced from realities of power. Lawmaking through the United Nations, created in 1945, was greatly constrained by the cold war confrontation between the United States and the Soviet Union. Advocates of international legal solutions to world problems emphasized their appropriateness for the world as it ought to be, as opposed to the realities of national self-interest. A United Nations Convention on the Prevention and Punishment of the Crime of Genocide nevertheless entered into force in 1951, following adoption by the General Assembly in 1948. The United States did not ratify the agreement (an act by the executive branch following approval by two-thirds of the Senate) until 1989. A 1948 Universal Declaration of Human Rights was passed by the United Nations General Assembly. The International Covenant on Civil and Political Rights and the International Covenant on Economic, Social, and Cultural Rights were opened for signature in 1966 and entered into force shortly after receiving their 35th ratification in 1976. The Untied States ratified the Covenant on Civil and Political Rights in 1992. Genocide, war crimes, and crimes against humanity were dealt with in the Rome Statute for an International Criminal Court in 1998. The Rome Statute entered into force in 2002. Additional United Nations human rights agreements include, among others, the International Convention on the Elimination of All Forms of Racial Discrimination (passed by the General Assembly in 1966), the Convention on the Elimination on all Forms of Discrimination Against Women (1979), the Convention Against Torture and Other Cruel, Inhuman, or Degrading Treatment or Punishment (1984), and the Convention on the Rights of the Child (1989). The United States ratified the Racial Discrimination and Torture Convention but not the others. U. S. ratifications have come with reservations, by which countries agree to treaties "except for" certain provisions. Advocates of reservations contend that treaty observance is more likely if countries are able to restrict their commitments. Examples include U.S. reservations to the International Covenant on Civil and Political Rights regarding free speech, allowing for broader protection of racist and militarist speech than that given under the covenant, and broad application of the death penalty.

Regional international legal protections of human rights are strongest in Europe but also exist in the Americas and in Africa. All three continents have courts of human rights. The United States and Canada are not parties to the American Convention on Human Rights, although cases involving the United States have been brought by the Inter-American Human Rights Commission. The United States is a member of the Organization of American States and therefore subject to decisions of the commissioners.

The United States was initially a major proponent of United Nations efforts to govern the ocean. Conventions emerged from successive United Nations Conferences on the Law of the Sea. These included the 1958 Geneva Conventions on the High Seas (entry into force, 1962), Territorial Sea, and Continental Shelf (both of which entered into force in 1964), and the 1982 Law of the Sea Treaty (entered into force, 1994). The United States is a party to the 1958 treaties but is not a party to the 1982 Law of the Sea treaty. The 1982 treaty includes an International Tribunal for the Law of the Sea, located in Hamburg, Germany, to settle disputes among parties. International environmental law includes a very successful ozone regime, including a treaty and later protocols with ever-stricter regulations on the production of ozone. A 1992 United Nations Framework Climate Change Convention (UNFCC; entry into force, 1994) seeks to regulate global warming, with specific guidelines set forth in a 1997 Kyoto Protocol (entry into force, 2005). The United States is a party to the convention but not to the protocol. Many of the environmental agreements, such as the UNFCC and Kyoto Protocol, are reviewed at periodic conferences of the parties.

International criminal law was administered after World War II at war crimes tribunals in Nuremberg and Tokyo, a major advance from attempts in Constantinople and Leipzig to prosecute war criminals after World War I. Subsequent tribunals have dealt with Rwanda, the former Yugoslavia, and Sierra Leone. In 1998, countries gathered in Rome to approve the Statute for an International Criminal Court. It did not permit reservations. In 2002, the Rome Statute entered into force. The United States is not a party.

An as yet uncompleted section of the Rome Statute will deal with aggression. Governments have been unable to agree on the relation to aggression of related terms such as terrorism, wars of national liberation, and preemptive war. Much of international law deals with whether countries are justified in going to war (*jus ad bello*) and the conduct of war (*jus in bellum*). Some uses of force have generally been legally permitted, especially when in self-defense or multilateral use of force, but others, such as preemptive war, are heavily criticized by international lawyers. Because of the growing importance of human rights law, some advocates would create an exception to prohibitions on the use of force for humanitarian intervention, but most lawyers and policy makers are skeptical.

U.S. officials have questioned the value of international law in promoting human rights and whether it serves U.S. interests. After the events of September 11, 2001, domestic and international critics of the George W. Bush administration charged the United States with widespread violations of international law. Administration supporters argued that an international war on terrorism justified curtailment of international human rights commitments.

Increasingly, international organizations, nongovernmental organizations, and individuals have been involved in the international legal process. States remain the primary actors, and the United Nations is structured around a leading role for states. But the emergence of a global civil society, whereby individuals associate across national boundaries, poses challenges to the state system. The challenges are evident in some applications of international law, such as nongovernmental tribunals (the Bertrand Russell and Permanent Peoples' Tribunal) and globalization whether from popular forces or from commercial interests.

See also RULE OF LAW.

Further Reading

Bartholomew, Amy, ed. *Empire's Law: The American Imperial Project and the "War to Remake the World"*. London; Pluto Press, 2006; Buergenthal, Thomas, and Murphy, Sean D. *Public International Law in a Nutshell*. St. Paul, Minn.: West Group, 2002; D'Amato, Anthony, and Jennifer Abbassi. *International Law Today: A Handbook*. Eagan, Minn.: Thomson-West, 2006; Glendon, Mary Ann. *A World Made New: Eleanor Roosevelt and the Universal Declaration of Human Rights*. New York: Random House, 2001; Joyner, Christopher. *International Law in the 21st Century: Rules for Global Governance*. Lanham, Md.: Rowman & Littlefield, 2005; Schulte, Constanze. *Compliance with Decisions of the International Court of Justice*. Oxford: Oxford University Press, 2004; Von Glahn, Gerhard, and L. Taulbee James. *Law among Nations: An Introduction to Public International Law*. 8th ed. Upper Saddle River, N.J.: Longman, 2006.

—Arthur W. Blaser

International Monetary Fund (IMF)

The International Monetary Fund (IMF), WORLD BANK, WORLD TRADE ORGANIZATION (WTO), and a handful of similar institutions have experienced unprecedented visibility recently, and these once obscure and relatively unfamiliar yet pivotal players in world economic affairs have become known even to those with no interest in finance and economics. During the past decade or so, the common association of the IMF with GLOBALIZATION initiatives has exposed the organization to unprecedented scrutiny from individuals and groups that had traditionally cared very little about the IMF and related institutions. Unfortunately, the politicization of globalization efforts and the associated resistance to those efforts from many circles has attracted controversy over the perceived role of the IMF in the global economy. Much of that controversy is fueled by misconceptions and propaganda intended to undermine liberalization initiatives around the world, and it has contributed to a widely misleading picture of what the IMF actually does and the power it has.

The IMF and some of its companion organizations were created from the agreements that emerged out of the Bretton Woods Conference during the last stages of World War II. Although this gathering of world leaders was a manifestation of broader plans to establish and secure geopolitical stability on conclusion of the war, its purposes and focus were rooted in problems that were unrelated to the war itself. The Bretton Woods Conference sought to address the financial instabilities and macroeconomic deficiencies of national, regional, and global systems that produced and perpetuated the financial and economic crises of the interwar period. More broadly, this meeting was a response to the structural and cyclical dislocations and transformations caused by mass industrialization and the consequent need to confront the inadequacies of pre-Keynesian solutions for the dilemmas of industrialization.

Above all, the Bretton Woods agreements were based on the conviction that conflict is avoidable through the facilitation of international economic cooperation and increased prosperity throughout the globe and that, therefore, the removal or gradual reduction of barriers to free and stable exchange is paramount. On the whole, the participants endorsed capitalist economic principles, though they disagreed regarding the proper level of state intervention and control over economic and financial mechanisms. Nevertheless, a consensus did exist concerning the Keynesian realization that industrialized economies require at least some degree of macroeconomic management and that the structural vulnerabilities of industrialized and industrializing nations must be remedied in some manner. In part, since domestic economic and financial stability was, among other things, a function of international economic and financial stability, domestic structural weaknesses would be countered through international processes established to pursue the above goals.

Despite the overarching economic objectives that animated all Bretton Woods negotiations and determinations, the primary reason for the existence of the IMF stems from financial concerns. The IMF's companion organizations, such as the World Bank Group, were conceived as a more direct reaction to economic priorities, particularly the needs of developing and structurally deficient economies, but the IMF sought to devise a methodology and set of mechanisms through which financial stability and cooperation, and especially currency viability, could be promoted and maintained. In fact, though the IMF's mission is broadly devoted to the implementation of free trade principles and politicoeconomic liberalization policies around the globe, its practical focus has been confined to the oversight, management, and regulation of currencies and the control of factors that ensure currency viability and financial stability.

As such, its principal areas of activity include financial supervision and assessment through which the IMF evaluates the capabilities, effectiveness, and performance of member and nonmember entities; lending and structural aid through currency support programs and financial liberalization efforts; and technical facilitation through training, knowledge management, and infrastructural development of many sorts. It is the second of these, financial restructuring and currency intervention, that has attracted so much notoriety among critics of globalization for its apparent advocacy of U.S. interests and Western cultural priorities. Regardless of its political connotations, this area of responsibility seems inherently driven by Western norms due to the assumptions upon which the IMF was founded, so criticisms such as the one above seem irrelevant.

The IMF is a large organization with headquarters in Washington, D.C., and a current subscription of 185 states, each of which has a seat on the board of governors. It is headed by a managing director, who serves a five-year term and answers to a 24-member executive board. Since 2004, the managing director has been Rodrigo de Rato of Spain, but he is expected to resign before his term expires. All too often, not least because of the relative size of the American subscription quota and the resulting influence the United States has over other members, managing directors have been viewed as the hand-picked representatives of the American government, although no American has ever served as the managing director of the IMF. Despite the manifest U.S. impact on the shaping of IMF policy and its organizational governance, the extent and effectiveness of any resulting influence over other members has frequently been overstated by the IMF's critics.

The IMF frequently works very closely with the World Bank and other development based organizations, but its mandate is largely limited to the stabilization of currencies and financial systems. Through loans and other forms of assistance to countries with substantial financial problems, the IMF attempts to restore, establish, or maintain sustainable, feasible, and equitable exchange rates in international markets. It monitors current-account relationships among member states and facilitates favorable balance of trade in regional and global markets. Although its lending programs and currency measures are mostly concerned with the financial aspects of domestic and international stability, intervention and assistance is normally contingent on structural reforms in target countries. However, it is important to remember that the IMF's involvement with development, though significant in particular regards, is secondary to its primary purpose of financial stabilization through the management of currencies and current accounts.

Some scholars have argued that the effective collapse of the Bretton Woods system precipitated by the abandonment of the gold standard in 1971 rendered the IMF all but irrelevant and that, therefore, its existence is problematic if not utterly unnecessary. The Bretton Woods system was based on an adherence to a fixed exchange rate mechanism, so the transition to a floating mechanism would indeed seem to undermine the viability of an organization whose major tasks were rooted in the desire to protect an established system of fixed exchange rates. Nonetheless, if the mission of the IMF is considered more broadly within the context of general financial stability and the structures required to maintain that stability, then the so-called collapse of the Bretton Woods system merely requires a reorientation of specific policy objectives to meet the demand of a mission that has remained mostly consistent throughout the last 60 years, the stabilization and coordination of world financial markets and currencies in order to promote an internationally viable financial system that promotes efficiency through balance and sustainability of trade, payments, and capital.

As has been true of the World Bank, the IMF has underwritten projects throughout the globe, especially in regions that are underdeveloped or experiencing serious structural difficulties, so it has been labeled by its critics a tool of Western expansionism and a supporter of the exploitation of DEVELOPING COUNTRIES by the industrialized world. To be fair, it must be admitted that the relationship between the IMF and the debtor states it assists in the developing world is intrinsically imbalanced, not least due to the economic and diplomatic leverage, to say nothing of military might, Western countries possess. In addition, the financial aid disbursed by the IMF does come with the proverbial strings, so that recipients of IMF financial largesse are often compelled to consider pro-Western structural reforms as the essential condition for assistance.

These observations notwithstanding, it would be altogether illogical and unwarranted to conclude that the causal links between assistance and restructuring are questionable or invalid. This essay is neither a defense nor a rejection of the IMF and its practices, so the debate between proglobalization and antiglobalization forces concerning the IMF should be resolved elsewhere, but the fact that the functional logic of the IMF depends on its ability to endorse and implement pro-Western capitalist norms cannot be forgotten. So people should not be surprised to discover that the IMF conditions its willingness to engage in specific projects on the reciprocal willingness of target states to implement those structural initiatives that will maximize the probability of success for IMF-sponsored projects. From a historical perspective, with respect to the definition and fulfillment of normative criteria, the IMF has always been an unashamedly Western club, and it has succeeded, at least in part, due to its commitment to that reality.

Further Reading
Federal Reserve Bulletin. Available online. URL: www.federalreserve.gov/pubs/bulletin/default.htm. Accessed July 2, 2007; Cesarano, Fillippo. *Monetary Theory and Bretton Woods.* New York: Cambridge University Press, 2006; Gilpin, Robert. *The Political Economy of International Relations.* Princeton, N.J.: Princeton University Press, 1987; Krugman, Paul. *Pop Internationalism.* Cambridge, Mass.: MIT Press, 1997; Udell, Gregory F. *Principles of Money, Banking, and Financial Markets.* New York: Addison Wesley Longman, 1999; Woods, Ngaire. *The Globalizers.* Ithaca, N.Y.: Cornell University Press, 2006.
—Tomislav Han

international trade

The famous French historian Ferdinand Braudel once noted: "No civilization can survive without mobility: all are enriched by trade and the stimulating impact of strangers." Indeed, international trade is as old as ancient history. Despite ups and downs, international trade has continued to grow throughout history. In 2005, total world merchandise trade was more than $10 trillion, accounting for nearly 20 percent of the total economic product of the world. The U.S. share of world exports in 2005 was 8.7 percent, and

WORLD MERCHANDISE TRADE (2005)

	Exports $ Million	Percentage of Total	Imports $ Million	Percentage of Total
World	10,392,567	100	10,652,542	100
Low-Income Countries	256,378	2.5	310,841	2.9
Middle-Income Countries	2,785,199	26.8	2,551,288	24
High-Income Countries	7,351,037	70.7	7,790,420	73.1
United States	904,289	8.7	1,732,706	16.3

the import share was 16.3 percent. The table above summarizes world trade. However, international economic exchange is larger than these numbers, which do not show foreign direct investment or the trade in services. The latter includes trade in intangible products such as banking, tourism, telecommunications, and exchange of professional services. Including trade in services would add another $2.4 trillion to world trade.

Economics presents trade purely in terms of an exchange of goods and services and its effects on the standards of living for people. However, religious, political, moral, and other sociocultural considerations have always been important in elevating or diminishing trade. One way of understanding these cultural considerations is to make explicit how trade is linked to everyday life and the cultural identity of people.

Trade is a natural component of human interactions. A few Greek and Roman writers understood the sea to be a way of promoting human interactions and facilitating commercial exchanges. The modern belief that interaction and exchange underlie prosperity and peace can then be traced back to such ideas. The late 18th-century political economist Adam Smith's notion of division of labor laid the basis of prosperity through trade inasmuch as he opined that gains from economic exchange accrue to those who specialize in producing things for which they are most suited. These ideas from the late 18th century formed the basis of doctrines of comparative advantage in trade in the 19th century. Similarly, political theorists had begun to argue that as nations exchanged goods, they would be less likely to go to war with each other.

This is best captured in French writer Frederick Bestiat's words that if trade does not cross frontiers, armies will.

But the case against trade is also made in economic and cultural terms. The economic rationale against trade rests on the thesis that economic specialization can make some nations too dependent on others or can result in an unequal exchange whereby one benefits at the cost of another. Cultural arguments against trade are many; the earliest ones were moral and philosophical. To the Greeks we owe the term *xenophobia*, or fear and dislike of foreigners. Christianity in general decried the profit motive that underlies commerce and trade. It was not until the modern era that such cultural notions regarding trade were questioned, but these arguments continue to be made. Trade wars are often portrayed in negative terms. Take, for example, the overly xenophobic tones in the United States against trade surpluses of East Asian countries. Many in the United States have fretted and fumed over Japanese trade surpluses from the mid-1970s to the mid-1990s, Chinese trade surpluses since the mid-1990s, and more recently the controversies regarding outsourcing of jobs to India. Fueling these controversies are numbers, such as the ones shown in the table above, where the total exports from the United States are $904 billion and imports are $1,733 billion, resulting in a merchandise trade deficit of $828 billion. But this trade deficit is reduced with the U.S. trade surplus on services and its earnings from its foreign enterprises. For example, around 25 percent of the total stock of foreign direct investment in the world comes from U.S. multinational corporations, which generate enormous amounts of earnings for the country. However, foreign direct investment is usually not considered part of international trade.

Historically, countries flip-flop between participating actively in international trade and following more inward-oriented strategies. In the 1800s, the United States did not actively participate in international trade, preferring instead to develop a manufacturing industry in New England. This led to a domestic conflict in the country whereby the Republican Northeast of the country supported protectionism in trade, while the cotton-producing South and the corn-producing Midwest supported free trade. This factored into the Civil War (1861–65) that ensued between the North and South, though the major issue in the war was abolition of SLAVERY. After the Civil War, a fall in navigation costs and improvements in agricultural technologies further made the United States quite competitive in agriculture. Cheap corn exports to Italy, for example, threw hundreds of thousands of Italian farmers out of jobs, accounting, in turn, for the first wave of Italian IMMIGRATION to the United States.

In the 20th century, the United States strengthened its export profile with manufactured exports, but two world wars, the interwar years, and the Great Depression were not favorable to trade. Nevertheless, it was at this time, unlike in the 19th century, that the United States began to express explicitly a preference for trade and also link it to causes of international peace. The famous Fourteen Principles (Points) espoused by President Woodrow Wilson before Congress in 1918 included freedom of the seas and free trade as steps toward international peace. President Franklin Roosevelt's secretary of state, Cordell Hull between the years of 1933 and 1944, was another strong advocate of free trade and, in a Wilsonian vein, believed it to be a force of world peace. Hull also supported the moves for the foundation of the UNITED NATIONS in 1945.

At the end of World War II, as the global community went about designing international institutions, the need for creating one on international trade was led by the United States. The General Agreement on Tariffs and Trade (GATT) was the de facto international trade institution created at the Havana Summit in 1947 by the 26 nations that met there. It is believed to have been enormously influential in boosting international trade. Between 1947 and 1994, GATT undertook eight rounds of multilateral trade talks among its member states to reduce tariffs or customs barriers. Starting with the Tokyo Round of 1974 to 1978, GATT also undertook reductions in nontariff barriers (NTBs) among nations. These NTBs included nontransparent trade laws, quotas and other quantitative restrictions, subsidies paid to domestic producers, and discriminatory government procurement practices.

GATT's Uruguay Round of trade talks, lasting eight years between 1986 and 1994, was important both for bringing new issues into the international trade agenda and also for strengthening GATT itself. Transforming GATT into the WORLD TRADE ORGANIZATION (WTO), which came into being in 1995, effected the latter. The WTO was given some teeth by the formation of a formal dispute settlement body to adjudicate and settle trade disputes among countries. The new issues pushed by the United States revealed the sources of the country's competitive advantage in the world. This included trade in services led by U.S. exports of telecommunications, banking, airline, hotels, and professional services. U.S. corporations also pushed for and received protections for intellectual property. The latter can be defined as creations of the human mind that go into the manufacture of any product. Intellectual property protections include patents, copyrights, and trademarks. The primary concern for the United States was global piracy of its products, ranging from luxury goods (such as fashion) to music and film videos.

The ninth round of multilateral trade talks is the one currently underway since November 2001, known as the Doha Round. However, at the time of this writing it has been slow going, chiefly because of factors within the United States and western Europe. In the United States, Congress has been under tremendous pressure from domestic agriculture and some manufacturing sectors to not allow any more tariff and nontariff reductions. These sectors now believe that the United States would lose jobs and that net gains would be little through further liberalization. The U.S. CONSTITUTION gives Congress the right to ratify trade treaties (Article I, Section 6). Even though historically U.S. presidents have favored free trade, Congress, in response to the local interests of its constituencies, has been more protectionist. While Congress has ratified all trade treaties submitted by the president, the fate of the Doha Round, even if it were to be concluded, remains uncertain.

Opposition to trade has also built up in other parts of the world. The EUROPEAN UNION (EU), which represents 25 European countries at the WTO, has dug in its heels on farm subsidies paid to farmers through an enormously entrenched measure called the Common Agricultural Policy (CAP). Despite calls to dismantle CAP, EU countries such as France, Austria, and Poland with powerful farm lobbies remain opposed. In mid-2006, the EU agreed to eliminate all farm subsidies by 2013, but since then there has been a lot of backpedaling.

Meanwhile, the developing world remains divided over the issue of trade. Historically, the developing world favored protectionism in seeking to boost its own industries and reach self-sufficiency. Nevertheless, by the late 1980s, it hesitatingly began to move in the direction of free trade. Since then a few countries such as Brazil, Argentina, and China have more or less embraced free trade, while smaller and poorer countries continue to seek preferential access to their products abroad while limiting their imports. The developing world's free trade coalition is made up of a group of nearly 20 countries (called the G20), while the other countries from Africa, the Caribbean, and the Pacific make up the APC, or G90. There are other groups as well. For example, a group of four African countries (Benin, Burkina Faso, Chad, and Mali—the G4) has asked the United States since 2003 to stop subsidizing its cotton producers, who keep the price of cotton artificially low in the United States and hurt cotton exports from the G4.

There have also been vehement protests against free trade from various other groups. As mentioned, the developing world remains ambivalent and divided on free trade. Furthermore, many labor, environment, and human rights groups argue that the competitiveness among nations, which forms the basis of trade, also dilutes labor and environmental standards as countries "race to the bottom" to reduce costs. The Doha Round was, in fact, supposed to be Seattle Round starting in 1999. However, protests in Seattle from advocacy groups delayed the start of the round.

Despite the slowdown in the Doha Round, world trade continues to grow. Between 2000 and 2005,

world exports of merchandise grew by 10 percent, far greater than the growth in national incomes. This leads economists to believe that not only will trade not diminish in the future but that it will also lead to economic growth. International trade rules such as those negotiated through GATT and WTO can facilitate the cause of trade, but negotiating these rules takes political will that has been forthcoming much more slowly in recent years. Ironically, international trade has grown despite the political slowdown.

Further Reading

Destler, I.M. *American Trade Politics*. 4th ed. Washington, D.C.: Institute for International Economics, 2005; Friedman, Thomas L. *The World Is Flat: A Brief History of the Twenty-First Century*. New York: Farrar, Straus & Giroux, 2005; Irwin, Douglas A. *Against the Tide: An Intellectual History of Free Trade*. Princeton, N.J.: Princeton University Press, 1996; Singh, J. P. *Negotiation and the Global Information Economy*. Cambridge: Cambridge University Press, 2008; Wolf, Martin. *Why Globalization Works*. New Haven, Conn.: Yale University Press, 2004; World Trade Organization. *World Trade Report 2007*. Geneva: World Trade Organization, 2007.

—J. P. Singh

liberal democracy

Liberal democracy is the basis for representative government that allows civil society, the economy, and political culture to evolve while maintaining transparent regulatory and administrative control for the provision of political goods: public order, public health, public welfare, institutions of JUSTICE, a free press, and the education of citizens. Citizens in liberal democracies assert vertical accountability in periodic elections for those who govern. Ideally, the renewal of leadership flows in this way from the society at large.

Liberal democracies also maintain horizontal accountability across centers of power to prevent institutions of governance from encroaching on one another and on the civil and political liberties of their citizens. Clear examples of horizontal accountability exist in the CHECKS AND BALANCES among the three branches of government enshrined in the U.S. CONSTITUTION and reflected in the workings of the federal government. The U.S. Congress's enormous power in authorizing and appropriating government funds is subdivided by specific functions reserved to the House of Representatives and the Senate. The president's power resides in the ratification or vetoing of legislation and in the control over the executive agencies of government. The U.S. Supreme Court determines if the laws of Congress or the actions of the president conform to the Constitution.

Liberal democracy in different states balances the power of government and civil society in ways reflecting the history and culture. The Republic of China, on Taiwan, maintains five branches of government (the executive, legislative, judicial, control, and examination yuan). Most parliamentary systems maintain a combined legislative-executive branch and a separate judiciary. All feature open processes for the redress of grievances administratively or before courts of law.

In liberal democracies, self-replicating, self-sustaining civil society institutions aggregate political and economic power to advance and defend the interests of their constituents. Examples include political parties, labor unions, and a myriad of associations at the national, municipal, and local levels. These institutions exert vertical and horizontal accountability and are subject to it themselves through internal regulation and accountability local and national law.

Liberal democracies generally recognize as the basis for international and domestic legitimacy of governments a respect for the civil and political liberties of citizens, regular elections in which candidates freely compete for the right to hold power, the rule of law (including an independent judiciary, codification of law, representation, and access for citizens sufficient to allow redress of grievances), and formal consent of the governed to those who govern, which can be granted and revoked in cycles of change not involving a resort to force or coercion.

Political scientist Robert Dahl lists the institutions required for liberal democracies to function: elected officials; free, fair, and frequent elections; freedom of expression; alternative sources of information; associational autonomy; and inclusive citizenship. Failure in any one of these institutions puts liberal democracy at risk, and the resolution of societal tensions and conflicts is thrown from the arena of regular and established procedures into contests of arms and other coercive means.

Not all democracies are liberal. Some maintain the forms of democratic governance but restrict citizens' rights to assembly, association, free expression, full participation in the electoral process by opposition parties or candidates, or the independence of the judiciary. These are commonly known as illiberal or electoral democracies. The rulers constrain vertical accountability exercised by the citizens on the government. In contrast, autocracies (authoritarian, totalitarian, or mixed regimes including oligarchies and monarchies) do not use electoral processes to choose leaders and actively suppress freedoms of assembly, association, and speech.

The following surveys and reports provide objective criteria for evaluating contemporary governments to determine whether a particular state qualifies as a liberal democracy: *Country Reports on Human Rights Practices*, submitted annually by the U.S. Department of State to Congress, examines internationally recognized individual, civil, political, and worker rights as proscribed in the United Nations Universal Declaration of Human Rights; *Freedom in the World*, issued annually by Freedom House, provides accurate summaries of the status of civil and political liberties on a country-by-country basis, with a scoring system for ready comparisons; *Handbook on Democracy Assessment*, produced by the International Institute for Democracy and Electoral Assistance, provides a methodology for assessing conditions of democracy and progress toward democratization; and *Index of Economic Freedom*, prepared and maintained online by the Heritage Foundation and the *Wall Street Journal*, provides objective criteria for measuring economic freedom in 161 countries.

Liberal democracy emerged from the European Enlightenment of the 18th century propelled by three competing and often conflicting strands of political thought: democratic, republican, and liberal. These principles shaped habits of mind in the political culture of the British colonies in North America and eventually across Europe for checking the accretion of centralized power, maximizing individual liberty, protecting the rights of minorities, and opening opportunities for the accumulation of personal wealth.

The ideal of citizens having a voice in the affairs of state and an obligation to advance their views in public originated in the *demos* (Greek for "people") of the Greek city-state (621 B.C. to 100 B.C.). The ideal of duty expressed in self-sacrificing public service by elites under the rule of law emerged in the commonwealth of Rome (250 B.C. to 27 B.C.). The Roman insistence on martial valor, no individual or institution standing above the law, and disciplined, self-sacrificing service to the state as the heart of the republican ideal (*res publica* is Latin for "public things") proved difficult to sustain. However, the historical appeal of a *pax Romana* (Latin for "Roman peace") based on republican virtues remained a guiding political principle from the fall of Rome (A.D. 464) to the modern period.

The sovereignty of an individual combined with protection of PROPERTY RIGHTS under contracts enforceable by law emerged during the European Enlightenment of the 18th century as LIBERALISM. The inspiration for the American and French Revolutions can be found in the political thought inherited from ancient Greece and Rome and the writings of JOHN LOCKE, Baron de Montesquieu, Jean Jacques Rousseau, and others. The American DECLARATION OF INDEPENDENCE (1776) against the British Crown proclaims "Life, Liberty, and the Pursuit of Happiness" as inalienable rights. These sentiments echoed in the rallying cry "Liberté, Egalité, Fraternité," and in the Rights of Man (1789) written during the French Revolution against the tyrannies of an unrestrained MONARCHY.

The intellectual revolutions of the 17th and 18th centuries laid the social groundwork for enforceable CONTRACT LAW and the political revolutions to follow. Liberal legal and political innovations made the engines of commerce available to harness scientific inquiry and drive the industrial and technological revolutions of the 19th century. The harnessing of social, political, and economic energy to state enterprises led to the consolidation of the European nation-state and drove British imperial expansion and eventually European colonization of technologically less-advanced African, Asian, and Middle Eastern cultures in the 18th and 19th centuries.

Ironically, this forced opening of non-Western cultures to the political, economic, and social influences of Europe led directly to the planetwide, revolutionary mid–20th–century decolonizations. The intellectual currents underlying the explosive democratizations of the late 20th century also trace their origins to this marriage of liberal social, political, and economic thought in the European Enlightenment.

In the late 20th century, exponential growth occurred in the number of governments formally and regularly accountable to their citizens. Samuel Huntington of Harvard University calculates three waves of democratization. The first rose from the American and French Revolutions and crested in the 1920s with some 30 countries, which declined to a dozen by 1942. The second wave rose and crested following World War II with 30 democracies or so, and then the number fell back.

A global tipping point was apparently reached in the mid-1970s with the revolution in Portugal against the Salazar dictatorship's failed colonial policies and domestic oppression. The third wave of democratization was broad and deep, cresting in the mid-1990s with more than 120 democracies in the world out of 190 nation-states. The fall of the Berlin Wall in 1989 marked the collapse of Marxism as the "last" ideological contender for social and political organization on the planet.

By 2005, 60 percent of the population of the planet lived under governments "produced by some form of open, fair, and competitive elections." Of the remaining 40 percent of humankind, nearly 80 percent live in the People's Republic of China and the rest in a swath of autocratic states across the Middle East and North Africa, Central Asia, and sub-Saharan Africa. Isolated Marxist regimes hold on in Cuba, the People's Democratic Republic of Korea (North Korea), and former republics of the Soviet Union. Some of these countries show signs of economic reform and perhaps early indicators of democratic development.

Liberal democracies distinguish themselves from states organized along other principles by their performance in the delivery of political goods. Liberal democracies enjoy higher rates of gross domestic product per capita, better infrastructure, greater social mobility, longer life spans, higher literacy rates and notably higher rates of female literacy, and correspondingly lower rates of infant mortality and persecution of minorities. Liberal democracies experience no famines or wars with other liberal democracies.

The empirical evidence of the comparative performance underscores the attentiveness given by elected officials to their voting constituencies compared to officials not subject to vertical accountability.

Authorities who seize power by extraconstitutional means or by subverting periodic and inclusive elections become isolated from citizens' concerns and insulated from the requirements for delivery of political goods. Often, resources to develop the economy or address social welfare concerns of citizens are diverted to private accounts or squandered on ill-considered schemes of aggrandizement or expansion. The further authorities remove themselves from direct accountability of voters, the greater the likelihood that inappropriate rent seeking, cronyism, and other forms of CORRUPTION will arise. Treating the state as a personal preserve even led some autocrats to assert the prerogatives of monarchy and bequeath their children political power (e.g., in Syria Hasan to Hasan, in North Korea Kim to Kim, in Iraq Hussein to Hussein, and in Egypt Mubarak to Mubarak). Finally, extraconstitutional regime changes compound the relative performance failures of autocracies by despoiling infrastructure, lives, and the wealth of the state.

Liberal democracy does not represent a panacea for the human condition but an administrative and regulatory mechanism that allows citizens a greater voice in government. Several autocratic governments in the mid and late 20th century using command economies (autarkies) proved capable of delivering high standards of public health, economic growth, and comparatively high rates of literacy. But the relative performance advantage of liberal democracy across all measures of human well-being settled for many the historical debate over organizing principles for human society.

"The End of History" metaphor proposed by Francis Fukuyama in his June 1989 article in *The National Interest* generated enormous confusion about the status of liberal democracy and future world order. Fukuyama stated that the Western concept of history as a dialectic between the forces of order and LIBERTY had come to an end with the collapse of Marxism and the resounding triumph of the West in the cold war. He never discounted the possibility of new wars, new social or religious movements, or even the reassertion of the forces of order in the future.

Fukuyama noted that healthy social orders require change and even pointed to the emergence of violent movements against oppressive governments and even liberal democracies should they fail in the delivery of political goods.

Jack Snyder and Harvey Mansfield demonstrated the cycle of political maturation for new democracies in their seminal work *Democratization and War*. The primitive politics of transitional democracies can drive elites to lowest-common-denominator appeals to win elections. Xenophobic or exclusionary election campaigns quickly turn into aggressive domestic and foreign policies. This phenomenon continues until voters abandon politicians who exploit primitive sentiment for those who articulate more realistic and attainable policies.

As the political culture matures, politicians who run for office on familial or cultural-linguistic ties begin to lose out to those who have the capacity to address broader segments of the population. Picking up garbage, organizing effective schools, delivering health care and other public services, and providing economic opportunity begin to gain traction in electoral campaigns and become more important than the passions of identity politics or manufactured threats of exploitation by "outsiders." Inclusive rather than exclusionary appeals win out.

Institutional failures or security challenges can overwhelm the capacity of an emerging government and literally collapse the state. Iraq and Afghanistan show the magnitude of security challenges that arise in transitions. In addition, political elites enjoy steep learning curves if the new democracy survives the early elections.

Liberal democracy manifested in representative government should be viewed as a self-sustaining, self-replicating system for the evolution of political culture. Regular elections on the African continent illustrate beneficent cycles of change, that occur even in the partially articulated institutions of less-developed countries. Steffan Linberg in *Democracy and Elections in Africa* shows that "Repeated elections—regardless of their relative freeness or fairness—appear to have a positive impact on human freedom and democratic values . . ." by linking elections and CIVIL LIBERTIES in the minds of voters and those officials charged with the administration of electoral processes. It is reasonable to assume that these phenomena occur in all states transitioning to democracy: Citizens become voters; democratic mechanisms begin to "lock in" as citizens believe they have a vested interest in the government; more citizens and political leaders accept and play by the democratic rules, thus becoming a self-fulfilling prophecy; civic organizations become stronger by providing protection of CIVIL RIGHTS and CIVIL LIBERTIES; law enforcement and judicial officials are given a formal role in the protection of political rights; and the MEDIA begin to play a new role as a "transmitters" for prodemocratic messages.

Liberal democracy generates representative governments that deliver political goods while engendering broader tolerance, understanding, compromise, and acceptance of the rule of law and the views of others. Extreme social and political movements, especially those that gain power through the persecution or exploitation of minorities and under the pressures of competitive politics retreat to the deoxygenated margins of political culture. Groups or movements that use exclusionary or intolerant appeals in liberal democracies tend to fade in prominence and eventually lack the financial resources to compete in elections.

Further Reading
Dahl, Robert. "What Political Institutions Does Large-Scale Democracy Require?" *Political Science Quarterly* 120, no. 2 (2005): 187–197; Fukuyama, Francis. "The End of History?" *The National Interest* (Summer 1989): 76–91; Fukuyama, Francis. *The End of History and the Last Man*. New York: Avon, 1992; Huntington, Samuel P. "After Twenty Years: The Future of the Third Wave." *Journal of Democracy* 8, no. 4 (1997): 4–12; ———. *The Third Wave of Democratization*. Norman: University of Oklahoma Press, 1991; International Institute for Democracy and Electoral Assistance. *Handbook on Democracy Assessment.* Stockholm, Sweden, 2002; International Institute for Democracy and Electoral Assistance. *The State of Democracy: An Assessment in Eight Nations Around the World.* Stockholm, Sweden 2003; Lindberg, Staffan I. *Democracy and Elections in Africa.* Baltimore: Johns Hopkins University Press, 2006; ———. "The Surprising Significance of African Elections." *Journal of Democracy* 17 (January 1, 2006): 139–151; Mansfield, Edward D., and Jack Snyder. "Democratization and War." *Foreign Affairs* 74, no. 3 (May/June 1995): 79–97; Mansfield, Edward D., and Jack Snyder. *Electing to Fight: Why Emerging Democracies Go to War.* Cambridge, Mass.: MIT Press, 2005; Navia, Patricio, and Thomas Zweifel. "Democracy, Dictatorships, and Infant Mortality Revisited." *Journal of Democracy* 11 (April 2, 2000): 99–114; O'Donnell, Guillermo. "Horizontal Accountability in Modern Democracies." *Journal of Democracy* 9 (July 3, 1998): 112–126; Przeworski, Adam. *Democracy and Development: Political Institutions and Well-Being in the World, 1950–1990.* Cambridge: Cambridge University Press, 2000; Sen, Amartya. *Development as Freedom.* New York: Knopf, 1999; Zakaria, Fareed. *The Future of Freedom: Illiberal Democracy at Home and Abroad.* New York: W.W. Norton, 2004.

—Robert E. Henderson

liberalism

During the 1950s, influential writers such as Louis Hartz described liberalism as the central defining characteristic of American public philosophy. However, since the 1980s, *liberal* is a term employed derisively by conservatives to smear those on the political left as hopelessly out-of-touch bleeding hearts. The tradition of liberalism is commonly understood to go back to the Whig opponents of the British monarch during the 17th century, yet the word *liberal* was never used politically until the early 19th century. As these two sets of conflicting pictures reveal, liberalism is an immensely complex concept, and its uses have varied greatly over time. Identifying one single commonality to liberalism can be tricky. Nevertheless, it is an essential keyword, and in the historical arguments over who or what is appropriately liberal, we can see in microcosm the historical development of American political thought since the end of the Civil War.

Liberal is a term with ancient roots, a translation of the Greek *eleutherios*, which rendered literally means "free." This word has been alternatively translated broadly as "civilized" or more narrowly as "generous." Its original usage in ancient Greece was in reference to the status of a free man, as opposed to women and slaves, as well as the capacity of one who is free to save and distribute his wealth, to generously give money and exercise restraint in accepting it from others. Likewise, the liberal arts or a liberal education described the proper development of a free man. Indeed, until the 18th century, acting with liberality was seen as a male capacity. By the 18th century, however, the term had gained additional salience as a description of an individual who held free and generous opinions and whose mind was unhampered by prejudice, virtues that could be exercised by both genders.

It was not until the early 19th century that the term *liberal* was used to designate a progressive political opinion. Originally, it was an insult uttered by British Tories at antiwar dissenters. It was meant to connote not so much a broadness as a laxness in principle and a foreignness of opinion—a reminder of the Spanish Liberales Party. To be a liberal, in other words, was to appear somehow un-British. Nevertheless, like many terms of ridicule, *liberal* was quickly adopted by those against whom it was aimed. Inevitably, by the second quarter of the 19th century, the neologism *liberalism* gained currency as a concept used to identify the political and theological doctrines of a liberal, which has given the term a far greater sense of coherence and unity than it, in fact, has. In the United States, the term *liberal* was a latecomer to the political vocabulary and did not become a familiar keyword until the arrival of the short-lived Liberal Republican Party (1872–76).

At the heart of liberalism stands the individual; it is securing the LIBERTY and personal autonomy of the individual that distinguishes liberal political philosophy from the communitarian aspirations of traditional conservatives on the right and socialists on the left. Liberalism is primarily a judicial mode of thought, and the protection of the individual is often conceptualized through the language of natural and CIVIL RIGHTS. Liberty is a status that one has under a government limited by the RULE OF LAW. One variant of this juridical philosophy is the tradition of SOCIAL CONTRACT theory, exemplified in JOHN LOCKE's *Second Treatise on Government* (1689). Locke imagined government and all social obligations as a result of a voluntary contract between free individuals who are born free and unencumbered by duties. Individuals are conceived as having been endowed by birth with NATURAL RIGHTS and in a state of freedom, which is also a state of insecurity. Government is an artifice

created by free individuals who grant it some share of their natural authority in exchange for protection of person and property.

Locke's theory, conceptualizing government as a contract for mutual interest, has had an extensive influence in the United States, although republican and religious influences were also critical during the Revolutionary Era of the 1760s and 1770s. This contractarian perspective leads to several important conclusions. First, the basis of all legitimate government derives from the voluntary consent of the governed. Popular sovereignty rather than tradition or divine right is the basis for liberal governments. Second, governments are not conceived as natural, sacred, or inviolable institutions, but rather as tools created by and for individual human beings, and they are to be judged by their capacity to protect individual freedoms and capacities. Traditionally, this has meant limited government, protections for individual religious conscience, and tolerance for diversity in religious faiths and practices. A third point derives from the first two. While individuals grant government some of their natural authority, they retain other rights, most importantly the right to unmake and remake government when it fails. Thus, a liberal polity may embrace everything from a spirit of experimentation in governing structures and policies to the right of revolution, famously exemplified by the DECLARATION OF INDEPENDENCE.

Within this theory of limited government and individual rights are found a number of philosophical tensions. On one hand, liberalism is founded on the universal principle that all human beings are equal, at least from a political standpoint, and that all should have equal rights under the law. These egalitarian assumptions bear a proclivity toward democracy; popular sovereignty requires democratic institutions of decision making. On the other hand, Locke saw the establishment of government caused by the desire of individuals to have protections for their property. If government is designed to permit the enjoyment of property, then liberal theory permits a great deal of social and economic inequality in the name of the freedom of individuals to acquire and enjoy their property. It is revealing to note, for example, that when James Madison speaks of protecting the rights of a minority in *Federalist 10*, he is speaking of creditors and others with wealth. Liberalism does not necessarily come out in favor of one side, either EQUALITY or individual liberty. Rather, liberalism provides the conceptual framework through which generations of Americans have debated (and tentatively resolved) how to balance these competing values.

In the last half of the 19th century, concern for the legal conditions of personal autonomy grew to encompass the social and economic contexts in which individual freedom and growth flourishes or withers. The impetus for these considerations was the increasing power and influence of corporations and banks in the decades after the Civil War. During this period that Mark Twain dubbed the Gilded Age, large-scale economic and financial institutions grew to dominate the market and influence government officials, while the opportunities for smaller entrepreneurs, farmers, and workers shrunk. As wealth and industrialization in the United States increased, so, too, did the gap between the rich and the poor. Throughout the large industrializing cities of the United States, slums and ghettos spread, inhabited by poor workers who were often unhealthy and illiterate. Under such conditions, liberal reformers argued, talk of abstract freedom rang hollow.

Liberal proposals attempted to improve workers' health and education, support immigrant communities, and establish MINIMUM WAGE and maximum hour laws as well as standards for cleanliness and safety in factories and other workplaces. Many of these measures were initially seen as voluntary and philanthropic, but increasingly liberals called for employing governmental powers, starting at the local and state levels. These reformist policies were developed in conjunction with a philosophical rethinking of the social nature of the individual and the conditions in which individual choices are made. A number of late Victorian British intellectuals, such as Thomas Hill Green, J. A. Hobson, and L. T. Hobhouse, raised the philosophical importance of these issues. The movement was called new liberalism, and these liberal philosopher-activists found American counterparts in the pragmatism articulated by William James and John Dewey. Pragmatism imparted an experimental and empirical take on the understanding of personal identity. Of significance is that these programs were not socialist in spirit, but rather they were animated by respect for the individual.

This new liberalism challenged the traditional concepts of limited government, as reformers excoriated the state's neglect of the poor and encouraged the use of police powers and economic regulations to redress these needs. In response, many business leaders and their advocates proposed a stricter form of laissez-faire economic individualism. They argued that governmental intervention was an assault on personal freedom. They also evidenced a suspicion toward reform. While some argued that reform was utopian and bound to fail, others went further, arguing that social progress required free competition and that by helping the losers in this struggle, government made society weaker. When social Darwinist William Graham Sumner considered *What Social Classes Owe to Each Other* (1883), his bottom-line answer was nothing. The U.S. SUPREME COURT, for a time, embraced large parts of this economic liberalism, for example, by invalidating minimum wage and maximum hour laws as violating the freedom of contract.

The conflict between social reformers and economic libertarians over the proper role of government in redistributing the burdens and benefits of CAPITALISM was, in many ways, a "family" debate between protagonists who were in agreement over some basic liberal propositions, for example, that the freedom of the individual was the most valuable social goal for the government to protect. In other words, both sides can be designated as liberal, marking the breadth of the liberal doctrine and distinguishing participants in this debate from communists and socialists on the left and from traditionalist opponents of technological progress on the right. Nevertheless, the differences between these two schools of thought were fundamental to an industrializing culture, and subsequently, the more common use of the term *liberal* would be to identify progressive reformers, while advocates of a market free of government regulation became known as conservatives or libertarians.

From the 1930s until the 1960s, the reformist tendencies of liberalism flourished as the ideological backdrop of American public policy. With the NEW DEAL in the 1930s, the U.S. federal government passed laws and designed programs that intervened in the economic life of the nation like never before. Americans, struck by the hardships of the Great Depression, embraced an ideal of "positive liberty," in which personal freedom was protected from the extreme crashes of a free market system by a set of economic safety nets. The liberal vision of fairness and equality further expanded in the 1960s under the GREAT SOCIETY of President Lyndon Johnson, who led a "War on Poverty" and directed the passage of a number of important pieces of antidiscrimination legislation such as the Civil Rights Act of 1964. At the same time, supporters of laissez-faire economics, who were by now calling themselves classical liberals, warned that the development of a welfare state was a slippery slope toward SOCIALISM. Classical liberals argued that welfare gave the government too much authority in the lives of individuals, stifled entrepreneurship, and made recipients dependent. In the words of Friedrich Hayek, the welfare state led down the "road to serfdom" and was therefore inherently antiliberal.

While the Great Society inscribed liberalism into the social policies of the federal government, the philosophical career of liberalism also received a shot in the arm as academic debates surrounding liberalism as a political and a moral creed grew in number and quality. At the heart of this resurgence in liberal theory were two texts each written by Harvard philosophy professors, John Rawls's *A Theory of Justice* (1971) and Robert Nozick's *Anarchy, State and Utopia* (1974). Rawls puts forth an expansive vision of SOCIAL DEMOCRACY. He uses a social contract experiment, asking individuals what type of society they would construct assuming they knew nothing about their own identity, interests, or status. Rawls argues that such rational actors would choose a society based on equal rights and committed to a system of redistributive justice, in which any social or economic inequality would benefit the least. Nozick's libertarian response attacks the idea of a liberal state committed to DISTRIBUTIVE JUSTICE and formulates a portrait of a minimal state designed to protect the PROPERTY RIGHTS of individuals. The debate between these two alternative visions of liberal justice reflects divisions within liberalism that have been evident since the Gilded Age.

Scholarly criticism of liberalism has come from a number of different positions, including critical race theorists, feminists, and communitarians on both the left and the right. One common theme is that contemporary liberalism has painted so abstract a picture of the rational and autonomous individual that it is incapable of actually reflecting the "situated self," the actual human being located in concrete communities. Self-described liberal theorists have responded in a number of ways. Will Kymlicka, reflecting the legalistic spirit of liberalism, has articulated a sophisticated theory of minority group rights designed to protect cultures against the potentially corrosive effects of mainstream culture. Other liberals, such as Rawls in his later writings, have embraced a theory of "political liberalism," arguing that liberal philosophy is based on political values and does not presuppose any particular metaphysical doctrine of the individual or of the good life.

These recent debates reveal that the traditions and concepts of liberalism remain a vital part of American political thought. Ironically, the vibrancy of recent liberal philosophy has occurred at the same time the term *liberal* has reached its nadir as a political label. Starting in the 1980s, American conservatives began to use the term *liberal* to evoke images of a group of out-of-touch elitists all too willing to spend other people's money. This period also marked a sharp upswing in conservative philosophy, combining free market values with a social reaction against the excesses of the 1960s counterculture. By the 1990s, the invectives had grown so powerful that many Democratic politicians refused to call themselves liberal, preferring to use the term *progressive*. It remains to be seen whether this avoidance of the "L word" reflects another vicissitude in the up-and-down career of liberalism or a permanent change in the American political vocabulary.

Further Reading
Arblaster, Anthony. *The Rise and Decline of Western Liberalism*. New York: Basil Blackwell, 1984; Dewey, John. *Liberalism and Social Action*. New York: G.P. Putnam's Sons, 1935; Hartz, Louis. *The Liberal Tradition in America*. New York: Harcourt, Brace, & World, 1955; Hayek, Friedrich A. *The Constitution of Liberty.* Chicago: University of Chicago Press, 1960; Kloppenberg, James T. *The Virtues of Liberalism*. New York: Oxford University Press, 1998; Kymlicka, Will. *Multicultural Citizenship: A Liberal Theory of Minority Rights*. New York: Oxford University Press, 1995; Rawls, John. *A Theory of Justice*. Cambridge, Mass.: Harvard University Press, 1971; Rawls, John.

Political Liberalism. New York: Columbia University Press, 1993; Sandel, Michael, ed. *Liberalism and Its Critics.* New York: New York University Press, 1984.
—Douglas C. Dow

market economy

A market economy is an economic system based on the unregulated exchanges between buyers and sellers as the determinant of decisions about what to produce and what prices should be charged. The central distinction between a market economy and all others, such as centrally directed, or command economies, and mercantilist systems, is that governments or other outside agencies do not control the major decisions of economic life.

Adam Smith's classic work, *An Inquiry into the Nature and Causes of the Wealth of Nations,* published in 1776, is the first theoretical study of market economies. Smith argues that market economies are more efficient than attempts by a government or a king to control economic life. Because markets are more efficient than other ways of organizing economic life, they produce greater good for more people and are therefore morally as well as economically superior.

A central question in any economic system is how much something is worth, that is, what is its value. The value of something you do not have, such as a particular item of clothing or an hour of a person's work, might be based on its usefulness to you. For example, on a cold day, a warm coat is worth more to you than a lightweight one. The value of something you do have might be based on how much time and energy it took you to make it. If you have spent hours and hours writing a song or creating a video, you might feel that it is worth quite a lot.

In a market economy, the value of something is expressed as its price. How much something is worth is determined by the price at which someone is willing to sell it and someone else is willing to buy it. The market price is not controlled by people who want to sell something nor by people who want to buy something. The market price is the result of buyers and sellers bargaining with each other until they make a deal.

A different way to think about the worth of something is to use a set of ethical values, morals, or beliefs that might be used to determine the value or price of something. For example, some people might think that an hour spent teaching children to read contributes more to society than an hour spent playing golf or making music videos and is thus worth more. In economies that are not based on market principles, they might try to impose their beliefs by trying to regulate the wages paid to people. The basic question of the worth of something then becomes a political issue to be resolved by control of the government or the distribution of power.

In a market economy, the value of something is ultimately determined by what people are willing to trade it for, the price they are willing to pay to buy it, or the price at which they will sell it. This leads directly to the principle of supply and demand as the determinant of what gets produced at what price across the entire economy. Producers create a supply of things and try to sell them at a given price, while buyers demand some number of things at a particular price. When the simple interaction of somebody looking to sell something and somebody looking to buy something is repeated time after time, a market exists. Markets are balanced and are in equilibrium when the supply of things at a given price equals the demand for those things at that same price. If the supply of goods being offered at a particular price and buyers willing to pay that price are not balanced, then people will be motivated to change. In the short run, if there are more items for sale at a given price than people want to buy, sellers will have to lower their prices.

Since a seller cannot become more efficient and make a profit selling items at a lower price, they will go out of business and be replaced by a new entrepreneur who can. In the short run, if there are more people who want to buy than there are items to buy, prices will go up. In the longer run, this imbalance in the market will encourage producers to make more of the items people want.

Since people are free to compete, if someone can figure out a less expensive way to make a product, then he or she can cut the price, sell more of the product, and still make a good profit. If someone figures out a way to produce something that does not currently exist but that people will want when they see it, then he or she will create a new product. People already selling products in the market are not going to sit idly by while newcomers take away their business but will try to improve their own products or lower their prices. The resulting competition among sellers tends to create efficiency and variety and improve quality. The market rewards efficient and clever producers and weeds out the inefficient and those slow to change their products.

In the most common alternatives to a market economy, politicians or bureaucrats decide what will be produced, in what varieties, and at what price. This can easily lead to inefficient businesses being allowed to survive or to an oversupply of things that people really do not want and an undersupply of things they do want.

Markets determine how many people do what kinds of jobs by the same interaction of supply and demand. People who need to hire other people to do a particular job offer a given level of wages. If people who have the skills and qualifications to do that job are willing to work for that wage, they take the job. If the people who can do the job are not willing to work for the offered wage, then the employer will have to raise the offer until the wages are enough to get the number of people needed for the job. Following the basic insight of Adam Smith and many other economists, the interaction of employers and job seekers, the supply of jobs at a given wage, and the supply of willing workers will balance out in the long run. Over time, the market will produce the most efficient and fairest distribution of jobs and salaries.

In a market economy, the primary roles of government in economic life are seen as maintaining a level playing field, guaranteeing that promises are kept and contracts are honored, and protecting PROPERTY RIGHTS. If either buyers or sellers in the market collude and try to affect supply or demand or manipulate prices, then the market will not function efficiently nor produce the best outcome. If people cannot be held accountable and be required to keep their promises, then contracts are useless. Only a government has the authority to act as a referee and the power to enforce its decisions.

Market economies in the real world do not always perform perfectly for a variety of reasons. Among the most prominent market failures are those that occur when the market takes too long to correct itself and those that result from what is known as the underproduction of public goods.

While Adam Smith argued and most American economists agree that in the long run the market produces the most efficient and best results, there can be serious consequences for people in the short run. For example, as supply and demand for goods and services moves toward the most efficient equilibrium, they can be seriously out of balance in the short run, producing alternating patterns of boom and bust and runaway inflation alternating with recession or even depression.

Private goods are things that can be consumed exclusively by an individual who has bought them. Public goods are things whose use or consumption cannot be limited to specific individuals who have paid for it. For example, the car you drive is a private good. You own it and can control who uses it. But the road you drive on is a public good. Some people helped pay for that road with their taxes, others did not, but anyone can use it. National defense is a public good. For example, people who pay taxes pay for the troops and weapons that keep the nation safe from outside attack, but people who do not pay their taxes and do not help pay for the national defense are still protected. This can easily lead to the underproduction of public goods. If you ask individuals, they would much rather spend their money on things they can own and consume by themselves instead of things they have to share with everyone else. Left to their own devices, people would spend far less than is needed on things such as roads, national defense, public education, and so on.

It is expected that government will intervene to correct market failures, to compensate for the worst effects of boom and bust, and to provide public goods by collecting taxes and spending them. The major debates about the role of the government in economic policy that divide conservatives, liberals, and libertarians revolve around the related questions of whether the market economy has, in fact, failed in a particular instance and, if it has, how the government can intervene in the most efficient and effective way to restore the market.

Debates about when and how government should intervene in a market economy to correct failures are common issues in American politics and presuppose that the market is the best way to organize economic life. Outside mainstream American economics and outside the United States, the fundamental assumption that markets create the most efficient and most moral results are directly challenged by Marxism and many socialist theorists. Islamic philosophical and economic thought is often skeptical of unbridled markets, as are major thinkers in Buddhist, Confucian, and Hindu traditions.

See also CAPITALISM.

Further Reading
Boyes, William, and Michael Melvin. *Economics*. 6th ed. Boston: Houghton Mifflin, 2005: Schiller, Bradley R. *Essentials of Economics*. 6th ed. Boston: McGraw Hill, 2007: Smith, Adam. *An Inquiry into the Nature and Causes of the Wealth of Nations*. Chicago: University of Chicago Press, 1976.

—Seth Thompson

nationalization

Nationalization is the taking of private assets by a state. Usually, nationalization is marked by a specific industry being taken over by the state, such as the oil, railroad, or energy industries. Such state ownership is in marked contrast to the private enterprise, or the free market, approach so often practiced in the contemporary context. The practice of nationalization is a development that emerged in the 20th century and was done for the purpose of social and economic equality. It was often seen as a principle of COMMUNISM or SOCIALISM. Nationalization became an attractive option for many nations in the post–World War II era as fears of price gouging, cartels, monopolies, and exploitation of workers and resources became important political issues for many nations in Europe and elsewhere. Nationalization is often undertaken because the state believes that some greater public purpose is at stake and that nationalization will serve a positive public purpose. For example, following World War II, Eastern European states nationalized all industry and agriculture. Common practice in noncommunist countries often follows the principle of EMINENT DOMAIN when nationalization occurs, which means that companies are compensated, at least in part, for assets seized by the state. However, in communist regimes, in which private ownership is opposed in principle, compensation usually does not occur. Often, foreign properties have been nationalized in underdeveloped

nations where resentment exists of foreign control of major industries.

Usually, but not always, when the state takes control of an industry or business, the private enterprise is compensated for the state takeover. Some forms of nationalization, such as when a nation takes control of the assets of a business owned by a foreign entity and the taking is not compensated for, may cause an international incident as the home country of the business being nationalized may be enjoined to come to the aid of the business being nationalized. For example, in 1938, Mexico nationalized several foreign-owned businesses, including major oil properties. Then-U.S. secretary of state Cordell Hull demanded that compensation for the state takeover be "prompt, effective and adequate." But Mexico, along with a number of other DEVELOPING COUNTRIES, often took a different view, arguing that the exploitation of a country's resources by a foreign private entity did not merit compensation.

In 1962, the UNITED NATIONS General Assembly adopted a resolution stating that when the nationalization of an industry or business occurs, the private owner is due compensation and "shall be paid appropriate compensation in accordance with international law." While this resolution established the principle that compensation was due, it did not go so far as to establish a procedure to guarantee due or market level compensation.

Sometimes a state will take over an important or large business enterprise when that business is in financial trouble and on the verge of bankruptcy. If a business is essential to national security or if a business employs a large number of workers who would otherwise become unemployed, the state may see an interest in taking over that failing business and putting it under state control. In the 1970s, when the British government took over the British-Leyland car maker, it was just such an effort. In fact, there was a wave of nationalization in Great Britain in the post–World War II era, as the government took over British Coal, British Gas, British Petroleum, British Rail, British Steel, and a host of other industries. Examples of nationalization in the United States included the creation of the Tennessee Valley Authority in 1939 (previously the Tennessee Electric Power Company) and more recently the creation of the Transportation Security Administration in 2001 following the

September 11, 2001, terrorist attacks, which nationalized the privately owned airport security industry.

In some cases, if certain industries perform at a subpar standards, pressure can be put on the government to reprivatize many of the same industries. Privatization is the reverse of nationalization. It marks the private ownership and control of a business or industry. In the 1980s, a wave of reprivatization occurred in Great Britain and elsewhere. This occurred because many of the nationalized industries did not perform up to industry standards; many were also perceived as inefficient or not serving the public interest. Also, as socialism and communism became discredited in the late 1980s and as market CAPITALISM swept the globe, the wave of capitalist and private ownership momentum became too powerful for most states to resist.

However, many developing nations believe that their natural resources, workers, and national integrity are being exploited by large commercial interests from abroad that come in, take control, and limit the sovereignty of the nation. Can small, less developed states resist these takeover ventures? Or is the power of the West, the force of the market, and the demands of consumer publics too powerful to resist? Most of the smaller and less-developed states feel unable to resist these forces even when they may want to. The dominant ideology, the rules of the game, and the reward and punishment mechanisms of the market are too powerful to fight. Thus, they either learn to make their awkward peace with the forces of market capitalism, or they can pay a heavy price. As GLOBALIZATION proceeds, these forces may be even more powerful in the future, leaving the sovereignty of small and less-developed states vulnerable to market forces and regime rules that may run counter to the interests or desires of the states.

In the past 20 years, nationalization has become a largely discredited notion. The wave of privatization so prevalent in the 1980s was only the beginning of a transformation that led to the rise of the ideology of market capitalism that swept the globe in the aftermath of the fall of communism. Adhering to the ideals of free market capitalism dominates in many countries, and because of this, few states would risk the political or economic fallout that would result if they tried to nationalize industries.

Therefore, even if a state wished to nationalize a particular industry, it is unlikely that such a nationalization would be politically viable, and the international rules of the game might make the overall cost of such a nationalization prohibitive. This puts many nations in a kind of prison, whereby the self-punishing mechanism of the market limits their flexibility and narrows their political as well as their economic options.

Internationally, the current political and economic trend clearly favors market capitalism, free enterprise, and private ownership as the regime model for the modern economic system, although it remains to be seen how long this trend will last. Globalization has propelled states to embrace market capitalism or be left behind. However, one notable recent exception has been the move to nationalize various industries, such as oil and communications, in Venezuela under the rule of President Hugo Chávez. The possible economic impact for various American corporations in these two fields has made this a prominent political issue for the United States in its diplomatic relations with Venezuela and other countries in the Latin American region.

Further Reading
Reid, Graham L., and Kevin Allen. *Nationalized Industries*. Harmondsworth, U.K.: Penguin, 1970; Sclar, Elliott D. *You Don't Always Get What You Pay For: The Economics of Privatization*. Ithaca, N.Y.: Cornell University Press, 2000; Tivey, Leonard, ed. *The Nationalized Industries since 1960: A Book of Readings*. London: Allen & Unwin, 1973.

—Michael A. Genovese

newly industrialized countries
The term *newly industrialized countries* (NICs) refers to a loose category of countries that have experienced some sustained economic development over the past two decades. A country's economy can be based on what economists refer to as the primary, agricultural, sector; the secondary, industrial, sector; or the tertiary, service, sector. The trajectory of economic development moves from reliance on agriculture to greater reliance on industry to greater reliance on the service sector. The primary sector of the economy is based on producing things: food and raw

materials. The industrial sector is focused on producing tangible things and products. The service sector largely produces intangible things, such as knowledge, ideas, technology, managerial skills, and entertainment.

In much of the world, agriculture means small-scale, often subsistence, farming, a form of economic life that relies heavily on human labor and does not produce a great deal beyond what is needed for people to survive. When an industrial sector is developed, the emphasis shifts from growing crops to manufacturing products in factories and a growing use of technology. Agrarian societies tend to have very small markets, and many people trade and barter for what they need rather than use money. As societies industrialize, markets expand, more people are working for wages, and the population tends to shift from living in rural villages to urban centers. The next stage of development is a shift from a primary focus on the industrial sector to a growing emphasis on the service sector of an economy, which often includes very sophisticated technology.

Some countries today have advanced capitalist economies. Countries such as the United States, France, Britain, and Germany are marked by growing reliance on the service sector as an economic base, widespread use of sophisticated technology, and the highest standards of living. These are the countries often referred to as the first world, the Global North, or the Global Rich. At the opposite end of the spectrum of economic development are the countries identified by the UNITED NATIONS that have experienced the worst economic performance in the past two decades and have the least prospects for future growth. These countries are categorized as the least developed, or the fourth world. The rest of the world, except for the former members of the Soviet bloc, is referred to as the third world or the global south. This is the largest and least homogenous group of economies in the world, including most of Asia except Japan, Latin America, Africa, and the Middle East (except for the few large oil-exporting countries in the latter region). Many of these countries have had some degree of success in beginning to develop their economies by shifting away from agriculture to a growing level of industrialization in the past two decades. Hence, they are newly industrialized countries.

Some examples will clarify the differences between advanced capitalist economies, newly industrialized economies, and fourth world states. The examples will also illustrate the breadth of the category "newly industrialized" and the differences among such countries. Comparing levels of employment in industry and agriculture will illustrate the differences in economic base. The gross domestic product per capita (GDP/cap) is a standard way of measuring and comparing standards of living in different countries.

South Korea, Mexico, and Egypt are all newly industrialized countries, although there are important differences in their levels of economic activity and standards of living. The United States is a good example of an advanced capitalist economy, and Bangladesh will serve as an example of a fourth world country.

In South Korea, which is now the 11th-largest economy in the world, only 6.4 percent of the labor force works in agriculture, while 26.4 percent works in industry. South Korea has been one of the most successful of all the newly industrialized economies and boasts GDP/cap of $20,000. Mexico is another newly industrialized country, although not as successful as South Korea. Some 18 percent of the Mexican workforce is employed in agriculture, while 24 percent is in the industrial sector. The Mexican GDP/cap is $10,000. Egypt is developed enough to be counted as a newly industrialized country, but there is a substantial gap between the South Korean, Mexican, and Egyptian levels of development. In Egypt, agriculture continues to employ 32 percent of the workforce, and industry only 17 percent. The Egyptian GDP/cap is $3,900. What these countries share is progress in shifting from agriculture as the most important part of the economy to an increasingly important industrial sector. Standards of living have risen, sometimes a great deal and sometimes only marginally. Despite good years and bad years, the general trend has been for improved economic performance.

Bangladesh, one of the least-developed countries, and the United States, an advanced capitalist country, provide sharp contrasts to the three newly industrialized countries. In Bangladesh, 63 percent of the work force has jobs in the agricultural sector, and only 11 percent in the industrial sector. In keeping with the low productivity of agriculture in most of the world, the Bangladesh GDP/cap is only $2,100, and there has been no sustained growth. In sharp contrast, a GDP/cap of $40,000 puts the United States near the top of the advanced capitalist economies in terms of standards of living. The fact that approximately 23 percent of all American workers are in the industrial sector is less important than the fact that only 0.7 percent of the American labor force is in agriculture. The standard of living, as measured by GDP/capita, has increased steadily.

There are two basic strategies that countries have pursued to achieve newly industrialized status: the Asian model and what is referred to as a neoliberal strategy. The Asian model has produced the "Asian tigers" of South Korea, Taiwan, Singapore, and Hong Kong, as well as "lesser tigers" such as Malaysia and Indonesia. Mainland China has pursued a similar strategy. The Asian model focuses on export-led development, that is, relying on a literate and controlled labor force to produce consumer goods to be shipped to consumers in North America and Europe. The strategy relies on strong governmental direction of economic activity, including active recruiting of foreign investment, protection of the local economy from foreign competition, and restrictions on political activity.

The strategies included in the neoliberal model are typically prescribed and supported by the advanced capitalist nations, international institutions such as the INTERNATIONAL MONETARY FUND and the WORLD BANK, and many professional economists. They include a strong emphasis on creating a MARKET ECONOMY with minimal government intervention, privatizing industries and some government functions, removing restrictions on foreign investment, sharply reducing government spending and taxes, and emphasizing export-oriented industries, particularly those that can take advantage of relatively low labor costs. Whereas the Asian model emphasizes the role of the government and political actors, the neoliberal model emphasizes economic factors and market forces. This has been the predominant model for economic development for most of the world outside of Asia.

The newly industrialized countries have been a major focus of U.S. foreign economic policy. As the largest consumer economy in the world, the United States has been a critical market for the exports from countries that are trying to industrialize and develop.

American consumers' purchases of a wide range of products, from toys to clothing to highly sophisticated electronics, have been a major force for economic success; lack of access to American and European markets has been a crippling obstacle. The fact that Americans have bought more from the newly industrialized countries than they have sold to them has provided stimulus and capital development. While economists disagree about the extent of the outsourcing of jobs and its long term consequences for the United States, when production or other jobs are moved out of the United States, they are relocated to newly industrialized countries.

When America buys more from the newly industrialized countries than it sells to them, a trade deficit is created. This has been a continuing problem for the United States. On both a country-by-country basis and in international settings such as the WORLD TRADE ORGANIZATION, the United States has strongly supported measures to open the domestic markets in the newly industrialized countries for American businesses.

The promotion of DEMOCRACY has long been an important goal of U.S. FOREIGN POLICY. The relationship between economic development and democracy remains controversial among political scientists and economists who study global development. There are some cases, such as South Korea and Taiwan, in which sustained economic development played a significant role in creating the conditions that led to the emergence of stable democratic regimes. There are also cases in which development has not led to increased democratization. There are cases in which relatively democratic regimes were causes of economic development and cases in which democratic regimes did not do well in promoting economic growth. At a minimum, the relationship is complex.

Further Reading

Bergston, C. Fred, ed. *The United States and the World Economy: Foreign Economic Policy for the Next Decade.* Washington, D.C.: Institute for International Economics, 2005; Goddard, C. Roe, et al., eds. *International Political Economy: State-Market Relations in a Changing Global Order.* Boulder, Colo.: Lynne Rienner, 2003; Siebert, Horst. *The World Economy.* London: Routledge, 2002.

—Seth Thompson

North American Free Trade Agreement
(NAFTA)

The North American Free Trade Agreement (NAFTA) is an agreement between the United States, Mexico, and Canada to expand economic activity by making it easier for a company located in one of the three countries to do business in the other two. This is to be accomplished by drastically reducing or eliminating tariffs (taxes) on goods shipped between countries and coordinating national and local regulations. Since its inception in 1994, NAFTA has been at the center of controversy.

Free trade areas and their more elaborate relatives called common markets are intended to spur economic growth and job creation by allowing businesses to treat all the citizens of two or more countries as a single economic unit. In most of the global economy, national borders contain and constrain trade and commerce. Governments use a number of devices, from tariffs (taxes on foreign goods) to rules and quotas, to regulate INTERNATIONAL TRADE. Some of those strategies are aimed at achieving fairness and balance. For example, if wages in one country are markedly lower than in its neighbor, a government may intervene to make sure the country is not swamped by artificially low-priced imports. Alternatively, a government may institute tariffs or other barriers to trade with another country because the home country's industry is very inefficient and its products cannot compete fairly against imports. The dividing line between intervening to make things fair and intervening to protect a weak and inefficient but politically potent industry is often extremely fuzzy.

Regardless of motive, tariffs and other barriers to trade make it more expensive to do business between two countries, introducing what economists call transaction costs. This is widely believed to reduce the overall level of economic activity and raise prices for consumers. A free trade area calls for the elimination of almost all barriers to trade between two or more countries. Governments will agree to drop tariffs against industries in each other's countries (and they may also agree to raise barriers to companies located outside the free trade area). Governments also agree to coordinate and standardize their labor laws and environmental regulations to facilitate trade and commerce across their borders. This was the logic that led the United States to pursue negotiations with Canada and Mexico beginning in the 1980s to create a North American Free Trade Area.

Even as negotiations were being completed, NAFTA became an issue in the 1992 presidential election. Third-party candidate Ross Perot made opposition to NAFTA a centerpiece of his campaign against incumbent president George H. W. Bush and the Democratic challenger, Bill Clinton. Perot charged that the primary effect of NAFTA would be the loss of jobs for Americans, and he often referred to "the giant sucking sound" of jobs moving south to Mexico. Perot was not the only critic of NAFTA, but in 1993 Congress approved the plan. Proponents of NAFTA cited overall growth in the economies of the United States, Canada, and Mexico and better products at lower prices for consumers. They also argued that there might be some short-term job losses in all three countries as inefficient companies went out of business, but that lost jobs would be quickly replaced by new jobs that were created as a result of expanding economies and growing demand.

NAFTA opponents raised a number of objections. The argument that NAFTA would cost jobs was made most often in the United States by critics who pointed out that a number of American manufacturing jobs had already moved to Mexico to take advantage of significantly lower wages and that the removal of barriers to imports from Mexico would accelerate that process. At the same time, some critics in Mexico worried about the ability of small Mexican farmers to compete against American agricultural imports. American and Canadian labor unions made a related argument when they objected to the fact that the NAFTA treaty did not include explicit guarantees for minimum labor standards and rights to join unions. A third line of argument against NAFTA came from American and Canadian environmentalists who decried the lack of environmental standards in the treaty and the danger that national environmental standards would be lowered or eliminated when the three countries negotiated common rules and standards. A final objection was more explicitly political: the loss of sovereignty. One of the hallmarks of a state in the modern international system is sovereignty, the right of each state to govern itself as it sees fit without external interference. This argument was made by citizens in all three countries, but most strongly in Mexico, where the fear was expressed that the government and citizens of Mexico would be forced by the United States and Canada to dramatically reform their economy and adopt a host of new laws. The Zapatista rebellion in Mexico's Chiapas province was launched on January 1, 1994, the day that NAFTA came into force, and fears of economic domination and exploitation by transnational corporations have figured prominently in the movement's anti-NAFTA, antiglobalization, and antipoverty rhetoric.

In response to some of the criticisms, the governments of Canada, Mexico, and the United States negotiated two comprehensive supplements to the original NAFTA treaty. The first was the North American Agreement for Environmental Cooperation. This agreement not only committed the three countries to maintaining environmental standards but also set up an institution for coordinating environmental issues and a source of financing for environmental projects, particularly in Mexico The second side agreement was the North America Agreement on Labor Cooperation. This agreement was designed to encourage the three countries to cooperate on resolving disputes over labor standards and to work toward convergence in national labor laws.

After more than 10 years of experience with NAFTA, the controversy has abated but not disappeared. Objective, scientific assessment of the impact of NAFTA on the Canadian, Mexican, and American economies is difficult because of the differences between the three countries and because of the difficulty of attributing specific effects to a single cause.

The first challenge to assessment is the difference in the size of the three national economies. The value of Canada's economy is $1.4 trillion, Mexico has an economy of $1.07 trillion, and the U.S. economy, at $12.4 trillion, is the largest in the world. Whatever impact an agreement such as NAFTA has on the United States will be relatively smaller than the impact on Canada or Mexico. The three countries also differ in the extent to which foreign trade contributes to their overall economic status. Canada and Mexico are relatively similar: In 2004, foreign trade contributed 62 percent of the Canadian gross domestic product (GDP, the standard measure of the size of an economy) and 58.5 percent of the Mexican GDP. Given that much reliance on foreign trade and the fact that the United States is the most important trading partner for both Canada and Mexico, the effects

of NAFTA are likely to be more pronounced than in the United States. In 2004, foreign trade amounted to only 20 percent of the U.S. GDP. Canada and Mexico ranked first and second as sources of imports to the United States and as markets for U.S. exports. These differences make it very difficult to generalize about the impact of NAFTA on the overall economic health of each country.

A second major problem in trying to weigh the effect of NAFTA on its members' economies is the fact that national economies are very large and very complex systems. Economic performance is affected by a wide range of variables, from global developments to government policies to the decisions of companies both large and small and the decisions of millions of individual consumers. Even skilled economists armed with very sophisticated tools of statistical analysis do not agree on the impact of single events or variables.

NAFTA has not inspired a host of followers, as some had hoped. The recently created Central American Free Trade Area is a much smaller economic unit than NAFTA and brings together even more dissimilar countries. While the United States has strongly advocated a free trade area of the Americas that would cover most of South America, it has met with a chilly reception from some key Latin American players. The United States has had more success with the more modest goal of negotiating free trade pacts with individual countries, such as Chile. While NAFTA remains a source of controversy for specific issues, the best assessment may be that it has been neither as beneficial as its most ardent proponents hoped nor as detrimental as its staunchest opponents feared. For most Americans, Canadians, and Mexicans, the most salient aspect of NAFTA may be the fact that products traded under NAFTA rules are labeled in English, French, and Spanish.

Further Reading

Acheson, Keith, and Christopher J. Maule. *North American Trade Disputes*. Ann Arbor: University of Michigan Press, 1999; Hakim, Peter, and Robert Litan, eds. *The Future of North American Integration: Beyond NAFTA*. Washington, D.C.: Brookings Institution Press, 2002; Hufbauer, Gary Clyde, et al. *NAFTA Revisited: Achievements and Challenges*. Washington, D.C.: Institute for International Economics, 2005; Schott, Jeffrey. *Free Trade Agreements: U.S. Strategies and Priorities*. Washington, D.C.: Institute for International Economics, 2004.

—Seth Thompson

North Atlantic Treaty Organization (NATO)

The North Atlantic Treaty Organization (NATO) was a quintessential product of the cold war, and its original purpose was aptly summarized by a British official who claimed that NATO existed to keep the United States in, the Soviet Union out, and Germany down. Such a characterization may be an anachronism in a post-Soviet world no longer animated by customary East-West polarities, but NATO was indeed established as a bulwark against Soviet expansionism in Europe and a guarantee against German military resurgence. As such, its mission and direction have been thrown into question, and its role in the geopolitical evolution of 21st-century Europe is unclear, nor is its ultimate relevance in a global diplomatic theater that has transcended and redefined traditional relationships and affinities.

Since the last round of enlargements in 2004, NATO has comprised 26 states from Europe and North America. Its headquarters is located in Brussels, Belgium, and its membership has grown considerably over the past decade. Contrary to what had been the case for most of its history, NATO now includes members from eastern and central Europe and is, thus, no longer an exclusive club for the United States, Canada, and their western European allies. Principal political authority lies with the North Atlantic Council, which is a deliberative decision-making body that acts through consensus instead of voting, thereby ensuring unity of purpose and strategic coordination for NATO initiatives. NATO is led by a secretary-general, who, as head of the North Atlantic Council, represents NATO in dealings with states and other international organizations. The alliance's political structure is complemented by a unified military command structure, which is controlled by American military personnel but supported by a staff that represents all member countries.

Despite NATO's obvious political role, it is, first and foremost, a military alliance. NATO exists to protect its members from attack by common enemies and to ensure the physical integrity of its territories.

The famous article 5 of the North Atlantic Treaty confirms that because an attack on one member will be considered an attack on all, the collective security of NATO countries depends on an appropriate response to military aggression by their enemies. Although article 5 does not specifically mandate a military response, the treaty clearly expresses the signatories' intent that NATO serve as a defense structure that leverages the military capabilities of its members. Above all, the historical setting from which NATO emerged demanded a military-based organization through which the security and territorial integrity of its participants could be ensured.

NATO was created in 1949 out of circumstances that may seem foreign to most Americans. In many ways, it was both a relic of a prewar European mentality that accepted the inevitability of conflict among great powers and a product of a postwar mindset that viewed conventional warfare as an increasingly ineffective, if not obsolete, means of achieving political objectives. From a geopolitical perspective, two goals seemed paramount to Western policy makers, particularly in the United States and the United Kingdom, immediately following World War II. First, the reconstruction of Europe, both physically and politically, had to be secured in a way that would promote the establishment and maintenance of long-term stability and prosperity in Western European states. Second, and just as significantly, European leaders needed to create an international, or at least regional, structure of some sort that would prevent the outbreak of future wars in Europe. The importance of both objectives was self-evident to contemporary politicians, inasmuch as stable democracies in Western Europe devoted to the implementation of free market principles and international cooperation appeared to be the keys to a minimization of conflict and the prevention of mutual aggression.

On both counts, that is, domestic political stability and international cooperation, the United States faced numerous challenges throughout Europe during the mid- to late 1940s. Internal political problems in countries such as Greece, Turkey, and Italy disturbingly illustrated that support among Europeans for ideologies, policies, and goals opposed by the United States was comparatively high in certain regions and that geopolitical alignment with the United States and its long-term trajectories could be

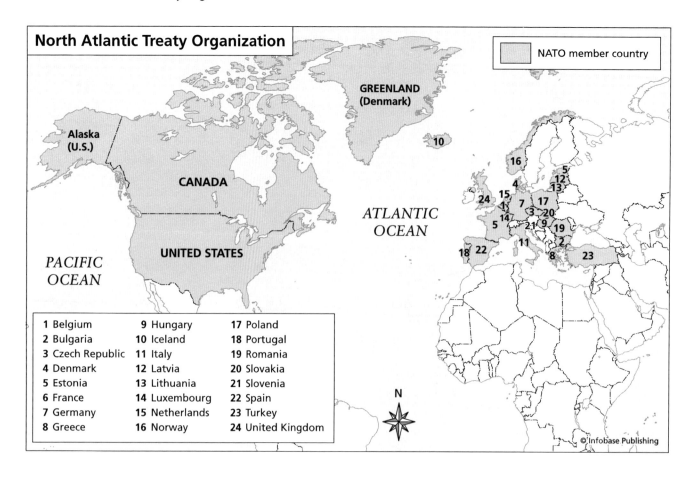

North Atlantic Treaty Organization

NATO member country

GREENLAND (Denmark)

Alaska (U.S.)

CANADA

ATLANTIC OCEAN

UNITED STATES

PACIFIC OCEAN

N

1 Belgium	9 Hungary	17 Poland
2 Bulgaria	10 Iceland	18 Portugal
3 Czech Republic	11 Italy	19 Romania
4 Denmark	12 Latvia	20 Slovakia
5 Estonia	13 Lithuania	21 Slovenia
6 France	14 Luxembourg	22 Spain
7 Germany	15 Netherlands	23 Turkey
8 Greece	16 Norway	24 United Kingdom

© Infobase Publishing

problematic. In addition, because of the spread of communist aggression and the fear of rejuvenated German militarism, visions of international cooperation and a reduction of mutual hostilities among European states seemed unworkable. As it turned out, both of these dilemmas, namely the difficulty of establishing pro-American, democratic regimes devoted to free markets in devastated regions and the implausibility of securing international comity and collaboration in Europe, were linked to the broader dilemma of Soviet expansionism after the war.

The United States and its Western European allies may not have shared unified aspirations regarding the political evolution and geopolitical alignment of postwar Europe, but they were unified in their apprehensions about perceived Soviet aggression and the growth of Soviet influence and power in Europe. Most Western European nations eventually accepted the reality that, along with the prospect of German rearmament, the threats posed by Soviet power were potentially the most destabilizing and destructive.

Within a few years following the end of World War II, America's European allies accepted the necessity of creating a substantial defense mechanism through which the safety and security of Western Europe could be assured.

By 1948, through the Treaty of Brussels, a core group of five Western European countries laid the foundations for future cooperation by formulating an effort to control a possible German resurgence. Although this treaty was confined largely to issues dealing with potential German rearmament, its signatories became convinced of the need to erect a similar yet more potent organ for the provision of anti-Soviet defense. The Europeans were operating on the premise that Europe had, by this time, become irrevocably divided between a pro-Soviet, communist East and pro-American, democratic West. In other words, NATO would be based on the assumption that such a geopolitical division was a fait accompli and that any resulting military alliance should be a response to this inherent division. (This is especially significant with respect to

NATO's role in today's world, since such a division is no longer a standard feature of European geopolitics.)

From the standpoint of the European states, U.S. membership in any anti-Soviet defense organization was a prerequisite, inasmuch as American military might was absolutely indispensable to deter or repel potential Soviet initiatives in the West. Obviously, the United States was also eager to secure European participation in a defense structure of some kind, not least because of prevailing balance-of-power theories and the fear that any losses in Europe would produce a redistribution of power between democratic and communist forces that favored the Soviet Union. American and European objectives for the protection of Europe and North America from communist aggression, and, to a lesser extent, German resurgence, were expressed through the North Atlantic Treaty, which was signed by the 12 founding members in April 1949.

The founding members included the five signatories to the Treaty of Brussels, which were Britain, France, and the Benelux countries (Belgium, the Netherlands, and Luxembourg); the United States and Canada as representatives of the western end of the Atlantic alliance; Denmark and Norway from the historically vulnerable Scandinavian territories; Portugal and Italy as strategically located outposts of antifascism and anticommunism in regions surrounded by antidemocratic regimes; and Iceland, which was permitted to join the alliance without a standing army. Spain was excluded because of the Franco dictatorship, the inherent uncertainties of Germany's and Austria's political situations disqualified them from inclusion, and others, such as Switzerland and Sweden, adhered to neutralist policies that precluded participation in military alliances.

By the early 1950s, the political climate in Greece and Turkey had stabilized, so that in 1952 these geopolitically critical states became members of NATO. As a counterweight to Soviet hegemony in the Balkans, eastern and central Europe, and also parts of the Arab Middle East, Greece and Turkey provided NATO with strategic options that enabled the alliance to check Soviet expansion and influence beyond established limits. In addition, by the mid-1950s, a long-term political settlement had been consolidated in West Germany, and it joined NATO in May 1955.

The most immediate consequence of West German membership was the emergence of the Warsaw Pact later that same month, a phenomenon that formalized, through these duly sanctioned oppositional military pacts, the existence of the cold war. The only other country to join NATO prior to the post-Soviet enlargements starting in the 1990s was Spain in 1982. On the whole, NATO's membership during its first 50 years reflected its origins as an anti-Soviet military alliance designed to prosecute the cold war and protect Europe from the expansionism and aggression of antidemocratic forces in the East.

Although NATO's primary geopolitical aims seemed unambiguous from the start, the means of realizing those aims were often disputable. The particular diplomatic objectives of its individual members frequently subverted the overall strategic and operational priorities of NATO as a whole, and the political gamesmanship among some states occasionally undermined the unity that was necessary for practical consensus and operational consistency. Perhaps the most significant division within NATO was one that paralleled diplomatic developments within the European Community (EC) and associated debates among EC members regarding the future of European foreign policy and defense strategy. EC foreign policy controversies centered on the question of whether the diplomatic and military viability of Europe would best be promoted through a continental strategy that revolved around a Franco-German geopolitical axis or an Atlantic one that optimized the leadership and capabilities of the United States and exploited the "special relationship" between the United States and Britain.

Likewise, a rivalry of sorts appeared within NATO that ultimately pitted a francophilic, Gaullist continentalism against an Anglo-American Atlanticism. This evolved into a formal split when, in 1966, France formally withdrew from NATO's unified military command structure, and it highlighted a tension that has waxed and waned over the decades but has never subsided. Some of this tension can be ascribed to French jealousy and President Charles de Gaulle's arrogant obstinacy in the face of American demands about French military and diplomatic compliance, yet the bulk of it has profoundly deeper roots and can be linked to an intrinsic Franco-American incompatibility that manifested itself not only within NATO but also in other areas that required cooperation between the two nations, such as Vietnam, the Middle East, and western Europe. Despite increased friction between the United States and France over the last few years as a result of controversial policies pursued by the George W. Bush administration, France has become increasingly cooperative and even compliant since the mid-1990s, but U.S. and French visions of a post-Soviet world will not be reconcilable any time soon, at least not from a long-term normative perspective.

These differences and related ones notwithstanding, during its first 40 years, NATO displayed remarkable solidarity and unity of purpose. After all, the cold war provided the organization and its members with an enviably uniform and uniquely definable set of objectives based on an ostensibly predictable system of geopolitical relationships according to which friends and enemies could be readily identified. In the end, although the particular manifestations of NATO policies and strategies varied from member to member, as did the benefits derived from those policies, the overarching objective of defeating or at least containing Soviet COMMUNISM and authoritarian aggression was relevant and meaningful to all members. So the definability and predictability of the cold war rendered NATO's purposes and operational tasks correspondingly definable and predictable, and most organizational dissent was inherently obviated or vitiated through the commonalty of those purposes.

With respect to purpose and organizational unity, the collapse of the Soviet Union and the dissolution of the Warsaw Pact confronted NATO with a crisis of conscience that it has been unable to address. Geopolitical logic appeared to dictate that the end of the cold war and the resulting irrelevance of cold war diplomatic paradigms demanded the abrogation of the North Atlantic Alliance and the dismantling of defense structures intended to fight the cold war. Without a doubt, an institution such as NATO, whose sole reason for being sprang from its almost single-minded ability to secure western Europe against Soviet-inspired aggression, seemed ill-equipped to survive in a geopolitical environment devoid of Soviet influence or a Soviet-based diplomatic or military foe. Nevertheless, NATO has somehow survived, though it has hardly thrived.

Since 1991, NATO has maintained its Atlantic focus by preserving the fundamental tie between North America and Europe, but the European part of the alliance has shifted its locus of activity eastward. By admitting former Warsaw Pact countries and erstwhile Soviet republics among its ranks, NATO has undermined some of the cultural and geographic solidarity that characterized the pre-1999 alliance. As a result, despite the support some of the eastern countries have demonstrated for U.S. policies, NATO policies have been undermined or weakened by the historical divisions that plagued the development of postwar Europe, especially the EC (and EUROPEAN UNION). In addition, the involvement of former Soviet satellites with NATO has alienated Russia, Ukraine, and Belarus, producing new geopolitical polarities between pro-Russian and anti-Russian forces in a region that is far from stable. Furthermore, according to many NATO observers, the accession of former Soviet satellites contradicts NATO's avowed support for democratic government, inasmuch as the commitment to (and the fate of) democratic governments in these one-time dictatorships is indeterminate at best.

Regardless of these limitations and concerns, NATO has endeavored to transform itself and to redefine its purpose beyond the comparatively narrow limits imposed on it by the cold war. As such, its mission has expanded to include geopolitical theaters outside Europe that appear central to European diplomatic and military interests. For instance, NATO has been spearheading operations in Afghanistan. Plus, NATO has enhanced its political role by increasing its diplomatic presence in various arenas and slowly shifting its practical focus to include greater predeployment capabilities. In fact, some scholars believe that NATO's continued viability lies in its readiness, willingness, and ability to morph from a military alliance into a diplomatic one.

As the political and economic integration of Europe has grown, not least through the emergence of the European Union (EU), and the geopolitical independence of Europe as a formidable economic and political global competitor has been secured, the institutional structures and organizational mechanisms of the European Union have increasingly served as both a counterweight and alternative to NATO's decreasingly relevant traditionalism. Viewed from another perspective, the EU and its more continental foreign policy, along with related initiatives to build an EU-specific defense capability, have appeared to offer a more logical and natural response to European defense and foreign policy needs than would be possible under a comparatively obsolete structure such as NATO's. Over time, the competition between NATO and the EU will inevitably increase, as will the amount of redundancy between them, and should the recent continentalist trend continue to prevail over the customary Atlanticist one, the case for NATO's ongoing utility and relevance will be a difficult one to maintain.

See also DIPLOMATIC POLICY.

Further Reading

Gaddis, John Lewis. *The Cold War*. New York: Penguin Books, 2006; Howorth, Jolyon, ed. *Defending Europe*. New York: Palgrave Macmillan, 2004; Kaplan, Lawrence S. *NATO Divided, NATO United*. Greenwood, Conn.: Praeger Paperbacks, 2004; LaFeber, Walter. *America, Russia, and the Cold War, 1945–2002*. Boston: McGraw-Hill, 2002; Sloan, Stanley R. *NATO, the European Union, and the Atlantic Community*. New York: Rowman & Littlefield, 2002; Udell, Gregory F. *Principles of Money, Banking, and Financial Markets*. New York: Addison Wesley Longman, 1999; Woods, Ngaire. *The Globalizers*. Ithaca, N.Y.: Cornell University Press, 2006.

—Tomislav Han

Organization of Petroleum Exporting Countries (OPEC)

The Organization of Petroleum Exporting Countries (OPEC) is an international organization whose members act as a cartel to try to manage the price of crude oil on world markets through coordinating their production. OPEC was created in 1960 by Iran, Iraq, Kuwait, Saudi Arabia, and Venezuela to try to counterbalance the dominance of global oil markets by the so-called Seven Sisters, the largest transnational oil companies. The founding members were ultimately joined by eight other countries, all of whom were less developed countries whose economies were dependent on revenues from oil sales in the global market.

In the 1960s, most of the world market for oil was controlled by an oligopoly of seven transnational corporations: Standard Oil of New Jersey (Esso), Royal Dutch Shell, British Petroleum, Standard Oil of New York (Socony), Texaco, Standard Oil of California (Socal), and Gulf Oil. The companies owned the right to drill and extract oil from countries, the shipping and transportation networks that brought the oil from wellheads to refineries, and the shipping and distribution networks that moved products from the refineries to the local gas station. The role of oil-rich third world countries was limited to passively collecting royalty payments from the companies at a rate largely determined by the companies themselves. Since the same corporation controlled the process from the time the oil left the ground until the time it was pumped into a motorist's gas tank, costs and profit could be assigned to different stages of the process to reduce taxes or royalties owed to different governments. The creation of OPEC was intended to give governments more control over their own national resources.

The price of a barrel of oil on the world market is affected by the quality of the oil and its location. Crude oil varies in the mix of chemicals and contaminants, especially sulfur, it contains and by the quality of the oil itself, both of which affect how easily and inexpensively it can be refined. The highest-quality crude oil with the fewest contaminants and least sulfur content is described as light and sweet. Oil from Saudi Arabia tends to be particularly light and sweet and is used as a benchmark. Oil from other countries is priced higher or lower than oil from Saudi Arabia depending on the quality of the oil, differences in costs of production, and the cost of transporting it to refineries and consumers.

For most of its first decade of existence, OPEC was ineffectual. The members lacked the information and expertise to manage oil production inside their own countries. The royalties paid to individual countries tended to be held as secrets by the transnational corporations and the countries themselves, so that national governments did not necessarily know if they were getting a better or worse return than their neighbors or other producers on other continents. The world market for oil over the past century has been cyclical, with periods of abundant supply alternating with shorter stretches of scarcity. During OPEC's first decade, there was plenty of oil available, and OPEC's members produced far less oil than did some of the major consuming nations, particularly the United States. OPEC members had no leverage, and the organization was inconsequential.

The situation changed dramatically in the late 1960s and early 1970s. First, several countries, beginning with Libya, started negotiating contingent royalty payments from the transnational corporations, with the amount one government would receive linked to payments to other governments. This gave governments of producing countries a little leverage to try to negotiate their returns upward. The second change was the most critical. A number of Arab countries, most of them also members of OPEC, had formed the Organization of Arab Petroleum Exporting Countries (OAPEC) and during and immediately after the 1973 war between Israel and its neighbors, sharply reduced their production of crude oil and imposed a boycott on the United States and Western Europe because of their support for Israel. The resulting sudden drop in the world oil supply at a time of growing demand led to sharply increased prices for oil and oil-based products. The boycott induced a shortage of gasoline in the United States that led to several months of long lines at gas stations and emergency procedures such as permitting gas purchases only on alternate days. By the time the boycott was ended, the balance of power in global oil had shifted, and OPEC emerged as a dominant player. Since then, OPEC members have transformed the world oil business by dramatically increasing their level of expertise and involvement in the actual production process in their countries, taking more direct control of their oil fields and reducing the role of transnational oil companies. In the global oil industry, as in other industries based on natural resources, the greatest profits come from processing and refining raw materials. OPEC member governments have become far more involved in what are termed "downstream" activities such as transporting crude oil, refining it, and distributing gasoline and other petroleum-based products to end users.

Today, there are 11 members of OPEC: Algeria, Indonesia, Iran, Iraq, Kuwait, Libya, Nigeria, Qatar, Saudi Arabia, the United Arab Emirates, and Venezuela. The OPEC international headquarters is located in Vienna, Austria. In 2005, average world oil produc-

tion was 84 million barrels per day. OPEC members produced 34 million barrels, about 40 percent of the world's total; in comparison, the United States produced about 10 percent of the total. But OPEC members exported about 78 percent of all the oil they produced, while the United States consumed all it produced and had to import around 12 million barrels of oil each day. The members of OPEC rely on revenues from their oil exports to finance their national budgets. For some OPEC members, oil is a major source of national income for investing in development as well as meeting annual government expenses; for others, it is virtually the only source of national income. Each member thus has a powerful need and desire for higher oil prices. At the same time, OPEC members are well aware that the higher the price of oil, the more likely oil consumers are to reduce consumption by finding alternatives to oil or by increasing the efficiency with which they use oil. OPEC members understand that if the price goes too high, it will undermine economic growth in the rest of the world. The impact of high oil prices on the richer countries of western Europe and North America can be measured in slower economic growth; the impact on less-developed countries is typically far more severe and may even lead to economic declines. OPEC long ago recognized that it and its customers shared an interest in a stable and predictable oil market.

The basic political division in OPEC has been between price hawks and doves. Price hawks are more interested in maximizing income through high prices and are those countries whose national budgets are stretched thin by the demands of a large and growing poor population and the need for long-term investment in economic development projects. The price doves are those countries, such as Saudi Arabia, Kuwait, and the United Arab Emirates, whose populations are much smaller compared to the amount of oil exported and whose national budgets are under far less stress. The doves tend to be more interested in the long-term stability of the market and the health of their customers' economies.

The oil or economics ministers of OPEC meet every six months to assess the oil market and set a target price. Each member is assigned a quota, which is a fixed number of barrels of oil that it can sell on the market. The target price and national quotas are typically balanced between the hawks' preference for immediate returns and the doves' preference for a stable and sustainable market. OPEC, like all international organizations, is a creature of its members and cannot directly enforce national quotas or punish nations who sell more than they are entitled to. In the past, Saudi Arabia has played a unique role in OPEC as a "swing producer." Saudi Arabia is unique within OPEC because of two factors. First, the kingdom's income from oil is very high, and its population is relatively small. The national budget is not under a great deal of stress, and government expenditures can be quite flexible if necessary. Second, Saudi Arabia typically has excess capacity, that is, the ability to produce more oil per day than its quota. Those facts have allowed Saudi Arabia to increase production when the global market was getting too hot and prices were rising too high or to decrease production when the market weakened and prices threatened to fall too low. The Saudis have also used the threat of ramping up production and lowering market prices to try to deter cheating on quotas by price hawks. Saudi Arabia's ability to play the role of swing producer has declined in the 21st century as world demand has grown sharply, OPEC's share of the world oil market has declined, and Saudi Arabia itself has begun to experience greater demands on its national budget.

The relationship between the United States and the members of OPEC is one of complex interdependence. The United States needs oil from OPEC, and the health of the American economy is affected by both the price of oil and the reliability of supplies. However, OPEC countries are not the largest source of oil imports to the United States. For example, in November 2006, non-OPEC countries provided 60 percent of all U.S. imports, with Canada and Mexico together accounting for almost 30 percent of U.S. imports. Of the 40 percent of oil imported from OPEC members, most of that came from Saudi Arabia (at nearly 12 percent), Venezuela (at nearly 10 percent), and Nigeria (at 7.5 percent). Oil imports are a major contributor to the American trade deficit with the rest of the world.

At the same time, OPEC in general, and some of its largest producing members in particular, rely heavily on the United States as a market. For example, exports of oil to the United States account for almost 19 percent of Saudi Arabia's income from INTERNA-

TIONAL TRADE, half of Venezuela's international exports, and a little less than half of Nigeria's. The health of their economies is very dependent on the economic well-being of the United States. Even OPEC members who do little or no business with the United States find their economic health dependent on the American economy because of the central role of the U.S. dollar in the global oil markets. The price of oil is set in world markets each day in terms of dollars, and OPEC members typically expect their customers to pay in dollars, even if their national currency is not. OPEC members, like most countries in the world, tend to hold dollars as their national reserve currencies, which is, in effect, their national wealth. Thus, even the staunchest price hawks who sell no oil to the United States find that they have a vested interest in the state of the American economy.

This complex interdependence has several effects on U.S. FOREIGN POLICY. It helps explain the close working relationship on both economic and security issues between the United States and Saudi Arabia, two countries that on the surface might seem to have little in common. It also explains important dimensions of the U.S. relationship with countries such as Nigeria and Indonesia. The relationship between the United States and Venezuela during the presidency of Hugo Chavez has been marked by increasing strains and pointed accusations on both sides. But the fact that the United States relies on Venezuela for about 10 percent of its oil imports, which amount to more than half of Venezuela's trade earnings, and the fact that Venezuela owns CITGO, a major refiner and distributor of petroleum products in the eastern United States, dramatically complicates the political equation for both governments.

OPEC's share of the global oil market has declined over the past two decades as producers such as Russia, Canada, and Mexico have played a larger role. But OPEC production is critical to world supplies, and the ability of some key members of OPEC to increase their oil production over the next few years will keep the organization at the center of petroleum economics and politics. OPEC will continue to affect the daily lives of Americans and will continue to be a focus of U.S. foreign policy. (General economic statistics are drawn from the *CIA World Factbook* at http://www.odci.gov/cia/publications/factbook/index.html. Data on oil production, imports and exports come from the Energy Information Administration of the U.S. DEPARTMENT OF ENERGY at http://www.eia.doe.gov.)

See also ENERGY POLICY.

Further Reading

Falola, Toyin, and A. Genova. *The Politics of the Global Oil Industry: An Introduction.* Westport, Conn.: Praeger, 2005; Parra, Francisco. *Oil Politics: A Modern History of Petroleum.* London: I.B. Tauris, 2004; Sampson, Anthony. *The Seven Sisters: The Great Oil Companies and the World They Shaped.* New York: Viking Press, 1975; Yetiv, Steve. *Crude Awakenings: Global Oil Security and American Foreign Policy.* Ithaca, N.Y.: Cornell University Press, 2004.

—Seth Thompson

social democracy

Social democracy is a term used to describe a political movement made up of union workers, farmers, and other nonelites that demands collective decision making in the social, economic, and educational institutions of a nation. It can also refer to the ideals and values of this movement and to the policies passed in its name. Social democrats seek to ameliorate the extreme effects of CAPITALISM and social inequality on the poor, but without challenging the fundamental system of private property and entrepreneurship. Therefore, while staying within the framework of a MARKET ECONOMY, social democracy challenges the classical defenses of a free market by expanding liberal ideals about political equality into areas traditionally designated as private and off limits to democratic accountability, such as the marketplace and the family. Whereas classical liberals see democratic participation as limited to voting for political representatives, social democrats expand the sphere of collective decision making to include social and economic institutions as well as the private familial sphere.

Social democracy stands somewhere between the poles of laissez-faire capitalism and SOCIALISM. While establishing policies of economic regulation and worker protections, social democracy falls short of socialist demands for economic centralization or state ownership of major industries. The proper ends of government are redescribed by social democrats to include the material welfare of its citizens, arguing that the conditions of individual autonomy and effective citizen participation presuppose a level of economic security and an EQUALITY of opportunity that transcends empty legal promises. To achieve true democracy, social democrats argue, requires addressing the highly unequal power gap that exists between workers and managers and owners and investors. Such an inequality that had broad effects on the personal autonomy of the poor could not be papered over by the illusion of legal equality, or any longer ameliorated by a further expansion of the West. It was the innovation of early European social democrats to break with Marxist COMMUNISM and argue that a workers' revolution could be achieved without overturning the state, but rather by transforming it from within by organizing POLITICAL PARTIES and using the advantages of universal SUFFRAGE.

For more than a century, social democracy has been a strong and permanent presence in the developed parliamentary democracies of western Europe. Major parties such as the Social Democrats in Germany and Sweden and Labour in the United Kingdom have successfully represented the interests of workers in parliaments both in and out of governing majorities. Social democratic parties in the United States have been present since the Gilded Age of the late 19th century, yet their presence has been far more tepid than their western European cousins. More commonly, as a result of the U.S. TWO-PARTY SYSTEM, social democratic aspirations are adopted by the progressive wing of one of the two major parties. Since the 1920s, that party has usually been the Democrats, although some early 20th-century progressives, such as Robert La Follette, were Republicans. Significantly, while some American social democrats have reached out to the writings of Karl Marx and Ferdinand Lasalle, the most successful bids for social democracy found in progressivism, the NEW DEAL and the GREAT SOCIETY, do not have deep genealogical ties to Marxism or European socialism.

Nevertheless, the United States has always had numerous unique cultural aspects sympathetic to social democratic values. The traditional place of prominence given to the individual farmer and the small proprietor in the American imagination were used as a wedge to attack the rise of large banks, railroads, and corporate monopolies during the Gilded Age. As well, religion has played a strong role in the American version of social democracy. The social gospel movement of the late 19th century involved many of the same middle-class Protestants who made up the backbone of the Progressive movement. Repulsed by the poverty caused by industrialization, these evangelicals sought a more egalitarian polity based on Christian values and rejected the competition and the worship of Mammon so prevalent in the Gilded Age. While among white Protestants this movement declined along with progressivism, its influence was still visible two generations later as African-American church leaders such as Martin Luther King, Jr., took leadership in the CIVIL RIGHTS MOVEMENT. Social democratic sympathies may also be seen at the center of American ideology, LIBERALISM. For example, the radically egalitarian values expressed in such canonical texts as the DECLARATION OF INDEPENDENCE have been used to attack racial discrimination and always left open the possibility of a democratic monitoring of social goods as requisite for a true pursuit of happiness.

The rise of social democracy lies at the intersection of an expanding franchise and a changing capitalist system. In Europe, revisionist socialists such as Edward Bernstein saw the opportunity for workers to use their newly acquired right to vote as a tool for entering government, using the state as an instrument for reform rather than trying to overthrow the state by revolution. Similarly, in the United States, each expansion of the franchise—first to poor white men, then (fleetingly) to African-American men after the Civil War, to newly arriving European immigrants, and eventually to women—has led to new demands made in the name of democratic equality. Soon after the Civil War, small farmers founded the Greenback and Populist movements to strike back at banking interests, and labor organizations took on more prominence by organizing strikes and demanding better wages and work conditions.

The American social democratic movement flowered during the first two decades of the 20th century, with a number of prominent national spokespersons. On the strength of his "Cross of Gold" speech, the DEMOCRATIC PARTY put forward William Jennings Bryan as its presidential candidate four times between 1896 and 1908. In 1901, Eugene V. Debs founded the Socialist Party, gathering together in one place many of the disparate parts of labor and trade unions as well as nonrevolutionary socialists. This era saw the spread of urban settlement houses, such as Jane Addams's Hull House in Chicago, and the founding of journals of progressive thought, such as *The New Republic* under Herbert Croly. Perhaps the high point of the Progressive movement came during the presidential elections of 1912, in which three of the four candidates for the office (Woodrow Wilson, Theodore Roosevelt, and Eugene V. Debs) ran as progressive reformists of one kind or another.

As diffuse as the Progressive movement was, there were several factors that gave early 20th-century social democrats a common identity. They broadly adopted pragmatic perspectives, embracing the use of social experiments to reduce waste, poverty, and ignorance and to keep competition alive. Unlike the New Deal reformers, who established national policies, progressive reformers tended to look to state or local governments for solutions, those "laboratories of democracy," as Louis Brandeis called them. Progressive policies called for labor laws that instituted minimum wages and maximum hours and laws to do away with child labor. They sought out CORRUPTION in government and called for the eradication of poverty and the establishment of progressive taxation. Progressives also campaigned for greater public support for education and other means of developing the mental and physical capacities of citizens. Reform was supposed to provide not just material benefits but an ethical renewal of a democratic spirit. It also expanded the tasks of government toward managing the economy, price stabilization, and brokering conflicts between labor and capital.

However, this brief success fell away rapidly. World War I, the Russian Revolution and the first domestic Red Scare, and a conservative-leaning U.S. SUPREME COURT all helped precipitate the decline of the Progressive movement in American politics, but not before the U.S. CONSTITUTION was twice amended to enact two progressive policy goals: women's suffrage and Prohibition. Both were monuments to the progressives' vision of rejuvenating the ethical character of American democracy by bringing in virtuous woman and expelling demon rum.

Social democratic movements would not return to the political center stage until the New Deal. However, once President Franklin D. Roosevelt and the Democratic Congress began tackling the problems of the Great Depression, the goals of social democracy had evolved, growing more centralized and more regulatory. No longer would it be adequate to promote fair competition and bust monopolies. The New Deal marked a new and highly experimental moment in American politics in response to overwhelming popular demands for the national government to intervene in defense of a sick economy. Roosevelt set about to use national planning and governmental spending in order to stabilize capitalism and make it fairer for the workers who had the least say. The federal government propped up the failing banking and lending organizations, insuring deposits with federal cash. It regulated agricultural and industrial production and growth and subsidized loans to farmers. It established minimal standards for industrial workers and instituted SOCIAL SECURITY. Most controversially, the New Deal adopted Keynesian economic techniques, using deficit spending on large public works projects and seeking not just to assist the needy but to actually employ them.

However, if New Deal era reforms were broader than those of the Progressive Era, they were also more conservative. The reforms of the 1930s were primarily administrative and did not possess the strong push toward social and personal transformation that so characterized the efforts of progressives. Rather than using the government as a catalyst for social change, the government adopted a new role of "broker state," brokering labor-management disputes that had led to so much violence and conflict in the past. Despite attempts such as Roosevelt's second bill of rights, the New Deal reforms did not result in a transformation of social relations. Reformers always had to fend off charges that their policies were a form of socialism or communism and thus un-American. Part of those challenges came not just from Republicans, but from the southern conservative wing of the Democratic Party. Nevertheless, as a result of the cautious approach of the New Deal Democrats, these new federal administrative powers were accepted by President Dwight Eisenhower's administration during the 1950s.

The greatest use of governmental power in pursuit of social democratic goals was President Lyndon B. Johnson's GREAT SOCIETY. The Great Society and Johnson's War on Poverty were partially inspired by Michael Harrington's *The Other America* (1962), which brought to light the existence of a seemingly permanent underclass in the United States who were not benefiting from the prosperity brought about by the postwar boom. Armed with a strong mandate in the 1964 presidential elections and a solid Democratic Congress, Johnson pushed through a flurry of legislation, signing into law programs meant to bring about greater equality of opportunity. Many programs, such as Job Corps and Head Start, focused on training and educational opportunities. Medicare and Medicaid brought affordable health insurance to millions, and a food stamp program was meant to do away with hunger in America. Johnson recognized that poverty and inequality in the United States was tied to race. As a result, Johnson's War on Poverty was conjoined with his ambitious CIVIL RIGHTS agenda, including legislation forbidding racial discrimination not only at the polls but in the workplace, in housing opportunities, and in public accommodations.

The most important philosophical defense of the principles of redistributive social democracy in the postwar era was John Rawls's *A Theory of Justice* (1971). Using a variation of the liberal contractual model for establishing governmental institutions, Rawls asked what kind of social rules for distributing social goods would individuals choose if they were unaware of what their position in society was. He went on to argue that under this "veil of ignorance," people would select a system based on a broad distribution of equal rights and liberties and the equal opportunity to compete for positions of social advance, and that any system of inequality would have to benefit the least well off.

It is somewhat ironic, however, that Rawls's classical liberal defense of social democratic policies was published at the very time that movement was slowly being eclipsed by a resurgence of both progressive and conservative political values. The Johnson administration found itself challenged on both its left and right. The 1960s saw the rise of the New Left, which, despite its name, took much of its ideas from the Progressive Era. Embodied by organizations such as Students for a Democratic Society (SDS), youth leaders sought to bring forth a commitment to a cultural renewal of egalitarian values. Building upon the Progressive Era, the 1960s also brought about the second wave of politically active feminism. The New Left criticized welfare programs for not going far enough in redistributing the benefits of American prosperity and for the degree of personal surveillance brought about by social workers administering welfare programs. Additionally, many civil rights leaders, such as King, broke with the liberal foundations of the Great Society during the late 1960s by questioning whether the great racial and economic divides in American society could be bridged merely through a focus on civil rights.

Many white voters felt that the benefits of the Great Society were going disproportionately to racial minorities. Republican candidates such as Richard Nixon, who won the presidency in 1968, successfully played up this racial element, using what was called a "southern strategy" to further fracture the Democratic coalition by dividing white southern Democrats from the national party. Emphasizing moral individualism, conservatives argued that government-subsidized safety nets weakened the incentives for personal savings and hard work. Welfare made people lazy and helped the undeserving poor. Indeed, the very term *welfare* took on a negative connotation in public speech. Libertarian voices attacked the economic wisdom of governmental regulation. They argued that high taxes led entrepreneurs and other owners of capital to take flight and invest in countries where building and maintaining a factory were cheaper due to lower employment costs and less regulation. Many white blue collar workers abandoned the Democratic Party during the 1970s and 1980s at a time when the strength of labor unions and the centrality of manual labor itself were on the wane.

Also important to the decline of social democracy has been the impact of GLOBALIZATION and international economic competition, which have created a labor market that is international rather than national. As a result, there has been both a decrease in the value of centralizing labor-management bargaining at the state level and a potential race to the bottom as the third world competes with the first world for investment. Globalization makes companies less dependent on home nations. Indeed, globalization rips at one of the founding premises of social democracy, that an economy is primarily national and controllable by the central government and that it is possible for sovereign governments to effectively manage in the national interest their nation's slice of the world economy.

The election of President Ronald Reagan in 1980, who famously argued that government was the problem and not the solution, marked the decline of social democracy as both a political movement and as a set of governing ideologies and helped bring about a revival of libertarian free market ideology, antagonistic to government regulation. The 1980s also saw the rise of the evangelical movement as a political force. This important movement had broken from the populist social gospel tradition of the Progressive Era and instead of pursuing social justice, preached personal salvation and traditional social values. By the 1990s, Democratic president Bill Clinton pledged to end "welfare as we know it" and signed into law a plan that significantly shrank aid to the unemployed. Social democracy as an ideal has never disappeared, but in the early 21st century its political fortunes have dimmed significantly.

Further Reading

Dewey, John. *The Public and Its Problems*. New York: Henry Holt, 1927; Fraser, Steve, and Gary Gerstle, eds. *The Rise and Fall of the New Deal Political Order, 1930–1980*. Princeton, N.J.: Princeton University Press, 1989; Harrington, Michael. *The Other America: Poverty in the United States*. New York: MacMillian, 1962; Kloppenberg, James T. *Uncertain Victory: Social Democracy and Progressivism in European and American Thought, 1870–1920*. New York: Oxford University Press, 1986; Laslett, John H. M., and Seymour Martin Lipset, eds. *Failure of a Dream? Essays in the History of American Socialism*. Berkeley: University of California Press, 1984; Rawls, John. *A Theory of Justice*. Cambridge, Mass.: Harvard University Press, 1971; Wright, Anthony. "Social Democracy and Democratic Socialism." In *Contemporary Political Ideologies*, edited by Roger Eatwell and Anthony Wright Boulder, Colo.: Westview Press, 1993.

—Douglas C. Dow

socialism

Socialism is a model of political economy centered on public control of significant means of production, stressing regulation of markets and reduction of material inequalities in order to expand possibilities for the free development of each individual. The modern movements for socialism have been driven primarily by the economic interests of workers and have been seen by socialists since the time of Karl Marx to be linked to class struggles between direct producers and appropriators of economic surpluses.

While the movements for socialism are unquestionably modern in origin, their fundamental elements were clearly present in the politics of the ancient world. Class struggle was well known to the ancient Greeks, for whom the most basic fact of political life was the ongoing rivalry between the *demos* (the ordinary working people) and the *aristos* (the land-owning elite). Attempts at constructing political solutions to the problems of class inequality were also recorded by ancient scholars and historians. In his *Politics*, Aristotle briefly described an effort by Phaleas of Chalcedon to prevent social conflict through the equal distribution of property. In Rome during the second century B.C., spiraling levels of material inequality led to two ill-fated attempts at land redistribution by Tiberius and Gaius Gracchus. Both were assassinated by opponents of their land reform plans.

Thomas More's *Utopia* (1516) stands as the first early modern meditation on the correction of social ills through the elimination of private property. The members of More's imaginary island community share all possessions equally, wear identical clothing, and trade houses on a regular basis to avoid either attachment or jealousy. But while More's vision of a society without property anticipates certain elements of the modern socialist critique of material inequality, its primary focus is on the ownership of personal possessions. The modern socialist movement, by contrast, would increasingly turn its attention to the forms of economic power rooted in the control of productive property. An early indication of this shift can be seen at the close of the English civil war, as Gerrard Winstanley and the Diggers occupied and cultivated rural waste grounds, building four small communes between 1649 and 1651. Stiff resistance from local land owners quickly ended the Diggers' experiments in communal living. In his published works, *The New Law of Righteousness* (1649) and *The Law of Freedom* (1652), Winstanley continued to promote the argument that social equality and economic betterment for the working class could be achieved only through common ownership of land.

Like the Diggers, Robert Owen and Charles Fourier held that socialism would take root in small, intentionally established rural communes. Owen began his career as the manager of a textile mill in Manchester, England, during the early years of the Industrial Revolution, then purchased his own factory at New Lanark, Scotland. There he implemented a series of reforms: housing for workers was improved, regular garbage collection was introduced, child labor was banned, and working hours were decreased. In 1825, Owen purchased land in Indiana for the founding of New Harmony, a commune based on his designs for "Villages of Cooperation." Initially, 800 residents moved to New Harmony, but the experiment survived only three years. Fourier's vision of a socialist community was first articulated in *The Theory of the Four Movements* (1808). Fourier maintained that communal villages (or "phalanxes") should be established, on which residents would live, work, and equally divide the proceeds of their labor. During the 1840s, a Fourierist movement developed in the United States that established communes in Massachusetts, New Jersey, and Colorado. As with the Owenite experiment at New Harmony, none lasted more than a few years.

At the beginning of the 19th century, a broader vision of socialist transformation was being developed by Claude Henri de Rouvroy Saint Simon. A member of the French aristocracy (who as a young man participated in the American Revolution), Saint Simon was an early exponent of the idea that industrialization would demand a sweeping reorganization of social and political life. Scientists, industrialists, and artists would plan and coordinate social order for the benefit of all. In *The New Christianity* (1825), Saint Simon argued for society to be restructured in such a way as to improve the lot of the poor. Yet, like Owen and Fourier, his vision of socialism was unconnected to the nascent political movements of the industrial working class.

This element of socialist theory would come to the fore in the work of Karl Marx, whose understanding of history was premised on the notion of class struggle as the primary driver of political change. Yet, while Marx was a key participant in the development of a European socialist movement, his work contains no blueprint for socialism. Unlike the earlier generation of utopian socialists, Marx and his coauthor Friederick Engels held that socialism could not be meticulously planned ahead of time but would emerge from the concrete development of its historical precursor, CAPITALISM. Marx's work does make clear, however, three aspects of socialism he believed to be of particular importance. First, socialism would be built not in small, rural communes but nationally and internationally through the achievement of working class political power. Second, though its technical procedures could not be rigorously specified in advance, socialism would involve public control of significant means of production. Third, the transition to socialism would begin with a lower stage of development in which material inequalities would continue to be patterned by differences in labor contributions before proceeding to an upper stage in which production and distribution would be based on the motto "From each according to ability, to each according to need." Marx's vision of socialism presupposed a high level of technological development and took as its central aim the reduction of time spent working to meet basic needs, so as to expand the time and resources available to pursue interests and desires.

At the end of the 19th century, the connection between socialism and working class political power was well established, but the precise path to be taken toward the achievement of both ends remained a topic for debate. The Russian socialist leader Vladimir Lenin held that under the repressive conditions of czarist Russia, a socialist transformation would require a revolutionary seizure of the state. In western Europe, by contrast, mass socialist parties increasingly pursued a legal, parliamentary route to power, outlined by Eduard Bernstein in *Evolutionary Socialism* (1898). But while such parties now began to contest elections and win seats in their national parliaments, the looming threat of war between European states challenged their expressed commitment to international working class solidarity. The decision in 1914 by most European socialist parties to support their national war efforts resulted in the eventual formation of rival communist parties by antiwar internationalists.

Both factions were represented in the United States. Between 1901 and 1918, the Socialist Party of America competed successfully in state and local elections in New York, Wisconsin, and Oklahoma. In 1912, Eugene V. Debs captured 6 percent of the popular vote as the Socialist Party's candidate for president. Convicted under the Sedition Act in 1918 for opposing U.S. entry into World War I, Debs continued his campaign for the presidency from prison. In 1919, mirroring the split in the European socialist movement, a communist faction broke from the Socialist Party to form the Communist Party of the United States of America. Despite being the target of government repression during the 1920s and 1950s, the Communist Party played vital roles in the organization of the Congress of Industrial Unions (CIO) and the movement for African-American CIVIL RIGHTS. Nonetheless, the American socialist parties remained marginal in comparison to the size and influence of their European counterparts. Scholars offered a variety of hypotheses to explain the phenomenon of American exceptionalism. Frederick Jackson Turner proposed that the American West's open frontier fed individualist dreams rather than class solidarity. Werner Sombart suggested that the high standard of living enjoyed by American workers gave them little reason to seek radical political or economic change. Louis Hartz maintained that having been founded on the liberal principles of legal equality and representative government, the United States lacked the deep-seated class divides that drove the European socialist movement. Despite some early predictions that they would vanish entirely after the collapse of the Soviet Union in 1991, socialist organizations remain a part of the American political landscape, albeit a minor one.

Two debates regarding elements of the socialist agenda are particularly important to both broader questions of political economy and more focused issues in public policy. The first concerns the problem of incentives. Advocates of market economies argue that the ability to accumulate private property ensures social productivity by overcoming the disincentive to labor. Lacking such an incentive, socialist economies (or nonmarket economic mechanisms) will tend toward stagnation. Though no socialist theorist since More has suggested the creation of pure equality or the elimination of personal property, socialist thought does generally advocate a reduction of material inequality. Yet, while unequal rewards can unquestionably act as incentives to labor, the relationship between rewards and incentives may be subject to declining marginal increases. Higher levels of statistical inequality in national economies, for example, do not necessarily correspond with higher levels of productivity.

A second debate considers the capacity of nonmarket mechanisms to cope efficiently with complex economic decisions. Markets arrive at supply and pricing choices through the uncoordinated actions of a large number of decentralized decision makers. The limited capacity of planning agencies to process information and make appropriate economic choices produced severe inefficiencies and a limited range of consumer goods in the Soviet Union. Oscar Lange and Alec Nove suggested various ways in which this problem might be overcome through the blending of socialist institutions and market mechanisms. More recently, Paul Cockshott and Allin Cottrell have argued that contemporary computing technology might now make possible the type of complex data analysis required by socialist planners. At a more fundamental level, Frederick von Hayek and Robert Nozick charged that any attempt at public economic planning would ultimately result in the rise of a totalitarian state. Planners charged with allocation decisions would simply express their economic preferences to the exclusion of all others. This critique struck deepest at the Soviet model of socialism, which attempted to remove market mechanisms altogether. The mixed economies of Sweden, Denmark, and Norway have demonstrated that socialist institutions are in no way incompatible with DEMOCRACY, while state-driven ventures in France and Japan have shown that government coordination of economic development need not produce crippling inefficiencies.

See also COMMUNISM; IDEOLOGY.

Further Reading

Bernstein, Eduard. *Evolutionary Socialism.* New York: Schocken Books, 1961; Cockshott, W. Paul, and Allin Cottrell. *Towards a New Socialism.* Nottingham, U.K.: Spokesman Books, 1993; Engels, Friederick. *Socialism: Utopian and Scientific.* New York: International Publishers, 1998; Foner, Eric. "Why Is There No Socialism in the United States?" *History Workshop Journal* 17 (1984): 57–80; Fourier, Charles. *The Theory of the Four Movements.* Cambridge: Cambridge University Press, 1996; Hayden, Delores. *Seven American Utopias: The Architecture of Communitarian Socialism, 1790–1975.* Cambridge, Mass.: MIT. Press, 1976; Hayek, F. A. *The Road to Serfdom.* Chicago: University of Chicago Press, 1994; Marx, Karl "Manifesto of the Communist Party" and "Critique of the Gotha Program." In *Later Political Writings*, edited by Terrell Carver. Cambridge: Cambridge University Press, 1996; Mészáros, István. *Socialism or Barbarism: From the "American Century" to the Crossroads.* New York: Monthly Review Press, 2002; Nove, Alec. *The Economics of Feasible Socialism Revisited.* London: Routledge, 1992; Ottanelli, Fraser M. *Communist Party of the United States: From the Depression to World War II.* New Brunswick, N.J.: Rutgers University Press, 1991; Salvatore, Nick. *Eugene V. Debs: Citizen and Socialist.* Champaign: University of Illinois Press, 1984; Sassoon, Donald. *One Hundred Years of Socialism.* New York: New Press, 1996; Shulman, George M. *Radicalism and Reverence: The Political Thought of Gerrard Winstanley.* Berkeley: University of California Press, 1989.

—Jason C. Myers

ugly American

Many believed that the phrase *ugly American* would be cast on the dustbin of history after the end of the cold war in 1989. In many ways, it seemed time- and context-bound, a relic of a different era, apropos to the conflict between the United States and the Soviet Union that so characterized international politics from the late 1940s until the late 1980s, but no longer descriptive of political reality or politics as practiced in a post–cold war world.

But no sooner had the phrase lost its cachet than it was brought back from the dead, and new life was breathed into the old phrase. In the midst of the international war against terrorism, the U.S. government was accused of engaging in actions—torture, extraordinary rendition, and other more extreme actions—that revived criticism of the United States and has brought back to political life the original meaning of the phrase *ugly American.*

Quite rightly, Americans are made uncomfortable when the phrase *ugly American* is used. It conjures up unattractive images of the most offensive variety and fosters feelings of guilt over past wrongs. That many Americans see at least a kernel of truth in the phrase likewise makes them feel uncomfortable, even guilty. The sobriquet *ugly American* is designed and intended to displease, as it is also intended to describe a particular way of being. And as a barometer of worldwide sentiment and opinion about the United States, it is a useful guide in helping determine how well or poorly Americans are thought of at any time around the globe.

While literally derived from the 1958 novel and best seller of the same name written by Eugene Burdick and William Lederer, the term *ugly American* is more often incorrectly associated with the novelist Graham Greene, who in 1955 wrote the book *The Quiet American*. Over time, the term *ugly American* has taken on a life of its own as an insulting description of the behavior of individual Americans while traveling abroad and also of the activities (often covert operations) of the U.S. government abroad.

The novel *The Ugly American* is a series of short stories connected around a common theme of how the United States was losing the international struggle against COMMUNISM because of the ignorance and arrogance of Americans abroad. Centered in Southeast Asia, the novel portrays a failure on the part of the American interlopers to adapt to or even try to understand the culture, history, or religions of the indigenous people. The assumption was that the native population was supposed to conform to the wishes of the American superpower, and there was no need for the United States to understand them. The action takes place in Sarkhan, a fictitious Southeast Asian country in the midst of a communist insurgent movement. In the novel, one of the locals laments that "A mysterious change seems to come over Americans when they go to a foreign land. They isolate themselves socially. They live pretentiously. They're loud and ostentatious." This is the behavior that has been characterized as "ugly."

Graham Greene's 1955 novel, *The Quiet American*, was centered in Indochina at a time when the French colonialists were leaving and the United States was taking over. Here, the American hero plays the locals as pawns in an international game of power politics. The Americans manipulate people and situations, care little for the native population, but rather see them as expendable and disposable.

Over time, the term *ugly American* has come to be used as an insult aimed at American tourists traveling abroad. In the post–World War II era, Americans, with their superior wealth and power, sometimes acted with an arrogance and conceit that struck many of the locals as rude and insulting. On top of that, some American travelers were quite loud and insistent on having things their way. Some demanded that the locals speak English, and when they did not, acted rudely. The actions of the few became the sobriquet applied to the many. The term *ugly American* caught on and was—and is—hard to break.

In political terms, *ugly American* has come to be a euphemism for the misuse of American power abroad. As the world's only remaining superpower, the United States has heavy burdens and responsibilities and at times overplays its hand or behaves as an international bully, even to its friends and allies. Those occasions in which the Untied States behaved badly invited criticism, and the term *ugly American* was often used as a catchphrase that conjures up images of powerful bullies browbeating and taking advantage of the less powerful.

In 2004 and 2005, the term was dusted off and reapplied to the policies of President George W. Bush. Bush often snubbed his nose at international agreements, pulled the United States out of international treaties, refused to sign on to many multilateral agreements, and in the war against Iraq, trampled on the UNITED NATIONS, and ignored the wishes of traditional allies, even going so far as to demonstrate open disdain for several traditional and long-standing allies. The alleged arrogance and bullying techniques of Bush served to revive the ugly American image, and polls demonstrated that the United States became very unpopular internationally, with the citizens of many nations citing the threats of American power as the greatest danger facing the planet. Measured by POLLING data from across the globe, the United States had declined dramatically in the estimation of citizens in other countries. In many nations—even European nations—the United States was seen as a dangerous, arrogant superpower that used its power unilaterally and against the interests of global peace. Amazingly, Bush was seen in many of these polls as more dangerous to world peace than was Osama bin Laden. While such attitudes reflect a multitude of factors, some are clearly directed at what is believed to be the arrogant and unilateral behavior of the United States internationally: the scandal at the Abu Ghraib prison, the rendition of suspects kidnapped from countries and taken to undetermined locations, the prison at Guantanamo Bay in Cuba, the denial of basic rights to many of those in detention, and torture at some locations. All these activities fueled the fire that was already smoldering and gave credibility to the view that, indeed, the United States considered itself above the law (both domestically and internationally) and that American power was out of control. Was this an American overreaction to the events of 9/11, or was this the ugly American writ large? Were these actions an accurate reflection of the real America, or an aberration? World opinion judged the United States harshly.

Is the image of the ugly American true? Clearly, there are times when the United States merits criticism, and at times it does seem to play into the worst elements associated with that term. But as the world's only superpower, the responsibilities of the United States require it to lead and take actions that to some seem ill advised. It is the occupational hazard of a superpower to be an inviting target of criticism, buts in the end, the true test of a superpower is whether it acts with wisdom and justice. Did it promote more than its own selfish interest and serve and protect the international community and its traditional friends and allies? Did it stand up for the right values, and did it have the courage of conviction to do the right thing in a complex world?

Further Reading
Greene, Graham. *The Quiet American*. New York: Penguin, 2004; Lederer, William J., and Eugene Burdick. *The Ugly American*. New York: W.W. Norton, 1999.

—Michael A. Genovese

United Nations
During the last years of World War II, the victorious Allied powers, particularly the United States, France, the United Kingdom, and the Soviet Union, created the United Nations (UN) "to save succeeding generations from the scourge of war." As was the League of Nations that preceded it, the UN was premised on the concept of "collective security," one component of the idealist or Wilsonian approach to international affairs. Convinced that the breakdown of the "balance of power" approach had contributed to World War I, world leaders resorted to crafting a treaty that would bind members to respond collectively to acts of aggression by rogue states, whether members or not. The League of Nations foundered due to less-than-universal membership (the U.S. Congress declined to back President Woodrow Wilson's plan) and the remaining members' insufficient commitment to curb the Japanese invasion of Manchuria (1931) and the Italian invasion of Ethiopia (1934). The drafters of the UN charter sought to create a structure that was more flexible in its decision making and more reflective of global power relations. The most palpable aspect of this was the designation of five permanent members of the Security Council that individually can block resolutions and actions through exercising a veto. At a series of meetings during the war (Moscow in 1943, Dumbarton Oaks in 1944, and Yalta in 1945), the United States, the United Kingdom, and the Soviet Union laid the groundwork for the organization. In San Francisco in April to June 1945, the UN charter was completed and signed. The subsequent ratifications became sufficient on October 24, 1945, and the UN came into being. October 24th is observed as UN Day around the world.

The charter mandated six major organs: the General Assembly (GA) composed of all members, the Security Council (to preserve the peace), the International Court of Justice (to hear disputes among nations), the Secretariat as the administrative body, the Economic and Social Council, and the Trusteeship Council (to foster the independence of trust territories). The goals of the UN, as enshrined in the preamble of the charter, include preventing war, reaffirming human rights, fostering respect for INTERNATIONAL LAW, and the promotion of social progress. Among the principles described in article 2 of the charter are the sovereign equality of all member states, the peaceful settlement of disputes among nations, support for UN enforcement actions as mandated by the Security Council, and noninterference in the domestic affairs of member states.

World leaders converge at the 62nd United Nations General Assembly. *(Getty Images)*

The GA is the primary deliberative organ of the United Nations, consisting of all 191 member states, each exercising one vote. Decisions are by simple majority vote except for matters deemed important questions (membership, peace and security actions if the Security Council deadlocks, and some budgetary matters), which require a two-thirds majority. Regular sessions of the GA begin on the third Tuesday in September and usually conclude by mid-December. Much of the GA's work is done through a series of committees: First (disarmament and security), Second (economic and financial), Third (social, humanitarian, and cultural), Fourth (decolonization), Fifth (administrative and budgetary), Sixth (legal), and the Special Political Committee (peace and security matters not handled by the First Committee).

The Security Council (SC) has 15 members, five of which are permanent (China, France, Russia, the United Kingdom, and the United States). The other 10 members are elected for two-year terms, with five elected in alternate years. In an effort to reflect global power at the time of its creation, the Security Council operates under the rule of "great power unanimity," generally referred to as "veto power" when one of the permanent members casts a negative vote, thereby blocking an action. Its functions include maintenance of peace and security, investigation and settlement of disputes or instructing the secretary-general (SG) to use good offices to this end, promotion of disarmament, application of economic or other nonmilitary sanctions, sending UN observer forces or armed forces in response to aggression and conflict, admission of new members, recommendation to the GA of the appointment of the SG, and with the GA election judges of the International Court. The SC may convene at any time to deal with crises.

The Economic and Social Council (ECOSOC) has 54 members who serve for three years, with 18 elected each year to staggered terms. It coordinates the economic and social work of the UN and serves as the liaison or reporting organ for most of the specialized agencies and affiliated intergovernmental organizations. It conducts studies, reports to the GA, and makes recommendations on issues ranging from economic concerns (poverty, development, and trade) through social issues broadly defined (human rights, including the rights of women and children, culture, education, and health). Two formal sessions occur annually for about two months each, one in New York and the other in Geneva. The actual work continues all year through commissions, committees, and the specialized agencies. A wide variety of international nongovernmental organizations (NGOs) maintain consultative status with ECOSOC, while an even larger number of national NGOs are affiliated through the Department of Public Information of the Secretariat. The specialized agencies, programs, and funds include a wide range of bodies from long-standing ones such as the International Labor Organization, the World Health Organization, and the United Nations Children's Fund, through newer ones such as the World Intellectual Property Organization. Also reporting to ECOSOC are functional commissions such as the Commission on the Status of Women and the Commission on Human Rights. Finally, somewhat more autonomous are the Bretton Woods organizations, named after the site of the 1944 conference on the international financial system. These include the World Bank Group, the International Monetary Fund, and the World Trade Organization (conceived at Bretton Woods but only in recent years supplanting the General Agreement on Tariffs and Trade). These financial bodies have decision-making structures dominated by member states with the world's stronger economies. Over the last few decades, they have come under criticism for implementing economic programs that are unduly free market oriented and "one-size-fits-all." Calls for greater flexibility and distribution of decision-making power have largely been ignored. In recent years, they have been criticized by leaders from some of the developing world and have become the target of grassroots anti-GLOBALIZATION protests.

The Trusteeship Council was created to supervise the administration of trust territories overseen by member states which, in turn, made up the council. The Trusteeship Council suspended its work in 1994 after the last trust territory, Palau, became independent. Under the ongoing reform and restructuring process, the Trusteeship Council almost certainly will be eliminated.

The International Court of Justice (ICJ) is a legacy of the Permanent Court of International Justice established in 1922 and continues to meet in The Hague. Under the 1945 charter provisions, it handles cases of disputes among sovereign nations, not cases involving private parties. Its 15 judges are elected for nine-year terms by the GA and SC. The judgeships are generally distributed on a regional basis, with the five permanent members almost always represented. The greatest constraint on the ICJ is that national sovereignty inherently impedes enforcement. While some nations commit in advance to the court's compulsory JURISDICTION, most do not. Generally, the two states must agree in advance to the court's jurisdiction, though one may initiate an action requesting the other's agreement. States usually comply with the decision. However, in two cases, the disappointed party demurred. One was the Corfu Channel case of 1947, when Albania refused to compensate the United Kingdom for damages in a shipping case, and the second was *Nicaragua v. U.S.A.*, when the ICJ ruled that the United States violated international law by mining Nicaraguan harbors. While the U.S. refused to acknowledge jurisdiction and blocked appeal to the Security Council, it did quietly assist in the removal of said mines.

The Secretariat is the administrative organ of the UN. It is charged with administering the daily affairs of organization (including the drafting of reports, verbatim records, translation of debates, and communication with the press and public), overseeing the operations of peacekeeping forces, attending to problems of refugees and human rights violations, and preparing studies of issues of concern to the body. The Secretary-General, appointed to a (renewable) five-year term by the GA upon recommendation of the SC, oversees this administration, brings to the SC threats to international peace and security, and may exercise good offices in the settlement of disputes. Secretary-General Kofi Annan (1997–2006) was especially active in advocating for the organization and using the influence of the office to encourage greater member state commitment to eradicating disease, alleviating poverty, and intervening in cases of human rights violations.

Member states are assessed obligatory dues for the regular budget and separately for the peace missions and international criminal tribunals; in addition, there are voluntary contributions to the funds and programs. The funding of the UN regular budget is based on contributions by member states, which are assessed an amount based on their "capacity to pay." This capacity is derived from national income, per capita gross national product, and foreign exchange earnings. Because of the wide range of difference in these capacities, limitations have been set for a "floor" and a "ceiling." In 1946, the assessment for the United States would have been around 50 percent of the total, but at the insistence of U.S. leaders it was capped at a ceiling of 40 percent, in 1973 further reduced to 25 percent, and ultimately cut to 22 percent of the regular UN budget, while in 1997 the lower limit was set at 0.001 percent. The other obligatory contributions are for the economic development programs and peacekeeping operations. The latter, in particular, have proven controversial when some countries were less than committed to UN actions, such as opposition by the Soviet Union to UN action during the Korean War. The United States has also contributed heavily to peacekeeping, though forcing reductions in giving down to 26.5 percent in recent years. Budget issues are a two-edged sword. While some would like to see the United States pay up to its full capacity, others are concerned that at present the United States, Japan, and Germany (with less than 10 percent of the world's population) account for about half the budget, and 10 members are responsible for 80 percent of it. A similar discrepancy exists regarding assessments versus voting numbers in the GA, where about 180 voting countries supply only about 25 percent of the budget. Despite the disproportion in voting strength in the largely exhortative GA, many of the poorer countries feel that wealthy ones, and the U.S. in particular, have wielded budget issues to force policies of reform that favor the economically and politically strong minority.

Voting patterns at the UN have shifted over the years as the membership has grown. During its early years, the UN consisted primarily of European and Latin American-Caribbean countries with Australia, New Zealand, and a few from Asia, the Middle East, and Africa that had gained their freedom, such as India, Iran, Iraq, Syria, and Liberia, as well as white-ruled South Africa. During the 1950s, additional states from the Middle East and Asia joined, and beginning in 1957 with Ghana, the decolonization of Africa and other parts of Asia led to a large influx of former colonies. This trend shifted the balance of votes in the GA in favor of developing, non-European nations. As a result, the majority that had voted overwhelmingly along the interests of the United States and western Europe was replaced by a larger bloc that strongly supported decolonization, development, and resistance to white rule in South Africa, often leaving the United States and some of its allies on the losing end. There was also a concomitant shift in the SC, despite the dominance of the permanent members. During the early years, votes tended to favor the so-called first world of U.S. and European market economies, leading the Soviet Union to exercise its veto frequently. As the agenda of the developing majority reached the SC, increasingly the United States invoked the veto to block resolutions calling for condemnation or action against apartheid in South Africa or Israeli policies toward Palestinians.

Several key issues that the UN has dealt with over decades serve well to reveal the challenges it has faced and some of the reasons for both its successes and failures. One of the first major crises it confronted was that of the Middle East. As decolonization of the region increased in the wake of World War II, the United Kingdom sought to unburden itself of its League of Nations mandate in Palestine. Arab aspirations for national independence of the region had been strong since the end of World War I, while over the same years some European Jews were striving to create a Jewish homeland in Palestine. The European powers had made conflicting promises to each. In the wake of the Nazi Holocaust, thousands of Jewish refugees were streaming into Palestine with the hope of creating a Jewish state. Increased violence between the Arab and Jewish communities, compounded by Jewish attacks on the British authorities seeking to curb IMMIGRATION, led Britain to transfer the problem to the fledgling UN. The GA, in November 1947, passed a partition plan to create two states, one Arab and one Jewish, in the area of the mandate, with the Jerusalem and Bethlehem areas to be *corpus separatum*, under international oversight. Each state was divided into three segments, contiguous only at small points. The Jewish state was slightly larger in territory, though it included much of the Negev Desert. Since the population of the area remained two-thirds Arab, the Arab state had a small minority of Jews, while the Jewish state had a very sizeable minority of Arabs. Some regarded the partition plan as a formula for disaster, but it was accepted by Jewish leaders but rejected overwhelmingly by the Arab states and the leaders of the Arab community in Palestine. In May 1948, with violence already having broken out between the two communities, Israel declared its independence. Several of its Arab neighbors responded with military attacks. When the war was over, Israel controlled about 80 percent of Palestine, having taken over large areas prescribed for the Arab state. A series of wars ensued in 1956 (over Suez), 1967, 1973, and subsequent Israeli incursions into Lebanon. Throughout this period, the UN supplied peacekeeping forces to help separate the belligerents, and the UN Relief and Works Agency provided sustenance to the Palestinian refugee population, which numbered in the hundreds of thousands. Since then, the UN has affirmed the right of refugees to return to their homes and/or gain compensation. It has also generally supported a "two-state" solution based on the borders that existed between 1948 and 1967 (after which Israel occupied the West Bank, Gaza Strip, Golan Heights, and the Sinai Peninsula, the last later returned to Egypt as a result of bilateral peace efforts). While the UN peacekeepers certainly served as a deterrent to escalation on many occasions, the Arab-Israeli conflict has been seen by many as a UN failure. If this is the case, it is in part because the strong pressure for Israeli withdrawal from the occupied territories expressed by the GA majority has led Israel to eschew the UN as a mediator. Instead, Israel sought its strong ally—the United States—as an intermediary, creating a dynamic that led the Arab states to default to a dominant U.S., not UN, role in the region. Were the United States more in line with the EURO-PEAN UNION, the other permanent SC members, and the GA majority, perhaps the UN would have proven a more successful peacemaker.

The contention over the representation of China at the world body also offers insights into constraints on the UN. In 1945, China was represented by the Nationalist (or Kuomintang) government. Less than four years later, Communist forces toppled the Nationalists, who fled to Taiwan. Standard UN prac-

tices in the case of regime change include an assessment of which party most effectively controls the territory and its infrastructure and a GA vote to recognize the credentials of the delegation representing the new government. Since the Communist victory represented an escalation of the cold war and the United States strongly resisted a second permanent seat being held by a communist government, it succeeded in getting the change in delegation deemed an "Important Question" requiring a two-thirds majority of the GA to shift the representation to the People's Republic government in Beijing. For 20 years, the SC lived with the anomaly of the displaced government in Taiwan wielding the powers of a permanent member. By 1971, with pressure from the new GA majority increasing and the Nixon administration initiating a détente with the People's Republic, U.S. opposition was relaxed, and the Beijing government gained its representation.

Most assessments of the UN's successes and failures focus almost exclusively on issues of peace and security, generally resulting in a mixed record. In some cases (Vietnam and Afghanistan) the cold war prevented the UN from exercising an effective role, while in others, the limited national interests of the great powers may have contributed to inaction or a belated response (Rwanda, Somalia, and the Sudan). Often overlooked are the successes of the UN in decolonization, democratic transitions, and nation building, such as the liberation of Southern Africa, the freedom of East Timor, and a somewhat less successful intervention in the Balkans.

The UN is probably most underappreciated in the areas that we today refer to as "unconventional security," such as human rights, global health and disease, environmental concerns, famine and disaster relief, and economic development. Through specialized agencies such as the World Health Organization, the Food and Agriculture Organization, and the UN Environment Program, the UN has eradicated diseases and fed starving populations, saving countless lives—something its critics frequently ignore. It has also served as the arena for crafting the Law of the Sea Treaty and the Kyoto Protocol on global warming. In response to human rights abuses, it has established the International Criminal Court (ICC) for the prosecution of those who commit genocides, crimes against humanity, and other criminal actions. While

United Nations service members boarding a plane *(United Nations)*

the ICC still lacks the support of the United States, it is proceeding to ensure that human rights violators know their actions may no longer go unpunished.

As the world has changed rapidly in the six decades since the UN's creation, the organization has struggled to reform itself to contend with new challenges and an ever-changing global balance of power. From the postwar years of dominance by the World War II Allies, through the bipolarity of the cold war, to the contemporary era with rising economic power exerted by the European Union, Japan, China, and India, the UN has been subjected to the shifting vicissitudes of its strongest members. As its 50th anniversary approached in 1995, the discussion over reform became more intense and urgent. The major areas of reform include streamlining the Secretariat and international civil service, demanding greater financial accountability by all units, exploring alternative modes of funding such as taxing arms sales or the exploitation of shared resources, developing a rapid response

and deployment capability for peacekeeping forces in international crises such as Rwanda, restructuring the Bretton Woods system to allow greater consultation with the poorer states, and considering expanded membership and changes in voting on the SC.

Looming over the entire discussion of reform is the challenge posed to the principle of multilateralism and collective security by the ideological and policy alternative of U.S. unilateralism and its refusal to allow U.S. forces to serve under UN command after the Somalia debacle of 1993. The administration of George W. Bush eschewed the vision of the UN as an effective broker of peace and security and regarded it in an instrumentalist fashion, as yet another tool for the achievement of U.S. FOREIGN POLICY goals. The August 2005 appointment of strident UN critic John Bolton to the U.S. ambassadorship through a recess appointment skirting SENATE opposition epitomized this stance, particularly as Bolton's objections nearly scuttled an omnibus reform program long under development. (Bolton left the post in late 2006 amid speculation that the Senate would not approve his permanent appointment.) Nevertheless, the reform process continues as the UN evolves and adapts to a changing global environment. With the political and economic ascension of the European Union, Japan, China, India, and other members states, it is likely that U.S. unilateralism will be increasingly untenable and may recede in the face of such challenges as arms proliferation, terrorism, the HIV-AIDS epidemic, global warming, economic development, and other issues that cross borders and demand the type of cooperation that can only be achieved through the United Nations.

See also DIPLOMATIC POLICY.

Further Reading

Baehr, Peter R., and Leon Gordenker. *The United Nations: Reality and Ideal.* 4th ed. New York: Palgrave/Macmillan, 2005; Childers, Erskine, with Brian Urquhart. *Renewing the United Nations System.* Uppsala: Dag Hammarskjöld Foundation, 1994; Fasulo, Linda. *An Insider's Guide to the UN.* New Haven, Conn.: Yale University Press, 2004; Gareis, Sven Bernhard, and Johannes Varwick. *The United Nations: An Introduction.* New York: Palgrave/Macmillan, 2005; Mingst, Karen A., and Margaret P. Karns. *The United Nations in the Post-Cold War Era.* 2nd ed. Boulder, Colo.: Westview Press, 2000; Moore, John Allphin, Jr., and Jerry Pubantz. *The New United Nations: International Organization in the Twenty-First Century.* Upper Saddle River, N.J.: Pearson/Prentice Hall, 2006; Weiss, Thomas G., David P. Forsythe, and Roger A. Coate. *The United Nations and Changing World Politics.* 4th ed. Boulder, Colo.: Westview Press, 2004; Yoder, Amos. *The Evolution of the United Nations System.* 3rd ed. Washington, D.C.: Taylor & Francis, 1997; Ziring, Lawrence, Robert E. Riggs, and Jack C. Plano. *The United Nations: International Organization and World Politics.* 4th ed. Belmont, Calif.: Thomson Wadsworth, 2005.

—Donald Will

United States Agency for International Development *(USAID)*

The Unites States Agency for International Development (USAID), created by an act of Congress in 1961, is an agency of the U.S. government that provides financial and technical assistance to developing nations. Its purpose is to help alleviate world poverty by assisting third world nations to accelerate their development. USAID funds programs in most major development sectors, including disaster relief, basic institution and services development, and specific global issues, such as HIV/AIDS and poverty.

Every U.S. president from Franklin Delano Roosevelt to George W. Bush has found that in order to serve American interests he has needed an agency able to work closely with the other nations of the world to promote their growth in the political, economic, and social sectors. USAID is the agency in the U.S. federal government that provides that capability. The logo of USAID, a handshake between an American and a citizen from the developing world, is known throughout the world and symbolizes the meeting of equals at the personal level to work together for a better world.

The concept of foreign assistance to less-fortunate nations has generally enjoyed bipartisan support, although that support has often been weak. The historical antecedent of foreign assistance was the Good Neighbor policy established by Franklin Roosevelt. After World War II and the destruction of much of Europe and Japan, those nations clearly needed U.S. assistance to rebuild, both as a defense against COMMUNISM and for general international stability. The United States quickly met the immediate need for disaster relief, most famously through the Committee for Relief in Europe (CARE). This relief work was a key factor in avoiding any major humanitarian crises in either Western Europe or Japan.

CARE packages became famous. It is worth noting that every post–World War II German chancellor, from Konrad Adenauer through Gerhard Schroeder, remembered with exceptional gratitude receiving American-provided food packages in the aftermath of World War II. For several it was their first taste of chocolate.

The Economic Cooperation Act, passed on April 2, 1948, initiated the Marshall Plan that started active American involvement in the reconstruction of Western Europe. Close cooperation with the recipient nations, the infusion of significant amounts of seed capital, and a sound institutional base resulted in a rapid reconstruction of Europe. Point Four followed and expanded programs for economic growth to the developing world. Point Four takes its name because it was the fourth point in President Harry S. Truman's 1949 inaugural address that focused on proposals to build a more prosperous, democratic, and stable world. President Truman's and Secretary of State George Marshall's vision of the nations of the world working together in peaceful collaboration and their competence in creating the institutions to achieve that collaboration, including what was to ultimately become USAID are widely acknowledged by historians today as a pivotal step in what became 50 years of progress.

The Mutual Security Agency (MSA), created by the Mutual Security Act of June 30, 1951, administered the foreign assistance program in post–World War II Europe. It also established the Foreign Operations Administration (FOA) as an independent agency outside the DEPARTMENT OF STATE in 1953. In 1953, the FOA and the MSA merged responsibilities.

As Western Europe stabilized and returned to sound government and economic prosperity, USAID and predecessor agencies expanded into Latin America, Africa, and Asia. Ultimately, USAID grew to concentrate almost exclusively on the newly independent nations of Africa, Asia, and the close American neighbors in Latin America. As one would anticipate, development in those nations was significantly slower than it had been in Western Europe. Western Europe had a solid history of democratically elected governments and strong industrial economies. Thus, Western European revitalization was primarily a case of recovering disrupted capacity rather than creating new capacity. In the developing world, there was little history of democratic or even transparent governance. Even more challenging, the newly independent African and Asian states had weak economies and little industrial base.

In the late 1980s with the disbandment of the Soviet Union and its empire, USAID shifted geographic focus again, this time into the countries of the former Soviet bloc. As those nations broke away, asserted their political independence, and embraced a liberal free enterprise economic model, many requested and received USAID assistance.

Historically, USAID has been exceptionally responsive to congressional direction; if Congress or a particular member of Congress is interested in primary education, funds flow in that direction. When congressional interest changes, so do funding priorities, which accounts for the vast range of projects and programs USAID has funded over the years. USAID is occasionally accused of being unfocused in its programs, and much of this diffusion comes from members of Congress mandating that USAID undertake projects in specific areas. Since the late 1960s, USAID has largely functioned as a bank. That is, USAID funds programs, projects, and activities that others then implement. USAID mainly makes grants, not loans.

While the concept of foreign assistance enjoys bipartisan support, that support often wanes during budget debates. USAID is a vulnerable target when there is a debate over domestic versus international priorities. Because of this vulnerability, USAID in the past 30 years has declined significantly in size. For example, in 1970, USAID had approximately 12,500 U.S. citizen employees working worldwide. By 2004, the entire USAID agency consisted of 2,000 citizen employees, of which roughly 900 work overseas.

USAID world headquarters is located in the Reagan Building in Washington, D.C. It operates under the policy direction of the secretary of state. USAID is organized into both geographical bureaus, including Africa, Latin America, newly emerging states (which includes former communist countries), and Asia, and technical bureaus, including economic growth, agriculture, and trade (EGAT), global health (GH), and democracy, conflict and humanitarian assistance (DCHA). USAID also occasionally creates bureaus or offices for special purposes. For example, the HIV/AIDS bureau was created in response to the pandemic. USAID also has specialized bureaus for planning, budgeting, participant training, congressional relations, and university relations.

There are three basic types of employees at USAID, including U.S. direct hires, third country nationals, and foreign service nationals. U.S. direct hires include foreign service officers (FSO), who are U.S. citizens and serve in both the United States and overseas. General schedule (GS) employees are also U.S. citizens and work mainly in Washington, D.C., although occasionally they spend short periods (one to six months) overseas. Third country nationals (TCN) are typically from the region in which they work but from a different country than the one in which they are actually working. Foreign service nationals (FSN) are citizens of the country in which they are actually working.

USAID implements most of its programs and projects through its bilateral missions. USAID has approximately 40 bilateral missions around the world. (Bilateral refers to working in a single country, for example, Nigeria, Kenya, or Indonesia). The number is approximate because USAID periodically changes to add new countries and subtracts as countries graduate for one reason or another. Reflecting the declining overall size of USAID, the bilateral missions have also shrunk considerably. Typically, now USAID missions are relatively small, having from 10 to 15 U.S. direct hire officers. FSNs or TCNs do more of the managerial and administrative work. With rare exceptions, now contractors or grantees implement the programs and projects.

As an economy of force measure, USAID has established several regional centers around the world. For example, in Africa there are centers in East, West, and southern Africa. These centers are generally somewhat larger than the bilateral missions they serve and often have specialists in areas such as law, accounting, and project design that the bilateral missions do not have. Circuit riding to the various bilateral missions in their regions can keep these specialists on the road for 50 percent to 75 percent of their time. In addition to providing staff support to the bilateral missions, regional centers often implement programs that have a regional dimension, such as regional family planning programs or regional agriculture research programs.

USAID now does exclusively grant financing, that is, funds go directly to an implementing agency for a specific purpose; the implementing agency does not have to repay these funds so long as it uses the funds for their intended purposes. Historically, the grants have gone primarily to the host country governments, which then have implemented the agreed-upon activities. Over the past 20 years, grants have often gone to universities or nongovernmental organizations (NGO).

Until the mid-1970s, USAID also made long-term concessional interest rate loans in Africa, Asia, and Latin America for capital projects, largely infrastructure—that is, roads, dams, and buildings. A concessional rate of interest is one that is lower than the market rate, typically from 1 to 3 percent. The WORLD BANK has assumed responsibility for most donor-funded capital projects in the developing world.

USAID has worked hard to cultivate positive relationships with universities throughout the United States, especially with the land grant colleges, which USAID often uses to implement agriculture, education, and university building programs in Africa and Asia. The presidents of three land grant universities have served as the administrator of USAID.

USAID often uses participating agency staffing agreements (PASA) with agencies or departments such as Treasury, the USDA, or the Internal Revenue Service to implement technical assistance projects such as building an agriculture extension service, a tax service, or a customs office. Typically, USAID provides the administrative support and program direction for the PASA team.

There are thousands of different types of NGOs working in the developing world, some indigenous, others international, and many American. Typically, USAID finances NGOs with a commitment to a specific purpose, be that family planning, cooperatives, or slowing global climate change.

Neither USAID nor the federal government as a whole could function without the contractors (for-profit firms) who do much of the basic work. There are thousands of firms that serve the needs of the three branches of government and those doing business with those institutions. A small number of these specialize in serving the needs of USAID. Overall, these firms have proven skillful in mobilizing teams to implement programs and projects in the areas of the world where USAID works.

Currently, the annual budget of USAID is approximately $11 billion, which is less than 1 percent of the federal budget. Actual funding varies from year to year. Geographically, sub-Saharan Africa is the largest recipient. Economic growth, agriculture, and trade (EGAT) funds programs in overall economic development, including education, agriculture, and trade promotion. Global health (GH) includes maternal-child health, family planning, and HIV/AIDS. Democracy, conflict and humanitarian assistance (DCHA) promotes democratic governance, conflict mitigation, and long-term humanitarian assistance. PL480 promotes the sale and distribution of basic U.S. agricultural commodities overseas. Disaster assistance provides short-term emergency help to nations suffering from natural disasters and other emergencies.

Throughout its history, USAID has financed programs in most major sectors, including infrastructure development, institutional development, agriculture, education, health, family planning, HIV/AIDS, natural resources management, human rights, trade, and promotion of democracy.

USAID has gone through a number of phases in implementing its programs. Initially, the emphasis was on direct relief in Europe and then on promoting reconstruction. The postcolonial era, beginning in the 1950s when the nations of Africa and Asia received independence, emphasized construction of basic infrastructure (for example, roads, schools, and hospitals) and building the capacity of the new governments to provide basic services. The greatest emphasis has been placed on agriculture, education, and health. While there have been some notable successes in places such as Botswana, Thailand, and South Korea, overall progress has often been very slow. Because of this, in the late 1970s, USAID began to emphasize private sector development, especially the development of for-profit businesses. In addition, USAID has emphasized family planning because it became clear that high population growth rates were partly responsible for slow per capita economic growth. By the late 1990s, it was clear that without improvements in governance, only possible through transparent democracies, neither the private sector nor the developing nations as a whole would flourish, hence the emphasis on promotion of DEMOCRACY.

USAID and predecessor agencies have achieved notable successes in several areas. One such example would be the reconstruction of Western Europe after World War II. World War II devastated Europe, and American intervention provided a vital impetus for Western Europe to reconstruct. The United States initially invited the Soviet bloc nations to participate in this process, but those nations chose not to participate, most critically in the Marshall Plan, and partly as a result lagged badly in reconstruction.

From 1950 until the late 1970s throughout Africa, Asia, and Latin America, USAID was instrumental in constructing the roads, schools, and hospitals that assisted nations such as Botswana, India, and South Korea to sustain their development to the point that they have achieved genuine prosperity. Partly because of these programs, life expectancy in the developing world has increased by approximately 33 percent over the past 40 years.

It has taken more than 20 years and approximately $12 billion, but gradually USAID has developed an effective methodology that assisted DEVELOPING COUNTRIES to reduce their fertility while allowing their male and female citizens to stay within the bounds of culturally appropriate behavior. More than 50 million couples now use family planning as a direct result of USAID's population program. In the 28 countries with the largest USAID-sponsored family planning programs, the average number of children per family had dropped from 6.1 in the mid-1960s to 4. 2 by 2001.

Almost from the date of the identification of the disease, USAID initiated HIV/AIDS prevention programs. Using an approach similar to that practiced for family planning, USAID has facilitated nations such as Uganda in making major reductions in their infection rates. Worldwide, more than 850,000 people have received education in how to prevent the spread of the HIV virus through USAID-sponsored programs.

USAID has also focused attention on disaster relief in the developing world. Whether it is volcanoes, droughts, or tsunamis, USAID got there quickly, organized things on the ground, and provided effective disaster relief. Hurricane Katrina provided an ironic testimony to the effectiveness of USAID disaster relief; the U.S. NGOs involved with Katrina lamented that FEMA lacked the professionalism, the clear procedures, and the sense of priorities and mission that they were accustomed to working with in USAID.

USAID has also worked on bringing about a "green revolution." Worldwide, the international agriculture research stations that provide the technical basis for the green revolution receive approximately 25 percent of their funding from USAID. At the bilateral level, USAID has been the leading funder of national agriculture research and the extension of that research on to farmers' fields. USAID and other donor investments in better seed and agricultural technologies over the past three decades have helped feed an extra billion people in the world.

Further Reading
United States Agency for International Development Web site. Available online. URL: www.usaid.gov. Accessed March 24, 2007; U.S. Overseas Loans and Grants (The Greenbook). Available online. URL: http://qesdb.usaid.gov/gbk. Bertotti, Timothy L. "History and Accomplishments of USAID." USAID/Columbia, 3 December 2001.

—Norman L. Olsen

welfare state

While often referred to today in a pejorative way, the welfare state began as an effort to soften the harsher edges of the system of CAPITALISM. With industrialization came urbanization as workers flocked to the urban areas in hopes of finding gainful employment, but many untrained workers had a difficult time finding affordable housing, making a living wage, and caring for their families. Over time, pressure built up on the government to help alleviate the problems of poverty, health care needs, housing shortages, and a host of other economic and human problems. One way governments attempted to address these problems came to be known as "the welfare state." In general, a welfare state is a system wherein the government strives to provide for the maximum of social and economic benefits for the citizen. Political scientist Andrew Hacker in the March 22, 1964, *New York Times Magazine* defined the welfare state as one "that guarantees a broad series of economic protections that any citizen can claim when he is no longer able to provide for himself. In a welfare state, the benefits an individual receives are political rights, not charity, and there should be no occasion for apology or embarrassment in applying for them. Moreover, the services made available by a welfare state will parallel in quality and coverage those open to individuals who are able to draw on private resources." The welfare state thus marks a shift away from the concept of government having a minimal role (safety and security) to a more positive role (providing for social services).

Today, *welfare state* means many different things to different people. It can be an ideal model of the provision of the tools and resources (welfare) necessary for decent living whereby the state is primarily responsible for the care of the citizen. It can also mean the state providing some minimal services and resources to the needy. In its grandest form, it can mean the state as the primary agent for providing goods and services.

In general, there are the minimalist model of the welfare state (for example, the United States) and the more robust model (such as can be found in northern Europe). At the minimalist level, the government is the provider of last resort, ensuring a basic safety net below which no civilized nation would let its citizens fall. At the more robust level, the state assumes greater responsibility for services, such as wages, jobs, and health care.

Most of the modern welfare states developed slowly over time, adding a piece here and a piece there, until the rudimentary elements of what we today call a welfare state became visible. In Europe, beginning in the late 19th and continuing into the 20th centuries, states began to become more and more involved in guaranteeing rights and services to their citizens. The state began to assume responsibilities previously handled by charities, churches, or local communities. One of the key steps in this process was the development of social insurance, established by Bismarck in Germany.

The United States is considered to have a low level of social welfare, especially in contrast to European states. This minimalist model assumes that the primary unit responsible for social welfare is the individual. The state is to play a minimal and not interventionist role. Thus, citizens of the United States do not have a "right" to health care (provided by the state), nor is the government responsible for ensuring jobs. Most of the social welfare function is in private hands or the responsibility of religious organizations. The state has a variety of minimal programs such as SOCIAL SECURITY, Medicare, and unemployment insurance, but these are small by the standards of most industrial nations. The individual is to be responsible for him- or herself, and the private sector is the chief vehicle for jobs and income. The welfare state in the United States came about as a result of the Great Depression of 1929. This led to the election of President Franklin D. Roosevelt and the creation of the NEW DEAL programs that marked the beginnings of social welfare in the United States. These programs were expanded during the 1960s during the GREAT SOCIETY era under President Lyndon B. Johnson. In the 1980s, efforts were made to put a cap on social welfare spending, but the programs proved resilient and fairly popular and were hard to trim.

During the so-called Republican Revolution of the mid-1990s, when the REPUBLICAN PARTY won control of both houses of Congress in 1994 (the first time in 40 years), the welfare state became one of the key targets of the party's resurgence. And one of the most visible features of the Republican "Contract with America" was the promise to reform and scale back federal welfare programs. But a Democrat, Bill Clinton, was still in the White House, and although politically wounded, he still could use the PRESIDENTIAL VETO pen.

In yet another instance of politics making strange bedfellows, Clinton actually worked closely with the Republican-controlled Congress, and together they passed a significant welfare reform bill. It cut back the welfare rolls and pushed power back to the states. It also had back-to-work features popular with voters. This shrinking of the welfare state demonstrated that FEDERALISM is alive and well in the United States and that the political system remains responsive to the will of the voters.

In the United Kingdom, the state has charted a middle course between the robust welfare state (often derisively referred to as "the nanny state") and the minimalist state. In fact, the first time the term *welfare state* was used was during World War II by Archbishop William Temple. And it was just after World War II that the British began to more fully develop their welfare system. In 1948, British politician Edward Hallett Carr enjoined his fellow citizens, "Let us substitute welfare for wealth as our governing purpose." It provides health care to all citizens as a right and pays for this service out of taxes. Asa Briggs identified three core elements of the welfare state as providing a guaranteed minimum income, social protection (safety net) in the event of job loss or other insecurity, and the provision of government-supplied life services. This soon became known as the "institutional model of welfare." The sociologist T. H. Marshall identified the welfare state as combining DEMOCRACY with capitalism. In the United Kingdom, coverage of the welfare state is fairly significant, but services are provided at a fairly low level.

In Sweden, a more robust form of the welfare state is in evidence. Some see this as the "ideal" form of the welfare state, whereby the government offers a wide safety net to its citizens. Sweden has a comprehensive social welfare state with redistributive and egalitarian goals. Such systems can be expensive. Many nations are not willing to pay the price, either in dollars or in state control, for such systems. Critics point to Sweden and argue that this "cradle-to-grave" welfare state makes the citizen dependent on the state, but most of the citizens of Sweden are pleased overall with their version of the welfare state.

Supporters of the more robust version of the welfare state argue that on humanitarian grounds, every citizen deserves a minimal standard of living that no civilized country should let its citizens fall below. They also argue that the robust welfare state is stable, secure, and not prone to rebellion or antisocial outbursts. They also argue that by investing in the social infrastructure, such as educational child care, health care, and so on, they are making their societies better, more economically advanced, more competitive, and better able to adapt to the demands of GLOBALIZATION. Further, many argue that a welfare state is the antidote to the predatory nature of capitalism and the crushing hand of SOCIALISM. It is thus seen as a "middle way" between two extremes. Finally, they argue that reliance on the private sector simply has not worked and that a more significant role of the state is necessary in the ups and downs of the business cycle.

Critics of the robust welfare state argue that such systems make citizens more dependent on the state and less free. They also argue that such systems are too costly. They further say that such systems are a drain, not a boon, to the state's economy. To the critics, the free market is a more just and more efficient way to distribute value. Often, critics see the rise of the welfare state as a prelude to socialism.

In terms of comparative social spending on welfare-related programs as a percentage of the gross domestic product (GDP), Denmark ranks first, spending more than 29 percent of GDP on its welfare-related programs. Next is Sweden (nearly 29 percent), followed by France, Germany, Belgium, Switzerland, Austria, and Finland. The United Kingdom ranks in the middle of the pack in 13th place (nearly 22 percent of GDP). The United States ranks near the bottom, in 26th place (out of 29), spending less than 15 percent of its GDP on social welfare programs. The United States ranks just ahead of Ireland, Mexico, and South Korea.

Further Reading
Coll, Blanche D. *Perspectives in Public Welfare: A History*. Washington, D.C.: U.S. Social and Rehabilitation Service, Intramural Research Division, U.S. Government Printing Office, 1969; Katz, Michael B. *In the Shadow of the Poorhouse: A Social History of Welfare in America*. New York: Basic Books, 1996;——— *The Undeserving Poor: From the War on Poverty to the War on Welfare*. New York: Pantheon Books, 1989.

—Michael A. Genovese

World Bank

First of all, to avoid confusion, what is commonly known as the World Bank must be distinguished from the larger organizational umbrella of which it is a part, the World Bank Group (WBG). WBG refers to a network of five institutions, two of which constitute the World Bank itself. The core of WBG is the World Bank, but over the past five decades the role of WBG has expanded beyond the customary focus on macroeconomic sustainability and poverty reduction through economic and financial assistance, education, and infrastructural development. What has become WBG originated with the creation of the International Bank for Reconstruction and Development (IBRD), one half of today's World Bank, during the Bretton Woods Conference at the end of World War II and eventually grew to include the International Development Association (IDA), which is the other half of the World Bank, the International Finance Corporation (IFC), the Multilateral Investment Guarantee Agency (MIGA), and the International Center for the Settlement of Investment Disputes (ICSID).

The ICSID provides dispute resolution for controversies between investors and member states through mediation, arbitration, and conciliation. It can play a role or even direct negotiations and resolutions of disputes concerning nonmember countries and issues that are not directly investment related but somehow invoke factors central to WBG initiatives and activities. MIGA can also offer some dispute resolution remedies, but its purpose is specifically tailored to help countries build a favorable environment for foreign direct investment (FDI). Since FDI is one of the keys to economic development in poor countries, MIGA provides guarantees and assistance to increase the probability and incidence of FDI in target countries. Its services supplement those of the IFC, which antedates MIGA by approximately 30 years and facilitates private investment and private sector development in countries that receive World Bank assistance of some sort.

As indicated, the central component of WBG is the World Bank itself, and it attracts the bulk of the public's attention. In fact, most people are utterly unfamiliar with the distinction between WBG and the World Bank, and, based on the information available through typical news sources, it would be difficult to avoid the conclusion that WBG does not exist. Much of this is due to the fact that the activities of ICSID, IFC, and MIGA seem obscure and are not readily understandable by laypersons. In addition, the services these three institutions provide do not seem as controversial as those of the World Bank itself, so they are not nearly as visible.

Institutions such as the World Bank have experienced unprecedented visibility recently, and they have become known even to those with no interest in development economics, poverty, or sustainability. During the past decade or so, the common association of the World Bank with GLOBALIZATION initiatives has exposed the organization to unprecedented scrutiny from individuals and groups that had traditionally cared very little about it. Unfortunately, the politicization of globalization efforts and the associated resistance to those efforts from many circles has attracted controversy over the perceived role of the World Bank in the global economy. Much of that controversy is fueled by misconceptions and propaganda intended to undermine liberalization programs around the world, and it has contributed to a widely misleading picture of what the World Bank actually does and the power it has.

As was the case with the INTERNATIONAL MONETARY FUND (IMF), the World Bank, originally consisting of only the IBRD, arose from the agreements that emerged out of the Bretton Woods Conference during the last stages of World War II. This gathering of Allied leaders was a manifestation of efforts to establish geopolitical stability upon the conclusion of the war and to formulate plans for the rebuilding of Europe and Japan. Much of the impetus for the meeting resulted from the desire to confront problems that were unrelated to the war per se but had been responsible, at least in part, for its outbreak. In that regard, the Bretton Woods Conference sought to address the macroeconomic deficiencies that produced and perpetuated the financial and economic crises of the interwar period and encouraged the spread of poverty and economic depression. More broadly, this meeting was a response to the structural and cyclical dislocations and transformations caused by mass industrialization and the consequent need to confront the inadequacies of pre-Keynesian solutions for the dilemmas of industrialization.

Above all, the Bretton Woods agreements were based on the conviction that conflict is avoidable through the facilitation of international economic cooperation and increased prosperity throughout the globe and that, therefore, the implementation and maintenance of sustainable development policies and the erection of viable economic infrastructures was paramount to Europe's survival. On the whole, the participants endorsed capitalist economic principles, though they disagreed regarding the proper level of state intervention and control over economic and financial mechanisms. Nevertheless, a consensus did exist concerning the Keynesian realization that industrialized economies require at least some degree of macroeconomic management and that the structural vulnerabilities of industrialized and industrializing nations must be remedied in some manner. Since domestic economic and financial stability was, among other things, a function of international economic and financial stability, domestic structural weaknesses would be countered through international processes established to pursue the above goals.

Despite the overarching economic objectives and normative criteria that animated Bretton Woods negotiations, the most immediate reason for the creation of the World Bank was the postwar reconstruction of Europe and Japan. Indeed, the largest loan (in real terms) ever issued by the bank was awarded to France shortly after the war. In addition, the newly established IBRD was charged with encouraging economic growth in the developing world by supporting infrastructure projects. As the rebuilding of Europe progressed from prospect to reality, the IBRD increasingly devoted its attention to less affluent parts of the globe. The IBRD has continued to provide low-interest loans to developing nations that have been categorized as middle income, and it eventually secured funding for projects in undeveloped and underdeveloped countries classified as the world's poorest. This was achieved through the creation of the IDA in 1960, thereby enabling the provision of no-interest loans and grants to the least capable countries around the globe.

Collectively, the World Bank's mission centers on the reduction of poverty, the formulation and implementation of sustainable economic development policies, the establishment or reform of economic infrastructures conducive to long-term growth, and the provision of humanitarian assistance following natural disasters or other emergencies. It has often sought to accomplish these goals through the simultaneous education and training of government officials in target countries and the restructuring of government programs or legal structures that pose obstacles to growth and the reduction of poverty. In most cases, its financial and economic assistance come through either investment or development policy loans, with the former category focusing on the emergence of long-term infrastructural capabilities that support and allow continued growth and the latter allocated for the creation and implementation of procedural systems through which markets and economic viability can be secured.

The World Bank is a sizable organization with headquarters in Washington, D.C., and a current membership of 185 states, each of which has a seat on the board of governors. It is headed by the bank president, usually nominated by the United States, who serves a five-year renewable term and answers to a 24-member board of executive directors. Since 2007, the president of the World Bank has been Robert Zoellick of the United States, who succeeded the embattled Paul Wolfowitz following his abortive term. Because of the size of the U.S. financial contribution to the development fund and the country's comparative influence over others, tradition has ensured that the bank president will always be an American citizen, although the extent and effectiveness of any resulting influence over other members has frequently been overstated by the bank's critics since the United States must carefully weigh and duly acknowledge the positions and priorities of key members of the board of directors.

As has been true of the IMF, the World Bank has underwritten projects throughout the globe and especially in regions that are underdeveloped or experiencing serious structural difficulties, so it has been labeled by its critics a tool of Western expansionism and a supporter of the exploitation of developing countries by the industrialized world. Although the relationship between the World Bank and the poor countries it assists in the developing world is intrinsically imbalanced, not least due to the economic and diplomatic leverage, to say nothing of military might, Western countries possess, such an imbalance should not serve as an a priori indictment of the World Bank and its initiatives.

In addition, despite the realization that the economic assistance and financial aid disbursed by the World Bank is predicated on certain prerequisites, so that recipients of aid are often compelled to implement pro-Western structural reforms as a consequence of that assistance, people should not be surprised to discover that the World Bank conditions its willingness to engage in specific projects on the reciprocal willingness of target states to implement those structural reforms that will maximize the probability of success for the World Bank's projects. In the end, as is the case with the IMF, the World Bank has always been an unashamedly Western club, and it has succeeded, at least in part, due to its commitment to that reality.

The normative question of whether Western sociocultural values and priorities should govern the practices, ideologies, and relationships of the World Bank cannot be settled in this essay, and the claims of antiglobalization and anti–free trade advocates should be explored elsewhere. However, the substantive debates concerning the bank's mission and purpose aside, it has witnessed its share of controversy over charges of malfeasance and corruption over the past few years. Recently departed bank president Paul Wolfowitz assiduously pursued corruption allegations against bank officials and member countries, though he was accused of selectively targeting people and states that did not endorse U.S. policy objectives. Wolfowitz's tenure was ultimately cut short by his own problems stemming from charges of unethical behavior regarding a girlfriend formerly employed by the World Bank. Moreover, his position seemed precarious from the outset because of his association with increasingly unpopular policies of the George W. Bush administration. Unfortunately, neither Wolfowitz's extensive background in public service nor his formidable intellect proved sufficient to rescue his beleaguered administration. World Bank observers hope that Robert Zoellick, a man with laudable international credentials and solid professional credibility, will be able to mend the reputation of an organization that plays a crucial role in global economic development and the alleviation of poverty.

Further Reading

Gilbert, Christopher L. The World Bank. New York: Cambridge University Press, 2006; Gilpin, Robert. The Political Economy of International Relations. Princeton, N.J.: Princeton University Press, 1987; Guide to the World Bank. Washington, D.C.: World Bank Publications, 2007; Krugman, Paul. Pop Internationalism. Cambridge, Mass.: MIT Press, 1997; Udell, Gregory F. Principles of Money, Banking, and Financial Markets. New York: Addison Wesley Longman, 1999; Woods, Ngaire. The Globalizers. Ithaca, N.Y.: Cornell University Press, 2006.

—Tomislav Han

World Trade Organization (WTO)

The World Trade Organization (WTO) is an international organization intended to contribute to the development of a global capitalist market system by removing barriers to free trade. In the aftermath of the Great Depression of the 1930s and the devastation of World War II, the United States led the way to the creation of a new international system that would rest on open markets and free trade. The INTERNATIONAL MONETARY FUND (IMF) and WORLD BANK were created in 1943 as part of the Bretton Woods system (named after the resort town in New Hampshire where the basic treaties were signed), which also included the UNITED NATIONS. The initial attempt to create a global trade organization was unsuccessful, and a temporary organization, the General Agreement on Trade and Tariffs (GATT) was established to fill the gap. It was not until 1995 that the WTO replaced GATT, and a fully functioning international organization devoted to removing barriers to free trade was inaugurated.

There are two major types of obstacles to a world market in which everyone could compete solely on the basis of the price and quality of their products: tariffs and "nontariff barriers" (NTBs). Tariffs are taxes imposed by governments on products imported from abroad. In the distant past, tariffs were a major source of government revenues; today they are primarily designed to protect a country's own businesses from foreign competition by explicitly making foreign products more expensive. The GATT and then the WTO have sponsored a series of very successful international negotiations in which governments agreed to reduce and even eliminate many tariffs. While many tariffs remain, especially those levied by third world countries to protect their own industries, the drive to reduce and eliminate them continues to make progress. As tariffs have dwindled in importance as barriers to free global trade, a new class of obstacles has emerged: nontariff barriers. Tariffs are part of a country's tax code and easy to identify. Nontariff barriers are far more pervasive in world markets today but far more difficult to identify because they are not formal taxes and are often defended by governments as reasonable health and safety regulations or part of a national culture. Conflicts over NTBs and other unfair trading practices such as dumping are likely to be major items on the international agenda for decades.

Three examples illustrate the sometimes ambiguous nature of NTBs. Toys produced in China and shipped to the United States, for example, have to meet U.S. standards for safety. This makes them more expensive to manufacture than if they merely had to meet China's own standards. This fact is not regarded as a nontariff barrier but a reasonable application of health and safety standards (known technically as phytosanitary regulations) by a national government. In 1995, the United States and the EUROPEAN UNION charged that South Korea was using taxes on imported whiskey as an NTB. Korean law levied a relatively high tax on whiskey and other distilled liquor, all imported from other countries, and a much lower tax on *soju*, a popular Korean alcoholic beverage. To the U.S. and European countries, the difference in tax rates was meant to give Korean *soju* producers an unfair advantage in the market. The Korean government argued that *soju* was part of the national culture, and even though its alcoholic content was similar to whiskey, it was really more like beer or wine than hard liquor. In the end, the World Trade Organization concluded that the different tax rates were not culturally determined but a deliberate nontariff trade barrier.

In contrast to the case of toy safety standards, which are widely accepted as not being an NTB, and the Korean *soju* case, in which it was determined that an NTB did exist, the differences between the way the United States and the European Union treat genetically modified foods is a good example of the difficulty of determining what is and is not an NTB. In the United States, genetically modified plants, such as new species of corn, are regulated by the DEPARTMENT OF AGRICULTURE with little distinction between species produced by manipulating genes in the laboratory and species produced by traditional cross-breeding. As long as there is no evidence of potential harm to consumers, they can be used in products and do not require special labeling. In the European Union, on the other hand, genetically modified corn is treated as a potential hazard and must be proven to be safe, or products containing it must carry prominent warning labels. European farmers do not grow genetically modified corn; American farmers do and would like to be able to export their crop to Europe. Large, mechanized American farms are more productive and efficient than European farms, and many crops can be grown in the United States, shipped to Europe, and still sell for less. But a European shopper, faced with two packages of cornflakes, one with all European corn and the other with genetically modified American corn and a big red warning label, is going to avoid the American product. The government of the United States has consistently argued that this is a blatant nontariff barrier, meant to discriminate against American crops by scaring consumers needlessly. The European Union has argued that it is better to be safe than sorry, that European consumers are not sure genetically modified corn is safe, and it is only fair to warn them.

The WTO is structured to offer solutions to disputes over unfair trade if the countries that belong to it choose to use it. The WTO does two things that contribute to a free and open world market. First, the WTO provides a setting for representatives of its 145 member countries as they try to negotiate mutually beneficial rules for conducting and regulating world trade. Some of those discussions are quite technical and involve very specific issues; others are broad and have sweeping implications for world trade. For example, the 2001 meeting of leading national officials in Doha, Qatar, began an ambitious effort to negotiate the phased elimination of the most important remaining global tariffs, those in agriculture. Contentious and difficult bargaining has continued at annual WTO sessions in Cancun, Geneva, and Hong Kong. When the WTO organizes meetings and the staff provides position papers and technical expertise, it is performing a function that is very similar to many other international organizations involved in promoting cooperation among nations.

The WTO also offers a way of resolving specific disputes among countries that is a distinctive contribution to international relations. The WTO dispute resolution process begins when one country brings an accusation of unfair trading or manipulation of NTBs against a second country. This usually happens after the two sides have tried to negotiate a settlement between themselves through diplomatic and political channels, but it can also be used if one country simply refuses to negotiate with the other. The WTO establishes a panel of impartial experts on INTERNATIONAL TRADE and economics who review the facts presented by both sides and arrive at a judgment. A significant weakness in the WTO process is that enforcement of its judgments is left to the countries involved. The WTO itself cannot force a country to change its laws or policies. Instead, the winning party in a WTO case is free to take steps of its own, perhaps instituting what are known as countervailing tariffs on products from the other country, to convince it to comply. More often than not, such measures do work, and countries do adjust their behavior.

The WTO has become a focus for controversy and PROTEST, often as part of larger campaigns against the perceived ills of GLOBALIZATION. The WTO's friends and supporters point to its success in reducing tariffs, opening up markets to both rich and poor countries, giving poor countries a voice in the rules of the global trading game, and expanding global wealth.

The WTO's critics charge that the rule-making meetings of the organization are inherently undemocratic, with the rich first world countries dominating the process and the meetings cloaked in secrecy. The outcomes, the critics say, are not fair and balanced global rules. Delegates to WTO rule-making sessions tend to come from national economic ministries and professional economists. The members of dispute resolution panels are picked for their expertise in economic analysis. As a result, the WTO's critics charge that critically important considerations, such as environmental issues, human rights, and standards for the treatment of workers get overlooked or deliberately ignored in favor of short-term, narrowly defined economic values.

In general, the charges leveled against the WTO and the defenses produced by its friends are embedded in the much larger set of issues and debates surrounding globalization. The WTO, along with the International Monetary Fund and World Bank, are the major international organizations at the heart of global economic patterns and the controversies surrounding the present and future of the global economy. As globalization continues to unfold around the world and its consequences, both positive and negative, become more apparent, the WTO will continue to be a very busy international organization and a controversial one.

Further Reading

Bhagwati, Jagdish, et al., eds. *The Uruguay Round and Beyond: Essays in Honor of Arthur Dunkel.* Ann Arbor: University of Michigan Press, 1998; Colgan, Jeff. *The Promise and Peril of International Trade.* Peterborough, Ont.; Orchard Park, N.Y.: Broadview Press, 2005; Dine, Janet. *Companies, International Trade, and Human Rights.* Cambridge: Cambridge University Press, 2005; Dowlah, Caf. *Backwaters of Global Prosperity: How Forces of Globalization and GATT/WTO Trade Regimes Contribute to the Marginalization of the World's Poorest Nations.* Westport, Conn.: Praeger, 2004; Everett, Simon, and Bernard Hoekman, eds. *Economic Development and Multilateral Trade Cooperation.* Houndmills, U.K.: Palgrave Macmillan, 2006; Jones, Kent. *Who's Afraid of the WTO?* New York: Oxford University Press, 2004.

—Seth Thompson

SELECTED BIBLIOGRAPHY

FOUNDATIONS AND BACKGROUND OF U.S. GOVERNMENT

Ackerman, Bruce A. *We the People: Foundations*. Cambridge, Mass.: Harvard University Press, 1991.

Bailyn, Bernard. *The Ideological Origins of the American Revolution*. Cambridge, Mass.: Harvard University Press, 1967.

Beard, Charles A. *An Economic Interpretation of the Constitution of the United States*. New York: Free Press, 1913.

Berkin, Carol. *A Brilliant Solution: Inventing the American Constitution*. New York: Harcourt, 2002.

Bliss, Robert M. *Revolution and Empire: English Politics and the American Colonies in the Seventeenth Century*. New York: Manchester University Press, 1990.

Bodenhamer, David J., and James W. Ely, Jr. *The Bill of Rights in Modern America after Two-Hundred Years*. Bloomingdale: Indiana University Press, 1993.

Dahl, Robert A. *How Democratic Is the American Constitution?* New Haven, Conn.: Yale University Press, 2002.

Dworkin, Ronald. *Law's Empire*. Cambridge, Mass.: Harvard University Press, 1986.

Elkins, Stanley, and Eric McKitrick. *The Age of Federalism: The Early American Republic 1788–1800*. New York: Oxford University Press, 1993.

Fehrenbacher, Don E. *The Slaveholding Republic*. Oxford: Oxford University Press, 2001.

Ferling, John. *A Leap in the Dark: The Struggle to Create the American Republic*. New York: Oxford University Press, 2003.

Friedman, Lawrence M. *A History of American Law*. New York: Simon & Schuster, 1985.

Frohnen, Bruce, ed. *The American Republic*. Indianapolis: Liberty Fund, 2002.

Gillman, Howard. *The Constitution Besieged: The Rise and Demise of Lochner Era Police Powers Jurisprudence*. Durham, N.C.: Duke University Press, 1993.

Hall, Kermit L. *The Magic Mirror: Law in American History*. Oxford: Oxford University Press, 1989.

Held, David. *Models of Democracy*. 3rd ed. Palo Alto, Calif.: Stanford University Press, 2006.

Henderson, H. James. *Party Politics in the Continental Congress*. Lanham, Md.: University Press of America, 2002.

Horton, James Oliver, and Lois E. Horton. *Slavery and the Making of America*. Oxford: Oxford University Press, 2005.

Hoffert, Robert W. *A Politics of Tensions: The Articles of Confederation and American Political Ideas*. Niwot: University Press of Colorado, 1992.

Jensen, Merrill. *The Articles of Confederation: An Interpretation of the Social-Constitutional History of the American Revolution*. Madison: University of Wisconsin Press, 1970.

Kahn, Paul W. *Legitimacy and History: Self-Government in American Constitutional Theory*. New Haven, Conn.: Yale University Press, 1993.

Kelley, J. M. *A Short History of Western Legal Theory*. Oxford: Oxford University Press, 1992.

Ketcham, Ralph. *The Anti-Federalist Papers*. New York: New American Library, 1986.

Levinson, Sanford. *Constitutional Faith*. Princeton, N.J.: Princeton University Press, 1988.

Levy, Leonard. *Origins of the Bill of Rights*. New Haven, Conn.: Yale University Press, 1999.

Locke, John. *Two Treatises of Government*. Edited by Peter Laslett. Cambridge: Cambridge University Press, 1987.

Madison, James, Alexander Hamilton, and John Jay. *The Federalist Papers*. New York: New American Library, 1961.

McDonald, Forrest. *States' Rights and the Union*. Lawrence: University Press of Kansas, 2000.

Nagel, Robert F. *The Implosion of American Federalism*. New York: Oxford University Press, 2002.

Reid, John Phillip. *Constitutional History of the American Revolution: The Authority of Rights*. Madison: University of Wisconsin Press, 1986.

Rossiter, Clinton. *1787: The Grand Convention*. New York: Macmillan, 1966.

Shearer, Benjamin F., ed. *The Uniting States. The Story of Statehood for the Fifty United States*. Volumes 1-3. Westport, Conn.: Greenwood Press, 2004.

Strong, Herbert J. *What the Anti-Federalists Were For*. Chicago: University of Chicago Press, 1981.

Whittington, Keith E. *Constitutional Construction: Divided Powers and Constitutional Meaning*. Cambridge, Mass.: Harvard University Press, 2001.

Wills, Garry. *Inventing America: Jefferson's Declaration of Independence*. Boston: Houghton Mifflin, 2002.

Wood, Gordon S. *The Creation of the American Republic*. Chapel Hill: University of North Carolina Press, 1969.

Wood, Gordon S. *The Radicalism of the American Revolution*. New York: Vintage Books, 1991.

Zuckert, Michael P. *Natural Rights and the New Republicanism*. Princeton, N.J.: Princeton University Press, 1994.

CIVIL RIGHTS AND CIVIC RESPONSIBILITIES

Abraham, Henry J., and Barbara A. Perry. *Freedom and the Court: Civil Rights and Liberties in the United States*. 8th ed. Lawrence: University Press of Kansas, 2003.

Abramson, Jeffrey. *We, the Jury: The Jury System and the Ideal of Democracy*. New York: Basic Books, 2000.

Alderman, Ellen, and Caroline Kennedy. *The Right to Privacy*. New York: Alfred A. Knopf, 1995.

Anderson, Terry H. *The Pursuit of Fairness: A History of Affirmative Action*. New York: Oxford University Press, 2004.

Baer, Judith A. *Our Lives before the Law: Constructing a Feminist Jurisprudence*. Princeton, N.J.: Princeton University Press, 1999.

Branch, Taylor. *At Canaans Edge: America in the King Years, 1965–1968*. New York: Simon & Schuster, 2006.

Branch, Taylor. *Parting the Waters: America in the King Years, 1954–1963*. New York: Simon & Schuster, 1988.

Branch, Taylor. *Pillar of Fire: America in the King Years, 1963–1965*. New York: Simon & Schuster, 1998

Butler, Judith. *Gender Trouble: Feminism and the Subversion of Identity*. New York: Routledge, 1990.

Cahn, Steven M., ed. *The Affirmative Action Debate*. New York: Routledge, 2002.

Chang, Gordon H., ed. *Asian Americans and Politics*. Stanford, Calif.: Stanford University Press, 2001.

Coetzee, J. M. *Giving Offense: Essays on Censorship*. Chicago: University of Chicago Press, 1996.

Cook, Timothy E., ed. *Freeing the Presses: The First Amendment in Action*. Baton Rouge: Louisiana State University Press, 2005.

Daniels, Roger. *Coming to America: A History of Immigration and Ethnicity in American Life*, 2nd ed. Princeton, N.J.: Perennial, 2002.

Gerstmann, Evan. *Same-Sex Marriage and the Constitution*. New York: Cambridge University Press, 2004.

Gutmann, Amy, ed. *Freedom of Association*. Princeton, N.J.: Princeton University Press, 1998.

Hammond, Phillip E. *With Liberty for All: Freedom of Religion in the United States*. Louisville, Ky.: Westminster John Knox Press, 1998.

Hoff, Joan. *Law, Gender, and Injustice: A Legal History of U.S. Women*. New York: New York University Press, 1991.

Hubbart, Phillip A. *Making Sense of Search and Seizure Law: A Fourth Amendment Handbook*. Durham, N.C.: Carolina Academic Press, 2005.

Israel, Jerold H., Yale Kamisar, Wayne R. LaFave, and Nancy J. King. *Criminal Procedure and the Constitution*. St. Paul, Minn.: Thomson West, 2006.

Jonakait, Randolph N. *The American Jury System*. New Haven, Conn.: Yale University Press, 2003.

Lee, Francis Graham. *Equal Protection: Rights and Liberties under the Law*. Santa Barbara, Calif.: ABC-CLIO, 2003.

Lehman, Godfrey D. *We the Jury: The Impact of Jurors on Our Basic Freedoms: Great Jury Trials of History*. Amherst, N.Y.: Prometheus Books, 1997.

Lewis, Anthony. *Gideon's Trumpet*. New York: Random House, 1964.

Lewis, Anthony. *Make No Law: The Sullivan Case and the First Amendment*. New York: Vintage Books, 1991.

Magee, James J. *Freedom of Expression*. Westport, Conn.: Greenwood Press, 2002.

Marable, Manning. *Race, Reform, and Rebellion: The Second Reconstruction in Black America, 1945–1990*. Jackson: University Press of Mississippi, 1991.

Mezey, Susan Gluck. *Disabling Interpretations: The Americans with Disabilities Act in Federal Court*. Pittsburgh: University of Pittsburgh Press, 2005.

Mohr, Richard D. *The Long Arc of Justice: Lesbian and Gay Marriage, Equality, and Rights*. New York: Columbia University Press, 2005.

Pember, Don R., and Clay Calvert. *Mass Media Law 2007–2008*. Boston: McGraw Hill, 2007.

Perry, Michael J. *We the People: The Fourteenth Amendment and the Supreme Court*. New York: Oxford University Press, 1999.

Rosen, Ruth. *The World Split Open: How the Modern Women's Movement Changed America*. New York: Penguin Books, 2000.

Segars, Mary C., and Ted G. Jelen. *A Wall of Separation? Debating the Public Role of Religion*. Lanham, Md.: Rowman & Littlefield, 1998.

Segura, Gary M., and Shaun Bowler, eds. *Diversity in Democracy: Minority Representation in the United States*. Charlottesville: University of Virginia Press, 2005.

Shull, Steven A. *American Civil Rights Policy from Truman to Clinton: The Role of Presidential Leadership*. Armonk, N.Y.: M.E. Sharpe, 1999.

Stuart, Gary L. *Miranda: The Story of America's Right to Remain Silent*. Tucson-University of Arizona Press, 2004.

Sunstein, Cass R. *Democracy and the Problem of Free Speech*. New York: The Free Press, 1995.

Wilkins, David E. *American Indian Politics and the American Political System*. Lanham, Md.: Rowman & Littlefield, 2002.

Witte, John, Jr. *Religion and the American Constitutional Experiment: Essential Rights and Liberties*. Boulder, Colo.: Westview Press, 2000.

POLITICAL PARTICIPATION

Alexander, Herbert E. *Financing Politics: Money, Elections, and Political Reform*. 4th ed. Washington, D.C.: CQ Press, 1992.

Ansolabehere, Stephen, and Shanto Iyengar. *Going Negative: How Attack Ads Shrink and Polarize the Electorate*. New York: The Free Press, 1995.

Asher, Herbert. *Polling and the Public: What Every Citizen Should Know*. 6th ed. Washington, D.C.: Congressional Quarterly Press, 2004.

Bagdikian, Ben H. *The New Media Monopoly*. Boston: Beacon Press, 2004.

Bennett, W. Lance. *News: The Politics of Illusion*. 6th ed. New York: Pearson Longman, 2005.

Campbell, Angus, Philip E. Converse, Warren E. Miller, and Donald E. Stokes. *The American Voter*. Chicago: University of Chicago Press, 1960.

Crigler, Ann N., Marion R. Just, and Edward McCaffery, eds. *Rethinking the Vote*. New York: Oxford University Press, 2004

Corrado, Anthony, Thomas E. Mann, Daniel R. Ortiz, and Trevor Potter. *The New Campaign Finance Sourcebook*. Washington, D.C.: Brookings Institution Press, 2005.

Downs, Anthony. *An Economic Theory of Democracy*. New York: Harper, 1957.

Dwyre, Diana, and Victoria A. Farrar-Myers. *Legislative Labyrinth: Congress and Campaign Finance Reform*. Washington, D.C.: CQ Press, 2001.

Edelman, Murray. *Constructing the Political Spectacle*. Chicago: University of Chicago Press, 1988.

Emery, Michael, and Edwin Emery. *The Press and America: An Interpretive History of the Mass Media*. 8th ed. Boston: Allyn & Bacon, 1996.

Fenno, Richard F., Jr. *Home Style: House Members in Their Districts*. Boston: Little, Brown, 1978.

Franklin, Mark N. *Voter Turnout and the Dynamics of Electoral Competition in Established Democracies since 1945*. Cambridge: Cambridge University Press, 2004.

Genovese, Michael A., and Matthew J. Streb, eds. *Polls and Politics: The Dilemmas of Democracy*. Albany: State University of New York Press; 2004.

Gierzynski, Anthony. *Money Rules: Financing Elections in America*. Boulder, Colo.: Westview Press, 2000.

Graber, Doris. *Mass Media and American Politics*. 7th ed. Washington, D.C.: Congressional Quarterly Press, 2006.

Hamilton, James T. *All the News That's Fit to Sell: How the Market Transforms Information Into News*. Princeton, N.J.: Princeton University Press, 2004.

Hernnson, Paul S. *Congressional Elections. Campaigning at Home and in Washington*. 4th ed. Washington, D.C., Congressional Quarterly Press, 2004.

Hernnson, Paul R., Ronald G. Shaiko, and Clyde Wilcox, eds. *The Interest Group Connection: Electioneering, Lobbying, and Policymaking in Washington*. Chatham, N.J.: Chatham House, 1998.

Hill, David B. *American Voter Turnout: An Institutional Perspective*. Boulder, Colo.: Westview Press, 2005.

Jacobson, Gary C. *The Politics of Congressional Elections*. New York: Longman, 2003.

Jamieson, Kathleen Hall, and Paul Waldman. *The Press Effect: Politicians, Journalists, and the Stories That Shape the Political World*. New York: Oxford University Press, 2003.

Kaid, Lynda Lee, and Anne Johnston. *Videostyle in Presidential Campaigns: Style and Content of Televised Political Advertising*. Westport, Conn.: Praeger, 2000.

Maisel, L. Sandy, and Kara Z. Buckley. *Parties and Elections in America: The Electoral Process*. 4th ed. New York: Rowman & Littlefield, 2005.

Malbin, Michael J., ed. *The Election after Reform: Money, Politics, and the Bipartisan Campaign Reform Act*. Lanham, Md.: Rowman & Littlefield, 2006.

Mayhew, David R. *Congress: The Electoral Connection*. New Haven, Conn.: Yale University Press, 1974.

Meyer, David S. *The Politics of Protest: Social Movements in America*. New York: Oxford University Press, 2006.

Page, Benjamin I., and Robert Y. Shapiro. *The Rational Public: Fifty Years of Trends in Americans' Policy Preferences*. Chicago: University of Chicago Press, 1992.

Paletz, David L. *The Media in American Politics: Contents and Consequences*. 2nd ed. New York: Longman, 2002.

Patterson, Thomas E. *Out of Order*. New York: Vintage Books, 1994.

Putnam, Robert. *Bowling Alone: The Collapse and Revival of American Community*. New York: Simon & Schuster, 2000.

Savage, Sean J. *JFK, LBJ, and the Democratic Party*. Albany: State University of New York Press, 2004.

Semiatin, Richard J. *Campaigns in the 21st Century*. New York: McGraw-Hill, 2005.

Wayne, Stephen J. *Is This Any Way to Run a Democratic Election?* 2nd ed. Boston: Houghton Mifflin, 2003.

Wayne, Stephen J. *The Road to the White House: The Politics of Presidential Elections*. 8th ed. Boston: Thomson Woodsworth, 2008.

West, Darrell M. *Air Wars: Television Advertising in Election Campaigns, 1952–2004*. 4th ed. Washington, D.C.: Congressional Quarterly Press, 2005.

LEGISLATIVE BRANCH

Baker, Ross K. *House and Senate*. 3rd ed. New York: W.W. Norton, 2001.

Berg, John C. *Unequal Struggle: Class, Gender, Race, and Power in the U.S. Congress*. Boulder, Colo.: Westview Press, 1994.

Brown, Sherrod. *Congress from the Inside: Observations from the Majority and the Minority*. 3rd ed. Kent, Ohio.: Kent State University Press, 2004.

Davidson, Roger H., Susan Webb Hammond, and Raymond W. Smock. *Masters of the House: Congressional Leadership over Two Centuries*. Boulder, Colo.: Westview Press, 1998.

Davidson, Roger H., and Walter J. Oleszek. *Congress & Its Members*. 10th edition. Washington, D.C.: Congressional Quarterly Press, 2006.

Fenno Richard F., Jr. *Homestyle: House Members in Their Districts*. Boston: Little, Brown, 1978.

Fenno, Richard P. *The Power of the Purse: Appropriations Politics in Congress.* Boston: Little, Brown, 1966.

Fiorina, Morris P. *Congress: Keystone of the Washington Establishment.* New Haven, Conn.: Yale University Press, 1989.

Fisher, Louis. *Constitutional Conflicts between Congress and the President.* 4th ed. Lawrence: University Press of Kansas, 1997.

Frisch, Scott A. *The Politics of Pork: A Study of Congressional Appropriation Earmarks.* New York: Garland, 1998.

Gertzog, Irwin N. *Women and Power on Capitol Hill.* Boulder, Colo.: Lynne Rienner Publishers, 2004.

Hamilton, Lee H. *How Congress Works and Why You Should Care.* Bloomington: Indiana University Press, 2004.

Lublin, David. *The Paradox of Representation: Racial Gerrymandering and Minority Interests in Congress.* Princeton, N.J.: Princeton University Press, 1997.

Mayhew, David R. *Congress: The Electoral Connection.* New Haven, Conn.: Yale University Press, 1974.

Mayhew, David R. *Divided We Govern: Party Control, Lawmaking, and Investigations 1946–1990.* New Haven, Conn.: Yale University Press, 1991.

O'Connor, Karen, ed. *Women and Congress: Running, Winning, and Ruling.* New York: Haworth Press, 2001.

Oleszek, Walter J. *Congressional Procedures and the Policy Process.* 6th ed. Washington, D.C.: Congressional Quarterly Press, 2004.

Rosenthal, Cindy Simon, ed. *Women Transforming Congress.* Norman: University of Oklahoma Press, 2002.

Sinclair, Barbara. *Unorthodox Lawmaking: New Legislative Processes in the U.S. Congress.* Washington, D.C.: Congressional Quarterly Press, 2000.

Wielen, Ryan J. *The American Congress.* 4th ed. Cambridge: Cambridge University Press, 2006.

EXECUTIVE BRANCH

Arnold, Peri E. *Making the Managerial Presidency.* Lawrence: University Press of Kansas, 1998.

Baker, Nancy V. *Conflicting Loyalties: Law and Politics in the Office of Attorney General, 1789–1990.* Lawrence: University Press of Kansas, 1993.

Burke, John P. *The Institutional Presidency.* Baltimore: Johns Hopkins University Press, 1992.

Cronin, Thomas E., and Michael A. Genovese. *The Paradoxes of the American Presidency.* 2nd ed. New York: Oxford University Press, 2004.

Edwards, George C. *On Deaf Ears: The Limits of the Bully Pulpit.* New Haven, Conn.: Yale University Press, 2003.

Edwards, George C. III. *The Public Presidency: The Pursuit of Popular Support.* New York: St. Martin's Press, 1983.

Eshbaugh-Soha, Matthew. *The President's Speeches: Beyond "Going Public."* Boulder, Colo.: Lynne Rienner Publishers, 2006.

Gelderman, Carol. *All the Presidents' Words: The Bully Pulpit and the Creation of the Virtual Presidency.* New York: Walker & Company, 1997.

Gergen, David. *Eyewitness to Power: The Essence of Leadership.* New York: Simon & Schuster, 2000.

Greenstein, Fred I. *The Presidential Difference: Leadership Style From FDR to George W. Bush.* 2nd ed. Princeton, N.J.: Princeton University Press, 2004.

Han, Lori Cox. *Governing from Center Stage: White House Communication Strategies during the Television Age of Politics.* Cresskill, N.J.: Hampton Press, 2001.

Hart, Roderick P. *The Sound of Leadership: Presidential Communication in the Modern Age*. Chicago: University of Chicago Press, 1987.

Hess, Stephen, and James P. Pfiffner. *Organizing the Presidency*. 3rd ed. Washington, D.C.: Brookings Institution, 2002.

Jones, Charles O. *The Presidency in a Separated System*. Washington, D.C.: Brookings Institution, 1994.

Kernell, Samuel. *Going Public: New Strategies of Presidential Leadership*. 4th ed. Washington, D.C.: Congressional Quarterly Press, 2007.

Kessel, John H. *Presidents, the Presidency, and the Political Environment*. Washington, D.C.: Congressional Quarterly Press, 2001.

Kumar, Martha Joynt, and Terry Sullivan, eds. *The White House World: Transitions, Organization, and Office Operations*. College Station: Texas A&M University Press, 2003.

Lammers, William W., and Michael A. Genovese. *The Presidency and Domestic Policy: Comparing Leadership Styles, FDR to Clinton*. Washington, D.C.: Congressional Quarterly Press, 2000.

Mayer, Kenneth R. *With the Stroke of a Pen: Executive Orders and Presidential Power*. Princeton, N.J.: Princeton University Press, 2001.

Nuestadt, Richard E. *Presidential Power and the Modern Presidents*. New York: Free Press, 1990.

Pfiffner, James P. *The Managerial Presidency*. College Station: Texas A&M University Press, 1999.

Skowronek, Stephen, *The Politics Presidents Make: Leadership from John Adams to George Bush*. Cambridge, Mass.: Belknap/Harvard Press, 1993.

Tulis, Jeffrey K. *The Rhetorical Presidency*. Princeton, N.J.: Princeton University Press, 1987.

Warshaw, Shirley Anne. *The Keys to Power: Managing the Presidency*. 2nd ed. New York: Longman, 2004.

Warshaw, Shirley Anne. *Powersharing: White House-Cabinet Relations in the Modern Presidency*. Albany: State University of New York Press, 1996.

JUDICIAL BRANCH

Abraham, Henry J. *Justices, Presidents, and Senators: A History of the U.S. Supreme Court Appointments from Washington to Clinton*. Lanham, Md.: Rowman & Littlefield, 1999.

Baum, Lawrence. *The Supreme Court*. 8th ed. Washington, D.C.: Congressional Quarterly Press, 2004.

Bedau, Hugo Adam, and Paul G. Cassell. *Debating the Death Penalty: Should America Have Capital Punishment? The Experts on Both Sides Make Their Best Case*. New York: Oxford University Press, 2004.

Bickel, Alexander. *The Least Dangerous Branch: The Supreme Court at the Bar of Politics*. New Haven, Conn.: Yale University Press, 1962.

Carp, Robert A., and Ronald Stidham. *The Federal Courts*. 4th ed. Washington, D.C.: Congressional Quarterly Press, 2001.

Fisher, Louis. *Military Tribunals and Presidential Power*. Lawrence: University Press of Kansas, 2005.

Hall, Kermit L., and Kevin T. McGuire, eds. *The Judicial Branch*. New York: Oxford University Press, 2005.

Hart, H. L. A. *The Concept of Law*. Oxford: Oxford University Press, 1961.

McCloskey, Robert G. *The American Supreme Court*. 2nd ed. Chicago: University of Chicago Press, 1994.

McGuire, Kevin T. *Understanding the U.S. Supreme Court: Cases and Controversies*. New York: McGraw Hill, 2002.

O'Brien, David M. *Storm Center: The Supreme Court in American Politics*. 7th ed. New York: W.W. Norton, 2005.

O'Connor, Sandra Day. *The Majesty of the Law: Reflections of a Supreme Court Justice*. New York: Random House, 2003.

Rehnquist, William H. *The Supreme Court: How It Was, How It Is*. New York: William Morrow, 1987.

Rosenberg, Gerald N. *The Hollow Hope: Can Courts Bring About Social Change?* Chicago: University of Chicago Press, 1991.

Segal, Jeffrey, et al. *The Supreme Court Compendium: Data, Decisions, and Developments*. 4th ed. Washington, D.C.: Congressional Quarterly Press, 2006.

Silverstein, Mark. *Judicious Choices: The New Politics of Supreme Court Confirmations*. 2nd ed. New York: W.W. Norton, 2007.

Ward, Artemus, and David L. Weiden. *Sorcerers' Apprentices: 100 Years of Law Clerks at the United States Supreme Court*. New York: New York University Press, 2006.

Warren, Kenneth F. *Administrative Law in the Political System*. 4th ed. Boulder, Colo.: Westview Press, 2004.

PUBLIC POLICY

Altman, Stuart, and David Shactman, eds. *Policies for an Aging Society*. Baltimore: Johns Hopkins University Press, 2002.

Balaker, Ted, and Sam Staley. *The Road More Traveled: Why the Congestion Crisis Matters More Than You Think, and What We Can Do about It*. Lanham, Md.: Rowman & Littlefield, 2006.

Beckett, Katherine. *Making Crime Pay: Law and Order in Contemporary American Politics*. New York: Oxford University Press, 1997.

Béland, Daniel. *Social Security: History and Politics from the New Deal*. Lawrence: University Press of Kansas, 2005.

Blanck, Peter, Eve Hill, Charles D. Siegal, and Michael Waterstone. *Disability Civil Rights Law and Policy*. St. Paul, Minn.: Thomson-West, 2004.

Blank, Rebecca, and Ron Haskins, eds. *The New World of Welfare*. Washington, D.C.: Brookings Institution Press, 2001.

Bodenheimer, Thomas S., and Kevin Grumbach. *Understanding Health Policy*. 3rd ed. New York: McGraw Hill, 2001.

Cahn, Matthew A. *Environmental Deceptions: The Tension between Liberalism and Environmental Policymaking in the United States*. Albany: State University of New York Press, 1995.

Daniels, Roger. *Coming to America: A History of Immigration and Ethnicity in American Life*. 2nd ed. Princeton, N.J.: Perennial, 2002.

DiNitto, Diana M. *Social Welfare: Politics and Public Policy*. 6th ed. Boston: Pearson, 2007.

Gaddis, John Lewis. *Strategies of Containment: A Critical Appraisal of Postwar American National Security Policy*. Rev. ed. New York: Oxford University Press, 2005.

Hochschild, Jennifer, and Nathan Scovronick. *The American Dream and the Public Schools*. New York: Oxford University Press, 2003.

Hoffman, Peter. *Tomorrow's Energy: Hydrogen, Fuel Cells, and the Prospects for a Cleaner Planet*. Cambridge, Mass.: MIT Press, 2001.

Jentleson, Bruce W. *American Foreign Policy: The Dynamics of Choice in the Twenty-First Century*. 2nd ed. New York: W.W. Norton, 2004.

Kotlifoff, Laurence J., and Scott Burns. *The Coming Generational Storm*. Cambridge, Mass.: MIT Press, 2004.

LaFeber, Walter. *The American Age: United States Foreign Policy at Home and Abroad*. 2nd ed. New York: W.W. Norton, 1994.

Levi, Michael A., and Michael E. O'Hanlon. *The Future of Arms Control*. Washington, D.C.: Brookings Institution Press, 2005.

McChesney, Robert. *The Problem of the Media: U.S. Communication Politics in the Twenty-first Century*. New York: Monthly Review Press, 2004.

Moe, Terry M., ed. *A Primer on America's Schools*. Stanford, Calif.: Hoover Institution Press, 2001.

Nye, Joseph. *The Paradox of American Power*. New York: Oxford University Press, 2002.

Rosen, Harvey. *Public Finance*. New York: McGraw Hill, 2004.

Rosenbaum, Walter A. *Environmental Politics and Policy*. 6th ed. Washington, D.C.: Congressional Quarterly Press, 2006.

Skidmore, Max J. *Social Security and Its Enemies: The Case for America's Most Efficient Insurance Program*. Boulder, Colo.: Westview Press, 1999.

Solinger, Rickie. *Pregnancy and Power: A Short History of Reproductive Politics in America*. New York: New York University Press, 2005.

Spitzer, Robert J. *The Politics of Gun Control*. Washington, D.C.: Congressional Quarterly Press, 2004.

Squires, Gregory D., and Sally O'Connor. *Color and Money: Politics and Prospects for Community Reinvestment in Urban America*. Albany: State University of New York Press, 2001.

Teske, Paul. *Regulation in the States*. Washington, D.C.: Brookings Institution Press. 2004.

Weaver, R. Kent. *Ending Welfare as We Know It*. Washington, D.C.: Brookings Institution Press, 2000.

STATE AND LOCAL GOVERNMENT

Axelrod, Donald. *Shadow Government: The Hidden World of Public Authorities—and How They Control Over $1 Trillion*. New York: John Wiley & Sons, 1992.

Benton, J. Edwin, and David R. Morgan. *Intergovernmental Relations and Public Policy*. Westport, Conn.: Greenwood Press, 1986.

Burns, Nancy. *The Formation of American Local Governments: Private Values in Public Institutions*. Oxford: Oxford University Press, 1994.

Christensen, Terry, and Tom Hogen-Esch. *Local Politics: A Practical Guide to Governing at the Grassroots*. Armonk, N.Y.: M.E. Sharpe, 2006.

Coppa, Frank J. *County Government: A Guide to Efficient and Accountable Government*. Westport, Conn.: Praeger, 2000.

Cronin, Thomas E. *Direct Democracy: The Politics of Initiative, Referendum, and Recall*. Cambridge, Mass.: Harvard University Press, 1989.

Cullingham, Barry, and Roger W. Caves. *Planning in the USA*. 2nd ed. New York: Routledge, 2003.

Dye, Thomas R., and Susan A. MacManus. *Politics in States and Communities*. 12th ed. Upper Saddle River, N.J.: Pearson Prentice Hall, 2007.

Ellis, Richard J. *Democratic Delusions: The Initiative Process in America*. Lawrence: University Press of Kansas, 2002.

Ferguson, Margaret R., ed. *The Executive Branch of State Government*. Santa Barbara, Calif.: ABC-CLIO, 2006.

Flanagan, Richard M. *Mayors and the Challenge of Urban Leadership*. Lanham, Md.: University Press of America, Inc., 2004.

Frug, Gerald E. *City Making: Building Communities without Walls*. Princeton, N.J.: Princeton University Press, 1999.

Gray, Virginia, Russell L. Hanson, and Herbert Jacob, eds. *Politics in the American States: A Comparative*

Analysis. 8th ed. Washington, D.C.: Congressional Quarterly Press, 2003.

Gross, Donald A., and Robert K. Goidel. *The States of Campaign Finance Reform.* Columbus: Ohio State University Press, 2003.

Hopkins, Lewis D. *Urban Development: The Logic of Making Plans.* Washington, D.C.: Island Press, 2001.

Judd, Dennis R., and Todd Swanstrom. *City Politics: Private Power and Public Policy.* New York: Longman, 2002.

Langer, Laura. *Judicial Review in State Supreme Courts: A Comparative Study.* Albany: State University of New York Press, 2002.

Leland, Suzanne M., and Kurt Thurmaier, eds. *Case Studies of City-County Consolidation: Reshaping the Local Government Landscapes.* Armonk, N.Y.: M.E. Sharpe, 2004.

Maddex, Robert L. *State Constitutions of the United States.* 2nd ed. Washington, D.C.: Congressional Quarterly Press, 2005.

Matsusaka, John G. *For the Many or the Few.* Chicago: University of Chicago Press, 2004.

Meador, Daniel J., and Frederick G. Kempin. *American Courts.* St. Paul, Minn.: West Publishing Company, 2000.

Meyer, Jon'a, and Paul Jesilow. *"Doing Justice" in the People's Court: Sentencing by Municipal Court Judges.* Albany: State University of New York Press, 1997.

Mikesell, J. L. *Fiscal Administration: Analysts and Applications for the Public Sector.* Belmont, Calif.: Thompson/Wadsworth. 2007.

Moncrief, Gary F., Peverill Squire, and Malcolm E. Jewell. *Who Runs for the Legislature?* Upper Saddle River, N.J.: Prentice Hall, 2001.

Morehouse, Sarah McCally, and Malcolm E. Jewell. *State Politics, Parties, and Policy.* Lanham, Md.: Rowman & Littlefield, 2003.

O'Toole, Laurence J., Jr., ed. *American Intergovernmental Relations.* 4th ed. Washington, D.C.: Congressional Quarterly Press, 2007.

Pelissero, John P., ed. *Cities, Politics, and Policy: A Comparative Analysis.* Washington, D.C.: Congressional Quarterly Press, 2003.

Ross, Bernard H., and Myron A. Levine. *Urban Politics: Power in Metropolitan America.* Belmont, Calif.: Thompson Wadsworth, 2006.

Rubin, Irene. *The Politics of Public Budgeting.* Washington, D.C.: Congressional Quarterly Press, 2005.

Saltzstein, Alan. *Governing America's Urban Areas.* Belmont, Calif.: Wadsworth-Thompson, 2003.

Smith, Kevin B., Alan Greenblatt, and John Buntin. *Governing States and Localities.* Washington, D.C.: Congressional Quarterly Press, 2005.

Syed, Anwar. *The Political Theory of American Local Government.* New York: Random House, 1966.

Thompson, Joel A., and Gary F. Moncrief. *Campaign Finance in State Legislative Elections.* Washington, D.C.: Congressional Quarterly Press, 1998.

Van Horn, Carl E., ed. *The State of the States.* Washington, D.C.: Congressional Quarterly Press, 2006.

Wesalo Temel, J. *The Fundamentals of Municipal Bonds.* New York: John Wiley & Sons. 2001.

INTERNATIONAL POLITICS
AND ECONOMICS

Acheson, Keith, and Christopher J. Maule. *North American Trade Disputes.* Ann Arbor: University of Michigan Press, 1999.

Arblaster, Anthony. *The Rise and Decline of Western Liberalism.* New York: Basil Blackwell, 1984.

Baehr, Peter R., and Leon Gordenker. *The United Nations: Reality and Ideal.* 4th ed. New York: Palgrave/Macmillan, 2005.

Bartholomew, Amy, ed. *Empire's Law: The American Imperial Project and the "War to Remake the World."* London; Pluto Press, 2006.

Bhagwati, Jagdish. *In Defense of Globalization.* Oxford: Oxford University Press, 2004.

Calvert, Peter, and Susan Calvert. *Politics and Society in the Third World.* 2nd ed. New York: Longman, 2001.

Cesarano, Fillippo. *Monetary Theory and Bretton Woods.* New York: Cambridge University Press, 2006.

Colgan, Jeff. *The Promise and Peril of International Trade.* Peterborough, Ont., and Orchard Park, N.Y.: Broadview Press, 2005.

D'Amato, Anthony, and Jennifer Abbassi. *International Law Today: A Handbook.* Eagan, Minn.: Thomson-West, 2006.

Destler, I. M. *American Trade Politics.* 4th ed. Washington, D.C.: Institute for International Economics, 2005.

Dine, Janet. *Companies, International Trade, and Human Rights.* Cambridge: Cambridge University Press, 2005.

Edwards, Lee. *The Collapse of Communism.* Stanford, Calif.: Hoover Institution Press, 2000.

Falola, Toyin, and A. Genova. *The Politics of the Global Oil Industry: An Introduction.* Westport, Conn.: Praeger, 2005.

Fasulo, Linda. *An Insider's Guide to the UN.* New Haven, Conn.: Yale University Press, 2004.

Friedman, Thomas L. *The World Is Flat: A Brief History of the Twenty-First Century.* New York: Farrar, Straus & Giroux, 2005.

Gaddis, John Lewis. *The Cold War.* New York: Penguin Books, 2006.

Gerven, Walter. *The European Union: A Polity of States and Peoples.* Stanford, Calif.: Stanford University Press, 2005.

Gilbert, Christopher L. *The World Bank.* New York: Cambridge University Press, 2006.

Gregory, Paul R. *Behind the Facade of Stalin's Command Economy.* Stanford, Calif.: Hoover Institution Press, 2001.

Hakim, Peter, and Robert Litan, eds. *The Future of North American Integration: Beyond NAFTA.* Washington, D.C.: Brookings Institution Press, 2002.

Howorth, Jolyon, ed. *Defending Europe.* New York: Palgrave Macmillan, 2004.

Huntington, Samuel P. *Third Wave: Democratization in the Late Twentieth Century.* Norman: University of Oklahoma Press, 1991.

Jones, Kent. *Who's Afraid of the WTO?* Oxford and New York: Oxford University Press, 2004.

Kaplan, Lawrence S. *NATO Divided, NATO United.* Greenwood, Conn.: Praeger Paperbacks, 2004.

Kegley, Charles W. *World Politics: Trends and Transformation.* 11th ed. Belmont, Calif.: Thomson Wadsworth, 2007.

Krugman, Paul. *Pop Internationalism.* Cambridge, Mass.: MIT Press, 1997.

LaFeber, Walter. *America, Russia, and the Cold War, 1945–2002.* Boston: McGraw Hill, 2002.

Mansfield, Edward D., and Richard Sisson, eds. *Evolution of Political Knowledge: Democracy, Autonomy, and Conflict in Comparative and International Politics.* Columbus: Ohio State University Press, 2004.

McGiffen, Steven. *The European Union: A Critical Guide*. Ann Arbor, Mich.: Pluto Press, 2005.

Parra, Francisco. *Oil Politics: A Modern History of Petroleum*. London and New York: I.B. Tauris, 2004.

Pei, Minxin. *China's Trapped Transition: The Limits of Developmental Autocracy*. Cambridge, Mass.: Harvard University Press, 2006.

Rawls, John. *Political Liberalism*. New York: Columbia University Press, 1993.

Sen, Amartya. *Development as Freedom*. New York: Anchor Books, 2000.

Siebert, Horst. *The World Economy*. London and New York: Routledge, 2002.

Steger, Manfred B., ed. *Rethinking Globalism*. Lanham, Md.: Rowman & Littlefield, 2004.

Udell, Gregory F. *Principles of Money, Banking, and Financial Markets*. New York: Addison Wesley Longman, 1999.

Woods, Ngaire. *The Globalizers*. Ithaca, N.Y.: Cornell University Press, 2006.

Yetiv, Steve. *Crude Awakenings: Global Oil Security and American Foreign Policy*. Ithaca, N.Y.: Cornell University Press, 2004.

APPENDICES

DECLARATION OF INDEPENDENCE

Action of Second Continental Congress, July 4, 1776.

The unanimous Declaration of the thirteen United States of America.

We hold these truths to be self-evident, that all men are created equal, that they are endowed by their Creator with certain unalienable Rights, that among these are Life, Liberty, and the pursuit of Happiness. That to secure these rights, Governments are instituted among Men, deriving their just powers from the consent of the governed. That whenever any Form of Government becomes destructive of these ends, it is the Right of the People to alter or to abolish it, and to institute new Government, laying its foundation on such principles and organizing its powers in such form, as to them shall seem most likely to effect their Safety and Happiness. Prudence, indeed, will dictate that Governments long established should not be changed for light and transient causes; and accordingly all experience hath shown, that mankind are more disposed to suffer, while evils are sufferable, than to right themselves by abolishing the forms to which they are accustomed. But when a long train of abuses and usurpations, pursuing invariably the same Object, evinces a design to reduce them under absolute Despotism, it is their right, it is their duty, to throw off such Government, and to provide new

Guards for their future security. Such has been the patient sufferance of these Colonies; and such is now the necessity which constrains them to alter their former Systems of Government. The history of the present King of Great Britain is a history of repeated injuries and usurpations, all having in direct object the establishment of an absolute Tyranny over these States. To prove this, let Facts be submitted to a candid world.

HE has refused his Assent to Laws, the most wholesome and necessary for the public good.

HE has forbidden his Governors to pass Laws of immediate and pressing importance, unless suspended in their operation till his Assent should be obtained; and when so suspended, he has utterly neglected to attend to them.

HE has refused to pass other Laws for the accommodation of large districts of people, unless those people would relinquish the right of Representation in the Legislature, a right inestimable to them and formidable to tyrants only.

HE has called together legislative bodies at places unusual, uncomfortable, and distant from the depository of their public Records, for the sole purpose of fatiguing them into compliance with his measures.

HE has dissolved Representative Houses repeatedly, for opposing with manly firmness his invasions on the rights of the people.

HE has refused for a long time, after such dissolutions, to cause others to be elected; whereby the Legislative powers, incapable of Annihilation, have returned to the People at large for their exercise; the State remaining in the mean time exposed to all the dangers of invasion from without, and convulsion within.

HE has endeavoured to prevent the population of these States; for that purpose obstructing the Laws of Naturalization of Foreigners; refusing to pass others to encourage their migrations hither, and raising the conditions of new Appropriations of Lands.

HE has obstructed the Administration of Justice, by refusing his Assent to Laws for establishing Judiciary powers.

HE has made Judges dependent on his Will alone, for the tenure of their offices, and the amount and payment of their salaries.

HE has erected a multitude of New Offices, and sent hither swarms of Officers to harass our People, and eat out their substance.

HE has kept among us, in times of peace, Standing Armies without the Consent of our legislatures.

HE has affected to render the Military independent of and superior to the Civil power.

HE has combined with others to subject us to a jurisdiction foreign to our constitution, and unacknowledged by our laws; giving his Assent to their Acts of pretended Legislation:

FOR quartering large bodies of armed troops among us:

FOR protecting them, by a mock Trial, from Punishment for any Murders which they should commit on the Inhabitants of these States:

FOR cutting off our Trade with all parts of the world:

FOR imposing Taxes on us without our Consent:

FOR depriving us in many cases, of the benefits of Trial by Jury:

FOR transporting us beyond Seas to be tried for pretended offences:

FOR abolishing the free System of English Laws in a neighbouring Province, establishing therein an Arbitrary government, and enlarging its Boundaries so as to render it at once an example and fit instrument for introducing the same absolute rule into these Colonies:

FOR taking away our Charters, abolishing our most valuable Laws, and altering fundamentally the Forms of our Governments:

FOR suspending our own Legislatures, and declaring themselves invested with power to legislate for us in all cases whatsoever.

HE has abdicated Government here, by declaring us out of his Protection and waging War against us.

HE has plundered our seas, ravaged our Coasts, burnt our towns, and destroyed the Lives of our people.

HE is at this time transporting large armies of foreign mercenaries to compleat the works of death, desolation and tyranny, already begun with circumstances of Cruelty & perfidy scarcely paralleled in the most barbarous ages, and totally unworthy the Head of a civilized nation.

HE has constrained our fellow Citizens taken Captive on the high Seas to bear Arms against their Country, to become the executioners of their friends and Brethren, or to fall themselves by their Hands.

HE has excited domestic insurrections amongst us, and has endeavoured to bring on the inhabitants of our frontiers, the merciless Indian Savages, whose known rule of warfare, is an undistinguished destruction of all ages, sexes and conditions.

IN every stage of these Oppressions We have Petitioned for Redress in the most humble terms: Our repeated Petitions have been answered only by repeated injury. A Prince, whose character is thus marked by every act which may define a Tyrant, is unfit to be the ruler of a free people.

NOR have We been wanting in attention to our British brethren. We have warned them from time to time of attempts by their legislature to extend an unwarrantable jurisdiction over us. We have reminded them of the circumstances of our emigration and settlement here. We have appealed to their native justice and magnanimity, and we have conjured them by the ties of our common kindred to disavow these usurpations, which would inevitably interrupt our connections and correspondence. They too have been deaf to the voice of justice and of consanguinity. We must, therefore, acquiesce in the necessity, which denounces our Separation, and hold them, as we hold the rest of mankind, Enemies in War, in Peace Friends.

WE, therefore, the Representatives of the UNITED STATES OF AMERICA, in GENERAL CONGRESS, Assembled, appealing to the Supreme Judge of the world for the rectitude of our intentions, do, in the Name, and by Authority of the good People of these Colonies, solemnly publish and declare, That these United Colonies are, and of Right ought to be FREE AND INDEPENDENT STATES; that they are Absolved from all Allegiance to the British Crown, and that all political connection between them and the State of Great Britain, is and ought to be totally dissolved; and that as FREE AND INDEPENDENT STATES, they have full Power to levy War, conclude Peace, contract Alliances, establish Commerce, and to do all other Acts and Things which INDEPENDENT STATES may of right do. And for the support of this Declaration, with a firm reliance on the Protection of Divine Providence, we mutually pledge to each other our Lives, our Fortunes and our sacred Honor.

JOHN HANCOCK.

Georgia
BUTTON GWINNETT
LYMAN HALL
GEO. WALTON

North Carolina
WILLIAM HOOPER
JOSEPH HEWES
JOHN PENN

South Carolina
EDWARD RUTLEDGE
THOMAS HEYWARD, JR.
THOMAS LYNCH, JR.
ARTHUR MIDDLETON

Maryland
SAMUEL CHASE
WILLIAM PACA
THOMAS STONE
CHARLES CARROLL
OF CARROLLTON

Virginia
GEORGE WYTHE
RICHARD HENRY LEE
THOMAS JEFFERSON
BENJAMIN HARRISON
THOMAS NELSON, JR.
FRANCIS LIGHTFOOT LEE
CARTER BRAXTON

Pennsylvania
ROBERT MORRIS
BENJAMIN RUSH
BENJAMIN FRANKLIN
JOHN MORTON
GEORGE CLYMER
JAMES SMITH
GEORGE TAYLOR
JAMES WILSON
GEORGE ROSS

Delaware
  CAESAR RODNEY
  GEORGE READ
  THOMAS M'KEAN

New York
  WILLIAM FLOYD
  PHILIP LIVINGSTON
  FRANCIS LEWIS
  LEWIS MORRIS

New Jersey
  RICHARD STOCKTON
  JOHN WITHERSPOON
  FRANCIS HOPKINS
  JOHN HART
  ABRAHAM CLARK

New Hampshire
  JOSIAH BARTLETT
  WILLIAM WHIPPLE
  MATTHEW THORNTON

Massachusetts-Bay
  SAMUEL ADAMS
  JOHN ADAMS
  ROBERT TREAT PAINE
  ELBRIDGE GERRY

Rhode Island
  STEPHEN HOPKINS
  WILLIAM ELLERY

Connecticut
  ROGER SHERMAN
  SAMUEL HUNTINGTON
  WILLIAM WILLIAMS
  OLIVER WOLCOTT

IN CONGRESS, JANUARY 18, 1777.

ARTICLES OF CONFEDERATION

Agreed to by Congress November 15, 1777 then ratified and in force, March 1, 1781.

Preamble

To all to whom these Presents shall come, we the undersigned Delegates of the States affixed to our Names send greeting.

Articles of Confederation and perpetual Union between the states of New Hampshire, Massachusetts-bay Rhode Island and Providence Plantations, Connecticut, New York, New Jersey, Pennsylvania, Delaware, Maryland, Virginia, North Carolina, South Carolina and Georgia.

ARTICLE I

The Stile of this Confederacy shall be "The United States of America".

ARTICLE II

Each state retains its sovereignty, freedom, and independence, and every power, jurisdiction, and right, which is not by this Confederation expressly delegated to the United States, in Congress assembled.

ARTICLE III

The said States hereby severally enter into a firm league of friendship with each other, for their common defense, the security of their liberties, and their mutual and general welfare, binding themselves to assist each other, against all force offered to, or attacks made upon them, or any of them, on account of religion, sovereignty, trade, or any other pretense whatever.

ARTICLE IV

The better to secure and perpetuate mutual friendship and intercourse among the people of the different States in this Union, the free inhabitants of each of these States, paupers, vagabonds, and fugitives from justice excepted, shall be entitled to all privileges and immunities of free citizens in the several States; and the people of each State shall free ingress and regress to and from any other State, and shall enjoy therein all the privileges of trade and commerce, subject to the same duties, impositions, and restrictions as the inhabitants thereof respectively, provided that such restrictions shall not extend so far as to prevent the removal of property imported into any State, to any other State, of which the owner is an inhabitant; provided also that no imposition, duties or restriction shall be laid by any State, on the property of the United States, or either of them.

If any person guilty of, or charged with, treason, felony, or other high misdemeanor in any State, shall flee from justice, and be found in any of the United States, he shall, upon demand of the Governor or executive power of the State from which he fled, be delivered up and removed to the State having jurisdiction of his offense.

Full faith and credit shall be given in each of these States to the records, acts, and judicial proceedings of the courts and magistrates of every other State.

ARTICLE V

For the most convenient management of the general interests of the United States, delegates shall be annually appointed in such manner as the legislatures of each State shall direct, to meet in Congress on the first Monday in November, in every year, with a power reserved to each State to recall its delegates, or any of them, at any time within the year, and to send others in their stead for the remainder of the year.

No State shall be represented in Congress by less than two, nor more than seven members; and no person shall be capable of being a delegate for more than three years in any term of six years; nor shall any person, being a delegate, be capable of holding any office under the United States, for which he, or another for his benefit, receives any salary, fees or emolument of any kind.

Each State shall maintain its own delegates in a meeting of the States, and while they act as members of the committee of the States.

In determining questions in the United States in Congress assembled, each State shall have one vote.

Freedom of speech and debate in Congress shall not be impeached or questioned in any court or place out of Congress, and the members of Congress shall be protected in their persons from arrests or imprisonments, during the time of their going to and from, and attendence on Congress, except for treason, felony, or breach of the peace.

ARTICLE VI

No State, without the consent of the United States in Congress assembled, shall send any embassy to, or receive any embassy from, or enter into any conference, agreement, alliance or treaty with any King, Prince or State; nor shall any person holding any office of profit or trust under the United States, or any of them, accept any present, emolument, office or title of any kind whatever from any King, Prince or foreign State; nor shall the United States in Congress assembled, or any of them, grant any title of nobility.

No two or more States shall enter into any treaty, confederation or alliance whatever between them, without the consent of the United States in Congress assembled, specifying accurately the purposes for which the same is to be entered into, and how long it shall continue.

No State shall lay any imposts or duties, which may interfere with any stipulations in treaties, entered into by the United States in Congress assembled, with any King, Prince or State, in pursuance of any treaties already proposed by Congress, to the courts of France and Spain.

No vessel of war shall be kept up in time of peace by any State, except such number only, as shall be deemed necessary by the United States in Congress assembled, for the defense of such State, or its trade; nor shall any body of forces be kept up by any State in time of peace, except such number only, as in the judgement of the United States in Congress assembled, shall be deemed requisite to garrison the forts necessary for the defense of such State; but every State shall always keep up a well-regulated and disciplined militia, sufficiently armed and accoutered, and shall provide and constantly have ready for use, in public stores, a due number of filed pieces and tents, and a proper quantity of arms, ammunition and camp equipage.

No State shall engage in any war without the consent of the United States in Congress assembled, unless such State be actually invaded by enemies, or shall have received certain advice of a resolution being formed by some nation of Indians to invade such State, and the danger is so imminent as not to admit of a delay till the United States in Congress assembled can be consulted; nor shall any State grant commissions to any ships or vessels of war, nor letters of marque or reprisal, except it be after a declaration of war by the United States in Congress assembled, and then only against the Kingdom or State and the subjects thereof, against which war has been so declared, and under such regulations as shall be established by the United States in Congress assembled, unless such State be infested by pirates, in which case vessels of war may be fitted out for that occasion, and kept so long as the danger shall continue, or until the United States in Congress assembled shall determine otherwise.

ARTICLE VII

When land forces are raised by any State for the common defense, all officers of or under the rank of colonel, shall be appointed by the legislature of each State respectively, by whom such forces shall be raised, or in such manner as such State shall direct, and all vacancies shall be filled up by the State which first made the appointment.

ARTICLE VIII

All charges of war, and all other expenses that shall be incurred for the common defense or general welfare, and allowed by the United States in Congress assembled, shall be defrayed out of a common treasury, which shall be supplied by the several States in proportion to the value of all land within each State, granted or surveyed for any person, as such land and the buildings and improvements thereon shall be estimated according to such mode as the United States in Congress assembled, shall from time to time direct and appoint.

The taxes for paying that proportion shall be laid and levied by the authority and direction of the legislatures of the several States within the time agreed upon by the United States in Congress assembled.

ARTICLE IX

The United States in Congress assembled, shall have the sole and exclusive right and power of determining on peace and war, except in the cases mentioned in the sixth article – of sending and receiving ambassadors – entering into treaties and alliances, provided that no treaty of commerce shall be made whereby the legislative power of the respective States shall be restrained from imposing such imposts and duties on foreigners, as their own people are subjected to, or from prohibiting the exportation or importation of any species of goods or commodities whatsoever – of establishing rules for deciding in all cases, what captures on land or water shall be legal, and in what manner prizes taken by land or naval forces in the service of the United States shall be divided or appropriated – of granting letters of marque and reprisal in times of peace – appointing courts for the trial of piracies and felonies commited on the high seas and establishing courts for receiving and determining finally appeals in all cases of captures, provided that no member of Congress shall be appointed a judge of any of the said courts.

The United States in Congress assembled shall also be the last resort on appeal in all disputes and differences now subsisting or that hereafter may arise between two or more States concerning boundary, jurisdiction or any other causes whatever; which authority shall always be exercised in the manner following.

Whenever the legislative or executive authority or lawful agent of any State in controversy with another shall present a petition to Congress stating the matter in question and praying for a hearing, notice thereof shall be given by order of Congress to the legislative or executive authority of the other State in controversy, and a day assigned for the appearance of the parties by their lawful agents, who shall then be directed to appoint by joint consent, commissioners or judges to constitute a court for hearing and determining the matter in question: but if they cannot agree, Congress shall name three persons out of each of the United States, and from the list of such persons each party shall alternately strike out one, the petitioners beginning, until the number shall be reduced to thirteen; and from that number not less than seven, nor more than nine names as Congress shall direct, shall in the presence of Congress be drawn out by lot, and the persons whose names shall be so drawn or any five of them, shall be commissioners or judges, to hear and finally determine the controversy, so always as a major part of the judges who shall hear the cause shall agree in the determination: and if either party shall neglect to attend at the day appointed, without showing reasons, which Congress shall judge sufficient, or being present shall refuse to strike, the Congress shall proceed to nominate three persons out of each State, and the secretary of Congress shall strike in behalf of such party absent or refusing; and the judgement and sentence of the court to be appointed, in the manner before prescribed, shall be final and conclusive; and if any of the parties shall refuse to submit to the authority of such court, or to appear or defend their claim or cause, the court shall nevertheless proceed to pronounce sentence, or judgement, which shall in like manner be final and decisive, the judgement or sentence and other proceedings being in either case transmitted to Congress, and lodged among the acts of Congress for the security of the parties concerned: provided that every commissioner, before he sits in judgement, shall take an oath to be administered by one of the judges of the supreme or superior court of the State, where the cause shall be tried, 'well and truly to hear and determine the matter in question, according to the best of his judgement, without favor, affection or hope of reward': provided also, that no State shall be deprived of territory for the benefit of the United States.

All controversies concerning the private right of soil claimed under different grants of two or more States, whose jurisdictions as they may respect such lands, and the States which passed such grants are adjusted, the said grants or either of them being at the same time claimed to have originated antecedent to such settlement of jurisdiction, shall on the petition of either party to the Congress of the United States, be finally determined as near as may be in the same manner as is before prescribed for deciding disputes respecting territorial jurisdiction between different States.

The United States in Congress assembled shall also have the sole and exclusive right and power of regulating the alloy and value of coin struck by their own authority, or by that of the respective States – fixing the standards of weights and measures throughout the United States – regulating the trade and managing all affairs with the Indians, not members of any of the States, provided that the legislative right of any State within its own limits be not infringed or violated – establishing or regulating post offices from one State to another, throughout all the United States, and

exacting such postage on the papers passing through the same as may be requisite to defray the expenses of the said office – appointing all officers of the land forces, in the service of the United States, excepting regimental officers – appointing all the officers of the naval forces, and commissioning all officers whatever in the service of the United States – making rules for the government and regulation of the said land and naval forces, and directing their operations.

The United States in Congress assembled shall have authority to appoint a committee, to sit in the recess of Congress, to be denominated 'A Committee of the States', and to consist of one delegate from each State; and to appoint such other committees and civil officers as may be necessary for managing the general affairs of the United States under their direction – to appoint one of their members to preside, provided that no person be allowed to serve in the office of president more than one year in any term of three years; to ascertain the necessary sums of money to be raised for the service of the United States, and to appropriate and apply the same for defraying the public expenses – to borrow money, or emit bills on the credit of the United States, transmitting every half-year to the respective States an account of the sums of money so borrowed or emitted – to build and equip a navy – to agree upon the number of land forces, and to make requisitions from each State for its quota, in proportion to the number of white inhabitants in such State; which requisition shall be binding, and thereupon the legislature of each State shall appoint the regimental officers, raise the men and cloath, arm and equip them in a solid-like manner, at the expense of the United States; and the officers and men so cloathed, armed and equipped shall march to the place appointed, and within the time agreed on by the United States in Congress assembled. But if the United States in Congress assembled shall, on consideration of circumstances judge proper that any State should not raise men, or should raise a smaller number of men than the quota thereof, such extra number shall be raised, officered, cloathed, armed and equipped in the same manner as the quota of each State, unless the legislature of such State shall judge that such extra number cannot be safely spread out in the same, in which case they shall raise, officer, cloath, arm and equip as many of such extra number as they judge can be safely spared. And the officers and men so cloathed, armed, and equipped, shall march to the place appointed, and within the time agreed on by the United States in Congress assembled.

The United States in Congress assembled shall never engage in a war, nor grant letters of marque or reprisal in time of peace, nor enter into any treaties or alliances, nor coin money, nor regulate the value thereof, nor ascertain the sums and expenses necessary for the defense and welfare of the United States, or any of them, nor emit bills, nor borrow money on the credit of the United States, nor appropriate money, nor agree upon the number of vessels of war, to be built or purchased, or the number of land or sea forces to be raised, nor appoint a commander in chief of the army or navy, unless nine States assent to the same: nor shall a question on any other point, except for adjourning from day to day be determined, unless by the votes of the majority of the United States in Congress assembled.

The Congress of the United States shall have power to adjourn to any time within the year, and to any place within the United States, so that no period of adjournment be for a longer duration than the space of six months, and shall publish the journal of their proceedings monthly, except such parts thereof relating to treaties, alliances or military operations, as in their judgement require secrecy; and the yeas and nays of the delegates of each State on any question shall be entered on the Journal, when it is desired by any delegates of a State, or any of them, at his or their request shall be furnished with a transcript of the said journal, except such parts as are above excepted, to lay before the legislatures of the several States.

ARTICLE X

The Committee of the States, or any nine of them, shall be authorized to execute, in the recess of Congress, such of the powers of Congress as the United States in Congress assembled, by the consent of the nine States, shall from time to time think expedient to vest them with; provided that no power be delegated to the said Committee, for the exercise of which, by the Articles of

Confederation, the voice of nine States in the Congress of the United States assembled be requisite.

ARTICLE XI

Canada acceding to this confederation, and adjoining in the measures of the United States, shall be admitted into, and entitled to all the advantages of this Union; but no other colony shall be admitted into the same, unless such admission be agreed to by nine States.

ARTICLE XII

All bills of credit emitted, monies borrowed, and debts contracted by, or under the authority of Congress, before the assembling of the United States, in pursuance of the present confederation, shall be deemed and considered as a charge against the United States, for payment and satisfaction whereof the said United States, and the public faith are hereby solemnly pleged.

ARTICLE XIII

Every State shall abide by the determination of the United States in Congress assembled, on all questions which by this confederation are submitted to them. And the Articles of this Confederation shall be inviolably observed by every State, and the Union shall be perpetual; nor shall any alteration at any time hereafter be made in any of them; unless such alteration be agreed to in a Congress of the United States, and be afterwards confirmed by the legislatures of every State.

CONCLUSION

And Whereas it hath pleased the Great Governor of the World to incline the hearts of the legislatures we respectively represent in Congress, to approve of, and to authorize us to ratify the said Articles of Confederation and perpetual Union. Know Ye that we the undersigned delegates, by virtue of the power and authority to us given for that purpose, do by these presents, in the name and in behalf of our respective constituents, fully and entirely ratify and confirm each and every of the said Articles of Confederation and perpetual Union, and all and singular the matters and things therein contained: And we do further solemnly plight and engage the faith of our constituents, that they shall abide by the determinations of the United States in Congress assembled, on all questions, which by the said Confederation are submitted to them. And that the Articles thereof shall be inviolably observed by the States we respectively represent, and that the Union shall be perpetual.

SIGNATORIES

In Witness whereof we have hereunto set our hands in Congress. Done at Philadelphia in the State of Pennsylvania the ninth day of July in the Year of our Lord One Thousand Seven Hundred and Seventy-Eight, and in the Third Year of the independence of America.

On the part and behalf of the State of New Hampshire:

Josiah Bartlett
John Wentworth Junior

On the part and behalf of the State of Massachusetts Bay:

John Hancock
Francis Dana
Samuel Adams
James Lovell
Elbridge Gerry
Samuel Holten

On the part and behalf of the State of Rhode Island and Providence Plantations:

William Ellery
John Collins
Henry Marchant

On the part and behalf of the State of Connecticut:

Roger Sherman
Titus Hosmer
Samuel Huntington
Andrew Adams
Oliver Wolcott

On the part and behalf of the State of New York:

James Duane
William Duer
Francis Lewis
Gouverneur Morris

On the part and in behalf of the State of New Jersey:

Jonathan Witherspoon
Nathaniel Scudder

On the part and behalf of the State of Pennsylvania:

Robert Morris
William Clingan
Daniel Roberdeau
Joseph Reed
John Bayard Smith

On the part and behalf of the State of Delaware:

Thomas Mckean
John Dickinson
Nicholas Van Dyke

On the part and behalf of the State of Maryland:

John Hanson
Daniel Carroll

On the part and behalf of the State of Virginia:

Richard Henry Lee
Jonathan Harvie
John Banister
Francis Lightfoot Lee
Thomas Adams

On the part and behalf of the State of No Carolina:

John Penn
Corns Harnett
Jonathan Williams

On the part and behalf of the State of South Carolina:

Henry Laurens
Richard Hutson
William Henry Drayton
Thomas Heyward Junior
Jonathan Matthews

On the part and behalf of the State of Georgia:

Jonathan Walton
Edward Telfair
Edward Langworthy

THE CONSTITUTION OF THE UNITED STATES OF AMERICA

We the people of the United States, in order to form a more perfect union, establish justice, insure domestic tranquility, provide for the common defense, promote the general welfare, and secure the blessings of liberty to ourselves and our posterity, do ordain and establish this Constitution for the United States of America.

ARTICLE I

Section 1. All legislative powers herein granted shall be vested in a Congress of the United States, which shall consist of a Senate and House of Representatives.

Section 2. The House of Representatives shall be composed of members chosen every second year by the people of the several states, and the electors in each state shall have the qualifications requisite for electors of the most numerous branch of the state legislature.

No person shall be a Representative who shall not have attained to the age of twenty five years, and been seven years a citizen of the United States, and who shall not, when elected, be an inhabitant of that state in which he shall be chosen.

Representatives and direct taxes shall be apportioned among the several states which may be included within this union, according to their respective numbers, which shall be determined by adding to the whole number of free persons, including those bound to service for a term of years, and excluding Indians not taxed, three fifths of all other Persons. The actual Enumeration shall be made within three years after the first meeting of the Congress of the United States, and within every subsequent term of ten years, in such manner as they shall by law direct. The number of Representatives shall not exceed one for every thirty thousand, but each state shall have at least one Representative; and until such enumeration shall be made, the state of New Hampshire shall be entitled to choose three, Massachusetts eight, Rhode Island and Providence Plantations one, Connecticut five, New York six, New Jersey four, Pennsylvania eight, Delaware one, Maryland six, Virginia ten, North Carolina five, South Carolina five, and Georgia three.

When vacancies happen in the Representation from any state, the executive authority thereof shall issue writs of election to fill such vacancies.

The House of Representatives shall choose their speaker and other officers; and shall have the sole power of impeachment.

Section 3. The Senate of the United States shall be composed of two Senators from each state, chosen by the legislature thereof, for six years; and each Senator shall have one vote. Immediately after they shall be assembled in consequence of the first election, they shall be divided as equally as may be into three classes. The seats of the Senators of the first class shall be vacated at the expiration of the second year, of the second class at the expiration of the fourth year, and the third class at the expiration of the sixth year, so that one third may be chosen every second year; and if vacancies happen by resignation, or otherwise, during the recess of the legislature of any state, the executive thereof may make temporary appointments until the next meeting of the legislature, which shall then fill such vacancies.

No person shall be a Senator who shall not have attained to the age of thirty years, and been nine years a citizen of the United States and who shall not, when elected, be an inhabitant of that state for which he shall be chosen.

The Vice President of the United States shall be President of the Senate, but shall have no vote, unless they be equally divided.

The Senate shall choose their other officers, and also a President pro tempore, in the absence of the Vice President, or when he shall exercise the office of President of the United States.

The Senate shall have the sole power to try all impeachments. When sitting for that purpose, they shall be on oath or affirmation. When the President of the United States is tried, the Chief Justice shall preside: And no person shall be convicted without the concurrence of two thirds of the members present.

Judgment in cases of impeachment shall not extend further than to removal from office, and disqualification to hold and enjoy any office of honor, trust or profit under the United States: but the party convicted shall nevertheless be liable and subject to indictment, trial, judgment and punishment, according to law.

Section 4. The times, places and manner of holding elections for Senators and Representatives, shall be prescribed in each state by the legislature thereof; but the Congress may at any time by law make or alter such regulations, except as to the places of choosing Senators.

The Congress shall assemble at least once in every year, and such meeting shall be on the first Monday in December, unless they shall by law appoint a different day.

Section 5. Each House shall be the judge of the elections, returns and qualifications of its own members,

and a majority of each shall constitute a quorum to do business; but a smaller number may adjourn from day to day, and may be authorized to compel the attendance of absent members, in such manner, and under such penalties as each House may provide.

Each House may determine the rules of its proceedings, punish its members for disorderly behavior, and, with the concurrence of two thirds, expel a member.

Each House shall keep a journal of its proceedings, and from time to time publish the same, excepting such parts as may in their judgment require secrecy; and the yeas and nays of the members of either House on any question shall, at the desire of one fifth of those present, be entered on the journal.

Neither House, during the session of Congress, shall, without the consent of the other, adjourn for more than three days, nor to any other place than that in which the two Houses shall be sitting.

Section 6. The Senators and Representatives shall receive a compensation for their services, to be ascertained by law, and paid out of the treasury of the United States. They shall in all cases, except treason, felony and breach of the peace, be privileged from arrest during their attendance at the session of their respective Houses, and in going to and returning from the same; and for any speech or debate in either House, they shall not be questioned in any other place. No Senator or Representative shall, during the time for which he was elected, be appointed to any civil office under the authority of the United States, which shall have been created, or the emoluments whereof shall have been increased during such time: and no person holding any office under the United States, shall be a member of either House during his continuance in office.

Section 7. All bills for raising revenue shall originate in the House of Representatives; but the Senate may propose or concur with amendments as on other Bills.

Every bill which shall have passed the House of Representatives and the Senate, shall, before it become a law, be presented to the President of the United States; if he approve he shall sign it, but if not he shall return it, with his objections to that House in which it shall have originated, who shall enter the objections at large on their journal, and proceed to reconsider it. If after such reconsideration two thirds of that House shall agree to pass the bill, it shall be sent, together with the objections, to the other House, by which it shall likewise be reconsidered, and if approved by two thirds of that House, it shall become a law. But in all such cases the votes of both Houses shall be determined by yeas and nays, and the names of the persons voting for and against the bill shall be entered on the journal of each House respectively. If any bill shall not be returned by the President within ten days (Sundays excepted) after it shall have been presented to him, the same shall be a law, in like manner as if he had signed it, unless the Congress by their adjournment prevent its return, in which case it shall not be a law.

Every order, resolution, or vote to which the concurrence of the Senate and House of Representatives may be necessary (except on a question of adjournment) shall be presented to the President of the United States; and before the same shall take effect, shall be approved by him, or being disapproved by him, shall be repassed by two thirds of the Senate and House of Representatives, according to the rules and limitations prescribed in the case of a bill.

Section 8. The Congress shall have power to lay and collect taxes, duties, imposts and excises, to pay the debts and provide for the common defense and general welfare of the United States; but all duties, imposts and excises shall be uniform throughout the United States;

To borrow money on the credit of the United States;

To regulate commerce with foreign nations, and among the several states, and with the Indian tribes;

To establish a uniform rule of naturalization, and uniform laws on the subject of bankruptcies throughout the United States;

To coin money, regulate the value thereof, and of foreign coin, and fix the standard of weights and measures;

To provide for the punishment of counterfeiting the securities and current coin of the United States;

To establish post offices and post roads;

To promote the progress of science and useful arts, by securing for limited times to authors and inventors the exclusive right to their respective writings and discoveries;

To constitute tribunals inferior to the Supreme Court;

To define and punish piracies and felonies committed on the high seas, and offenses against the law of nations;

To declare war, grant letters of marque and reprisal, and make rules concerning captures on land and water;

To raise and support armies, but no appropriation of money to that use shall be for a longer term than two years;

To provide and maintain a navy;

To make rules for the government and regulation of the land and naval forces;

To provide for calling forth the militia to execute the laws of the union, suppress insurrections and repel invasions;

To provide for organizing, arming, and disciplining, the militia, and for governing such part of them as may be employed in the service of the United States, reserving to the states respectively, the appointment of the officers, and the authority of training the militia according to the discipline prescribed by Congress;

To exercise exclusive legislation in all cases whatsoever, over such District (not exceeding ten miles square) as may, by cession of particular states, and the acceptance of Congress, become the seat of the government of the United States, and to exercise like authority over all places purchased by the consent of the legislature of the state in which the same shall be, for the erection of forts, magazines, arsenals, dockyards, and other needful buildings;—And

To make all laws which shall be necessary and proper for carrying into execution the foregoing powers, and all other powers vested by this Constitution in the government of the United States, or in any department or officer thereof.

Section 9. The migration or importation of such persons as any of the states now existing shall think proper to admit, shall not be prohibited by the Congress prior to the year one thousand eight hundred and eight, but a tax or duty may be imposed on such importation, not exceeding ten dollars for each person.

The privilege of the writ of habeas corpus shall not be suspended, unless when in cases of rebellion or invasion the public safety may require it.

No bill of attainder or ex post facto Law shall be passed.

No capitation, or other direct, tax shall be laid, unless in proportion to the census or enumeration herein before directed to be taken.

No tax or duty shall be laid on articles exported from any state.

No preference shall be given by any regulation of commerce or revenue to the ports of one state over those of another: nor shall vessels bound to, or from, one state, be obliged to enter, clear or pay duties in another.

No money shall be drawn from the treasury, but in consequence of appropriations made by law; and a regular statement and account of receipts and expenditures of all public money shall be published from time to time.

No title of nobility shall be granted by the United States: and no person holding any office of profit or trust under them, shall, without the consent of the Congress, accept of any present, emolument, office, or title, of any kind whatever, from any king, prince, or foreign state.

Section 10. No state shall enter into any treaty, alliance, or confederation; grant letters of marque and reprisal; coin money; emit bills of credit; make anything but gold and silver coin a tender in payment of debts; pass any bill of attainder, ex post facto law, or law impairing the obligation of contracts, or grant any title of nobility.

No state shall, without the consent of the Congress, lay any imposts or duties on imports or exports, except what may be absolutely necessary for executing its inspection laws: and the net produce of all duties and imposts, laid by any state on imports or exports, shall be for the use of the treasury of the United States; and all such laws shall be subject to the revision and control of the Congress.

No state shall, without the consent of Congress, lay any duty of tonnage, keep troops, or ships of war in time of peace, enter into any agreement or compact with another state, or with a foreign power, or engage in war, unless actually invaded, or in such imminent danger as will not admit of delay.

ARTICLE II

Section 1. The executive power shall be vested in a President of the United States of America. He shall hold his office during the term of four years, and, together with the Vice President, chosen for the same term, be elected, as follows:

Each state shall appoint, in such manner as the Legislature thereof may direct, a number of electors, equal to the whole number of Senators and Representatives to which the State may be entitled in the Congress: but no Senator or Representative, or person holding an office of trust or profit under the United States, shall be appointed an elector.

The electors shall meet in their respective states, and vote by ballot for two persons, of whom one at least shall not be an inhabitant of the same state with themselves. And they shall make a list of all the persons voted for, and of the number of votes for each; which list they shall sign and certify, and transmit sealed to the seat of the government of the United States, directed to the President of the Senate. The President of the Senate shall, in the presence of the Senate and House of Representatives, open all the certificates, and the votes shall then be counted. The person having the greatest number of votes shall be the President, if such number be a majority of the whole number of electors appointed; and if there be more than one who have such majority, and have an equal number of votes, then the House of Representatives shall immediately choose by ballot one of them for President; and if no person have a majority, then from the five highest on the list the said House shall in like manner choose the President. But in choosing the President, the votes shall be taken by States, the representation from each state having one vote; A quorum for this purpose shall consist of a member or members from two thirds of the states, and a majority of all the states shall be necessary to a choice. In every case, after the choice of the President, the person having the greatest number of votes of the electors shall be the Vice President. But if there should remain two or more who have equal votes, the Senate shall choose from them by ballot the Vice President.

The Congress may determine the time of choosing the electors, and the day on which they shall give their votes; which day shall be the same throughout the United States.

No person except a natural born citizen, or a citizen of the United States, at the time of the adoption of this Constitution, shall be eligible to the office of President; neither shall any person be eligible to that office who shall not have attained to the age of thirty five years, and been fourteen Years a resident within the United States.

In case of the removal of the President from office, or of his death, resignation, or inability to discharge the powers and duties of the said office, the same shall devolve on the Vice President, and the Congress may by law provide for the case of removal, death, resignation or inability, both of the President and Vice President, declaring what officer shall then act as President, and such officer shall act accordingly, until the disability be removed, or a President shall be elected.

The President shall, at stated times, receive for his services, a compensation, which shall neither be increased nor diminished during the period for which he shall have been elected, and he shall not receive within that period any other emolument from the United States, or any of them.

Before he enter on the execution of his office, he shall take the following oath or affirmation:—"I do solemnly swear (or affirm) that I will faithfully execute the office of President of the United States, and will to the best of my ability, preserve, protect and defend the Constitution of the United States."

Section 2. The President shall be commander in chief of the Army and Navy of the United States, and of the militia of the several states, when called into the actual service of the United States; he may require the opinion, in writing, of the principal officer in each of the executive departments, on any subject relating to the duties of their respective offices, and he shall have power to grant reprieves and pardons for offenses against the United States, except in cases of impeachment.

He shall have power, by and with the advice and consent of the Senate, to make treaties, provided two thirds of the Senators present concur; and he shall nominate, and by and with the advice and consent of the Senate, shall appoint ambassadors, other public ministers and consuls, judges of the Supreme Court, and all other officers of the United States, whose appointments are not herein otherwise provided for,

and which shall be established by law: but the Congress may by law vest the appointment of such inferior officers, as they think proper, in the President alone, in the courts of law, or in the heads of departments.

The President shall have power to fill up all vacancies that may happen during the recess of the Senate, by granting commissions which shall expire at the end of their next session.

Section 3. He shall from time to time give to the Congress information of the state of the union, and recommend to their consideration such measures as he shall judge necessary and expedient; he may, on extraordinary occasions, convene both Houses, or either of them, and in case of disagreement between them, with respect to the time of adjournment, he may adjourn them to such time as he shall think proper; he shall receive ambassadors and other public ministers; he shall take care that the laws be faithfully executed, and shall commission all the officers of the United States.

Section 4. The President, Vice President and all civil officers of the United States, shall be removed from office on impeachment for, and conviction of, treason, bribery, or other high crimes and misdemeanors.

ARTICLE III

Section 1. The judicial power of the United States, shall be vested in one Supreme Court, and in such inferior courts as the Congress may from time to time ordain and establish. The judges, both of the supreme and inferior courts, shall hold their offices during good behavior, and shall, at stated times, receive for their services, a compensation, which shall not be diminished during their continuance in office.

Section 2. The judicial power shall extend to all cases, in law and equity, arising under this Constitution, the laws of the United States, and treaties made, or which shall be made, under their authority;—to all cases affecting ambassadors, other public ministers and consuls;—to all cases of admiralty and maritime jurisdiction;—to controversies to which the United States shall be a party;—to controversies between two or more states;—between a state and citizens of another state;—between citizens of different states;—

between citizens of the same state claiming lands under grants of different states, and between a state, or the citizens thereof, and foreign states, citizens or subjects.

In all cases affecting ambassadors, other public ministers and consuls, and those in which a state shall be party, the Supreme Court shall have original jurisdiction. In all the other cases before mentioned, the Supreme Court shall have appellate jurisdiction, both as to law and fact, with such exceptions, and under such regulations as the Congress shall make.

The trial of all crimes, except in cases of impeachment, shall be by jury; and such trial shall be held in the state where the said crimes shall have been committed; but when not committed within any state, the trial shall be at such place or places as the Congress may by law have directed.

Section 3. Treason against the United States, shall consist only in levying war against them, or in adhering to their enemies, giving them aid and comfort. No person shall be convicted of treason unless on the testimony of two witnesses to the same overt act, or on confession in open court.

The Congress shall have power to declare the punishment of treason, but no attainder of treason shall work corruption of blood, or forfeiture except during the life of the person attainted.

ARTICLE IV

Section 1. Full faith and credit shall be given in each state to the public acts, records, and judicial proceedings of every other state. And the Congress may by general laws prescribe the manner in which such acts, records, and proceedings shall be proved, and the effect thereof.

Section 2. The citizens of each state shall be entitled to all privileges and immunities of citizens in the several states.

A person charged in any state with treason, felony, or other crime, who shall flee from justice, and be found in another state, shall on demand of the executive authority of the state from which he fled, be delivered up, to be removed to the state having jurisdiction of the crime.

No person held to service or labor in one state, under the laws thereof, escaping into another, shall, in consequence of any law or regulation therein, be discharged from such service or labor, but shall be delivered up on claim of the party to whom such service or labor may be due.

Section 3. New states may be admitted by the Congress into this union; but no new states shall be formed or erected within the jurisdiction of any other state; nor any state be formed by the junction of two or more states, or parts of states, without the consent of the legislatures of the states concerned as well as of the Congress.

The Congress shall have power to dispose of and make all needful rules and regulations respecting the territory or other property belonging to the United States; and nothing in this Constitution shall be so construed as to prejudice any claims of the United States, or of any particular state.

Section 4. The United States shall guarantee to every state in this union a republican form of government, and shall protect each of them against invasion; and on application of the legislature, or of the executive (when the legislature cannot be convened) against domestic violence.

ARTICLE V

The Congress, whenever two thirds of both houses shall deem it necessary, shall propose amendments to this Constitution, or, on the application of the legislatures of two thirds of the several states, shall call a convention for proposing amendments, which, in either case, shall be valid to all intents and purposes, as part of this Constitution, when ratified by the legislatures of three fourths of the several states, or by conventions in three fourths thereof, as the one or the other mode of ratification may be proposed by the Congress; provided that no amendment which may be made prior to the year one thousand eight hundred and eight shall in any manner affect the first and fourth clauses in the ninth section of the first article; and that no state, without its consent, shall be deprived of its equal suffrage in the Senate.

ARTICLE VI

All debts contracted and engagements entered into, before the adoption of this Constitution, shall be as valid against the United States under this Constitution, as under the Confederation.

This Constitution, and the laws of the United States which shall be made in pursuance thereof; and all treaties made, or which shall be made, under the authority of the United States, shall be the supreme law of the land; and the judges in every state shall be bound thereby, anything in the Constitution or laws of any State to the contrary notwithstanding.

The Senators and Representatives before mentioned, and the members of the several state legislatures, and all executive and judicial officers, both of the United States and of the several states, shall be bound by oath or affirmation, to support this Constitution; but no religious test shall ever be required as a qualification to any office or public trust under the United States.

ARTICLE VII

The ratification of the conventions of nine states, shall be sufficient for the establishment of this Constitution between the states so ratifying the same.

Done in convention by the unanimous consent of the states present the seventeenth day of September in the year of our Lord one thousand seven hundred and eighty seven and of the independence of the United States of America the twelfth. In witness whereof We have hereunto subscribed our Names,

G. WASHINGTON: Presidt. and deputy from Virginia

New Hampshire: JOHN LANGDON, NICHOLAS GILMAN

Massachusetts: NATHANIEL GORHAM, RUFUS KING

Connecticut: Wm: SAML. JOHNSON, ROGER SHERMAN

New York: ALEXANDER HAMILTON

New Jersey: WIL LIVINGSTON, DAVID BREARLY, WM. PATERSON, JONA: DAYTON

Pennsylvania: B. FRANKLIN, THOMAS MIFFLIN, ROBT. MORRIS, GEO. CLYMER, THOS. FITZSIMONS, JARED INGERSOLL, JAMES WILSON, GOUV MORRIS

Delaware: GEO: READ, GUNNING BEDFORD JUN, JOHN DICKINSON, RICHARD BASSETT, JACO: BROOM

Maryland: JAMES MCHENRY, DAN OF ST THOS. JENIFER, DANL CARROLL

Virginia: JOHN BLAIR—, JAMES MADISON JR.

North Carolina: WM. BLOUNT, RICHD. DOBBS SPAIGHT, HU WILLIAMSON

South Carolina: J. RUTLEDGE, CHARLES COTESWORTH PINCKNEY, CHARLES PINCKNEY, PIERCE BUTLER

Georgia: WILLIAM FEW, ABR BALDWIN

BILL OF RIGHTS

The Conventions of a number of the States having, at the time of adopting the Constitution, expressed a desire, in order to prevent misconstruction or abuse of its powers, that further declaratory and restrictive clauses should be added, and as extending the ground of public confidence in the Government will best insure the beneficent ends of its institution;

Resolved, by the Senate and House of Representatives of the United States of America, in Congress assembled, two-thirds of both Houses concurring, that the following articles be proposed to the Legislatures of the several States, as amendments to the Constitution of the United States; all or any of which articles, when ratified by three-fourths of the said Legislatures, to be valid to all intents and purposes as part of the said Constitution, namely:

AMENDMENT I

Congress shall make no law respecting an establishment of religion, or prohibiting the free exercise thereof; or abridging the freedom of speech, or of the press; or the right of the people peaceably to assemble, and to petition the government for a redress of grievances.

AMENDMENT II

A well regulated militia, being necessary to the security of a free state, the right of the people to keep and bear arms, shall not be infringed.

AMENDMENT III

No soldier shall, in time of peace be quartered in any house, without the consent of the owner, nor in time of war, but in a manner to be prescribed by law.

AMENDMENT IV

The right of the people to be secure in their persons, houses, papers, and effects, against unreasonable searches and seizures, shall not be violated, and no warrants shall issue, but upon probable cause, supported by oath or affirmation, and particularly describing the place to be searched, and the persons or things to be seized.

AMENDMENT V

No person shall be held to answer for a capital, or otherwise infamous crime, unless on a presentment or indictment of a grand jury, except in cases arising in the land or naval forces, or in the militia, when in actual service in time of war or public danger; nor shall any person be subject for the same offense to be twice put in jeopardy of life or limb; nor shall be compelled in any criminal case to be a witness against himself, nor be deprived of life, liberty, or property, without due process of law; nor shall private property be taken for public use, without just compensation.

AMENDMENT VI

In all criminal prosecutions, the accused shall enjoy the right to a speedy and public trial, by an impartial jury of the state and district wherein the crime shall have been committed, which district shall have been previously ascertained by law, and to be informed of the nature and cause of the accusation; to be confronted with the witnesses against him; to have compulsory process for obtaining witnesses in his favor, and to have the assistance of counsel for his defense.

AMENDMENT VII

In suits at common law, where the value in controversy shall exceed twenty dollars, the right of trial by jury shall be preserved, and no fact tried by a jury, shall be otherwise reexamined in any court of the United States, than according to the rules of the common law.

AMENDMENT VIII

Excessive bail shall not be required, nor excessive fines imposed, nor cruel and unusual punishments inflicted.

AMENDMENT IX

The enumeration in the Constitution, of certain rights, shall not be construed to deny or disparage others retained by the people.

AMENDMENT X

The powers not delegated to the United States by the Constitution, nor prohibited by it to the states, are reserved to the states respectively, or to the people.

OTHER AMENDMENTS TO THE CONSTITUTION

AMENDMENT XI

(1798)

The judicial power of the United States shall not be construed to extend to any suit in law or equity, commenced or prosecuted against one of the United States by citizens of another state, or by citizens or subjects of any foreign state.

AMENDMENT XII

(1804)

The electors shall meet in their respective states and vote by ballot for President and Vice-President, one of whom, at least, shall not be an inhabitant of the same state with themselves; they shall name in their ballots the person voted for as President, and in distinct ballots the person voted for as Vice-President, and they shall make distinct lists of all persons voted for as President, and of all persons voted for as Vice-President, and of the number of votes for each, which lists they shall sign and certify, and transmit sealed to the seat of the government of the United States, directed to the President of the Senate;—The President of the Senate shall, in the presence of the Senate and House of Representatives, open all the certificates and the votes shall then be counted;—the person having the greatest number of votes for President, shall be the President, if such number be a majority of the whole number of electors appointed; and if no person have such majority, then from the persons hav-

ing the highest numbers not exceeding three on the list of those voted for as President, the House of Representatives shall choose immediately, by ballot, the President. But in choosing the President, the votes shall be taken by states, the representation from each state having one vote; a quorum for this purpose shall consist of a member or members from two-thirds of the states, and a majority of all the states shall be necessary to a choice. And if the House of Representatives shall not choose a President whenever the right of choice shall devolve upon them, before the fourth day of March next following, then the Vice-President shall act as President, as in the case of the death or other constitutional disability of the President. The person having the greatest number of votes as Vice-President, shall be the Vice-President, if such number be a majority of the whole number of electors appointed, and if no person have a majority, then from the two highest numbers on the list, the Senate shall choose the Vice-President; a quorum for the purpose shall consist of two-thirds of the whole number of Senators, and a majority of the whole number shall be necessary to a choice. But no person constitutionally ineligible to the office of President shall be eligible to that of Vice-President of the United States.

AMENDMENT XIII

(1865)

Section 1. Neither slavery nor involuntary servitude, except as a punishment for crime whereof the party shall have been duly convicted, shall exist within the United States, or any place subject to their jurisdiction.

Section 2. Congress shall have power to enforce this article by appropriate legislation.

AMENDMENT XIV

(1868)

Section 1. All persons born or naturalized in the United States, and subject to the jurisdiction thereof, are citizens of the United States and of the state wherein they reside. No state shall make or enforce any law which shall abridge the privileges or immunities of citizens of the United States; nor shall any state deprive any person of life, liberty, or property, without due process of law; nor deny to any person within its jurisdiction the equal protection of the laws.

Section 2. Representatives shall be apportioned among the several states according to their respective numbers, counting the whole number of persons in each state, excluding Indians not taxed. But when the right to vote at any election for the choice of electors for President and Vice President of the United States, Representatives in Congress, the executive and judicial officers of a state, or the members of the legislature thereof, is denied to any of the male inhabitants of such state, being twenty-one years of age, and citizens of the United States, or in any way abridged, except for participation in rebellion, or other crime, the basis of representation therein shall be reduced in the proportion which the number of such male citizens shall bear to the whole number of male citizens twenty-one years of age in such state.

Section 3. No person shall be a Senator or Representative in Congress, or elector of President and Vice President, or hold any office, civil or military, under the United States, or under any state, who, having previously taken an oath, as a member of Congress, or as an officer of the United States, or as a member of any state legislature, or as an executive or judicial officer of any state, to support the Constitution of the United States, shall have engaged in insurrection or rebellion against the same, or given aid or comfort to the enemies thereof. But Congress may by a vote of two-thirds of each House, remove such disability.

Section 4. The validity of the public debt of the United States, authorized by law, including debts incurred for payment of pensions and bounties for services in suppressing insurrection or rebellion, shall not be questioned. But neither the United States nor any state shall assume or pay any debt or obligation incurred in aid of insurrection or rebellion against the United States, or any claim for the loss or emancipation of any slave; but all such debts, obligations and claims shall be held illegal and void.

Section 5. The Congress shall have power to enforce, by appropriate legislation, the provisions of this article.

AMENDMENT XV

(1870)

Section 1. The right of citizens of the United States to vote shall not be denied or abridged by the United States or by any state on account of race, color, or previous condition of servitude.

Section 2. The Congress shall have power to enforce this article by appropriate legislation.

AMENDMENT XVI

(1913)

The Congress shall have power to lay and collect taxes on incomes, from whatever source derived, without apportionment among the several states, and without regard to any census of enumeration.

AMENDMENT XVII

(1913)

The Senate of the United States shall be composed of two Senators from each state, elected by the people thereof, for six years; and each Senator shall have one vote. The electors in each state shall have the qualifications requisite for electors of the most numerous branch of the state legislatures.

When vacancies happen in the representation of any state in the Senate, the executive authority of such state shall issue writs of election to fill such vacancies: Provided, that the legislature of any state may empower the executive thereof to make temporary appointments until the people fill the vacancies by election as the legislature may direct.

This amendment shall not be so construed as to affect the election or term of any Senator chosen before it becomes valid as part of the Constitution.

AMENDMENT XVIII

(1919)

Section 1. After one year from the ratification of this article the manufacture, sale, or transportation of intoxicating liquors within, the importation thereof into, or the exportation thereof from the United States and all territory subject to the jurisdiction thereof for beverage purposes is hereby prohibited.

Section 2. The Congress and the several states shall have concurrent power to enforce this article by appropriate legislation.

Section 3. This article shall be inoperative unless it shall have been ratified as an amendment to the Constitution by the legislatures of the several states, as provided in the Constitution, within seven years from the date of the submission hereof to the states by the Congress.

AMENDMENT XIX

(1920)

The right of citizens of the United States to vote shall not be denied or abridged by the United States or by any state on account of sex.

Congress shall have power to enforce this article by appropriate legislation.

AMENDMENT XX

(1933)

Section 1. The terms of the President and Vice President shall end at noon on the 20th day of January, and the terms of Senators and Representatives at noon on the 3rd day of January, of the years in which such terms would have ended if this article had not been ratified; and the terms of their successors shall then begin.

Section 2. The Congress shall assemble at least once in every year, and such meeting shall begin at noon on the 3rd day of January, unless they shall by law appoint a different day.

Section 3. If, at the time fixed for the beginning of the term of the President, the President elect shall have died, the Vice President elect shall become President. If a President shall not have been chosen before the time fixed for the beginning of his term, or if the President elect shall have failed to qualify, then the Vice President elect shall act as President until a President shall have qualified; and the Congress may by law provide for the case wherein neither a President elect nor a Vice President elect shall have qualified, declaring who shall then act as President, or the manner in which one who is to act shall be selected, and such person shall act accordingly until a President or Vice President shall have qualified.

Section 4. The Congress may by law provide for the case of the death of any of the persons from whom the House of Representatives may choose a President whenever the right of choice shall have devolved upon them, and for the case of the death of any of the persons from whom the Senate may choose a Vice President whenever the right of choice shall have devolved upon them.

Section 5. Sections 1 and 2 shall take effect on the 15th day of October following the ratification of this article.

Section 6. This article shall be inoperative unless it shall have been ratified as an amendment to the Constitution by the legislatures of three-fourths of the several states within seven years from the date of its submission.

AMENDMENT XXI

(1933)

Section 1. The eighteenth article of amendment to the Constitution of the United States is hereby repealed.

Section 2. The transportation or importation into any state, territory, or possession of the United States for delivery or use therein of intoxicating liquors, in violation of the laws thereof, is hereby prohibited.

Section 3. This article shall be inoperative unless it shall have been ratified as an amendment to the Constitution by conventions in the several states, as provided in the Constitution, within seven years from the date of the submission hereof to the states by the Congress.

AMENDMENT XXII

(1951)

Section 1. No person shall be elected to the office of the President more than twice, and no person who has held the office of President, or acted as President, for more than two years of a term to which some other person was elected President shall be elected to the office of the President more than once. But this article shall not apply to any person holding the office of President when this article was proposed by the Congress, and shall not prevent any person who may be holding the office of President, or acting as President, during the term within which this article becomes operative from holding the office of President or acting as President during the remainder of such term.

Section 2. This article shall be inoperative unless it shall have been ratified as an amendment to the Constitution by the legislatures of three-fourths of the several states within seven years from the date of its submission to the states by the Congress.

AMENDMENT XXIII

(1961)

Section 1. The District constituting the seat of government of the United States shall appoint in such manner as the Congress may direct: A number of electors of President and Vice President equal to the whole number of Senators and Representatives in Congress to which the District would be entitled if it were a state, but in no event more than the least populous state; they shall be in addition to those appointed by the states, but they shall be considered, for the purposes of the election of President and Vice President, to be electors appointed by a state; and they shall

meet in the District and perform such duties as provided by the twelfth article of amendment.

Section 2. The Congress shall have power to enforce this article by appropriate legislation.

AMENDMENT XXIV

(1964)

Section 1. The right of citizens of the United States to vote in any primary or other election for President or Vice President, for electors for President or Vice President, or for Senator or Representative in Congress, shall not be denied or abridged by the United States or any state by reason of failure to pay any poll tax or other tax.

Section 2. The Congress shall have power to enforce this article by appropriate legislation.

AMENDMENT XXV

(1967)

Section 1. In case of the removal of the President from office or of his death or resignation, the Vice President shall become President.

Section 2. Whenever there is a vacancy in the office of the Vice President, the President shall nominate a Vice President who shall take office upon confirmation by a majority vote of both Houses of Congress.

Section 3. Whenever the President transmits to the President pro tempore of the Senate and the Speaker of the House of Representatives his written declaration that he is unable to discharge the powers and duties of his office, and until he transmits to them a written declaration to the contrary, such powers and duties shall be discharged by the Vice President as Acting President.

Section 4. Whenever the Vice President and a majority of either the principal officers of the executive departments or of such other body as Congress may by law provide, transmit to the President pro tempore of the Senate and the Speaker of the House of Representatives their written declaration that the President is unable to discharge the powers and duties of his office, the Vice President shall immediately assume the powers and duties of the office as Acting President.

Thereafter, when the President transmits to the President pro tempore of the Senate and the Speaker of the House of Representatives his written declaration that no inability exists, he shall resume the powers and duties of his office unless the Vice President and a majority of either the principal officers of the executive department or of such other body as Congress may by law provide, transmit within four days to the President pro tempore of the Senate and the Speaker of the House of Representatives their written declaration that the President is unable to discharge the powers and duties of his office.

Thereupon Congress shall decide the issue, assembling within forty-eight hours for that purpose if not in session. If the Congress, within twenty-one days after receipt of the latter written declaration, or, if Congress is not in session, within twenty-one days after Congress is required to assemble, determines by two-thirds vote of both Houses that the President

is unable to discharge the powers and duties of his office, the Vice President shall continue to discharge the same as Acting President; otherwise, the President shall resume the powers and duties of his office.

AMENDMENT XXVI
(1971)

Section 1. The right of citizens of the United States, who are 18 years of age or older, to vote, shall not be denied or abridged by the United States or any state on account of age.

Section 2. The Congress shall have the power to enforce this article by appropriate legislation.

AMENDMENT XXVII
(1992)

No law varying the compensation for the services of the Senators and Representatives shall take effect until an election of Representatives shall have intervened.

INDEX

Note: Page references in **boldface** refer to encyclopedia entries. Page references in *italic* refer to figures or tables.

and social security 855

State of the Union addresses 648, 649

Supreme Court appointments 745

telecommunication policy 863

transition 652–653

treaties 655

triangulation strategy of 57

and veto power 427, 664

vice president of 363, 667

welfare reform 788, 839, 875, 878, 968, 1,049, 1,065

and women in government 216

Clinton v. City of New York (1998) 664–665

Clinton v. Jones (1997) 361

cloture 379, 381–382, 402, 420, 434

CNN effect 267

coalition(s) **232–234**, 268. *See also* caucus

Coast Guard, U.S. 775

coattails **477–479**

Code of Federal Registration 679

code of legislative ethics **352–354**, 421

Coercive (Intolerable) Acts 37

COINTELPRO program 313

Coke, Sir Edward 22, 62, 72–73, 79, 149, 237

Colby, Bainbridge 201

cold war. *See also* North Atlantic Treaty Organization (NATO)

and armed forces, need for 642

and bureaucracy, growth of 463

CIA and 468, 469

and conservative tradition 238–239

covert operations in 469–470, 574

and developing nations 1,004

ending of 801, 1,026

FDR legacy and 246

ideology and 253

and international law 1,017

nuclear arms control efforts 757–759

and presidential disability 535–536

and presidential power 547, 801

and presidential war powers 481

propaganda in 309

soft power and 579

UN and 1,058

and U.S. policy 120, 766, 769, 770, 801

Coleman, William T., Jr. 528, 720

collective bargaining **759–762**, 833

colonial governments **15–17**, 21, 161, 926

colonialism 1,003–1,004, 1,025

colonial legislatures 16–17

colonies

capitalism in 993

dissatisfaction with British rule 37

population 15

and virtual representation 87–88

Colorado, gay and lesbian rights in 173

Columbine massacre *806*, 808

Comit;aae Maritime International (CMI) 724

command economy **995–996**, 998, 1,026. *See also* communism

commander in chief **479–482**, 498

Commentaries on the Laws of England (Blackstone) 164, 167–168, 696, 952

commerce clause **17–20**

and federal jurisdiction 527

and federal supremacy 25

Supreme Court on 17–20, 57, 105, 108, 109, 154, 596, 817, 872

Commerce Court 588

commercial aviation, history of 493

Commercial Space Launch Act of 1984 529

commission(s), types and functions 679

commission-administrator model of government 909–910

commissioner 703

commission-executive form of government 910, 912–913

commission form of government 897, 909, 943

Commission on Economy and Efficiency. *See* Taft Commission

Commission on Organization of the Executive Branch. *See* Hoover Commission

Commission on Presidential Debates 488

committee(s), congressional. *See also* appropriations committees; Ways and Means Committee

ad hoc, defined 354

authorizing 354–355

and career ladder for Congresspersons 355, 356

chairpersons 355, 357

conference 335, 340, 354

cozy triangles and 484–486, 556

executive branch testimony before 556

functions of 354

history 367

House 356

in legislative process 401–402, 419

partisan structure of 355

and pork-barrel spending 415–416

resistance to reform 355

resolutions establishing membership of 424

riders and 427–428

select, defined 354

Senate 356, *433*

seniority rankings in 356

shirking 356

staff for 367

standing 354–355

turf wars between 355

Committee for Relief in Europe (CARE) 1,060

Committee of the Permanent Representatives of the Member States (COREPER) 1,011

Committee on Economic Development 835

Committee on Foreign Affairs 466

Committee on Government Reform (House of Representatives) 452

Committee on Homeland Security 355

Committee on House Administration 346

Committee on Public Information 308, 770

Committees of Safety 37

committee system. *See also* committee(s), congressional

in colonial governments 16–17

in Congress **354–357**

in state and local legislatures 928, 932–933, 976

Common Agricultural Policy (CAP) 1,023

Common Cause 485

common law **20–23**, 148, 237–238

common property 950

Commonwealth, common law heritage 20–21

Commonwealth of Independent States (CIS) 759

Communicable Disease Center 507

Communications Act of 1934 486, 564, 565

Communications Decency Act 864

Communications Satellite Act of 1962 565

communism **996–999**. *See also* command economy

communist state, characteristics of 998–999

developing countries and 1,004–1,005

and freedom of religion 997

and freedom of speech 166, 195–196

and labor unions 518

principles of 997–998

Red Scare deportations 518

in Soviet Union 997–999

Communist Manifesto (Marx and Engels) 996–997

I

L